THE CAMBRIDGE COMPANION TO
CHRISTIAN LITURGY

Throughout the long history of Christianity, Christians have celebrated their faith in a myriad of ways. This *Companion* offers new insights into the theological depths of the liturgical mysteries that are the essence of Christian worship services, rituals, and sacraments. It investigates how these mysteries order time and space, and how they permeate the life of the Churches. The volume explores how Christian liturgy, as a corporeal and communal set of activities, has had a profound impact on spiritualities, preaching, pastoral engagement, and ecumenical relations, as well as encounters with religious others. Written by an international team of scholars, it also explores the intrinsic connections between liturgy and the arts, and why liturgy matters theologically. Ultimately, *The Cambridge Companion to Christian Liturgy* demonstrates the inextricable link between theology and liturgy and provides incentives for critical and constructive reflections about the relevance of liturgy in today's world.

Joris Geldhof is Catherine F. Huisking Professor of Theology at the University of Notre Dame, Indiana, USA. Previously, he was Professor of Liturgy and Sacramental Theology at the Catholic University of Leuven, Belgium. The Past President of the international ecumenical *Societas Liturgica*, he is the author of *Liturgy and Secularism: Beyond the Divide*, *Liturgical Theology as a Research Program*, and *Monotheism in Christian Liturgy*.

THE CAMBRIDGE COMPANION TO
CHRISTIAN LITURGY

Edited by

Joris Geldhof
University of Notre Dame

Shaftesbury Road, Cambridge CB2 8EA, United Kingdom

One Liberty Plaza, 20th Floor, New York, NY 10006, USA

477 Williamstown Road, Port Melbourne, VIC 3207, Australia

314–321, 3rd Floor, Plot 3, Splendor Forum, Jasola District Centre, New Delhi – 110025, India

103 Penang Road, #05-06/07, Visioncrest Commercial, Singapore 238467

Cambridge University Press is part of Cambridge University Press & Assessment, a department of the University of Cambridge.

We share the University's mission to contribute to society through the pursuit of education, learning and research at the highest international levels of excellence.

www.cambridge.org

Information on this title: www.cambridge.org/9781009186667

DOI: 10.1017/9781009186650

© Cambridge University Press & Assessment 2025

This publication is in copyright. Subject to statutory exception and to the provisions of relevant collective licensing agreements, no reproduction of any part may take place without the written permission of Cambridge University Press & Assessment.

When citing this work, please include a reference to the DOI 10.1017/9781009186650

First published 2025

Cover image: Baptismal font, Saint Oswald Church, Seefeld in Tirol, Tyrol, Austria. Photo: DEA / ALBERT CEOLAN / Contributor / De Agostini / Getty Images

A catalogue record for this publication is available from the British Library

A Cataloging-in-Publication data record for this book is available from the Library of Congress

ISBN 978-1-009-18666-7 Hardback
ISBN 978-1-009-18664-3 Paperback

Cambridge University Press & Assessment has no responsibility for the persistence or accuracy of URLs for external or third-party internet websites referred to in this publication and does not guarantee that any content on such websites is, or will remain, accurate or appropriate.

For EU product safety concerns, contact us at Calle de José Abascal, 56, 1°, 28003 Madrid, Spain, or email eugpsr@cambridge.org

Contents

List of Tables page vii
List of Contributors ix
Acknowledgments xi

Introduction 1
JORIS GELDHOF

Part I **Liturgy Throughout the Ages**

1 Liturgy in Early Christianity 7
   HARALD BUCHINGER

2 Liturgy in the Middle Ages 24
   JORIS GELDHOF

3 Liturgies and the Reformation 42
   JAN SCHNELL

4 Liturgies Beyond the Reformation 61
   MELANIE C. ROSS

5 Liturgy in Eastern Christianity 80
   STEFANOS ALEXOPOULOS

6 The Liturgical Movement 98
   KATHERINE E. HARMON

Part II **The Celebration of the Liturgy**

7 The Eucharist 117
   PATRICK PRÉTOT

8 Liturgy and the Sacraments 133
   CLARE V. JOHNSON

9 Liturgy of the Hours 155
   LIBORIUS OLAF LUMMA

10 The Liturgical Year 173
    MARYANN MADHAVATHU

Part III Liturgy and the Arts

11 Liturgical Music and Singing   195
    DOROTHEA HASPELMATH-FINATTI

12 Liturgy and Architecture   214
    GILLES DROUIN

13 Liturgy, Icons, and Images   232
    NATALIE CARNES

Part IV Liturgy and the Life of the Churches

14 Liturgy, the Body, and the Senses   251
    BRIDGET NICHOLS

15 Liturgy, Spirituality, and Piety   268
    JOB GETCHA

16 Liturgy and Pastoral Ministry   283
    SAMUEL GOYVAERTS

17 Liturgy and the Proclamation of the Word   299
    CAS WEPENER

18 Liturgy and Ecumenism   317
    THOMAS POTT

19 Liturgy and the Religions of the World   335
    MARIANNE MOYAERT

Part V The Study of Liturgy

20 Liturgical Texts   355
    JULIETTE J. DAY

21 Liturgy as Ritual (and Prayer)   369
    KIMBERLY HOPE BELCHER

22 Liturgical Theology   389
    NATHAN G. JENNINGS

Bibliography   405
Names Index   415
Concepts and Places Index   419

Tables

3.1 Family Tree of High-Impact Reformation Liturgies   43
3.2 Reformation Liturgies of Luther, Zwingli, Calvin, and Cranmer   46
10.1 Periods of the Roman Liturgical Year   186
10.2 Periods of the East Syrian Liturgical Season   187
10.3 West Syrian Liturgical Cycles   187
10.4 Seasons of the Armenian Liturgical Year   188
10.5 Seasons of the Maronite Liturgical Year   190
21.1 Adapted from the List of Ritual Characteristics in Grimes, *Ritual Criticism*   372

Contributors

Stefanos Alexopoulos, Catholic University of America
Kimberly Hope Belcher, University of Notre Dame
Harald Buchinger, Universität Regensburg
Natalie Carnes, Duke University
Juliette J. Day, University of Helsinki
Gilles Drouin, Institut Catholique de Paris
Joris Geldhof, University of Notre Dame
Job Getcha, Metropolitan of Pisidia
Samuel Goyvaerts, Tilburg University
Katherine E. Harmon, Saint John's University
Dorothea Haspelmath-Finatti, Universität Wien
Nathan G. Jennings, Seminary of the Southwest
Clare V. Johnson, Australian Catholic University
Maryann Madhavathu, Mount Carmel Generalate
Marianne Moyaert, Katholieke Universiteit Leuven
Bridget Nichols, University College Dublin
Liborius Olaf Lumma, Universität Innsbruck
Thomas Pott, Pontificio Ateneo Sant'Anselmo
Patrick Prétot, Institut Catholique de Paris
Melanie C. Ross, Yale University
Jan Schnell, Wartburg Theological Seminary
Cas Wepener, Stellenbosch University

Acknowledgments

First and foremost, I would like to express an immense amount of gratitude to all the authors who have contributed to the *Cambridge Companion to Christian Liturgy*. All of them initially reacted to my invitation with enthusiasm. That enthusiasm enabled me to continue to work on the volume, which, as always, turned out to be more complicated once underway than expected at the beginning. It was a great delight to read the authors' texts as their first reader and to learn from their insights and wisdom. I am convinced that their reflections will enlighten many more people, for whom this book is actually written.

I also owe a lot of gratitude to Ana Ashraf, who assisted me with the preparation of the manuscript. Her sense of detail and fine talent for language were indispensable. In the same vein I thank the members of my research group at the Faculty of Theology and Religious Studies at Katholieke Universiteit Leuven, who were, and still are, always understanding and supportive of what I'm doing. It is a privilege to have worked in an environment with so many opportunities for intellectual growth and academic liberty.

In a special way I am additionally mindful of the priest serving the old Saint Paul parish in Ghent, now part of a larger pastoral where my daughters were baptized and where I still go for the Eucharist on Sunday on a regular basis, as long as it lasts, and when I am in the country, . . . If anywhere, I think my liturgical home is there.

Introduction
JORIS GELDHOF

The relevance of Christian liturgy can hardly be underestimated. Christians are present in most of the world's cultures and societies today. Sometimes they are only tiny minorities. Sometimes these minorities are well respected, but the opposite can be equally true. Sometimes they are suppressed and even persecuted. In other cases Christians occupy a majority position, which enables them to celebrate and live their faith in the public realm. This position, which can but may not necessarily go back several centuries, also allows them to be in power and to staff the decision-making bodies at many levels of socio-economic and political life. Still other historical circumstances cause Christians to look back on an influential past and a lost impact. This often results in a fragmented situation with an uncertain outcome, which obviously comes with many challenges, not least for Christians themselves. This scenario is particularly the case in so-called secular cultures, characterized by sometimes dramatically rapid processes of pluralization and detraditionalization. The point, however, is that Christians in all these different situations have somehow inherited ways of celebrating their faith and continue to develop ritual practices, worship patterns, and a corresponding prayer life. What unites Christians in so many cultures and societies is not so much what and how they think but rather a consistency of a certain liturgical praxis. In a way, liturgy more than doctrinal contents or moral convictions determines Christian identity. The liturgy's relevance consists in nothing other than constituting the deepest core of the Christian religion.

In the light of these observations, the present *Cambridge Companion to Christian Liturgy* aims to provide a comprehensive study of the meaning of Christian worship by shedding light on the intriguingly complex history it went through (with a focus on the Mediterranean and European regions, where it has historically been the strongest), the fundamental and constitutive elements of which it consists, its embodiment in concrete practices and artistic expressions, and its unique importance for the life of the Churches, as well as its creative potential for theological thinking and research. The volume deliberately combines a solid introduction into the basics of the liturgy with a wealth of impetuses for independent thinking. It moreover opts for a consistent and synthetic *theological* approach. This means at least three things. First, it considers liturgy not only from a neutral or outsiders' perspective or from a mere historical or anthropological viewpoint but also as a reality in close relation to divine revelation and a wide variety of ecclesial traditions. Second, it subscribes to a broad and inclusive vision about theologians actively engaging with other areas of expertise, whereby interdisciplinarity is not a contemporary academic fashion but something actually, and fruitfully, practiced all over the line. Third, it overcomes denominational, methodological, and ideological narrowmindedness by relying on decent academic scholarship and thoroughgoing dialogue among experts.

For there is no reason in denying that, in recent decades, the field of liturgical studies has undergone a rapid development of constructive exchanges with other areas, such as ritual studies, social sciences, gender studies, performance arts, postcolonial discourses, critical theories, socio-economic and moral issues, practical and empirical theologies, and so on. These interactions have achieved many interesting insights and results, and they have undoubtedly enriched the study of Christian worship. At the same time, however, they have also raised the critical question about the specificity of liturgical studies, its primary objects and its methods: What is it that liturgical scholars – with their different capacities and competences as historians, systematicians, and practitioners – can uniquely contribute to the conversation about the meaning and role of Christianity for humanity and the world? Correspondingly, while realizing the deep impact and crucial import of multiple approaches and various discourses in contemporary academia from which liturgical studies cannot stay absent, the present volume first and foremost centers on *the specifics of Christian liturgy* itself.

The distinctively theological approach for which the present volume opts is made concrete throughout the individual parts and contributions inasmuch as the authors have paid sufficient attention to one or more of several clusters:

(i) liturgy as both commemoration (*anamnesis*) and imitation (*mimesis*) or, in other words, liturgy as the enactment of past events by way of memorial actions and imitations, implying a distinctive understanding of "time";

(ii) the pervasive idea of "mystery" and the multiple ways in which it is embodied in matter, actions, sounds, texts, images, gestures, and habits;
(iii) liturgy as standing at the intersection of an upward movement (*anabasis*) and a downward movement (*katabasis*), including human actions directed toward the divine and the belief that God equally works for humankind, or, put differently, liturgy as meant to be worshiping God and sanctifying the world simultaneously;
(iv) liturgy as representing – and maybe even illuminating – fundamental tensions within the human condition – for example, between memory and hope, the already and the not-yet, the present and the promise, the actual and the unfulfilled, pain and relief, boundedness and liberation, creation and redemption;
(v) liturgy also as incarnating (and undergoing) tensions between reality and eschatological norms – that is, between how things are (lived) and how things should be (ideally);
(vi) liturgy as naturally involving various human faculties, including not only the cognitive ones, such as reason and the intellect, but also the imagination, the senses, affections, emotions, passions, and desires.

Furthermore, it is crucial for the set-up of the present volume that certain conceptual and ideological binaries are overcome. Certain debates and controversies over liturgy (e.g., over what is a "good" versus a "bad" service, or over the value of traditional forms) are not avoided but named with a view to clarifying the rationale behind various theories, standpoints, and opinions. The authors of individual contributions, however, do not give evidence of any partisanship promoting one vision over against another one. Rather, they seek common ground in the realization that the one who deals with liturgy deals with a very delicate and deeply human matter, and that people's attachment to liturgical forms above anything else deserves respect. In other words, ossified oppositions between conservative versus liberal ideas, between liturgy as mere conviviality versus liturgy as solemn ceremony, or between pro and contra inculturation have no place in the present volume. Instead, the authors advocate an open and tolerant view, based on profound academic scholarship, and an overall irenic attitude vis-à-vis liturgical variety and diversity.

The material covered in the present book is subdivided into five parts with twenty-two contributions in total. The logic behind these five parts is the following. Each contribution is based on a sound survey of the major events and developments that determined the history of Christian worship, which is the major focus of Part I. The four constitutive dimensions of which the liturgy consists (Eucharist, sacraments, hours, year) are presented in a systematic fashion in Part II. In addition, it is shown how these four axes and the ethos around them have always been embodied in artistic forms, auditive as well as visual and tactile, and in buildings, which explains the central attention for the connection between art and liturgy in Part III. In and through these multiple shapes and forms and celebrations, the liturgy establishes an encompassing reality which in many and diverse ways impacts people's lives and personal identities, their communities and self-perceptions, and the role Christians (want to) play in the world and in society at large. Therefore, the multiple relations between the liturgy and the life of the churches form the subject of Part IV. This encompassing liturgical reality requires due study and understanding, not only through the texts liturgical traditions have yielded or through the appearance of Christian rituals and prayer services but also theologically. Part V closes this volume with a threefold focus on text, ritual, and theology.

Part I

Liturgy Throughout the Ages

1 Liturgy in Early Christianity
HARALD BUCHINGER

The origins and early development of Christian liturgy are mostly shrouded in darkness due to a significant dearth of sources. Liturgical manuscripts do not emerge before the fourth century and remain rare throughout Late Antiquity. Prayers preserved on papyri attest to a great diversity of traditions; hymns are attributed to authors of the fourth and subsequent centuries, especially in Latin, Greek, and Syriac. In some cases – especially Armenian and Georgian translations of texts from Late Antique Jerusalem, the "mother of all churches" – the contents of later books can be confidently dated to the fifth to seventh centuries. For most celebrations, however, one can look for scattered hints in patristic works. Apocrypha – not least acts of apostles – contain descriptions of rituals that may often mirror early Christian practice. Particularly valuable are catechetical and mystagogical expositions of the sacraments of Christian initiation, including the Eucharist, which emerge in the later fourth century along with homilies for various liturgical feasts.

The so-called (pseud-)apostolic Church Orders writings constitute a uniquely informative and at the same time problematic genre that proliferated from earliest times onward. These were intended to regulate community life, often with special attention to liturgy. While they contain the first extant prayer texts, account must be taken of a tension between description and prescription, and in many cases it is unclear when and where, if at all, the proposed texts and rituals were actually observed. Governing ecclesial practice was also the task of synodal and conciliar documents, which frequently dealt with liturgical questions. Although monks and nuns often abstained from the liturgical life of secular congregations, some monastic rules and lives are key documents of liturgical history.

Even where clearer pictures emerge, diversity is certainly the most important characteristic of early liturgy; almost every witness can be complemented with evidence of divergent practice and theology. Still more important is the observation that the formative phases of early Christian liturgy are the effect of several categorical disruptions: The destruction of the Temple in Jerusalem compelled Christians and Jews alike to reconceptualize their worship in un-cultic categories; for the former, the death of Christ and the belief in his resurrection constituted a qualitatively new relation to God. In this period, some basic patterns of Christian liturgy emerge (1). When Christianity acquired freedom of religion and became the public cult of the Roman Empire after the Constantinian Turn, not only did its liturgy grow and develop through the influx of large masses of new Christians and the expansion of its format, but it also had to assume the unprecedented socio-religious task of securing the well-being of the commonwealth through proper veneration of God. This new function and the concern about orthodoxy fostered tendencies of standardization of some liturgical forms within ongoing diversity (2). Regional and linguistic variety, political history, doctrinal dissociations, and hierarchical divisions resulted in the consolidation of differentiated rites in East and West with distinctive shapes and forms in their rituals and texts. Only at the end of this process do comprehensive codifications of liturgical corpora occur; extant witnesses are often the result of a transregional reception process that mostly involved on the one hand a wishful construction of the received tradition and on the other its hybridization with other local liturgies and also later developments (3).

In addition to elucidating basic patterns of Christian worship, this chapter therefore explores the interplay between continuity and discontinuity in early liturgical history. Methodologically, "comparative liturgy" aimed at reconstructing common roots underlying received traditions and at disclosing patterns of liturgical development (traditionally but misleadingly labeled "laws"). Furthermore, the "genetical method" that illuminates the shape of liturgy that has grown throughout history has to be complemented with a "critical method," which investigates streams of tradition that have dried up or have been stopped, thus revealing alternatives to historically successful developments. Moreover, liturgical sources are not only aids for the execution of certain services; they may be biased products of certain authorities and need not necessarily mirror actual practice. Last, but not least, formalized liturgy is only a small part of the ritual life of Christians; the "lived religion" of what has been labeled the "Second Church" always encompassed practices beyond hierarchical control. These include those denounced as "syncretistic" or even "magic" – foreign appellations that never matched the self-conception in historical reality. Liturgical historiography should not only expound the intended experience of competent subjects of celebrations implied in the official codification but also investigate the actual experience of the concrete historical subjects.

TOWARD A DISTINCTIVELY CHRISTIAN LITURGY

Un-Cultic Conceptualization of Early Christian Liturgy and Its Cultic Reinterpretation

Christianity did not originate as a separate religion from the outset. Although according to Acts 11:26, "the disciples were first called Christians in Antioch," it took a while until they dissociated from Judaism and integrated converts from the Gentiles. Of the first believers it is written that they "continued day by day with one accord in the temple and broke bread in their homes."[1] In this context, the practice of characteristic rituals or the act of lending distinct interpretations to established rituals did not necessarily imply abandoning traditional practices. Even the typological application of elements from the biblical and Jewish cult to the new Christian reality does not devalue their original meaning. On the contrary, the fact of their being transferred confirms their importance.

Nevertheless, for Jesus' followers, his crucifixion and their belief in his resurrection changed everything. On the one hand, they had to make sense of the horrible event of the passion within the belief in the God of Israel, whom Jesus had called his father. This implied turning to religious institutions, especially the cult at the Temple in Jerusalem, its biblical elements and foundations: sacrifice and expiation, Passover and atonement, (high-) priesthood. On the other hand, the uniqueness of the Christ-event[2] made every cultic mediation "once for all" (Hebr 7:27, 9:12, 10:10) and in principle obsolete – a productive thought not least in view of the destruction of the Second Temple by the Romans in 70 CE and the cessation of its cult. It is, however, important to acknowledge that the reconceptualization of a templeless religion was a challenge and an achievement not only for and of early Christianity but also for and of contemporary Judaism. The so-called Parting of the Ways was a complex process that in recent research is not conceived in terms of a mother–daughter relation but rather with the metaphor of twin sisters.

---

[1] Acts 2:46.
[2] Cf. Hebr 7–10.

It is striking that cultic terms are never applied to Christian rituals in the New Testament. Terms and concepts related to either the Jewish temple in Jerusalem or the Greco-Roman sanctuaries, their inventory, especially altars, their personnel – particularly priests – and their various sacrifices and other performances are never used to refer to Christian ritual practice. They occur only in different ways. In objective language, they continue to be used to describe exactly these Jewish or pagan cults. Metaphorically, they are adduced as biblical means of theological interpretation, on the one hand for Christ and the Christ-event, especially the passion, and on the other for the Christians and the new reality of their life and conduct (temple, sacrifice, unleavened breads, reasonable service ...).

Only in a second, albeit early, move were cultic elements from the Bible – that is, the later so-called Old Testament – employed to interpret Christian rituals. Cultic reinterpretation of Christian liturgy of this kind can first be observed when the Eucharist is addressed as "pure offering" with reference to Mal 1:11 in Didachè 14, thus metaphorically applying biblical terminology to the service of breaking bread and giving thanks as a whole. From the middle of the second century onward, the designation of the Eucharist as "offering" can relate to the service in its entirety, the nonverbal act of bringing the gifts, and the verbal act of the Eucharistic prayer. While Christian prophets and teachers are called "your high priests" in Didachè 13 in order to justify the non-metaphorical command to give them the first fruits, and the bishops and deacons are subsequently said to "serve (*leitourgéō*) the service of prophets and teachers,"[3] a first attempt to interpret the Christian offices of bishops, presbyters, and deacons in the light of the biblical cult is not undertaken until 1 Clement 40–42, 44. Only in the allegorical exposition of every Christian reality in cultic terms by the Alexandrian theologians, especially Origen (d. after 250 CE), clergy too were reconceived as "priests" in the biblical sense (along with the Christians, the soul, and so forth). In the same period, bishops were first described as "high priests" in writings that promoted their authority (especially in the Syriac *Didascalia*) – a typology that became prominent in later ordination prayers.

The Passover had long been used to make sense of Christ's passion (1 Cor 5:7; John 19:36) before it lent not only its name but also its motifs and theology to the oldest, central, and in fact for a long time sole Christian feast: Easter. The reinterpretation of the church building as

---

[3] Didachè 15.

temple and of its sanctuary as Holy of Holies and altar began only after the Constantinian Turn in the fourth century. While Eusebius, a theological grandson of Origen, was well aware that he was giving an allegorical interpretation, in later authors this hermeneutical frame collapsed, and temple categories were used in plain objective language to describe the Christian church building and its furniture. Mystery language further contributed to a cultic reinterpretation of Christian initiation from the second century on and particularly of the Eucharist in later periods. From earliest times, the complex interplay between cultic and un-cultic perceptions has been one of the most productive tensions in Christian liturgical theology.

Baptism
Almost all strands of early Christian writings presuppose baptism as a fundamental initiation ritual. While various kinds of ablutions and immersions existed in the biblical religion and Second Temple Judaism, its closest parallel is the baptism preached and practiced by John the Baptist, from which Christian baptism also took the notion of remission of sins. A variety of baptismal theologies occur already in the writings that were to become the New Testament, most significantly rebirth and dying (and rising) with Christ; later on, illumination became a prominent metaphor.

From the earliest sources, several fundamentally different types of ritual can be distinguished. The Mediterranean tradition, which soon became common in East and West, celebrates the transition from a past and an environment perceived as sinful to the new reality of Christian life. Therefore, in this context, baptism is preceded by an increasingly complex phase of detachment later solemnized as catechumenate and accompanied with exorcistic rites, which culminates in renouncing Satan and his realm. By contrast, in the Syrian tradition, a predominantly positive concept modeled on Christ's baptism and on adoption by God gives prominence to a messianic unction of the head which often preceded and sometimes even replaced water baptism. Only as a result of intricate, non-monolinear developments and cross-fertilization did the classical shape of initiation become increasingly common in the post-Constantinian church, in which an anointment of the whole body precedes the water ritual of baptism, which in turn is followed by a consignation and unction of the head. Whereas baptismal foot washing was practiced in certain regions and defended as an integral part of the "mystery" by Ambrose of Milan (d. 397) with reference to John 13, it is doubtful if it was ever conceived as an independent ritual of initiation.

Eucharist

Early Christian meals share ritual patterns with Late Antique Greco-Roman culture; the earliest instances of the Eucharistic celebration belong to the symposium type. The structure of the meal, with its ritual elements and the prayers codified in Didachè 9–10, resembles conventions palpable in later Jewish sources to an extent that a genetic relationship cannot be denied. However, the *"birkat ha-mazon* (blessing of the meal)" and earliest Christian after-table prayers have a fundamentally different function in the logic of the ritual than Eucharistic prayers that precede the consumption of the sanctified food. A second type emerges in the second century: In the mass-type celebration, the meal is reduced to a symbolic token; the various rituals of breaking bread and sharing the cup are contracted to a single ritual action of taking bread and wine together, thanksgiving, (breaking the bread), and distribution of the gifts. The concentration of Eucharistic praying before communion affected its character (and, by implication, the role of the presider): Only in this position can the central speech-act of thanksgiving assume the function of changing the matter of the Eucharist. In the mass-type celebration, the Eucharistic action is furthermore preceded by a Liturgy of the Word consisting of reading Scripture, expounding it, and reciting a common prayer, and is often concluded with a kiss of peace.

The distinction between symposium and mass-type celebrations of the Eucharist is, however, not a simple dichotomy: Further occasions and diverse ritual frameworks are provided by the baptismal Eucharist in which initiation culminated, the paschal Eucharist marking the breaking of the fast at Christianity's most ancient and important feast, and Eucharistic meals at tombs; "ascetic Eucharists" and the integration of or abstention from certain foodstuffs confirm and contradict sympotic patterns.

Earliest Eucharistic prayer texts are transmitted in pseudapostolic Church Orders, most notably the Didachè and the so-called *Apostolic Tradition*. Along with scattered hints in patristic sources, particularly important and diverse evidence comes from apocryphal acts of apostles (especially those of John and Thomas); liturgical manuscripts emerge only from the fourth century on. Although "conventions" are referred to already in the third century by Origen, early Eucharistic prayers could have a variety of forms and be addressed not only to God the Father but also to the Son and to the Holy Spirit. Basic elements – not necessarily all in combination from the outset – include thanksgiving, praise, and petition; in the course of the third century, expressions of offering have been added. The "Lord's Day" is the original occasion for the "Lord's Supper"; from the earliest sources on, baptism and, if necessary, repentance are prerequisites of participation.[4]

Feasts

The weekly celebration of the "Lord's Day" goes back to earliest times, as does the practice of fasting on Wednesday and Friday.[5] Since Jesus' crucifixion occurred on the eve of Passover (John) or on the day after (synoptics), it made sense to identify him with the Passover lamb[6] and also to generate meaning in the cruel and outwardly desperate event through typological exegesis. Nevertheless, an annual Christian Easter feast is not documented before the second century, when some churches continued to celebrate on the Jewish date, the Fourteenth of Nisan (hence "Quartodecimans"), while others observed the "first day of the week," that is, the "Lord's Day" or Sunday, on which all gospels agree that the empty tomb was found. Regardless of the date, breaking the fast was the core symbol of the celebration. Whereas for the "dominical" tradition, the transition "from darkness to light" seems to be constitutive,[7] the Quartodeciman practice, being an "anti-Pascha" in opposition to the Jewish celebration, could contrast fasting with the Jewish banquet and the beginning of the Christian feast with its end. While a fast of variable duration is a universal constituent of every Christian Easter celebration, a subsequent joyful Pentecost period of fifty days belongs to its dominical version.

Feasts of martyrs occur typically at the exact place of the burial and on the date of the martyrdom, which was understood as the heavenly birthday. Only secondarily did their exchange become a means of networking between different regions and communities.

Daily Prayer

The exhortation to "pray without ceasing"[8] and the search for biblical precedents of pious practice soon led to various patterns that highlighted morning and evening as hinges between day and night. In addition, there were prayer moments at the third, sixth, and ninth

---

[4] Cf. Didachè 14.
[5] Didachè 14 and 8.
[6] 1 Cor 5:7; Jn 19:36 quoting Ex 12:10.46.
[7] Melito, Pasch. 68; cf. the Passover Haggadah.
[8] 1 Thess 5:17.

hours along with prayer at night. However, no universally accepted order is to be assumed in the early centuries.

Further Celebrations

Along with practices of daily penance, a solemn reconciliation of sinners who had separated themselves from the church was established and increasingly accepted, though not without rigorist resistance. While laying on of hands and prayer are mentioned already in New Testament writings, formal ordination formularies appear only centuries later, at first in the so-called Apostolic Tradition. Church participation in weddings took a while to become standard and remained controversial for centuries. Song and prayer accompanied Christian funerals. A few witnesses suggest that dance-hymns belonged to the ritual repertoire of Early Christians. Less spectacular but much more relevant are the widely found phenomena of so-called popular or lived religion, private devotion, and religious practice beyond formalized congregations and the control of the official church and its clergy.

THE CONSTANTINIAN TURN AND THE ESTABLISHMENT OF AN IMPERIAL CHURCH

Although the precise character of the Constantinian Turn is debated in historiography, its impact on liturgical history cannot be overestimated. Under Constantine (d. 337), Christian liturgy became public in a double sense: Through the Milan protocol of 313 it profited from freedom of cult after periods of persecution. In subsequent legislation, the emperor also imposed onto Christian worship a new socio-religious function formerly attributed to the public cults of Greco-Roman religion: securing the well-being of the public commonwealth. Although it took centuries even after Theodosius I (d. 395) declared Christianity the state religion and ordered the closing down of "pagan" temples, the new format and function profoundly transformed Christian liturgy. Larger spaces with monumental furniture accommodated a hierarchically stratified congregation with highly differentiated ranks and roles; movement developed into solemn processions both within the church and in the public space. The clergy was professionalized and received privileges of court ritual: Not only gestures of reverence and distinctive vestments and badges but also the use of light and incense were adopted from civic ceremonies. Speech-acts had to be formalized, and not only for acoustic reasons; the care for efficacy and concerns about the orthodoxy of the new public cult furthered its standardization at the expense of freedom and improvisation.

The gradual abolition of the ancient Greco-Roman cults and the transferal of their function to Christian liturgy boosted the cultic reinterpretation and sacralization of the latter and stimulated the application of mystery language, especially to the sacraments of initiation and the Eucharist. In parallel with the identification of Christian worship as public cult, expressions of personal piety and rituals of "lived religion" flourished: pilgrimage, the use of relics, and practices of veneration, intercession, and healing that involved appeals not only to deceased but also to living saints.

Initiation

The influx of masses of converted people into the church only superficially, if at all, required standardized procedures for instructing converts and securing a minimum of knowledge and ritual competence through pre-baptismal catechesis and post-baptismal mystagogy. The developed catechumenate can be seen as symptomatic not only of a flourishing but also of crisis in the system of Christian initiation.

At the same time, several mystagogies convey a fairly complete picture of baptism and Eucharist; whereas no texts of sacramental prayers for the blessing of water (and oils) are transmitted in these contexts, Eucharistic prayers are outlined or even quoted in extenso. In spite of significant variety and diverse developments, common patterns of baptismal and pre- and post-baptismal rites emerge: Exorcisms, unctions, and ultimately a renunciation of Satan prepare the initiate for baptism. Like the receiving of white garments, the handing over of lit candles may illustrate the metaphor of "enlightening." As a result, nearly all rites adopt an unction of the head with perfumed oil, which is interpreted as a "seal" and can be understood in a Pneumatological sense. Lasting differences include one relating to a verbal core element: Whereas in much of the West a trinitarian interrogatory confession of faith accompanies the threefold water-rite, a common element in the East is a passive baptismal formula invoking the name of the Trinity.

During Late Antiquity, the spread of infant baptism further detached personal faith from the celebration of the sacrament. In most places, there was hardly any attempt to adapt the ritual designed for the initiation of adults for the subjects that could not speak for themselves. Almost all baptismal formularies transmitted in later manuscripts therefore contain a fossilized liturgy in which much of the meaning has collapsed, along with the existential process of conversion and the belief that it had once accompanied and informed.

Eucharist

The post-Constantinian century saw the almost universal reception of the mass-type Eucharistic celebration. Although it took time for the reading orders accompanying the establishment of festal cycles to gradually evolve, in the Liturgy of the Word, fixed structures of readings do appear. Psalmody, often with a refrain, occurs as part of the readings block. Further chants accompany processions: at first during communion, later on also for the entrance at the very beginning, and for the transfer of the gifts in the East and their collection and preparation in the West at the beginning of the liturgy of the Eucharist.

A progressive standardization of Eucharistic prayers can be observed within diverse patterns; designations such as "Antiochene" and "Alexandrian" anaphoras signify typological rather than regional varieties. Praise culminates in the biblical Sanctus in all traditions from the fourth century on. Summaries of salvation history are integrated into the anamnetic part, which in the developed liturgies almost invariably include the institution narrative. Assuring the identity of the celebration with Jesus' iteration, "Do this in remembrance of me," may have become a catechetic need. The integration of credal formulae and an emphasis on the role of the Holy Spirit in the epiclesis reflect doctrinal developments and the concern for orthodoxy. At various structural points of the Eucharistic prayer, intercessions for various categories of the living and the dead articulate the communion either of the recipients or of those offering the gifts. While thanksgiving after receiving communion may appear to be the heir of pristine after-table prayers, other minor prayers at other points in the mass accrue only gradually.

In Eucharistic theology, the interpretation of the Eucharist not only as offering but also as sacrifice became widespread, as did the interpretation of the Eucharistic table as altar, of the church building as temple, and of the presiding bishop or presbyter as priest in the common religious sense. It appears that often the awareness ceded that these categories apply to Christian liturgy only secondarily, by way of exegetical interpretation and thus in a metaphorical way. Applying the notion and terminology of an "awe-inspiring mystery" went along with erecting physical barriers between nave and sanctuary and – especially in the East – with hiding significant moments behind curtains. Ancient Eucharistic prayer traditions, most notably the anaphoras, are always formulated in the first person plural of the assembled church that is the subject of the celebration. However, in some late accretions to the minor prayers of the Eucharist, presiders sometimes no longer pray in the name of the assembled congregation as a whole but in the name of the officiating clergy making the offering for the people.

Festal Cycles
Soon after the Constantinian Turn, imperial building activity in Jerusalem and its environs turned the holy city and Palestine into a memorial landscape; pilgrims seeking to celebrate "according to time and place" gave rise to a categorically new way of commemorating particular moments of salvation history. Taking the Bible not only as a guidebook to sacred sites but also as a calendar according to which the narrative could be recalled and reenacted in annual repetition, various feasts and celebrations were invented. Insofar as elements of the biblical story are imitated in dramatic rituals, this innovative style has been labeled "mimetic." Although progressive historicization, particularization, and materialization can in the course of time be observed in these celebrations, liturgy is always more than a historicizing reenactment: In liturgical commemoration, the narrative is reflected through intertexts from both testaments. Psalmody, in which the congregation participates with refrains, allows identification with and appropriation of biblical experiences. Hermeneutically sophisticated intertextuality and dramatic rituals are interwoven with sacramental celebrations that imply different modes of participation in the theological contents.

This has resulted in three partially overlapping festal cycles: The Easter cycle moves with the Easter date that is determined to be the Sunday after the full moon following the spring equinox, and feasts centered around the Nativity have their fixed date in the calendar, as have the saints' celebrations that over time become increasingly numerous and in many places even inflationary. The creation of lectionaries providing appropriate readings and psalms for the various occasions is an art often inspired by typological exegesis; hymnography and chant become popular means of expounding the differentiated festal contents. Proper prayers add to the complexity of liturgical formularies, though not in all rites.

Along with the popularity of pilgrimage and the cultural transfer that came in its wake, catechetical convenience may have contributed to the success of the liturgical year; it may be no coincidence that the major feasts of the annual cycle celebrate the same basic contents of Christian faith that became integrated into the Eucharistic prayers in the same period and thus were recapitulated every Sunday.

Celebration at various places identified with biblical sites in or around Jerusalem – or at locations representing them in other contexts – is a driving force in the development of stational liturgy characteristic of urban Christianity. In large cities where different congregations gather in various churches – most notably Rome – presiding at different places in the course of the year is a way for the bishop to demonstrate and implement his superintendence over the whole local church. A third formative principle of stational liturgy is the celebration of saints' days at their tombs. When this urban liturgy is later exported to lesser contexts, churches are sometimes represented by altars; more often, the stational system collapses into a mere calendar: Places become dates, and many feasts become mere formularies in the calendar.

Liturgy of the Hours

Although frequent prayer, not least at key hours of day and night, was a concern of numerous third-century authors, a formalized Liturgy of the Hours emerges only after the Constantinian Turn. The classic distinction between "Cathedral" – that is, urban congregational office – and "Monastic" Liturgy of the Hours is of heuristic value, although they rarely occur in pure form. Late Antique monasticism is a multifaceted phenomenon of different life- and prayer-styles ranging from solitary hermitism to strictly organized communal life, and the hybrid liturgy of urban monastics serving at regular churches is of particular importance. While the relevance of more extensive horaria of "everlasting praise" and "sleepless" monks and nuns is not to be underestimated, the formal curriculum of seven canonical hours per day (justified with Ps 119 [118]:164) in addition to nocturnal vigils becomes standard in East and West: the "cardinal" hours of Lauds and Vespers at morning and evening, Prime, Terce, Sext, and None as little hours during the day, Compline as its conclusion at bedtime, and the vigil at the beginning, in the middle, or toward the end of night. Whereas the regular night watch is a typical exercise of ascetics and has an eschatological flavor, secular congregations also celebrated vigils on Sundays in commemoration of the resurrection or on the occasion of martyrs' and other important saints' feasts, along with Easter – the "mother of all holy vigils"[9] – Epiphany, Christmas, or Pentecost. In many traditions, these nights – most significantly Easter – have become regular occasions for baptism.

---

[9] Augustine, *Sermo* 219.

Vigils are apt occasions for reading substantial portions of the Bible. Otherwise, the twofold structure of psalmody complemented with prayer forms the backbone of all offices. Different choices and hermeneutics can be discerned according to the distinction between "Monastic" and "Cathedral" – that is, congregational daily worship. In the "Cathedral office," select psalms appropriate to the time of day are repeated daily: Ps 51 (50); 63 (62) and 148–150 – the "Lauds" that gave the office its name – in the morning, Ps 141 (140) and in several traditions Ps 104 (103) in the evening. The "Monastic office" tends to recite psalms regardless of their content in their biblical sequence; in many orders, it becomes the rule to consider the psalter as a pensum that is to be persolved in regular turns, at least once in the course of a week.

Especially in secular and hybrid usage, nonverbal symbols of kindling light in the evening – accompanied by verbal elements, most prominently the hymn "O Gladsome Light" – and burning incense in ritualization of Ps 141 (140):2 become widespread and give Vespers a characteristic flavor. The ritualization of the metaphor that the believer's "prayer should be set forth before you, and the lifting up of my hands as an evening sacrifice" underscores the cultic dimension of the Liturgy of the Hours.

CODIFICATION OF DIFFERENTIATED RITES IN EAST AND WEST

In the course of Late Antiquity, the diversity of observances takes concrete form in various rites of East and West that have a distinctive character but also share common ritual patterns.

Consolidation and Dissociation of Local Churches, Denominations, and Uses

The liturgical life of the early church is characterized by great regional diversity. Its development was determined by geographical and historical circumstances, with cultural centers exerting influence on their hinterlands. Megalopolises such as Alexandria and Antioch in the East and Rome in the West coined liturgical styles: Alexandrian liturgy spread south along the Nile from Lower to Upper Egypt and to Ethiopia, which, however, developed a rite peculiar to itself. Much of the rest of the Christian East belongs to the Antiochene realm, which reached east as far as India and, at times, China and Mongolia.

Significant borders also affect liturgical history: The Syriac-speaking Church of the East in Sasanian Persia outside the empire underwent a largely independent development and maintained pristine traditions and a semitic flavor. Likewise, the Armenian Rite found its own identity between Jerusalem and Antioch on the one hand and the Church of the East on the other, not without integrating Western influences from the Crusades onward. In turn, political power increased the impact of a local use: The rite of the Eastern capital Constantinople, originally a variant of the West–Syrian liturgical realm of Antioch, became dominant throughout the empire in a long process that lasted well into the second millennium. In the West, the hegemony of the Roman Rite was partly a consequence of secular power policy: When the Carolingians aimed at supplanting older Gallican usages with the Roman Rite, a hybridized Romano–Frankish liturgy became standard in much of the West. Its propagation on the Iberian peninsula followed the Reconquista and the centralist church–political agenda of the centralist reforms of Pope Gregory VII (d. 1085). Only in Milan and – to a restricted extent – in Toledo did local non-Roman Rites survive into modern times, not least on account of respect to profiled archbishops of the sixteenth-century reform era. However, local variants of the Roman Rite persisted in many places centuries after the council of Trent, though the revival of neo-Gallican liturgies in eighteenth-century France is an idiosyncratic phenomenon that in its own way was determined by political interests. Within these coordinates, Late Antique Jerusalem played its own part, especially in the development of festal liturgies that originated in mimetic celebrations "according to time and place."

Geographical, historical, and political circumstances were not the only conditions for the differentiation of various rites. Agreement or disagreement with doctrinal decisions, especially of the great ecumenical councils, led to the separation of churches: The Church of the East did not accept the councils of Ephesus (431) and Chalcedon (451). Dissensus about the latter was the cause for the consolidation of non-Chalcedonian churches in the West–Syrian and Coptic realm as well as – eventually, as a result of a complex historical process – in the Armenian church. While for those not following the doctrine adopted by the empire, their innate liturgy became an identity-marker. The "Melkites" – that is, those accepting the emperor's decisions – took over the Byzantine Rite at later points in history. Hierarchical divisions (and, much later, unions) contribute to the complexity of the situation. Rites, churches, and languages are therefore not coextensive. The same rite can be celebrated not only in many diverse languages but also in separated churches. Conversely, various rites are often celebrated in the same language or in churches united by hierarchy.

Last, but not least, liturgical history is not only a matter of secular churches ruled by bishops. Solemn rituals at cathedrals have a different form from celebrations presided over by presbyters in lesser places in the same rite. Monasticism of various types has always added to liturgical diversity. Eremitic, semi-eremitic, and coenobial – that is, communitarian monastic ascetics – generated or adapted their own ways of worship. Whereas, for example, in the East, abstention from non-biblical hymnography can be observed in early Eastern monasticism (before monks became the avant-garde of hymnographic compositions), in the West, the monastic rule attributed to St. Benedict became the backdoor through which "Ambrosian" hymnography entered the Roman Rite.

Genuine diversity affects all aspects of liturgy; within common patterns, distinctive styles especially of chanting and praying (not only in the Eucharistic anaphora) led to differences between the various rites. In the Eucharistic liturgy especially, the famous "soft points"[10] were particularly prone to characteristic ritual development: firstly, at the beginning; secondly, between the Liturgy of the Word and the anaphora; and, thirdly, around communion.

In most cases, comprehensive documentation in the form of liturgical books emerges only in the Middle Ages. The formative phase in which the Eastern and Western rites took their shape is a kind of latency period of liturgical history not directly elucidated by sources. Apart from scattered hints and very rare manuscripts, only the methods of "comparative liturgy" afford inferences on the actual shaping of the received traditions.

The Early Medieval Codification of Established Traditions and Its Multiple Hybridization

In most places, liturgical manuscripts only survive from a period when the dissociation and consolidation of liturgical rites had come to a certain completion. This is of course not to suggest that the pace of change stopped at any point. On the contrary, codification more often attests to development and hybridization than it does to pure preservation of a certain past. It is an irony of history that from most major centers no physical books at all are transmitted from much of the first millennium and in some

[10] Robert F. Taft, "How Liturgies Grow: The Evolution of the Byzantine Divine Liturgy," in *Beyond East and West: Problems in Liturgical Understanding*, ed. Robert F. Taft (Rome: Pontifical Oriental Institute, 2001), 203–232.

instances well into the second (which naturally does not mean that inferences from other places or later documents would not allow one to reconstruct the forms and texts used in these centers in earlier periods). Liturgical codification is therefore to a great extent a result of interplay between centers and peripheries. While peripheral witnesses can be more conservative than testimonies from centers of innovative developments, they often also attest to hybridization with earlier regional traditions. Episcopal liturgy can attract peculiar rituals; but at the same time, its rarer celebration and particular stabilization can preserve pristine elements.

The exceptionally well-documented liturgy of Late Antique Jerusalem, for example, is mostly accessible through manuscripts from the closer (Judaean desert and Sinai) or farther periphery (Caucasus), and to a large extent (lectionary, earliest hymnography, much of euchology) exclusively or at least predominantly not in its original Greek but in Armenian and Georgian. In the second millennium, the Rite of the Holy City was hybridized with and ultimately replaced by the Byzantine Rite.

The Byzantine Rite obviously took its shape in a repeated interchange with Palestine before the earliest extant documentation emerges; various ecclesial institutions within the capital certainly followed diverse uses, although their concrete shape is mostly unknown until the end of the first millennium. Again, the earliest manuscripts come from the periphery.

The same is true of Rome. Although, of course, the existence of liturgical manuscripts is attested, all extant early medieval manuscript witnesses of the Roman Rite were written in the Carolingian realm with the aim of the adoption and propagation of Roman papal liturgy. Along with remarkable fidelity to its transmission, its hybridization with earlier Gaulish traditions and its complementation with innovative elements can be observed; although the Frankish construction of Romanness involves creative appropriation, the Romanization and to a certain degree unification of liturgy in the Carolingian realm is an astonishing cultural achievement and a watershed in the history of Western liturgy. This remarkable success came at the expense of the almost total extinction of the older Gaulish Rite insofar as its elements were not absorbed into the Romano–Frankish synthesis; only very few purely Gaulish manuscripts survive. While distinctive lectionary and chant manuscripts from the "Ambrosian" Rite of Milan do exist, most presiders' books betray significant hybridization with the Roman Rite.

Other local liturgies died out without leaving manuscript testimonies at all (which, of course, does not imply that such manuscripts did not exist); this is true, for example, for the Latin liturgy of Roman

North Africa. In still other cases, comprehensive codification appears as a phenomenon of crisis under cultural pressure or the threat of extinction: Extant documentation of the Old Hispanic Rite comes from the period of its successive replacement by the Roman Rite, but ironically even the few manuscripts transmitting the "Old Roman" version of Roman chant come from a period when the Frankish version of the same repertoire known as "Gregorian" – but which in fact mirrors a profound stylistic transformation that went along with its reception by the Carolingians – had become dominant in the whole Latin West.

Tradition is always multifaceted and in constant change. Liturgical history is an interplay between standardization and differentiation; between enrichment, hybridization, and displacement; between growth and impoverishment. Liturgical historiography therefore does not only explain what has come into being and why; it also pays attention to what has been lost – and should acknowledge the manifold ritual expressions of religious life beyond the borders of formal congregations.

For Further Reading

Bärsch, Jürgen, and Benedikt Kranemann (eds.), *Geschichte der Liturgie in den Kirchen des Westens. Rituelle Entwicklungen, theologische Konzepte und kulturelle Kontexte. 1: Von der Antike bis zur Neuzeit* (Münster: Aschendorff, 2018).

Bradshaw, Paul F., *The Search for the Origins of Christian Worship: Sources and Methods for the Study of Early Liturgy* (London: SPCK, 2002).

Bradshaw, Paul F., and Maxwell E. Johnson, *The Origins of Feasts, Fasts and Seasons in Early Christianity* (London/Collegeville, MN: SPCK/Liturgical Press, 2011).

Bukovec, Predrag, *Die frühchristliche Eucharistie* (Tübingen: Mohr Siebeck, 2023).

Ferguson, Everett, *Baptism in the Early Church: History, Theology, and Liturgy in the First Five Centuries* (Grand Rapids, MI: Eerdmans, 2009).

Frank, Georgia, *The Memory of the Eyes: Pilgrims to Living Saints in Christian Antiquity* (Berkeley: University of California Press, 2000).

Heil, Uta (ed.), *From Sun-Day to the Lord's Day: The Cultural History of Sunday in Late Antiquity and the Early Middle Ages* (Turnhout: Brepols, 2022).

Mazza, Enrico, *Mystagogy: A Theology of Liturgy in the Patristic Age* (New York: Pueblo, 1989).

McGowan, Andrew B., *Ancient Christian Worship: Early Church Practices in Social, Historical, and Theological Perspective* (Grand Rapids, MI: Baker, 2014).

Uro, Risto, Juliette J. Day, Richard E. DeMaris, and Rikard Roitto (eds.), *The Oxford Handbook of Early Christian Ritual* (Oxford: Oxford University Press, 2019).

2 Liturgy in the Middle Ages
JORIS GELDHOF

THE REPUTATION OF MEDIEVAL LITURGY: A STILL COMMON STANDARD INTERPRETATION

There are still a lot of biases regarding the Middle Ages in general and medieval liturgy in particular.[1] Even the term "Middle Ages" itself is witness to this: It is said to be an intermediate period, a preferably quickly bridged buffer between two other, more elevated eras. That a time of approximately one thousand years in European history, from about 500 to 1500 CE, is, however, still so called is actually shocking. This is, at least partially, a result of the way rulers and intellectuals in the early modern era looked at the period behind them. People then spoke of a dark time, which fortunately had come to an end. Classical Antiquity was idealized, and people longed to be able to relate directly to the high level of civilization that Greco-Roman culture had achieved. Only in between were those pesky "Middle Ages," with barbarism, illiteracy, chaos, violence, wars, rudeness, unstructuredness, incompetence, and so on.

As for Christian liturgy specifically, many theologians and historians have fallen into the trap of a similar predominantly negative portrayal of the Middle Ages. People still talk about the medieval liturgy with much lack of knowledge and with even less appreciation. There is still a strong prejudice against the liturgy of the medieval period, in particular, that there was in fact a kind of standstill-and-thus-decline in the period between the fall of the Western Roman Empire (late fifth century, 476 to be precise) and that of the Eastern Roman Empire (with

---

[1] I owe a great amount of gratitude to Andrew J. M. Irving from the University of Groningen, who read this chapter's first draft and gave many excellent suggestions on how to improve it.

the fall of Constantinople in the mid-fifteenth century, 1453 to be precise). This has partly but certainly not exclusively to do with a glorification of the fourth century as the golden age of the liturgy, particularly as a result of the Constantinian Turn, when the Christian religion was "finally" able to grow and flourish under the leadership of the Church Fathers in several areas around the Mediterranean basin – that is, especially in the Roman Empire.

Leading scholars, including representatives and advocates of the Liturgical Movement, propagated several variations of this view. A striking example is Theodor Klauser, who, in his widely disseminated and accessibly written survey of the historical development of liturgy in the West, bluntly writes about the period between Popes Gregory the Great and Gregory VII (590–1073): "There is no trace of any real advance in the development of the Roman liturgy during this period."[2] Here and there the liturgical year was indeed tampered with, but "[t]he other things that were undertaken are of little importance."[3] Indeed, according to Klauser, "Gregory's reform was of necessity confined to details of little importance."[4] He criticizes this quasi-stagnation mainly because, in his view, there was essentially a drastic "change in the relationship of the people to the liturgy."[5] "The liturgy," he goes on to explain, "which was once and always should be the common act of the priest and people, became now exclusively a priestly duty."[6] More recently, the famous and able French liturgical historian Marcel Metzger, who even speaks explicitly of a "golden age" of liturgy in Late Antiquity, represents the same view:

> As far as rituals are concerned, by the eighth century, the essentials had been established, and the innovations of the following centuries could affect only secondary or peripheral aspects: development of entrance rites, addition of prayers and songs, decoration of sanctuary, and so on.[7]

---

[2] Theodor Klauser, *A Short History of the Western Liturgy: An Account and Some Reflections*, 2nd ed., trans. John Halliburton (Oxford: Oxford University Press, 1979), 46.
[3] Ibid., 46.
[4] Ibid., 94.
[5] Ibid., 97.
[6] Ibid.
[7] Marcel Metzger, *History of the Liturgy: The Major Stages*, trans. Madeleine Beaumont (Collegeville, MN: Liturgical Press, 1997), 112. Recently, Metzger published a revised version of the French original of his book: *La liturgie dans l'histoire: De la dernière Cène au concile Vatican II* (Paris: Desclée de Brouwer, 2024). Metzger is also the

According to Metzger, the story of the liturgy after Late Antiquity can be quickly told. In essence, it is a matter of solidification and growing rigidity. "Liturgy was becoming a codified worship; pastoral care was no longer its inspiration."[8]

This chapter attempts to undermine prevailing prejudices regarding the medieval liturgy, or at least to avoid discussing it on the assumption that that era was merely a conduit between two culturally, spiritually, and intellectually more advanced periods. After first briefly evoking the immense complexity of the liturgy in the Middle Ages, especially given the multiplicity of historical contexts, the following topics are discussed in turn: the development of liturgical books; the forms of the sacraments of baptism, penance, and the Eucharist after the evaporation of the overarching structure of the Christian initiation of adults; and the veneration of saints and relics.[9] This choice obviously cannot do justice to the Middle Ages as a whole, but we do claim that through this selection of themes, a better understanding of the liturgy in this period can be given.

A DAZZLINGLY COMPLICATED OVERALL PICTURE

The Middle Ages were a whirlwind period with many changes in people's lives, socially, economically, politically, intellectually, administratively, and spiritually. In what follows no more can be done than to point out some salient factors that had a demonstrable impact on the Church's liturgical life. We limit ourselves to five such factors, which obviously are not unrelated but have mutually influenced each other.

First, it should be noted that the spread of Christianity in Europe has had a bumpy history with considerable regional differences.[10] While

---

author of a massive two-volume study on the evolution of Church, its discipline and its worship in the Roman empire.

[8] Metzger, *History of the Liturgy*, 121.

[9] Within the constraints of the present chapter, it is impossible to also look at the development of theological interpretations of the liturgy and the sacraments. For that we refer to compendia in the area of sacramental theology and its history, such as, for example, *The Oxford Handbook of Sacramental Theology*, ed. Hans Boersma and Matthew Levering (Oxford: Oxford University Press, 2015), where there is ample attention to the corresponding evolutions in the Middle Ages.

[10] Peter Heather, *Christendom: The Triumph of a Religion, AD 300–1300* (London: Allen Lane, 2022). It is a pity that Heather does not look specifically at liturgy and does not have a more positive view of faith, but his account of how Christianity "conquered" large parts of Europe in always different and difficult circumstances is definitely well informed and interesting.

Christianity had gained a foothold in most parts of what was the Roman Empire, that was not the case in areas we know today as the Low Countries, large parts of Germany, Scandinavia, Hungary, the Czech Republic, Slovakia, Poland, and the Baltic states. However, Christianity did penetrate Ireland and the British Isles before the fifth century CE, and it was through missionary waves from there that important steps were taken to spread Christianity into northwestern and central Europe, and later further east and north. With that spread of faith into new lands came profound sociocultural upheavals, which greatly influenced the face of liturgy, pastoral, church leadership, and even the design of church buildings, both inside and out.

Second, there was some shifting of the primary bearers of culture, knowledge, and scholarship. This was extended over several centuries; in other words, it did not happen everywhere at the same time and with the same consequences. Whereas monasteries and abbeys were the primary centers where faith and knowledge – as well as liturgy – were preserved and passed on in the early Middle Ages, cities gradually became more and more important. Abbeys were often located in the countryside, cities at crossroads of important trade routes, both overland and via rivers. It was in cities that new religious congregations settled, education was organized, and forms of religious celebration developed, which had previously differed greatly. A certain tension between rural and urban contexts for liturgy is recognizable even today in many places.

Third, far-reaching political decisions put the history of the liturgy and sacraments in a definitive fold. At least two of these should be mentioned here.[11] At the end of the eighth century, there was a request to the pope from Charlemagne to provide him with an authoritative liturgical document for dissemination in his empire. In this way, a uniform liturgy became an instrument in the emperor's policy of unification. Only, with the book he received, he could not do much because it was aimed purely at celebrations in the context of the papal court in Rome and was not fully equipped to be introduced in the context of villages, towns, and abbeys for the whole of an entire liturgical year. So elements were added and changed, all neatly written down. It has been noted that the codification of the liturgy under Charlemagne

---

[11] Pablo Argárate, "Les réformes liturgiques carolingienne et grégorienne," *Questions Liturgiques* 93 (2012): 157–70. For a recent book covering the more general historical picture, without referring to the liturgy specifically, see Steven Vanderputten (ed.), *Rethinking Reform in the Latin West, 10th to Early 12th Century* (Leiden: Brill, 2023).

marked the definitive end of the oral tradition on which the liturgy was based in earlier times.[12]

In the eleventh century, a bitter conflict raged between the emperor and the pope known as the investiture controversy.[13] That included the power to appoint abbots and bishops, which was a sensitive issue at a time when the precise powers of church and state had not yet been defined as they would be later in the modern period. In any case, the pope succeeded in rigging a veritable reform of the ecclesiastical household, as a result of which celibacy for priests was introduced as compulsory, simony was outlawed, papal control of worship was tightened, and Latin was further promoted as the sole language of that worship. A centralization of papal authority went hand in hand with a sacralization of the liturgy. Priests became primarily the ministers and dispensers of the sacraments, while the private mass, which had earlier roots, now became the standard model for the celebration of the Eucharist (see "Baptism, Penance, and the Eucharist after the Disappearance of Christian Initiation").

Fourth, it should be pointed out that the Middle Ages were quite a vibrant time intellectually. To explain the various currents and tendencies, an appeal is usually made to the Christianized legacies of Plato and Aristotle. While there is no doubt that these great philosophers of Greek Antiquity left an indelible mark on the intellectual life of European cultural history, perhaps the terms (Christian) Platonism and (Christian) Aristotelianism are a little too schematic.[14] At any rate, it is not the case that for a time there was first the influence of Plato alone, which gave rise to beautiful mystical and metaphysical speculations, and that this was suddenly succeeded at a certain time by the influence of Aristotle, which then led to a tighter and drier line of reasoning.

---

[12] Metzger, *History of the Liturgy*, 118. This very interpretation, however, needs to be nuanced, particularly in view of what we know about the origins and evolutions of Gregorian chant, where one observes various and flexible patterns of codification. See, for example, Daniel J. DiCenso, "Revisiting the *Admonitio generalis*, in *Chant, Liturgy and the Inheritance of Rome*, ed. Daniel J. DiCenso and Rebecca Maloy (Woodbridge: Boydell & Brewer, 2017), 315–71, and Susan Rankin, *Sounding the Word of God: Carolingian Liturgical Books for Singers* (Notre Dame, IN: University of Notre Dame Press, 2022).

[13] Kathleen G. Cushing, *Reform and Papacy in the Eleventh Century: Spirituality and Social Change* (Manchester: Manchester University Press, 2005).

[14] Lydia Schumacher, "Christian Platonism in the Medieval West," in *Christian Platonism: A History*, ed. Alexander J. B. Hampton and John Peter Kenney (Cambridge: Cambridge University Press, 2020), 183–206; Jos Decorte, *Waarheid als weg: Beknopte geschiedenis van de middeleeuwse wijsbegeerte* (Kapellen and Kampen: Pelckmans and Kok Agora, 1992).

Rather it is the case that in different contexts work was done with different constellations and from composite influences that do not simply bear the stamp of either (neo-)Platonic or Aristotelian.

Nevertheless, the stereotypical explanations outlined still have an impact on the story of what the interpretation of the liturgy and the development of sacramental doctrine looked like in the Middle Ages. That story goes more or less like this: As soon as the underlying Platonic view of humanity and the world began to wane and the knowledge of Greek dramatically faded away, all sorts of allegorical interpretations of the liturgy emerged, culminating in the *Liber officialis* of Amalarius of Metz (c. 830).[15] Because those allegories were (considered) at odds with reason and logical thinking, it took a while to find an adequate framework for liturgical interpretation and a theological thinking that was reconcilable with an increasingly emancipating philosophy.[16] That balance was eventually found in scholasticism, and in particular in Thomas Aquinas, whom many still regard as the greatest theologian of all time.[17] The unfortunate consequence of pushing scholasticism forward, however, was that a more experience-oriented and spiritually driven direction in theology lost out.[18] For some, this may explain why the theology of the liturgy has not really taken off in the West since, say, the early eleventh century, and, in fact, until the twentieth century, with perhaps some precursors in the nineteenth century. Whatever the case, it is not wise to draw a dividing line too sharply between scholastic theology and liturgical allegory, since in practice they often went hand in hand.

Moreover, in order to understand the intellectual framework of the Middle Ages, and thus Christian worship and ceremonies, it is necessary to mention four outstanding thinkers who set the stage. First and

[15] Herbert Schneider, "Roman Liturgy and Frankish Allegory," in *Early Medieval Rome and the Christian West: Essays in Honour of Donald A. Bullough*, ed. Julia M. H. Smith (Leiden: Brill, 2000), 341–54. This contribution is followed by an edition of the so-called Büdingen Fragment, which is compared to Hanssen's standard critical edition of Amalarius's *Liber Officialis* dating from the late 1940s.

[16] This generalizing story about the emergence of liturgical commentaries in the Middle Ages does not sufficiently take into account other factors, such as the immense variety in biblical exegeses and the variegating audiences for which the commentaries were put together. Sometimes, they had a simple edifying or moral purpose; sometimes, they were meant to be highly sophisticated treatises.

[17] For a recent and comprehensive study, see Donald S. Prudlo, *Thomas Aquinas: A Historical, Theological, and Environmental Portrait* (New York: Paulist Press, 2020).

[18] Hans Geybels, *Cognitio Dei experimentalis: A Theological Genealogy of Christian Religious Experience* (Leuven: Leuven University Press, 2007).

foremost, there is Augustine, to whom virtually all definitions of liturgy and sacraments in the Middle Ages go back.[19] In fact, his fundamental idea that liturgy consists of visible signs communicating divine grace still stands. Second, there is Pseudo-Dionysius the Areopagite, of whom it was assumed that he had heard Paul himself preach at Athens, and who for that reason enjoyed enormous prestige. Among other things, the so-called *corpus areopagiticum* contains the basis for speculations about the celestial and ecclesiastical hierarchy, including a penetrating interpretation of the liturgy.[20] Third, there is Boethius, thanks to whom medievalists had access to parts of Aristotle's logic in Latin.[21] Fourth, mention should be made of Isidore of Seville, who produced the vastly influential *Etymologiae*, which can be interpreted as a kind of basic encyclopedia of all there is to know.[22] In many medieval theological treatises, traces of these four thinkers can be found alongside – and in complex and varying ways interwoven with – influences of Platonic and Aristotelian origin.

Fifth, it is important to realize that the Middle Ages were a period of noticeable developments on the spiritual plane, too, which interacted strongly with cult and worship. The founding of the Benedictine order by Benedict of Nursia (480–547) naturally counts as a milestone. From the mother monastery Montecassino, where also the famous Rule of Benedict originated,[23] monasteries were systematically founded all over Europe. Monastic life provided a balance of communal (i.e., liturgical) prayer, manual labor, and community life under the guidance of an abbot.[24] Gradually, the Benedictine way of life won

---

[19] Allan D. Fitzgerald et al. (eds.), *Augustine through the Ages: An Encyclopedia* (Grand Rapids, MI: Eerdmans), s.v. "Christian Worship," 156–64.

[20] Hanns Peter Neuheuser, "Zur Problematik der Pseudo-Dionysius-Rezeption in der hochmittelalterlichen Liturgiehermeneutik," in *Kulturkontakte und Rezeptionsvorgänge in der Theologie des 12. Und 13. Jahrhunderts*, ed. Ulrich Köpf and Dieter R. Bauer (Münster: Aschendorff, 2011), 45–101.

[21] Margaret Gibson (ed.), *Boethius: His Life, Thought and Influence* (Oxford: Blackwell, 1981).

[22] Andrew Fear and Jamie Wood (eds.), *A Companion to Isidore of Seville* (Leiden: Brill, 2019).

[23] On a website maintained by the Benedictine Order, one can find many editions, translations and resources of the *Regula Benedicti*: https://osb.org/our-roots/the-rule.

[24] However, the Benedictines were not the only form of monastic life in the early Middle Ages. Well known are the monasteries founded by and living according to the rule of the Irish missionary Columbanus (540–615), including those of Luxeuil and Marmoutier in France and Bobbio in Italy. For some background, see Conor Newman, Mark Stansbury, and Emmet Marron (eds.), *Columbanus and Identity in Early Medieval Europe: Formation and Transmission* (Rennes: Presses Universitaires

the confidence of rulers, leading monasticism to flourish. Well known is the development of Cluny, the abbey in Burgundy that became so powerful and wealthy during the ninth and tenth centuries that a little later a reform movement started from within. Known as the Cistercian reform, named after the founding of the Abbey of Cîteaux in 1098, it grafted monastic life back onto frugality, humility, effective manual labor, and prayer at regular intervals under the motto "simplicity and poverty." The most famous Cistercian monk of the Middle Ages is probably St. Bernard of Clairvaux (1090-1153). Concerning the liturgy, the Cistercians mainly advocated austerity in externals, a reduction in the number of feasts, and an internalization of the encounter with Christ.

Later, in the twelfth, but especially in the thirteenth, century, many more new religious congregations saw the light, the so-called mendicant orders. Perhaps the best known are the Franciscans and the Dominicans, both named after their founders, Francis of Assisi (1181-1226) and Dominic de Guzman (1170-1221) respectively. Unlike the monastic orders, members were not bound by the vow of stability, which in fact made them very mobile. Inspired by apostolic zeal and motivated to serve Christ and his Church through an ideal of poverty, they traveled throughout Europe to found monasteries and communities, especially in the cities.[25] Because there was a need for a certain uniformity for their worship services, in particular the hours and the Eucharist, these new developments in spiritual life also had an immediate impact on the liturgy.[26] In addition to the Franciscans and Dominicans, by the way, there were also the Augustinians, the Carmelites, the Servites, the Minims, the Mercedarians, and the Trinitarians, among other new branches of the Benedictines apart from the Cistercians, many female religious movements including the beguines and the Bridgettines (founded in the fourteenth century), Carthusians, Premonstratensians, military orders involved in the Crusades, mystics, lay associations,

---

de Rennes, 2022), and for an introduction into monastic rules of the early Middle Ages, Adalbert de Vogüé, *Les règles monastiques anciennes (400-700)* (Turnhout: Brepols, 1985).

[25] Caroline Bruzelius, *Preaching, Building, and Burying: Friars in the Medieval City* (New Haven, CT: Yale University Press, 2014).

[26] Stephen J. P. Van Dijk (ed.), *Sources of the Modern Roman Liturgy: The Ordinals of Haymo of Faversham and Related Documents (1243-1307)* (Leiden: Brill, 1963). Haymo of Faversham was an English Franciscan who became Superior General of the order in 1240.

fraternities, and so on. All, in their own way and according to their own charism, gave color to the religious life of the Middle Ages.[27]

THE DEVELOPMENT OF LITURGICAL BOOKS

It is against the background of all these developments that the production of liturgical books must be framed. This was a huge logistical and economic challenge because the publication of a liturgical manuscript required a high degree of stability as well as the necessary craftsmanship, from the drying of animal skins to the neat application of ink. Consequently, a liturgical book had a huge monetary value to a community (only exceptionally was it owned by an individual or family), in no way comparable to what a printed book is worth today, even to a seasoned bibliophile.

The usual way of representing liturgical books from the Middle Ages refers to the user, that is, the corresponding actor in the liturgical event.[28] This is not only a convenient way to classify or catalog a copious amount of material, but it also says something about the liturgy as essentially practical in nature. In other words, the origin of the liturgical books is not in the quest for knowledge or the need to inform, even about the Bible or Jesus Christ, but in the respectful performance of liturgical acts in line with tradition and Scripture. Specifically, the liturgical books were compiled with an eye toward performing the various roles in worship, and as these evolved or changed, so did the need to adapt the books. Further, the need for liturgical books also taps into the tendencies toward codification and clericalization that increased during the Middle Ages, especially since the eleventh century.

---

[27] See, for example, Jennifer Kolpacoff Deane and Anne E. Lester, *Between Orders and Heresy: Rethinking Medieval Religious Movements* (Toronto: University of Toronto Press, 2022).

[28] Essential literature about medieval liturgical books are two undisputed reference works: Cyrille Vogel, *Medieval Liturgy: An Introduction to the Sources*, trans. William G. Storey and Niels Krog Rasmussen (Washington, DC: The Pastoral Press, 1986), and Éric Palazzo, *A History of Liturgical Books from the Beginning to the Thirteenth Century*, trans. Madeleine Beaumont (Collegeville, MN: Liturgical Press, 1998), amplified by two more recent publications: Andrew J. M. Irving and Harald Buchinger (eds.), *On the Typology of Liturgical Books from the Western Middle Ages. Zur Typologie liturgischer Bücher des westlichen Mittelalters*, LQF 115 (Münster: Aschendorff, 2023), and Cassian Folsom, *The Liturgical Books of the Roman Rite: A Guide to the Study of their Typology and History*, vol. 1: *Books for the Mass* (Naples: EDI, 2023). I refer to these publications for references to primary sources as well as secondary literature.

For the earliest history of liturgical books in the West, reference must be made to the city of Rome, and the specific situation that had arisen there. Indeed, in addition to the liturgy in the city's titular churches or parishes, a whole celebratory cycle of the pope and his entourage, the so-called stational liturgy, had also developed.[29] Actually, these were two virtually separate circuits, which became intertwined only at a later stage. Both cycles, each with their accompanying documents, were soon transported to areas outside Rome and Italy, initially to Gaul (southern France) but also to the Iberian peninsula and later to the Germanic areas along the Rhine, following the shifting political powers in Western Europe at the time. In all these regions liturgical mixtures arose, with Roman and Gallican elements. At some point, around the turn of the first and second millennia, the liturgy thus grown and composed, was reintroduced in the city of Rome under the reign of the Ottonian kings. And once the popes and their curia had regained prestige and authority, the Roman liturgy gradually became the model for Christian worship throughout Europe. Among other things, the widespread practice of pilgrimage and the rapid expansion of mendicant orders played a key role in this. While there was a great variety in local feasts and saints, a certain unity of the Roman Rite was nevertheless evident in the basic structures of the Eucharist, the praying of the hours, and the administration of the sacraments.

As for the books for the celebration of the Eucharist or "the Mass" (*missa*), mention must be made in the first place of the *sacramentaria*. These are the books containing the prayers uttered by the presiding minister (priest), which originated from collections of disparate prayer forms known as *libelli*. The *Sacramentarium Veronense* is a collection of these. The *Sacramentarium Gelasianum vetus*, most probably representing the presbyteral liturgy at Rome, dates from the late seventh century; later all manner of Gallican additions were made to it: These are the so-called Gallican *Sacramentaria Gelasiana vetera*. The *Sacramentarium Gregorianum*, on the other hand, reflected the papal liturgy in Rome. A version of it, the *Hadrianum*, was delivered to Charlemagne for diffusion throughout his empire. Before that could be done successfully, however, major modifications had to be made to it.

---

[29] Folsom, *The Liturgical Books*, 44–54. Forms of stational liturgy also developed elsewhere, such as in Constantinople and Jerusalem. See John F. Baldovin, *The Urban Character of Christian Worship: The Origins, Development, and Meaning of Stational Liturgy* (Rome: Pontificium Institutum Studiorum Orientalium, 1987).

That was the work of, among others, Benedict of Aniane, disciple of Alcuin of York, at the beginning of the ninth century.[30]

The liturgical books for reading from Scripture originated from *capitularia*, lists of pericopes to be read at certain times during the liturgical year. In fact, originally, it was simply from the Bible itself that readings were made; indeed, in some early manuscripts of the Bible one finds indications that a reading should be begun at a certain point, as well as an indication of where the reading should stop. Later, a need developed to provide separate books for the reading from Paul's corpus of letters, the *epistolaria*, as well as from the gospels, the *evangeliaria*. Indeed, in the celebration of the liturgy, the reading of both of these pieces came to belong to a different function, the subdeacon and the deacon, respectively. Later, all the readings at Mass were sometimes compiled into one volume, the *lectionarium*. Well-known early examples are the *capitularium* of Wüzburg and the lectionaries of Luxeuil and Sélestat and to some extent even the Lindisfarne Gospels; of an ulterior date are, for example, the gospel books of Constance and Milan, the lectionary of Beuron, and that of Chartres.

A similar history exists with the liturgical books for singing, the *antiphonalia*, *cantatoria*, or *gradualia*, which technically are not the same.[31] Indeed, originally there were no separate books for these; explicit annotations for musical melodies, neumes, are found only at the earliest from the late ninth century (with a lot of uncertainty regarding when this practice started) and developed gradually. The parts of the mass that were sung were centered around the so-called *ordinarium* (including the Kyrie, Gloria, Credo, Sanctus, and Agnus Dei) and the *proprium* (with the Introitus, responsorial psalm or *graduale*, *alleluiaticum*, *offertorium*, and communion song). There were further refinements with, for example, the *tractus* instead of the alleluia in Lent and the extensive development of *sequentia* in the second millennium.[32]

---

[30] Hans Bernhard Meyer, "Benedikt von Aniane (ca. 750–821): Reform der monastischen Tagzeiten und Ausgestaltung der römisch-fränkischen Meßfeier," in *Liturgiereformen: Historische Studien zu einem bleibenden Grundzug des christlichen Gottesdienstes. Teil I: Biblische Modelle und Liturgiereformen von der Frühzeit bis zur Aufklärung*, ed. Martin Klöckener and Benedikt Kranemann (Münster: Aschendorff, 2002), 239–61.

[31] There is indeed some terminological complexity involved here, at least since Amalarius of Metz; see Folsom, *The Liturgical Books*, 99.

[32] Eugenio Costa, Jr., *Tropes et séquences dans le cadre de la vie liturgique au Moyen Âge* (Roma: CLV – Edizioni Liturgiche, 1979).

As time progressed, the need arose to integrate the various components of the celebration of Mass – orations, readings, and chants – into one book. This was due in part to the greater focus on the figure of the presiding priest as well as the spread of the private Mass. The book in which everything came together is known as the missal (*missale*). The first missals date from the tenth century, but it was not until the thirteenth century – perhaps with the exception of Rome – that the *sacramentaria* in particular fell into disuse and were completely replaced by the missal.[33] From that time until the first printed copy of the *Missale Romanum* (which ironically happened not in Rome but in Milan in 1474), the history of the missal, including the *ordo missae*, can be accurately documented.[34]

In addition to the liturgical books for the Mass, other written material arose to accompany Christian worship. In the regime of the hours, of course, one knows the *breviarium*, which does not necessarily refer to an abbreviated book. The breviary can be compared to the missal in that it is an integration of different sources for the purpose of streamlining liturgical performance. The various components of the breviary were the *psalterium*, with indications for the recitation of the psalms, an *antiphonale* (but a different one than the one for the Mass),[35] a compilation of hymns, or *hymnale*, and *homiliaria*. These were anthologies of homilies by the Church Fathers (or excerpts from them) brought together for the purpose of being read aloud, especially in Matins (the nocturnal office), now reading office.

All kinds of instructions concerning the effective performance of the liturgy were collected in yet another type of book, the so-called *Ordines Romani*, to which the name Michel Andrieu will undoubtedly

---

[33] This development, however, was more complicated, as recent research has convincingly shown. There were integrated "missals" at a much earlier stage, and there was also a great geographical difference between the Italian peninsula and regions north of the Alps. See Andrew J. M. Irving, "Mass by Design: Design Elements in Early Italian Mass Books," in *Scribes and the Presentation of Texts (from Antiquity to c. 1550)*, ed. Barbara A. Shailor et al. (Turnhout: Brepols, 2021), 251–74.

[34] Daniel McCarthy, "Seeing a Reflection, Considering Appearances: The History, Theology and Literary Composition of the Missale Romanum at a Time of Vernacular Reflection," *Questions Liturgiques* 94 (2013): 109–43; Cesare Giraudo (ed.), *Il Messale Romano: Tradizione, traduzione, adattamento* (Rome: CLV and Edizioni Liturgiche, 2003).

[35] A famous one is the Antiphonary of Bangor, which goes back to the late seventh century.

be forever attached.³⁶ Around the middle of the twentieth century, he published an extensive collection of them,³⁷ which significantly increased our understanding of the origins and early development of the structures of the liturgy in the West. Unlike what their name suggests, the *Ordines Romani* are by no means all about the liturgy of the city of Rome, with its special provisions for the pope and the papal court, but also, for example, about daily arrangements of prayers and meals in monasteries, about ordination to various ministries and functions in the life of the church, the consecration of church buildings, aspects of the liturgical year, the liturgy surrounding the death of Christians, and so on.³⁸ Moreover, they reflect a lot of material from and adaptations to other regions as well, such as the Frankish lands, and they cover a period from about Gregory the Great to the invention of printing in the fifteenth century.

From elements of the *ordines* and *sacramentaria*, especially those that did not relate to the Eucharist, grew in the later Middle Ages the books still known, at least since Trent, as the *Rituale* and the *Pontificale*. The first collected the liturgical celebrations, sacraments, and blessings at which a priest presided, such as infant baptism and the anointing of the sick. The second collected the texts, prayers, and customs for those liturgical celebrations at which a bishop presided, such as the ordination of priests or the dedication of a church. Essential steps in the development of the *Pontificale* were the renowned Romano-Germanic Pontifical,³⁹ the Roman Pontificals of the twelfth century, and the Pontifical of William Durandus of Mende, which dates from the last decade of the thirteenth century.

BAPTISM, PENANCE, AND THE EUCHARIST AFTER THE DISAPPEARANCE OF CHRISTIAN INITIATION

To now gain a view of the practical ways in which the liturgy was celebrated in the Middle Ages, a certain thematic limitation enforces

---

[36] Marcel Metzger, "Les éditions critiques de documents liturgiques. Les contributions strasbourgeoises," *Revue des sciences religieuses* 88 (2014): 191–206.

[37] Michel Andrieu (ed.), *Les Ordines Romani du haut Moyen Âge*, 5 vols. (Louvain: Spicilegium sacrum Lovaniense, 1931–1961).

[38] A neat survey of the contents of the *Ordines Romani* can be found in Vogel, *Introduction to the Sources*, 135–224.

[39] Henry Parkes, *The Making of Liturgy in the Ottonian Church: Books, Music and Ritual in Mainz, 950–1050* (Cambridge: Cambridge University Press, 2015).

itself, confining my discussion to the sacraments of Baptism, Penance, and Eucharist because they can be meaningfully taken together. What these sacraments have in common is that, as a result of the collapse of Christian initiation as a consistent and overarching ritual whole around the fifth century, they took on a very different liturgical shape and theological interpretation. In all three cases, this evolution led to what, at the risk of falling into an anachronism or a gross generalization, might be called descriptively – not judgmentally – individualism. That is, the focus of the celebration came to be on the individuals who either "administered" or "received" the sacrament, and it derived much less of its meaning from the gathering of the community or from its actual celebration. Along with this individualization of sacramental ministry came a kind of professionalization – again at the risk of an anachronism – in which the assignment of roles and the definition of functions were captured in an increasingly strict legislative system.

As far as the Eucharist in the Middle Ages is concerned, the first point to note is the emergence of the private Mass, of which the earliest roots presumably already lay in the seventh century.[40] There is a plausible theory that this must be situated in the growth of monasteries and in the idea that monks were ideally also priests.[41] Thus there came to be many more priests who had to say Mass on a regular basis (promptly daily) than an abbey community actually needed. The spontaneous solution to this problem was that Masses could be said simultaneously in the abbey church, which can be easily ascertained in the architecture of medieval church buildings, with their numerous side chapels, among other practical arrangements. From the monastic world, then, practices were copied in the realm of secular clergy, with parishes and dioceses. Nevertheless, the Church has always pointed out that the Mass should never be a purely individual (religious) exercise, and thus, in principle, there should always be at least one other person present in addition to the priest, preferably an altar server.[42]

Over the centuries, the private Mass has unfolded as the model or ideal type of the Eucharist in the West, with only minor adjustments to

---

[40] Arnold Angenendt and Thaddäus A. Schnitker, "Die Privatmsesse," *Liturgisches Jahrbuch* 33 (1983): 76–89.

[41] Angelus A. Häußling, *Mönchskonvent und Eucharistiefeier: Eine Studie über die Messe in der abendländischen Klosterliturgie des frühen Mittelalters und zur Geschichte der Meßhäufigkeit*, LQF 58 (Münster: Aschendorff, 1973); Cyrille Vogel, "La multiplication des messes solitaires au Moyen-Âge: Essai de statistique," *Revue des sciences religieuses* 55 (1981): 206–13.

[42] Thomas P. Rausch, "Is the Private Mass Traditional?," *Worship* 64 (1990): 237–42.

its ritual composition – as Klauser and Metzger rightly pointed out. An intimate connection grew with the figure of the priest, whose identity was, and sometimes still is, almost exclusively dependent on his ability to "say" Mass. Very important in this context is the development of an underlying complex of ideas, the main ingredients of which are that Christians can pray for each other, even beyond the boundaries of death, and that salvation mediated through the celebration of Mass is somehow accumulable.[43] A double consequence of this development is that the Eucharist was valued more for what it yielded in terms of individual benefits (salvation of one's own or somebody else's soul) and less intensely for how it intertwined with the cycle of Christian feasts and the rhythm of the year. This in turn gave rise to the emergence of many local customs and devotions concerning the body and blood of Christ. The undisputed highlight of these is the feast of Corpus Christi, instituted as a universal solemnity by Pope Urban IV in 1264 and for which Thomas Aquinas wrote most of the liturgical prayer material.[44]

The history of baptism in the Middle Ages was also marked by the disintegration of Christian initiation. Both demographic evolutions, with larger groups converting en masse to the Christian faith under the guidance of their rulers (e.g., Clovis in Reims), and theological developments shaped the practice of baptism. In particular, the ideas, inspired by Augustine, that baptism washes away original sin and that it is best done as soon as possible after birth, had a tremendous impact. At the ritual level, baptism was initially still linked to the celebration of Easter, with the so-called seven scrutinies ritual as an intermediate stage. In this, the various steps of Christian initiation were compressed into the week before Easter, with an emphasis on the exorcisms. This expansion was probably not long-lived, however, and in practice crumbled even further, eventually leaving only one preparatory ritual for baptism proper on Holy Saturday, although it must be said that uniformity in baptismal rites was far from the norm. Around the eleventh century, even the connection with Easter was dissolved, and the

---

[43] Thomas O'Loughlin, "Treating the 'Private Mass' as Normal: Some Unnoticed Evidence from Adomnan's *De locis sanctis*," *Archiv für Liturgiewissenschaft* 51 (2009): 334–44.

[44] Miri Rubin, *Corpus Christi: The Eucharist in Late Medieval Culture* (Cambridge: Cambridge University Press, 1991); Jan-Heiner Tück, *A Gift of Presence: The Theology and Poetry of the Eucharist in Thomas Aquinas*, trans. Scott G. Hefelfinger (Washington, DC: The Catholic University of America Press, 2018).

ritual became more and more a matter of the priest administering it individually to newborn children.[45]

A similar evolution took place in the practice of penance. While in Late Antiquity there had been a genuine *ordo paenitentium*, whereby penitents could be reintegrated into the Eucharistic community after a long period of time, but only once and only after a serious sin or crime, the culture concerning the consciousness of sin and the constant need for repentance changed radically under the influence of the form that Christianity took in the British Isles and in the context of the spread of monasteries.[46] More specifically, there was a shift from public penance to individual confession of sins, which had a major impact on the ritual nature of the sacrament. Moreover, there was a meticulous increase in what was understood to constitute sin, and this was recorded in penitential books (*paenitentialia*), listing a certain compensation for each sin. Later, these books developed into veritable manuals that served as guides for priests, who were responsible for listening to and granting forgiveness to penitent sinners. On the theological level, Thomas Aquinas stressed that sincere repentance (*contritio*) is ultimately sufficient to obtain God's forgiveness, although all sins must be explicitly confessed (*confessio*), and, if possible, there must also be a kind of restitution (*satisfactio*).[47] The doctrine of penance has had a gigantic impact not only on moral and sacramental theology but also on the religious and social history of Western Europe and beyond.[48]

SAINTS, RELICS, PILGRIMAGES

To understand even better the overall picture of the liturgy in the Middle Ages, it is also necessary to point out the many forms of devotional practices related to the liturgy that developed during this period. Among these, the veneration of saints flourished.[49] It was born out of profound recognition for the martyrs, but afterwards the realization

---

[45] Pierre-Marie Gy, "Du baptême Pascal des petits enfants au baptême 'quamprimum'," in *Haut Moyen-Âge: Culture, éducation et société: Études offertes à Pierre Riché*, ed. Michel Sot (Nanterre: Érasme, 1990), 353–65.

[46] Rob Meens, *Penance in Medieval Europe: 600–1200* (Cambridge: Cambridge University Press, 2014).

[47] Maria C. Morrow, "Reconnecting Sacrament and Virtue: Penance in Thomas's *Summa Theologiae*," *New Blackfriars* 91 (2010): 321–34.

[48] Jean Delumeau, *L'aveu et le pardon: Les difficultés de la confession XIIIe–XVIIIe siècle* (Paris: Fayard, 1992).

[49] Robert Wisniewski, Raymond Van Dam, and Bryan Ward-Perkins (eds.), *Interacting with the Saints in the Late Antique and Medieval Worlds* (Turnhout: Brepols, 2023).

grew that a quasi-perfect Christ-centered way of life was also possible by courageously bearing witness to the faith without a violent death having to follow. St. Martin of Tours (c. 316–397), who had already gained enormous prestige during his lifetime with his advocacy of an ascetic lifestyle, was exemplary in this evolution.[50] In addition, the cult concerning relics was also of great importance to the medieval liturgical system. To Ambrose of Milan goes back the idea of an intimate connection between an altar and a relic (of a martyr), and thus of Christ, Eucharist, and veneration of saints. The practices of placing a relic in every altar, of keeping a few relics in every church, and of building entire churches and monasteries around tombs of saints have strongly shaped the face of Christianity in Europe. As a result, an almost inseparable bond grew between popular devotion and liturgy, as people were strongly attracted to the proximity and accessibility of tangible holiness. It may not even be an exaggeration to say that the real presence of Christ in the gifts of bread and wine had a strong parallel with the salvific efficacy that was assumed to emanate from the relics of his saints.[51] Moreover, pilgrimage centers developed around important centers where relics were kept and venerated. Among other reasons related to penance, masses of people went on pilgrimage, and even the phenomenon of the Crusades can be explained at least in part as a kind of pilgrimage.

CONCLUDING NOTE

This chapter has shown that there is no good reason to neglect, let alone to look down upon, medieval liturgy. The Middle Ages were not just a period where things were transferred-yet-deterred from Antiquity to modernity. To the contrary, they were constitutive of the outline and the structures of liturgical forms and arrangements we still know today. Moreover, there was a vast amount of variety and diversity of liturgies and liturgical expressions in the Middle Ages, embedded in local contexts and closely connected to the mentalities and temperaments of different peoples. To tell the story of liturgy in the Middle Ages is to become increasingly aware of its complexity and, in and through that, of its enduring significance and beauty.

---

[50] Olivier Guillot, *Saint Martin, apôtre des pauvres* (Paris: Fayard, 2008).
[51] Of course, there were also relics related to Christ himself; see Nicolas Guyard, *Les reliques du Christ: Une histoire du sacré en Occident* (Paris: Cerf, 2022).

For Further Reading

Angenendt, Arnold, "Liturgie im Frühmittelalter," 273–92; Martin Klöckener, "Liturgische Quellen des Frühmittelalters," 293–328; Jürgen Bärsch, "Liturgie im Hoch- und Spätmittelalter," 329–76, in *Geschichte der Liturgie in den Kirchen des Westens: Rituelle Entwicklungen, theologische Konzepte und kulturelle Kontexte*, vol. 1, ed. Jürgen Bärsch and Benedikt Kranemann (Münster: Aschendorff, 2018).

Bricout, Hélène, and Martin Klöckener (dir.), *Liturgie, pensée théologique et mentalités religieuses au haut Moyen Âge: Le témoignage des sources liturgiques*, LQF 106 (Münster: Aschendorff, 2016).

Gittos, Helen, and Sarah Hamilton (eds.), *Understanding Medieval Liturgy: Essays in Interpretation* (Burlington, VT: Ashgate, 2016).

Harper, John, *The Forms and Orders of the Western Liturgy from the Tenth to the Eighteenth Century: A Historical Introduction and Guide for Students and Musicians* (Oxford: Clarendon Press, 1991), esp. part II.

Irving, Andrew J. M., and Harald Buchinger (eds.), *On the Typology of Liturgical Books from the Western Middle Ages. Zur Typologie liturgischer Bücher des westlichen Mittelalters*, LQF 115 (Münster: Aschendorff, 2023).

Irving, Andrew J. M., and Daniel DiCenso (eds.), *Medieval Latin Liturgy: A Research Guide* (Leiden: Brill, forthcoming).

Larson-Miller, Lizette (ed.), *Medieval Liturgy: A Book of Essays* (New York: Garland Publishing, 1997).

Levy, Ian Christopher, Gary Macy, and Kristen Van Ausdall (eds.), *A Companion to the Eucharist in the Middle Ages* (Leiden: Brill, 2012).

Monti, James, *A Sense of the Sacred: Roman Catholic Worship in the Middle Ages* (San Francisco, CA: Ignatius Press, 2012).

Thibodeau, Timothy, "Western Christendom," in *The Oxford History of Christian Worship*, ed. Geoffrey Wainwright and Karen B. Westerfield-Tucker (Oxford: Oxford University Press, 2012), 216–53.

Vogel, Cyril, *Medieval Liturgy: An Introduction to the Sources*, trans. William G. Storey and Niels Krog Rasmussen (Washington, DC: The Pastoral Press, 1986).

3 Liturgies and the Reformation
JAN SCHNELL

INTRODUCTION

The scope of this chapter is confined to liturgies and liturgical developments in sixteenth-century Western Europe, with implications and reflections raised for global, contemporary Christianity. "Reformation," for the purposes of this chapter, is defined as a sixteenth-century Western European reform movement that responded to abuses in the medieval Catholic church and resulted in the emergence of Protestant churches. The Reformation brought about a crucial restoration of the voice, visibility, and vocation of assemblies. Primary attention is given to the developments centered around the reformer Martin Luther, with key developments from other reformers in Switzerland, France, and England identified. The chapter concludes by considering the impacts Reformation developments may have for today.

LITURGICAL DEVELOPMENTS IN CONTEXT AND CONTRAST

Starting from Martin Luther's liturgical reform efforts in relation to the medieval Catholic church (the dominant Christian influence of the time and region), developments will be highlighted in conjunction with key actors without harmonizing theologies or practices.

Luther among Emerging Liturgies

Table 3.1 shows a family tree of liturgies that mutually informed one another, whether through emulation or distinction. All these Reformation liturgies were developed in conversation also with the Roman Rite celebrated in their region. The table is limited to reformers who lived, at least for a time, in Wittenberg, Zurich, Geneva, Strasbourg,

Table 3.1 *Family Tree of High-Impact Reformation Liturgies*

Year	Author	Place	Title or Description
1523	Martin Luther	Wittenberg	Formula Missæ
1524	Diebold Schwartz	Strasbourg	German Service
1525	Huldrych Zwingli	Zurich	Act or Custom of the Supper
1526	Martin Luther	Wittenberg	Deutsche Messe
1529, 1533	Guillaume (William) Farel	Neuchâtel, published Genève, introduced	*Manière et fasson* (French Service)
1539	Martin Bucer	Strasbourg	The Psalter with Complete Church Practice
1542	Jean Calvin	Geneva and Strasbourg	The Form of Church Prayers
1549	Thomas Cranmer	Canterbury	Book of Common Prayer, 1st
1552	Thomas Cranmer	Canterbury	Book of Common Prayer, 2nd
1556	John Knox	Geneva	The Forme of Prayers and Administration of the Sacraments, etc.
1564	John Knox et al.	Edinburgh	The Book of Common Order

and Canterbury. For the purposes of this chapter, I highlight liturgies from Luther, Zwingli, Calvin, and Cranmer from this family tree.

For Luther's part, while he had many reforming ideas regarding liturgical theology – baptism, Eucharist, congregational singing, biblical translation – he was hesitant to change much in the Roman Rite itself. Luther's reforms of liturgical rites represent no dramatic dismantling of the service of the Mass; he was not so much a liturgical composer as an editor and translator. Liturgical reforms he did make in the 1523 Formula Missæ and the 1526 Deutsche Messe point to Christ throughout the liturgies – Christ is the reforming center. One particular criterion guided Luther's reforms of liturgies – a true encounter with the God who justifies: "Experiencing Christ's justification through God's promises and activity in Word and sacrament was the primary goal."[1] Justification by grace through faith was the doctrine that helped him assess consistency with the gospel.[2] Luther considered the Formula Missæ to be a report on

---

[1] Martin J. Lohrmann, email message to author, March 29, 2023.
[2] Bryan D. Spinks, "'Berakah', Anaphoral Theory and Luther," *Lutheran Quarterly* 3 (1989): 274.

the state of liturgies in Wittenberg and not a general liturgical reform.³ It was no new composition; it was an edited version of the Latin Mass, with the express purpose of revealing the clarity of the gospel of Jesus Christ (that is justification by grace) by removing accretions to the liturgy that occluded this central promise. More revealing than the words of the service itself is this note from Luther after the Offertory:

> From here on almost everything smacks and savors of sacrifice. And the words of life and salvation [institution narrative] are imbedded in the midst of it all, just as the ark of the Lord once stood in the idol's temple next to Dagon. ... Let us, therefore, repudiate everything that smacks of sacrifice, together with the entire Canon and retain only that which is pure and holy.⁴

For Luther, liturgy is gift, not sacrifice; he advises getting rid of anything that hinders witnessing and receiving the gift of the promise of Christ. Luther strove to make clear justification by grace through faith in Jesus Christ, foundation in Scripture, and active assembly participation so that Christ was known.

Three years later, as multiple vernacular liturgies were appearing, Luther argued for contextualization by insisting that his Deutsche Messe was limited and simply a German Mass for sixteenth-century Germans in Wittenberg.⁵ "[Luther] wanted each region to draw up its own worship order according to its local needs, rather than have every region uniformly use one dictated by him."⁶ While anyone was free to use the Wittenberg liturgy, people in other places and times were not bound to this contextual iteration. The liturgy would be wrongly used if it became a law and work of righteousness, or, as Luther put it, "We will want to beware lest we make binding what should be free ... [Christians] are free to change [these rites] how and when ever

---

[3] See, Martin Luther, *Luther's Works*, 55 vols., ed. Jaroslav Pelikan and Helmut T. Lehmann (Philadelphia, PA: Fortress Press, 1955), 53:62 (hereafter cited as *LW*).

[4] Luther, *LW*, 53:26. Robin A. Leaver identified two examples of Lutheran Reformation-era liturgies with full Eucharistic prayers: the liturgy for Pfaltz-Neuberg (1543) and the Swedish order of 1576. See *Luther's Liturgical Music: Principles and Implications*, Lutheran Quarterly Books (Grand Rapids, MI: Eerdmans, 2007), 189.

[5] Robin A. Leaver notes that before Deutsche Messe was published, there were already vernacular masses in cities such as Nuremberg, Strasbourg, Augsburg, and Allstedt, but these were translations of the Roman Mass with minimal innovations beyond language ("Luther and Bach, the 'Deutsche Messe' and the Music of Worship," *Lutheran Quarterly* 15 [2001]: 317).

[6] Vernon P. Kleinig, "Lutheran Liturgies from Martin Luther to Wilhelm Löhe," *Concordia Theological Quarterly* 52.2 (1998): 127.

[sic] they may wish."⁷ His choices to hear people speak and sing aloud more than in the Roman Rite and to declutter what obscured the proclamation of grace in Jesus followed his theological commitments to grace, gift, and promise.

Of particular interest in these two liturgies is what surrounds the *verba testamenti* (words of institution) and what conclusions that evidence suggests. Luther believed the words of institution were not prayer but proclamation; therefore, the assembly needed to hear them: "The whole power of the mass consists of the words of Christ, in which he testifies that forgiveness of sins is bestowed on all those who believe that his body is given and his blood poured out for them. This is why nothing is more important for those who go to hear mass than to ponder these words."⁸ Luther's Formula Missæ includes a Eucharistic prayer with praise and thanksgiving before the words of institution; in the Deutsche Messe, the words of institution stand alone, followed by a sanctus or hymn. Could this imply that Luther moved theologically away from the inclusion of a full Eucharistic prayer? No, the evidence does not support this conclusion for a number of reasons. The Formula Missæ, with its Eucharistic prayer, remained Wittenberg's main service throughout Luther's lifetime. In sixteenth-century Germany, there are many examples of Eucharistic prayers in contextualized liturgies against which Luther says nothing, and Luther does not indicate in the Deutsche Messe that a practice of only words of institution should be replicated elsewhere.⁹ Any ambivalence observed in Luther's various practices is likely because he was less concerned about what human prayers seem proper than about people truly receiving Christ in the Eucharist through words of promise and the gift of faith.

Proliferation of Reformation Liturgies

Table 3.2 outlines five Reformation liturgies from key leaders Martin Luther, Huldrych Zwingli, Jean Calvin, and Thomas Cranmer. They are

---

[7] Martin Luther, "An Order for Mass and Communion for the Church at Wittenberg." These statements are not understood as welcoming just any proliferation of liturgies. As Luther also noted, "Now the nearer our Masses are to the first Mass of Christ, the better they undoubtedly are; and the further from Christ's Mass, the more dangerous" (*LW*, 35:81).

[8] Ibid., 36:57.

[9] Joseph Herl, "Luther and the Liturgy in Wittenberg," in *Worship Wars in Early Lutheranism: Choir, Congregation and Three Centuries of Conflict* (Oxford: Oxford Academic, 2010). Accessed March 10, 2023, at https://doi.org/10.1093/acprof:oso/9780195365849.003.0001.

Table 3.2 *Reformation Liturgies of Luther, Zwingli, Calvin, and Cranmer*

Martin Luther's 1523 Formula Missæ Wittenberg	Huldrych Zwingli's 1525 Act or Custom of the Supper Zurich	Martin Luther's 1526 Deutsche Messe Wittenberg	Jean Calvin's 1542 The Form of Church Prayers Geneva and Strasbourg	Thomas Cranmer 1552 2nd Book of Common Prayer Canterbury
Introit	Collect (preparatory)	Psalm or Hymn (sung)	Psalm 124:8	Lord's Prayer
Kyrie (sung)	1 Cor 11:20–29	Kyrie (sung)	Confession	Prayer (prep)
Gloria (sung)	Gloria		Absolution with Scripture	Decalogue Confession
Collect	Salutation	Collect		Collects
Epistle	Gospel		Psalm	Epistle
Alleluia (sung) or Gradual	Absolution	German Hymn (sung)	Decalogue (Strasbourg, sung)	
Veni Sancte Spiritus or Sancti Spiritus			Prayer for Illumination	
Gospel		Gospel	Scripture	Gospel
Nicene Creed	Apostles' Creed	Creed		Creed
Sermon		Sermon	Sermon	Sermon
				Offertory and Offering
			Intercessions	Intercessions
				Exhortation
				Invitation
Sursum Corda (sung)				
	Exhortation			Confession and Absolution
	Lord's Prayer	Lord's Prayer	Lord's Prayer	Scripture, comforting

Liturgy 1	Liturgy 2	Liturgy 3	Liturgy 4	Liturgy 5
Preface			Prayer of Preparation	Preface
Words of Institution	Pastoral Prayer for Assembly's Strength	Exhortation	Apostles' Creed	Sanctus (sung)
Sanctus (sung)	Words of Institution	Words of Institution	Words of Institution	Prayer of Humble Access
Benedictus (sung) and Elevation				Consecration Prayer
Optional Prayer			Exhortation	
Lord's Prayer				
Peace				
Distribution +Agnus Dei, sung	Distribution with John 13	Elevation and Distribution +Agnus Dei or Hymn	Distribution	Distribution
Collect	Psalm 113	Sanctus	Psalm(s) or Scripture during Distribution	Lord's Prayer
Benedicamus (sung)	Prayer of Thanks	Prayer of Thanks	Prayer of Thanks	Prayer of Thanks
			Canticle of Simeon (Strasbourg, sung)	Gloria (sung)
Benediction	Dismissal with Peace	Benediction	Benediction (Number 6:24–26)	Benediction[1]

[1] Chart constructed through extant liturgies in addition to "Reformation Liturgies." Accessed March 3, 2023, at https://reformationworship.com/liturgies/

presented side by side so readers are able to study similarities and differences in the shapes of these liturgies and reference them. A few distinguishing characteristics are discussed below.

Huldrych Zwingli (1484–1531), a reformation leader in Zurich, Switzerland, published a Latin Mass in 1523 and a German service called *Act or Custom of the Supper* in 1525. The Zurich city council approved the German service but without the antiphonal reading of Creed and Psalms that Zwingli preferred. He removed song and music from the service even as artwork and organs were removed from Swiss churches. In addition, preaching no longer followed a lectionary but was based on the continuous reading of a book of the Bible, which loosened connection to the church year and minor festivals.[10] Four months before his death, Zwingli wrote "Exposition of the Christian Faith" in which he describes his liturgy, including the practice of distributing communion: "Each person takes a piece of the bread with his own hand, and then passes the rest to his neighbor."[11] Receiving communion in this manner, Zwingli witnessed congregants who had been separated by enmity become reconciled through the sacrament.

Jean Calvin (1509–1564) was serving a French-speaking congregation in German-speaking Strasbourg and had access to Zwingli's liturgy in addition to Guillaume (William) Farel's French service and Martin Bucer's German service as he adapted a service in French. In 1542, he published *The Form of Church Prayers* in Geneva (1545 revision), to which he had returned, and his successor published it in Strasbourg (1547, 1549, 1552, 1553, 1559, 1561 revisions). In relation to the Roman Mass, Calvin retained the sacraments of baptism and Eucharist, the Lord's Day, and some music. He introduced the use of a vernacular psalter, but rejected saints' days, minor festivals, images, processions, choirs, and musical instruments.[12] Calvin included a Prayer for Illumination before the reading of Scripture and sermon to call on God to send the Spirit to illumine people's hearing of the Word Jesus Christ. He emphasized preaching in the vernacular in order to

---

[10] Frank C. Senn, "Reformation Liturgies," in *Oxford Research Encyclopedia of Religion* (Oxford: Oxford University Press, 2015). Accessed February 15, 2023, at https://bit.ly/4k2kmpg.

[11] Huldrych Zwingli, "Exposition on the Christian Faith" (1531), as reprinted "Zwingli Archives" Christian History Institute. Accessed February 14, 2023, at https://christianhistoryinstitute.org/magazine/article/archives-replacing-the-mass.

[12] John Calvin, "Order of Worship (1542) and Genevan Liturgy in Strassborg (Strasbourg)," in *A Puritan's Mind*. Accessed February 7, 2023, at www.apuritansmind.com/puritan-worship/john-calvins-order-of-worship-1542/.

instruct and support the faith of the assembly. "Calvin would have preferred to celebrate Holy Communion every Sunday, following the usage of the patristic church, but the consistory was not prepared to depart from the pattern of quarterly communion observed in the Swiss Reformed cantons."[13] In Calvin's liturgy, several elements, such as the call to worship and the benediction, come directly from Scripture.

Thomas Cranmer (1489–1556) was Archbishop of Canterbury when the English Parliament passed the 1534 Act of Supremacy, which declared King Henry VIII the head of the Church of England and recognized his marriage to Anne Boleyn (and his divorce from Catharine of Aragon). In addition, the act eliminated several feast days and provided occasion for some limited liturgical reforms. A decade later, in 1544, Cranmer introduced the first officially sanctioned vernacular liturgy – the Great Litany – which he composed drawing on resources from John Chrysostom, Martin Luther, and the Sarum (Salisbury) Rite. King Edward VI, who ascended to the throne in 1547, was more open to liturgical reform than his father, and it is under his reign that *The Booke of Common Prayer and Administration of the Sacraments, and Other Rites and Ceremonies of the Churche, after the Use of the Churche of England* was published following Parliament's Act of Uniformity, which established Cranmer's liturgy as the one legal form of worship in England. This first Book of Common Prayer included rites for Sundays as well as throughout the week:

- Calendar of Psalms and lessons
- Matins (Matins and Lauds) and Evensong (Vespers and Compline)
- Introits, Collects, Epistle, and Gospel readings for communion services
- Holy Communion service
- Baptism
- Confirmation
- Marriage
- Visitation and communion with the sick
- Funeral
- Purification of Women
- Prayers for Ashwednesdaie (Ash Wednesday)
- Rationale for leaving out and retaining certain ceremonies
- Notes

---

[13] Senn, "Reformation."

Cranmer requested critiques of the Book of Common prayer from many, including Martin Bucer, whose reply Cranmer found helpful, and in 1552 he published a significantly revised Book of Common Prayer. The Holy Communion service was reordered: The Lord's Prayer, Gloria, Confession, and "Comfortable Words" were moved; the Decalogue, Dialogue, Preface, and Sanctus were added.

During her five-year reign, Queen Mary I (Mary Tudor) tried to restore medieval Catholicism and reverse the English Reformation. Parliament resisted many of her attempts, but Mary Tudor condemned over three hundred "heretics," including Thomas Cranmer, to be burned at the stake. In 1558, Elizabeth I ascended to the throne upon her half-sister's death. A Protestant, Queen Elizabeth quickly called for a vote in Parliament that named her supreme head of the Church of England and reintroduced the Book of Common Prayer. The Elizabethan Settlement was a political and religious attempt to settle religious turmoil, slow down religious persecution, and increase religious tolerance. Queen Elizabeth's emphasis on the via media (middle way) not only mediated a path between Catholic and Puritan positions, but it also engrained in the collective consciousness of Anglicans that the Book of Common Prayer can serve the whole Church of England even though differing theological interpretations exist.

BAPTISM

Luther saw baptism as central to the whole Christian life.[14] Although performed only once, it is neither merely a rite of Christian initiation nor a transactional form of securing forgiveness. Rather, Luther maintained, baptism is a daily renewal in Christian living because the promises of baptism grant daily freedom from sin and death so people can live in the newness of life.[15] In baptism, the God of all living promises moves toward people and lavishes them with the promise of justification. Therefore, human efforts toward achieving right living can add nothing to baptism's efficacy.

Although all the gracious and efficacious work is God's, Luther continued to affirm Christian acts of justice toward creation and

---

[14] Luther's clearest writings on baptism can be found in his "The Holy and Blessed Sacrament of Baptism" (1519), "The Babylonian Captivity of the Church" (1520), "Concerning Rebaptism" (1528), "Ten Sermons on the Catechism" (1528), "Small and Large Catechisms" (1529), and "Sermon at the Baptism of Bernhard von Anhalt" (1540), in which he affirms a sacramental life centered on the Word, Jesus Christ.

[15] See for example LW, 36:68–69.

neighbor. Lutheran historian Martin J. Lohrmann writes, "Faith receives the promises of baptism. Love lives out these promises 'in righteousness and purity,' not as impossible standards required so that God will love us, but as effects of what it means to be loved by God and live as people washed and clothed in God's grace."[16] Baptismal living daily delivers free promises God alone confers; living out of free grace looked to Luther like love for neighbor and world.

The reasons for Luther writing on baptism shifted across his lifetime from initially distinguishing his position from that of medieval Catholic theologians to later differentiating himself from other reformers' positions, especially those of Andreas Karlstadt and Huldrych Zwingli. In contrast to the medieval Catholic accent on *opus operatum* (the objective efficacy of the sacrament performed regardless of relationship to recipient), an early Luther emphasized the role of the Word and faith present in the relationship between God and recipient.

Later, Luther's writings became responses to other reformers; for example, he disagreed with Zwingli's assertion that without faith the water of baptism does nothing. Zwingli said he relied on Scripture alone and believed scholars prior to him had been mistaken when they "ascribed to the water a power which it does not have and the holy apostles did not teach."[17] Zwingli emphasized the baptismal covenant as dependent upon the baptized person's obedient response and not the water. "Zwingli defined baptism as a symbol of the Old Testament covenant between God and God's people and a ritual that bound the community together as all of the participants and witnesses remembered the significance of their own baptisms. Neither physical nor spiritual purification was part of baptism for Zwingli."[18] Regarding baptism, Zwingli emphasized faith and incorporation into the church community.

Calvin distanced himself from Zwingli's more static understanding of baptism and emphasized God's unconditional promise to people.[19] A sacrament, he said, is "a testimony of God's grace toward us, declared

---

[16] Martin J. Lohrmann, "Faith and Love in Luther's Small Catechism," in *Teaching Reformation: Essays in Honor of Timothy J. Wengert*, ed. Martin J. Lohrmann and Luka Ilić (Minneapolis, MN: Fortress Press, 2021), 231.

[17] Huldrych Zwingli, "Of Baptism," in *Zwingli and Bullinger*, trans. and ed. G. W. Bromiley (Philadelphia, PA: Westminster Press, 1953), 130.

[18] Karen E. Spierling, "Baptism and Childhood," in *Reformation Christianity*, ed. Peter Matheson (Minneapolis, MN: Fortress Press, 2010), 126.

[19] Bryan D. Spinks, "Luther's Timely Theology of Unilateral Baptism," *Lutheran Quarterly* 9 (1995): 25.

to us by an outward sign, with a reciprocal attestation of our piety toward [God]."[20] While he agreed with Zwingli that baptism involves Christian initiation into community, Calvin critiqued Zwingli by emphasizing baptism's purifying role: "Baptism promises us no other purification than by the sprinkling of the blood of Christ; which is emblematically represented by water, on account of its resemblance to washing and cleansing."[21] Baptism grafts one into the life, death, and resurrection of Christ through a death to sin and a new life in Jesus. Luther's position, when addressing Zwingli, was similar to Calvin's. He clarified that the water of baptism is a visible sign of God's grace apart from anything a human does. "Note well, therefore, that baptism is water with the Word of God not water and my faith. My faith does not make the baptism but rather receives the baptism, no matter whether the person being baptized believes or not; for baptism is not dependent upon my faith but upon God's Word."[22] For both Luther and Calvin, God's promise in baptism simultaneously incorporates and declares Jesus' resurrection.

Luther also addressed Karlstadt's rejection of infant baptism, which Anabaptist theologians further developed and even radicalized. Anabaptist leader Balthasar Hubmaier wrote, "Since Christ has instituted the baptism of water only for the faithful,[23] one should baptize only the faithful, i.e., those who openly and verbally confess their faith ... infant baptism is no baptism, nor it is worthy of the name."[24] In his response to the Anabaptist view, Luther again refined his baptismal theology:

> There is quite a difference between having faith, on the one hand, and depending on one's faith and making baptism depend on faith, on the other. Whoever allows himself to be baptized on the strength of his faith ... denies Christ, because he trusts in and builds on something of his own, namely, on a gift which he has from God, and not on God's Word alone.[25]

---

[20] Jean Calvin, *Institutes of the Christian Religion*, trans. Ford Lewis Battles (Grand Rapids, MI: Eerdmans, 1975), 87.
[21] Ibid., 478.
[22] *LW*, 51:186.
[23] Matt 28; Mark 16.
[24] Balthasar Hubmaier, "A Christian Catechism" (1526), in *A Reformation Reader: Primary Texts with Introductions*, ed. Denis R. Janz (Minneapolis, MN: Fortress Press, 2008), 204.
[25] Martin Luther, "Concerning Rebaptism" (1528), in *Martin Luther's Basic Theological Writings*, ed. William R. Russell (Minneapolis, MN: Fortress Press, 2012), 255.

Faith is crucial, but, at the same time, lack of faith does not spoil God's promises. Luther based his critiques in his teachings on justification: Baptism must remain based in the saving work of Jesus and not in human belief lest faith become another good work attempting to earn salvation, which would be a mockery of the free promise and gift of the gospel.

EUCHARIST

Four contextual Eucharistic concerns of the Reformation include the distribution of wine, Mass as sacrifice, real presence, and transubstantiation. The reformers were in lively, transnational conversations with one another – through tracts, disputations, sermons, and more – as they distinguished themselves from the medieval Catholic church and each other.

Wine Distribution

Against the medieval Catholic practice of the assembly receiving only the bread at communion while priests received both bread and wine, Luther argued for the whole assembly to also receive wine. Since he understood the sacrament to belong to everyone and not priests alone, Luther saw this differentiation in communion as an intolerable example of clericalism: "It is wicked and despotic to deny both kinds to the laity."[26] Even though he affirmed that reception of either bread or wine alone is fully efficacious, he deemed access to the reception of both forms as important due to its biblical basis: "Matt. [26:26–28], Mark [14:22–24], and Luke [22:19f] agree that Christ gave the whole sacrament to all his disciples. That Paul delivered both kinds is so certain that no one has ever had the temerity to say otherwise. In addition, Matt. [26:27] reports that Christ did not say *of the bread*, 'eat of it, all of you,' but *of the cup*, 'drink of it, all of you.'"[27] For Luther, "all" meant the entire assembly.

Sacrifice

Thomas Cranmer criticized the way the Roman Rite was practiced as a sacrifice offered to God by priests on behalf of the people: "The greatest

---

[26] Martin Luther, "That these words of Christ, 'This is my body,' etc., still stand firm against the fanatics," in *The Annotated Luther*, vol. 3, ed. Paul W. Robinson et al. (Minneapolis, MN: Fortress Press, 2016), 28.

[27] Ibid., 22. (Italics added.)

blasphemy and injury that can be against Christ, and yet universally used through the Popish kingdom, is this, that the priests make their mass a sacrifice propitiatory, to remit the sins as well of themselves, as of other[s] both quick and dead."[28] This was similar to Luther's statement that the "most wicked abuse of all"[29] and "the greatest and most horrible abomination"[30] was practicing the Mass as a sacrifice and monetizing on people's fear of hell. For him, Mass was being treated as a sacrifice because that was both the common understanding of the people[31] and the position of medieval Catholic priests.

Luther opposed a sacrificial liturgical theology because it suggested humans could accomplish salvific "good works" on their own apart from God's promise.[32] This debate between Luther and medieval Catholic theologians often revolved around the theological concept of *ex opere operato* ("by the work having been worked") – but it was more precisely a debate over just one aspect of it. In the Reformation world, Lutheran, medieval Catholic, and Reformed theologians alike accepted the part of *ex opere operato* that had been clarified by the Donatist controversy – namely that the efficacy of sacramental grace was not dependent on the faithfulness of the celebrant. The portion Luther contested was the Catholic understanding that the Eucharist confers grace by being celebrated faithfully. Luther held that a priestly act does not itself intrinsically offer grace, since only God and God's words of promise free people:[33] "The Mass is a promise of the forgiveness of sins made to us by God, and such a promise as has been confirmed by the death of the Son of God."[34] It is this promise, Luther affirmed, that faith receives as a gift on account of the saving work of Jesus who died once

---

[28] Thomas Cranmer, "*A Defence of the true and Catholick doctrine of the Sacrament of the body and blood of our Saviour Christ: with a confutation of Sundry errors concerning the same*" (1550), 229. Accessed March 2, 2023, at https://bit.ly/4mm5q6L.

[29] Luther, "This is my body," 38.

[30] Martin Luther, Smalcald Articles, article 2. Accessed December 29, 2022, at www.gutenberg.org/files/273/273-h/273-h.htm.

[31] Luther, "This is my body," 53.

[32] Ibid., 41–42. See also "Luther on the Reform of Worship" in *Lutheran Quarterly* 13 (1999): 315-33, where scholar Helmar Junghans clarifies that "[Luther's] contemporaries understood [good works] much more as particular acts of piety than as works of love for the neighbor" (320–21).

[33] See *LW*, 35:45–74, "Sermon on the Blessed Sacrament of the holy and True Bod and Blood of Christ," Luther, Smalcald Articles, article 2, and Luther, "This is my body," 40, n. 91.

[34] Luther, "This is my body," 41.

and for all. Jean Calvin, too, wrote that Christ was sacrificed only once. His *Institutes* say, "The body of the Lord was once offered as a sacrifice for us, so that we may now feed upon it, and, feeding on it, may experience within us the efficacy of that one sacrifice; and that his blood was once shed for us, so that it is our perpetual drink."[35] The Eucharist does not re-sacrifice Christ for worshippers but, rather, feeds people with salvific promise.

Christ's Presence

A point of divergence in Eucharistic theology between Reformed theologians and Luther centers around the presence of Christ. As Jesus instituted the Lord's Supper, he said, "This is my body." How could these words be understood while also acknowledging that Christ sits at the right hand of God? Zwingli articulated that Eucharistic bread and wine *signify* Christ's presence. In his letter to Joachim Vadian, Zwingli sounded exasperated with Luther, who was saying different things in various conversations: "[Luther] conceded that the body of Christ is finite. He conceded that the Eucharist may be called a 'sign' of the body of Christ."[36] In a report from the Marburg Colloquy, Zwingli acknowledges Scripture does not say, "This is a *sign* of my body," but that reading John 6 supports Zwingli's interpretation.[37] After talking about his flesh and blood, Jesus interprets, "It is the spirit that gives life; the flesh is useless. The words that I have spoken to you are spirit and life" (John 6:63). Citing Augustine, Zwingli asserts that Christ remains at the right hand of God: "The body of Christ must be in one place, and that it is at the right hand of God, they did not withdraw it thence to submit it for mastication to the foul teeth of men."[38] Along with Martin Bucer from Strasbourg, Zwingli believed that Jesus "sitting at the right hand of the Father" meant that he could only be in one place and does not come down from heaven to inhabit the bread. Zwingli consistently argued for interpretations that followed what the senses actually perceive.

---

[35] Calvin, *Institutes*, 526.
[36] Huldrych Zwingli, "Zwingli's Letter to Vadian" (1529), in *A Reformation Reader*, 196.
[37] "The Marburg Colloquy: Another Report" (1529), in *A Reformation Reader*, 197.
[38] Huldrych Zwingli, "An Account of the Faith of Huldereich Zwingli Submitted to the Roman Emperor Charles" (July 3, 1530), trans. S. M. Macauley, in *The Latin Works and Correspondence of Huldreich Zwingli*, vol. 2 (Philadelphia, PA: Heidelberg Press, 1922), 42–56. Accessed March 27, 2023, at https://pages.uoregon.edu/sshoemak/323/texts/zwingli.htm.

Later Calvin developed a concept of the "spiritual union" with Christ that recipients of the Eucharist experience as they are drawn to commune with Christ.[39] He writes,

> By the corporeal objects which are presented in the sacrament, we are conducted, by a kind of analogy, to those which are spiritual. So, when bread is given to us as a symbol of the body of Christ, we ought immediately to conceive of this comparison, that, as bread nourishes, sustains, and preserves the life of the body, so the body of Christ is the only food to animate and support the life of the soul.[40]

Along with Zwingli, Calvin considered it a nonsensical error to suppose Christ is attached to Eucharistic elements: "The bond of this union, therefore, is the Spirit of Christ, by whom we are conjoined, and who is, as it were, the channel by which all that Christ himself is and has is conveyed to us."[41] Communion with Christ occurs on a spiritual plane via a bond with the Holy Spirit. Calvin's and Zwingli's Eucharistic theology and practices were similar enough that an agreement on intercommunion was reached between Calvin and Zwingli's successor Heinrich Bullinger. Fourteen years after Calvin published his *Institutes*, which articulated this view, Thomas Cranmer was teaching a similar view. People "come to this holy communion with such a lively faith in Christ, and such an unfeigned love to all Christ's members, that as they carnally eat with their mouth this sacramental bread and drink the wine, so spiritually they may eat and drink the very flesh and blood of Christ, which is in heaven, and sitteth on the right hand of his Father."[42] Cranmer's writings suggest that Christ remains in heaven and communes spiritually with those who receive the Eucharist.[43] In contrast to these views, Luther said,

---

[39] Calvin's concept of spiritual union was a rejection of the Lutheran idea of "mystical union" – the physical presence of Christ in and with the elements of bread and wine.
[40] Calvin, *Institutes*, 527.
[41] Ibid., 535.
[42] Cranmer, *A Defence*, 18.
[43] It is noteworthy that some people in the Church of England tradition have interpreted Cranmer's doctrine of spiritual presence to imply that Christ is present through the Spirit. This position is based on one writing where Cranmer says, "baptism, wherein we receive not only the spirit of Christ, but also Christ himself, whole body and soul, manhood and Godhead, unto everlasting life, as well as in the holy communion." (*Writings and Disputations of Thomas Cranmer, Archbishop of Canterbury, Martyr, 1556, Relative to the Sacrament of the Lord's Supper*, ed. John Edmund Cox [Cambridge: The University Press, 1844], 25.)

Scripture teaches us, however, that the right hand of God is not a specific place in which a body must or may be, such as on a golden throne, but that it is the almighty power of God, which at one and the same time can be nowhere and yet must be everywhere. ... the power of God cannot be so circumscribed and determined [as to be in only one place], for it is immeasurable and cannot be grasped with the senses, beyond and above all that is or may be.[44]

For Luther, the right hand of God is not any one place but is the power of God, which has the capacity to be truly present throughout creation. He maintains that the Eucharist is more than a sign of Christ's body and blood because in it Jesus is truly present to recipients.

Transubstantiation

While Luther agreed with the medieval Catholic view that Christ is truly present in the Eucharist, he challenged transubstantiation, a change that meant, "by the consecration of the bread and wine there takes place a change of the whole substance of the bread into the substance of the body of Christ our Lord and of the whole substance of the wine into the substance of his blood."[45] Luther relied again on his understanding of the right hand of God as God's ubiquitous power as he addressed transubstantiation. Jesus' body is present in the Eucharist "as well as at all other places ... although there need be no transubstantiation or conversion of the bread into his body, it can well be present nonetheless, just as the right hand of God does not need to be converted into all things even though it is surely present and in them."[46] Luther resisted describing *how* Christ was present in the Eucharist, which was based, he believed, in a wayward desire to quantify or rationally explain the holy mysteries of Christ's presence. Instead, Luther wanted people to have liturgical liberty to "believe either one view or the other without endangering one's salvation."[47] He argued that both biblical witness and common understanding allowed for bread to mean bread and wine

---

[44] Luther, "This is my body," 204.
[45] Council of Trent (1551), *Catechism*, 1376. Accessed March 20, 2023, at www.catholiccrossreference.online/catechism/#!/search/1376-1377. "Transubstantiation became the dominant (but never entirely exclusive) way to describe the real presence in the Fourth Lateran Council (1215), which was then expanded upon using Aristotelian categories by Thomas Aquinas" (Martin Lohrmann, email message to author, March 29, 2023). See also Edward Schillebeeckx, *The Eucharist* (London: Bloomsbury Publishing Plc, 2005), 54 ff.
[46] Luther, "This is my body," 210.
[47] Ibid., 32.

to mean wine. People's consciences did not need the burden of professing that bread means the "accidents of bread" in order to be right before God or the church.[48]

The liturgies edited and endorsed by the reformers were developed in conversation with the Roman Rite and with each other's services. In relation to one another, they honed and clarified their liturgical theologies, especially in relation to baptism, the Eucharist, and the role of the assembly. For all the changes this era brought, including liturgical theology's role in reformers distinguishing themselves from one another, liturgies themselves enjoyed remarkable stability, with shared care for biblical origins and early church practices.

IMPACT OF REFORMATION DEVELOPMENTS TODAY

While the sixteenth-century Reformation era is past, impacts of Reformation principles, processes, and liturgical practices are present and ongoing. How do the worship developments described above stimulate reflection and conversation today and continue earnest discernment of liturgical reform? The major questions of the Reformation remain pertinent: How do Christians announce and live out of the promises that Jesus meets us in communal worship, God's grace sets people free, and freedom makes space to serve earth and world at the intersections of profound gift and need? Palestinian Bishop Emeritus Munib A. Younan calls on Christians to "never give up our theological conviction that human actions in this world cannot bring us salvation. Nevertheless, we could stress more that we have been placed on this earth together with all humans precisely to be stewards of the earth and of each other."[49] The gospel is relevant to the human condition; lives of faith and acts of love can be stewarded without supposing that such living or acting secures salvation.

There is much to learn from both the limitations and excellence of the reformers. In contrast to the patriarchal worldview of the reformers and Reformation liturgies, attention is currently needed to confront systems of dominance so that liturgies and surrounding practices become increasingly antiracist, decolonial, and inclusive. A low view of human capacity needs to be exchanged for a more

---

[48] See Thomas Aquinas, *Summa Theologiae*, III, 77, and Luther, "This is my body," 33.
[49] Munib A. Younan, "Beyond Luther: Prophetic Interfaith Dialogue for Life," in *The Global Luther: A Theologian for Modern Times*, ed. Christine Helmer (Minneapolis, MN: Fortress Press, 2009), 62.

positive theological anthropology. Pastor Vernon Kleinig reports that, for Luther, "The [Deutsche Messe] is a simplification of the liturgy for uneducated laity. ... He believed ... that [legislating its use] would lead to a great liturgical impoverishment."[50] While understanding that all people are limited, it is simultaneously true that assemblies have an immense capacity for liturgical imagination and deep and faithful participation. Liturgical leaders get to accompany assemblies into the worlds where liturgies suggest Christians live – worlds where the abundant Eucharistic table critiques spaces of structurally sanctioned scarcity, where daily baptismal renewal suggests investment in practices of restorative justice.

The reformers model some excellence that matters today: liturgical nuance, clarity, and contextual specificity with flexibility. Unconditional gifts of promise through baptism, the Eucharist, and God's Word remain free grace from God to God's beloved. Liturgical leaders display pastoral sensitivity to people in context even while liturgies, through practices such as the Prayers of Intercession, turn people toward the wideness of God's mercy for the life of the world. Scripture creates faith and guides reflective nuance as liturgical leaders figure out how to speak in local vernaculars. Both the foibles and the brilliance of various reformers teach across centuries that liturgies both express faith and form it.

For Further Reading

Dahill, Lisa E., Jim B. Martin-Schramm, and Bill McKibben, *Eco-Reformation: Grace and Hope for a Planet in Peril* (Eugene, OR: Wipf & Stock, 2016).

The Global Luther: A Theologian for Modern Times, ed. Christine Helmer (Minneapolis, MN: Fortress Press, 2009).

These multi-authored books consider current crushing issues in light of Reformation histories and theologies. They produce dialogues and focus attention on sites of needed ongoing reformation in the life of the church and the world. By looking with particularity at ecology, interfaith engagement, hope in frayed contexts, and the power of music, they offer methodologies and examples of how to employ a Reformation theologian's lens to the issues that most threaten one's community today.

Bainton, Roland H., *Women of the Reformation, from Spain to Scandinavia* (Minneapolis, MN: Augsburg Publishing House, 1977).

---

[50] Kleinig, "Lutheran Liturgies," 134.

Women of the Reformation in France and England (Minneapolis, MN: Augsburg Publishing House, 1973).

Women of the Reformation in Germany and Italy (Minneapolis, MN: Augsburg Publishing House, 1971).

Stjerna, Kirsi Irmeli, *Women and the Reformation* (Malden, MA: Blackwell, 2009).

From Italy to England, women of the Reformation had a steady influence on liturgical theology and praxis, which has been under-recorded in scholarship. Through these four publications, Stjerna and Bainton fill in gaps in Reformation research by highlighting the leadership and contributions of Reformation women. The impact of women on liturgies of the Reformation should not be underestimated; they protected more famous reformers, taught the story of the Reformation at table and in church groups, disseminated information, urged greater listening to differing viewpoints, and sang the faith. Using their indexes, one can easily pinpoint discussions related to liturgical challenges and developments.

4 Liturgies Beyond the Reformation
MELANIE C. ROSS

Liturgical scholar James F. White famously noted a problem in the study of Protestant liturgy: "Non-sacramental" traditions have not received sufficient scholarly attention in liturgical studies because their worship was considered too deviant from the standards set in either Catholic and Orthodox thinking or in mainstream Protestant theologies rooted in Lutheranism, Calvinism, and Anglicanism. "Most Protestant worship, historically and at present, has not made the eucharist its central service," he observed, therefore "to focus solely on the eucharist means to ignore what happens on almost every Sunday during the year."[1] Indeed, many post-Reformation Protestants avoid the term "sacrament" (a non-biblical word that seems to ascribe semi-mechanical efficacy to certain human actions, independent of the faith of believers) in favor of "ordinances" (which emphasize Jesus' institution and the obedient response of believers).[2] They pay almost no attention to the liturgical year and have evolved their own functional cycles of marking time.

However, post-Reformation Protestants also contribute unique gifts to the ecumenical worship mosaic. Quakers wait silently on God, and Pentecostals burst forth in ecstatic speech. Evangelicals and Pentecostals may devote literally half their worship time to music.

---

[1] James F. White, *Protestant Worship: Traditions in Transition* (Louisville, KY: Westminster/John Knox Press, 1989), 14.

[2] George Hunsinger et al., *Twentieth Century and Contemporary Protestant Sacramental Theology* (Oxford University Press, 2016), 398. Some Baptists, however, now acknowledge the historical value of the term "sacrament" to indicate an oath of allegiance, and some have even argued for a kind of "Baptist sacramentalism." For example, see Stanley K. Fowler, *More Than a Symbol: The British Baptist Recovery of Baptismal Sacramentalism*, vol. 2 (Eugene, OR: Wipf & Stock, 2007).

Love-feasts and watch-night services have played an important role in Methodist worship. Many Anabaptist congregations have retained the tradition of foot washing. White rightly insisted that liturgical scholars pay more careful attention to these traditions, arguing that any attempts to find consensus will not succeed if they ignore the diversity of what Christians actually do when they worship.

This chapter surveys the liturgical practices of five traditions that emerged during the so-called radical Reformation or after the historic Reformation: Quakerism, Anabaptism, Methodism, Pentecostalism, and Evangelicalism. I will focus more attention on baptism and the Lord's Supper – the two areas where theological distinctives become most apparent – than on other sacraments, and I will pay less attention to the liturgical structure of time in hours or years, since these are generally not priorities for Christians in these traditions. For several of these groups, music has taken on a quasi-sacramental role and will therefore be discussed in detail.

QUAKERS

Early Quakers were members of a small denomination (today known formally as the Religious Society of Friends) founded by George Fox in England in the seventeenth century. The name "Quaker" was originally intended as a slur. It referred to the way that Quakers (who called themselves the "Friends of Truth" or "Society of Friends") supposedly shook as they worshipped, preached, and wrestled with their calling "under the Light."[3] Quakers contended that the "Inward Light" of Christ dwelt in every person, regardless of religion, gender, race, or social status. They accepted women as itinerant evangelists and were among the earliest Anglo-American critics of the transatlantic slave trade. The major event leading to the founding of the Society of Friends was the English Civil War (1642–1652), which climaxed the struggle between the Royalists and the Puritans. When the monarchy and the Church of England were restored in 1660, Quaker worship was banned, leading to the imprisonment of over one-tenth of the 50,000 Friends in England.[4]

---

[3] Dan Graves, "Singing Out of the Silence: A Survey of Quaker Choral Music," *Choral Journal* 34.5 (1993): 15.

[4] Hugh Barbour and J. William Frost, *The Quakers* (New York: Greenwood Press, 1988), 60.

Historical Liturgy

The whole medieval apparatus of worship and most Protestant adaptations of it disappeared in Quaker worship. In contrast to some of the earliest Puritans who had been ordained as Roman Catholic priests, Quaker leaders had no direct connection with Catholicism. Furthermore, Quakers went further than other Protestants in their reforms. Although many Quakers in the seventeenth century would have been familiar with the Book of Common Prayer, the more abbreviated Directory for the Publique Worship of God, and an assortment of Christian expressions of worship, they rejected service books, outward and visible sacraments, preaching, choirs, and organs. Quakers were determined to strip worship "to the fundamental simplicity of waiting together for the Spirit's direction in a silence that reflected the silence of heaven (Revelation 8:1)."[5] In 1653, Francis Higginson, a Cumberland clergyman, described his attendance at a Quaker gathering:

> The places of their Meetings are for the most part, such private houses as are most solitary and remote from Neighbours ... their Speakers ... standing ... with his hat on, his countenance severe, his face downward, his eyes fixed mostly towards the earth, his hands & fingers expanded, continually striking gently on his breast ... If ... their chiefe Speaker be ... absent, any of them speak that will pretend a revelation; sometimes girles are vocal. ... Sometimes ... there is not a whisper among them for an houre or two together.[6]

During the nineteenth century, a number of splits occurred within Quakerism, and today several vastly different branches exist. The Quaker belief in the individual's direct experience of God means that they have no central creed, no set doctrine, and no ritual sacraments that are accepted by all Friends. Jewish Friends, Universalist Friends, Evangelical Christian Friends, and Atheist Friends all lay claim to the title "Quaker."[7]

Today Quaker worship falls into three general (and sometimes overlapping) categories: unprogrammed, programmed, and semiprogrammed.

---

[5] David L. Johns, "Worship and Sacraments," in *The Oxford Handbook of Quaker Studies*, ed. Stephen W. Angell and Pink Dandelion (Oxford: Oxford University Press, 2013), 261.
[6] Francis Higginson, *A Brief Relation of the Irreligion of the Northern Quakers* (London: n.p., 1653), 12–14; quoted in Adrian Davies, *The Quakers in English Society, 1655–1725* (Oxford: Clarendon, 2000), 77.
[7] Graves, "Singing Out of the Silence," 15.

Unprogrammed worship, also known as "open worship" or "traditional" worship, is composed of four simple movements or stages: gathering, settling into silence, expectant waiting, and closing. Each of these is more or less informal, and there is usually no announcement of passage from one movement to the next.

While unprogrammed worship is the form closest to that of the early Friends, the majority of Quakers in the world – especially in the United States, most of Africa, and South America – practice a form of programmed worship. Programmed worship has a gathering and a closing, but in between there can be a wide variety of conventions, including hymn-singing, preaching, Scripture reading, and public prayers.

Semi-programmed worship combines elements of both categories. In addition to hymns, prayers, and a sermon, worship will also include periods of unprogrammed worship that may range from a few moments to ten or fifteen minutes or longer.

Silence

At the heart of Quaker worship is the belief that "the inner light is accessible to all and that the purpose of worship is common waiting upon God in stillness and quietness."[8] Many Christian liturgies, including the Roman Catholic Mass, allow for brief periods of silence. However, silence in the Quaker tradition is of a different type. In recent decades, Quakers have regularly used the phrases "waiting worship" or "expectant waiting," which reflect the method and theological intention of this component of worship. This period of expectant waiting will often be punctuated by vocal ministry, such as a brief homily, meditation, prayer, or testimony. One scholar has drawn parallels between the Quaker practice of silence and the Pentecostal practice of speaking in tongues:

> One doesn't plan ahead of time what to say, just as one doesn't invent a tongue in which to speak. There is rather a sharing out of the depths of one's self, or differently described, a speaking that is prompted by the leading of the Spirit. It is almost universally felt in Quaker circles that rational analysis and argument over what is spoken "out of the silence" is inappropriate. One is not to analyze or judge but rather to listen and obey. As in the case of glossolalia, the process of speaking out of the silence and listening in the silence

[8] James F. White, *Protestant Worship*, 137.

involves a resting of the analytical mind, a refusal to let deliberative, objective thinking dominate the meeting for worship.[9]

Silence is not passive inaction but rather an active discipline of waiting with expectation for the Spirit who animates the faithful.[10]

Baptism and Lord's Supper

Early Quakers believed that "the coming of Christ put an end to the old dispensation of outward observances," including sacred objects and liturgical rites.[11] The symbols and representations of Christ that were important in the past are no longer satisfying now that the living Christ is coming. Worship in the new era is "in spirit and in truth,"[12] a phrase that frequently appears in Friends' writings. Consequentially, most Friends have not incorporated the rites of baptism or communion into their worship. Friends often refer to worship itself as being communion. In their response to the ecumenical document *Baptism, Eucharist and Ministry*, Quakers explained,

> In silence, without rite or symbol, we have known the Spirit of Christ so convincingly present in our quiet meetings that his grace dispels our faithlessness, our unwillingness, our fears, and sets our hearts aflame with the joy of adoration. We have thus felt the power of the Spirit renewing and recreating our love and friendship for all our fellows. This is our eucharist and this is our communion.[13]

While acknowledging that "the words and symbolic actions of the eucharist are experienced by very many Christians as a most powerful means of grace, a grace which shines forth clearly in their lives," Quakers believe that the grace of God cannot be restricted to any particular form of Eucharistic liturgy and that "the reality of God's presence may be known in worship that retains none of the traditional elements that are central to the life of many churches."[14] Furthermore, they worry that "separating a particular sacrament and making it a focal

---

[9] Richard A. Baer, Jr, "Silent Worship, Glossolalia, and Liturgy: Some Functional Similarities," *Quaker Religious Thought* 41.1 (1975): 30.
[10] Johns, "Worship and Sacraments," 264.
[11] Ibid., 269.
[12] John 4:24.
[13] Part of the Epistle from London Yearly Meeting 1928, *Quaker Faith and Practice* 26.15 (1995).
[14] *To Lima with Love: The Response from the Religious Society of Friends in Great Britain to the World Council of Churches Document Baptism, Eucharist and*

point in worship can obscure the sacramental validity of the rest of creation and human life."[15]

ANABAPTISTS

Anabaptists are a notoriously difficult group to define. Even figuring out what to call this group has been problematic. Their contemporaries called them enthusiasts, spiritualists, fanatics, Anabaptists, and baptists. Luther preferred the term *Schwärmer* – a German word that calls to mind the uncontrollable buzzing of bees around a hive. Calvin called them "fanatics," "deluded," "scatter brains," "scoundrels," and "mad dogs." The term that won out in history – "Anabaptist" – is unfortunate because it is somewhat misleading. It means "re-baptizers," and, strictly speaking, Anabaptists did not believe in re-baptizing: They advocated adult baptism or believers baptism and were convinced that infant baptism was invalid. Therefore, they claimed that baptism was not a rebaptism but the *only* one. Anabaptists today include Mennonites, the Amish, Hutterites, Church of the Brethren, and the Bruderhof.

Early Anabaptism was both geographically and theologically diverse. There were at least three identifiable streams of Anabaptism in Europe in 1520. It is not clear whether their beginnings were connected, although later on they may have influenced each other. Geographically, they may be distinguished as the South German/Austrian stream (Thomas Müntzer), the Swiss stream (Conrad Grebel, Felix Manz), and the North German/Dutch stream (Melchior Hoffman, Menno Simons). Although Anabaptism was not a unified movement, there were several motifs its members held in common: a rejection of infant baptism, a memorialist view of the Lord's Supper, and an emphasis on cross-bearing and martyrdom. The latter was no doubt prompted by the ferocity with which Anabaptists were hounded and killed by Catholics, Lutherans, and the Reformed. Death by drowning or being burned at the stake was not uncommon for Anabaptist leaders.

Worship and Ecclesiology

Early Anabaptists agreed with sixteenth-century reformers that salvation is God's gift, freely given and made available solely through faith in

---

Ministry (London: Quaker Home Service for London Yearly Meeting of the Religious Society of Friends [Quakers], 1987).

[15] Ibid.

Jesus Christ as Lord. However, unlike other reformers of the era, Anabaptists did not attempt to reform the structure of the church or its liturgy. Instead, they denied the efficacy and importance of sacramental objects, ceremonial acts, and liturgical seasons altogether.[16] They also interpreted scripture and the nature of the church differently from many of their contemporaries in the Roman Catholic and emerging Protestant traditions. Anabaptists recognized the practical necessity of some political order; however, they understood their true citizenship to be in the kingdom of God.

Anabaptists hoped to recover the pure church of apostolic times: a goal that seemed nearly impossible at a time when everyone was forced to belong to a state-controlled church. Indeed, during the sixteenth century, it was almost impossible for most people to imagine a Christian community existing outside of a particular relationship with the state. As Valerie Rempel notes, the church of that time performed civil functions as well as theological functions: It kept marriage and death records and provided birth records through the practice of infant baptism. Anabaptists did more than merely challenge the theology of infant baptism as a means of salvation: They were also challenging the very structure of the communities in which they were embedded.[17] Even today, Anabaptists refuse to fly any national flags in their sanctuaries, lest their allegiance to God be seen in any way as being blurred with allegiance to the state.

Baptism

According to their interpretation of John 5:7–8, Anabaptists believed that Christians undergo three baptisms: the baptism of water (a sign of the forgiveness of sins), the baptism of the Holy Spirit (which released spiritual gifts in the believer for the building up of the church), and the baptism of blood (an acknowledgment that living the way of Christ would entail suffering, hardship, and possibly death for the sake of the gospel).[18] Anabaptists questioned whether an infant or young child

---

[16] Walter Klaassen, *Anabaptism: Neither Catholic nor Protestant* (Waterloo, ON: Conrad, 1973), 12–14.

[17] Valerie G. Rempel, "Anabaptist and Mennonite Practices of Worship," in *Historical Foundations of Worship (Worship Foundations): Catholic, Orthodox, and Protestant Perspectives*, ed. Melanie Ross and Mark Lamport (Grand Rapids, MI: Baker Academic, 2022), 228.

[18] Rebecca Slough, "Baptismal Practice among North American Mennonites," in *Baptism Today: Understanding, Practice, Ecumenical Implications*, ed. Thomas F. Best, vol. 207 (Collegeville, MN: Liturgical Press, 2008), 91.

could fulfill the both joyful and difficult calling of being a disciple of Christ. Article one of the Schleitheim Confession (1527), one of the first Anabaptist writings on church order, explains that baptism is a particular event within a larger process wherein a person hears the gospel, confesses, repents, is forgiven, is regenerated, requests baptism, is incorporated into the church, and remains a disciple:

> Baptism shall be given to all those who have been *taught* repentance and the amendment of life and [who] *believe truly that their sins are taken away* through Christ, and to all those who *desire to walk* in the resurrection of Jesus Christ and be buried with Him in death, so that they might rise with Him; to all those who with such an understanding themselves *desire and request* it from us.[19]

Lord's Supper

When early Anabaptists were interrogated about their views of the Lord's Supper, most took the view that it was a simple memorial meal.[20] Anabaptists rejected the notion that specially sanctified persons, places, and things put humanity in touch with God. (At this point, they clearly followed their teacher Huldrych Zwingli.) This theology is demonstrated in their observance of the Lord's Supper. Anabaptists believed that the *act* of breaking bread and drinking wine, not the elements themselves, was sacramental. They placed greater significance on the horizontal dimensions of the meal, which often took place in their homes, regarding it as a time to be reconciled with each other and to commit themselves afresh to the community. In an effort to dissociate themselves completely from the sacramental words of the Catholic Mass, the Anabaptists insisted on the non-sacred function of words. Conrad Grebel wrote that only the words from the gospels or 1 Corinthians were to be used for the observance of the supper, with no additions. Until the mid-twentieth century, most Anabaptist groups also practiced foot washing as part of the celebration of the Lord's Supper: an act that called for humility and could function as a means of reconciliation for members who had been at odds with each other.

---

[19] The Schleitheim Confession, in *Legacy of Michael Sattler*, trans. and ed. John Howard Yoder (Scottdale, PA: Herald Press, 1973), 37.

[20] Some Anabaptists did use sacramental language. See John D. Rempel, *The Lord's Supper in Anabaptism: A Study in the Christology of Balthasar Hubmaier, Pilgram Marpeck, and Dirk Philips*, vol. 33 (Harrisonburg, VA: Herald Press, 1993).

Anabaptist worship today reflects its sixteenth-century theological roots. Anabaptists continue to baptize adult believers, share in the Lord's Supper as a memorial of Christ's death, offer mutual aid, and practice an "ethic of love in all relationships: an agape stance affirming even adversaries, seeking justice, building peace, reconciling relationships, confronting waste, living simply, honoring ecology, giving relief, sharing faith."[21]

METHODISM

Methodism began in the late eighteenth century when a group of men including John Wesley and his brother, Charles Wesley, sought to drive reforms from within the Church of England. While attending Oxford, the brothers established a weekly student meeting. Participants prayed, studied scripture, celebrated communion, and occasionally visited the sick or imprisoned. Fellow students derisively called the group the Holy Club, Sacramentarians, Methodists, or Bible Moths. "Methodist" was the name that stuck: a reference to their method of practicing the Christian faith. This group began a tradition that, generations later, would have a strong global presence and would become the second-largest Protestant denomination in the United States.

On May 24, 1738, John Wesley had a transforming experience of grace at an Anglican society meeting on Aldersgate Street, after which he wrote in his journal, "About a quarter before nine, while he was describing the changes which God works in the heart through faith in Christ, I felt my heart strangely warmed. I felt I did trust in Christ, Christ alone, for salvation; and an assurance was given me that He had taken away my sins, even mine, and saved me from the law of sin and death."[22] Soon thereafter, Wesley began evangelistic work, which quickly expanded throughout the British Isles. It is estimated that he rode over 250,000 miles on horseback and preached over 40,000 sermons. Wesley trained other circuit riders and organized new converts to groups for fellowship, accountability, and Bible study. Methodist societies were formed all over Great Britain.

Charles Wesley also preached widely, but his most enduring contribution to the Methodist movement was writing hymns that are still

---

[21] "An Anabaptist Theology of Worship," *WorshipTraining*. Accessed May 21, 2023, www.worshiptraining.com/media/an-anabaptist-theology-of-worship/.

[22] "Extracts from John Wesley's Journal," in *John and Charles Wesley*, ed. Frank Whaling (New York: Paulist, 1981), 107.

sung widely today, including "Love Divine, All Loves, Excelling" and "O for a Thousand Tongues to Sing." The Methodist movement was also a Eucharistic renewal movement, and the Wesleys' 166 *Hymns on the Lord's Supper*, published in 1745, are a rich treasure of Eucharistic piety. It has been argued that none of Charles Wesley's other hymns compare in quality and theological depth to those included in that selection.[23]

Methodism was countercultural in its day: While the Enlightenment downplayed sacramental worship, Wesley insisted on frequent communion, where zeal was encouraged. Methodists were accused of enthusiasm, and the introduction of hymn singing gave Methodism a warmth that was lacking in the staid worship of the Anglican state church.[24]

Anglican Roots

John Wesley, who was an ordained Anglican, loved the Book of Common Prayer. In September 1784, he declared, "I believe there is no liturgy in the world, either in ancient or modern language, which breathes a more solid, scriptural, rational piety, than the Common Prayer of the Church of England."[25] Consequently, Wesley wanted the people called the Methodists to attend worship in their local Anglican parish and "imbibe the Prayer Book's liturgies," which for Sunday morning usually consisted of "Morning Prayer, the Litany, and the first part of the Order for Holy Communion inclusive of the sermon or homily (the 'antecommunion') that was prior to the sacramental section."[26] Supplemental Methodist "preaching" services, which consisted of Scripture reading, preaching, prayer, and song, were also held early in the morning and late in the afternoon, so as not to interfere with "church hours" on Sundays. Watch-night services (from approximately eight p.m. to past midnight) and love-feasts (a service of sharing food, prayer, religious conversation, and hymns) were also important components of Methodist worship.

---

[23] Kenneth Cracknell and Susan J. White, *An Introduction to World Methodism* (Cambridge: Cambridge University Press, 2005), 180.

[24] James F. White, *A Brief History of Christian Worship* (London: Abingdon Press, 2010), 145.

[25] John Wesley, *The Letters of the Rev. John Wesley, A.M. – Standard Edition*, ed. John Telford, vol. VII (London: The Epworth Press, 1931), 239.

[26] Karen B. Westerfield Tucker, "Mainstream Liturgical Developments," in *The Oxford Handbook of Methodist Studies*, ed. William J. Abraham and James E. Kirby (Oxford: Oxford University Press, 2009), 296.

North American Developments

Wesley had no intention of splitting off from the Church of England: Instead, he hoped to revitalize it from the inside. However, within his own lifetime, Methodism would come to function like an independent movement, ultimately answerable to no one but its founder. Lester Ruth writes,

> With respect to Methodist worship, what John Wesley intended was not what he got. Although Wesley desired for Methodist worship to supplement the worship of the Church of England, which he wanted Methodists to attend, instead he sparked a movement whose members preferred their own Methodist practices and kept a tenuous connection to Anglicanism.[27]

A prime illustration of this tension can be found in the fate of Wesley's 1784 liturgical book, "The Sunday Service of the Methodist in North America with Other Occasional Services." Wesley's service – the first Methodist worship book – was clearly based on the Book of Common Prayer. Wesley abridged the prayer book, removing what he thought to be "unscriptural" material and taking into account what he perceived to be the liturgical needs of the Methodist communities in the newly emancipated American colonies. The book included texts for morning and evening prayer (for Sunday use only), the Lord's Supper, infant and adult baptism (but no rite of confirmation), marriage, burial, and ordination. As James F. White comments,

> Every page of the "Sunday Service" bears marks, not of a casual reviser, but of one who had read or heard the prayer book daily throughout eight decades, and who is determined to retain all that wore well and to discard only that which proved inadequate in his own experience.[28]

In a letter, Wesley specified how he expected American Methodists to utilize his redacted version of the prayer book (which was sent across the Atlantic alongside *A Collection of Psalms and Hymns for the Lord's Day*):

> [I have] prepared a Liturgy little differing from that of the Church of England (I think, the best constituted national Church in the world),

---

[27] Lester Ruth, "Liturgical Revolutions," ed. William J. Abraham and James E. Kirby (Oxford: Oxford University Press, 2009), 313.

[28] John Wesley and James F. White, *John Wesley's Prayer Book: The Sunday Service of the Methodists in North America* (Franklinville, NJ: OSL Publications, 1991), 3.

which I advise all the travelling preachers to use on the Lord's Day in all the congregations, reading the Litany only on Wednesdays and Fridays, and praying extempore on all other days. I also advise the elders to administer the Supper of the Lord, on every Lord's Day.[29]

The Lord's Supper would have been administered much less frequently in the Church of England at the time, so Wesley's admonition is notable. However, Wesley's liturgical disciplines were not greatly valued by his American followers. American Methodists "politely accepted" the 1784 book, but it was probably never widely used.[30] In the year after Wesley's death in 1791, the 314 pages of his "Sunday Service" were quietly laid aside in favor of thirty-seven pages of "Sacramental Services, &c." in the *Discipline* of that year. Simply put, "Wesley's love for the Book of Common Prayer, his emphasis on frequent eucharists, his affection for the church year – none of these survived passage across the Atlantic."[31] Reflecting on this history, Karen Westerfield Tucker suggests that Methodist worship today "may be identified as ordered and flexible, particular and catholic, traditional and contemporary, spiritual and worldly, local and global, pragmatic and perfectionist. Each of these poles, and indeed each pair of them, is valuable."[32]

PENTECOSTALISM

Pentecostalism is often traced back to the grassroots revival that broke out in Los Angeles, California, at the Azusa Street Mission under the leadership of African American Holiness preacher William J. Seymor.[33] The Azusa Street revival (1906–1908) engendered what came to be described as "classical" Pentecostalism associated with denominations such as the Assemblies of God, the Church of God in Christ, and the

---

[29] *The Letters of John Wesley*, vol. 7, ed. John Telford (London: Epworth, 1931), 239.
[30] Bryan D. Spinks, "Anglicans and Dissenters," in *The Oxford History of Christian Worship*, ed. Karen B. Westerfield Tucker and Geoffrey Wainwright (Oxford: Oxford University Press, 2006), 521.
[31] White, *Protestant Worship: Traditions in Transition*, 158.
[32] Karen B. Westerfield Tucker, "Sunday Worship in the World Parish: Observations," in *The Sunday Service of the Methodists: Twentieth-Century Worship in Worldwide Methodism*, ed. K. B. Westerfield Tucker (Nashville: Kingswood Books, 1996), 324.
[33] See Cecil M. Robeck, *The Azusa Street Mission and Revival: The Birth of the Global Pentecostal Movement* (Nashville: Thomas Nelson, 2006). American Pentecostal scholarship revolves around whether the ministries of Charles F. Parham (Topeka, 1901) or William H. Seymour (Azusa, 1906) constitute the origins of Pentecostalism.

Church of God (Cleveland, Tennessee). "Classical" Pentecostalism tended to emphasize an experience of grace and sanctification, subsequent to and distinct from salvation, which was evidenced by speaking in tongues.

Some fifty years after the Azusa Street revival, a new wave of Pentecostalism began in mainline Protestant churches. The second wave – which came to be known as the charismatic movement – began on a Sunday morning in 1959, when Reverend Dennis Bennett, pastor of an Episcopal Church in Van Nuys, California, announced to his congregation that he had been baptized with the Holy Spirit and had spoken in tongues. Bennett's story hit the local media, then *Time* and *Newsweek*, and then national television. Soon after, the movement spread to Baptist, Methodist, Presbyterian, Lutheran, and Roman Catholic churches. Like first-wave Pentecostals, Charismatics emphasize the work of the Holy Spirit and the continued operation of "miraculous" gifts. In contrast to the first wave, however, Charismatics did not separate into new denominations, but chose instead to remain within their existing liturgical and theological structures.

The "Third Wave" or "Neo-Charismatic" movement followed and gained momentum in the 1980s through the ministry of leaders such as Chuck Smith and John Wimber. Missiologist Peter Wagner explained the Third Wave as "a gradual opening of straightline evangelical churches to the supernatural ministry of the Holy Spirit without the participants becoming either Pentecostals or Charismatics."[34] The Third Wave stressed that after conversion there was hope for more than one filling with the Holy Spirit, which could include events like receiving healing, casting out demons, or announcing prophecies. Those who were "Spirit-filled" adamantly shunned the idea that they were spiritually elite, or better than other kinds of Christians.[35] Koinonia Vineyard is an example of a "Third Wave" church.

Worship Distinctives

Despite theological differences between the three waves of Pentecostalism, all three share a worldview that is radically open to God doing something different and new. Harvey Cox submits that Pentecostalism is "a protest against 'man-made creeds' and the

---

[34] C. Peter Wagner, "Healing Without Hassle," *Leadership* 6 (Spring 1985): 114.
[35] Athony C. Thiselton, *The Holy Spirit – in Biblical Teaching, Through the Centuries, and Today* (Grand Rapids, MI: Eerdmans, 2013), 422.

'coldness' of traditional worship."[36] Worship services include elements such as spontaneous prayers, "praise and worship" music with loud keyboard music, clapping of hands, dancing, and kinetic gestures such as hand raisings, prostrations, kneeling, and weeping. Some worshipers may be "slain in the Spirit" when hands are laid upon them and they fall to the floor under the "intoxicating" influence of the anointing Spirit.[37]

Pentecostals reject the idea that God has withdrawn the "dispensations" (miracles, tongues) that he once granted: The gifts of the Spirit are for all time and for all believers. Pentecostals see direct continuity between Israel, the early church, and the church in the twenty-first century. Accordingly, Pentecostal worship celebrates the healing – supernatural and natural, spiritual, social, psychological, and bodily – that God effects in the present day. Key biblical texts for Pentecostal worship include 2 Corinthians 3:17, "where the Spirit of the Lord is, there is freedom," and Galatians 5:1, "for freedom Christ has set us free."[38]

A particularly noteworthy aspect of Pentecostal worship is glossolalia: the Spirit-inspired utterances that Pentecostals believe must accompany the baptism in the Holy Spirit following conversion. The gift of tongues allows people to pray in non-rational meditative language that is not mediated.[39] There are biblical precedents for tongues: Paul does not forbid the use of tongues in the assembly and teaches that spontaneous prophecy could be delivered in tongues and interpreted in the context of corporate worship. Furthermore, Paul's reference to prayer as "inarticulate groanings too deep for words" in Romans 8:26–27 may be understood as referring primarily to glossolalia.

Musical Theology

Finally, Pentecostal musical theology has had a profound impact on all branches of Christian worship. In 1946, Pentecostal preacher Reg Layzell began teaching that corporate praise is the means by which

---

[36] Harvey Cox, *Fire from Heaven: The Rise of Pentecostal Spirituality and the Reshaping of Religion in the 21st Century* (Boston: Da Capo Press, 2009), 14.

[37] J. Kwabena Asamoah-Gyadu, *Contemporary Pentecostal Christianity: Interpretations from an African Context* (Eugene, OR: Wipf & Stock, 2013), 21.

[38] Telford Work, "Pentecostal and Charismatic Worship," in *The Oxford History of Christian Worship*, ed. Karen B. Westerfield Tucker and Geoffrey Wainwright (Oxford: Oxford University Press, 2006), 576.

[39] Walter J. Hollenweger, *The Pentecostals* (London: SCM, 1972), 272.

God becomes manifestly present in worship.⁴⁰ Many influential megachurches today, including Hillsong, Bethel, and Elevation, are heirs to this theology. They believe that the gifts of the Spirit are for today and that congregations should expect some sign of God's manifest presence when they worship. Some scholars have even argued that worship music in these communities plays an analogous role to that of sacraments in liturgical communities. Glenn Packiam suggests that sacramental imagination is the link between contemporary and liturgical worship: "Both believe that the Spirit communicates the presence of God to us through our senses and emotions, through the physiology of sound and sight, through the chemical activity in our brains when people sing together, and more."⁴¹ Emily Snider Andrews similarly argues that in congregations like Bethel, the experience of modern worship has become "an undergirding 'sacramental principle'" through which participants encounter God's presence.⁴²

EVANGELICAL MEGACHURCHES

In the 1980s, observers of American Christianity began to take note of a new phenomenon: Large congregations were attracting crowds of 2,000 or more worshippers on a weekly basis. These congregations were able to place gifted orators in their pulpits, supply professional musicians for worship, incorporate new developments in audio visual technology, and offer a wide array of classes, programs, and recreational activities on Sunday and throughout the week. Megachurches were beginning to remake the American religious landscape.

In 2020, The Hartford Institute for Religion Research defined megachurches as "Protestant churches with regular attendances pre-pandemic of 2,000 or more adults and children."⁴³ There are

---

40   See Lester Ruth and Lim Swee Hong, *A History of Contemporary Praise and Worship: Understanding the Ideas That Reshaped the Protestant Church* (Ada, MI: Baker Academic, 2021), 7ff.
41   "Why Contemporary Worship Isn't Actually Ruining the Church – Missio Alliance." Accessed March 18, 2023, www.missioalliance.org/why-contemporary-worship-is-not-ruining-the-church/.
42   Emily Snider Andrews, "Exploring Evangelical Sacramentality: Modern Worship Music and the Possibility of Divine-Human Encounter," (Ph.D. diss., Fuller Theological Seminary, 2020), 245.
43   "Megachurch Research." Accessed March 20, 2023, http://hirr.hartsem.edu/megachurch/research.html.

approximately 1,750 megachurches in the United States.[44] The majority of their participants are white and college educated, although this racial makeup is rapidly changing. In 2010, only 21 percent of megachurches were multiracial. Today, more than half (58 percent) report being multiracial, defined as having 20 percent or more minority presence in their congregation. Most megachurches are led by a long-tenured pastor. Although megachurches experience a constant churn – new people flow in the front door while others slip quietly out the back – the most recent data suggests that two-thirds of megachurch attendees have been at their churches for more than five years and are permanent, committed, and active participants.

Ritual Patterns

One of the great challenges megachurches face is that of making a Sunday morning worship experience engaging – even entertaining – for thousands of churchgoers without watering down the theological message. James K. Wellman, Jr., Katie E. Corcoran, and Kate J. Stockly address precisely this dilemma in their seminal work, *High on God: How Megachurches Won the Heart of America*. Integral to their argument is the work of sociologist Emile Durkheim, who posits a fundamental paradox: As *homo duplex*, humans desire to be unique autonomous beings, but we can only accomplish this in and through community. Megachurches "work" not because they help people reason their way out of the tension between individuality and community but because they meet their "emotional needs."[45] After their five-year study of twelve megachurches across the United States, the authors argue that megachurch leaders create an environment and a set of emotion-laden interactions that pull visitors in and keep them coming back.

Specifically, the authors detail their theory of a "Megachurch Ritual Cycle," which includes six megachurch practices linked to six core emotional desires: (1) Belonging and acceptance are provided by inviting

---

[44] While this section focuses on megachurches in the United States, it is important to note that there are significant numbers of megachurches throughout the world, especially in Korea, Brazil, and several African countries. The largest megachurch in American averages 60,000 in attendance; however, many global churches are much larger, including one church in Korea that claims over 250,000 attendees. See "The Definition of a Megachurch from Hartford Institute for Religion Research." Accessed March 18, 2023, http://hirr.hartsem.edu/megachurch/definition.html.

[45] James Wellman, Jr., Katie Corcoran, and Kate Stockly, *High on God: How Megachurches Won the Heart of America* (Oxford: Oxford University Press, 2020), 25.

websites, familiar architecture, and an "ultra-friendly welcome team"; (2) a "wow" factor is achieved through the music and lighting of worship services; (3) a reliable leader is established by the charismatic pastor in the talk or sermon; (4) deliverance is obtained through the altar call; (5) purpose is met through service groups; and (6) a recharge of emotional energy is attained through mid-week small groups.[46] Megachurches succeed because they understand how to create, motivate, and charge their congregations with emotional energy that stimulates intense loyalty and a visceral desire to keep returning for a recharge.

Music

The sonic experience of the music significantly contributes to the "wow factor" of worship. The music of the megachurch is typically of the Contemporary Worship Music (CWM) genre. Ethnomusicologist Monique Ingalls defines CWM as "a global Christian congregational song repertory modeled on mainstream Western popular music styles."[47] CWM is created to sound like commercial popular music. It features driving, fast-paced rhythms; simple harmonic structures; significant repetition; use of the major mode; and loud accompaniment.[48] Lyrics are generally drawn from one of two sources: excerpts of scriptural praise or narratives of religious experience. Music takes up a significant portion of megachurch services, with several songs following each other.

For many participants, part of the appeal of megachurches is that they are surrounded by many people in a vast space. However, the music allows each person to experience the service on a personal, intimate, visceral level. Kevin McElmurry calls this mode of worship "Alone/Together." People may be alone, but they experience the emotions of those around them. Indeed, the presence of other congregation members is "a deeply affective and effective way of socializing those who are 'outsiders' to experience the emotion of the insiders, to be close and witness another who is caught up in a 'moment.'"[49] This is why megachurches work so hard on getting the "unchurched" into their venues: They know that the joy and the "wow" of their services can

---

[46] Ibid., 83.
[47] Monique M. Ingalls, *Singing the Congregation: How Contemporary Worship Music Forms Evangelical Community* (New York: Oxford University Press, 2018), 5.
[48] John D. Witvliet, "The Blessing and Bane of the North American Mega-Church: Implications for Twenty-First Century Congregational Song," *Jahrbuch für Liturgik und Hymnologie* 37 (1998): 198.
[49] Wellman, Jr., et al., *High on God*, 109.

only be experienced in person, as the crowd and its emotion create a sense that something is happening here that happens nowhere else.[50]

Critics frequently charge megachurches with being a kind of religious "Disneyland" – a form of entertainment with little spiritual challenge from the pulpit and no sense of group belonging. Research shows something else: Megachurches succeed because they have created a system that responds to the deepest longings in the human spirit through acceptance; a sense of joy; a leader who inspires and offers deliverance; and a community that accepts, equips, and sends people out to serve.

CONCLUDING THOUGHTS

Quakers, Anabaptists, Methodists, Pentecostals, and Evangelicals – along with other post-Reformation Protestant groups – offer a minority yet significant witness within the church as a whole. They speak in a distinctive, sometimes disruptive voice, reminding other Christians of liturgical emphases that have sometimes received less historical attention. Quakers have always seen a clear connection between worship and justice: They were the first to oppose slavery and to achieve the equality of women. Anabaptists discovered profundities in believer's baptism as a life-and-death commitment that had rarely been known in traditional Christianity since the early church.[51] Methodists remind believers of all stripes about the dangers of formalism in worship and the power of heart-warming experiences. Pentecostals meet in the expectation that the presence of God will fall powerfully on those gathered. Evangelicals understand the importance of making public worship hospitable and presenting the gospel in a clear and compelling fashion. Ultimately, these post-Reformation churches challenge all Christians to question where battles of the past are still relevant and to ask if there are places where new common ground might be discovered.

For Further Reading

Dandelion, Pink, *The Liturgies of Quakerism* (Aldershot: Ashgate, 2005).
Ellis, Christopher J., *Gathering: A Theology and Spirituality of Worship in Free Church Tradition* (London: SCM Press, 2004).

---

[50] Ibid., 109.
[51] White, *Protestant Worship: Traditions in Transition*, 91.

Rempel, John D., *The Lord's Supper in Anabaptism: A Study in the Christology of Balthasar Hubmaier, Pilgram Marpeck, and Dirk Philips* (Waterloo, ON: Herald Press, 1993).

Ross, Melanie C., *Evangelical Worship: An American Mosaic* (New York: Oxford University Press, 2021).

Ruth, Lester, and Swee-Hong Lim, *A History of Contemporary Praise and Worship: Understanding the Ideas That Reshaped the Protestant Church* (Grand Rapids, MI: Baker Academic, 2021).

Westerfield Tucker, Karen, *American Methodist Worship* (New York: Oxford University Press, 2011).

White, James F., *Protestant Worship: Traditions in Transition* (Louisville, KY: Westminster/John Knox Press, 1989).

5 Liturgy in Eastern Christianity

STEFANOS ALEXOPOULOS

INTRODUCTION

Liturgy is at the heart of Eastern Christianity. The liturgical life and experience of each of the Eastern Christian Churches is the ritual expression and celebration of the gospel message of salvation in Christ, formed, evolved, and conveyed in each case through the culture, history, and artistic expression of each of the Eastern Christian Churches. It is a fact that there is a growing awareness of and interest in Eastern Christianity among Western Christians, in part because of the ecumenical movement in the last seventy years or so but also in part because of the plight of Eastern Christians in many parts of the world and their flight to countries of the Western world. Eastern Christian communities have been established throughout the world, some of them a couple of centuries old and quite integrated into mainstream society and others consisting of recent immigrant communities hosting Eastern Christian refugees who flee religious violence and lack of opportunities.[1]

---

[1] This chapter is based on Stefanos Alexopoulos and Maxwell Johnson, *Introduction to Eastern Christian Liturgies* (Collegeville, MN: Liturgical Press Academic, 2022), and Stefanos Alexopoulos, "Die Liturgie in den östlichen Kirchen," in *Handbuch der Liturgiewissenschaft Gottesdienst der Kirche* 1.1, ed. Martin Klöckener and Reinhard Meßner (Regensburg: Verlag Friedrich Pustet, 2022), 206–67. See also Ephrem Carr, "Liturgical Families in the East," *Handbook for Liturgical Studies*, vol. 1, *Introduction to the Liturgy*, ed. Anscar J. Chupungco (Collegeville, MN: Liturgical Press, Pueblo, 1997), 11–24; Christine Chaillot, "The Ancient Oriental Churches," in *The Oxford History of Christian Worship*, ed. Geoffrey Wainwright and Karen Westerfield Tucker (Oxford: Oxford University Press, 2006), 131–69; Lucas Van Rompay, "Excursus: The Maronites," in *The Oxford History of Christian Worship*, 170–74; Alexander Rentel, "Byzantine and Slavic Orthodoxy," in *The Oxford History of Christian Worship*, 254–306; Sebastian Brock, *Fire from Heaven*:

The exposure of the West to Eastern Christianity, however, was not something new in theological circles. Especially after the Reformation, and with the assistance of the printing press, Eastern Christianity was studied, initially and primarily for polemical reasons, both within the post-Reformation Catholic–Protestant conflict but also in the context of Catholic and Protestant missionary activity among Eastern Christians. The patristic, liturgical, and ecumenical movements gradually led to a greater appreciation of Eastern Christian traditions, with the Second Vatican Council marking the turning point in the changing attitudes toward Eastern Christianity.[2] Since then much progress has been made, which led Pope John Paul II to state that "the Church must breathe with her two lungs,"[3] while Sebastian Brock recently offered a corrective, adding the Syriac Orient as the "third lung" to the two lungs of Latin (Catholic) and Greek (Byzantine Orthodox) traditions.[4] Central to this appreciation and respect for Eastern Christianity is its theologically rich and ritually impressive liturgical rites.

The liturgical rites of Eastern Christian Churches broadly speaking represent four ecclesial communities. (1) Orthodox autocephalous churches all follow the Byzantine liturgical tradition and recognize the Patriarch of Constantinople as their first among equals. The mutual

---

Studies in Syriac Theology and Liturgy, Variorum Collected Studies Series 863 (Aldershot: Ashgate Publishing, 2006); Bryan Spinks, "Eastern Christian Liturgical Traditions: Oriental Orthodox," in *The Blackwell Companion to Eastern Christianity*, ed. Ken Parry (Oxford: Wiley-Blackwell, 2007), 339–67; Gregory Woolfenden, "Eastern Christian Liturgical Traditions: Eastern Orthodox," in *The Blackwell Companion to Eastern Christianity*, 319–38; Paul Naaman, *The Maronites: The Origins of an Antiochene Church*, Cistercian Studies 243 (Collegeville, MN: Cistercian Publications, 2009); Bishop Mar Awa Royel, *Mysteries of the Kingdom: The Sacraments of the Assyrian Church of the East*, 3rd ed. (Modesto, CA: Edessa Publications, 2018); Baby Varghese, *The Early History of the Syriac Liturgy: Growth, Adaptation and Inculturation* (Wiesbaden: Harrassowitz Verlag, 2021); Nina Glibetić, "History of Orthodox Worship," in *Historical Foundations of Worship: Catholic, Orthodox, and Protestant Prespectives*, ed. Melanie Ross and Mark Lamport (Grand Rapids, MI: Baker Academic, 2022), 85–97; Baby Varghese, "From the East to the West: Introduction of the West Syrian Liturgy Among the Saint Thomas Christians of South India," *The Syriac Annals of the Romanian Academy* 2 (2022): 197–224. For a more complete bibliography, see Alexopoulos and Johnson, *Introduction to Eastern Christian Liturgies*, 389–419.

[2] See its decree on Ecumenism, especially para. 14–18, "Unitatis redintegratio," Vatican: The Holy See, 2023, bit.ly/4jHMaiA.

[3] John Paul II, "Ut unum sint," par. 54; Vatican: The Holy See, 2023, bit.ly/44lh3yP.

[4] Sebastian Brock, "Variety in Institution Narratives in the Syriac Anaphoras," in *The Anaphoral Genesis of the Institution Narrative in Light of the Anaphora of Addai and Mari*, Orientalia Christiana Analecta 295, ed. Cesare Giraudo (Rome: Edizioni Orientalia Christiana, 2013), p. 65, n. 1.

excommunication of 1054 is traditionally given as the date of the schism between what we call today the Catholic West and the Orthodox East, but by all accounts, the pivotal point was the sack of Constantinople by the Fourth Crusade in 1204 and its ensuing pillaging and atrocities. (2) Oriental Orthodox churches, that is the churches that emerged out of those who did not accept the Council of Chalcedon in 451, include the Armenian Church, the Coptic Church, the Syriac Church, the Ethiopian Church, and the Eritrean Church; they all have their own liturgical rites but are in communion with one another. (3) The Church of the East is the Church that emerged out of those that did not accept the Council of Ephesus in 431; this church has its own liturgical rite. (4) The Eastern Catholic Church includes groups from the Orthodox, Oriental Orthodox or Church of the East who have entered into communion with Rome while maintaining their own liturgical rites. A unique member of this group is the Maronite Church, which follows its own Maronite Rite and does not have a counterpart among the Orthodox or the Oriental Orthodox, as it claims it was always in communion with Rome.

Correspondingly, there are seven extant liturgical rites of the Christian East: Armenian, Byzantine, Coptic, Ethiopian, East Syrian, West Syrian, Maronite. The Hagiopolitan Rite, the liturgical tradition of Jerusalem, while extinct, has exerted great influence in all Eastern (and Western for that matter) liturgical traditions. Special attention must be paid to the naming of these traditions. Historically, there is great variety in how these liturgical traditions are named; there are different ways, sometimes even overlapping, as some are based on confession, others on language, and others on political labels. Some are named after people, while others are geographical.[5]

Up to now, there have been two primary methodological approaches to examining Eastern liturgies: (1) philology and (2) comparative liturgy. The philological approach is centered primarily on the critical editions of original texts, which is absolutely necessary for the study of Eastern liturgies. On the other hand, the origins and evolution of liturgical rites are studied by the approach called comparative liturgy, founded by Anton Baumstark and incarnated in the work of Juan Mateos, Robert Taft, Gabriele Winkler, Paul Bradshaw, and their students.[6] More

---

[5] See Alexopoulos and Johnson, *Introduction to Eastern Christian Liturgies*, xvi–xviii.
[6] On the method of comparative liturgy, see Robert Taft, "Comparative Liturgy Fifty Years after Anton Baumstark (d. 1948): A Reply to Recent Critics," *Worship* 73 (1999): 521–40; Fritz West, *The Comparative Liturgy of Anton Baumstark* (Nottingham:

recently, (3) a third approach is complementing the previous two, which involves the use of ritual studies and the social sciences. This third method has been primarily applied to the Byzantine Rite and demonstrates the centrality of liturgy in understanding the history and culture of any Eastern Christian tradition.[7]

LITURGY AND EASTERN CHRISTIAN CHURCHES

"Liturgy is the soul of the Christian East."[8] The notion of liturgy is not just texts, rites, and rituals; rather, it is the ritual celebration of salvation in Christ; it is encountering the mystery of God, the now-and-not-yet of the Christian experience; it is the visible expression of the faith of a community, the incarnation of the Christian message in a particular time, place, culture, and people. The history of liturgy is a story of people at prayer, and the different liturgical traditions express particular cultural incarnations of a people at prayer. For liturgy is at their center as it expresses their faith, their life, their spirituality, their piety, their heritage, and their experience of God. Central to the identity, conscience, and liturgical practice of Eastern Christian traditions is the celebration of the Eucharistic liturgy. The Divine Liturgy (Byzantine), *Qurbana* (Syriac), *Badarak* (Armenian), *Prosfora* (Coptic), *Qedussah*

Grove Books Limited, 1995). In 1998 a conference tribute to Baumstark and his methodology took place; see Robert Taft and Gabriele Winkler (eds.), *Comparative Liturgy Fifty Years after Anton Baumstark (1872–1948): Acts of the International Congress, Rome, 25–29 September 1998*, OCA 265 (Rome: Pontificio Istituto Orientale, 2001); Anton Baumstark, *Comparative Liturgy*, ed. Bernard Botte (Westminster: Newman Press, 1958); and Anton Baumstark, *On the Historical Development of the Liturgy* (Collegeville, MN: Liturgical Press, 2011), introduction, translation, and annotation by Fritz West, and its preface by Robert Taft, xv–xxiv. Robert Taft, "The Structural Analysis of Liturgical Units: An Essay in Methodology," in *Beyond East and West: Problems in Liturgical Understanding* (Rome: Pontifical Oriental Institute, 1997), 187–202. See also Alexopoulos and Johnson, *Introduction to Eastern Christian Liturgies*, xix–xxi.

[7] See, for example, Robert Taft, *Through Their Own Eyes: Liturgy as the Byzantines Saw It* (Berkeley, CA: InterOrthodox Press, 2006); Derek Krueger, *Liturgical Subjects: Christian Ritual, Biblical Narrative, and the Formation of the Self in Byzantium* (Philadelphia, PA: University of Pennsylvania Press, 2014); the ongoing "Euchologia Project" of the Austrian Academy of Sciences, headed by Prof. Claudia Rapp; see www.oeaw.ac.at/en/imafo/research/byzantine-research/communities-and-landscapes/euchologia-project; and *Studia Patristica* 108, vol. 5 (2021), which contains papers of the Euchologia Project team presented at the Eighteenth International Conference on Patristic Studies held at Oxford in 2019.

[8] Taft, "Response to the Berakah Award," in *Beyond East and West*, 286. This part draws heavily upon Alexopoulos and Johnson, *Introduction to Eastern Christian Liturgies*, xxiv–xxv.

(East Syrian), or *Keddase* (Ethiopian), and worship as a whole, are seen respectively as the expression and summation of the faith of the Church. It is through worship that Scripture is taught, as Scripture permeates every aspect of Eastern worship,[9] and the worship space is filled in many traditions with an iconic representation of the Divine Economy (scenes from the Old and New Testaments) and the life of the Church (martyrs and saints).

Among Eastern Christians there is a sense of ownership of their liturgical tradition, as it connects them as a community with their historical, cultural, and theological roots. Eastern Christians have a very strong sense of community, fostered by communal liturgical celebrations. In these communities clergy have a role of liturgical, spiritual, and communal leadership. Because Eastern Christians have survived in contexts hostile to Christianity (and many still do), the notion and sense of martyrdom is very real for them. The martyrs of the early Church and the neo-martyrs of recent centuries are sources of inspiration and courage, giving a strong eschatological flavor to their liturgy and spirituality. This reality heightens their sense and awareness of the responsibility to hand down their tradition to the coming generations. Finally, Eastern liturgies have a sense of transcendence: "The liturgy is transcendent but not distant, hieratic but not clericalized, communal but not impersonal, traditional but not formalistic."[10]

It is within this context that the Eastern Christian understanding of sacraments and sacramental theology is articulated and understood. In speaking about sacraments, Eastern Christians usually use the term "mysteries," from the Greek word *mysterion*, and its equivalent in other Eastern languages. The sacramental life of the Church is about participating in the sacraments, not just "receiving" the sacraments.[11] It is through the celebration of and participation in the sacraments that the faithful enter into communion with the triune God, where the community experiences the presence of God; in other words, through sacramental participation they enter into the mystery of salvation. While most Eastern Churches talk about "seven" sacraments, this

---

[9] Stefanos Alexopoulos, "The Use of the Bible in Byzantine Liturgical Texts and Services," in *Oxford Handbook of the Bible in Orthodox Christianity*, ed. Eugen Pentiuc (Oxford: Oxford University Press, 2022), 243–60.

[10] Taft, "Sunday in the Byzantine Tradition," *Beyond East and West*, 67.

[11] Michael Fahey, "Sacraments in the Eastern Churches," in *The New Dictionary of Sacramental Worship*, ed. Peter Fink (Collegeville, MN: Liturgical Press, Michael Glazier, 1990), 1123–30, at 1125.

number has been superimposed on them through direct or indirect scholastic Western influence.[12] Historically, the lists of sacraments of Eastern Churches include – in addition to the standard seven (baptism, chrismation, Eucharist, ordination, penance, marriage, unction) – funerals, the tonsure of monks, the blessing of waters on Epiphany, and the consecration of a church.

EASTERN CHRISTIAN LITURGICAL RITES

What follows is a short survey of the seven extant Eastern Christian liturgical rites (Armenian, Byzantine, Coptic, Ethiopic, East Syrian, West Syrian, Maronite),[13] beginning, however, with the now extinct Hagiopolite Rite (the liturgy of Jerusalem and Palestine), which has liturgically influenced, to a greater or lesser degree, almost all of the liturgical traditions of the Christian East and even Western rites.

Hagiopolite Liturgy

In the fourth century, and with the help of imperial patronage, Jerusalem became *the* pilgrimage center of the Christian world, establishing its own liturgical identity and developing its own ritual tradition, which is called in the documents "Hagiopolite" (Jerusalem was now called *Hagia Polis* – Holy City, hence the term "Hagiopolite"). The heyday of the Hagiopolite Rite was the period between the fourth and the sixth centuries. Persian and then Arab invasions and conquests in the seventh century and later halted its development. The ninth century marks the beginning of the Byzantinization of the Hagiopolite Rite,

---

[12] Thomas Hopko, as quoted by D. Smolarski, *Sacred Mysteries: Sacramental Principles and Liturgical Practice* (New York: Paulist Press, 1995), 1; Christiann Kappes, "A New Narrative for the Reception of Seven Sacraments into Orthodoxy: Peter Lombard's *Sentences* in Nicholas Cabasilas and Symeon of Thessalonica and the Utilization of John Duns Scotus by the Holy Synaxis," *Nova et Vetera* 15, English ed. (2017): 383–419; see also Yury Avvakumov, "Sacramental Ritual in Middle and Later Byzantine Theology: Ninth–Fifteenth Centuries," in *The Oxford Handbook of Sacramental Theology*, ed. Hans Boersma and Matthew Levering (Oxford: Oxford University Press, 2015), 249–66, at 253–54; Stefanos Alexopoulos, "'The Savior Accomplished the Sacraments in Himself:' Symeon of Thessalonike's Christological Approach to the Seven Sacraments," in *LET US BE ATTENTIVE! Proceedings of the Seventh International Congress of the Society of Oriental Liturgy*, ed. Martin Lüstraeten, Brian Butcher, and Steven Hawkes-Teeples (Münster: Aschendorff, 2020), 11–21.

[13] This section summarizes material from Alexopoulos and Johnson, *Introduction to Eastern Christian Liturgies*, xxv–xli.

a process that was completed by the thirteenth century.[14] Although the language of the Hagiopolite Rite was Greek,[15] its most important sources have survived in other languages such as Latin, and in Armenian and Georgian translations of Greek sources.[16] Equally important for understanding the Hagiopolite Rite is the parallel development of the significant monastic life of the Judean desert.[17] The Divine Liturgy of St. James is the Eucharistic liturgy associated with the Hagiopolite Rite.[18]

The Armenian Rite

The roots of the Armenian Rite can be traced to Syria (Edessa) in the south and Cappadocia (Caesarea) in the west. Armenia became the first nation in history to become Christian at the very beginning of the fourth century (301 AD), and the invention of the Armenian alphabet in the early fifth century and the subsequent translation of the Bible and

---

[14] On the Byzantinization of the Hagiopolite Rite, see Daniel Galadza, *Liturgy and Byzantinization in Jerusalem* (Oxford: Oxford University Press, 2018).

[15] See for example, *Lectures on the Christian Sacraments: The Procatechesis and the Five Mystagogical Catecheses Ascribed to St Cyril of Jerusalem*, trans. Maxwell E. Johnson (Yonkers, NY: St Vladimir's Seminary Press, 2017); Michel Aubineau, *Les homélies festales d'Hesychius de Jérusalem*, vol. 1: *Les homélies I–XIV*, Subsidia hagiographica 59 (Brussels: Societé des Bollandistes, 1978); Papadopoulos-Kerameus, "Τυπικὸν τῆς ἐν Ἱεροσολύμοις Ἐκκλησίας (Cod. XLIII S. Crucis)," in Ἀνάλεκτα Ἱεροσολυμιτικῆς Σταχυολογίας, vol. 2, 1–254 (St. Petersburg, 1891).

[16] Anne McGowan and Paul F. Bradshaw, *The Pilgrimage of Egeria: A New Translation of the Itenerarium Egeriae with Introduction and Commentary*, ACC 93 (Collegeville, MN: Liturgical Press, 2018); Athanase Renoux, *Le codex arménien Jérusalem 121*, I: *Introduction* (Patrologia Orientalis 35, fasc. 1, no. 63, 1969), II: *Édition* (Patrologia 36, fasc. 2, no. 168, 1971); for the Georgian Lectionary, see Michel Tarchnischvili, *Le grand lectionnaire de l'Église de Jérusalem (Ve–VIIIe siècle)* (Louvain: Secrétariat du Corpus scriptorium Christianorum orientalium, 1959–1960); Charles Renoux, *L'hymnaire de Saint-Sabas (Ve–VIIIe siècle): Le manuscript géorgien H2123. III. De la nativité de notre seignur Jésus-Christ au Samedi de Lazare*, Patrologia Orientalis 58.2 (Turnhout: Brepols, 2021), 389 [149] – 405 [165].

[17] Joseph Patrich, *Sabas, Leader of Palestinian Monasticism: A Comparative Study in Eastern Monasticism* (Washington, DC: Dumbarton Oaks Research Library and Collection, 1995).

[18] For the text tradition, see B. Ch. Mercier, *La liturgie de saint Jacques: édition critique du texte grec avec traduction latine* (Paris: Typographie Firmin-Didot, 1946); Alkiviadis Kazamias, Ἡ Θεία Λειτουργία τοῦ Ἁγίου Ἰακώβου τοῦ Ἀδελφοθέου καὶ τὰ νέα Σιναϊτικὰ Χειρόγραφα (Thessaloniki: Ἱερὰ Μονὴ Θεοβαδίστου Ὄρους Σινᾶ, 2006); Lili Khevsuriani, Mzekala Shanidze, Michael Kavtaria, Tinatin Tseradze, and Stéphan Verhelst, *Liturgica Ibero-Graeca Sancti Iacobi: Editio – translatio – retroversio – commentarii*. Jerusalemer Theologisches Forum 17 (Münster: Aschendorff Verlag, 2011).

Christian literature opened the next phase of Armenian liturgical history. Together with its early Syrian[19] and Cappadocian roots,[20] and the later Byzantine influence,[21] the Armenian Rite developed in close connection with Jerusalem.[22] Finally, the presence of the Crusaders between the twelfth and fifteenth centuries resulted in a very intriguing cultural exchange, which also influenced liturgical practice. All these elements are incorporated organically and creatively within the same liturgical tradition, while maintaining ancient liturgical uses otherwise lost.[23] The theology emanating from the Armenian Rite is strongly incarnational, inspired and influenced by the Christology of Cyril of Alexandria.[24] The Armenian Rite is the liturgical expression of the Armenian Church and its Catholic counterpart.

The Byzantine Rite

The Byzantine Rite as it survives and is celebrated today is a hybrid rite, the result of the synthesis and fusion of the liturgy that was celebrated (1) in the Great Church of Hagia Sophia in Constantinople and in the streets of the city in the context of liturgical processions and (2) with the liturgical tradition of the Anastasis Cathedral and Palestinian monasteries, particularly Hagios Sabas, in the Judean desert. The Byzantine Rite – in other words, the liturgy of the Orthodox Patriarchate of Constantinople – was gradually adopted by the Chalcedonian Patriarchates of Alexandria, Antioch, and Jerusalem, who were thus "byzantinized."[25] As a result, the Byzantine Rite is the common liturgical expression of Orthodox Churches, and the largest communion among Eastern Churches and their Eastern Catholic counterparts. Important turning points in the history of the Byzantine Rite,

---

[19] See Gabriele Winkler, *Das armenische Initiationsrituale. Entwicklungsgeschichtliche und liturgievergleichende Untersuchung der Quellen des 3. Bis 10. Jahrhunderts*, OCA 217 (Rome: Pontificio Istituto Orientale, 1982).

[20] See M. Daniel Findikyan, *The Commentary on the Armenian Daily Office by Bishop Step'anos Siwnec'I (d. 735): Critical Edition and Translation with Textual and Liturgical Analysis*, OCA 270 (Rome: Pontificio Istituto Orientale, 2004), 511–15.

[21] See Charles Renoux, "Un bilan provisoire sur l'héritage grec du rite arménien," *Le Muséon* 116 (2003): 53–69.

[22] See Charles Renoux, *Le lectionnaire de Jérusalem en Arménie: le Čašoc*, Patrologia Orientalis 44.4 (Turnhout: Brepols, 1989).

[23] Alexopoulos and Johnson, *Introduction to Eastern Christian Liturgies*, xxix–xxx.

[24] Robert Taft, "The Armenian Liturgy: Its Origins and Characteristics," in *Treasures in Heaven: Armenian Art, Religion, and Society*, papers delivered at the Pierpont Morgan Library at a Symposium organized by Thomas F. Mathews and Roger S. Wieck, May 21–22, 1994 (New York, 1998), 13–30, at 22–23.

[25] See Galadza, *Liturgy and Byzantinization in Jerusalem*.

which influenced its evolution and celebration, are Iconoclasm (726–842) and its aftermath, the sack of Constantinople by the Fourth Crusade (1204), the Fall of Constantinople in 1453, and the invention of the printing press.[26] The Byzantine Rite is the liturgical expression of the Eastern Orthodox Churches and their Catholic counterparts.

The Coptic Rite

Tracing its roots back to the missionary work of St. Mark the Evangelist in Egypt, Christianity initially grew among the Hellenistic Jewish communities and the Greek-speaking coastal area of Egypt, but it quickly spread in the south among the Coptic-speaking indigenous population. The fifth-century Christological controversies were a pivotal point for Christianity in Egypt; the Greek-speaking coastline, centered around Alexandria, accepted Chalcedon, while the Coptic-speaking hinterlands refused Chalcedon and were persecuted, their leadership taking refuge at the monastery of St. Macarius. Thus monastic culture significantly influenced Coptic liturgy. As a consequence of the Arabic conquest of 640, Coptic was replaced by Arabic as the language of the people, but the use of Coptic continues to be used as the liturgical language of the Coptic Church to this day.[27] The Coptic Rite is the liturgical expression of the Coptic Church and its Catholic counterpart.

The Ethiopian Rite

The Ethiopian Rite has traditionally been seen as a variant of the Coptic Rite, but in fact it has its own fascinating and distinct history and development,[28] going back to at least the fourth century, when Frumentius and Edesius converted the emperor's son, leading to

---

[26] See the classic outline of the history of Byzantine Liturgy: Robert Taft, *The Byzantine Rite: A Short History* (Collegeville, MN: Liturgical Press, 1992). Parts of this outline have been challenged by Stig Frøyshov, "The Early History of the Hagiopolitan Daily Office in Constantinople," *Dumbarton Oaks Papers* 74 (2020): 351–82. For a response, defending Taft's outline, see Stefano Parenti, "The Beginning of the Hagiopolite Liturgy in Constantinople: New Narrative or Historical Novel? About an Article by Stig R. Frøyshov," *Medioevo Greco* 22 (2022): 399–427. The dust has not yet settled on this.

[27] Alexopoulos and Johnson, *Introduction to Eastern Christian Liturgies*, xxxiv–xxxv.

[28] On Ethiopian Christianity, see Hebtemichael Kidane, "Ethiopian (Ge'ez) Worship," in *The New Westminster Dictionary of Liturgy & Worship*, ed. Paul Bradshaw (Louisville, KY: Westminster/John Knox Press, 2003), 169–72; Aziz S. Atiya, *History of Eastern Christianity* (Notre Dame, IN: University of Notre Dame Press, 1968), 146–66; Adrian Hastings, *The Church in Africa: 1450–1950* (Oxford: Clarendon Press, 1994), chs. 1, 4, and 6; Elizabeth Isichei, *A History of Christianity in Africa from Antiquity to the Present* (London: SPCK, 1995).

Christianity being declared the imperial religion by 330. The Ethiopian tradition bears the marks of Coptic and Syriac influence and is unique among Eastern Christian traditions for the presence of unique Old Testament practices, whose origins still puzzle scholars. Finally, the Ethiopian Rite is also characterized by a number of its own particular features, such as its highly refined system of hymnography and hymnology composed of twelve hymnographic forms. The city of Axum is considered to be the cradle of Christianity in Ethiopia. The Ethiopian Rite is the liturgical expression of the Ethiopian and Eritrean Churches and their Catholic counterparts.[29]

The East Syrian Rite

The East Syrian Rite is the ritual expression of Mesopotamian Christianity. Its theological and intellectual centers since the second century were the cities of Edessa (Urfa, Turkey) and, after the Council of Ephesus, Nisibis (Nusyabin, Syria) within the Persian Empire. Associated with the Christology of Nestorius, and thus isolated from the Byzantine (Greek) world, it developed its unique liturgy with clearly Semitic features preserving ancient practices. One of the characteristics of the East Syrian Rite is its emphasis on the glory and praise of God with an eschatological outlook. A number of East Syrian prayers do not contain a petition; their main objective is simply praising and worshiping God:

> Thou, O my Lord, art in truth the quickener of our bodies and thou art the good savior of our souls and the constant preserver of our lives: thee, O Lord, we are bound to confess and adore and glorify at all times, Lord of all, Father and Son and Holy Ghost, for ever.[30]

The East Syrian Rite is the liturgical expression of the Ancient (Assyrian) Church of the East and its Catholic counterparts, the Chaldean Catholic Church and the Syro-Malabar Catholic Church in India.[31]

The West Syrian Rite

The early liturgical traditions of Antioch and Jerusalem lie at the heart of the West Syrian Rite. The West Syrian Rite is connected to the

---

[29] Alexopoulos and Johnson, *Introduction to Eastern Christian Liturgies*, xxxvi–xxxvii.
[30] F. E. Brightman (ed.), *Liturgies, Eastern and Western: Being the Texts, Original or Translated, of the Principal Liturgies of the Church*, vol. 1. *Eastern Liturgies* (London: Oxford University Press, 1965), 255.
[31] Alexopoulos and Johnson, *Introduction to Eastern Christian Liturgies*, xxxvii–xxxviii.

Christians of the geographical region of Syria who rejected the Council of Chalcedon. It was originally bilingual, with both Greek and Syriac in use, but gradually Syriac became the predominant language, with Arabic becoming significant after the Arab conquest. The West Syrian Rite is the ritual expression of the Syrian Orthodox Church and its Catholic counterpart, the Syrian Catholic Church, and of the Malankara Orthodox Church in India and its Catholic counterpart, the Syro-Malankara Church.[32]

The Maronite Rite

The Maronite Rite is part of the Syrian family of rites,[33] with liturgical influence from West Syrian, East Syrian, and Jerusalem, but it is defined by its own particular context, as the Monastery of St. Maron became associated with the defense of Christology of the Council of Chalcedon in the area. After the tenth century, Mount Lebanon became the heartland of the Maronite Church. Their contact with the Crusades and the ensuing relationship with the Roman Catholic Church resulted in massive Latin influence, which resulted in some pushback.[34] It is only recently, after Vatican II, that there has been a move to discover the Syrian origins of this rite, thus moving toward a restoration of Maronite liturgy, architecture, and iconography.[35] The Maronite Rite is the liturgical expression of the Maronite Church.[36]

THE SPIRIT OF EASTERN CHRISTIAN LITURGIES

For Eastern Christians, liturgy and identity are intimately connected.[37] Their identities are formed in liturgical celebrations experienced as occasions of comfort, consolation, peace, strength, and courage, especially in times of distress, repression, persecution, and expulsion. Rooted in the ancient liturgical centers of the Eastern Christian world, and despite unfortunate divisions due to the Christological controversies, political

---

[32] Ibid., xxxviii–xxxix.
[33] It was William Macomber who first made the strong case that the Maronite Rite is a distinct rite. See William Macomber, "A Theory on the Origins of the Syrian, Maronite, and Chaldean Rites," *Orientalia Christiana Periodica* 39 (1973): 235–42.
[34] Lucas van Rompay, "Excursus: The Maronites," in *The Oxford History of Christian Worship*, ed. Wainwright and Westerfield Tucker, 170–74, at 171.
[35] Abdo Badwi, *The Liturgical Year Iconography of the Syro-Maronite Church* (Kaslik: Publications de l'Université Saint-Esprit de Kaslik, 2006).
[36] Alexopoulos and Johnson, *Introduction to Eastern Christian Liturgies*, xl–xli.
[37] This section summarizes Alexopoulos and Johnson, *Introduction to Eastern Christian Liturgies*, 355–88.

tensions, and historical events, the liturgical traditions of Eastern Christianity present a remarkable unity in diversity, in expressing the one Christian faith in diverse cultural contexts. In spite of division going back to the Councils of Ephesus (431) and Chalcedon (451), recent theological encounters in the context of the ecumenical dialogue among the Churches has shown a remarkable unity in the expression of faith.[38] The realization has become stronger that liturgy is the authentic expression of faith articulated, prayed, lived, and taught in each tradition. A close reading of liturgical texts of the various Eastern Christian traditions reveals a common and shared foundational faith that emerges as a surprising unifying factor in spite of centuries-old divisions.[39]

Pivotal to the liturgical life of Eastern Christians is the celebration of and participation in the mysteries, and particularly of the Eucharist. In these there is a strong sense not only of God's initiative in worship but also of our response. For example, Nicholas Cabasilas, a fourteenth-century spiritual author of the Byzantine tradition, wrote in *The Life in Christ*,

> There is an element which derives from God, and another which derives from our own zeal. The one is entirely His work, the other involves striving on our part. However, the latter is our contribution only to the extent that we submit to His grace and do not surrender the treasure nor extinguish the torch when it has been lighted.[40]

---

[38] Sebastian Brock, "The Origins of the Qanona 'Holy God, Holy Mightly, Holy Immortal' According to Gabriel of Qatar (Early 7th Century)," *The Harp: A Review of Syriac and Oriental Studies* 21 (2019): 173–86; Sebastian Brock, "The Syriac Churches and Dialogue with the Catholic Church," *Heythrop Journal* 44 (2004): 466–76; Christine Chaillot (ed.), *The Dialogue Between the Eastern Orthodox and Oriental Orthodox Churches* (Volos: Volos Academy Publications, 2016).

[39] See, for example, Sebastian Brock, "The 'Nestorian' Church: A Lamentable Misnomer," *Bulletin of the John Rylands Library* 78 (1996): 23–35; Robert Taft, "Mass Without the Consecration? The Historic Agreement on the Eucharist between the Catholic Church and the Assyrian Church of the East Promulgated 26 October 2001," *Worship* 77 (2003): 492–509; Mar Awa Royel, "A Survey of the Christology of the Assyrian Church of the East as Expressed in the *Khudra*," unpublished paper, available at bit.ly/433MYHu (last visited November 20, 2020); Stefanos Alexopoulos, "Greek Scholarship on the Coptic Liturgical Tradition: An Assessment," in ΣΥΝΑΞΙΣ ΚΑΘΟΛΙΚΗ: *Beiträge zu Gottesdienst und Geschichte der fünf altkirchlichen Patriarchate für Heinzerd Brakmann zum 70. Geburtstag*, Orientalia-Patristica-Oecumenica 6.1, ed. Diliana Atanassova and Tinatin Chronz (Berlin: Lit Verlag, 2014), 1–11.

[40] Nicholas Cabasilas, *The Life in Christ* (New York: St Vladimir's Seminary Press, 1974), 48–49.

Our salvation necessitates our own response to God's invitation, and that encounter primarily takes place in Eastern Churches within the liturgical life and experience. The outcome of this encounter is newness of life, unity with Christ, becoming one with Christ, lived and experienced in the sacramental life. This is how Cabasilas puts it:

> In the sacred Mysteries, then, we depict His burial and proclaim his death. By them we are begotten and formed and wondrously united to the Savior, for they are the means by which, ... "in him we live, we move, and have our being" (Acts 17:28). Baptism confers being and, in short, existence according to Christ. It receives us when we are dead and corrupted and first leads us into life. The anointing with Chrism perfects him who has received new birth by infusing into him the energy that befits such a life. The Holy Eucharist preserves and continues this life and health. It is therefore by this Bread that we live and by the chrism that we are moved, once we have received being from the baptismal washing.[41]

And the purpose of sacramental participation is salvation:

> What then could be a greater proof of kindness and benevolence than that He who washes with water should set the soul free from uncleanness? Or that He by anointing it with chrism should grant it to reign in the heavenly kingdom? Or that He as the Host of the banquet should provide His own Body and Blood? And moreover, that men should become Gods (cf. Jn 10:35) and sons of God (cf. Rom 8:14). And that our nature should be honoured with God's honour, and that dust should be raised to such a height of glory as to become equal in honour and dignity to the divine nature?[42]

In the sacramental life the Holy Spirit plays a pivotal role, connecting it with Divine Economy and thus making every Christian a part of salvation history. The fourth-century Saint Ephrem the Syrian writes in a poem,

> See, Fire and Spirit are in the womb of her who bore You;
> see, Fire and Spirit are in the river in which You were baptized.
> Fire and Spirit are in our baptismal font,
> in the Bread and the Cup are Fire and Holy Spirit.[43]

---

[41] Ibid., 49–50.
[42] Ibid., 51–52.
[43] Sebastian Brock, *The Luminous Eye: The Spiritual World Vision of Saint Ephrem*, 2nd ed. (Kalamazoo: Cistercian Publications, 1992), 108. I am grateful to Alex Neroth van Vogelpoel for bringing this hymn to my attention.

Sacramental life, with Eucharistic participation at its core and its apex, is the process through which Christians grow into the mystery of God and allow themselves to be assumed by that mystery that can only be approached by faith rooted in salvation history and the apostolic experience. A tenth-century Coptic author wrote about the Eucharist,

> When he wanted to redeem us through himself and to raise us up to heaven, he established for us an economy, so that he would remain with us forever, just as he was with his disciples. He commanded us to take the bread (from which comes our flesh as well as his flesh) and the water and wine (from which comes our blood as well as his blood), to raise them up on the holy altar, and to ask him in his name for what he taught us, so that he might descend upon them through his Holy Spirit, through whom he descended upon the flesh and blood of Mary, and so that he might transform them into his body and blood. [He did this] so that he might truly come to be with us in a visible, comprehensible, and tangible way, just as he was with the apostles – so that he might die for our sakes, just as he died for the people at that time; that he might be twisted up by being torn and discarded on the plate, just as he was wrapped up in linen bands and discarded in the tomb, and that he might pour out his blood for our sake in the cup, just as he poured out his blood on Golgotha.[44]

Participation in the Eucharist leads to one's unity with Christ. Saint Ephrem the Syrian puts it in the following way:

> In a new way his body has been fused with our bodies,
> and his pure blood has been poured into our veins.
> His voice, too, is in our ears and his splendor in our eyes.
> The whole of him with the whole of us is fused by his mercy.
> And because he loved his Church greatly, he did not give her the manna of her rival;
> He became the Bread of Life for her to eat him.

He then highlights the sacramental potential of all creation and its participation in the Economy of Salvation:

> Wheat, olive and grape that were created for our use,
> these three in three ways serve you in symbol.

---

[44] Pseudo-Sawirus ibn al-Mugaffa', *Book of Elucidation*, as presented in Stephen Davis, *Coptic Christology in Practice: Incarnation and Divine Participation in Late Antique and Medieval Egypt* (Oxford: Oxford University Press, 2008), 298. I am grateful to Fr. Arsenius Mikhail for bringing this text to my attention.

> With three medicines you have cured our sickness;
> humanity was weak, suffering and failing;
> you have strengthened it with your blessed Bread,
> you have consoled it with your sober Wine,
> and you have given it joy with your holy Anointing.[45]

Eastern Christians participate in the Eucharist with a deep sense of their personal unworthiness, with a profound faith in God's loving-kindness and forgiveness, and with the awareness that it is a continuous call to holiness. An Armenian Eucharistic hymn notes:

> The Medicine of Life flew from on high to reside in those worthy of it.
> Let us make holy our souls and thoughts in honor of His glory.
> We hold God in our hands: let there be no blemish in our bodies.
> Once He has entered, He takes up residence with us,
> so let us make ourselves holy within.[46]

But this emphasis on the sacramental life, so evident in the liturgical life of Eastern Christian churches, does not mean that they are not biblical, of which they are sometimes accused. They are *both* liturgical *and* biblical! Both the Old and New Testaments are central to the faith, worship, and life of all Eastern Christian traditions and define every aspect of their life. Not only is the worship of Eastern Christians replete with Scriptural texts, but the book of Psalms is the foundation (both structurally and thematically) to hymnography, and prayers and hymns are full of direct quotations, paraphrases, and allusions to Scripture.[47]

An example of the use of Scripture in hymnology, which in the context of the liturgical year also offers a hermeneutic to Scripture, is the entrance hymn for the feast of the Cross on September 14 in the Maronite liturgical tradition. This hymn offers a glimpse into the soul of Eastern Christians who hold the Cross dearly in their hearts and affords us the opportunity to see how through hymnography the Scripture is taught and interpreted:

> Alleluia! Lord, your cross was taken from the tree in Eden, and your death upon the cross has granted new life to all the world. In its

---

[45] Adapted from Robert Murray, *Symbols of Church and Kingdom: A Study in Early Syriac Tradition* (Cambridge: Cambridge University Press, 1975), 77.
[46] Brock, *The Luminous Eye*, 112–13.
[47] See Alexopoulos and Johnson, *Introduction to Eastern Christian Liturgies*, 359–66.

shadow refuge can be found for the rich and poor. All the prophets and the martyrs sing its praises. On this day we join them in giving glory. Alleluia! The cross is our light!

Alleluia! When they crucified the Lord, our great Redeemer, and he died upon the cross for our salvation, all was fulfilled. Joseph, his disciple, with great love came to bury him. He beheld and touched the body of the Savior. On this day we join with him in giving glory. Alleluia! The cross is our light!

Alleluia! With the cross we bless ourselves for Christ's protection. When the Tempter comes to us with his deception and sees the cross; far from it he flees and hides himself in the darkest depths, for the holy cross is mighty and defends us. On this day we raise it up in exaltation. Alleluia! The cross is our light![48]

Redemption through the Cross is central to how Eastern Christians have faced the reality and experience of persecution and martyrdom throughout the centuries.[49]

A question that is often posed relates to the potential contribution of Eastern Christianity and its liturgical traditions to the modern world. In other words, is the value of Eastern Christianity its "other worldliness," or does it have something to offer? One way to approach this question is through the monastic perspective of Eastern Christian Churches. Asceticism and its various expressions have left their imprint on both the liturgy and spirituality of Eastern Christianity. For example, the ascetical practice of fasting, embedded in the liturgical cycles of the liturgical year and in some cases covering two-thirds of the whole year, is a prophetic voice in today's world, which is plagued by consumerism and individualism (among other things). In the Eastern Christian tradition fasting is not only about self-control but also about turning one's attention to one's neighbor and attending to their needs, a prophetic call to social justice. The following hymn from the first Wednesday of Great Lent puts it this way:

> Come, faithful ones, as we fast bodily, let us also fast in spirit. Let us undo every tie to injustice; let us break all stifling covenants with violence; let us burst every wrongful contract; let us give bread to

---

[48] *Book of Offering: According to the Rite of the Antiochene Syriac Maronite Church* (Bkerké: Maronite Patriarchate, 2012), 606–7.
[49] Alexopoulos and Johnson, *Introduction to Eastern Christian Liturgies*, 369.

the hungry and bring the poor and homeless in our houses, that we may receive from Christ His great mercy.[50]

The monastic tradition stands as a pillar pointing to the centrality of God in one's life, to the calling to live according to the gospel in every aspect of life, and to witnessing the gospel by one's way of life.[51] A prayer that is recited every day during the Great Lent in the Byzantine tradition, accompanied by full prostrations, and which is ascribed to St. Ephrem the Syrian, summarizes one way to see what lived Christian life is all about:

> O Lord and Master of my life!
> Take from me the spirit of sloth,
> faint-heartedness, lust of power, and idle talk.
> But give rather the spirit of chastity,
> humility, patience, and love to Your servant.
> Yes, Lord and King! Grant me to see my own errors
> and not to judge my brother,
> for You are blessed unto the ages of ages. Amen.[52]

Finally, the experience of the modern world unquestionably poses challenges to Eastern Christian Churches. The three most important are (1) that Eastern Christian Churches need to define their identity, especially the relationship between religion and nation; (2) that Eastern Christian Churches need to promote the study of their own liturgical traditions; and (3) that Eastern Christian Churches need to engage with Western culture and the modern world.[53] In other words, Eastern Christian Churches face the challenge of new encounters in a new world with new problems. The discussions about their identity in new contexts, new questions that new contexts place before them, and the study of their own heritage and tradition will hopefully allow Eastern Christian Churches to define and redefine their place, role, and contribution to an ever-changing world. Refusal to engage with the challenge of new encounters will make Eastern Christian Churches irrelevant and will lead to their demise.

---

[50] Translation from *The Lenten Liturgies* (Belmont, CA: Narthex Press, 1995), 40.
[51] Alexopoulos and Johnson, *Introduction to Eastern Christian Liturgies*, 370.
[52] Adapted from "Lenten Prayer of St. Ephrem the Syrian," *Greek Orthodox Archdiocese of America Celebrating 100 Years!* Accessed July 24, 2023, at www.goarch.org/-/lenten-prayer-of-st-ephrem-the-syrian.
[53] For a discussion of these, see Alexopoulos and Johnson, *Introduction to Eastern Christian Liturgies*, 380–88.

For Further Reading

Alexopoulos, Stefanos, and Maxwell E. Johnson, *Introduction to Eastern Christian Liturgies* (Collegeville, MN: Liturgical Press Academic, 2022).

Glibetić, Nina, "History of Orthodox Worship," in *Historical Foundations of Worship: Catholic, Orthodox, and Protestant Perspectives*, ed. Melanie Ross and Mark Lamport (Grand Rapids, MI: Baker Academic, 2022), 85–97.

Taft, Robert, *The Byzantine Rite: A Short History* (Collegeville, MN: The Liturgical Press, 1992).

6 The Liturgical Movement
KATHERINE E. HARMON

INTRODUCTION: THE LITURGICAL MOVEMENT AND SOCIAL CHRISTIANITY

The Liturgical Movement refers to a complex series of theological, social, and spiritual forces that converged over the course of the modern period. Early initiatives resulted in ritual revisions and recommendations on a more limited scale among Catholic,[1] Protestant,[2] and Anglican[3] Christians. These revisions sought to improve accessibility of texts, attended to participation, and expressed ecclesial identity. Yet, all Christian Churches were impacted by the conditions of the nineteenth century, which introduced powerful socio-cultural shifts, including (1) a significant remapping of how Western society was organized following industrialization and changing economic patterns; (2) separation of the Church from the State, to the point that the State actively reduced or oppressed the Church; (3) an Enlightenment rationalism ready to critique and reject religious practices, particularly ones that

---

[1] See Herman Wegman, *Christian Worship in East and West: A Study Guide to Liturgical History*, trans. Gordon Lathrop (New York: Pueblo, 1985), 346–51; J. D. Crichton, *Lights in the Darkness: Fore-Runners of the Liturgical Movement* (Collegeville, MN: Liturgical Press, 1996); and Keith Pecklers, "History of the Roman Liturgy from the Sixteenth until the Twentieth Centuries," in *Introduction to the Liturgy*, vol. 1, *Handbook for Liturgical Studies*, ser. ed. Anscar J. Chupungco (Collegeville, MN: Liturgical Press, 1997), 153–78.

[2] Frank C. Senn, "Liturgy in the Age of Romanticism," in *Christian Liturgy: Catholic and Evangelical* (Minneapolis, MN: Fortress Press, 1997), 568–608, and James F. White, *Protestant Worship: Traditions in Transition* (Louisville, KY: Westminster/John Knox Press, 1989).

[3] Owen Chadwick, *The Mind of the Oxford Movement* (London: A. & C. Black, 1960), and Christopher Irvine (ed.), *They Shaped Our Worship: Essays on Anglican Liturgists* (London: SPCK, 1998).

were controlled by an elite clergy; and (4) an emphasis upon personal relationships with God and private piety[4] as keys to salvation, rather than ecclesial affiliation or practices.[5] In addition to these challenges, the established Churches had remained strangely silent in the face of rampant social upheaval and suffering, and were even seen as buoying up systems of social oppression.[6]

In response, reform-minded Christians took up these challenges by emphasizing their commitment to alleviate suffering, looking to the person of Jesus and the kingdom of God as theological models, and advocating for concrete social change. This response is described as Social Christianity.[7] Its earliest iterations included the abolitionist movement and first-wave feminism,[8] the Social Gospellers,[9] and strains within the Oxford, or Tractarian, movement.[10] For Roman Catholics, women religious pioneered the development of social structures responding to the needs of the most vulnerable, while the emergence of Catholic Social Teaching with Pope Leo XIII's (1810–1903) *Rerum Novarum* (1891) responded directly to the deplorable working conditions amongst the poor working class.[11]

---

[4] See Oto Gründler, "Devotio Moderna," in *Christian Spirituality II: High Middle Ages and Reformation*, vol. 17 of *World Spirituality: An Encyclopedic History of the Religious Quest*, ed. Jill Raitt (New York: Crossroad, 1987), 176–93, and Salvatore Marsili, "Spiritualità liturgica," in *I segni del mistero di Cristo: Teologia liturgica dei sacramenti*, BEL Subsidia 42, ed. Michele Alberta (Rome: CLV Edizioni Liturgiche, 1987), 451–516.

[5] See Conrad L. Donakowski, "The Age of Revolutions," in *The Oxford History of Christian Worship*, ed., Geoffrey Wainwright and Karen B. Westerfield Tucker (New York: Oxford University Press, 2006), 351–94.

[6] See Emma Griffin, *Liberty's Dawn: A People's History of the Industrial Revolution* (New Haven, CT: Yale University Press), 20.

[7] See Shailer Mathews, "The Development of Social Christianity in America during the Past Twenty-Five Years," *The Journal of Religion* 7.4 (July 1927): 376–86; Martin E. Marty, *Protestantism and Social Christianity* (Munich: K. G. Saur, 1992); Ralph William Franklin, "Response: Humanism and Transcendence in the Nineteenth Century Liturgical Movement," *Worship* 59.4 (1985): 342–53.

[8] J. Philip Wogaman, "Nineteenth-Century Slavery and Feminist Controversies," in *Christian Ethics: A Historical Introduction*, 2nd ed. (Louisville, KY: Westminster John Knox Press, 2011), 191–201.

[9] See Ronald C. White and C. Howard Hopkins, *The Social Gospel: Religion and Reform in Changing America* (Philadelphia: Temple University Press, 1976): 5–25.

[10] See Donald Gray, *Earth and Altar: The Evolution of the Parish Communion in the Church of England to 1945*, Alcuin Club Collections, no. 68 (Norwich: Canterbury Press Norwich, 1986), and William George Peck, *Social Implications of the Oxford Movement* (New York: C. Scribner's Sons, 1933).

[11] See Wogaman, "The Social Encyclicals," in *Christian Ethics*, 223–30; Aaron Ignatius Abell, *American Catholicism and Social Action* (Notre Dame, IN: University of Notre Dame, 1960).

The Liturgical Movement, realized across numerous Christian denominations, is best interpreted out of this context. Liturgical Movement advocates identified participation in liturgical worship as a source for spiritual transformation, which would establish social solidarity as Christ's body in the world. Driven by a nineteenth-century Romanticism[12] interested in the retrieval of sources, the emerging field of liturgical scholarship was pioneered by Reformed and Roman Catholic scholars alike. As with ecumenical efforts within Social Christianity,[13] efforts of Liturgical Movement advocates eventually resulted in an ecumenical convergence that had never before been experienced by Christian denominations.

Interpreting the Liturgical Movement as a social movement has been difficult because of its immense diversity of iterations (e.g., scholarship, the arts, ritual and symbol, catechesis), because of differing opinions within the movement itself,[14] and because its "success" began to be measured by ecclesial recognition and the adoption of concrete liturgical ritual revisions. However, in concert with social–historical evaluations,[15] this essay offers a brief introduction to the major contours of the Liturgical Movement by keeping in mind its foundational hope to promote active participation and spiritual formation of all the faithful, so that they might become agents of social restoration in the modern world.

Adequately addressing the complexities of each ecclesial denomination[16] in the West touched by the Liturgical Movement, not to mention Eastern Christians,[17] presents a challenge beyond the scope of this piece. The Liturgical Movement is far from uniquely Roman Catholic,[18]

---

[12] Thomas O'Meara, "The Origins of the Liturgical Movement and German Romanticism," *Worship* 59 (1985): 326–42, and Joris Geldhof, "German Romanticism and Liturgical Theology: Exploring the Potential of Organic Thinking," *Horizons* 43 (2016): 282–307.

[13] See Wogaman, *Christian Ethics*, 216.

[14] Gavin Brown, "From Stages to Strands: Re-Interpreting the Liturgical Movement," *Pacifica* 23 (2010): 58–83.

[15] See David J. O'Brien, *The Renewal of American Catholicism* (New York: Oxford University Press, 1972), 65–66; Marvin L. Krier Mich, *Catholic Social Teaching and Movements* (Mystic, CT: Twenty-Third Publications, 1998), 62–75.

[16] See Senn, *Christian Liturgy*, 632–92; and John Fenwick and Bryan Spinks, *Worship in Transition: The Liturgical Movement in the Twentieth Century* (New York: Continuum, 1995).

[17] See Olivier Rousseau, "Pastoral Liturgy and the Eastern Liturgies," in *The Assisi Papers* (Collegeville, MN: Liturgical Press, 1957), 113–27.

[18] Gordon Lathrop, "The Study of Liturgy: An Ecumenical Rejoinder," *Worship* 92 (Jan. 2018): 46–53; Michael Moriarty and Henry Breul, *The Associated Parishes for*

but focusing on Roman Catholic experiences allows at least two patterns to emerge. First, while, in general, Liturgical Movement initiatives moved from calls for social transformation through liturgical formation to advocacy for Church renewal through liturgical reform,[19] the interests in holistic human formation (often described as living the "Christ-life"[20]), active participation, and social regeneration remained constant. Second, Christians who sought to live out the duties inscribed by Christian baptism, embrace communal experiences of worship (especially those found in the Lord's supper), and become agents for unity in the modern world eventually looked to realizing unity with each other.[21] The efforts of liturgical renewal could only result in ecumenical hopes, and some realities.

NINETEENTH-CENTURY FOUNDATIONS FOR LITURGICAL RENEWAL

The Liturgical Movement's strategies for inviting the faithful to embrace the liturgical life are perhaps most deeply marked by efforts of spiritual and intellectual formation. Efforts of *ressourcement*,[22] borrowings from biblical scholarship,[23] and contemplating the mystery of Christ through ecclesial and sacramental participation as experienced through liturgical rite and text[24] inspired Liturgical Movement advocates such as liturgical theologian Aemiliana Löhr, OSB (1892–1972), to describe the liturgy as food that allowed "baptismal life" to rise to "new

---

Liturgy and Mission, 1946–1991: The Liturgical Movement in the Episcopal Church (Ph.D. diss., University of Notre Dame, 1993); David Ray Moores, *Principles and Goals for Liturgical Renewal Movement from a Reformed Perspective* (Ph.D. diss., Fuller Theological Seminary, 1975); Ray Billington, *The Liturgical Movement and Methodism* (London: Epworth, 1969).

[19] See Mark Searle, Barbara S. Searle, and Anne Y. Koester, *Called to Participate: Theological, Ritual, and Social Perspectives* (Collegeville, MN: Liturgical Press, 2006), 2–12.

[20] See Gerald Ellard, "A Papal Motto and Its Meaning," *Orate Fratres* 1.5 (1927): 141–45, at 143.

[21] Keith F. Pecklers articulates this succinctly in his entry "The History of the Modern Liturgical Movement," in *Oxford Research Encyclopedia of Religion* (New York: Oxford University Press, 2015).

[22] Gabriel Flynn and Paul D. Murray, eds., *Ressourcement: A Movement for Renewal in Twentieth-Century Catholic Theology* (Oxford: Oxford University Press, 2012), 23–25.

[23] The journal *Bibel und Liturgie* expressly supported this interest, founded out of Klosterneuburg in Austria.

[24] See Odo Casel, *Das christliche Kultmysterium*, 4, durchges. u. erw. Aufl. (Regensburg: Verlag Friedrich Pustet, 1960).

heights of power and beauty" and made "life in Christ more fruitful, strong, [and] invincible."[25] The Liturgical Movement's growth and development were propelled by centers for liturgical scholarship, academic and pastoral publications, and opportunities for the faithful (lay and cleric) to receive and share in the spirituality of the liturgy through conferences, retreats, and formation. Many of these centers were Benedictine.[26]

The first of these centers appeared in post-Revolutionary France, in Solesmes, the monastery refounded by Dom Prosper Guéranger, OSB (1805–1875), in 1833. Frequently identified as a beginning point[27] for the Liturgical Movement, the work of Guéranger marked the first identification of the "liturgy" as inspiring a social "movement." Despite the limitations of Guéranger's scholarship,[28] Solesmes's reestablishment "awakened the passion for liturgical studies" in several European countries, and Benedictine abbeys became particular locations for this restoration with the production of resources and the establishment of liturgical conferences or weeks and partners for liturgical education.[29] Guéranger, for example, served as spiritual director to Mother Cécile Bruyère, OSB (1845–1909), first abbess of St. Cecile, who counseled her nuns in liturgical spirituality and worked with her neighbors at Solesmes to train her nuns in singing chant and in understanding the meaning of the Mass, the Divine Office, and the liturgical year.[30] Guéranger paired his *Institutions liturgiques* (begun in 1841), intended for a more scholarly audience, with the pastorally oriented *L'année liturgique*, beginning in Advent of 1841, which introduced the liturgical year as a point for spiritual reflection and anticipated the continual significance of the liturgical year as a catechetical tool.[31]

---

[25] Aemiliana Löhr, *The Year of Our Lord: The Mystery of Christ in the Liturgical Year*, trans. A Monk of St. Benedict (New York: P. J. Kenedy & Sons, 1937), 160–61.

[26] See Ralph William Franklin, "The Nineteenth Century Liturgical Movement," *Worship* 53 (1979): 12–39.

[27] See Bernard Botte, *From Silence to Participation: An Insider's View of Liturgical Renewal*, trans. John Sullivan (Washington, DC: The Pastoral Press, 1988).

[28] For some evaluation of Guéranger, see *The Liturgical Movement*, trans. Lancelot Sheppard, vol. 115, *Twentieth Century Encyclopedia of Catholicism*, ser. ed. Henri Daniel-Rops (New York: Hawthorn Books, 1964), 10–12.

[29] Gabriel Braso, *Liturgy and Spirituality* (Collegeville, MN: Liturgical Press, 1960), 51.

[30] See Guy Marie Oury, *Light and Strength: Mother Cecile Bruyère, First Abbess of Sainte-Cecile of Solesmes*, trans. M. Cristina Borge (Hulbert, OK: Our Lady of Clear Creek Abbey, 2012).

[31] Cuthbert Johnson, *Prosper Guéranger (1805–1875): A Liturgical Theologian: An Introduction to His Liturgical Writings and Work*, Studia Anselmiana 89 (Rome: Pontificio Ateneo S. Anselmo, 1984), 343, fn. 11.

While Guéranger's work was widely circulated and influential,[32] the more critical-historical work of discovering the "roots" of Christian worship were advanced by fellow French priest Louis Duchesne (1843–1922), whose 1889 *Origines du culte chrétien* laid "the foundations for a movement that could no longer be stopped."[33] Reformation Churches likewise pursued scholarly study, including that by Germans Theodor Kliefoth (1810–1895) and Wilhelm Löhe (1808–1872), who composed a collection of orders of service, *Agende für christliche Gemeinden des lutherischen Bekenntnisses* (1844).[34] English Tractarians likewise attended to texts accompanying the celebration of the liturgy, including the revision of the temporal cycle, the Order of Holy Communion, the use of lectionary pericopes, the translation and use of traditional hymns, and a retrieval of the Geneva psalter.[35]

In Germany, the wider context of Romanticism shaped the intellectual pursuits of the movement, with Beuron's founding in 1863 by Fathers Maurus (1825–1900) and Placidus Wolter, OSB (1928–1908). Beuron served as an early champion of liturgical art[36] and acknowledged the significance of the lay faithful's access to the liturgical rite by publishing the first German–Latin missal in 1884 by Anselm Schott, OSB (1843–1896), *Das Messbuch der Heiligen Kirche*.[37] Maria Laach, refounded in 1893, followed as a significant center for liturgical scholarship in Germany, becoming home to many Roman Catholic scholars who significantly impacted liturgical renewal, including Abbot Ildefons Herwegen, OSB (1874–1946), and Odo Casel, OSB (1886–1948). Maria Laach also partnered with the neighboring Abbey of the Holy Cross at Herstelle, home to several prominent liturgists, including Löhr and Agape Kiesgen, OSB (1899–1933). The sisters at Herstelle served as conversation partners for the development of Casel's *Mysterientheologie*.[38]

---

[32] See Bouyer, *Liturgical Piety*, 54–57; Pecklers, "History of the Roman Liturgy," 166.
[33] Wegman, *Christian Worship*, 352.
[34] Ibid., 352.
[35] Ibid.
[36] In the United States, the *Liturgical Arts Society Journal* and the *Liturgical Arts Quarterly* would devote themselves to the development of the liturgical arts. See Susan J. White, *Art, Architecture, and Liturgical Reform: The Liturgical Arts Society, 1928–1972* (New York: Pueblo, 1990).
[37] *The Liturgical Movement*, trans. Sheppard, 14; Pecklers, "History," 168.
[38] Teresa Berger, "The Classical Liturgical Movement in Germany and Austria: Moved by Women?" *Worship* 66 (1992): 231–50, and Teresa Berger, *Liturgie und Frauenseele: Die liturgische Bewegung aus der Sicht der Frauenforschung* (Stuttgart: Verlag W. Kohlhammer, 1993).

A prominent center for Roman Catholic liturgical scholarship, Maria Laach's publications included *Ecclesia Orans* (1918) and *Jahrbuch für Liturgiewissenschaft* (1921). Parallel to these German Catholic locations, Reformed and Evangelical Lutheran scholars, including Friedrich Schleiermacher (1768–1834) and Johann A. W. Neander (1789–1850), pioneered historical work that would become critical for subsequent liturgical scholarship.[39]

In Italy, Abbot Emmanuele Caronti, OSB (1882–1966), served as a leading figure, composing not only his *La pietà liturgica* (1921) but an Italian missal for use by the faithful.[40] *Ephemerides liturgicae* first appeared in 1887, and *Rivista liturgica* (1914) offered an exchange for Italian Catholic liturgical advocates. Societies for liturgical study and resources for scholars also developed in Great Britain, following interest in and energy surrounding ancient and medieval texts. Of particular relevance for liturgical study, the Surtees Society in Durham began in 1834, while the Henry Bradshaw Society (1890) and the Alcuin Club Collections (1897) were founded to promote liturgical scholarship in the English language.[41]

The significance of scholarship and resources as propelling the movement necessarily pair with concrete experiences of and access to worship on the part of the faithful. Translations of the missal and commentaries on the liturgical year, for example, would be among the first and most widely impactful resources for the lay faithful.[42] And Damasus Winzen, OSB (1901–1971), understood the beginning of the Liturgical Movement (at Maria Laach in Germany) to be "when a group of Catholic laymen, university teachers, doctors, and lawyers went to the Abbot of Maria Laach [Herwegen] in the year 1914 to ask him about ways and means to best promote the more active participation of the faithful in the mass."[43]

---

[39] Lathrop, "A Rejoinder," 50.
[40] Keith Pecklers, *The Unread Vision: The Liturgical Movement in the United States of America: 1926–1955* (Collegeville, MN: Liturgical Press, 1998), 17–18, and Franco Brovelli, *Ritorno alla liturgia: Saggi di studio sul movimento liturgico* (Rome: Edizioni Liturgische, 1989), 231–32.
[41] Pecklers, "History of the Roman Liturgy," 167–70, and Ralph W. Franklin, *Nineteenth-Century Churches: The History of a New Catholicism in Württemberg, England, and France* (New York: Garland, 1987).
[42] Louis Bouyer, *Liturgical Piety* (Notre Dame, IN: University of Notre Dame Press, 1955), 64.
[43] Damasus Winzen, quoted in Ernest B. Koenker, *The Liturgical Renaissance in the Roman Catholic Church* (Chicago: University of Chicago Press, 1954), 12. See also Maisie Ward, "Changes in the Liturgy: Cri de Coeur," *Life of the Spirit* 16 (1961): 129.

The Belgian Liturgical Movement would also be marked by pastoral efforts. Maredsous, founded from Beuron in 1872, published one of the earliest translations of the missal for the laity, in French and Latin, *Missel des fidèles* by Gérard van Caloen, OSB (1853–1932).[44] Mont César was founded from Maredsous in 1899. In 1903, Pope Pius X's (1835–1914) *motu proprio*, "Tra le Sollecitudini," appeared. While focused on sacred music, Pope Pius X invited consideration of participation in liturgical worship as a source for the true Christian spirit and, in 1905, followed with his *Sacra Tridentina Synodus*, which called the Roman Catholic faithful to frequent sacramental reception of communion.[45] These documents, stressing active participation and sacramental communion, would provide critical force for the Liturgical Movement as a social and spiritual movement.

In Belgium, interest in the lay faithful's participation was tightly tied to a burgeoning tradition of Catholic Social Teaching surrounding labor and economics. The Belgian "worker priest" movement captured the attention of young Lambert Beauduin (1873–1960), who, upon entering the Monastery at Mont César, was captivated by the possibility of spiritual renewal flowing from the liturgy. At the 1909 Malines National Congress of Catholic Works (*Congrès national des oeuvres catholiques*), which was intended to discuss social, economic, and political concerns, Beauduin maneuvered to have a paper read titled "La vraie prière de l'église," which promoted Pope Pius X's instruction: that the liturgy provided the true source of social transformation.[46] The resolutions of the congress included the promotion of liturgical renewal and resources. Following this, Mont César became a leading figure in promoting the Liturgical Movement, beginning with series in both French and Flemish editions for the faithful (*La vie liturgique*, 1909) and for clergy (*Questions liturgiques*, 1910), and inaugurating its *sémaines liturgiques*, beginning in 1912.[47]

By the twentieth century, multiple denominations had turned to a retrieval of liturgical worship as food for social restoration, emphasizing participation in the Lord's Supper, the significance of baptism, and a retrieval of scripture. But it is difficult to evaluate to what extent the

---

[44] *The Liturgical Movement*, trans. Sheppard, 1.
[45] See Joseph Dougherty, *From Altar-Throne to Table: The Campaign for Frequent Holy Communion in the Catholic Church* (Lanham, MD: Scarecrow Press, 2010).
[46] Sonya Quitslund, *Beauduin: A Prophet Vindicated* (New York: Newman Press, 1973), 20–24, and Bouyer, *Liturgical Piety*, 60–61; Cf. also Bouyer, *Dom Lambert Beauduin: Un homme d'Église* (Paris: Cerf, 2009).
[47] Pecklers, *Unread Vision*, 8–9.

various denominations were inspired by the work of one another. Interdenominational tensions remained taut, and Beaduin's ecumenical efforts even resulted in his censure.[48] Yet, the field of liturgical scholarship would prove to be a point of increasing exception as common interest in retrieval of liturgical texts and their meaning resulted in a growing desire, even expectation, that Christian Churches would embrace ecumenism and unity.[49]

TRAJECTORIES FOR THE TWENTIETH-CENTURY LITURGICAL MOVEMENT

For Roman Catholics of the twentieth century, the new Catholic intellectual scene encouraged by Leo XIII enabled Catholics to agree, both due to natural reason and supernatural revelation, that all humans had unalienable rights, providing a springboard for Catholic and, increasingly, lay Catholic inclusion in early social justice movements that blossomed in the late 1910s and 1920s.[50] The retrieval of Thomism and Catholic philosophical and cultural vision, which had burst on the European stage, significantly shaped the work of American counterparts.[51]

Early liturgical initiatives in North America occurred in specific instances, such as in the work of Justine Bayard Cutting Ward (1879–1975) in establishing the Pius X School of Liturgical Music (in Manhattanville, New York) in 1916 with Mother Georgia Stevens, RSCJ (1870–1946), in order to promote the use of liturgical chant. But the Liturgical Movement in the United States became more formally organized in 1926, when Virgil Michel, OSB (1890–1938), and a team of editors, supported by St. John's Abbey in Collegeville, Minnesota, launched both the journal *Orate Fratres*, as a means to connect and spread news about the Liturgical Movement, and the Liturgical Press, to produce resources for teaching the faithful. Michel's desire to found the

---

[48] See Quitslund, *Beauduin: A Prophet Vindicated*.
[49] See Eugene L. Brand, "Reflections on the Ecumenical Aspects of the Liturgical Movement," *Worship* 51.1 (1977): 49–55, and John St. H. Gibaut, "The Liturgical Movement: Cradle of Ecumenical Culture," *Ecumenism* 122 (1996): 4–11.
[50] Jay P. Dolan, *Transforming Parish Ministry: The Changing Roles of Catholic Clergy, Laity, and Women Religious* (New York: Crossroad, 1989), 24–25.
[51] See Margaret Mary Reher, "The Path to Pluralism, 1920–1985," in *Catholic Intellectual Life in America: A Historical Study of Persons and Movements*, Makers of the Catholic Community Series, ed. Christopher J. Kauffman (New York: Macmillan Publishing Company, 1989), 114–41.

Liturgical Movement in the United States resulted from his experiences in European liturgical centers and especially his conversations with Beauduin.[52] Michel, himself a philosopher and deeply influenced by the emerging field of Catholic Social Teaching, summed up the possibilities of liturgical worship with a syllogism:

> Pius X tells us that the liturgy is the indispensable source of the true Christian spirit; Pius XI says that the true Christian spirit is indispensable for social regeneration. Hence the conclusion: The liturgy is the indispensable basis of Christian social regeneration.[53]

The founding of the US Liturgical Movement also paired liturgical publishing (scholarly and pastoral) with pastoral outreach. Advocates for the Liturgical Movement gravitated toward promoting the use of the missal as a means for facilitating participation. Whether published in bound editions with Latin/English columns or as a disposable *Leaflet Missal* (founded by Paul C. Bussard [1903–1983] in 1929), a premier object of the Liturgical Movement became the continued production, distribution, and use of a variety of versions of the missal by laymen, laywomen, and parochial school children. Numerous accounts from the pages of *Orate Fratres* in the later 1920s and early 1930s testify to the use of the missal in study clubs[54] and the possibility for the missal to inspire people not only to love the Mass but to participate in it, directly leading to participation in the wider goals of social regeneration.[55]

In the 1930s, Liturgical Movement efforts began appearing in South American contexts, also with strong pastoral interests. In Rio de Janeiro, in 1933, Martinho Michler, OSB; Beda Kecheisen, OSB; Polycarpo Armstalden, OSB; and Hildebrando Martins, OSB, among others, founded the movement and began publishing a weekly bulletin, *Folheto litúrgico* (1934), founded in Sao Paulo. This resource initially simply included the texts for Sunday in order to promote the dialogue Mass but eventually included more instructions for promoting a better

---

[52] Pecklers, *Unread Vision*, 19.
[53] Virgil Michel, "Liturgy the Basis of Social Regeneration," *Orate Fratres* 9 (1935): 536–45, at 545.
[54] See Katharine E. Harmon, *There Were Also Many Women There: Lay Women in the Liturgical Movement in the United States, 1926–59* (Collegeville, MN: Liturgical Press, 2013), 113–25.
[55] See William Busch, "The Missal and the Breviary, or the Mass and the Hour-Prayers, as Sources of Spiritual Life," *Orate Fratres* 3.11 (1929): 340–47.

understanding of the liturgy.[56] In Argentina, the *Revista Liturgica Argentina* (established in 1935 by Andrés Azcárate Esparza, OSB [1891–1981]) served as a liturgical clearinghouse to connect persons interested in the liturgy.[57] Likewise, an Argentinian Liturgical Week was held at La Plata, organized by the Argentine Catholic Action Youth, in 1937. Twelve archbishops and bishops participated, evidencing stronger hierarchical engagement than even the United States would experience in its own liturgical weeks, which began meeting in 1940.[58] Also in 1937, a joint pastoral letter issued by all Chilean bishops stressed the need for education in the liturgical life and the crucial role played by lay people in the spiritual life of the Church.[59] Shortly afterwards, the Bishops of Peru issued a similar national program of "liturgical activity," which raised hopes in the United States for a more programmatic approach to officially supporting liturgical efforts that had been approved at a more individual level.[60]

The Second World War impacted the trajectory of the Liturgical Movement, surprisingly, by increasing the exchange of ideas between German and French liturgists. J. D. Chrichton observed that this new relationship gave rise to the Pastoral Liturgical Movement, which stressed that the liturgy was "not a clerical possession" but belonged to the "whole Christian community."[61] The *Centre de Pastorale Liturgique* was established in 1943 and hosted annual congresses that served as the forerunners to international congresses that met later, such as at Lugano (1953) and Assisi (1956), the first liturgical international meeting in which authorities from Rome were directly involved.[62] The postwar Liturgical Movement saw the increasingly close collaboration of liturgists with "scripture experts, systematic theologians, historians, and even sociologists," as well as increasing interest in the use of the vernacular[63] and in ecumenism.

---

[56] Pecklers, "History of the Roman Liturgy," 171. See also José Ariovaldo da Silva, *O Movimento Litúrgico no Brasil: Estudo Histórico* (Petrópolis: Vozes, 1983).

[57] See Ernesto J. A. Maeder, "El Abad Azcárate y la Revista Litúrgica Argentina: Una Labor Precursora (1935–1960)," *CuadMon* 159 (2006): 485–92.

[58] "Liturgical Brief: Liturgical Week La Plata," in "The Apostolate," *Orate Fratres* 11 (1937), 474.

[59] "Liturgical Brief: Bishops' Pastoral," in "The Apostolate," *Orate Fratres* 11 (1937), 474.

[60] "Another Revolution in South America," in "The Apostolate," *Orate Fratres* 13 (1939), 416–18.

[61] Chrichton, *Light in the Darkness*, 155.

[62] Ibid., 155.

[63] For a discussion of the Vernacular Society see Pecklers, *The Unread Vision*, 63–66.

Efforts for the liturgical formation of the lay faithful continued to flourish, even amid the adoption of older forms of spiritual revival, such as the parish mission. One such event took place in Halifax, Nova Scotia, during November 1935, with themes attentive to theological models central to the Liturgical Movement, including the Mystical Body of Christ, the excellence of "life-in-Christ," active participation in the Mass, and the structure of the liturgical year.[64] National Liturgical Weeks hosted in the United States also boasted numerous pastoral and practical topics, though members often also drew on the latest in Catholic theology.[65] Beginning in 1940 and lasting through the Council era, these weeks were unabashedly interested in social transformation and the responsibility of the "great corporate act of the Mystical Body," in living out "our oneness, our corporateness, our living organic wholeness in Christ," as Msgr. Reynold Hillenbrand (1904–1979) had described.[66] The 1943 National Liturgical Week, among others, focused on the liturgy's intersection with the "racial problem," the "rural problem," and the "labor problem."[67]

As had been the case in parts of Europe and South America, Catholic Action groups and study clubs in the United States were encouraged to make use of the missal,[68] including nationally organized groups for Catholics such as the National Council of Catholic Women.[69] The Liturgical Movement and Catholic Action were tightly intertwined, and this was readily recognized.[70] But, whether part of formalized Catholic Action or not, lay Catholics interested in an active life of faith fed by liturgical worship identified the Mass in radically new ways.

[64] Charles F. Curran, "Liturgical Mission at St. Joseph's Parish, Halifax, Nova Scotia," in *Orate Fratres* 83–87, at 84.
[65] Godfrey Mullen, *Participation in the Liturgy: The National Liturgical Weeks 1940–1962* (Ph.D. diss., University of Notre Dame, 2003).
[66] Reynold Hillenbrand, "The Spirit of Sacrifice in Christian Society," in *1943 National Liturgical Week Proceedings* (Ferdinand, IN: The Liturgical Conference, 1944), 100–9, at 102–3.
[67] In the United States, liturgy and social issues appeared frequently in the *National Liturgical Week Proceedings, Orate Fratres, The Catholic Worker*, publications by the Grail Movement (Loveland, Ohio), and journals such as the short-lived *Liturgy and Sociology*.
[68] See William Busch, "The Liturgy, a School of Catholic Action," *Orate Fratres* 7 (1932): 9; John Fitzsimons and Paul McGuire (eds.), *Restoring All Things: A Guide to Catholic Action* (New York: Sheed & Ward, 1938); and John J. Griffin, "Catholic Action and the Liturgical Life," *Orate Fratres* 9.1 (1934): 360–71.
[69] See Agnes M. Marceron, "Study Club on the Mass," in "The Apostolate," *Orate Fratres* 7 (1933), 570.
[70] Leo R. Ward, "Living the Liturgy," in *Catholic Life, U.S.A.: Contemporary Lay Movements* (St. Louis: B. Herder Book Co., 1959), 10.

Writing to Dorothy Day (1897–1980) in the *Catholic Worker* in January of 1943, a young lady ("L. I.") described herself as a Japanese-American girl who had fled Shanghai the previous year on a crowded boat, full of Protestant missionaries and Catholic Sisters and fathers, representing nations from China to Germany and Russia. As "L. I." related, on Christmas Eve, refugee Protestants and Catholics alike gathered together for Mass. She explained, "[N]ations may fight and men misunderstand each other, but in prayer they speak and understand a common language and in Him they find a common refuge. It is not Pearl Harbor we should remember, but Christ on the Cross!"[71]

While scholarly resources were developed and used by more "professional" persons, a significant amount of literature was explicitly created for use in colleges or high schools (e.g., Gerald Ellard, SJ's [1894–1963] *Christian Life and Worship* [1933] and Mary Perkins Ryan's [1912–1993], ed., *The Sacramental Way* [1948]), as well as in grade schools. In the United States, a discussion of liturgy and education would not be possible without considering the scores of religious women involved in adopting liturgical theology and practice within the realms of education, especially through introduction to the missal, the liturgical year, and chant.[72] Dominican Sisters of Grand Rapids, Sr. Estelle Hackett, OP (1888–1948), and Jane Marie Murray, OP (1896–1987), partnered with Michel to develop the experimental *Christ Life Series in Religion* (1934–1935) for use in Catholic schools. Catholic colleges and high schools were encouraged to augment their liturgical programs by offering formal courses on the liturgy utilizing liturgical publications – a practice viewed as one of the "chief means towards the revival of Catholic literature in the United States."[73]

Eventually, Catholics who had been exposed to a liturgically formed education would be far readier to receive and interpret post-Conciliar reforms. Farsighted activists, such as Australian Archbishop Sir Guilford Young (1916–1988), had become interested in the Liturgical Movement after meeting Godfrey Diekmann, OSB (1908–2002), of St. John's in Collegeville, Minnesota, in Rome. Young then brought the Liturgical Movement to his home Archdiocese of Hobart. By 1960, Archbishop Young had ensured that "every Mass in the archdiocese

---

[71] L. I. "From an American-Japanese Girl," *The Catholic Worker* (Jan. 1943): 5. I am grateful to my student at Marian University, Sarah Getman, for this reference.

[72] In the United States, the statistics and discussions recorded at the *National Liturgical Week Proceedings* and in the "Author Index" of *Orate Fratres* reveal the significant number of women religious.

[73] "The Apostolate," *Orate Fratres* 8 (1934): 182.

featured the active participation of the laity," including use of the dialogue Mass, laymen reading the Epistle and Gospel (in vernacular), and a common set of hymns chosen for whole dioceses so the faithful could be familiar with music (and sing) regardless of where they attended Mass.[74]

The arts served as important media for liturgical renewal, and liturgical artists such as Ade Bethune (1914–2002), who created the iconic images featured in the American *The Catholic Worker* and served as liturgical architectural consultant, adopted the emphases of the Liturgical Movement for social transformation through the liturgy.[75] Others, such as Hiltrudis Powers, CPPS (1920–2011), long-time director of the ecclesiastical arts department in O'Fallon, Missouri, which was famous for its production of liturgical vestments, took seriously the Liturgical Movement's retrieval of the symbolic in the production of its art.[76]

Meanwhile, the interface of liturgy and culture – and the desire for a liturgically informed spirituality that might transform culture – inspired the Grail Movement. Founded in Holland before the outbreak of the Second World War as a lay apostolate for young working women, the Grail moved its center to the United States (Loveland, Ohio) during wartime, forming a small community in which members might experience the radical social implications of the Mystical Body through group prayer and work.[77] The Grail Movement relied heavily on active participation and ownership of liturgical prayer.[78]

One of the last social spheres to receive robust attention within the Liturgical Movement was the first unit of society, the family.[79] A significant amount of literature provided resources for the whole

---

[74] Clare V. Johnson, "Transcending Text: Liturgy as Medium of Evangelisation 50 Years after Vatican II," in *Australian Journal of Liturgy* 13 (2013), 100–17, at 102.

[75] See Harmon, *There Were Also Many Women There*, 191–220.

[76] Mary Cecile Gunelson, "The Ecclesiastical Art Department O'Fallon, Missouri History" (February 1996), 4. Archives of the Sisters of the Most Precious Blood, O'Fallon, MO.

[77] Debra Campbell, "Reformers and Activists," in *American Catholic Women: A Historical Exploration*, ed. Karen Kennelly, *The Bicentennial History of the Catholic Church in America*, ser. ed. Christopher J. Kauffman (New York: Macmillan, 1989), 175–76.

[78] Lydwine Van Kersbergen, "The Restoration of Sunday: Goal of the Modern Lay Apostolate, Grailville, Loveland, Ohio," *1949 Liturgical Week Proceedings* (Conception, MO: The Liturgical Conference, 1950), 35.

[79] See Mary Perkins Ryan, "Liturgy and the Family Arts," *1946 Liturgical Week Proceedings* (Highland Park, IL: The Liturgical Conference, 1947), 106–7, and Harmon, *There Were Also Many Women There*, 242–325.

Christian family, including Florence Berger's (1909–1983) *Cooking for Christ: A Year in the Liturgical Kitchen* (1949); Mary Reed Newland's (1917–1989) *The Year and Our Children* (1954); Therese Mueller's (1905–2002) *Family Life in Christ* (first appearing as a series in *Orate Fratres* in 1939); and Perkins Ryan's *Beginning at Home* (1955), to name just a few. Such resources frequently relied on the liturgical year, incorporated reflection on liturgical symbol and sacrament, and provided lenses for reading everyday family life as resonating with a life in Christ, despite its imperfections.[80]

CONCLUSION: REVISION OF RITES

Liturgical scholarship began inspiring the development of new rites long before the post-Conciliar revisions for Catholic or Reformed traditions. For example, the Anglican Church of South Africa produced two revised baptismal rites in 1926 and in 1930, borrowing from the British *Book of Common Prayer 1928* and influenced by the retrieval work of liturgical scholarship.[81] And, in 1947, the newly created Church of South India, uniting some dioceses of the Anglican Church of India, Pakistan, Burma, and Ceylon; the South India Province of the Methodist Church; the South India United Church (a Presbyterian/Congregational union); and the Basel mission developed an entirely new rite inspired by liturgical scholarship, with an emphasis upon full congregational participation. While lacking an attentiveness to inculturation that would mark later developments of rites, these projects pioneered ecumenical possibilities driven by liturgical scholarship.[82]

In terms of numbers and population density, as well as systemic implementation of renewal principles worldwide, the Roman Catholic Church became home to the most widely implemented and experienced liturgical renewal through its revised liturgical forms.[83] More specifically, the implementation of reforms began with the papacy of Pope Pius XII (1876–1958), whose encyclical pairing of Mystici Corporis (1943) and Mediator Dei (1947) affirmed central theological and pastoral thrusts of the Liturgical Movement. He established the Pian Commission, which

---

[80] See Eileen Nutting, "A Mother and Her Children," *Orate Fratres* 24.7 (1950): 318.
[81] Andrew-John Bethke, "Tracing the Theological Development of the South African Baptismal Rites: The Journey to an Anglican Prayer Book 1989 and Beyond," *Anglican Theological Review* 99.1 (2017): 45–64.
[82] Fenwick and Spinks, 53–59, at 58. See also Paul Puthanangady, "Liturgical Renewal in India," *Ephemerides Liturgicae* 91 (1977): 350–66.
[83] Wegman, 346.

inaugurated some of the first major reforms for the Latin Rite, beginning with the pastorally and theologically significant Easter Vigil and Holy Week. When Pope Pius XII restored the Vigil in 1951, the first step in what would become a series of restorations of Holy Week liturgies between 1951–1957,[84] Liturgical Movement advocates interpreted his decision as an unprecedented and profoundly pastoral response to the spiritual needs of people in the modern world. The Vigil's restoration underlined several important pastoral initiatives for liturgical renewal in the first half of the twentieth century, including an insistence that ritual participation could inform spiritual transformation; the role of the liturgical year in shaping a liturgically formed spirituality; and the necessity of intelligible and accessible texts to aid the faithful's active participation. In much sharper relief, Liturgical Movement advocates realized that restoring all in Christ might demand reformed rituals, as well as a renewed spirit.[85]

In interpreting these ritual revisions, remembering that the various Christian Churches were all responding to a similar social problem is important. By 1951, the World Council of Churches' report of the Faith and Order Commission on Worship observed, "In the course of this enquiry we have been struck by the extent to which a 'liturgical movement' is found in churches of widely differing traditions."[86] The hopes and, indeed, expectations for liturgical renewal on an ecumenical plane were reflected in the permeable boundaries of scholarship used across denominations and, after the Second Vatican Council, in significant revisions of rites and lectionaries;[87] in the founding of and membership in new organizations for liturgical study, such as the North American Academy of Liturgy (1975); and in the expanding ecumenical nature of the Liturgical Conference (beginning in 1979).

---

[84] Pius XII, *Decretum de facultativa celebratione instauratae Vigiliae paschalis ad triennium prorogata* (January 11, 1952) [AAS 44 (1952), 48–63]; Pius XII, *Liturgicus Hebdomadae Sanctae Ordo Instauratur* (November 16, 1955) [AAS 47 (1955), 838–41]; Pius XII, *Circa Ordinem Hebdomadae Sanctae Instauratum* (February 1, 1957) [AAS 49 (1957), 91–95].

[85] See Godfrey Diekmann, *The Masses of Holy Week and the Easter Vigil*, Popular Liturgical Library (Collegeville, MN: Liturgical Press, 1956), and Katharine E. Harmon, "Awaiting the 'Mother of All Vigils': The 1951 Provisional Restoration of the Easter Vigil in the United States," *Worship* 91 (2017): 131–48.

[86] Pehr Edwall, ed., *Ways of Worship: The Report of a Theological Commission of Faith and Order* (New York: Harper, 1951), 16.

[87] See, for example Horace T. Allen, "Lectionaries," in *The New Westminster Dictionary of Liturgy and Worship*, ed. Paul Bradshaw (Louisville: Westminster John Knox Press, 2002), 274–77.

While concrete revisions of liturgical texts or ecclesial documents detailing liturgical reform might seem to evidence the outcomes of the Liturgical Movement, focusing on liturgical revisions and reform confuses the means and the end. The Liturgical Movement was – and remains – a social and spiritual movement.[88] Remembering this premise explains the essential link between liturgy and justice, which has been difficult to maintain in the aftermath of post-Conciliar revisions and rightly illustrates consistent interest across Christian denominations in the retrieval of Christian worship as key to supporting the grace-filled life of the individual, called by baptism, to participate in the body of Christ in its social, communal dimensions.

The Liturgical Movement's vision for a restored society in Christ has not yet been met. Despite significant ecumenical efforts in some areas, unity amongst Christian Churches has been sorely tested by divisions in ideology, liturgical aesthetics, and, for Catholics, even in the reception of liturgical reforms. The ultimate hope, which remains an "unread vision," as liturgical historian Keith Pecklers has described it,[89] is transformation of the world in the light of Christ. We continue to await the day when all might be one.

For Further Reading

Berger, Teresa, *Liturgie und Frauenseele: Die liturgische Bewegung aus der Sicht der Frauenforschung* (Stuttgart: Verlag W. Kohlhammer, 1993).

Botte, Bernard, *From Silence to Participation: An Insider's View of Liturgical Renewal*, trans. John Sullivan (Washington, DC: The Pastoral Press, 1988).

Brovelli, Franco, *Ritorno alla liturgia: Saggi di studio sul movimento liturgico* (Rome: Edizioni Liturgiche, 1989).

Bugnini, Annibale, *The Reform of the Liturgy 1948–1975*, trans. Matthew J. O'Connell (Collegeville, MN: Liturgical Press, 1990).

Harmon, Katharine E., *There Were Also Many Women There: Lay Women in the Liturgical Movement in the United States, 1926–59* (Collegeville, MN: Liturgical Press, 2013).

Pecklers, Keith F., *The Unread Vision: The Liturgical Movement in the United States of America: 1926–1955* (Collegeville, MN: Liturgical Press, 1998).

---

[88] See Virgil Michel, "Foreword" to *Orate Fratres* 1.1 (1926): 1–4.
[89] Pecklers draws upon T. S. Eliot's poem, "Ash Wednesday."

Part II

The Celebration of the Liturgy

7 The Eucharist

PATRICK PRÉTOT

INTRODUCTION

The celebration and theological interpretation of the Eucharist has been one of the Roman Catholic Church's major projects since the beginning of the twentieth century. The main manifestation of this renewal was the publication of a revised *Ordo Missae* on April 3, 1969,[1] followed by a new edition of the entire Roman Missal in 1970. The third typical edition, the current one, was published in 2008.[2] But it must be emphasized immediately that the link between the new *Ordo Missae* and Catholic Eucharistic doctrine is expressed above all in the General Instruction of the Roman Missal (GIRM), a text that combines doctrinal aspects, liturgical prescriptions, and pastoral indications.[3] However, these fundamental sources cannot be separated from the great current of historical and theological research in this field.

Indeed, under the impetus of a major investigation into the history of the liturgy, the Liturgical Movement has restored to the *lex orandi*, that is, the celebration itself, its status as the primary source – *theologia prima* – for understanding the Church's Eucharistic faith. In a work published in 1966, Louis Bouyer laid down the principle of this new approach: Whereas in the past theology had been made *about* the

---

[1] *Ordo Missae, editio typica* (Città del Vaticano: Typis Polyglottis Vaticanis, 1969).
[2] *Missale Romanum, editio typica tertia*, reimpressio emendata (Città del Vaticano: Typis Vaticanis, 2008). The second *editio typica* was published in 1975. Henceforth reference will be made to *The Roman Missal*, English translation according to the third typical edition for use in the dioceses of the United States of America (Collegeville, MN: Liturgical Press, 2011).
[3] For an excellent edition of the text and commentary, see Edward Foley, Nathan D. Mitchell, and Joanne M. Pierce (eds.), *A Commentary on the General Instruction of the Roman Missal* (Collegeville, MN: Liturgical Press, 2007).

Eucharist, for him it was now a question of making theology *of* the Eucharist.[4] And in so doing, this theologian, who contributed to the elaboration of the missal of 1970, considered the Eucharistic prayers as the first place of understanding of the Eucharistic action, an investigation that would be extended by researchers such as Enrico Mazza and Cesare Giraudo.[5]

Shifts in the Catholic Church's teaching on the liturgy as a whole, and on the Eucharist in particular, were far reaching and in line with the desire of Pope John XXIII, which was taken up by the fathers gathered at the Second Vatican Council. They aimed at a renewal of the whole life of the Church, involving an adaptation of institutions, the search for union "of all those who believe in Christ," and a new missionary impetus.[6]

At the same time, these shifts provoked rejection and even ruptures that persist today, despite numerous attempts to overcome them.[7] We should also point out that, in fact, the accelerated erosion of Sunday practice (at least in Western Europe) and the estrangement of other religious groups (particularly in Africa and Latin America), as well as the practices that emerged in the wake of the Covid-19 health crisis,[8] mean that these twentieth-century transformations are still often misunderstood by many of the faithful.

Without claiming to cover the subject exhaustively, it is possible to infer from these premises that historical and theological research in the twentieth century – the general significance of which will be the subject of the first part of this chapter – gave rise to three major shifts in our approach to the Mass. Studies on the Eucharistic prayer have enabled us to rediscover the Eucharist as a memorial, updating God's work of salvation in human history, as discussed in the second section of the chapter. By giving pride of place to the Word of God in the celebration, the liturgy of the Word as a way of encountering the Risen Lord has been

---

[4] Louis Bouyer, *Eucharist: Theology and Spirituality of the Eucharistic Prayer*, trans. Charles U. Quinn (Notre Dame, IN: University of Notre Dame Press, 2006).

[5] Enrico Mazza, *The Celebration of the Eucharist: The Origin of the Rite and the Development of Its Interpretation*, trans. Mathew J. O'Connell (Collegeville, MN: Liturgical Press, 1990); Cesare Giraudo, *In Unum Corpus: Traité mystagogique sur l'Eucharistie*, trans. Éric Iborra and Pierre-Marie Hombert (Paris: Cerf, 2014).

[6] Pope John XXIII, *Gaudet Mater Ecclesia*, the famous address he gave on October 11, 1962, some words of which are referred to in *Sacrosanctum Concilium*.

[7] Cf. Pope Benedict XVI's motu proprio *Summorum Pontificum*, July 7, 2007, and Pope Francis' motu proprio *Traditionis custodes*, July 16, 2021.

[8] Hans-Jürgen Feulner and Elias Haslwanter (eds.), *Gottesdienst auf eigene Gefahr? Die Feier der Liturgie in der Zeit von Covid-19* (Münster: Aschendorff, 2020).

highlighted in section three. Finally, section four explores the Eucharist as a ritual journey that not only accompanies the assembly but transforms it: It builds up the Body of Christ, the sign of the Risen One who proclaims in this world the Kingdom to come.

A RENEWAL OF TRADITION WITH AN ECUMENICAL VOCATION

The twentieth-century shift toward the Eucharist was fostered by a resourcing of tradition that took three main directions. The first was the study of liturgical sources from Antiquity and the Middle Ages, predating the post-Tridentine Roman Missal published by Pope Pius V in 1570.[9] The second was a rereading of the works of the Church Fathers, especially the great mystagogical catecheses (Cyril of Jerusalem, John Chrysostom, Theodore of Mopsuestia, Ambrose of Milan, and Augustine of Hippo).[10] The third was an appreciation of the different traditions of Christianity, particularly those of the Christian East.

This was a real turning point, because in the Latin West, since the eleventh century, following a profound crisis in language to account for faith in the presence of the Lord, theology had adopted as its starting point categories external to action, borrowed in particular from Aristotle's philosophy. These scholastic categories (matter, form, substance, accidents) had the advantage of giving the transformation of the Eucharistic species a rational interpretation that responded to the questions and aspirations of the time. However, by isolating the ritual aspect from theology, they no longer allowed for the Eucharistic action itself. This was to become the object of an essentially disciplinary preoccupation, supported by an increasingly restrictive prescriptive arsenal (the rubrics).

In addition, the investigations of biblical scholars and patrologists, and of specialists in Jewish sources, made it possible to rediscover the roots of the Eucharist in the biblical tradition, as well as in the ritual heritage of Israel. Christian forms have developed gradually over the

---

[9] Martin Klöckener, "Liturgische Quellen des Frühmittelalters," in *Geschichte der Liturgie in den Kirchen des Westens*, vol. 1, ed. Benedikt Kranemann and Jürgen Bärsch (Münster: Aschendorff, 2018), 293–328.

[10] Jean Daniélou, *The Bible and the Liturgy* (Notre Dame, IN: University of Notre Dame Press, 2014); François Cassingena-Trévedy, *Les Pères de l'Église et la liturgie: Un esprit, une expérience, de Constantin à Justinien* (Paris: Desclée de Brouwer, 2009).

course of history. Depending on encounters with other cultures, firstly those of the Hellenistic and Roman worlds, they have transformed those received from Judaism by the first generations. But above all, they were obliged to reinterpret the tradition because of the completely new understanding of worship implied by the paschal event, as witnessed in particular by the letter to the Hebrews: The curtain of the Temple was torn at the Lord's death on the cross.[11]

However, this major project has remained dependent on a focus on complex early documentation – particularly that of the first millennium – at the risk of sometimes losing our way in analyses that are constantly being challenged.[12] What is more, focusing on the Eucharistic part (and especially the euchological corpus) makes it impossible to give a true account of the ritual process from the Word to the Eucharist. At the same time as it highlighted the Eucharistic prayer as the summit of the action, notably by proclaiming it aloud in the vernacular, the liturgical reform of Vatican II restored the liturgy of the Word to its fundamental place in the celebration of the Mass.

By reemphasizing the biblical category of memorial, this research also rediscovered, in its own way, Dom Odo Casel's great insight into the notion of the liturgical mystery.[13] The Eucharist is a celebration of God's covenant with humanity. As the doctrine enshrined in *Sacrosanctum Concilium* invites us to understand, it is indeed the same mystery that is celebrated in the liturgy of the Word and in the liturgy of the Eucharist. This places the categories affirmed by the Council of Trent (sacrifice, sacrament, and real presence) in a broader perspective, that of the actualization of the paschal mystery.

In terms of both liturgical institutions and doctrine, contemporary developments are the result of a desire not only to encourage the active participation of the faithful, as has often been emphasized, but also to take greater account of the whole of tradition. In so doing, the aim was to overcome the aporias in which medieval debates, and then the stiffening caused by sixteenth-century polemics, had trapped Catholic doctrine. The ecumenical dimension is therefore essential, not only with Christian denominations that emerged from the Reformation

---

[11] Mt 27:50–51.
[12] Paul F. Bradshaw, *Eucharistic Origins* (London: SPCK, 2004); cf. also Paul F. Bradshaw, *The Search for the Origins of Christian Worship* (London: SPCK, 1992), and, more recently, Paul F. Bradshaw and Maxwell Johnson, *The Eucharistic Liturgies: Their Evolution and Interpretation* (Collegeville, MN: Liturgical Press, 2012).
[13] Dom Odo Casel, "Das Mysteriengedächtnis der Messliturgie im Lichte der Tradition," *Jahrbuch für Liturgiewissenschaft* 6 (1926): 113–204.

movements of the sixteenth century but also with Churches of the East. The Liturgical Movement, supported by the great biblical, patristic, and ecumenical revivals, has ultimately sought to reconnect with the foundations of the great Christian tradition in order to overcome deep-seated separations.

A NEW UNDERSTANDING OF EUCHARISTIC DYNAMICS

Studies of Eucharistic prayers have profoundly renewed approaches to the theology of the Eucharist.[14] The diversity of Eucharistic prayers brought to light by investigation of ancient sources opened the door to the expression of diverse models of understanding.[15] And the reform of the Mass at Vatican II consisted primarily in abandoning the uniqueness of the Roman canon and introducing a set of formularies into the missal.[16]

This made it easier to grasp the plural nature of tradition. There is in fact not one but many theologies of the Eucharist, rooted in the very diversity of New Testament documentation. Debates over the paschal character of the Last Supper or its unfolding are indicative of the impossibility of harmonizing the different versions of the institution narrative.[17] In this respect, the differences between Eucharistic Prayer I (the ancient Roman Canon) and Eucharistic Prayer II inspired by the Apostolic Tradition, a canonical–liturgical document dating from the early third century,[18] are a major sign that it is impossible to reduce the theology of the Eucharist to a single vision. This is moreover in no mean way confirmed by the recognition of the validity of which the anaphora of Addai and Mari – a form that does not contain the words of the

---

[14] For a synthesis, see Andreas Heinz and Heinrich Rennings (eds.), *Gratias agamus: Festschrift Balthasar Fischer* (Freiburg: Herder, 1992).

[15] Anton Hänggi and Irmgard Pahl (eds.), *Prex eucharistica*, 3rd ed. (Fribourg: Presses Universitaires, 1998); Geoffrey J. Cuming and Ronald C. D. Jasper (eds.), *Prayers of the Eucharist: Early and Reformed*, 4th ed., ed. Paul F. Bradshaw and Maxwell E. Johnson (Collegeville, MN: Liturgical Press, 2019).

[16] *Les nouvelles prières eucharistiques*, special issue of *La Maison-Dieu* 94 (1968); Otto Nussbaum, *Die eucharistischen Hochgebete II–IV: Ein theologischer Kommentar* (Münster: Regensberg, 1971); cf. also my article, "La prière eucharistique dans la réforme de l'Ordo Missae: Du Canon romain aux prières eucharistiques," *La Maison-Dieu* 298 (2019): 21–53.

[17] Giraudo, *In Unum Corpus*, 137–53 and 155–96.

[18] Matthieu Smyth, "L'anaphore de la prétendue 'tradition apostolique' et la prière eucharistique romaine," *Revue des sciences religieuses* 81 (2007): 95–118.

institution to which the Latin tradition attributes the virtue of realizing Eucharistic consecration – are two major signs.

For centuries, the Mass has been presented in terms of the words of Christ (*verba Christi*) pronounced by the priest at the altar, thus exercising a priestly power received through ordination and thus realizing "consecration." It is this transformation of gifts into the body and blood of Christ, a conviction of faith attested by the earliest Christian literature, that found a precise expression in the doctrine of "transubstantiation," and to which medieval theologians gave a metaphysical meaning. It was canonized by the Council of Trent in a context of polemic against the Protestant reformers.[19]

This made the Mass, and especially the "canon" (the "canonical" prayer said by the priest at the altar), the moment par excellence for assuring the presence of Christ in action. In this vision, there is an essential link between the understanding of the role of the ordained minister, on the one hand, and that of consecration and sacramental presence, on the other. In this respect, one can speak of an interpretative system that was reinforced by a whole range of ceremonial aspects (orientation, gestures and postures of the priest, silence of the canon, ringing of bells, kneeling of the faithful, etc.). All this tended to isolate a moment understood as the climax of the action. The rest of the canon then appeared as a ceremonial wrapping for the consecration, a set of prayers necessary for its legality (and as such a serious obligation for the priest) but not really for its validity. What was essential was the conjunction of Eucharistic material (host and chalice contents), form (words of consecration), and the minister's intention to ensure the effectiveness of the action.

Without denying this dogmatic heritage, certain aspects of which were reaffirmed by Pope Paul VI in his encyclical *Mysterium fidei* (September 3, 1965), the 1969 GIRM now designated a process that extends from the presentation of the gifts to the communion of the faithful via the Eucharistic prayer. Referring to Christ's actions at the Last Supper, it emphasizes that "the Church has arranged the entire celebration of the Liturgy of the Eucharist in parts corresponding to precisely these words and actions of Christ:

1. At the Preparation of the Gifts, the bread and the wine with water are brought to the altar, the same elements that Christ took into his hands.

---

[19] André Duval, *Des sacrements au Concile de Trente* (Paris: Cerf, 1985), 21–59.

2   In the Eucharistic Prayer, thanks is given to God for the whole work of salvation, and the offerings become the Body and Blood of Christ.
3   Through the fraction and through Communion, the faithful, though they are many, receive from the one bread the Lord's Body and from the one chalice the Lord's Blood in the same way the Apostles received them from Christ's own hands."[20]

Such a presentation thus underlines the four verbs of the New Testament accounts of the Last Supper: to take, to bless, to break and to give the bread, to take, to bless and to give the cup.[21] The Eucharistic action cannot be separated from the presentation of gifts, nor from the communion toward which it tends. Within this overall dynamic, the GIRM presents the Eucharistic prayer as "the center and summit of the entire celebration," which is then the site of the Church's Eucharistic offering – a sacrifice of thanksgiving.

Since the sixteenth century, the Mass has been interpreted as a cult in which the Church represents the sacrifice Christ made to the Father on the altar of the cross. In this context, the priest offers the sacrifice of the cross to God, so that its fruits may be poured out on humankind. Considering the Eucharistic prayer as a "prayer of thanksgiving and sanctification," it now appears as the place of a double movement of acceptance of the gift and offering of the life of the faithful. It is thus one of the major expressions of the covenant and of the great dialogue between God and humankind, an exchange manifested in the initial dialogue that precedes the preface and which is now part of the Eucharistic prayer, a dialogue whose source is the divine initiative, as Pope Francis emphasized in *Desiderio desideravi*.[22]

The GIRM thus makes a distinction between the elements that make up the Eucharistic prayer, a prayer in which the whole assembly, together with the minister, gives thanks (particularly in the preface) for the work of creation and salvation, while the acclamation of the Sanctus, "which is part of the Eucharistic Prayer itself, is sung or said by all the people with the priest." At the same time, the intercessions express the fact that the concrete assembly celebrates "in communion with the entire Church, of

---

[20] *GIRM*, 72. See Foley et al., *A Commentary*, 162–65.
[21] Gregory Dix, *The Shape of the Liturgy*, new ed. (London et al.: Bloomsbury/T&T Clark, 2015).
[22] Pope Francis, *Desiderio desideravi*, 4: "No one had earned a place at that Supper. All had been invited. Or better said: all had been drawn there by the burning desire that Jesus had to eat that Passover with them."

heaven as well as of earth, and that the offering is made for her and for all her members, living and dead, who have been called to participate in the redemption and salvation purchased by Christ's Body and Blood."[23]

However, it is the movement from anamnesis to offering ("remembering ... we offer you") that is particularly highlighted as the fundamental structure of the Eucharist. Certainly, in the account of the institution and consecration, we are reminded,

> [B]y means of words and actions of Christ, the Sacrifice is carried out which Christ himself instituted at the Last Supper, when he offered his Body and Blood under the species of bread and wine, gave them to his Apostles to eat and drink, and left them the command to perpetuate this same mystery.[24]

But the text emphasizes that it is by fulfilling the order received from Christ the Lord through the apostles that the Church remembers (*anamnesis*) Christ himself, "recalling especially his blessed Passion, glorious Resurrection, and Ascension into heaven." And "in this very memorial, the Church ... offers in the Holy Spirit the spotless Victim to the Father."[25]

Furthermore, the study of Eucharistic prayers in the Christian East has contributed to rebalancing the relationship between pneumatology and the Eucharist, notably by restoring a decisive place to epiclesis.[26] For the GIRM, through the epiclesis, "the Church implores the power of the Holy Spirit that the gifts offered by human hands be consecrated, that is, become Christ's Body and Blood, and that the spotless Victim to be received in Communion be for the salvation of those who will partake in it."[27] It should be noted here that, while venerable ancient formularies such as the Anaphora of St. Basil placed the epiclesis after the institution narrative, linking the request for the transformation of the gifts to that of the assembly, the elaboration of Eucharistic Prayer II of the 1970 Missal reshaped the anaphora of the Apostolic Tradition. This was done in order to preserve a Latin tradition that, since Ambrose of Milan, has privileged the pronunciation of Christ's words as the determining act.[28]

---

[23] *GIRM*, 79. See Foley et al., *A Commentary*, 174, 178–79.
[24] Ibid., 176.
[25] Ibid., 177.
[26] Dom Fernand Cabrol, "Le Canon Romain et la Messe," *Revue des sciences philosophiques et théologiques* 3 (1909): 490–524.
[27] *GIMR*, 79. See Foley et al., *A Commentary*, 174–75.
[28] Pierre-Marie Gy, "Doctrine eucharistique de la liturgie romaine dans le haut moyen âge," in Pierre-Marie Gy, *La liturgie dans l'histoire* (Paris: Cerf, 1990), 187–204, esp. 196–97.

In the Eucharist, the Church remembers God's first gift through creation and salvation history. In so doing, it fulfills Christ's command to "Do this in memory of me,"[29] in order to continue proclaiming and realizing the Kingdom that is already here and yet awaits its full realization. In this respect, the ritual itinerary symbolizes the three aspects of the Paschal Mystery, of which the Eucharistic memorial is a form of fulfillment. The eschatological dimension of the Eucharist is closely linked to the rediscovery of the Paschal Mystery, of its intrinsic unity, which combines the memory of passion and death, the confession of resurrection, and the session of Christ at the right hand of the Father in the expectation of his coming in glory. The memorial acclamation of the Eucharistic prayer thus synthesizes this actualization of the mystery with the memory of the work of salvation (past), the presence of the mystery celebrated (present), and the eschatological expectation of its full realization (future):

> We proclaim your death, O Lord,
> and profess your Resurrection,
> until you come again.[30]

WORD AND EUCHARIST

The post-Vatican II reform of the Mass has largely been seen in terms of the deployment of a liturgy of the Word. The homily, profession of faith, and universal prayer form its integral part. To speak of a liturgy of the Word (and no longer of "readings") implies that the liturgical action is centered on the public proclamation of the Scriptures in the vernacular, in a dialog-like structure that includes a responsorial psalm. This innovation was accompanied by a major pastoral effort to open up "the treasures of the bible ... more lavishly, so that richer fare may be provided for the faithful at the table of God's word."[31] It has resulted in the publication of a new *Ordo Lectionum Missae* and various other lectionaries, and an Introduction to the Lectionary for Mass, a text of high theological density that echoes the conciliar constitution *Dei Verbum*.

The liturgy of the Word is an act of celebration, not just an act of teaching, and this liturgical "action" in its own right implies a diversity

---

[29] Lk 22:19.
[30] *The Roman Missal*, 641, 647, 652, 659.
[31] *Sacrosanctum Concilium*, 51; cf. also 24 and 35.

of ministers (readers, cantor for the psalm, but also presider for the homily):

> The main part of the Liturgy of the Word is made up of the readings from Sacred Scripture together with the chants occurring between them. The homily, Profession of Faith, and Prayer of the Faithful, however, develop and conclude this part of the Mass.[32]

The transformation of the "readings," which were previously usually read by the priest himself at the altar (in Latin, with his back to the people), into the "liturgy of the Word" is therefore an essential shift in the *Ordo Missae*, which configures the Mass around two poles: liturgy of the Word and Eucharistic liturgy, two forms of celebration of the same mystery, which the Dominican Yves Congar presented shortly before Vatican II as the "two forms of the bread of life"[33] in Tradition.

The liturgical reform has thus brought about what, in an ecumenical context, has been identified as a "conversion to the Word of God," expressed by a threefold renewal: (1) wider and deeper access to the entire biblical corpus through a renewal of the lectionaries; (2) more direct access to the Word of God thanks to proclamation in the vernacular; and (3) maximum enhancement of the relationship between Word and sacrament, since every sacramental celebration includes a proclamation from the Scriptures. In addition, the relationship between the homily (formerly known as the sermon) and the readings was enhanced, and the ambo became the place of the Word in the church building.

Despite the success of publications designed to make liturgical readings more accessible to the faithful, these impulses are encountering real difficulties at the pastoral level, which is linked to the gap between contemporary culture and biblical sources. But as the Gospel parable of the sower itself attests, it is in the nature of proclamation to encounter such difficulties. However, without forgetting these obstacles, the essential thing is undoubtedly the rediscovery of Scripture as the Word addressed to a liturgical assembly:

> For in the readings, as explained by the homily, God speaks to his people, opening up to them the mystery of redemption and salvation, and offering them spiritual nourishment; and Christ himself is present in the midst of the faithful through his word.

---

[32] GIRM, nr. 55. See Foley et al., *A Commentary*, 147.
[33] Yves Congar, "Les deux formes du pain de vie dans l'Évangile et dans la Tradition," in *Parole de Dieu et Sacerdoce, Etudes présentées à Mgr Weber*, ed. Eugène Fischer and Louis Bouyer (Paris: Desclée et Cie, 1962), 21–58.

By their silence and singing the people make God's word their own, and they also affirm their adherence to it by means of the Profession of Faith. Finally, having been nourished by it, they pour out their petitions in the Prayer of the Faithful for the needs of the entire Church and for the salvation of the whole world.[34]

In the light of the conciliar Constitution *Dei Verbum*, the unity of "Word" and "Sacrament" has thus been rediscovered. The apostolic exhortation *Verbum Domini* (September 30, 2010) sets out the fundamental theological consequences of this rediscovery. Pope Benedict XVI develops a reflection on the sacramentality of the Word proclaimed in celebration, which invites us to transform our approaches:

> Word and Eucharist are so deeply bound together that we cannot understand one without the other: the word of God sacramentally takes flesh in the event of the Eucharist. The Eucharist opens us to an understanding of Scripture, just as Scripture for its part illumines and explains the mystery of the Eucharist.[35]

One of the difficulties in this area is to understand the council's affirmation of Christ's presence in his Word, "since it is He Himself who speaks when the holy scriptures are read in the Church."[36] This gives this part of the Mass a sacramental dimension that Pope Benedict XVI has decisively highlighted and which had previously been expounded by theologians, notably by Louis-Marie Chauvet.[37] Since, as Thomas Aquinas famously held in the *Summa theologiae*, the sacraments "operate what they signify," the presence of Christ through the proclamation of the Word in the liturgical site must be understood as a "*viva vox evangelii*" (a living voice of the gospel).[38] Discussed at the Council, this affirmation sometimes gives rise to the fear of reducing faith in the real presence, which results from the transformation of the species and toward which a cult of adoration is exercised.

In unfolding this doctrine of the modalities of the Lord's presence through the repetition of the formula "*praesens adest*" (he is present

---

[34] GIRM, 55. See Foley et al., *A Commentary*, 147–48.
[35] *Verbum Domini*, 55.
[36] *Sacrosanctum Concilium*, 7.
[37] Louis-Marie Chauvet, *Symbol and Sacrament: A Sacramental Reinterpretation of Christian Existence*, trans. Patrick Madigan and Madeleine Beaumont (Collegeville, MN: Liturgical Press, 1995), 190–227.
[38] Paul De Clerck, "Au commencement était le Verbe," *La Maison-Dieu* 189 (1992): 19–40, esp. 35–36.

there), the council links the presence in the Eucharistic action: (1) in the sacrifice of the Mass, (2) in the person of the minister, and (3) "especially" (*tum maxime*) under the species, with his presence in the sacraments, in the prayer of the hours, and above all in the Scriptures proclaimed in the liturgy. Christ's presence in the Word cannot therefore be isolated from the other modalities with which it enters into symphony. Ultimately, the presence of Christ through the mediation of the Word is a presence that cannot be understood outside the celebrating assembly. The liturgical assembly is the place where the Word takes shape: It is the proclamation that establishes the assembly as a body receiving the Word. This listening assembly is the recipient of a presence offered as a gift. At the same time, it makes itself present through its attention to the mystery unfolding in the liturgy. Presence in the Word is a contemplative dynamic of giving and receiving.

In this area, in a postmodern world marked by the search for immediate satisfaction (in the primary sense of "without mediation"), we witness the emergence of Eucharistic representations that privilege what is perceptible to the senses, rather than views illuminated by the depth of the mystery. Thus, in our practices, and in our singing, we see forms of thought that tend to assign the Lord's presence to a place (tabernacle, monstrance), which is contrary to classical doctrine. What is more, these postmodern representations of the Lord's presence can be said to find a foundation in post-medieval Eucharistic piety, which is all the more unquestionable in that it is based on a tradition canonized by councils and the testimony of saints and enshrined in the teaching of catechisms. There are therefore approaches to sacramental presence that, in fact, challenge the conciliar doctrine of presence in the Word. This tendency is all the more prevalent inasmuch as the Word is associated with the ephemeral, and therefore not with a lasting presence.

From now on, it is nevertheless essential to think of the Eucharist in terms of the ritual process, as a complex journey in which Word and Sacrament are in constant interaction, and which opens up to an experience of encounter. The place of the Word is not limited to the liturgy of the Word: It runs through the entire Eucharistic action from the beginning of the Mass to the dismissal. This is not only because liturgical words are inspired by, and even woven from, the Scriptures but, far more profoundly, because the Eucharistic mystery is the manifestation of God's work in human history, God's work of which the Bible is the great narrative, and which culminates in Christ's Passover, God's new and eternal covenant with humankind.

The story of the pilgrims to Emmaus thus remains a fundamental reference point for an understanding of the Eucharist that is in tune with the challenges of a time marked by social networking and consumerism as a way of life.[39] The Lucan story reminds us that Christ's presence in the Word and in the Eucharistic sharing is a gift that is always to be received and can never be assimilated to a "thing" over which we can exercise power and control.

AN ASSEMBLY INTO THE BODY OF CHRIST

Retrieving patristic accents, the GIRM emphasizes the unity of the assembly over which the priest presides:

> The priest invites the people to lift up their hearts to the Lord in prayer and thanksgiving; he unites the congregation with himself in the prayer that he addresses in the name of the entire community to God the Father through Jesus Christ in the Holy Spirit. Furthermore, the meaning of the Prayer is that the entire congregation of the faithful should join itself with Christ in confessing the great deeds of God and in the offering of Sacrifice.[40]

By emphasizing the role of the assembled ecclesia as the "integral subject of liturgical action," Yves Congar highlighted how Vatican II had profoundly renewed the ecclesiology of Eucharistic action. In so doing, the council endorsed a fundamental shift, which remains at large a program which is yet to be executed. Whereas, since the Middle Ages, the Eucharistic celebration has been considered the action of the priest offering the sacrifice for the good of the faithful, and often without the latter taking part at the Eucharistic table, the Liturgical Movement, especially with the pioneering work of Dom Lambert Beauduin, has brought back into focus the necessary "active participation" of the faithful. This is particularly evident at the beginning of the chapter on the Eucharist (ch. II) of the Conciliar Constitution on the Liturgy. This text constitutes a masterly synthesis of the progress made on this point over the course of the twentieth century:

> The Church, therefore, earnestly desires that Christ's faithful, when present at this mystery of faith, should not be there as strangers or silent spectators; on the contrary, through a good understanding of

---

[39] Lk 24:13–35.
[40] *GIRM*, nr. 78. See Foley et al., *A Commentary*, 171–72.

> the rites and prayers they should take part in the sacred action conscious of what they are doing, with devotion and full collaboration. They should be instructed by God's word and be nourished at the table of the Lord's body; they should give thanks to God; by offering the Immaculate Victim, not only through the hands of the priest, but also with him, they should learn also to offer themselves; through Christ the Mediator, they should be drawn day by day into ever more perfect union with God and with each other, so that finally God may be all in all.[41]

This passage brings together what, since the end of the patristic era, various practices and often theological productions had separated. The Eucharistic synaxis is presented as a sacrifice and a fraternal table where people come to restore themselves. It is both the gift of a word and the sharing of the same bread. It is also a place of spiritual sacrifice for Christians, as the apostle expresses in the Letter to the Romans.[42]

Last but not least, it is communion beyond all divisions, a communion whose source is the Passover, for this gift of communion with God and between participants is the fruit of a sacrifice, that of Christ who died on the cross "to gather into one the dispersed children of God."[43] In other words, the active participation of the faithful in the Eucharist is not based on a principle of role distribution, according to which one must "do something" in order to truly participate. In fact, active participation is the translation into liturgy of an essential affirmation of ecclesiological doctrine set out in Vatican II's Constitution on the Church, *Lumen gentium*, namely the exercise of the common priesthood of the baptized in the celebration.[44] The GIRM makes this vision explicit with regard to the functions of the People of God in the Eucharistic celebration:

> In the celebration of the Mass the faithful form a holy people, a people whom God has made his own, a royal priesthood, so that they may give thanks to God and offer the spotless Victim not only through the hands of the priest but also together with him, and so that they may learn to offer themselves. They should, moreover, to make this clear by their deep religious sense and their charity

---

[41] *Sacrosanctum Concilium*, 48. See also Joris Geldhof, "On Interiorizing the Mystery of the Eucharist: A Reflection on *Sacrosanctum Concilium*, 48," *Questions Liturgiques* 97 (2016): 123–40.
[42] Cf. Rom 12:1.
[43] Jn 11:52.
[44] *Lumen Gentium*, 11.

toward brothers and sisters who participate with them in the same celebration. Thus, they are to shun any appearance of individualism or division, keeping before their eyes that they have only one Father in heaven and accordingly are all brothers and sisters to each other.[45]

If the first epiclesis, before the narrative, is a request for the transformation of gifts, the second concerns the assembly, the sign of the Church in a given place and at a given time. Or, as the third Eucharistic prayer of the *Missale Romanum* has it: "Grant that we, who are ... filled with his Holy Spirit, may become one body, one spirit in Christ."[46] This is the fundamental dynamic of the Eucharist, reflected in the adage "the Eucharist makes the Church," which the encyclical *Ecclesia de Eucharistia* takes up by saying that "the Eucharist builds up the Church."[47]

Such an approach draws on the formulas of Augustine of Hippo: "you are the body of Christ"; "receive what you are"; "it is your mystery that is represented on the altar"; and "let your amen be your signature."[48] It distances itself from a medieval theology that emphasized sacramental efficacy by focusing on the mere transformation of the species into the body and blood of Christ. The Eucharist is above all the actualization of the paschal work, the foundation of communion with God and between the members of his people, in the expectation that God will be all in all.[49]

CONCLUSION

The recent health crisis, which has shaken the whole world, has demonstrated the extent to which the relationship with the Eucharist has been perceived as a vital dimension of Christian life. Eucharistic celebrations through social networks should call for real discernment. They do, however, point to a thirst for the Eucharist that characterizes a contemporary world in search of ritual landmarks and emotionally dense experiences. In a context marked by forms of individualism and

---

[45] GIRM, 95. See Foley et al., *A Commentary*, 205–6.
[46] *The Roman Missal*, 653.
[47] *Ecclesia de Eucharistia*, ch. II; 26. Cf. also Laurent de Villeroché, *L'Église fait l'Eucharistie, l'Eucharistie fait l'Église: Un paradoxe en sacramentaire* (Paris: Cerf, 2021).
[48] Augustine, *Sermo*, 272.
[49] 1 Cor 15:28.

consumerism, the question is how to make Eucharistic faith resonate: The celebration of the Eucharist is by its nature a communal act, a celebration of the Church, a ritual act in which the Church remembers the salvation that came through the Passover of her Lord. The Eucharist is therefore inseparable from Easter faith: The risen Christ is alive, present to his Church as it journeys through history.

For Further Reading

Bouyer, Louis, *Eucharist: Theology and Spirituality of the Eucharistic Prayer*, trans. Charles U. Quinn (Notre Dame, IN: University of Notre Dame Press, 2006).

Foley, Edward, John F. Baldovin, Mary Collins, and Joanne M. Pierce (eds.), *A Commentary on the Order of Mass of the Roman Missal* (Collegeville, MN: Liturgical Press, 2011).

Foley, Edward, Nathan D. Mitchell, and Joanne M. Pierce (eds.), *A Commentary on the General Instruction of the Roman Missal* (Collegeville, MN: Liturgical Press, 2007).

Giraudo, Cesare, *In Unum Corpus: Traité mystagogique sur l'Eucharistie*, trans. Éric Iborra and Pierre-Marie Hombert (Paris: Cerf, 2014).

Grillo, Andrea, *Eucaristia: Azione rituale, forme storiche, essenza sistematica* (Brescia: Queriniana, 2019).

Jungmann, Joseph A., *The Mass of the Roman Rite: Its Origins and Development (Missarum Sollemnia)*, 2 vols. (Notre Dame, IN: Ave Maria Press, 2012).

Kilmartin, Edward J., *The Eucharist in the West: History and Theology*, ed. Robert J. Daly (Collegeville, MN: Liturgical Press, 2004).

Mazza, Enrico, *The Celebration of the Eucharist: The Origin of the Rite and the Development of Its Interpretation*, trans. Mathew J. O'Connell (Collegeville, MN: Liturgical Press, 1990).

The Eucharistic Prayers of the Roman Rite, trans. Mathew J. O'Connell (Collegeville, MN: Liturgical Press, 2004).

Stuflesser, Martin, *Eucharistie: Liturgische Feier und theologische Erschließung* (Regensburg: Friedrich Pustet, 2013).

8 Liturgy and the Sacraments
CLARE V. JOHNSON

Ritual celebrations of sacraments are at once profound human experiences and mysterious acts of divine grace that affect the life of the individual and the ecclesial community, having both immediate and remote effects and ramifications. The church enacts its sacramental doctrine in liturgical celebration. Through symbolic ritual actions that have evolved over centuries of practice, theological reflection, and official articulation, the gathered assembly of the faithful expresses and enacts the Christian sacraments in the presence and under the headship of Christ. As "powers that come forth from the body of Christ"[1] and actions of the Holy Spirit, sacraments utilize elements of creation symbolically to reveal different aspects of the Paschal Mystery and invite the faithful to embrace and participate in God's acts of grace to individual, ecclesial, and global benefit.

Recognizing the rich diversity of Christian sacramental rites and traditions, this chapter considers the Christian sacraments (other than the Eucharist)[2] from a predominantly Roman Catholic perspective. It begins with an exploration of the principle of sacramentality and an outline of key theological aspects of sacraments, and then considers the ritual definition, enactment, and expected outcomes of six ecclesial sacraments.

[1] *Catechism of the Catholic Church*, 1116, www.vatican.va/archive/ENG0015/_P30.HTM (hereafter *CCC*). All Catholic Church documents referenced in this chapter are sourced from the www.vatican.va website. Individual document URLs are not listed.

[2] Patrick Prétot considers the Eucharist in Chapter 7.

DEFINING SACRAMENTS

Sacramentality

The broad concept of "sacramentality" is the foundation on which considerations of individual Christian sacraments rest. Scripture teaches that God created all that is and saw that "indeed it was very good."[3] Christian sacramentality is a biblically inspired worldview that holds that God's good creation is the medium in and through which humans (as the pinnacle of creation[4] and called to have dominion over it)[5] can know, offer worship to, and interact with the creator.[6] Viewed through the lens of sacramentality, creation itself is seen as revelatory of the Triune God's ongoing presence[7] and action and is to be valued and respected as its locus. As creatures living symbiotically with creation, humans utilize created matter drawn from everyday life to "name, experience, and worship"[8] God's creative telos is to commune in personal relationship with his creatures, who are transformed upon willingly receiving his self-expression in order to respond, return, and impart his love to others. The principle of sacramentality presupposes that our transcendent God desires continued interaction with creation (especially humans) and chooses to be present imminently and symbolically in "mediated immediacy"[9] through the things of this earth (water, light, salt), the products of human work (bread, wine, oil, clothing), and preeminently in the incarnation of the Son, the "human externalization of the Trinity."[10]

In Jesus Christ, God – fully divine and fully human – entered creation historically, redeeming it, transforming it, promising the ongoing presence of the Holy Spirit to continue sanctifying it, and (through his death and resurrection) opening a path to salvation[11] for all who believe.

---

[3] Gen 1:31.
[4] Gen 1:27.
[5] Gen 1:28.
[6] Wis 13:5.
[7] The notion that God shares Godself with humanity via creation by reaching out in gratuitous loving self-gift is known as "uncreated grace," the natural expression of Godself, who is uncreated. Such grace is accessible to all.
[8] Kevin W. Irwin, *The Sacraments: Historical Foundations and Liturgical Theology* (New York: Paulist, 2016), 211–12.
[9] Edward Kilmartin, "Sacraments as Liturgy of the Church," *Theological Studies* 50 (1989): 536.
[10] Joseph Martos, *The Sacraments: An Interdisciplinary and Interactive Study* (Collegeville, MN: Liturgical Press, 2009), 140.
[11] Pope Francis, "*Laudato Si*: Papal Encyclical on 'Care for Our Common Home'," (May 24, 2015), 9, 70, 71 (hereafter *LSi*).

Christ's promise of presence found expression in the tangible observable reality of the church, which continued to meet in his name post-Ascension, to engage in symbolic ritual actions in his memory as he instructed, employing earthly things and his efficacious word. In their ritual celebrations the early Christians experienced Christ's ongoing presence,[12] which strengthened and inspired them to live his way[13] for the benefit of all. In the living church was found "the persisting presence of the incarnate Word in space and time."[14] Experiencing Christ's presence in the celebration of sacred rites centered, motivated, and transformed the early church, which treasured, protected, comprehended, and passed on in these rites core expressions of their faith and identity as members of Christ's body called to extend his witness and works in the world throughout the ages.

Over centuries of practice the church has understood that within ecclesial life are certain privileged moments of intense sacrality wherein God's ongoing presence is manifested, revealed, and encountered in particular ways via created matter in liturgical action, for the benefit of those who freely answer God's call to participate in personal and communal relationship and to foster communion among humankind and all creation.[15] The church names such privileged moments "sacraments."

Sacraments

The ritual enactment and theological definition of sacraments have both evolved considerably over the course of Christian history. Augustine (d. 430 CE) provided a touchstone description of a sacrament as "a sign of a sacred thing,"[16] a "visible form of an invisible grace," and "visible words,"[17] applying the term "sacrament" to hundreds of sacred realities. Augustine's basic sacramental description is still used within

---

[12] Lk 24:13–35; Pope Leo the Great explains, "What was visible in our Lord has passed over into the sacraments." Sermon 74, 2: *Patrologia Latina*, vol. 54, ed. J. P. Migne, 398.

[13] Mk 10:52.

[14] Karl Rahner, "The Theology of the Symbol," *Theological Investigations Vol 4: More Recent Writings*, trans. Kevin Smyth (New York: Crossroad, 1982), 240.

[15] Second Vatican Council, *Lumen gentium*, "Dogmatic Constitution on the Church" (November 21, 1964), 1 (hereafter *LG*).

[16] Augustine, *City of God*, x. 10 c. 5.11,1, www.gutenberg.org/files/45304/45304-h/45304-h.htm#Page_388.

[17] Augustine, "Answer to Faustus, a Manichean," 19.16, *Works of Saint Augustine* vol. 1/20, trans. Roland Teske, SJ, ed. Boniface Ramsay (New York: New City Press, 2007), 246–47.

church teaching,[18] though conceptualizations and definitions of "sign" have gained precision in their application to sacraments.

Understanding signs and symbols is critical to apprehending sacraments in their liturgical context.[19] Signs point to something, ideally convey one straightforward concept, and do not participate in the reality they signify (e.g., smoke is a sign of fire, but not fire itself).[20] Symbols (such as sacraments) are a category of sign that do participate in what they signify as multivalent, complex concepts that exceed their surface appearances, bringing together[21] "something beyond" with what is sensually apparent. The ultimate Christian symbol and sacrament is Christ, a tangible person who both points to God and is God. As symbols, sacraments are mysterious[22] means of "mediating supernatural life,"[23] ritual word-acts in which the natural and the supernatural are united. In their celebration God grants created grace[24] to a willing human recipient–participant within a communal faith context. Vatican II's inclusion of scripture in every sacramental celebration was intended to highlight the efficaciousness of God's Word spoken in liturgy, with the understanding that "when God speaks, things happen."[25]

Augustine's hundreds of sacraments were abridged by Peter Lombard in the twelfth century to a list of seven ecclesial sacraments (Baptism, Confirmation, Eucharist, Penance, Extreme Unction, Matrimony, Holy Orders), which were declared Catholic doctrine by the Councils of Lyons II (1274), Florence (1439), and Trent (1547). Lombard's list was accepted in Eastern Orthodoxy, but sixteenth-

---

[18] *CCC*, 1131.
[19] Pope Francis, *Desiderio Desideravi*, Apostolic Letter "On the Liturgical Formation of the People of God," (June 29, 2022), 27.
[20] Semiotician Charles Sanders Peirce identified three categories of sign: icon, index, symbol. See: *Philosophical Writings of Peirce*, ed. Justus Buchler (New York: Dover, 1955), 98–119.
[21] *Syn + bole* (Gk) means "to throw together."
[22] *Mysterion* (Gk) means "sacred or hidden mysteries." Its later Latin equivalent, *sacramentum* (from *sacrare*: "to make or be holy/sacred, consecrate, dedicate"), was not exact. Tertullian employed *sacramentum*'s meaning as a "sacred oath" that soldiers made when committing to serve a ruler, as a cognate for the commitment one makes to Christ in Baptism. See Tertullian, *Ad martyras* 3, www.newadvent.org/fathers/0323.htm.
[23] *LSi*, 235.
[24] Created grace is an intentional operation of God within the soul, a supernatural gift of divine life distinct from Godself, gratuitously granted and made present to a person open to its reception.
[25] Irwin, *The Sacraments*, 252.

century Protestant Reformers only accepted Baptism, Eucharist, and a form of Penance as sacraments, due to their verifiable scriptural origins. The question of "institution" of the sacraments by Christ was addressed variously by the different denominations – where Protestants sought historical scriptural evidence of institution, Roman Catholics argued that "a sacrament can only be 'instituted' by him who has the power to produce its effect" and that each sacrament had a different process of institution.[26] Vatican II sees each sacrament as "instituted" in and through its celebration as an act of Christ, who is present and whose power alone effects the sacraments.[27]

Today various strong convergences exist among different Christian denominations regarding sacraments. Baptism and Eucharist are broadly accepted as central to the ritual praxis and faith life of many Christian communities, and the importance of the Word as sacramental has wide ecumenical consensus.[28] Mainstream Christian denominations accept the validity of each other's Baptism, provided the matter and the form, and the intention of minister and recipient, indicate a valid conferral.[29] For Catholics (with the sui generis churches in communion) and Eastern Orthodox Christians, sacraments are seen as "constituent elements of the church representing the apex of its liturgical life,"[30] and the seven ecclesial sacraments are celebrated. The major Protestant churches (Lutherans, Anglicans, Reformed, Methodists) emphasize "the Word proclaimed, which is invested with sacramental significance,"[31] and celebrate the sacraments of Baptism and Eucharist on account of their scriptural attestation. Protestant churches with Anabaptist origins (Mennonites, Baptists, Pentecostals) emphasize "the role of personal faith, as commitment, over ecclesiastical faith" and recognize an "ordinance" (rather than a sacrament) as "a response of the believer that 'confirms the faith' that God has already given"[32] them. Both Roman Catholics and Protestants believe the

---

[26] Jorge A. Scampini, "The Sacraments in Ecumenical Dialogue," in *The Oxford Handbook of Sacramental Theology*, eds., Hans Boersma and Matthew Levering (Oxford: Oxford University Press, 2015), 687.
[27] Second Vatican Council, *Sacrosanctum Concilium*, "Constitution on the Sacred Liturgy," (December 4, 1963), 7, (hereafter *SC*).
[28] See Lizette Larson-Miller, *Sacramentality Renewed: Contemporary Conversations in Sacramental Theology* (Collegeville, MN: Liturgical Press, 2016), 23.
[29] Catholic Church, *Code of Canon Law*, Canon 869§2.
[30] Scampini, "The Sacraments in Ecumenical Dialogue," 676.
[31] Ibid., 676.
[32] Ibid., 676. Cf. also Melanie Ross's discussion in Chapter 4.

church plays a vital "ministerial and instrumental role in the proclamation of the Word and the celebration of the sacraments."[33]

The Scholastic Sacramental Legacy

The scholastics of the twelfth and thirteenth centuries (especially Hugh of Saint Victor [d. 1141], Thomas Aquinas [d. 1274], and Duns Scotus [d. 1308]) developed a sophisticated sacramental system based on Aristotelian philosophy that "provided an intellectual framework for explaining the meaning and purpose of the church's sacramental worship."[34] Much of current Roman Catholic sacramental doctrine still relies on scholastic theological formulae and explanations, which necessitates understanding its philosophical base.

Aristotle (d. 322 BCE) theorized that everything in existence is constituted of matter and form. Matter is the sensible or tangible aspect of a thing (what can be perceived with the senses). Form is the intelligible aspect of a thing (what can be conceived with the mind). Aquinas applied this theory to sacraments, proposing that there are sensible (matter) and conceptual (form) aspects of sacraments and that every sacramental rite needs to contain both aspects for it to be valid. For example, in Baptism, the matter is water (used in observable symbolic action), and the form is the Trinitarian formula based on Mt 28:19: "I baptize you in the name of the Father, and of the Son, and of the Holy Spirit." This theory safeguards the validity of every Catholic sacrament.

In articulating how sacraments work, the scholastics utilized another Aristotelian duality: sign and cause. As signs, sacramental rites point to the operation of unseen realities (such as grace), and, as causes, sacraments have supernatural effects on the individual subject and consequently on the ecclesia. The valid celebration and reception of sacraments effects sanctifying grace because sacraments as acts of the Church are instrumental causes[35] of grace, with Christ being the instigator or "efficient" cause of grace.

The scholastics posited that sacraments achieve their effect *ex opere operato* (from the working of the work) and not *ex opere operantis* (by the work of the worker), which makes the sacramental celebration

---

[33] Scampini, "The Sacraments in Ecumenical Dialogue," 689.
[34] Martos, *The Sacraments*, 131.
[35] Gloria Frost explains: "*Instrumental causes* are employed by another cause, called a principal cause, to reach its end." "Efficient Causes Which Act Through Another Cause's Power," in *Aquinas on Efficient Causation and Causal Powers* (Cambridge: Cambridge University Press, 2022), 206–27.

"intrinsically efficacious"[36] and not dependent on the sanctity of the minister because Christ's power is at work as principal agent or final cause. Hence, when performed validly with a willing subject and intention, sacraments accomplish their stated purpose.

According to the scholastic system, three sacraments convey an indelible "character" on the soul of the sacramental subject, which means they are deemed unrepeatable and their effect permanent: Baptism, Confirmation, Holy Orders. Following its codification by Trent, the scholastic approach to sacraments informed the Catholic Church's theological, rubrical, and juridical thought until the mid-twentieth century.

Sacraments in the Era of Vatican II

With the rediscovery of early church liturgical sources, the Liturgical Movement of the nineteenth and early twentieth centuries considered approaches to sacramental theology beyond scholasticism.[37] Embracing the ancient category of "mystery,"[38] Liturgical Movement thinkers recovered "the unity of liturgy and sacramental theology," opening "a new paradigm for sacramental theology, but without relinquishing ways to think about sacramental efficaciousness."[39] Considering sacraments from a liturgical perspective facilitated the exploration of them as ritual experiences formative of faith, and the essential role of the assembly as active participants.

The Second Vatican Council taught that "Christ is always present in his Church, especially in her liturgical celebrations" and that "by his power he is present in the sacraments so that when a man baptizes it is really Christ himself who baptizes."[40] Prior to the Council, Edward Schillebeeckx[41] and Karl Rahner[42] articulated a new approach to

---

[36] Nathan D. Mitchell, *Meeting Mystery: Liturgy, Worship, and Sacraments* (Maryknoll, NY: Orbis, 2009), 37.

[37] Cf. Katharine E. Harmon's discussion in Chapter 6.

[38] See Odo Casel, *The Mystery of Christian Worship and Other Writings* (Westminster, MD: Newman Press, 1962).

[39] Patrick Prétot, "The Sacraments as 'Celebrations of the Church': Liturgy's Impact on Sacramental Theology," in *Sacraments: Revelation of the Humanity of God – Engaging the Fundamental Theology of Louis-Marie Chauvet*, eds. Philippe Bordeyne and Bruce T. Morrill (Collegeville, MN: Liturgical Press, 2008), 26–27.

[40] SC, 7.

[41] Edward Schillebeeckx, *Christ the Sacrament of Encounter with God* (Kansas City, MO: Sheed & Ward, 1963).

[42] Karl Rahner, *The Church and the Sacraments*, trans. W. J. O'Hara (New York: Herder & Herder, 1963).

sacramental theology, which the conciliar church embraced. According to this view Christ is *Ursakrament* (primordial sacrament) – the sacrament of God – while the institutional church is *Grundsakrament* (ground/root sacrament) – the sacrament of Christ.[43] The seven sacraments then, are acts of the Church, which was instituted by Christ to continue the work of salvation "by means of sacrifice and sacraments around which the entire liturgical life revolves."[44]

Vatican II depicted sacraments primarily as liturgical events, celebrated by the entire body of Christ.[45] In emphasizing the importance of the active participation of all the faithful in the celebration of liturgy[46] and stating that in the liturgy the real nature of the true church is manifested,[47] Vatican II "retrieved the ancient tradition that the ecclesia is the subject of liturgical action."[48] Vatican II's embrace of *ressourcement* (return to authoritative sources) and *aggiornamento* (bringing up-to-date/contextualization) paved the way for a new generation of scholars to begin to bridge the chasm that had appeared between liturgy and sacramental theology from the early medieval period onward,[49] where sacraments were studied primarily as an aspect of dogmatic theology while liturgics principally studied rubrics. New methods for studying liturgy (e.g., liturgical theology and ritual studies) emerged in the latter part of the twentieth century, informed by dialogue with other human sciences (e.g., anthropology, psychology, sociology) that took seriously the experiential nature of sacramental rites.[50] Given subsequent scholarly engagement with emerging philosophical and theological trends in the twenty-first century (e.g., affective science and ecological theology), it is doubtful whether any comprehensive sacramental theology is possible today separate from the sacraments' nature as enacted liturgical rites.[51]

---

[43] Kilmartin describes the church as "the social situation of the abiding presence of Jesus Christ" (*The Sacraments*, 533).

[44] SC, 2. Kilmartin explains, "Because of the unity between Christ and the Church, the mediated immediacy made possible by the one Spirit of Christ, the sacramental celebrations of the Church, root sacrament, are efficacious signs of Christ, primordial sacrament in both senses" (*The Sacraments*, 536).

[45] LG, 1 and 9, and SC, 7.

[46] SC, 14.

[47] Ibid., 2.

[48] Yves M. J. Congar, "L'Ecclesia ou communauté chrétienne, sujet intégrale de l'action liturgique," in *La Liturgie après Vatican II*, ed. J. P. Jossua and Y. Congar (Paris: Cerf, 1967), 241.

[49] Irwin, *The Sacraments*, 3.

[50] Cf. Kimberly Hope Belcher's discussion in Chapter 21.

[51] See Larson-Miller, *Sacramentality*, 20, 34.

Recent versions of the sacramental ritual books represent a distillation of current official ecclesial teaching on the celebration of sacraments informed by deliberations on the revised rites of Vatican II following decades of praxis around the world.

LITURGICAL ENACTMENT OF CHRISTIAN SACRAMENTS

Christian beliefs about sacraments are conceived, embodied, and voiced in liturgy, the celebration of which forms Christian identity and conforms celebrants to Christ. While theological explanations provide a rationale for sacraments and rubrics, and *praenotandae*[52] assure their validity, sacraments exist only in ritual enactment.

The seven ecclesial sacraments are grouped into three categories: Sacraments of Initiation (Baptism, Confirmation, Eucharist), Sacraments of Healing (Penance and Anointing of the Sick), and Sacraments at the Service of the Communion (Matrimony and Holy Orders).

Sacraments of Initiation
Baptism
Celebrating Baptism, the pre-requisite for all other sacraments,[53] ritualizes a person's preexisting relationship with God (who knows them from before they were born)[54] and marks their official entry into the church as a member of the body of Christ.[55] Washed clean of all sin[56] through the salvific waters symbolizing their entry into Christ's death and resurrection,[57] which brings with it the promise of eternal life,[58] the baptized person is born again as a child of God,[59] receiving the "Spirit of filial adoption,"[60] and is "configured to Christ by an indelible character."[61]

---

[52] See John Huels, "Assessing the Weight of Documents on the Liturgy," *Worship* 70 (2000): 118, fn. 2.
[53] Canon, 842§1.
[54] Jer 1:4; Gal 1:15.
[55] 1 Cor 12:13.
[56] Original sin and all personal sin. See Catholic Church, "Christian Initiation: General Introduction," *Rite of Christian Initiation of Adults* (Strathfield: St Pauls, 1986/2003), 5 (hereafter CIGI).
[57] Rom 6:3–11.
[58] Jn 3:5; Mk 16:16.
[59] 1 Jn 3:1.
[60] CIGI, 1.
[61] Canon 849.

In Baptism a person becomes a temple of the Holy Spirit[62] incorporated into communion with the Holy Trinity, whose name is invoked in the baptismal formula[63] accompanying the immersion or pouring of the blessed water (sacramental matter). The baptized person becomes part of a royal priesthood and a holy nation.[64] A validly celebrated Baptism (i.e., where correct matter and form are used) cannot be repeated.

Anyone who desires Baptism is eligible to receive the sacrament. Following ancient traditions,[65] adults seeking initiation into the Catholic Church must be instructed in the faith and duties of a Christian and ideally will receive formation in the catechumenate through the Rite of Christian Initiation of Adults (RCIA, meanwhile OCIA or Order of Christian Initiation of Adults). In the RCIA catechumens learn about the faith, reflect on scriptures, and receive mentoring from a sponsor[66] through a staged faith formation process. The RCIA incorporates liturgical rites (rite of acceptance into the order of catechumens, rite of election/enrollment of names, preparation rites on Holy Saturday), which leads to the celebration of the sacraments of Baptism, Confirmation, and Eucharist in one ceremony usually at the Easter Vigil and ideally conducted by the bishop.[67] A post-baptismal period of catechesis and mystagogy follows for the neophytes as they become accustomed to their new Christian life. A simplified form of the RCIA is offered for children of catechetical age.[68]

Christians in the East and West have always baptized infants.[69] Anabaptists do not recognize the validity of infant baptism, teaching that only those who freely confess their faith in Christ and request baptism are to be baptized. Among Christian denominations that baptize infants, parents stand as faith proxies for their infant,

---

[62] 1 Cor 3:16.
[63] Mt 28:19.
[64] 1 Pt 2:9.
[65] See: Maxwell E. Johnson, *The Rites of Christian Initiation: Their Evolution and Interpretation*, rev. ed. (Collegeville, MN: Liturgical Press, 2007).
[66] See Canons, 872–74.
[67] Other ordinary ministers of Baptism are priests and deacons. In imminent danger of death, "any member of the faithful (indeed any person who has the requisite intention, can and sometimes must administer baptism" using the correct method (matter and form). See *Order of Baptising Children*, 2nd typical ed. (Totowa, NJ: Catholic Book Publishing Company, 2020), 16–17 (hereafter *OBC*). See RCIA 384–99 for the ritual process for unconfirmed adults and Christians baptized in another denomination and seeking to join the Roman Catholic Church. Eastern Christians seeking to become Roman Catholic simply make a profession of Catholic faith (RCIA, 388).
[68] RCIA, 242–306.
[69] Congregation for Divine Worship, *Pastoralis Actio* "Instruction on Infant Baptism," (October 20, 1980), 4.

requesting baptism and making a promise to raise their child in the faith with the support of godparents and the faith community. In the Roman Catholic tradition infants do not receive the other initiatory sacraments until after the age of reason. In Eastern Catholic and Orthodox traditions, infants receive all three initiatory sacraments in one ceremony.

Ideally infants will be baptized within the first few weeks after birth.[70] Baptism takes place in a church or oratory either within the context of a Ritual Mass (the church's preference) or as a stand-alone rite, normally on a Sunday. The infant, their parents, and their godparents are welcomed, and the parents are asked what name they have given their child, and what they ask of the church (they answer "Baptism," or another term). The celebrant seeks assurance that they understand the responsibility they are undertaking and ascertains that the godparents are ready to help the parents in their duty.

The celebrant welcomes the infant to the church with great joy and signs them with the Sign of the Cross, inviting parents and godparents to do the same. A biblical reading and responsorial psalm, homily, prayer of the faithful, and litany of the saints follow. After a prayer of exorcism, the infant is anointed with the oil of catechumens for strength. Outside of Easter time, the celebrant blesses the "natural and clean water"[71] to be used for Baptism and invites the parents and godparents to renounce sin and profess their faith. The parents reaffirm their will that their infant should receive Baptism. The immersion or pouring of water occurs three times as the baptismal formula is prayed.

Explanatory rites follow: anointing with Chrism (indicating the indelible mark of baptism), clothing with a white garment,[72] handing on of a lighted candle (representing the eternal light of Christ), and the *ephphatha* rite (the celebrant touches the ears and mouth, praying that the infant may receive God's word and profess the faith). The newly baptized infant is processed to the altar for praying of the Lord's Prayer, after which the celebrant blesses the parents and blesses and dismisses the assembly.[73]

As members of the faithful, the baptized have various rights (detailed in Canon Law) and responsibilities, such as worshiping God and working to build up the body of Christ in the world. The church

---

[70] Canon, 867.
[71] CIGI, 18.
[72] Gal 3:27.
[73] For further details see the *OBC* introduction, 1–31.

entrusts infants who die without Baptism to the mercy of God,[74] and if their parents had intended to have them baptized, they are granted a Catholic funeral.[75]

Confirmation

The second sacrament of Christian initiation is Confirmation.[76] This sacrament seals[77] Baptism and more fully conforms the faithful to Christ, strengthening them to bear Christian witness and build up the church in faith and charity.[78] The seal of Confirmation conveys an indelible character on the soul such that it cannot be repeated. Jesus promised to send the Holy Spirit of truth from the Father[79] to help the disciples after he ascended and promised that this Spirit would remain with them forever.[80] At Pentecost the Spirit descended and filled the disciples with missionary zeal.[81] Through laying hands on the newly baptized, the apostles and leaders of the church indicated an additional gifting of the Holy Spirit beyond that received in Baptism.[82]

Over the centuries, the sacrament of Confirmation has accrued to itself various interpretations and emphases, depending on the context of its celebration and the circumstances of the candidate. Within the RCIA an adult candidate (accompanied by a sponsor) is initiated (ideally by a bishop, but often by a priest) during the Easter Vigil in one continuous Baptism–Confirmation–Eucharist rite. In this celebration, Confirmation is clearly a sealing of Baptism and reflects the descent of the Holy Spirit on Jesus immediately following his Baptism by John.[83]

Children who have reached the age of reason (seven years)[84] can be confirmed, though bishops' conferences can set a more mature age if this seems suitable to allow for a longer period of faith formation, provided reception of the Eucharist is not unduly delayed. The baptized who possess reason are encouraged to celebrate the sacrament of

---

[74] "The Hope of Salvation for Infants Who Die Without Being Baptised," International Theological Commission (April 19, 2007).
[75] Catholic Church, *Order of Christian Funerals* (Sydney: E. J. Dwyer, 1989), 237.
[76] *CCC*, 1212. Eastern Christians call this sacrament Chrismation.
[77] See Ibid., 1285.
[78] Catholic Church, *Order of Confirmation* (Strathfield: St Pauls, 2015), 2 (hereafter *OC*).
[79] Jn 15:26.
[80] Jn 14:16.
[81] Acts 2:1–13.
[82] Acts 8:15–17.
[83] Mk 1:9–11.
[84] Canon, 11.

Penance prior to being confirmed. Often children confirmed at around seven years[85] also receive the Eucharist concurrently or shortly thereafter. Unbaptized children of catechetical age can receive Baptism, Confirmation, and the Eucharist in the same ritual celebration. Confirmation can also be conferred on a baptized person who is in danger of death.[86] Confirmation is celebrated to mark entry into full communion with the Catholic Church for those baptized in another Christian denomination.

The Confirmation liturgy is ideally celebrated for a group of candidates, their families, friends, and the local faith community and is to have a festive and solemn character. Candidates should be supported by a sponsor (ideally their baptismal godparent) for the celebration and beyond.

Confirmation takes place within Mass or without Mass, and its proper minister is the bishop (though he can delegate this responsibility to another priest).[87] After the Liturgy of the Word, the bishop preaches a homily in which the mystery of Confirmation is addressed. A renewal of baptismal promises using the interrogatory form of the Creed precedes the Confirmation rite. The bishop lays hands (from a distance) while praying for the Holy Spirit to free the recipients from sin and send the seven spiritual gifts.[88] Then the bishop anoints the individual candidates with Chrism (the sacramental matter) and traces the Sign of the Cross on the forehead while praying (the sacramental form): "N., be sealed with the Gift of the Holy Spirit." The bishop exchanges a sign of peace with the confirmed. The Universal Prayer follows and Mass proceeds as usual, or, if celebrated outside Mass, the Lord's Prayer, the Blessing, and the Prayer over the People conclude the rite.

Sacraments of Healing
Penance

The sacrament of Penance serves to heal those whose relationship with God and the church has been weakened, damaged, or even severed on account of sin. When the faithful freely choose to turn away from God[89] and engage in acts contrary to what is morally right, sin is committed,

---

[85] The age of confirmation varies considerably in local praxis around the world from seven years through the teenage years.
[86] Canon, 891.
[87] *OC*, 7–8.
[88] Isa 11:2.
[89] Catholic Church, "Rite of Penance," *The Rites of the Catholic Church, Vol. 1* (Collegeville, MN: Liturgical Press, 1990), 5 (hereafter *RP*).

and harm to others can result. Every sin has a personal and communal consequence. What is done to or by one member of Christ's body is done to all and affects all.[90] The purpose of Penance is to restore the repentant sinner's relationship with God and full communion with the church so that they may make right any harm done, return to spiritual health, and participate fully in the church's life and activities.

Christ the healer is encountered in this sacrament as the one who forgives the penitent and restores them to health[91] and right relationship. The church through the priestly minister[92] welcomes the forgiven person back into communion.[93] Grace as the opposite of sin sanctifies the sinner as they move through the four stages of this sacrament: (1) the sinner understands their actions as sinful and in need of God's forgiveness, and feels contrition as they accept responsibility for their sin; (2) the sinner confesses their sins in number and kind to a priest;[94] (3) the sinner asks for and accepts God's forgiveness (absolution) with the intention of not sinning again; and (4) the forgiven person engages in expiation for sins committed (penance) and makes any reparations necessary to remedy the harm caused. The sacrament is complete when penance has been carried out.

Penance can be celebrated using one of three ritual options. In the first rite the priest welcomes the penitent, inviting them to trust in God, and reads a short text from scripture proclaiming God's mercy. The penitent prays a general formula of confession before confessing their sins. Sometimes the priest helps the penitent to "make an integral confession" and provides suitable counsel.[95] The priest invites the penitent to express their sorrow in an Act of Contrition. The priest extends his hands over the penitent's head and prays the Prayer of Absolution through which God forgives the penitent.[96] The sacrament concludes with the priest offering a word of praise and thanks to God from among several options. The matter of Penance is the penitent's contrition, confession, and penance, and the form is the Prayer of Absolution.

The Second Rite of Penance occurs within a communal celebration consisting of Introductory Rites, Liturgy of the Word, communal Examination of Conscience, General Confession of Sins (*Confiteor* or

---

[90] 1 Cor 12.
[91] Mt 9:2–8.
[92] John 20:23.
[93] Lk 24:47.
[94] See Canons, 967–75, and Ibid., 991.
[95] *RP*, 44.
[96] Rom 5:10.

similar), Litany, the Lord's Prayer, Individual Confession and Absolution, Proclamation of Praise for God's Mercy, Concluding Rite. The Third Rite of Penance is for use in situations of grave necessity only[97] and repeats all the elements of the Second Rite but adds a general absolution (omitting individual confession and absolution). For those conscious of serious sins, the general absolution is contingent upon their intent to celebrate individual reconciliation at the soonest possible opportunity.[98]

Those members of the faithful who have reached the age of reason, understand the difference between right and wrong, and can diagnose their own actions as a mistake, an accident, or an intentional act are eligible to participate in Penance and are bound to confess any grave sins at least once a year.[99] Children over seven years are required to celebrate Penance prior to receiving their first Eucharist.[100] Adults initiated through the RCIA do not celebrate Penance until they have a need after completing initiation. Penance can be the first of a sacramental continuum celebrated for those facing death: Penance – Apostolic Pardon – Anointing of the Sick – Viaticum.[101]

Penance is celebrated frequently for devotional reasons, and the faithful are encouraged to confess venial sins regularly. Those who have committed grave sins are bound to confess them in number and kind after an examination of conscience.[102] Penance is usually celebrated in a church or oratory and can be celebrated on any day of the liturgical year, though the seasons of Lent and Advent are apt times for its celebration. Penance can be repeated as often as needed.

Anointing of the Sick

Jesus showed concern for the bodily and spiritually sick[103] and personally experienced illness[104] and suffering.[105] The Letter of James 5:14–16 calls for the sick to be anointed with oil and prayed over with the prayer

---

[97] Canon, 961.
[98] Ibid., 962.
[99] Ibid., 989.
[100] Pius X, *Quam Singulari*, "Decree on First Communion" (August 8, 1910).
[101] See Catholic Church, *Pastoral Care of the Sick: Rites of Anointing and Viaticum* (New York: Catholic Book Publishing Company, 1983), *editio typica* 1972, 239–56.
[102] Canon, 988§1.
[103] For example, Lk 5:12–26, Mk 5:1–20, Lk 19:9.
[104] Mt 25:36.
[105] Jn 19:1–3, 18–28.

of faith, while Mark 6:12–13 recounts the disciples anointing the sick and curing them.

Pastoral Care of the Sick: Rites of Anointing and Viaticum (*PCS*) instructs that the sacrament of Anointing is for "those whose health is seriously impaired by sickness or old age,"[106] those with some types of mental illness,[107] those facing surgery for serious illness,[108] sick children of the age of reason (seven years, "if they have sufficient use of reason to be strengthened by the sacrament"),[109] and unconscious Christian believers who would have requested the sacrament if able.[110] It is not to be administered to those who have died,[111] as sacraments are for the living,[112] nor to "anyone who remains obdurately in open and serious sin."[113] When unable to access a Catholic priest, Catholics can be anointed by a minister of an Eastern Church,[114] and Catholic priests may anoint Eastern Christians who freely request the sacrament.[115] Anointing is to be celebrated as soon as the right time comes and can be repeated as needed.[116]

As a liturgy and thus a public ritual,[117] even *in extremis*, the ecclesia is represented by the presiding priest, who is the proper minister of this sacrament,[118] though ideally it will be celebrated with family of the sick person or a small group of the faithful, as a prayer of the church and an encounter with Christ.[119] The oil of healing (olive or plant oil consecrated by the bishop during the Chrism Mass in Holy Week) is the sacramental matter, and the sacramental form is the prayer spoken by the priest while anointing. The scriptural gesture of laying on of hands is employed as a sign of blessing.[120] The rite is flexible, according to the condition of the sick person, but, celebrated outside of Mass, it consists

---

[106] *SC*, 73, *PCS*, 8.
[107] *PCS*, 53.
[108] Ibid., 10.
[109] Ibid., 12. See also Canon 1005.
[110] Ibid., 14.
[111] *PCS*, 15; the sacrament for the dying is Viaticum (Ibid., 26–7).
[112] Ibid., 166.
[113] Ibid., 15. The case of voluntary euthanasia would constitute such a situation.
[114] Pontifical Council for Promoting Christian Unity, *Directory for the Application of Principles and Norms on Ecumenism* (January 1, 1998) (hereafter *DAE*), 123.
[115] Ibid., 125.
[116] *PCS*, 11, and Ibid., 102, respectively.
[117] *SC*, 26.
[118] *PCS*, 16.
[119] Ibid., 99.
[120] Lk 4:40; *PCS*, 106.

of: Greeting, Sprinkling with Holy Water, Instruction, Penitential Rite, Reading, Response (silence or homily), Litany, Laying on of Hands, Prayer over the Oil, Anointing, Prayer after Anointing, The Lord's Prayer, Blessing.

The sacrament is enacted as follows: "The community, asking God's help for the sick, makes its prayer of faith in response to God's word and in a spirit of trust."[121] The priest lays hands on the head of the sick person in silence. The priest prays in thanksgiving over the blessed oil (or blesses it if it is unblessed). The priest generously anoints the sick person on the forehead with the blessed oil saying, "Through this holy anointing may the Lord in his love and mercy help you with the grace of the Holy Spirit."[122] Then anointing their hands, he says, "May the Lord who frees you from sin save you and raise you up." Silent anointing of additional parts of the body can follow if appropriate. The oil is not wiped off after the anointing. One of the selection of prayers after anointing is prayed. *PCS* provides for a continuous rite where the sacrament of Penance precedes Anointing and is followed by Holy Communion, if appropriate.

There are various possible outcomes of the sacrament of Anointing of the Sick: (1) a gift of grace from the Holy Spirit bringing strength, peace, and courage to overcome the difficulties of being ill, old, or in danger of death; (2) union with Christ's passion – the sick person is configured to Christ in suffering; (3) forgiveness of sins (if unable to celebrate Penance); (4) restoration of health (when it is conducive to the salvation of the soul); (5) an ecclesial grace – the sick contribute to the good of the ecclesia as symbols of God's presence and care; and (6) preparation for death.

Sacraments at the Service of Communion

Matrimony

The Catholic sacrament of Matrimony is an exclusive, indissoluble, intimate partnership of life and love, for which Christians are "fortified and consecrated" by Christ.[123] Grounded on "the conjugal covenant of irrevocable personal consent,"[124] in which the spouses "are no longer

---

[121] James 5:14–15; *PCS*, 105.
[122] *PCS*, 107.
[123] *CCC*, 2364; Ibid., 1535.
[124] Catholic Church, *Order of Celebrating Matrimony* (Strathfield: St Pauls, 2015), 2 (hereafter *OCM*).

two, but one flesh,"[125] it is envisioned as a singular, free, faithful, and fruitful relationship of equals.[126] Ordered both to the wellbeing of the spouses and the procreation and upbringing of children, marriage is directed toward serving others and in so doing contributes to the personal salvation of the individual and to building up the church.[127] Based on the biblical view of humankind created biologically male and female in the image and likeness of God, the sacrament of Matrimony is open to baptized and confirmed,[128] single, legally capable, sane,[129] uncoerced, potent,[130] male–female couples of an age customarily accepted in the region.[131] Canon law details a range of circumstances that prohibit some from participation in this sacrament.[132] A valid marriage between the baptized "is always a sacrament"[133] because it "presupposes and demands faith."[134] Sacramental marriage is repeatable if one of the spouses dies.

The *Order of Celebrating Matrimony* teaches that God's call to marriage extends beyond the sacramental rite.[135] As a way of life to be lived rightly and witnessed publicly, marriage requires an ongoing daily commitment that is strengthened by God's presence so that "where there is one flesh, there is also one spirit."[136] The proper ministers of Matrimony are the couple themselves, as they are the only ones who can declare their personal consent to enter the marriage covenant. A priest, deacon, or delegated assisting layperson presides at the rite and witnesses the couple's exchange of consent on behalf of the church and (in many places) on behalf of the state.[137]

Both the matter and form of Matrimony are found in the free exchange of consent, which must be offered in words or equivalent signs with internal consent of the mind presumed.[138] The exchange of consent conveys the couple's willingness to consummate their relationship

---

[125] Mt 19:6.
[126] *OCM*, 2–3. See also: Pope Paul VI, *Humanae vitae*, "On the Regulation of Birth," papal encyclical (July 25, 1968), 9.
[127] *CCC*, 1534.
[128] Gen 1:27; *OCM*, 18.
[129] Canon, 1095.
[130] Ibid., 1084 §1.
[131] Ibid., 1072; see also Ibid., 1083.
[132] See Canons, 1073–94.
[133] *OCM*, 7.
[134] Ibid., 16, *SC*, 59.
[135] *OCM*, 11.
[136] Tertullian, *Ad uxorem*, II, VII: CCL 1, 393.
[137] See *OCM*, 118–151.
[138] Canon, 1104§2; Ibid., 1101§1.

physically, which makes their bodies a medium of sacramental completion. Upon exchange of consent, God joins the spouses in an indissoluble bond.[139] Christ "abundantly blesses" the love that binds them,[140] and in the marriage covenant the married couple symbolizes the bond between Christ and the Church and is called to "bear true witness to Christ before all."[141]

The sacrament of Matrimony should normally occur within a Ritual Mass that reflects a marital focus, and the rite provides for the inclusion of appropriate local cultural customs. The rite begins when the bride and bridegroom individually answer formal questions ascertaining that they are entering into marriage without coercion, freely and wholeheartedly; are prepared to love and honor each other for as long as they both shall live; and are prepared to accept children lovingly from God and bring them up according to the law of Christ and the church.[142] They join their right hands and publicly declare their consent, either as a promissory statement or by replying affirmatively to ministerial questions.[143] The first form of the declaration includes a promise "to be faithful" to the spouse in good times and bad, in sickness and health, and to love and honor them all of life's days. Being faithful refers not only to sexual fidelity but also to the baptismal grounding of sacramental marriage. The blessing and mutual giving of rings provide tangible symbols of the love, fidelity, and inner bond of the spouses. The Nuptial Blessing consecrates the married couple with an explicit epiclesis.[144] The Catholic rite of Matrimony emphasizes marriage as a partnership of complementary equals, from the greeting of the entire bridal party at the door of the church ahead of their procession down the aisle together[145] to the mutual giving and receiving of rings and the inclusion of a Nuptial Blessing option that focuses equally on the husband and wife.[146]

Holy Orders

The laying on of hands has always been the ritual gesture Christians use to indicate choice, setting apart, and commissioning of a communal

---

[139] Mk 10:9.
[140] OCM, 59.
[141] Ibid., 74.
[142] OCM, 60.
[143] In scripture the right hand symbolizes strength (Ex 15:6), comforting (Isa 41:13), authority, and choosing (Gen 48:14; Mt 25:32–34).
[144] OCM, 74 and 242.
[145] This is the first form of the entrance presented. Other forms are also permitted.
[146] Ibid., 9, 45, 242.

leader.[147] The earliest Church Orders describe the bishop (the proper minister of Holy Orders) imposing hands and praying to indicate God's empowerment of a leader for the church, who is conformed to Christ.[148] The laying on of hands, which communicates the gift of the Holy Spirit, constitutes the matter of Holy Orders, and the form of the sacrament is the prayer of ordination for each order (deacon, priest, bishop) recited by the presiding bishop. The gift of the Holy Spirit conveyed in Holy Orders marks the candidate with an indelible character on the soul, which constitutes them permanently as a sacred minister of the church with different duties according to each degree of the sacrament.

In the bishop is found the fullness of the sacrament of Holy Orders, and bishops are ordained chief teachers, leaders of worship, and governing shepherds of the church. In the exercise of their power, priests are dependent upon their bishop and are linked to him "in sacerdotal dignity," consecrated to preach the gospel, shepherd the faithful, and celebrate divine worship in the image of Christ.[149] Deacons are ordained to "serve the People of God in the *diakonia* of liturgy, word, and charity, in communion with the Bishop and his Presbyterate."[150] Those to be ordained for priesthood serve a period as transitional deacons, while others are admitted to the permanent diaconate.

Holy Orders is to be celebrated in the cathedral, within a Ritual Mass on a Sunday or holyday of obligation to enable the greatest number of attendees. The Ritual Mass for the Ordination of a Bishop takes place as usual up to the reading of the Gospel. The rite of ordination commences with the singing of *Veni Creator Spiritus* (or equivalent), after which the bishop-elect is led by assisting priests to the ordaining bishop. The Apostolic letter mandating the candidate for the episcopacy is read, and the assembly offers an acclamation. The ordaining bishop gives a homily. The bishop-elect is called forward to make a variety of promises related to his duties.[151] The Litany of the Saints is sung while the bishop-elect lies prostrate.

For the ordination, the bishop-elect kneels before the ordaining bishop, who lays hands on his head in silence, and all the attending bishops do likewise. Two deacons hold the Book of the Gospels over the

---

[147] Acts 6:6, 13:3; 1 Tim 4:14; 2 Tim 1:6.
[148] See *Apostolic Tradition*, pts. 1, 2 (bishop), 8 (presbyter), 9 (deacon).
[149] LG, 28.
[150] Ibid., 29.
[151] Catholic Church, "Ordination of a Bishop," *Ordination of a Bishop, of Priests, and of Deacons* (Washington DC: ICEL, 2018), 40 (hereafter *OBPD*).

bishop-elect's head (emphasizing the importance of his preaching), while the ordaining bishop recites the prayer of ordination (required to validate the act). All attending bishops join him in praying,

> Now pour forth upon this chosen one the power that is from you, the governing Spirit, whom you gave to your beloved Son Jesus Christ and whom he gave to the holy Apostles, who established the Church in each place as your sanctuary, to the glory and unfailing praise of your name.[152]

The ordaining bishop concludes the prayer. Then the new bishop is anointed on the head with Chrism as a sign of his "distinctive share in the Priesthood of Christ"[153] and presented with the Book of the Gospels, a ring symbolizing his fidelity to the church, the pallium as a sign of his authority as a metropolitan and his communion with the pope; the miter signifying his resolve to pursue holiness; and the crozier (pastoral staff) indicating his shepherding and governing role. If the ordination has been celebrated in the new bishop's own cathedral, he is invited by the ordaining bishop to take his seat in the cathedra. Rising and putting aside his crozier, the new bishop receives the fraternal kiss from the ordaining bishop and other attending bishops as Psalm 95(96) is sung. The mass proceeds as usual until the concluding rites, when the new bishop (in miter and with crozier) is led through the church by two bishops and blesses everyone during the singing of the *Te Deum* (or other suitable song), after which he briefly addresses the assembly. The Mass concludes with a blessing and dismissal. The rites for ordaining a priest and deacon follow a similar but simpler structure, with the key sacramental elements of the laying on of hands and the Prayer of Ordination as the focal point.

The immediate outcome of the sacrament is that the deacon/priest/bishop can serve as a leader within the church to fulfil the duties and responsibilities afforded him according to his degree of Holy Orders. Candidates for Roman Catholic priesthood must be baptized and confirmed, be male, be at least 25 years old, be free from any irregularity or impediment,[154] and must have fulfilled the requirements outlined in canon law.[155] Transitional deacons and priests are required to make a public commitment to celibacy.

---

[152] Ibid., 25.
[153] Ibid., 26.
[154] See Canons, 1040–49.
[155] See Ibid., 1026–39.

CONCLUSION

As part of a living faith tradition open to the fluid circumstances of history and culture, the liturgical celebration of sacraments has clearly changed over time. The introduction of instituted catechists, lectors, and acolytes of both genders, investigations into the question of women deacons, and the development of new inculturated liturgies (such as an Amazonian Rite) indicate that the process of liturgical evolution continues.[156] Considerations of other areas of potential development in the praxis and theology of the church's liturgy and sacraments will ensure that the needs of Christ's faithful are well served into the future.

For Further Reading

Chauvet, Louis-Marie, *Symbol and Sacrament: Sacramental Reinterpretation of Christian Existence*, trans. Madeleine Beaumont (Collegeville, MN: Liturgical Press, 1994).

Cooke, Bernard, *Sacraments and Sacramentality* (Mystic: Twenty-Third, 1994/2004).

Depoortere, Kristiaan, "From Sacramentality to Sacraments and Vice Versa," in *Contemporary Sacramental Contours of a God Incarnate*, ed. Lieven Boeve and Lambert Leijssen (Leuven: Peeters, 2001).

Holcomb, Justin S., and David A. Johnson (eds.), *Christian Theologies of the Sacraments: A Comparative Introduction* (New York: New York University Press, 2017).

Kelleher, Margaret Mary, "Sacraments and the Ecclesial Mediation of Grace," *Louvain Studies* 23 (1998): 180–97.

Morrill, Bruce (ed.), *Sacramental Theology: Theory and Practice from Multiple Perspectives* (Basel: MDPI, 2019).

---

[156] See Pope Francis, *Antiquum ministerium* (May 10, 2021); *Christus domini* (January 10, 2021).

9 Liturgy of the Hours
LIBORIUS OLAF LUMMA

THE *ECCLESIA ORANS* IN THE COURSE OF THE DAY

In Christianity, the *Liturgy of the Hours*[1] represents the liturgical – thus best communally performed – form of daily prayer in certain stable ritual orders. In the Liturgy of the Hours, the Christian community articulates itself as *ecclesia orans* ("praying Church").[2] In this prayer, the Church follows the daily repeated natural rhythm of time and offers a spiritual interpretation to the continuously recurring sequence of light and darkness. The Liturgy of the Hours also takes up the rhythm of the year with its feast days and seasons. In some liturgical traditions or on certain occasions, the impact of the liturgical year on the Liturgy of the Hours is so strong that the expression of the time of day recedes into the background or disappears almost completely. The Liturgy of the Hours establishes and expresses connections between the Christian faith and the natural rhythm of creation. It assumes that the order of nature is divine revelation in itself, thus nature and (biblical) tradition give testimony to the same content, like two sides of the same coin. The rhythm of creation can therefore be a source of experiencing, understanding, and

---

[1] Also called *Office* or *Divine Office*, the term *Liturgy of the Hours* was adopted by the Roman Catholic Church after the Second Vatican Council (1962–1965) and is used in this chapter as a generic term for all variations of the Office. The abbreviation LotH often refers specifically to the current Roman Catholic order of the Liturgy of the Hours; thus it will not be used here. For further explanation regarding the adoption of the name Liturgy of the Hours in the Roman Catholic Church, see Stanislaus Campbell, *From Breviary to Liturgy of the Hours: The Structural Reform of the Roman Office, 1964–1971* (Collegeville, MN: Liturgical Press, 1995), 74–76, and Annibale Bugnini, *La riforma liturgica (1948–1975). Nuova edizione riveduta e arricchita di note e di supplementi per una lettura analitica*, Ephemerides Liturgicae Subsidia 30 (Rome: Edizioni Liturgiche, 1997): 503–4.

[2] Also translated as "the Church at prayer" or "the Church praying."

deepening faith. As the Christian community expresses itself in this liturgy, it is united over and over again in prayer. The *ecclesia orans* relates to the rhythm of creation, which in turn relates to divine revelation.[3]

In its first step, this chapter intends to specify the topic by showing how to recognize the Liturgy of the Hours from the outside and how to distinguish it from other forms of Christian worship. The next step will elaborate on the distinction between "monastic" and "cathedral" types of the Liturgy of the Hours: a well-established differentiation that is most helpful to understand liturgical elements and patterns. The succeeding short paragraph explains key contents of the Liturgy of the Hours to specify the intention of this liturgical tradition in all its richness. Afterward, three paragraphs are dedicated to practical observations, which are helpful for the understanding of historical development: first, certain differences between the theological aspiration of the Liturgy of the Hours and its reality in Christian lives; second, the relation between the Liturgy of the Hours and the real daily course of hours; and, eventually, the historically developed liturgical hours and their most common English names. On this basis, a brief overview of the Liturgy of the Hours in various Eastern and Western traditions will provide orientation over the state of the Liturgy of the Hours in current Christianity. A short theological summary concludes the chapter.

THE PHENOTYPE OF THE LITURGY OF THE HOURS

The Liturgy of the Hours can be identified by various elements; however, not all of them must be present at the same time.[4] Clearly given is always a high proportion of biblical texts, which are proclaimed (read or sung) by individual lectors, choirs, or the entire assembly. Among these, different categories of biblical texts can be found:

(1) In many traditions – especially those of the monastic type – psalms take up by far the largest portion of the Liturgy of the Hours.
(2) Canticles are the biblical texts similar to psalms that are taken from sources other than the Book of Psalms itself. Among the

---

[3] See the incarnational approach to the Liturgy of the Hours in George Guiver, *Company of Voices: Daily Prayer and the People of God* (New York: Pueblo, 1988), 7.

[4] For the following cf. the slightly different definition in: Achim Budde, *Gemeinsame Tagzeiten. Motivation – Organisation – Gestaltung*, Praktische Theologie heute 96 (Stuttgart: Kohlhammer, 2013), 215–16.

large number of Old Testament canticles, the *Benedicite* (Dan 3:52–90, either the full text or excerpts from it) is probably the most common in Eastern and Western Christianity as a chant of joy and salvation. The New Testament offers only a limited number of canticles, but some of them have gained a prominent position in many liturgical traditions. The *Nunc dimittis* (Lk 2:29–32) is widely used as a canticle leading into the night's rest, while the *Magnificat* (Lk 1:46–55) as a hymn of thanksgiving and praise to the God of Israel came to prominence in Western traditions as a canticle for sunset.

(3) In the Liturgy of the Hours biblical readings are usually either significantly shorter or significantly longer than readings in the Eucharist. In the short outline, the readings have a "food-for-thought" character. In the long outline, they serve as extensive contemplations of larger biblical narratives and/or argumentative contexts.

(4) Additionally, we find hymns – that is, Christian songs – based on biblical or contemporary philosophical, mythological, or poetic motifs, referring to the time of day, to a feast day, or to the respective liturgical season. Although hymns were controversial in earliest times and were even sometimes banned for their non-biblical origin, they prevailed and gained significant popularity. The *Phos hilaron* ("*Joyful Light*") – a Christological interpretation of sunset that can presumably be traced back to the second century – is still one of the most commonly sung hymns in the Byzantine tradition, while hymnody in the Latin world was largely influenced by Ambrose of Milan's strophic poetry in the fourth century. The non-strophic *Te Deum* ("We praise thee, o God") can be traced back to even earlier Latin prototypes. It is still in use today as a hymn for Sundays and feast days and is also known in vernacular versions. Even today new hymns are written, composed, and introduced into Christian liturgies.

(5) Prayers, at least in the form of collects but often as Universal Prayer, can also be found. Rituals specific to the time of day can be added, the most conspicuous being the lighting of lights (*lucernarium*) at sunset and the burning of incense, especially in the evening accompanied by Psalm 141 (140).[5]

---

[5] With reference to the famous *Itinerarium Egeriae* as evidence for the high value of the lucernarium and the use of incense in late fourth-century Jerusalem – a practice that remains alive mainly in Eastern traditions to this day – cf. Paul F. Bradshaw, *Daily*

The phenotype of the Liturgy of the Hours also includes regularity and positioning in the daily schedule as such. The most widespread hours for celebration are sunset and sunrise (or daybreak). In addition, there is nocturnal prayer, which, however, can differ considerably between a prominent Sunday/feast day and a less emphasized weekday practice. Depending on the denominational tradition, other hours are added to the daily cycle. Not all Christian traditions celebrate the same set of daily hours. All this results in an extensive sequence of recurring daily prayer times, in which the Christian Church constitutes itself as a praying community according to the natural rhythm of light and darkness, waking and sleeping, activity and rest.

In its artistic and ritual expression, the Liturgy of the Hours can take on such different styles that the structural similarities can be barely recognizable at first glance. This applies to gestures and postures, ways of reciting and singing, the distribution of liturgical offices and services among different people, and even more so to the almost dramatic difference between the celebration in public assembly and the texts being read in private.

Some other Christian prayer forms – some of which are extremely popular – are also characterized by frequent repetition, and some of them were created in deliberate imitation of the Liturgy of the Hours. However, since they lack the above-mentioned elements, they are usually not regarded as Liturgy of the Hours in the academic discourse or in official declarations by the respective churches. Among these prayer forms, the rosary, the *Angelus* (primarily Roman Catholic), and the Jesus Prayer (primarily Orthodox) are presumably the most popular. Simply put, when we find regular, more or less well-ordered Christian liturgical prayer spread throughout the day, comprising a combination of psalms, other biblical texts, hymns, prayers, and elements specific to the time of day – or at least a combination of most of these elements – we are dealing with the Liturgy of the Hours. If the Liturgy of the Hours is celebrated in a public assembly, it is usually performed in the same places of worship where the Eucharist takes place. Occasionally, however, there are liturgical spaces specifically designed for the Liturgy of the Hours that emerged mainly from the context of Western monastic or clerical communities.

Prayer in the Early Church: A Study of the Origin and Early Development of the Divine Office (Eugene, OR: Wipf & Stock, 1981), 72–92.

MONASTIC AND CATHEDRAL TYPES

The distinction between monastic and cathedral types of the Liturgy of the Hours is widely established.[6] It should not be misunderstood as a comprehensive description of the historical genesis of the Liturgy of the Hours but rather as a systematic approach to different liturgical elements in their larger framework. The term "monastic" refers to the individual motivation – paradigmatically found in Christian eremitism – to be inwardly shaped by the word of the Holy Scripture as much as possible, independent of personal inclinations and desires, and originally even independent of the time of day. This attitude is realized in techniques of prayer and meditation, by which biblical texts – especially psalms – are memorized, recited, murmured, and mentally comprehended and contemplated in their canonical biblical order.[7] The retreat from everyday urban life into eremitism is motivated by the intention to devote oneself entirely to the Word of God, with experienced hermits passing on their knowledge and techniques to the younger generation. The monastic type of the Liturgy of the Hours – be it within or outside a monastic community – can be identified wherever smaller or larger sequences of psalms are read in biblical order, generally without any direct reference to the time of day. This monastic idea has left its mark on all major Christian liturgical traditions.

The cathedral type is based on life in urban Christian communities. It tries to do justice to different situations, such as motivational situations, intellectual prerequisites, phases of life, and artistic competences. The cathedral type is characterized by a selection of hymns, prayers, readings, and rather fewer than more psalms clearly related to the time of day, to a feast day, or to a liturgical season, as well as ritual elements with a high community-building effect, such as the *lucernarium* in the evening or – in more recent times – rites of

---

[6] See the brief and concise definition in Robert Taft, *The Liturgy of the Hours in East and West: The Origins of the Divine Office and Its Meaning for Today*, 2nd ed. (Collegeville, MN: Liturgical Press, 1993), 211–13. Taft gives the elaborated theological explanations of the "spirits" of cathedral and monastic offices in the same source on pp. 347–65. Also see the substantial introduction by Paul Bradshaw, *Two Ways of Praying: Introducing Liturgical Spirituality* (London: SPCK, 1995), 13–26.

[7] See the patristic evidence in Gabriel Bunge, *Irdene Gefässe: Die Praxis des persönlichen Gebetes nach der Überlieferung der heiligen Väter*, 5th ed. (Beuron: Beuroner Kunstverlag, 2017), 38–45, 91–98.

baptismal commemoration.[8] Like monastic elements, cathedral elements are found in all major denominational traditions today. More recently, they have been reinforced by pastoral liturgical efforts that focus the communally celebrated liturgy more on internal, intuitively experienced consistency and artistic quality than on quantity of biblical texts.

Most traditions in Christian history can be classified as combinations of monastic and cathedral approaches. Sometimes the monastic and cathedral patterns are still clearly discernible. Other traditions merge monastic and cathedral elements into so closely interwoven mixed types that a clear assignment can be difficult in individual cases. This development is typical of many patterns in Western Christianity, among which the Rule of St. Benedict (presumably originating in the middle of the sixth century, based on preceding models in Italian monasteries and in the papal liturgy in Rome) became most influential and is the best documented testimony.

KEY CONTENTS OF THE LITURGY OF THE HOURS

No consistent single *leitmotif* can be attributed to the Liturgy of the Hours. Psalms speak of persecution, fear, despair, thanksgiving, joy, rejoicing, lamentation, mourning, and confidence – sometimes even in narrative breaks – and thus refer the Christian assembly to all these emotions and experiences in the Liturgy of the Hours. At the same time, stable aspects arise from the theological and spiritual interpretation of light and darkness based on biblical references and shine through in all different traditions of the Liturgy of the Hours. In the evening with its transition of daylight into darkness, death and mortality come before the eyes of the worshippers,[9] as well as the motif of forgiveness and healing[10] or the motif of divine protection amidst all the darkness of human existence.[11] The night hours are for conscious waking and waiting.[12] The time of sunrise is celebrated especially in the light of

---

[8] In its 2004 hymnal, the Old Catholic Church of Switzerland introduced a rite of "sanctification of the diurnal work," which is a ritualized commemoration of baptism at the end of the morning prayer. *Gebet- und Gesangbuch der Christkatholischen Kirche der Schweiz* (Basel: Christkatholischer Schriftenverlag, 2004), 51–52.

[9] Lk 2:29–30.

[10] Lk 4:40.

[11] Ps 4:9.

[12] Matt 26:1–13.

resurrection.[13] The daytime hours – the usual time for human work – stand in relation to the Passion of Jesus Christ[14] or to the motif of the pilgrim church.[15] Other motifs can complement, or sometimes even overlap or completely marginalize, the ones mentioned above, which is particularly noticeable of feast days.

However, the Liturgy of the Hours is always shaped by the Christian belief in the resurrection. For the Catholic Church, the Second Vatican Council speaks of the Liturgy of the Hours as the "hymn which is sung throughout all ages in the halls of heaven."[16] In the Liturgy of the Hours, the everyday human world is rhythmized, ritualized, and "sanctified."[17] It is placed in an existential relationship with the heavenly reality. In turn this should and can have a retroactive effect on the lives of those who step out of their everyday life into the liturgical ritual and thereby interpret their everyday life, deepen their faith, and walk a common path as a community of the faithful, as God's people.

ASPIRATION AND REALITY

In many Christian denominations, the Liturgy of the Hours is part of the normative liturgical canon; it is prescribed in more or less the same detail. Its reordering is the responsibility of the respective ecclesiastical authorities rather than at the arbitrary discretion of individuals or congregations. Particularly in those denominations whose self-understanding is based mostly on historical continuity with the first millennium, the Liturgy of the Hours is regarded as an important *locus theologicus*: an authentic witness to Christian faith and a core source of theological knowledge. With its many regional and denominational differences, the corpus of the Liturgy of the Hours is one of the richest and most diverse testimonies of Christian identity and spiritual and artistic tradition.

At the same time, the practical reality of the Liturgy of the Hours is significantly different. Performing regular – especially communal – prayer several times a day at fixed hours requires not only a high level of self-motivation but also corresponding routines in daily life. It is not compatible with every profession, every phase of life, or every

---

[13] Eph 5:14.
[14] Mk 15:25.33.34.
[15] Ps 121(120).
[16] *Sacrosanctum Concilium*, 83.
[17] Ibid., 88.

individual spiritual inclination. Thus the Liturgy of the Hours is and has always been shared by different people in different ways. Certain occupations and obligations make it impossible for most people to share the hours with their fellow Christians in a liturgical gathering.

Against this background, monasticism inevitably had to establish itself as the main carrier of the Liturgy of the Hours and became most influential in establishing its patterns and contents, although only a very small proportion of the Christian population is and has been monastic. The Liturgy of the Hours has always been the central element structuring everyday monastic life in all Christian denominations, insofar as they know monasticism at all. Depending on the authority monasticism enjoys in the different traditions, its influence on the development of the Liturgy of the Hours has varied and still varies.

Generally a very influential position of monasticism can be observed in Eastern Churches, despite all the differences in detail. Outside monastic communities, only a small portion of the Liturgy of the Hours is practiced – for example, on Sundays and feast days. But when it is celebrated, it follows the same structural elements and the same texts as in the monastic liturgy. In other words, monasticism has adopted a normative position and carries the Liturgy of the Hours in its full extent. Other Christians participate in congregational practice, but to a lesser extent.

In the first one and a half millennia, the Western world saw a different development: Monasticism was joined by all clerics as the central bearers of the Liturgy of the Hours. Since the High Medieval Church of the Latin West, all clerics have been obliged to integrate the Liturgy of the Hours into their daily life and work, even when they live individually outside of a monastery or other type of clerical fraternity. Thus the Liturgy of the Hours – which had been highly influenced by monastics up to the Carolingian era – became a "reader for clerics"[18] (later known as the breviary), a mere sequence of texts to be dutifully performed by individuals. Lay people participated only to a very limited extent, even when the Liturgy of the Hours remained normative and kept a certain presence in parishes on Sundays and feast days, for example. Essentially, the Liturgy of the Hours transformed from a

---

[18] See the brief historical overviews in Campbell, *From Breviary to Liturgy of the Hours*, 1–15; Josef Andreas Jungmann, *Der Gottesdienst der Kirche: Auf dem Hintergrund seiner Geschichte kurz erläutert* (Innsbruck: Tyrolia, 1962), 167–98; and Reinhard Meßner, *Einführung in die Liturgiewissenschaft*, 2nd ed. (Paderborn et al.: Ferdinand Schöningh, 2009), 275–79 (with additional references).

communal celebration to an individual clerical duty. Even in monasteries, the practice of reading the breviary in private became customary, at least to a certain extent.

Different directions were taken in Western Europe from the sixteenth century onward: The Protestant branch of Western Christianity was largely critical of the compulsory nature of the Liturgy of the Hours, as it was to clerical celibacy and monasticism in general. It developed its own cultural and liturgical identity in the service of the Word of God through, for example, denominational hymns, spiritual literature, new emphases in church interior design, and the development of denominational schools and other educational agencies. In the course of this dynamic, the Liturgy of the Hours adopted very different roles. In some Protestant churches, it was almost completely marginalized. It remained at best a set of prayer suggestions in hymnals. At the same time, Anglican congregations rediscovered and continued the Liturgy of the Hours, which remained or was developed as a culturally significant and artistically rich ritual tradition and, at least in certain parts, as a widespread and popular form of congregational worship, especially in the High Church tradition.

For a long time, the Roman Catholic Church continued the breviary in Latin as an obligational reader for clerics. In the late nineteenth century, the Liturgical Movement rediscovered the Liturgy of the Hours as a spiritual and liturgical resource for the entire church beyond clerical duties. Communal worship in monasteries was given new value as a model for the liturgical renewal of Roman Catholicism. The twentieth century witnessed two comprehensive Roman Catholic reforms, accompanied by several minor steps.[19] The reform of the Roman breviary published by Pope Pius X in 1911 primarily served to shorten the compulsory workload for clerics.[20] Thus, its starting point was still the individual cleric with his individual workload. The new Roman breviary rearranged the psalms to a considerably abridged one-week cycle and slightly shortened the other elements of the Liturgy of the Hours.

The Second Vatican Council reformed the entire Liturgy of the Hours in its Constitution on the Sacred Liturgy *Sacrosanctum*

---

[19] Campbell, *From Breviary to Liturgy of the Hours*, 16–77.
[20] For a comprehensive insight into the liturgical reforms by Pope Pius X, see Honoré Vinck, *Pie X et les réformes liturgiques de 1911–1914: Psautier, bréviaire, calendrier, rubriques*, Liturgiewissenschaftliche Quellen und Forschungen 102 (Münster: Aschendorff, 2014), 102.

Concilium (1964).²¹ As a result, the Liturgy was simplified²² and again shortened, the psalms were again completely rearranged to a four-week-cycle,²³ and vernacular languages were generally permitted for liturgical use.²⁴ Nevertheless the Liturgy of the Hours continued to spread hardly, if at all, as a communal service. In contrast to the Eastern Churches mentioned above, the Roman Catholic Church today has various normative Liturgies of the Hours, following the Council's differentiation between the needs of monastic and similar religious communities on the one hand and those of clerics and laypeople on the other.²⁵

RELATION TO THE TIMES OF DAY

Deviations between "liturgical time" and "real time" are widespread in most Christian traditions. A precise correlation between liturgically described time and real, astronomical time is common, for example, for the scheduling of the Jewish Sabbath service or the fasting rules in the Islamic month of Ramadan. In Christianity, such a minute-by-minute correlation is the exception, cultivated almost exclusively in hermitism and in monasteries with strictly reduced contact with the outside world. Moreover, not only are standardized times common (for example, daily evening prayer at six p.m., regardless of the position of the sun), but so also is the anticipation of hours at an earlier time or even an earlier day, as well as the merging of several hours to one combined service. This phenomenon is well known in the Western and in the Eastern world and might be motivated by the need to find time for extensive liturgies as well as for work – pastoral or practical – and for restful sleep. Thus, evening prayer can be performed on the preceding morning, and nocturnal prayer can be performed in the evening, so that there remains enough time for sleep. Breviary practice in the Western world produced even more extreme variants.²⁶ The Second Vatican Council instructed the Roman Catholic Church to pay attention that the liturgies be "genuinely related to the time of the day when they are prayed, as far as this may be possible."²⁷

---

[21] *Sacrosanctum Concilium*, 83–101.
[22] Ibid., 34.
[23] Ibid., 91.
[24] Ibid., 36.
[25] Ibid., 89e, 95, 101.
[26] For further evidence, see, Michael Kunzler, *Liturge sein: Entwurf einer ars celebrandi* (Paderborn: Bonifatius, 2007), 601–3.
[27] *Sacrosanctum Concilium*, 88.

THE HOURS AND THEIR COMMON ENGLISH NAMES

All Christian traditions know the prayer at the time of sunset or – in the broader sense – at the end of the working day and the transition from light into darkness. The name Vespers, from the Latin *vespera*, was adopted for this hour. "Vespers" originally meant the evenstar (planet Venus) but later also became an expression for the cardinal direction west and for the time around sunset or evening. There is early evidence that Vespers was concluded *before* sunset to leave time for dinner and the indispensible work that followed in monasteries.[28] The most prominent psalm for Vespers is Ps 141(140), especially in Eastern liturgies.[29] In the further selection of psalms and other elements, Vespers can have quite different thematic emphases, especially on feast days. There can be references to Jesus' burial in the evening but also to thanksgiving at the end of the (feast) day, to the healing of suffering associated with the evening hour,[30] and to general expressions of praise and adoration, as in the *Magnificat*,[31] for example. The latter is the daily climax of Vespers in almost all Western traditions.

Compline, from the Latin *complere* (to conclude), was established in early monasticism as a "prayer on the edge of the bed," that is, a communal prayer in the dormitory concluding the day and opening the nocturnal silence.[32] Its most important and most widespread psalm is Ps 91(90).[33] Compline focuses on the forgiveness of sins but even more on surrendering one's life into God's hands. Since the Carolingian era at the latest, the *Nunc dimittis* (Lk 2:29–32) has been established as the New Testament climax of Compline almost all over Western Christianity. In the Byzantine tradition, the *Nunc dimittis* has always been part of Vespers.

Almost all liturgical families today know these two evening prayers with much in common: Vespers and Compline, the latter being of specific monastic origin and of much simpler ritual arrangement. A combination of Vespers and Compline, *Evensong* is a festive communal liturgy, which both concludes the (working or festive) day and leads

---

[28] Cf. *Rule of the Master* 34:12–13 and *Rule of St Benedict* 41:8–9.
[29] Taft, *The Liturgy of the Hours in East and West*, 355f.
[30] Lk 4:38–41.
[31] Lk 1:46–55.
[32] Cf. *Rule of the Master* 30, and *Rule of St Benedict* 42.
[33] Cf. Liborius Olaf Lumma, *Die Komplet: Eine Auslegung des römisch-katholischen Nachtgebets* (Regensburg: Pustet, 2017), 87–91, 167–83.

into the peace of the night.³⁴ Such combinations of Vespers and Compline into one ritual were already known in the Middle Ages, especially outside monastic communities. The contemporary (mostly Anglican) Evensong follows from old traditions when Compline did not even exist and Vespers was the only evening prayer, concluding the day and at the same time leading into the night.

The nocturnal prayer – usually named Vigil(s) after *vigilia* ("guard duty," especially in the military) – shows a large variation in patterns. Vigil can be a festive liturgy in the night from Saturday to Sunday or in the nights preceding feast days, mirroring the Easter Vigil, arranged with great musical effort, extensive biblical and non-biblical readings, and in clear reference to central beliefs such as the mystery of resurrection. But Vigil also occurs as an extensive, but rather simply arranged, recitation of biblical and non-biblical texts. It can be scheduled at the beginning or the very end of the night, where it can merge with Lauds (see below) and adopt the name *Matins*. The Second Vatican Council abolished the Vigil (under the name Matins) almost completely – leaving it largely to monastics – and transformed it into the newly established Reading Office.³⁵ The contemporary Roman Catholic Reading Office continues the heritage of long biblical and non-biblical nocturnal readings, but it no longer has any reference to a specific time of day. It is arranged as a "contemplation book" for the Roman Catholic Church.

The morning prayer at daybreak or sunrise is called Matins (from the Latin *matutina*, morning star/morning hour) as well as, in the Western tradition, Lauds (from *laudes matutinae*, morning psalms of praise, whereby *laudes* became the generic term for Pss 148–50 in ancient Christian Latin³⁶). Besides Pss 148–50, Pss 51(50) and 63(62) are of great importance in the history of Lauds. Matins/Lauds regards the sunrise as a daily experience of life's victory over the darkness of death in Christ's resurrection. Lauds almost always has a paschal, clearly doxological, and grateful character, which is replaced by other motifs only on special occasions around repentance and grief. While Vespers is more important for contemporary communal practice than Lauds, the latter was regarded as much more important, at least in certain prominent sources such as Western monasticism.³⁷

---

[34] Sometimes the term "Evensong" is used for Vespers alone.
[35] *Sacrosanctum Concilium*, 89c.
[36] See the evidence for the occurrence of Pss 148–150 in early Western lauds in Campbell, *From Breviary to Liturgy of the Hours*, 4–9.
[37] In the *Rule of St Benedict*, Lauds contains more psalms than Vespers; the psalms for Lauds are provided in detail for every day of the week, while Vespers is simply filled

A Western peculiarity is the prayer at the first hour of the day (Prime) as distinct from Lauds, which existed in the Roman Catholic Church for many centuries but was abolished by the Second Vatican Council.[38] The prayers at the third, sixth, and ninth hours of the day (Terce, Sext, None) – that is, in the morning, at noon, and in the afternoon – are widespread in most Christian traditions. The summarizing name *Little Hours* makes it clear that these liturgies are shorter and less significant than those of Vespers, Vigils, and Lauds.[39] As mentioned above, the chronology of the Passion of Jesus is an important background,[40] but this is not recognizable in every individual case, certainly not on feast days. Another important motif of the Little Hours is the pilgrimage to Jerusalem, mirroring the course of the faithful in their everyday lives toward eternity and salvation.

MONASTIC AND CATHEDRAL HOURS TODAY

In the current state of the Liturgy of the Hours, both monastic and cathedral elements are clearly recognizable. An outstanding example of an almost purely monastic pattern is the Coptic Liturgy of the Hours, which is uniquely unaffected by feast days or liturgical seasons and is performed daily in an unchanged form.[41] Each hour follows the same pattern and contains twelve (Terce, Sext, None, Vespers, Compline) or twelve plus seven (Lauds) psalms. Over the course of the day, almost the entire book of Psalms is read according to the biblical order. In addition, there are almost always the same opening and closing elements, including Ps 51(50) for every hour. Only a few elements are specific to the time of day, especially the short Gospel readings such as Lk 9:10–17 for None, Lk 4:38–41 for Vespers, and Lk 2:25–32 for Compline. The Vigil follows

---

with the series of Pss 110(109)–47 over the seven days of the week. While Vespers is scheduled *before* sunset, Lauds must always be precisely celebrated at daybreak. *Rule of St Benedict* 8:4, 12, 13, 18:12–17, 41:8.

[38] *Sacrosanctum Concilium*, 89d.
[39] Sometimes Compline is also subsumed under the Little Hours.
[40] Alexander Zerfass, "Offizium und Innerlichkeit. Die Passionschronologie und die Horen des Stundengebets," in *Die Dynamik der Liturgie im Spiegel ihrer Bücher: La dynamique de la liturgie au miroir de ses livres. Festschrift für Martin Klöckener. Mélanges offerts à Martin Klöckener*, ed. Hélène Bricout, Benedikt Kranemann, and Davide Pesenti (Münster: Aschendorff, 2020), 525–43.
[41] A brief and concise analysis can be found in Taft, *The Liturgy of the Hours in East and West*, 249–59, and in Stefanos Alexopoulos and Maxwell E. Johnson, *Introduction to Eastern Christian Liturgies* (Collegeville, MN: Liturgical Press, 2022), 186–88.

an extended and different pattern. It is by far the most extensive hour of the daily cycle.

It seems obvious that such a large prayer workload cannot be incorporated into the everyday lives of most people. It is therefore only partially performed in Coptic parishes, mostly on Sundays and feast days. Only in a church like the Coptic, where monasticism is the central authority for faith and theology, can such a pure monastic liturgy be established and continue to exist today. At the other end of the contemporary spectrum are newly developed cathedral patterns in Western churches or in ecumenical communities. Renouncing the monastic claim to read the complete Psalter regardless of occasions or personal interests, these liturgies seek to focus on the thematic cohesion of the elements. The liturgy is meant to be immediately and intuitively accessible even to people who are not familiar with the Bible in its entirety or with complex liturgical traditions.[42]

Such focus may arise from the time of day, from a feast day, from a public event, or from an ecumenical gathering with a specific purpose. Some cathedral arrangements have become part of denominational hymnals and have thus gained normative character in, for example, Anglican, Lutheran, Old Catholic, or Roman Catholic churches. Rarely are such pure cathedral liturgies meant to be repeated on a daily basis. However, the clearly cathedral arrangements by the ecumenical brotherhood of Taizé in France (founded in 1940) have developed with worldwide appeal. Based on their experience as hosts of young people from all over the world, the brothers of Taizé have introduced a pattern of three daily gatherings with short, often repeated texts (psalms, biblical verses, prayers) in appealing musical arrangements, long periods of silence, and a combination of simple melodies for the entire assembly and sophisticated melodies for well-trained cantors.[43]

All other denominational traditions move between the two aforementioned extremes of the almost purely monastic Copts and certain almost purely cathedral contemporary Western liturgies. In the Byzantine hours, there are both clearly cathedral and clearly monastic elements.[44] Among the monastic ones, the reading of the twenty kathismata might be the best known: The Psalter is divided into twenty

---

[42] Budde, *Gemeinsame Tagzeiten*, 197–275.
[43] Richard Mailänder, *Die Gesänge aus Taizé*, in *Basiswissen Kirchenmusik 1. Theologie – Kirchengesang*, ed. Hans-Jürgen Kaiser and Barbara Lange (Stuttgart: Carus, 2009), 174–79.
[44] Taft, *The Liturgy of the Hours in East and West*, 273–91.

sections (each called a "kathisma") and then read in the course of a week at Vespers and Orthros (= Lauds), beginning with Vespers on Saturday evening (at the start of Sunday) and ending with Orthros on Saturday morning. Additional kathismata are read in the Little Hours, while Lent knows an increased number of psalms in general. This arrangement gives the first kathisma (Pss 1–8) a prominent place in Byzantine communities, since Vespers at the beginning of Sunday is widespread in congregational practice.[45] Cathedral elements are found in the famous ancient hymn *Phos hilaron*; the series of Pss 141(140), 142 (141), 130(129), and 117(116); and the *lucernarium* as textual and ritual elements of Vespers that can be traced back to the early church.[46] The Byzantine Rite is also characterized by a strong emphasis on hymnody. Non-biblical hymnodic songs give every day its own character, since each day is dedicated to certain saints or events of Salvation history. Based on the emphasis on hymnody and saints, the kathismata are often shortened in practical performance; on some solemn occasions the psalms are completely replaced by hymnody.

In Western Christianity, the Rule of St. Benedict stands paradigmatic for the typical mixture of monastic and cathedral elements in the Liturgy of the Hours. Benedict places high value on the psalms as such: Each psalm has to occur at least once a week.[47] At the same time, Benedict assigns certain psalms and Old Testament canticles to the same hour every day or at least once a week.[48] This pattern is combined with hymns and other elements that are specific to the time of day or the feast day. Benedict himself was not the inventor of this typical Western pattern,[49] and he was open to different opinions and new developments,[50] but his monastic rule stands as the best available source of the Latin liturgy with an extensive history of influence.

Despite the great Western propensity for reform of any kind, contemporary occidental liturgies still reveal the basic pattern that was formed in and around Rome in the first centuries and continued in the Rule of St. Benedict. Each hour is composed of the same elements, although the Little Hours lack some of them, and the exact sequence can vary. For the Roman Catholic liturgy, the Second Vatican Council

---

[45] Gregory W. Woolfenden, *Daily Liturgical Prayer: Origins and Theology* (Aldershot: Ashgate, 2004), 52–57.
[46] Ibid., 55–58, 280.
[47] *Rule of St Benedict* 18:22–25.
[48] Ibid., 9–13, 18.
[49] Campbell, *From Breviary to Liturgy of the Hours*, 1–5.
[50] *Rule of St Benedict* 18:22–25.

standardized the sequence for all hours. Opening and closing elements are short, and hymns and readings are either related to the time of day or to a feast day or season. Some hours have core elements that remain unchanged for every day, such as the aforementioned *Magnificat* in Vespers, the *Nunc dimittis* in Compline, or the *Benedictus* (Lk 1:68–79) in Lauds. The middle section of every hour is taken up by the psalmody with a mixture of cathedral and monastic principles. Some psalms – as well as biblical canticles – are selected specifically for the time of day or feast day; all others fill in the remaining gaps according to their biblical order. Thus the liturgy maintains the requirement that all psalms are read within a certain period of time – one week (in some monastic orders to this day), for example; four weeks (in the post-Vatican II Roman Catholic Liturgy of the Hours); or thirty days (in some Anglican traditions). A Western specificity is "antiphonal" singing (or recitation or reading), which goes back to the early Middle Ages: The biblical verses are recited alternately by two groups (e.g., choir and congregation).[51]

THE PRAYING CHURCH

In the Liturgy of the Hours, the church is the *ecclesia orans*: The praying church enters into a close, explicit, public relationship to God. According to Christian faith and philosophical conviction, creation owes itself and stands in eternal relationship to God. In the Liturgy of the Hours, the church partakes in this relationship by relating the natural rhythms of creation to faith. Thus the Liturgy of the Hours becomes a deeply and literally "ecological" expression of faith and of Christian identity. Creation and Bible, nature and liturgy, time and dogma are two sides of the same coin.

Sunset, night, and sunrise play a greater role than the daylight hours. The liturgical calendar can sometimes override the daily course, sometimes even displacing it altogether. In congregational practice, certain hours on certain days occupy a much more significant place than others. Nevertheless, in contrast to the celebration of the Eucharist

---

[51] Overviews about the most important denominational traditions that are not discussed in detail in this chapter can be found in Alexopoulos and Johnson, *Introduction to Eastern Liturgies*, 166–80 and 190–212; in Taft, *The Liturgy of the Hours in East and West*, 219–71 and 319–26; and in Woolfenden, *Daily Liturgical Prayer*, 121–200 and 255–76.

or to liturgies for individual occasions such as baptism, the Liturgy of the Hours is by its very nature the "everyday life" of the church, for which no other reason is needed than the natural rhythm of time.

In the Liturgy of the Hours, the praying church is above all a listening church: listening to the Word of God (with a particularly prominent place for the Book of Psalms) and listening to creation. Next, the church is also praising, supplicating, and creative: producing hymns, collects, and intercessory prayer. In all these acts, the church is fully with itself, constituting itself anew as a praying community in relation to God, to creation, and to Salvation history. In this way, the church becomes at the same time a missionary church: It is a sign before the world and for the world.

The history of the Liturgy of the Hours shows a certain discrepancy between aspiration and reality. Only very small inner-church circles fully support it; others participate to varying degrees. This is not a deficit a priori: It can also show that Christianity has room for different approaches even in its public practice. The liturgy is capable of adapting to different circumstances. As praiseworthy as it is when certain Christians live entirely with and from the Liturgy of the Hours, it is not to be condemned when others do not or cannot. The Liturgy of the Hours includes traditional forms that resist any reform and adaptation and therefore give the liturgy and the church a distinctive diachronic identity, as well as newly designed arrangements that try to integrate today's rhythms of life, musical styles, symbolism, and so on. Thus a great abundance of phenotypes of the Liturgy of the Hours emerges. At first glance some of them have very little in common, but they all go back to the same core idea that the Second Vatican Council attempted to define as "sanctification of time."[52]

For Further Reading

Bradshaw, Paul F., *Daily Prayer in the Early Church: A Study of the Origin and Early Development of the Divine Office* (Eugene, OR: Wipf & Stock, 2008).

Budde, Achim, *Gemeinsame Tagzeiten: Motivation – Organisation – Gestaltung*, Praktische Theologie heute 96 (Stuttgart: Kohlhammer, 2013).

Campbell, Stanislaus, *From Breviary to Liturgy of the Hours: The Structural Reform of the Roman Office, 1964–1971* (Collegeville, MN: Liturgical Press, 1995).

---

[52] *Sacrosanctum Concilium*, 88.

Klöckener, Martin, and Heinrich Rennings, *Lebendiges Stundengebet* (Freiburg: Herder, 1989).

Taft, Robert, *The Liturgy of the Hours in East and West: The Origins of the Divine Office and Its Meaning for Today*, 2nd ed. (Collegeville, MN: Liturgical Press, 1993).

Woolfenden, Gregory W., *Daily Liturgical Prayer: Origins and Theology* (Aldershot: Ashgate, 2004).

10 The Liturgical Year

MARYANN MADHAVATHU

INTRODUCTION

The liturgical year is not merely a calendar but a theological entity that transmits the saving mystery of Christ into the life of the Church. The overall structure of the liturgy of any liturgical Church is related to the concept of the liturgical year.[1] The liturgy serves the Church with prayers of rhythmic structure to help participants assimilate the salvation mystery into their daily life. The liturgical year mediates the Paschal Mystery, which is both origin and center of the liturgical year. The presence of God and the saving grace made accessible in liturgical services throughout the year allow participants to enter into the realm of unending life. Thus, the liturgical year moves beyond history and functions as an image of the eternal sign of God.

This chapter is a theological reflection of the present structure of the liturgical year through its evolution of the celebrations of Sunday, Easter, Christmas, the cult of saints, and Marian feasts. It begins by analyzing the concept of time in both a historical and a liturgical sense. Then it analyzes the growth of Christian liturgical celebrations in daily, weekly, and annual rhythms. It concludes with a presentation of the structure of the liturgical year in diverse liturgical traditions.

---

[1] Churches that have liturgical worship with a rigid structure, a certain order, specific words, and particular prayers for worship are known as liturgical churches. Non-liturgical churches have informal worship, which is not structured and may involve a range of Bible readings, prayers, and reflections.

LITURGICAL TIME: DAILY, WEEKLY, AND ANNUAL RHYTHMS

Time is a very complex and mysterious concept with multifaceted dimensions.[2] Time in its ordinary linear sense is understood in relation to the token-reflexive expressions "the past," "the present," and "the future." The concept of time is closely related to humankind's capacity for memory. One of the characteristics of liturgical time is that it encompasses the past and the present as well as the future. The liturgy recalls or remembers past events, relives them in the present, and renews the Church. Each time, it drives the participants toward the eschatological future.

Therefore, liturgical time could be considered an entity that goes beyond the boundaries of an ordinary sense of time. Explicitly, the liturgical time of the Church has a more cyclical nature than historical time. The liturgical year and calendar have special features when compared to ordinary year and time calculations made according to the civil or Gregorian calendar. The Church year is shaped by the celebration of the mysteries of salvation.[3] The Paschal Mystery of Christ is the point around which the entire liturgical year turns.[4] Every festival, every Sunday is rooted primarily in the Paschal Mystery celebrated in the Eucharist, which from the beginning and always proclaims the Lord's death until He returns.[5]

The liturgical year is an annual, year-long contemplation and celebration of the salvation of the human race in Jesus Christ.[6] The celebration of the salvation mysteries is carried out according to daily, weekly, and yearly cycles. The first is the natural cycle of the day; the second is

---

[2] J. J. C. Smart, "Time," in *The Encyclopedia of Philosophy*, ed. Paul Edwards (New York Macmillan, 1972), 126; J. M. Quinn, "Time," in *New Catholic Encyclopedia*, ed. Berard L. Marthaler et al. (Detroit, MI: Thomson/Gale, 2003), 77.

[3] The system of annual liturgical celebration received its outline only in the thirteenth century, and as a unity this celebration of an annual cycle was called "the year of the Church" or later "the Christian year." Prosper Guéranger used the expression "liturgical year" in his famous work *L'année liturgique* in the nineteenth century. Matias Augé, "The Liturgical Year in the Roman Rite," in *Handbook for Liturgical Studies: Liturgical Time and Space*, vol. 5, ed. Anscar J. Chupungco (Collegeville, MN: Liturgical Press, 2000), 135.

[4] Adolf Adam, *The Liturgical Year: Its History and Its Meaning after the Reform of the Liturgy* (New York: Pueblo, 1981), 23.

[5] Thomas J. Talley, *The Origins of the Liturgical Year* (New York: Pueblo, 1986), 237.

[6] For a study of the theology of the liturgical year, see Maryann Madhavathu, "A Comparative Study of the Theology of the Liturgical Year in the Roman and the Syro-Malabar Rite," *Questions Liturgiques* 96 (2015): 102–20.

the cycle of the week, with a special emphasis on the importance of Sunday; and the third is the yearly cycle.[7] Though the current structure of the liturgical year basically took shape in the sixth century, it was only in the sixteenth that the celebrations of the annual cycle came to be understood as a unity, namely "the year of the Church."[8]

The liturgical calendar originated to commemorate the Paschal Mystery of Christ in the course of one year. The weekly celebration of the salvific mystery on Sunday paved the way for the origin of the celebration of the various aspects of the Paschal Mystery over the span of one year. The primitive liturgical cycle was of extreme simplicity, reflecting the basic eschatological understanding of liturgy.[9] For the most ancient calendar of the Church, the historical commemoration was of little significance. The primitive liturgical calendar consisted of the observance of two annual feasts, namely Pascha and Pentecost, and of the Lord's Day on Sunday. In the first half of the third century, these feasts of the paschal mystery served as the main content of the liturgical calendar.[10] The Nativity–Epiphany cycle of feasts also had a place in the liturgical calendar of various Churches as early as the fourth century. For the first three centuries there was no particular Christian calendar. Pascha was the only feast, commemorated on Sundays and once per year on the anniversary of Christ's crucifixion.

SUNDAY: THE DAY OF THE LORD

According to *Sacrosanctum Concilium*, Sunday is the foundation and kernel of the Christian liturgical year.[11] Sunday is an innovation of Christians not inherited from the Hebrew cult. The Christian shaping of the week, giving primary place to Sunday as the Lord's Day, was probably already adopted in most regions of the Church by the end of

---

[7] Reinhard Meßner, *Einführung in die Liturgiewissenschaft* (Paderborn: Schöningh, 2001), 288; Anscar J. Chupungco, *What, Then, Is Liturgy?: Musings and Memoir* (Collegeville, MN: Liturgical Press, 2010), 83; Jesús Castellano Cervera, "Liturgy and Spirituality," in *Handbook for Liturgical Studies: Fundamental Liturgy*, vol. 2, ed. Anscar J. Chupungco (Collegeville, MN: Liturgical Press, 1997), 61.

[8] Matias Augé, "The Liturgical Year in the First Four Centuries," in *Handbook for Liturgical Studies: Liturgical Time and Space*, vol. V, ed. Ansgar J. Chupungco (Collegeville, MN: The Liturgical Press, 2000), 135.

[9] Gregory Dix, *The Shape of the Liturgy* (London: Dacre Press, 1945; A. & C. Black, reprint 1986), 335.

[10] Ibid., 335.

[11] See *Sacrosanctum Concilium*, 106.

the first century.[12] Early Christians paid special attention to Sunday mainly because it was the day of the resurrection of the Lord.[13] It was the day for specially commemorating the Lord and his Paschal Mystery, and they came together to celebrate the "breaking of bread." In the fourth century in the early Jerusalem cathedral office, both the passion and the resurrection accounts were read every Sunday during the morning office of the readings.[14] According to the Jewish calendar, the resurrection occurred on the first day of the week. It was the usual expression for Sunday in Syriac-speaking circles.[15] Greek-speaking communities preferred the term "Lord's Day" (kuriakè hèmera). The Latin West had the equivalent term *Dominica*. As early as Tertullian and Cyprian, *Dominica* is the ordinary name for Sunday.[16] While making the Christian day of worship a civil day of rest, Emperor Constantine referred to it as "Dies solis."[17]

There were other reasons for celebrating Sunday. Gentile Christians took up the Jewish understanding of the first day of the week as the day of creation. From ancient times onward Sunday has been considered the eighth day, being the image of the eschatological day.[18] It is the day on which God inaugurated a new world, and it serves as an image of the age to come. Later writers speak about more historical events commemorated on Sunday, including when God established light and rained manna in the wilderness, and when the Lord poured out the Holy Spirit upon his disciples.[19]

It seems likely that Sunday was from its beginnings a Christian observance independent of the Sabbath.[20] Many modern scholars believe that the first Christians chose Sunday as their Sabbath day in order to differentiate themselves from other Jews, and the Christian

---

[12] Thomas J. Talley, "Liturgical Calendar," in *New Dictionary of Sacramental Worship*, ed. Peter E. Fink (Collegeville, MN: Liturgical Press, 1990), 154.
[13] Cheslyn Jones et al. (eds.), *The Study of Liturgy* (London: SPCK, 1992), 457; Acts 20:1; 1 Cor 16:2.
[14] Paul F. Bradshaw, "The Use of the Bible in Liturgy: Some Historical Perspectives," *Studia Liturgica* 22 (1992): 36–43.
[15] Jones et al. (eds.), *The Study of Liturgy*, 456.
[16] Joseph A. Jungmann, *The Early Liturgy: To the Time of Gregory the Great*, trans. Francis A. Brunner (London: Darton, Longman & Todd, 1959), 21.
[17] Jones et al. (eds.), *The Study of Liturgy*, 456–57.
[18] P. Jounel, "The Year," in *The Church at Prayer*, vol. IV: *The Liturgy and Time*, trans. M. J. O'Connell, ed. A. G. Martimort et al. (Collegeville, MN: Liturgical Press, 1986), 18; Jungmann, *Early Liturgy*, 21.
[19] Jones et al. (eds.), *The Study of Liturgy*, 457.
[20] Adam, *The Liturgical Year*, 7–8.

Eucharist was usually celebrated on Saturday evening.²¹ In the East, at the end of the third century, the Eucharist was celebrated not only on the day of resurrection but also on Saturday.²² Scholars agree that Christians first began to observe Sunday not as a substitute for the Sabbath but as their day for corporate worship.²³

Early Christians likely celebrated Sunday not as a day of rest but as a festival. It is eschatological in its significance, as representing the inauguration of the "world to come," and only secondarily a memorial of the historical fact of the resurrection of Jesus.²⁴ Later, Sunday was considered a day of rest, with participants abstaining from worldly affairs for the sake of prayer. Sunday was the day of the gathering and breaking of bread. In Didachè, Sunday is the normal day of the Christian assembly. From as early as Rev 1:10, the Christian day for the Eucharistic assembly was known as "the day of the Lord."²⁵

Three central themes regarding Sunday date from the beginning: resurrection, meals, First Day, and Eighth Day. Attendance at the weekly assembly was regarded as obligatory even in times of persecution.²⁶ To abstain from this meal was to separate oneself from the Lord. The Sunday meal is that which we take in common with the Lord and the community.²⁷ The Church was very much conscious of the necessity of the Sunday celebration. Because of Sunday's unique importance, there developed a vigil office. It became a day of baptism other than the Easter vigil and Pentecost vigil.²⁸ Sunday was seen as the day for the manifestation, or epiphany, of the Church. During the rest of the week the Church was dispersed and hidden, as its individual members went about their life and work in different places. But on Sunday the *ecclesia* came together and revealed itself in the celebration of the Eucharist.²⁹

---

²¹ Paul F. Bradshaw, *The Search for the Origin of Christian Worship* (Oxford: Oxford University Press, 2002), 178.
²² Alexander Schmemann, *Introduction to Liturgical Theology*, trans. Asheleigh E. Moorhouse (London: Faith Press, 1966), 154–55.
²³ D. A. Carson (ed.), *From Sabbath to Lord's Day: A Biblical, Historical and Theological Investigation* (Grand Rapids, MI: Zondervan, 1982); Bradshaw, *The Search for the Origins*, 193.
²⁴ Dix, *The Shape of the Liturgy*, 336–37.
²⁵ Talley, "Liturgical Calendar," 153.
²⁶ Jones et al. (eds.), *The Study of Liturgy*, 457.
²⁷ Ibid., 457.
²⁸ Ibid.
²⁹ P. Bradshaw, *Early Christian Worship: A Basic Introduction to Ideas and Practice* (London: SPCK, 1996), 78.

From the ninth century onward, the saints' days were allowed to take precedence over Sunday in the West. The East has maintained the privileged position of Sunday more consistently: Only a few feasts, and those connected with the mysteries of Christ, are celebrated on a Sunday.[30] In later years the prime importance of Sunday as the controlling rhythm of the liturgical year was overshadowed by other calendrical developments, such as the cycle of saints' days.[31] The council teaches, "Other celebrations, unless they be truly of the greatest importance, shall not have precedence over Sunday."[32]

EASTER: THE HEART OF THE LITURGICAL YEAR

Pascha or Passover is the undisputed center of the liturgical year. It was celebrated once every week as Sunday, and once every year as Easter.[33] For the first three centuries, all celebrations in the Church were based on the Pascha. "Passover" refers to the whole complex of the spring festival, the Passover as well as the Feast of Unleavened Bread. The primitive Church celebrated Pascha in the form of a nocturnal festival. A vigil was held from the evening of Saturday until dawn on Sunday. In the second century, it was a unitive commemoration of the death and resurrection of our Lord, a nocturnal celebration of a single night, constituting the Christian Passover.[34] The Church celebrates the memory of the Lord's resurrection once every year at Easter, the most solemn of all feasts.[35] The entire mystery of Christ – namely his incarnation, passion, death, resurrection, glorification, and the outpouring of the Spirit on the Church – is celebrated during the Pascha.[36]

In the second century the Pascha was celebrated as a distinct Christian feast. It combined the commemoration of both the death and resurrection of Christ and the celebration of both baptism and the Eucharist.[37] According to Gregory Dix, the primitive Pascha has the character of a liturgy of "Redemption" rather than a commemoration of the historical fact of the resurrection of Jesus. Like the Jewish Passover,

---

[30] Jones et al. (eds.), *The Study of Liturgy*, 458.
[31] Richard F. Buxton, "Sunday," in *The New SCM Dictionary of Liturgy and Worship*, ed. Paul F. Bradshaw (London: SCM, 2013), 452.
[32] *Sacrosanctum Concilium*, 106.
[33] Adam, *Liturgical Year*, 63.
[34] Jones et al. (eds.), *The Study of Liturgy*, 459.
[35] *Sacrosanctum Concilium*, 102.
[36] Talley, "Liturgical Calendar," 154.
[37] Dix, *The Shape of the Liturgy*, 459.

it commemorated a deliverance from bondage, in the case of Christians from the bondage of sin and from time and mortality into the glorious liberty of the children of God and the everlasting kingdom of our Lord.[38] Pascha, being the feast of the redemption, was considered the most suitable occasion for the conferring of the sacraments.[39]

Christians observed a paschal fast before the Pascha that was extended to the cockcrow, the hour for the sacramental consummation of the vigil, unlike the Jewish fast, which was broken with the eating of the Passover meal and festivity.[40] At the time of Irenaeus (202 CE), the paschal fast took place during the last days of the Holy Week. In the third century, the paschal fast was extended to six days of the Holy Week. The six-week fast might be considered an extension of the paschal fast of six days. After the Council of Nicaea, a fast of forty days before paschal baptism became common. In the seventh century, there was a general tendency to extend the paschal fast so that the total number of fast days would total forty. In fact, the theme of Jesus' fast as the motivating factor for the paschal fast was only a later introduction. This association of the Lord's fast in the wilderness was attached to the season of Lent only after it had come into existence in connection with the preparation of candidates for baptism.[41]

Eastern Churches start with Lent on the Monday before Ash Wednesday of the Western tradition. For the Easterners, Lent consists of forty days, excluding the Sunday of the first week, Lazarus Saturday, and the Holy Week.[42] In celebrations of the Holy Week in Jerusalem specific celebration of the day was in the afternoon, usually at the ninth hour, with a service of readings that extended to and most often connected with the evening office, *lucernarium*[43] which was not celebrated until around seven in the evening.[44]

Originally the Pascha was a unitive celebration, but the Holy Week celebration made the Pascha the Feast of Resurrection. The first testimony concerning Good Friday comes from Jerusalem at the end of the fourth century.[45] The last of the first four days of the Great Week, the afternoon synaxis included the Eucharist. A second celebration of

---

[38] Ibid., 338.
[39] Ibid., 339.
[40] Talley, *The Origins of the Liturgical Year*, 27.
[41] Dix, *The Shape of the Liturgy*, 340.
[42] Jounel, "The Year," 69.
[43] It is the evening office where the service of lighting candles occurs.
[44] Talley, *The Origins of the Liturgical Year*, 42–43.
[45] Jounel, "The Year," 49.

the Eucharist was in the Church of Golgotha, the chapel behind the Cross. Thereafter, a third Eucharist was celebrated in the "Upper Room." This celebration forged a connection between the afternoon service and a vigil stretching through the entire night. On the morning of Good Friday, the wood of the Cross was venerated until noon, followed by prayers that concluded the Liturgy of the Word and preceded the distribution of communion. From noon until three in the afternoon there were readings in the courtyard before the Cross. A vigil through the night from Friday to Saturday was kept at the tomb. The two most striking features of the Good Friday liturgy in the West are the veneration of the Cross and the Mass of the Pre-Sanctified.[46]

Holy Saturday is called "the great Saturday" in the East. It commemorates the repose of Jesus in the tomb, as well as his descent into Sheol.[47] On the Saturday of the Great Week normal services were conducted, and the vigil began with the evening office, specifically with the IDEM: *lucernarium*, the lighting of the lamp. A total fast was kept on Holy Saturday. It was a completely a-liturgical day, meaning that the Eucharist was never celebrated on that day – a tradition that has been preserved both in East and West.[48] The custom was to prolong the celebration of the Pascha for one week. In the fourth century, the central feature of the liturgical arrangement of this week was the explanation of the mysteries to the newly baptized.[49] The Church taking up the Old Testament Pentecost replaced the commemoration with the events recorded in Acts 2 and also with her own character as the People of the New Covenant. Pentecost was considered another ordinary occasion for the celebration of baptism and confirmation.[50] In the first century itself there are clear signs that the fiftieth day was being regarded as a festival with its own proper content, not just as the conclusion of a festal season.[51]

Already in the second century, the celebration of the resurrection was continued for fifty days. This period was one of unbroken rejoicing.[52] In the course of the fourth century, the Christian Pentecost celebrated Christ's ascension and the sending of the Holy Spirit onto the Church. Ascension was not a separate feast; it was included in the

---

[46] Jones et al. (eds.), *The Study of Liturgy*, 461.
[47] Jounel, "The Year," 50–51.
[48] Jones et al. (eds.), *The Study of Liturgy*, 462.
[49] Talley, *The Origins of the Liturgical Year*, 54–55.
[50] Dix, *The Shape of the Liturgy*, 341.
[51] Talley, *The Origins of the Liturgical Year*, 59.
[52] Jounel, "The Year," 17.

celebration of the Pascha. For Christians, these fifty days symbolized the fact that "in Christ" they had already entered into the Kingdom of God. The fifty days manifested the world to come.[53]

Days of fasting have been significant in the formation of the Christian calendar. The preparation for feasts like Christmas and Easter included fasting. Christians were directed to fast on Wednesdays and Fridays. There were regular services of the Word at the ninth hour (about three p.m.) on these days.[54] All Wednesdays and Fridays outside the "great fifty days" were fast days in the East from the second century. According to Schmemann, they were days commemorating the days of Christ's betrayal and death.[55]

The Roman Church introduced its own system of corporate fasts. These were the seasonal fasts of the Ember Days,[56] on the Wednesday, Friday, and Saturday of the weeks that marked the chief agricultural operations of the year in Italy. These seasonal fasts were assigned to the first, fourth, seventh, and tenth months. The observance consisted in a solemnization of the regular weekly fasts on Wednesday and Friday, an extension of the Friday fast through Saturday, and a vigil through the night from Saturday to Sunday, concluding with the Eucharist early Sunday morning.[57] Fasting was the "station" of the Church herself, the people of God standing in readiness, awaiting the parousia of the Lord.[58] When there was Eucharist on such days in the evening, the communion would terminate their fast or vigil.[59] Besides the forty days of fasting before Easter there were other fasts of forty days, before Christmas beginning on November 11, for example, which was referred to as St. Michael's Lent.[60] Now let us see how the Christmas cycle was developed in the Church. The multiplication of festivals – a characteristic feature of the fourth century – was due to the Church's need to replace pagan festivals.[61]

ORIGIN OF THE CHRISTMAS AND EPIPHANY CLUSTER

For the first three centuries there was no particular Christian calendar. Pascha was the only feast, commemorated on Sundays and once per year

---

[53] Dix, *The Shape of the Liturgy*, 340.
[54] Bradshaw, *Early Christian Worship*, 78–79.
[55] Schmemann, *Introduction to Liturgical Theology*, 157.
[56] Talley, "Liturgical Calendar," 151. Cf. Jounel, "The Year," 29.
[57] Talley, "Liturgical Calendar," 151.
[58] Schmemann, *Introduction to Liturgical Theology*, 157.
[59] Ibid., 158.
[60] Talley, "Liturgical Calendar," 158.
[61] Schmemann, *Introduction to Liturgical Theology*, 174.

on the anniversary of Christ's crucifixion. According to Schmemann "the multiplication of feasts went hand in hand with the great theological controversies and was in a way a reflection of the results attained in these controversies."[62] The earliest Christians seem to have had little interest in events like the Nativity. Every feast was a manifestation of Christ and salvation in him, not a commemoration of a particular event. Thus the Nativity or Epiphany is the feast of divine manifestation, not of the birth of Jesus. Christmas is simultaneously the feast of the triumph over the darkness of paganism as the manifestation of the "sun of truth" and of the triumph of Nicaea over Arianism, as well as the affirmation of the divine nature of Christ.[63]

Scholars find a highly hypothetical connection between the Feast of Tabernacles and Epiphany.[64] Epiphany was the oriental festival of nativity, parallel to December 25. Both festivals celebrated the nativity of Christ. But Epiphany also celebrated the baptism of Jesus, the miracle at Cana, the visit of the Magi, and even, in one source, the Transfiguration.[65] Later Jesus' baptism became the sole content of Epiphany. The Feast of the Nativity was introduced in Jerusalem only in the sixth century. It celebrated both the Nativity and baptism on Epiphany. In the course of time in many places Epiphany came to represent the *tria miracula*: the visit of the Magi, the baptism in the Jordan River, and the first miracle at Cana.[66]

The development of the Nativity cycle was connected on the one hand with the necessity to Christianize the dates of the great pagan feasts of December 25 and January 6 and on the other hand with the fight for Nicene orthodoxy, for *homoousion*.[67] The birthday celebration of Christ, the true Sun of Righteousness, was substituted for a very popular pagan feast in Rome.[68] Whatever other reasons there were for the selection of December 25, it is important to note that the day was thought of as more than just a commemoration of the birthday of Jesus.[69] What was being celebrated was not just the historical event of the Nativity but belief in the reality of the incarnation of the Son

---

[62] Ibid., 176.
[63] Ibid.
[64] Talley, "Liturgical Calendar," 155–56.
[65] Ibid., 156.
[66] Ibid., 157.
[67] Schmemann, *Introduction to Liturgical Theology*, 176.
[68] Bradshaw, *Early Christian Worship*, 86. Cf. Talley, "Liturgical Calendar," 156.
[69] For a detailed study of the structure of the Christmas season, see Susan K. Roll, *Toward the Origins of Christmas* (Kampen: Kok Pharos, 1995), 43–46.

of God. Hence there was a strong doctrinal or apologetic purpose shaping the festival and not merely a popular piety.⁷⁰

In all major traditions, the Feast of the Nativity is preceded by a more or less extended season of fasting. There was a season of fasting from the feast of St. Martin (November 11) until Christmas. The real motive behind such fasting was the fact that Epiphany was a day for baptism.⁷¹ The season of Advent makes its appearance in Rome only in the second half of the sixth century. *Adventus* was understood in the biblical and eschatological sense of *parousia*. Actually, Advent fostered a joyful expectation of the Feast of the Nativity, but the aim was to direct the thoughts of Christians to the glorious return of the Lord at the end of time.⁷² In the Syrian rites, the weeks before Christmas are weeks of annunciation. In the West Syrian liturgical year, there are five annunciations, whereas, in the East Syrian liturgical year, there are four. The Presentation of the Lord (February 2) and the Annunciation of the Lord (March 25) could be considered two Christmas feasts outside the Christmas cycle.⁷³

Between 700–1700 CE we find the origin and development of many feasts of ideas. These feasts do not focus on the particular events of salvation but have as their object truths of faith, special aspects of Christian teaching and piety, as well as various titles of the Lord, his mother, or a saint. The idea-feasts are also called "devotion feasts" or dogmatic, thematic, and static feasts.⁷⁴ Feasts of the Trinity, Corpus Christi, the Sacred Heart of Jesus, Christ the King, the Precious Blood, the Holy Name, and the Holy Family, as well as many feasts of Mary, are examples of idea feasts. They are rooted in concepts more than in specific events. Their holidays were set apart as the expression and affirmation of separate elements in the Church's doctrine. This kind of development of feast days weakened the idea of the Church year as a liturgical whole. When the liturgical year is divided into a series of festal cycles, it becomes inwardly disunified and less harmonious.⁷⁵ In addition, many of these feasts were unnecessary duplications.⁷⁶

---

⁷⁰ Bradshaw, *Early Christian Worship*, 87.
⁷¹ Adam, *Liturgical Year*, 130.
⁷² Jounel, "The Year," 93. Cf. Jones et al. (eds.), *The Study of Liturgy*, 468.
⁷³ Adam, *Liturgical Year*, 149–54.
⁷⁴ Ibid., 25.
⁷⁵ Schmemann, *Introduction to Liturgical Theology*, 177.
⁷⁶ Adam, *Liturgical Year*, 25.

VENERATION OF SAINTS AND MARIAN FEASTS

The cult of saints is more ancient than the Feast of the Nativity. The witnessing of martyrs is a sign of the continued reality of Christ's Pascha. Memorial days of the martyrs and other saints are included in the annual cycle. By celebrating their anniversaries, the Church proclaims achievement of the Paschal Mystery in the saints who have suffered and been glorified with Christ.[77] The veneration of martyrs started by the middle of the second century, and their memorial days were assigned to the dates of their death. These are known as their *dies natalis*, their birthday into the Kingdom of Heaven.[78] There was the commemoration of all the martyrs at Nisibis on the Friday after Easter. On May 13, 609, Boniface IV dedicated the old Pantheon to the Blessed Virgin Mary and all the martyrs. It remained the Feast of All Martyrs until 835 CE, when Gregory IV introduced the Feast of All Saints on November 1.

After the Peace of Constantine, the cult of the martyrs gained external solemnity. Within three centuries the number of saints' days had more than doubled.[79] There has been a substantial change with regard to the understanding of the feast of a martyr. The second century word for a martyr's feast was always his or her birthday in heaven. But by the fourth century the martyrs' feasts were no longer designated their "birthdays" but their burials (*depositiones*). The earthly event became the object of the liturgical celebration. The primary interest of the calendar shifted from eternity to time and earthly history.

The liturgical cult of Mary originated in Jerusalem with the feast of August 15 as its foundation. All Churches of the East welcomed the Feast of the Dormition of Mary. In Ethiopia, the death of the Mother of God was commemorated on January 16, and the Assumption on August 15. East Syrians celebrate the Feast of the Congratulations of the Mother of God on December 26, the Annunciation on March 25, and the Presentation of the Lord on February 2, which is called *Hypopante* (Meeting).[80] Ethiopia has over thirty feasts of Mary.[81] Down through the centuries, numerous feasts in the veneration of Mother Mary had

---

[77] *Sacrosanctum Concilium*, 104.
[78] Talley, "Liturgical Calendar," 152.
[79] Jones et al. (eds.), *The Study of Liturgy*, 482.
[80] Adrien Nocent, *The Liturgical Year: Lent, the Sacred Paschal Triduum, Easter Time*, vol. 2, trans. Matthew J. O'Connell, ed. Paul Turner (Collegeville, MN: Liturgical Press, 2014), 475.
[81] Jounel, "The Year," 131–32.

developed. However, the liturgical veneration of Mary would have value and meaning only if it fit harmoniously into the celebration of salvation history. It is relative to the Christ event from which it derives its meaning.[82] After the Second Vatican Council the cult of Mary was revised and reduced to its essential forms,[83] and the council taught that the Holy Church honours with especial love the Blessed Mary, Mother of God, who is joined by an inseparable bond to the saving work of her Son.[84] With the renewal of the liturgy, the commemoration of Christ's mother in the annual cycle must now be made in more organic fashion.[85]

As we have seen, history witnessed drastic changes to the Church year. Whenever the feasts and the seasons deviated from the original spirit of the calendar, it resulted in an aberration from the real purpose of the liturgical year. Vatican II has admonished the Church to go back to the ancient custom of giving more importance to the calendar. The seasons are to be given preference over feasts of saints.[86]

DIFFERENT CALENDARS IN THE CHURCH

Various Church traditions have different structures for the liturgical year. A brief sketch of the structure of the major liturgical traditions of the West and East is presented below.

Roman/Latin Liturgical Year

The daily cycle of the liturgical year is based on the Liturgy of the Hours. The weekly cycle of the liturgy begins by elaborating Christ's resurrection, celebrated on Sunday, the first day of the week. As Sunday is the weekly memorial of the resurrection, Friday is the day commemorating Jesus' Passion and Death. The first Sunday of Advent is the beginning of the yearly cycle of the liturgy. In the Roman rite, the liturgical year consists of three different periods. Table 10.1 itemizes the distribution of the different periods of the Roman liturgical year.

---

[82] Ignazio M. Calabuig, "The Liturgical Cult of Mary in the East and West," in *Handbook for Liturgical Studies: Liturgical Time and Space*, vol. 5, ed. Anscar J. Chupungco (Collegeville, MN: Liturgical Press, 2000), 227.

[83] Pierre Jounel, "The Veneration of Mary," in *The Church at Prayer: The Liturgy and Time*, vol. 4, ed. A. G. Martimort (Collegeville, MN: Liturgical Press, 1986), 148.

[84] *Sacrosanctum Concilium*, 103.

[85] Pope Paul VI, Apostolic Exhortation *Marialis Cultus* (1974), §2.

[86] *Sacrosanctum Concilium*, 108 and 111.

Table 10.1 *Periods of the Roman Liturgical Year*

No.	Name	Time	Duration
1	Christmas cycle	From the first Sunday of Advent to the Sunday after Epiphany	6 weeks
2	Easter cycle	From Ash Wednesday to Pentecost	13 ½ weeks
3	Ordinary time	Two time periods between the Christmas and Easter Cycles	33–34 weeks

The liturgical year today consists of the seasonal cycle (*Proprium de tempore*) and the sanctoral cycle (*Proprium de sanctis*). The two cycles of feasts, ordinary time, and other solemnities and feasts celebrating the mystery of redemption are known as the "temporal cycle" or "Proper of the Time." The calendar of saints' feasts is called the "sanctoral."[87] The Easter cycle begins on Ash Wednesday and ends thirteen and a half weeks later on Pentecost. The annual commemoration of Christ's birth begins with the first Sunday of Advent and ends on the Sunday after Epiphany, which is the feast of Christ's baptism.[88]

East Syrian Liturgical Year

The earliest document of evidence divides the liturgical year of the East Syrians into nine seasons.[89] *Hudra*, the book of Choral Service, divides the year into nine periods of approximately seven weeks each.[90] These nine periods of the liturgical season, along with their duration, are presented in Table 10.2.

Within this framework, the liturgical year also adds feasts of saints. Sundays are reserved as the days of the Lord, while Wednesdays are devoted to the veneration of Mary. Fridays are dedicated to the commemoration of saints and other departed members of the Church.[91]

West Syrian Liturgical Year

Table 10.3 gives a general picture of the liturgical cycles of the West Syrian Church.

---

[87] Adam, *Liturgical Year*, 19
[88] Ibid., 20–21.
[89] John Moolan, *The Period of Annunciation–Nativity in the East Syrian Calendar: Its Background and Place in the Liturgical Year* (Kottayam: Oriental Institute of Religious Studies, 1985), 1.
[90] Ibid., 11.
[91] Ibid., 53.

Table 10.2 *Periods of the East Syrian Liturgical Season*

No.	Name of the Season	Duration
1	*Subara* (Weeks of Annunciation)	6 weeks
2	*Denha* (Weeks of Epiphany)	7 weeks
3	*Sawma Rabba* (Weeks of Great Fast/Lent)	7 weeks
4	*Qyamta* (Weeks of Resurrection)	7 weeks
5	*Sliha* (Weeks of Apostles)	7 weeks
6	*Qaita* (Weeks of Summer)	6 weeks
7	*Eliyah-Sliba* (Weeks of Elias–Cross)	5 weeks
8	*Muse* (Weeks of Moses)	3 weeks
9	*Qudas-Edta* (Weeks of Dedication of the Church)	4 weeks

Table 10.3 *West Syrian Liturgical Cycles*

No.	Season	Meaning
1	*Suboro*	Annunciation
2	*Yaldo–Danho*	Nativity–Epiphany
3	*Sawmo Rabo*	Great Fast
4	*Qyomtho*	Easter
5	Pentecost/*Sleeho*	Apostles
6	Transfiguration	Transfiguration
7	*Sleebo*	Cross

The yearly liturgical cycle of the West Syrian liturgical tradition consists of seven liturgical seasons arranged on the basis of the salvific events of Christ. Within the yearly cycle, the Church unfolds the whole saving mystery of Christ through various liturgical seasons. The liturgical year begins with the season of Annunciation. The West Syrian liturgical year sets apart two Sundays prior to the season of Annunciation for the sanctification and renewal of the Church.[92] Being sanctified/consecrated through the two Sundays, the Church enters into the liturgical year.[93]

---

[92] Joseph Thankachan and S. Simon, "Liturgical Calendar of the Syriac Orthodox Church," *Syriac Orthodox Resources*, 4th Syriac Computing Forum, 2003. Accessed March 15, 2023, at https://syriacorthodoxresources.org/Calendar/index.html.

[93] Gabriel Mar Gregorios Metropolitan, "Liturgical Year & Seasons," *The Malankara Orthodox Syrian Church*. Accessed March 15, 2023, at http://mosc.in/the_church/liturgy/liturgical-year-seasons.

Armenian Liturgical Year

The Armenian Church divides the year into seasons based upon the Great or Tabernacle Feasts. The five seasons of the liturgical year are shown in Table 10.4.

Table 10.4 *Seasons of the Armenian Liturgical Year*

No.	Name	Time
1	Advent	Fifty days from the Sunday nearest November 25 through the Saturday following January 6
2	Eastertide	Nine weeks before Easter Day and fifteen weeks after Easter
3	Transfigurationtide	between Eastertide and Assumptiontide
4	Assumptiontide	Four weeks from the Assumption of the Virgin Mary through the Exaltation of the Holy Cross (*Khachverats*)
5	Exaltationtide	From the Exaltation of the Cross through the beginning of Advent

Byzantine Liturgical Year

In the Byzantine Church, the Church year differs from the civil calendar. It begins with the first day of September, which is called the Indiction, marks the beginning of the liturgical year, and thus ends with the thirty-first day of the following August. The Orthodox Churches generally use the Julian calendar, not the Gregorian calendar, to calculate when Easter is. This is the calendar that was officially implemented by Julius Caesar and was in use primarily between 45 BCE and 1582 CE.[94] The Fathers of the first Ecumenical Council in Nicaea in the year 325 adopted the first of September as the opening of the new Church year. The Byzantine (Constantinopolitan or Constantinian) indiction became mandatory throughout the Roman Empire. Justinian I (527–565) made dating by indiction compulsory for all legal documents. Later, when the first day of September was designated as the beginning of the Church year, it assumed a religious character and became a feast of the Church, a day, that is, which had its own special liturgical service. On this day the Church commemorates the day on which Christ entered the synagogue in Nazareth and read from the scrolls the words

---

[94] The Gregorian calendar is the calendar currently in use to determine the date in most of the Western world as well as in some other parts of the globe. It replaced the Julian calendar. An average year in the latter is 365.25 days, while an average year in the former is 365.2425 days.

of the prophet Isaiah. No reliable evidence exists to indicate when the beginning of the indiction became a feast of the Church; we do know, however that it already existed in the eighth century.[95] Four main periods of fasting in the East are the Great Fast, which begins seven weeks before Easter; the Fast of the Apostles, starting on the Monday eight days after Pentecost and lasting until June 28; the Dormition Fast of two weeks, from August 1 through August 14; and the Christmas fast of forty days, from November 15 to December 24.[96]

Maronite Liturgical Year

The Maronite church, one of the largest Eastern Rite churches, is prominent in modern Lebanon. The church is in canonical communion with the Roman Catholic Church and is the only Eastern Rite church that has no counterpart outside that union. The church retains the ancient West Syrian liturgy, often delivered in Syriac, even though the vernacular tongue of modern Maronites is Arabic. The Maronite Church has six seasons, details of which are given in Table 10.5 on the next page.

Coptic Liturgical Year

The Coptic calendar is based on the ancient Egyptian calendar and is used by the Coptic Orthodox Church for its liturgical readings and for the determination and commemoration of dates for fasts and feasts. The calendar has thirteen months – twelve months of thirty days each and one month of five to six days, depending on whether the year is a leap year or not. The Coptic year starts on September 11, or September 12 in the year before leap years, according to the Gregorian calendar. Every day the Coptic Church celebrates the salvation and the life of victory in Christ the Good Saviour. Every Sunday, the Church celebrates Christ's birth, suffering, death, and resurrection. The Church has fourteen Feasts for the Lord, seven major and seven minor ones. On average the Church commemorates three martyrs every day of the year. The Church commemorates the Annunciation, Nativity, and Resurrection of the Lord on the twenty-ninth day; the Virgin Mary on the twenty-first day; and the Archangel Michael on the twelfth day of each Coptic month. Dates for the feasts and fasts of the Coptic Orthodox Church change every year.[97]

---

[95] Julian Katrij, *A Byzantine Rite Liturgical Year* (Toronto: Basilian Press, 1992), 11–16.
[96] Timothy Ware, *The Orthodox Church: An Introduction to Eastern Christianity* (New York: Penguin, 1993), 300.
[97] Lois M. Farag (ed.), *The Coptic Christian Heritage: History, Faith and Culture* (Abingdon: Routledge, 2013), 132–59.

Table 10.5 *Seasons of the Maronite Liturgical Year*

No.	Name	Time	Important Features
1	Season of Christmas	After the Sundays of the Church and extends to the day before the Feast of the Epiphany	Preparation time in expectation of the second and final coming of Jesus.
2	Season of Epiphany	From January 6 until the Sunday of the Dead	The Season focuses on Jesus as "the Light of the World." Color of season: Blue
3	Season of Lent	Starts on Ash Monday and extends to the beginning of Holy Week	Preparation time with awareness of sins and reconciliation
4	Season of Easter	From Easter Sunday to the day before Pentecost Sunday	Resurrection of Jesus, the source of all hope
5	Season of Pentecost	From Pentecost Sunday extending to the day before the Feast of the Triumph of the Cross	Role and the power of the Spirit in the life of the Church
6	Season of Cross	From the Feast of the Triumph of the Cross until the Sundays of the Church	Life on this earth is a journey to God's Heavenly Kingdom, and the cross is the sure sign of risen glory

CONCLUSION

In the course of the year, the Church unfolds the whole mystery of Christ from the incarnation and nativity to the ascension, to Pentecost and the coming of the Lord. Many historical and theological reasons have contributed to the evolution and formation of present liturgical calendars. Nevertheless, the Paschal Mystery of Christ is commemorated in its various aspects at various feasts and seasons. Every feast originated as a manifestation of Christ and salvation in him, not as a commemoration of a particular event. The faithful are provided with all sorts of possibilities to enter into the manifold aspects of the mystery of salvation. The liturgical year provides a framework for the annual celebration and manifestation of the mystery of Christ. Liturgical time has a symmetrical nature with the Christian structure of time, which spirals toward eternity. Since liturgy offers the actualization of the Paschal Mystery at a specific moment, the liturgical year manifests a mysterious and sacramental character. In other words, the liturgical year could be called a sacrament of the Paschal Mystery. Hence it is a sign of the mystery of Christ that transmits the person of Christ Himself and his saving grace throughout the church year. This cyclic progression of the liturgical year is oriented toward the fullness of salvation in the eschaton. Consequently the liturgical year is not just about recalling events from the past but about a living encounter with Christ. In other words, the liturgical calendar itself proclaims the centrality of Christ and his paschal mystery.

For Further Reading

Adam, Adolf, *The Liturgical Year: Its History and Its Meaning after the Reform of the Liturgy*, trans. Matthew J. O'Connell (New York: Pueblo, 1981).

Chupungco, Anscar J., "The Liturgical Year: The Gospel Encountering Culture," *Studia Liturgica* 40 (2010): 46–64.

Geldhof, Joris, "The Philosophical Presuppositions and Implications of Celebrating the Liturgical Year," *Studia Liturgica* 40 (2010): 197–207.

Johnson, Maxwell E. (ed.), *Between Memory and Hope: Readings on the Liturgical Year* (Collegeville, MN: Liturgical Press, 2000).

Neunheuser, Burkhard, "Odo Casel and the Meaning of the Liturgical Year," *Studia Liturgica* 15 (1983): 210–13.

Nocent, Adrian, *The Liturgical Year*, trans. by Matthew J. O'Connell, 3 vols. (Collegeville, MN: Liturgical Press, 2013).

Taft, Robert F., "The Liturgical Year: Studies, Prospects, Reflections," *Worship* 55 (1981): 2–23.

Talley, Thomas J., *The Origins of the Liturgical Year* (New York: Pueblo, 1986).

Part III

Liturgy and the Arts

11 Liturgical Music and Singing
DOROTHEA HASPELMATH-FINATTI

Sing Praise to God who reigns above, the God of all creation![1]

This is a hymn that, like many others, has traveled back and forth between countries and denominations. It has been received into many churches and families, like my own. While living in Germany, as a Lutheran family, we first encountered the hymn while on holiday at Salisbury Cathedral. We took it with us back to Germany and later to our other countries. The hymn is of German origin, was translated into English in the nineteenth century, and was given a new melody in England in the twentieth century. The song has thus "traveled" from Lutheran Germany to Anglican England and back again. It is one of many hymns and songs that are continually being taken up in new places, in other languages and denominations. The same is true of other musical elements of the liturgy. Bach's organ music, for example, has long been part of the liturgies of many countries and denominations.

This chapter aims to clarify the reasons why human beings tend to embrace music and singing, as seemingly aimless activities, in their liturgies. Through human history and evolution, rituals and liturgies are almost always musical or include musical features. Music making is a human activity that conjoins body and mind, the individual and the many, in exemplary ways. This chapter suggests following the path of liturgical theology, which has already taken up the dialogue with the natural sciences, aiming to better understand the role of music and singing in human ritual behaviors and liturgies.

---

[1] The hymn "Sing Praise to God Who Reigns Above" is a translation by Francis A. Cox of a German hymn by Johann Jakob Schütz, "Sing Praise to God," no. 447 in *The New English Hymnal* (Norwich: The Canterbury Press, 1986). The twentieth-century tune in the same hymn book is "Palace Green" by Michael Fleming.

Liturgical theology takes the liturgical celebration as the primary place where the assembly can experience God's healing and transforming presence through the manifold and richly interwoven strands of liturgical actions, such as music and singing.[2] This experience is made possible by the interplay between the various aesthetic aspects of the liturgical celebration, which include music and words, and the biological constitution of the human being, which combines physical, mental, and communal aspects.

Studies in neuroscience and evolutionary biology are now delving ever more deeply into the rich complexity of the human mind-and-body relationship, which is paramount to activities such as singing and instrumental music making. The dialogue between theology and the human sciences can help theologians to better understand the complex and dynamic human condition and such activities as music making and singing in worship and liturgies.

Therefore, in the first section, this chapter will present two different but resonating concepts of this dialogue as developed by systematic theologian Markus Mühling and liturgist Giorgio Bonaccorso. The second section will explore relevant contemporary research into music and the act of singing from various fields of the humanities. These insights can constructively contribute to a better understanding of the functioning of music and singing in the human body, mind, and environment. What becomes increasingly evident in this context is that through music and singing healing, compassion, and cooperation can grow.

However, the role of liturgical singing and instrumental music has been discussed controversially within the history of Christian (and other) faith traditions. Some Church fathers, like Augustine, already feared the capacity music has to occupy the primary place in the human heart – a place that in their view should belong to faith alone. Thus, the third section will present diverse and sometimes conflicting approaches to liturgical music and singing between different traditions. An insight into the research on music in interreligious encounters will open this topic.

---

[2] Cf. Alexander Schmemann, *Introduction into Liturgical Theology* (Crestwood, NY: St Vladimir's Seminary Press, 1966); David Fagerberg, *Theologia Prima: What Is Liturgical Theology?* (Chicago: Hillenbrand Books, 2004); Andrea Grillo, *Einführung in die liturgische Theologie: Zur Theorie des Gottesdienstes und der christlichen Sakramente* (Göttingen: Vandenhoeck & Ruprecht, 2006); Dorothea Haspelmath-Finatti, *Theologia Prima – Liturgische Theologie für den evangelischen Gottesdienst* (Göttingen: Vandenhoeck & Ruprecht, 2014).

Finally, I suggest that the ecumenically developed concepts of justification and sanctification can be illustrated with the help of research into singing and music. Liturgical music and singing can be understood as a divine gift and a precondition for the celebration of liturgy through which individuals and communities can experience faith and healing.

THE DIALOGUE BETWEEN THEOLOGY AND OTHER DISCIPLINES

As a liturgical theologian, Giorgio Bonaccorso has engaged extensively with the dialogue between theology and the natural sciences. His insights can help to uncover the interplay and functioning of the diverse and interconnected aesthetic strands of liturgy.

In his books *L'estetica del rito* and *Il corpo di Dio*, Giorgio Bonaccorso has investigated the complex relationship between art and ritual, brain and body.[3] He found how in the arts and in rituals, interwoven aesthetic strands, or "languages," like sound, image, smell, and movement, and the interwovenness of human sensible brain- and body-activities, correspond to each other[4] and how these richly interwoven activities can lead to experiences of transcendence. In rituals and liturgy, mythical and faith stories are woven into the aesthetic strands of the ritual. Precisely through the aesthetic context, faith stories can unfold their message and move minds and bodies.

In his more recent book *Critica della ragione impura*,[5] Giorgio Bonaccorso emphasizes that there is no such thing as "pure reason." On the contrary, there are always conditions, and these are never "pure" but always embodied and thus "impure." As human beings, we *are* bodies; we are always part of the reality being described. We are always "immersed" in different layers of reality and its evolution. While for natural sciences, research into the simplest components is essential and cannot be abandoned, it is equally necessary to understand the complexities of reality as a whole – which is where the humanities, including theology, can come in. With Bonaccorso, the complex aesthetic structure of liturgical activity, as witnessed in music and singing,

---

[3] Giorgio Bonaccorso, *L'estetica del rito: Sentire Dio nell'arte* (Cinisello Balsamo: Edizioni San Paolo: 2013), and Giorgio Bonaccorso, *Il corpo di Dio: Vita e senso della vita* (Assisi: Citadella Editrice, 2006).
[4] Bonaccorso, *L'estetica*, 99.
[5] Giorgio Bonaccorso, *Critica della ragione impura: Per un confronto tra teologia e scienza* (Assisi: Citadella Editrice, 2016).

corresponds to the many interconnections discovered in human biology and evolutionary research. What is true for evolutionary development is also true for the development of worship: Unexpected levels of complexity can emerge at any time.

Within the German-speaking academic context, Markus Mühling is one of the first theologians to engage with the international dialogue between theology and neurosciences, and evolutionary theories. While he does not refer to liturgy, his insights into the relationship between brain and body, humankind and evolution can contribute to a deeper understanding of liturgical aesthetics. In his book on neurobiology, evolution, and theology with the title *Resonances*,[6] Mühling engages with recent research in the fields of brain studies and evolutionary theory. He introduces the epistemological concept of the ecological brain.[7] Here, the functions of the brain appear to be interrelated not only with the entire body, but also with the environment.

Further, the subject of interrelatedness can also be found in evolution theories. While Darwinian theory is based on the adaptation of individuals to pressures of selection, more recent concepts focus on types of interactions called "niche construction" activities.[8] It is not only organisms that change, but also the environment that changes and is changed through the organisms' niche constructing activities. Both theories, the "ecological brain" and "niche construction," are described as open systems, or "open loops."[9] Here, I propose taking Mühling's twofold "open loops" as a way of describing what happens in the context of music and singing. While singing, our brain functions within the body, words are pronounced, melodies are brought forth while the sound already reaches our ears, and our bodies receive the sounds, vibrating. We breathe in and out while singing. We produce and receive emotions. Our brain functions as an "open loop," in connection with the entire body and with the environment.

The niche construction theory can illustrate the communal experience of worship singing. We sing within our church community. In singing, our liturgical assembly is all "open loops." Our community is linked to other communities, to humankind and creation. We can experience music and singing as God's transforming gift that comes to

---

[6] Markus Mühling, *Resonances: Neurobiology, Evolution and Theology – Evolutionary Niche Construction, the Ecological Brain and Relational-Narrative Theology* (Göttingen: Vandenhoeck & Ruprecht, 2014).
[7] Ibid., 71–85.
[8] Ibid., 144–66.
[9] Ibid., 81.

us through the music of the others. Through music, we can already praise God as one church, as one humanity, and as one with creation.

STUDIES FROM HUMAN SCIENCES ON MUSIC, SINGING, AND SYNCHRONY

In recent decades, studies on singing and music have been conducted in the fields of neurobiology and evolutionary anthropology. For many liturgists, and not only those from Protestant traditions, language seems to be the foundation of worship, while music is only meant to support the linguistic message. Liturgy is primarily understood as an active expression of faith. The theoretical concepts presented above already show in how many ways human mental activity is dependent on the interplay between body, brain, and environment, and the condition of evolutionary developments.

The following four studies engage with several aspects of the human interaction with music and singing both physically and mentally, fostering the thesis that, in liturgy, as in other cultural expressions, music and singing are foundational to human reasoning and wellbeing. The first study by Brandt et al. deals with the musical condition of children's language acquisition. The second study by Vickhoff et al. on choir singing finds joint singing to be beneficial for wellbeing. The third study by Epel et al. links mental and cellular healing to regular chanting exercises, while the fourth study discovers the connection between children's joint singing and prosocial behavior.

Singing for Language Learning

In their study *Music and Early Language Acquisition*,[10] Anthony Brandt, Molly Gebrian, and L. Robert Slevc joined their competences in music performance, musicology, and brain imaging to put forward their hypothesis: Music precedes language in human development. They describe music as a kind of "scaffolding" for language acquisition:

> Language is typically viewed as fundamental to human intelligence. Music, while recognized as a human universal, is often treated as an ancillary ability – one dependent on or derivative of language. In contrast, we argue that it is more productive from a

---

[10] Anthony Brandt, Molly Gebrian, and L. Robert Slevc, "Music and Early Language Acquisition," *Frontiers in Psychology* 3 (2012): 1–17.

developmental perspective to describe spoken language as a special type of music.[11]

The authors show how speech uses sound in a creative way; while speech is referential, "symbolic," and used for communication, "sound is the bearer of the message."[12] Children, while learning to speak, play with sounds. When children listen to language they first listen to the sound, to the musical aspect of language. In the same way, while learning to use language actively, they first use the musical aspects: They cry, or they use vowel sounds, and they continually increase the spectrum of musical expressions. "Infants use the musical aspects of language (rhythm, timbral contrast, melodic contour) as a scaffolding for the later development of semantic and syntactic aspects of language."[13] In the contexts of this study, the authors present language acquisition as a process that starts as a mainly passive and thus "receiving" activity. Language learning starts before birth. Prenatal infants are immersed in sounds and the musical features of language.[14] They recognize voices and musical styles, and they react to rhythms.

What children can grasp at first is the "music of the speech," the prosody. Only later do they learn to understand the referential meaning of language into the musical "scaffolding." And only afterward do music and language develop more separately. As the authors demonstrate, music is necessary and central to human development; it is learned and trained.[15] However, music does not serve a clearly defined purpose. Music is non-referential. As creative play, music can be understood as a gift to humankind, the prerequisite for such other purpose-led human activities as the use of language.

Thus, the musical aspects of liturgy can be seen as the non-referential "scaffolding" for the purposeful use of language. Not only when children are learning to speak but also in liturgy are musical aspects fundamental to language. Music is the "carrier of the message" and cannot be understood as mere ornamentation. Since the learning of music begins before birth, it is clear that music is a primary gift. This also applies to its role in the liturgy. Further studies have shed more light on the role of liturgical music. Music is not only a prerequisite for speech, but it can also realize what is proclaimed and preached in

[11] Ibid., 1.
[12] Ibid., 3.
[13] Ibid., 6.
[14] Ibid., 3.
[15] Ibid., 5.

messages of faith, namely individual and communal healing. Studies on the functions of singing now suggest that singing and music can promote health and prosocial behavior. Some of these studies are presented here.

Choir Singing for Health and Wellbeing

In their interdisciplinary study on the relationship between choir singing and wellbeing, Björn Vickhoff et al. explored the experiences of wellbeing often reported in the context of choir singing.[16] They hypothesized that one important reason for these positive effects of communal singing could lie in the fact that "singing demands slower than normal respiration, which may in turn affect heart activity."[17]

To validate their hypothesis, the authors focused "on the interplay between two oscillators, the respiratory organ and the heart, while singing."[18] The relationship between respiration and heart rate variability (HRV) plays an important role. While both are irregular, the pronounced coupling of the two has calming effects both subjectively and biologically and is "beneficial for cardiovascular function."[19] By contrast, if the coupling is weak, circulatory complications may occur. Therefore, guided breathing, as in yoga, can have regulating effects on blood pressure and heartrate.

During the study, groups of choir singers were asked to engage in three consecutive singing tasks: humming while breathing individually, joint hymn singing with free breathing, slow mantra singing while breathing only between phrases. Results showed that hymn and mantra singing had significantly more influence on heart rate variability than humming. This leads to the observation, that "music structure guides respiration for singers."[20] Building on further studies, the authors conclude:

> "Choir singing coordinates the neurophysiological activity for timing, motor production on words and melody, respiration and HRV. It has been proposed that joint action leads to joint perspectives ... and joint intentions .... In other words: singers may change their ego-centric perspective of the world to a *we-perspective* which causes them to perceive the world from the same point of view."[21]

---

[16] Björn Vickhoff et al., "Music Structure Determines Heartrate Variability of Singers," *Frontiers in Psychology* 334 (2013): 1–16.
[17] Ibid., 1.
[18] Ibid., 1.
[19] Ibid., 1.
[20] Ibid., 12.
[21] Ibid., 13.

Here, religious rituals, as widely performed in different ways around the globe, come into play: Interestingly, coordinated respiratory activity, irrespective of whether it is caused by yoga breathing, mantra chanting, praying, or singing, is ritually performed in most religions. This is a common factor, more so than the semantic content of beliefs.[22] This study presented by Vickhoff and his colleagues shows how the seemingly aimless activity of singing proves to strengthen health and wellbeing, not only for individuals but also for entire groups of singers.

Chanting for Mental Health and Longevity

Helen Lavretsky and her colleagues conducted research into the effects of yogic meditation on people engaged in caring for a family member with dementia.[23] The researchers worked with a group of caregivers who were themselves affected by mild symptoms of depression. For eight weeks, one part of the group participated in a brief daily yogic meditation, consisting of a chanted mantra (with the words "birth-life-death-rebirth") accompanied by repetitive finger movements and the visualization of light. A control group listened to a CD with relaxing instrumental music for the same time span each day. As the results proved, the chanting group showed "significantly lower levels of depressive symptoms and greater improvements of mental health"[24] compared to the music listening group. The results can be understood in the context of family dementia caregiving: The task of caring for a mentally impaired family member exposes caregivers to an especially high level of stress. Resilience to stress decreases with age, and caregivers are often of an advanced age. In addition, chronic stress leads to a higher risk of developing depression.

The study confirms a number of positive effects of traditional chanting meditation, even after brief (twelve minutes) daily practice, and in comparison with the control group. Mental health and cognitive abilities improved more in the meditation group than in the music listening group. The most impressive result is found in the influence of meditation on cellular aging: The "telomerase activity"[25] improved

---

[22] Ibid., 13.
[23] Helen Lavretsky et al., "A Pilot Study of Yogic Meditation for Family Dementia Caregivers with Depressive Symptoms: Effects on Mental Health, Cognition, and Telomerase Activity," in *International Journal of Geriatric Psychiatry* 28 (2013). Author manuscript 2014.
[24] Ibid., 1.
[25] "A telomere is a region of repetitive DNA sequences at the end of a chromosome, which protects the end of the chromosome from deterioration. Shortened telomere

by 43.3 percent in the meditation group, compared to 3.7 percent in the music listening group.[26]

This study strengthens the hypothesis that singing, in a context of repetition and ritual, is beneficial for mental as well as physical health. It underlines how both are interrelated. Some of the benefits, especially the decrease of depression and anxiety, may also be achieved by the regular exercise of listening to relaxation music. However, telomerase activity, responsible for cell health and linked to longevity, was found to increase much more in the chanting group.

Research on Buddhist chant can help provide a deeper understanding of the effects of worship singing. Religious or traditional song or chant is an activity that interrupts the usual daily occupations. While there is no purpose, there may well be an outcome: the chanting activity improves mental health and reduces depression. It furthers cognitive abilities and leads to the slowdown of cellular aging through telomerase activity. It is obvious that ritual singing has healing affects. Further, this kind of singing activity does not only help the singers to live up to a stressful and demanding task, but it improves cell health and life expectancy through telomerase activity, in ways that exceed typical states of cell aging in healthy people who are not exposed to stressful situations. This study shows that more than only listening to relaxing music, the regular chanting of words that signify life, death, and rebirth can strengthen the singers, help them to assist others, and even add new spans of life where, without the singing, life expectancy would be reduced. As Bonaccorso has shown, the layering and interlacing of aesthetic activities can augment the probability of experiences of transcendence or faith.

Regular ritual chanting and singing can then function in similar ways to the sacraments, as the sacraments are believed to transform the lives and actions of those who take part in them. Through the workings of the sacraments, transcendence can be experienced, faith can be strengthened, and those who suffer or assist others in need are believed to receive new strengths and hope for life to be restored.

Music and Singing for Prosocial Behavior

Michael Tomasello and Sebastian Kirschner, psychologists at the Department of Developmental and Comparative Psychology at the

---

length and reduced telomerase (the cellular enzyme primarily responsible for telomere length and maintenance) are associated with premature mortality and predict a host of health risks and diseases." Ibid., 2.

[26] Ibid., 1.

Max Planck Institute for Evolutionary Anthropology in Leipzig, explored the effects of joint music making, in this case in young children.[27] They hypothesized "that music evolved into a tool that fosters social bonding and group cohesion, ultimately increasing prosocial ingroup behaviour and cooperation."[28] In order to test their hypothesis, they compared the behavior of two groups of children with nearly identical tasks, with "the same level of social and linguistic interaction."[29] The only difference between the two playful activities the children engaged in was that one group used music. As a result, the study showed clearly that joint music making "increases subsequent spontaneous cooperative and helpful behaviour."[30]

Kirschner and Tomasello developed two games to be played by the children in both groups. The first game included a situation where children would benefit from mutual help. The second game offered possibilities of cooperative problem solving. The children involved in the musical version of the game had sung together and jointly used simple percussion instruments. As a result, the active engagement in joint music making significantly improved their helping behaviors in the first game and in the second game helped them to cooperate more than members of the "non-musical" group.[31] The second, "spontaneous cooperative problem solving" game arrived at similar results. However, within the music-making group, the second game was accompanied by a much higher frequency of verbal communication between the cooperating players than in the group without music. As a result, the study leads to "clear evidence for music and dance functioning as behavioural tools for mutual social bonding."[32] One main reason for these astonishing results may be the "joint intentionality" in music making, which can even be found in contemporary Western cultures, where music is used for "social bonding" during many public occasions, such as sporting events, worship, and weddings, supporting an understanding of music as a collectively intended activity.

Compared to the use of language, which is most effective in mobilizing joint intentionality for goal-directed behavior, music might be

---

[27] Sebastian Kirschner and Michael Tomasello, "Joint Music Making Promotes Prosocial Behavior in 4-Year-Old Children," in *Evolution and Human Behavior* 31 (2010): 354–64.
[28] Ibid., 354.
[29] Ibid., 354.
[30] Ibid., 354.
[31] Ibid., 360.
[32] Ibid., 361.

more efficacious in mobilizing joint intentionality per se – in the sense of feeling a "we" unit, thus getting people to experience each other as coactive, similar, and cooperative members of a group.[33] Joint music making then, for the authors of the study, is an "expressive mode that is beyond the referential and propositional use of words in language."[34] While there seems to be no goal in joint music making, the joint activity creates group experiences. It promotes the possibility of common feelings and emotions. As the study shows, the likelihood of finding readiness for mutual help among participants is higher in the music-making group than in the "non-singing" group. However, this help is not a necessary consequence of the joint singing experience – its probability is only increased by it. The children do not sing *in order* to then help each other. Their singing is an aimless activity.

This study compares two similar enactments of children's games, only one of them containing joint singing, instrumental rhythmical music, and dance. Here, I suggest comparing the musical game to liturgy: Liturgy, in many traditions, contains joint singing and instrumental rhythmical music. In his seminal work *The Spirit of the Liturgy*, Romano Guardini famously emphasized that liturgy is a game-like, aimless activity.[35]

The activity of joint singing gives rise to an enhanced readiness for prosocial behavior, at least among young children. Here, joint music making and singing are linked to social bonding and spontaneous cooperation. The music-making children seem to act more in the ways of the "open loops" described by Mühling in the niche-construction theory than do children in the non-music-making group. Joint music making brings forth prosocial behavior.

Excursion: Interreligious Music and Singing

Verena Grüter is a German theologian and musicologist specializing in intercultural theology. For her book *Klang – Raum – Religion*, Grüter has analyzed an interreligious music festival in a small town in Bavaria.[36] She joined extensive empirical studies with insights from theology, religious studies, musicology, and sociology. For her analysis,

---

[33] Ibid., 362.
[34] Ibid., 357.
[35] Romano Guardini, *The Spirit of the Liturgy* (New York: Crossroad, 1998), 61–72.
[36] Verena Grüter, *Klang – Raum – Religion: Ästhetische Dimensionen interreligiöser Begegnung am Beispiel des Festivals Musica Sacra International* (Zurich: Theologischer Verlag Zürich, 2017).

she has delved into the history of "functions and styles"[37] of religious music. Different religions show different approaches to music, and, in addition, religious attitudes to music are subject to changes through history. In various religious contexts, periods when the use of music was limited or even prohibited were followed by eras of a new endorsement of music.

In her interviews with festival musicians and organizers, Grüter focused on the question of religious experience. When referring to experiences of singing, some of the respondents would speak of experiences of "sharing" and of "faith springing up from singing."[38] When people of different religious affiliations sang together, mutual enrichment could be experienced. From the perspective of theoretical interreligious dialogue, such sharing still appears to be a relatively distant vision.[39] However, in the joint singing and listening of the festival, transformations of relationships could be witnessed. These experiences of sound affected the bodies of the participants and brought them into states of vibration or resonance. The sound vanishes, but the effects on the body can persist.[40] Grüter describes the joint musical experience as an interruption, a liminal "turn" experience, a destruction of order that opens new freedoms and rights, if only for a short amount of time. However, when the destabilizing experience is repeated time and again, a new kind of order can emerge.[41] Music, as performed and experienced in the context of this festival, can open new doors for interreligious understanding.

SINGING AND MUSIC IN CHRISTIAN DENOMINATIONS

Verena Grüter's insights into the dynamics of religious music history can add new dimensions to any comparative approach to music in liturgy and worship between Christian denominations. The approach to music and to musical styles changes throughout history within each church and community. This is also true for the churches that are most indebted to their early roots and traditions. While Roman Catholic and Lutheran traditions experienced times of some restrictions to musical

---

[37] Grüter, "Funktionen und Stile religiöser Musik im Rahmen des Festivals," in *Klang - Raum - Religion*, 77–115.
[38] Grüter, *Klang - Raum - Religion*, 162.
[39] Ibid., 163f.
[40] Here, Grüter refers to insights from performance theories as presented by Erika Fischer-Lichte. Ibid., 310.
[41] Ibid., 316.

styles, the use of instrumental music was never banned from the liturgies. Orthodox and Reformed traditions, however, have known eras without instrumental music or, in the case of the Zurich reformation, without music at all. However, music has since returned to Reformed liturgies, and, in the context of Orthodox churches, some organ music can be found.

This section gives some insights into the understanding and development of music in Christian denominations. In the Christian East, liturgical singing has played a vital role throughout history, while the use of instrumental music does not play a part in Orthodox traditions. However, more recent developments, namely in the North American context, have brought forth arguments in favor of more diversity in the field of Orthodox liturgical music.

Harrison Russin, musicologist at St. Vladimir's Seminary in New York, remarks that "a careful balance between orthodoxy and diversity – a balance which often seems contrary or even paradoxical to modern eyes – defines much of the Orthodox inheritance from the Greek tradition."[42] As Harrison shows, arguments against instrumental music are now often linked to the question of language and communication. As instruments cannot communicate words, they are not found fit for Orthodox liturgies.[43] However, "Worship in Orthodox churches is not composed entirely of concrete, logically formulated ideas; the essence of iconography is, in fact, that it is not concrete, that it responds to the viewer."[44] Harris' argument could foment discussions in other denominations, as no worship can do without nonverbal ways of expression. However, Harrison's understanding of the role of iconography in the Orthodox liturgical context is not uncontested. In Orthodox theology, icons can be understood as the "gospel of the illiterate,"[45] thus functioning in the same way as language, conveying concrete ideas.

Nevertheless, they can also be described as mystical, as Hilarion Alfeyev writes: "Icons reflect the mystical experience of the whole

---

[42] Harrison Russin, "Organs in Orthodox Worship: Debate and Identity," *Journal of the International Society for Orthodox Church Music* 4 (2020): 98–108, at 100.

[43] Ibid., 105. Here, Russin refers to Johann von Gardner, *Russian Church Singing, Volume I: Orthodox Worship and Hymnography*, trans. Vladimir Morosan (Crestwood: St Vladimir's Seminary Press, 1980), 22.

[44] Russin, "Organs." Here, Russin refers to Anna Kartsonis, "The Responding Icon," in *Heaven on Earth*, ed. Linda Safran (University Park: The Pennsylvania State University Press, 1998), 58–80.

[45] Hilarion Alfeyev, *Orthodox Christianity, Volume III: The Architecture, Icons and Music of the Orthodox Church* (Yonkers, NY: St Vladimir's Seminary Press, 2014), 211.

fulness of the Church and not only of some individual members."[46] Individuals, however, can be drawn into mystical experiences through the presence of icons in the liturgy. Alfeyev cites Archimandrite Sophrony (Sakharov), who describes mystical experience in the life of Saint Siluan the Athonite:

> During vespers, in the church ... to the right of the royal gates where the icon of the Savior is situated, he saw the living Christ. ... It is impossible to describe the condition in which he was at that time. ... We know from the words and writings that he was taken from this world and in spirit transported into heaven where he heard unutterable speech.[47]

Here, the liturgical experience of iconography is depicted as a movement that links heaven and earth in ways that cannot be described with human language, as it contains "unutterable speech." As a nonverbal way of expression, iconography enables experiences of transcendence. Liturgies, including those from the context of the churches of the Reformation that feel indebted to the verbal dimensions of faith, contain more than words and concepts. The architecture of the meeting space, sounds, voices, smells, light, perhaps works of art – as well as the co-presence of others – are prerequisite to the liturgical experience. Liturgies are basically multidimensional.

In the Christian West, rich musical styles emerged during the late Middle Ages and in the times leading up to the Reformation. While Martin Luther endorsed the use of liturgical music and hymn singing, the Swiss Reformers, in the tradition of Southwest German sermon-centered worship styles, were much more critical of music in worship. Lutheran liturgical music found its unrivalled summit in the music of Johann Sebastian Bach. Enlightenment times, however, soon restricted the style and scope of music in Lutheran worship. Biblical texts should now be read and no longer chanted in recitation mode.[48] Liturgical compositions should follow the taste of the time, emphasize texts, and avoid repetitions and complexities.

From the beginning, Swiss Reformed tradition demanded that liturgy should be as simple and as focused on the essential content of the

---

[46] Ibid., 234.
[47] Here, Alfeyev cites Archimandrite Sophrony (Sakharov), who describes mystical experience in the life of Saint Siluan the Athonite. Ibid., 235, fn. 49.
[48] *Jakob Georg Christian Adlers Schleswig-Holsteinsche Kirchenagende 1797*, in Wolfgang Herbst, *Evangelischer Gottesdienst: Quellen zu seiner Geschichte* (Göttingen: Vandenhoeck & Ruprecht, 1992), 158–65, at 159.

faith as possible. Ralph Kunz calls this a reductionist approach and a "grammar orientated culture."[49] As Kunz points out, present-day Reformed liturgists are facing a dilemma: On the one hand, they tend to defend the simple and concentrated form of the worship service of their inheritance; on the other hand, many of them bemoan the aesthetic poverty of Reformed worship, as compared to the richer liturgical traditions found in other denominations.[50]

A trained musician himself, Zwingli famously objected to the use of music in the worship service. He promoted a liturgy consisting of biblical teaching and listening. For Kunz, it is important to stress that Zwingli's main objective was not to restrict, but, on the contrary, to enable liturgical experience. The faithful are not asked to abstain from anything; instead, they are called to gain access to the central experience of faith, namely the spiritual encounter with God.[51] For Zwingli, no sacrament can achieve what Christ did for humankind; neither can music fill this role. For him, music cannot be sacred and should thus not be used in worship.[52] For Kunz, however, the present-day church needs to contradict Zwingli's approach: Banning physical signs and actions from worship results in a liturgy without an outer form, but faith cannot live without form.[53] Jean Calvin may already have sensed similar insights. While the ban of instrumental music persisted, Calvin had experienced congregational psalm singing in Strasbourg and in consequence introduced this way of singing into Reformed worship[54]. Hymn singing in the tradition of the Genevan Psalter has since spread to the liturgies of many other denominations.

Throughout history, Anglican church music has been dependent on the confessional state of the governing monarchs. Since the Reformation, "catholic" kings and queens supported rich musical styles, and many composers dedicated their work to church music compositions. "Protestant" monarchs tended to prefer simple worship styles with little or virtually no music. During the "Puritan takeover,"

---

[49] Ralph Kunz, *Gottesdienst evangelisch reformiert* (Zurich: Pano Verlag, 2001), 3.
[50] Ibid., 4.
[51] Ibid., 128.
[52] Ibid., 132.
[53] Ibid., 149.
[54] David Plüss and Dorothea Haspelmath-Finatti, "Singing/Embodiment/ Resonance," in *International Handbook of Practical Theology: A Transcultural and Transreligious Approach*, ed. Birgit Weyel et al. (Berlin: De Gruyter, 2022), 533–46, at 534f.

beginning with an ordinance of Parliament in 1643,[55] the arts were banned from worship, organs were destroyed, Catholicism was persecuted.[56] Church musicians and organ builders left the country. After the Restoration, musicians and music gradually returned. But it was only with the Oxford Movement that cathedral music, with choir schools, could grow again and come to the flourishing that has since fomented liturgies and music not only in Anglican churches worldwide but in other countries and denominations.[57]

The history of Roman Catholic church music shows several turning points. On the eve of the Council of Trent, theological statements emphasized the serving role of liturgical music: Music should be subordinate to the dogmatic dimensions of faith. The music should not obscure the words of faith[58] but rather serve as a "maid" to the liturgy.[59] Restoration efforts such as the *Cecilian Movement* in the nineteenth century promoted Gregorian choral and mass compositions in the style of classical vocal polyphony.[60]

The Second Vatican Council brought a new turn. Liturgical music is now understood as an integral part of the liturgy. Here, music has more than a serving role.[61] While council texts, such as *Sacrosanctum Concilium*, emphasized the importance of quality musical education, many congregations in many regions of the world now finally felt free to incorporate a wide variety of musical styles into their liturgies without too much concern for quality issues.

---

[55] See Roy Strong, *A Little History of the English Country Church* (London: Jonathan Cape, 2007), 151.

[56] "Two years later Parliament ordered the destruction of all vestments and all other 'popish' ornaments, such as screens, organs and fonts. ... In addition, visitations of commissioners set out to smash anything that would remotely remind the congregation of its Catholic past." Ibid., 151.

[57] Hanna Rijken, *My Soul Doth Magnify: The Appropriation of Choral Evensong in the Netherlands* (Amsterdam: VU University Press, 2020).

[58] Friedrich Nausea, bishop of Vienna, demanded in a letter to Pope Paul III that only biblical texts should be sung during the liturgy. R. F. Hayburn, *Papal Legislation on Sacred Music: 95 A.D. to 1977 A.D.* (Collegeville, MN: Liturgical Press, 1979), 25–27. Cf. Stefan Kopp, Marius Schwemmer, and Joachim Werz, *Bestandteil, Dienerin oder Museumsstück der Liturgie?, Mehr als nur eine Dienerin der Liturgie: Zur Aufgabe der Kirchenmusik heute*, ed. Stefan Kopp, Marius Schwemmer, and Joachim Werz (Freiburg im Breisgau: Herder, 2020), 9–17, at 11, fn. 10.

[59] Cf. the title of the book: "Mehr als nur eine Dienerin."

[60] Ibid., 13.

[61] Wilfried Haunerland, "Participatio actuosa und musica sacra. Gesang und Instrumentalmusik als liturgisches Handeln," in Ibid., 58–71, at 58.

RECEIVING LITURGY AS JUSTIFICATION THROUGH MUSIC AND SINGING, ECUMENICALLY

Finally, these findings lead to the conviction that music is not only one feature of worship and liturgies but that worship music can induce experiences of transcendence and faith; it can foster healing and promote prosocial behavior. In addition, music can transform human relationships. It can foster understanding between diverse groups of church and society, with healing consequences for the entire environment. Likewise, ecumenical, interreligious, and intercultural understanding can grow.

The gravest dividing line between some Christian denominations has long been the question, "What saves us?" Is it faith or good works? Is it the word of God or adherence to rules and tradition?[62] Research on music and singing provides new insights into the relationship between faith and good works. It shows that there is no reason to choose between them. Rather, the two turn out to be closely linked: Faith can be seen as an experience of transcendence brought about through activities that connect mind, body, and community, such as liturgical singing and music making. In the context of biblical texts, faith is understood as something that brings redemption and healing to the mind and body. Studies on singing and music show that singing and music have healing capacities.

What are called good works in the religious context can be understood as prosocial behavior. Research on singing and music has identified activities – such as singing in a group – that can bring about spontaneous prosocial behavior. The exploration of singing and music can strengthen ecumenical efforts. New light can be shed on the relationship between justification and sanctification. Singing as an experience of faith has been shown to foster a willingness to help others and work together. Activities such as liturgical singing and music can bring about experiences of sanctification. As human beings, we can only receive God's justifying and sanctifying work on us. Liturgy is, with Romano Guardini, a "divinely ordained game" that we can learn to play. Singing the hymns we encountered in some holy place is one such

---

[62] In recent times, ecumenical and liturgical theologians have already found ways to bridge the divide. Cf. among others, Martha Moore-Keish, *Do This in Remembrance of Me: A Ritual Approach to Reformed Eucharistic Theology* (Grand Rapids, MI: Eerdmans, 2008).

playful activity. Through singing and music we can experience liturgy as a gift that we receive together with all humankind and creation.

Furthermore, the study of evolutionary niche construction can show the ways in which human life is conditioned by evolutionary history. As a species, we are drawn into more and more interactions not only with other humans but also with other species and with our environment. This observation might explain why humans tend to seek shared aesthetic – and often musical – experiences, even in a non-religious atmosphere.

Some questions remain. The most important is that of abuse. As music making promotes bonding between group members, music can strengthen groups with hostile intentions. Music, as one strand in the fabric of song, supports the sung words and augments the message. This remains true when the words are destructive.[63] How can such abuse be prevented? Insights into the functions of music and singing do not explicitly answer the question of choice. Which music should be used, which hymns should be sung? However, the observation that music works in such ways that liturgy can be perceived as a divine gift, as a gift that can heal und promote prosocial behavior, might help to find new criteria for worship music preparation – and a renewed regard for the labor of church musicians. Then, new generations can sing,

> Be joyful in the Lord, my heart! Both soul and body bear your part! To God all praise and glory![64]

For Further Reading

Bonaccorso, Giorgio, *L'estetica del rito: Sentire Dio nell'arte* (Cinisello Balsamo: Edizioni San Paolo: 2013).

Gelineau, Joseph, *Les chants de la messe dans leur enracinement rituel* (Paris: Cerf, 2001).

---

[63] Cf. as one of many examples Luther's hymn "Erhalt uns, Herr, bei deinem Wort." The original lyrics call for the death of the pope and the Turks: "und steur' des Papst und Türken Mord." The current version, to be found in the hymn book for the German-speaking Evangelical Churches, *Evangelisches Gesangbuch*, still calls for the assassination of God's enemies: "Erhalt uns, Herr, bei Deinem Wort und steure Deiner Feinde Mord."

[64] Cf. "Sing Praise to God," no. 447 in *The New English Hymnal* (Norwich: The Canterbury Press, 1986), verse 4. "Sei Lob und Ehr dem höchsten Gut," Nr. 326, in *Evangelisches Gesangbuch. Ausgabe für die Evangelisch-Lutherischen Kirchen in Niedersachsen und für die Bremische Evangelische Kirche* (Hannover: Verlagsgemeinschaft für das Evangelische Gesangbuch Niedersachsen/Bremen, 1994).

Grüter, Verena, *Klang – Raum – Religion: Ästhetische Dimensionen interreligiöser Begegnung am Beispiel des Festivals Musica Sacra International* (Zurich: Theologischer Verlag Zürich, 2017).

Klomp, Mirella, *The Sound of Worship: Liturgical Performance by Surinamese Lutherans and Ghanaian Methodists in Amsterdam* (Leuven: Peeters, 2011).

Rijken, Hanna, *My Soul Doth Magnify: The Appropriation of Choral Evensong in the Netherlands* (Amsterdam: VU University Press, 2020).

Robert, Philippe, *Chanter la messe* (Paris: Bayard, 2016).

12 Liturgy and Architecture
GILLES DROUIN

CHURCHES TO WELCOME GOD TODAY

"God is not, until it's made of stone / You need a house to pray in."[1] In writing these verses, the renowned French writer Victor Hugo bore witness to the fascination that the Middle Ages exerted on intellectuals in the heyday of Romanticism, through the Romanesque and especially Gothic religious edifices with which they studded the West. In fact, this fascination with the Middle Ages and the associated imagery was, thanks to the great Protestant and Catholic missionary movements of the nineteenth and twentieth centuries, widely transplanted to all five continents and remains deeply associated with a certain idea of Christianity. But the poet goes further, deliberately associating God and stone, God and his manifestation in stone, in a direct, immediate way, through a kind of rhetorical short-circuit. This is not the classic association, based on the identity of words, between the Church as an institution or mystery and the church as a building, but between God himself and the building, as if what some call the religion of the Book had become for Christianity not a religion of the Word but a religion of stone.

In so doing, the poet has grasped in his own way the extent to which, in Christianity at least, the spaces of prayer manifested a certain idea that those who conceived, constructed, and built them had and still have of God, of the relationship that humans have with him, both personally and as a community, a community that is as much religious as it is cultural and/or political. The theologian, often less perceptive but, for better or worse, more conceptual than the poet, would say today

---

[1] *Œuvres complètes de Victor Hugo, Poésie III*, Collection Bouquins (Paris: Gallimard, 1974), 973. Translation by the editor.

that these prayer spaces, these buildings, are authentic theological places. It is this approach that I would like to develop in this chapter, a resolutely theological approach to architecture, or more precisely, to the space of Christian liturgy. This approach does not, of course, exclude any of the other disciplines; instead it draws on them. It obviously calls on history, of which liturgical studies is a daughter, largely emancipated but which cannot and must not deny its origins. It calls on anthropology, insofar as "living," in the sense of inhabiting, and "praying" are deeply rooted, if not universal, human realities.[2]

After three years of working on the restoration of Notre-Dame Cathedral in Paris, I've had the opportunity to experience just how many different – and potentially conflicting – ways there are to envisage such an operation.[3] At Notre-Dame, the state as owner is first and foremost the guarantor and guardian, vigilant if not fussy, of a heritage approach. This is a dimension that, if one is not careful, tends to become dominant, if not exclusive, in a society worried about the solidity of its anthropological and cultural foundations. The Church, as the exclusive, perpetual, and gratuitous assignee under French law,[4] is the guarantor of an approach that I have described as liturgical–symbolic. This means that the Church is the institution and the community that established the building and that for 850 years has ensured its habitation for the purpose for which it was built – a rare occurrence in many older buildings, most of which are no longer used for the purpose for which they were originally built. Last but not the least, all the players involved are concerned by a functionalist approach, or how to welcome the 12 million visitors who flock to an edifice with a variety of motivations, often far removed from those for whom the cathedral was built and transformed over the ages.

This singular experience of Notre-Dame reinforced my conviction that the theological discipline is a crossroads science above all because its object is in some way homogeneous to that which enables us to enter into the understanding of a space designed for liturgy. God, as Victor Hugo rightly saw, was a relevant if not royal way to initiate an understanding of a monument designed to celebrate the liturgy of the Church. The reciprocal is not to be dismissed too quickly: Theology should

---

[2] Bernard Klasen, *Habiter: Une philosophie de l'habitat* (Paris: Salvator, 2018).
[3] Gilles Drouin, "Enjeux théologiques d'une restauration," in *La Cathédrale immortelle?* ed. Pascale Bermond and Dominique Poirel (Turnhout: Brepols, 2023), 201–18.
[4] Law of April 13, 1908, amending the law of December 9, 1905, on the separation of Church and State, known as the law on the conservation of religious buildings.

indeed take into account non-textual corpora, in particular the arts, and what specialists in these disciplines have to say. For they can be said to be more sensitive seismographs than many theoretical treatises for grasping the movements and deep edges of the ever-shifting relationship between God and an era, a culture, a society. Consequently, in a resolutely theological approach, I will deal successively with the space of celebration

- as a mirror and matrix of the kind of Church "we" want to be and share;
- as a sign of Christ's presence, that is, as a place where the unique mystery of Christ is actualized, in a Caselian conception nourished by Pauline images of the Church as the body and bride of Christ;
- as an irruption and openness to the radical condescension of God, who gives himself even in the cosmic dimension of his personal and communal manifestation.

EPIPHANY OF THE CHURCH

It was Romano Guardini who originated what became – in the Catholic world, following the many magisterial revivals up to Popes John Paul II and Francis – an adage: the liturgy as epiphany of the Church. Guardini perceived that the space of celebration itself had an epiphanic dimension. He did not do this by proposing a particular type of space, designed specifically for liturgy or for a particular type of liturgy, but by proposing a series of ways of inhabiting a space that was a priori neutral. I'm obviously referring to the work carried out with architect Rudolf Schwarz in the Knights' Hall (*Rittersaal*) at Burg Rothenfels.[5] This work has all too often been reduced to the invention of the enveloping plan – a brilliant invention, even if the reformers had glimpsed it four centuries earlier – and it still leaves its mark on the spaces inherited from the Liturgical Movement, particularly in German-speaking countries.

Guardini and Schwarz proposed numerous ways of inhabiting the Knights' Hall, depending on its use (liturgical or otherwise) and the type and size of the assemblies present: They thus enriched the "auditorium" design that had become widespread in both the Protestant and Catholic worlds from the seventeenth century onward by rediscovering features close to its medieval counterpart. But they also proposed new

---

[5] Bert Daelemans, "Rothenfels, le théologien et l'architecte," in *L'espace liturgique, un espace d'initiation*, ed. Gilles Drouin (Paris: Cerf, 2019), 137–78.

configurations that were enveloping and open. In so doing, both of them offered a range of solutions to the problem of the Knights' Hall and revived the fundamental option long taken by Christians when, after the Constantinian Turn, they built large and lasting buildings for worship: It is the congregation that, under Christian rule, determines the choice of building for celebrating the "new" worship.

When Christians moved out of the "church house" inherited both from the practices of the first three centuries and from the memory of the original liturgical site of their central rite, the Eucharist was born not from the liturgy of the Temple or the synagogue, but from a domestic liturgy celebrated by Christ with the group of Twelve in the Upper Room. So, not only did they enlarge the house to the dimensions of the growing community – with rare exceptions[6] – but they also chose a place designed to receive large numbers of people for secular activities: the basilica. Thus, they "broke away" from the strictly domestic spaces they so far had inhabited as well as from the other model: the temple considered as *Domus Dei*, with a central *cella*, or in the case of the Temple of Jerusalem, a Holy of Holies, the place where the divinity dwells, accessible only to special personnel, the priests, subject to extremely rigorous and codified purification procedures.

The choice of a basilica is at least as much a functional choice, a theological choice. The word "choice" is not to be taken in the sense of a centralized decision but rather as the testimony of a kind of obviousness that has imposed itself throughout the Mediterranean basin. In the basilica, the interior space initially reserved for the divinity is the space that welcomes the assembly. Expressed in theological terms, in this case Augustinian (cf. the famous *sermo* nr. 272), it is the assembly that gathers to commemorate the death and resurrection of its Lord, which becomes what it receives: the body of Christ. It is this body, gathered for the anamnesis of the saving event, that becomes sign and reality, symbol in the sense given to it by Louis-Marie Chauvet of the presence of the divinity, in this case Christ present in his body, indissociably Eucharistic and ecclesial.

Benedictine architect and theologian Philippe Marckiewicz, using the example of Ravenna, points out that the Christian basilica presents an inversion in iconographic terms in comparison with the pagan temple. The interior of the building is now covered in mosaics,

---

[6] In Aquileia, for example, there are still traces of a vast church house built at the time of the great basilicas in the middle of the fourth century.

becoming a kind of showcase for the assembled ecclesial body, while the exterior, overlooking the city, remains extremely sober. The author goes so far as to describe this inside-outside relationship as a metaphor for the interiority proper to Christian worship.[7] The basilica as the site of the Eucharist, along with the funerary-inspired choice of the centered-plan building for the baptistery or the various *memoriae*, provides the building blocks for fifteen centuries of Christian liturgical architecture.

However, one must not absolutize this Paulino–Augustinian-inspired choice of the basilica model, already partly adopted by the synagogue for similar reasons,[8] and overlook the influence of the Temple of Jerusalem in the design of Christian buildings from the patristic "golden age" onwards. I'm referring not so much to the formal revivals of Leviticus-inspired cultic and priestly vocabulary, which would gradually flourish and eventually invade medieval allegory, as to a tension between a Pauline-inspired conception of liturgy and one more marked by the interpretation of the Letter to the Hebrews regarding Christ's sacrifice and its relationship with the Temple Liturgy for Yom Kippur.

This tension – which François Cassingena-Trévedy, in a very different context, conceptualizes in terms of the duality of celebratory "ethos"[9] – was a very early feature of the Christian liturgical space, which, although fundamentally basilical, accentuated the distinction between a nave reserved for the baptized and a sanctuary reserved for clerical ministers. Nonetheless, the Roman basilica and its variations retain the epiphanic dimension of a body rich in an abundant pluriministeriality, with the strong distinction between the place of the Word, monumental and accessible to a plurality of ministers, often located in the middle of the nave in Gaul in particular, and the place of the Eucharist, the altar, absidal, with its schola, often located at the front of the altar and separated from the nave by low chancels, accessible to the many ministers of song and, in some cases, of the Word. Moreover, it has a *synthronon* where the bishop presides, not alone but "in his presbyterium," according to an ecclesiology inherited from Ignatius of

---

[7] Ferrante Ferranti and Philippe Markiewicz, *Les pierres vivantes: L'église revisitée* (Paris: Ed. Philippe Rey, 2005).

[8] Louis Bouyer, *Liturgy and Architecture* (Notre Dame, IN: University of Notre Dame Press, 1965).

[9] François Cassingena-Tévedy, *Te igitur: Le missel de saint Pie V: Herméneutique et déontologie d'un attachement* (Geneva: Ad Solem, 2007), passim.

Antioch, and which Vatican II's constitution on the liturgy attempted to recover.[10]

From a leap of several centuries, we find ourselves on the threshold of the second millennium in a Christendom that is covered with the white mantle of churches so dear to Cluniac monk Raoul Glaber. The very long period we are spanning remains generally faithful to the basilica model inherited from Rome but has seen it evolve through a double movement of complexification and fragmentation. The fragmentation of spaces has too often been unilaterally linked to the clericalization of liturgy, which characterizes the gradual shifts that became evident with the Carolingian and then Gregorian reforms. The rood screen has often been singled out as a late but spectacular example of this clericalizing fragmentation. But this is to overlook the compenetration between Church and society that characterized this period of the classical Middle Ages, as highlighted by historian Dominique Iogna-Prat.[11]

From then on, the distribution of space, particularly on either side of rood screens – which were not generalized until late in the thirteenth century – was the subject of constant negotiation between clerics and lay notables, betraying a strong porosity of space, as evidenced by incessant trials right up to the Tridentine period in the Catholic world. That said, the phenomenon of fragmented spaces remains no less real, with the basilica sometimes reintegrated into a system directly descended from the domestic church – I am referring here to the monastery – and the Cistercian plan, which, although late in its development, represents the epitome of a micro-Christianity seeking to live out a form of evangelical perfection, organized around the atrium, a legacy of the Roman house allegorized as a paradisiacal figure.

The fragmentation of spaces reflects the specialization of clerical bodies, for example, in the progressive enclosure of large canonical bodies in collegiate churches and then cathedrals from the twelfth century onward. Very early on, it took on the form of specific itineraries for the veneration of relics by the faithful, often distinct from liturgical itineraries, with vertical specialization of spaces, as in Gregory the Great's Vatican basilica, a device destined to have great posterity, or multiple forms of horizontal specialization that would blossom in the great Romanesque and Gothic ambulatories. The rise of devotion, often

---

[10] See *Sacrosanctum Concilium*, 41.
[11] Dominique Iogna-Prat, *Cité de Dieu, cité des hommes: L'Eglise, l'architecture et la société* (Paris: Presses Universitaires de France, 2016).

associated with family or fraternal communities, led to the proliferation of chapels, which eventually included the most prestigious or best-endowed buildings. Finally, with the mendicants, it took on the form imposed by the development of popular urban preaching, with, for example, the double churches of the Dominicans, a space for religious doubled with a space for preaching. It was on the interpenetration of this Church with the society of its time, whose spaces of celebration bore multiple stigmata, that the multi-faceted assaults of modernity in the time of the reforms would come to bear.

In his *Quinto libro d'architettura*, sixteenth-century architectural theorist Sebastiano Serlio developed a rare break with the basilica and a return to the ancient figure of the temple.[12] This theorist, who was close to Christian Platonic circles, even considered that the basilica was merely a degraded form, a kind of degeneration of the temple, which he saw as a circular edifice centered on the altar. These considerations had little posterity, at least before the utopias of deist-inspired eighteenth-century architects Boullée and Ledoux in France, but they testify to the depth of the upheaval that followed, in certain circles, the rediscovery of pagan Antiquity.

While abandoning the term "church" for "temple" in the French-speaking world to distinguish itself from the dominant Catholicism, the Protestant Reformation remained fundamentally faithful to the heritage of basilicas, which it associated with a vigorous theology of the assembly and a reunion with that of the common priesthood. After some hesitation, the Catholic reform rehabilitated the basilica by ridding it of its many medieval fragmentations. First and foremost it removed the rood screen, to make it a unified space, oriented by the tabernacle altar, an ingenious invention that combines the sign of sacrifice and that of presence, two dimensions highly valued by Tridentine theology in controversy with the reformers.

This space is now clearly separated from the profane space, from the outside, by a screen facade, which becomes the cipher of a change in the conception of the relationship between a sacred universe and a henceforth profane universe over which the Roman Church no longer has a monopoly in the management of its sacrality. Above all, this "Tridentine" space, which is entirely eschatological, is structured by the only distinction that holds sway in a Church that now sees itself as a perfect society, between a space reserved for clerics, the sanctuary, and a

---

[12] Sebastiano Serlio, *Il quinto libro d'archittetura* (Venetia: a presso Giovanni Battista e Marchio Sessa Fratelli, 1559).

space reserved for the laity, the nave. These two spaces, the first of which, in majesty, is visible to all but accessible only to those authorized to approach, touch, and, of course, consecrate the Eucharistic body of Christ, are now separated by a low barrier, the baluster, which is much less porous than medieval rood screens were, despite their monumentality. The baluster, also known as the communion table, materializes the point of contact between the ecclesial body and the Eucharistic body of Christ, the latter being entirely in the hands of the priests, who master its manufacture and use.

In fact, it was at this time that "Domus Dei" appeared on the pediment of some Catholic churches, without specifying the sacred or Eucharistic conception of the formula. Despite the many revivals of the following centuries (neo-classicism, neo-Gothic, neo-Romanesque, and other Roman–Byzantine or Roman–Andalusian speculations, etc.), the Tridentine formula is characterized by its unfailing robustness and plasticity. In fact, these multiple styles clothed a model of spatial organization whose robustness testified to the solidity, even rigidity, of an ecclesiology and liturgy now firmly established on their Tridentine foundations.

Surprisingly, the Council of Trent, with its dual doctrinal and reformist aims, produced neither a treatise on ecclesiology nor indeed a treatise on liturgy. It would be the task of the biblical, liturgical, and ecumenical movements of the nineteenth and twentieth centuries to lay, often in reaction, the theoretical foundations for a profound *aggiornamento* in these matters, an *aggiornamento* from which liturgical spaces would not emerge unscathed this time, not so much in their somewhat early acceptance of the most contemporary trends in the art of their time but rather in their structures. The emblematic experience of Rothenfels, which has the force of a manifesto, is a case in point. Evolutions would be slow and never linear.

In the Catholic world, the Second Vatican Council led to profound changes in the space for celebration, even though it had not legislated in this direction, any more than had Trent before it. In most cases, the demand for active participation has meant that the altar and nave have been brought closer together and turned around to celebrate versus populum. This being the case, little has changed in terms of the form of the assembly, not only in buildings inherited from the medieval and Tridentine periods but more surprisingly in many of those built after the liturgical reform. There have certainly been a few inspired evolutions of the enveloping plan and, more rarely, a few attempts to more profoundly modify the articulation between nave and sanctuary, such as the various versions of the *Kommunioraum*, but it has to be said that after more than a century of the Liturgical Movement and half a century of liturgical reform, the face-to-face model, inspired by the university auditorium or the theater, and sometimes radicalized by the influence of the television model, where the person or persons on the podium are more like presenters than ministers, remains the structuring element in most spaces, including the most recent.

SIGN OF CHRIST'S PRESENCE

"For the accomplishment of such a great work, Christ is always present with his Church, especially in liturgical actions."[13] Number 7 of Vatican II's Constitution on the Sacred Liturgy lists seven ways in which Christ is present in liturgical action. The category of presence that is so important in Catholic theology but sometimes overwhelmed by its Eucharistic form, the Real Presence, is successively considered in the sacrifice; in the person of the minister, "especially under the Eucharistic species";[14] in the celebration of the sacraments; in the act of proclaiming the Word; and in the communal singing of the psalms.

This text is not directly concerned with liturgical space, a question that the Council did not address for its own sake. However, it is probably the most important place to consider both what may have followed the liturgical reform in celebration spaces and what might be aimed for when one imagines spaces according to Vatican II. The text draws on a theology of the actualization of the mysteries through and in the liturgy and affirms that the liturgy continues the work of salvation inaugurated by God in the Old Testament and brought about in Christ in his Paschal Mystery.

Architecturally, we can associate each of the modes of presence listed by SC 7 with a place or sign in the space of celebration: the altar for the sacrifice; the chair for the person of the minister; the tabernacle for the presence that the council does not describe as real, but which it does qualify with the expression "especially"; and the ambo for the Word. As far as the sacraments are concerned, there remains what can be interpreted as a lack of a fixed place for baptism, which is still very common in Catholic circles, as well as a place for reconciliation, as the confessional has generally not found a post-conciliar successor. The same could be said of the Liturgy of the Hours, which, despite having

---

[13] See *Sacrosanctum Concilium*, 7.
[14] Ibid., 7.

been defined by the council as the prayer of the whole Church, has not found its place in most of the buildings designed or constructed after Vatican II.

Although we must be cautious not to hypostasize too quickly each mode of Christ's presence in the liturgy, the parallelism between SC 7 and the signs of Christ's presence in liturgical action reveals certain difficulties in the architectural reception of the liturgical movement and reform, which is far from complete. The failure to take into account the place of baptism and the possibility of celebrating the Liturgy of the Hours in most post-conciliar creations shows the extent to which most church designs remain almost exclusively Eucharistic. Moreover, within the liturgy of the Mass, even if they are often reduced to satellite desks of the altar, the ambos generalized by the reform testify to a certain acceptance of the revaluation of the Word and the proper density of the Liturgy of the Word brought about by the council.

Clearly, we are a long way from the monumental ambos of the first millennium, and even from the Middle Ages in Italy: A better articulation of the ambo with both the altar and the congregation, which would probably require an exit from the sanctuary space and a form of autonomization of the ambo, is an encompassing task that remains before us. The Order of Christian Initiation of Adults (OCIA) and, more broadly, the rediscovery of the catechumenate of adults in the various Christian churches should help us to think of spaces that are in movement, anchored on signs, and reflections of a Christian life with its source in baptism, as nourished by the Word and whose form and horizon are Eucharistic. The establishment of such an axis, stretched between its baptismal source and its Eucharistic horizon, with a central ambo, should make it possible, even in our very elongated Western basilica buildings, to move away from a strictly theatrical face-to-face approach, to restore movement to our liturgies, and, above all, to set the place of the assembly of the faithful between the two major places of the *sacramentum* that makes the Christian, that is, the baptistery and the altar. It should thus be symbolically extricated from the status of a parterre of foreign and mute spectators of what is happening in front, on stage.

In fact, these limits to the reception-in-space of some of the major intuitions of the Liturgical Movement and Reform point, in a hollow way, to a "great forgotten," including in number 7 of *Sacrosanctum Concilium*. In this paragraph, the minister is a sign of Christ's presence, but not the assembly itself. The text does not even mention the assembly, except through the Pauline image of the Bride in its conclusion. The design of liturgical spaces according to Vatican II should be considered from the assembly,[15] whereas all too often it is reduced to the installation of an altar, an ambo, and a presider's seat on a central podium. Except perhaps in the case of spaces created for monastic communities and their guests, its dynamics is considered as an invariant that cannot be touched except to ensure a minimum of visibility of what is happening at the altar and ambo, on the stage.

So, perhaps it is the lack of a genuine theology of the assembly that reveals the difficulties in receiving the Liturgical Movement in terms of celebration space. It is not enough to repeat after Congar that "*ekklesia* is the integral subject of liturgical action"[16] to take into account in all its theological depth what is meant by active participation, which is merely the liturgical version of the exercise of the faithful's baptismal priesthood. As far back as the thirteenth century, Thomas Aquinas used the notion of *character* to account for the non-repeatability of certain sacraments of the *septenarium*. In a cultic context, the priestly characters enabled the expression of the baptismal, as it was necessary for some to be ordained so that all could render to God the new worship due to Him. As defined in *Sacrosanctum Concilium*, active participation is not reduced to its functional dimension of "doing something" but is thought of through the human part, irreducibly articulated between the assembly and the presidency, of a liturgy envisaged by the council, following the Liturgical Movement, as a theandric action.[17]

Questions about the shape of the assembly, its relation with other liturgical spaces – altar, baptistery, and ambo in the first instance – and its mobility have only been raised marginally, notably in a few spaces that are variants of the *Kommunioraum* or plural spaces where assembly and ministers wander from the space of the Word to the Eucharistic space. Yet it is only by taking the assembly seriously that one can epiphanize the liturgy as the true action of *Christus totus*, head and body finally rearticulated.

The concept of presence, mobilized by the council for the reasons outlined above in the Catholic tradition, even if it suffers from a lack of dynamic character, remains relevant for thinking about a liturgical

---

[15] Julien Sauve, "Partir de l'assemblée: L'assemblée liturgique selon Vatican II et sa réception selon Jean-Marie Duthilleul," *La Maison-Dieu* 301 (2020): 151–73.

[16] Yves Congar, "The Ecclesia or Christian Community as a Whole Celebrates the Liturgy," in *At the Heart of Christian Worship: Liturgical Essays of Yves Congar*, trans. and ed. Paul Philibert (Collegeville, MN: Liturgical Press, 2010), 15–67. This text originally appeared in French in 1966.

[17] *Sacrosanctum Concilium*, 48.

space, but it cannot do without an integrated, systemic approach to the various places that are signs of Christ's presence, a system precisely envisaged for and based on the assembly, both sign and reality of the presence of Christ's ecclesial body. In architecture as in theology, the non-resorption of the medieval divide between the ecclesial and sacramental dimensions of understanding the body of Christ still weighs heavily on our representations and thus ultimately dictates architectural choices that relegate consideration of active participation to the implementation of liturgical technical devices.

A HABITABLE PART OF THE COSMOS

The ecological crisis raises anew the traditional question of the cosmic dimension of Christian liturgy. In his letter on liturgical formation, *Desiderio desideravi*, Pope Francis used Irenaean accents to consider the sacramental destiny of the great signs of the Christian liturgy: water, light, oil, bread, and wine, each considered by the Creator on the horizon of their sacramental fulfillment. This reunion with a liturgical approach to creation is bound to have implications for the design of our celebration spaces.

Based on the thought of John Scotus Eriugena, theologian Arnaud Montoux in *Réordonner le cosmos* shows how the Cluniacs summoned the whole of creation, including some deformed or even monstrous aspects, in their buildings, to reveal its ordered, or "reordered," aspect through a redemption that they considered to be wide ranging, never reduced to human beings alone.[18] The church was like the image or anticipated realization of what creation was called to, groaning in pains of a birth that is still going on. Since modernity, it has been difficult for us to envisage, as the ancients did, what is now described as nature as a cosmos, an ordered universe. Blaise Pascal, a modern, captured better than anyone the distress of the human condition lost between two infinities:

> Then, returning to himself, let man consider his own being compared with all that is; let him regard himself as wandering in this remote province of nature; and from the little dungeon in which he finds himself lodged, I mean the universe, let him learn

---

[18] Armand Montoux, *Réordonner le cosmos: Itinéraires érigéniens à Cluny* (Paris: Cerf, 2016).

to set a true value on the earth, on its kingdoms, its cities, and on himself. What is a man in the infinite?[19]

Four centuries later, human beings' distress and even anguish is no longer measured solely by their solitude in a space, but by the prospect of a near future in which the universe is likely to become uninhabitable. The break with the conceptions of the ancients is now radical: Disorder and chaos have a dual spatial and temporal dimension. It is in such a world that the Church celebrates liturgy today. One can no longer adopt the meditations of Maximus the Confessor in his *Mystagogy*, in which the church building, conceived by him as a Chalcedonian association between a nave and a sanctuary, was the cipher of man and the world as a whole. It is difficult for us to make, as Teilhard de Chardin did at the beginning of the twentieth century, a Christological reading of the universe and its history.[20] And yet we still read Scripture in our liturgies, which Maximus envisaged as the scriptural body of Christ that the Church and the liturgy give to the baptized as the key to understanding the cosmos and its history. The hypothesis I am proposing here is a modest one: Couldn't the Church's liturgy, and subsequently its space of celebration, offer some resources for making the universe and its history, into which we are often thrown and swept as if in spite of ourselves, perhaps not intelligible but simply habitable?

Using Norberg-Schulz's concept of the genius of place, Frédéric Debuyst shows how the Christian Church is situated in a place.[21] Indeed, the Christian Church is not "out of place": In the logic of the incarnation, the liturgy is celebrated in a given time and place, and it is in this time and place and nowhere else that one makes a double remembrance of a past event and its eschatological fulfillment. As far back as the twelfth century, Abbé Suger, though steeped in a Christian Neoplatonism inherited from Pseudo-Denys, marveled at the fact that oak trees from the forests of what was not yet the Ile de France, stones from the nearby Pontoise quarries, and even gems from across the seas found their place in the great work he was overseeing.[22] But Suger's

---

[19] Blaise Pascal, *The Thoughts of Blaise Pascal*, trans. C. Kegan Paul (London: George Bell & Sons, 1901), 19–20.
[20] Pierre Teilhard de Chardin, "The Mass on the World," in Pierre Teilhard de Chardin, *The Heart of the Matter*, trans. by René Hague (San Diego, New York, London: Harcourt et al.), 119–34.
[21] Frédéric Debuyst, *Le génie chrétien du lieu* (Paris: Cerf, 1997).
[22] Suger, *Ecrits sur la consécration de Saint-Denis*, in Suger (abbé), *Œuvres I*, Les Belles Lettres, 17–19.

abbey church, while taking on the elements of creation to give divine thanks to divine propitiation, was nonetheless a space apart, a kind of heaven on earth.

Debuyst's vision of the relationship between church and place, including its cosmic dimension, is quite different. His concern for the church's integration into a place often translates into a fairly wide opening of the celebration spaces to the outside world, to nature in the modern sense of the term, a portion of nature that is usually preserved or even reconstituted. The Cistercian monastery of Pra'd Mill in Piedmont is just one example, while the abbey church of Boscodon on the French side of the Alps is another.

The celebration space in the parish church of Saint François de Molitor, in the heart of Paris, opens out onto a garden that is explicitly envisaged as an image of a paradise – whether a lost paradise or an anticipation of the garden city of the Apocalypse remains to be seen. Still in an urban setting, the church of Saint Paul de la Plaine, north of Paris, attempts to open up almost immediately to the city, its buildings and its activities, with a meager garden providing a transition deliberately envisaged more as a connection than a distance. In this type of building, it is both creation that invites itself into the liturgy and the liturgy that expands to the dimensions of a nature that is fairly framed, carefully chosen, or even reconstructed. This interaction between nature and church is not the same as that mediated by Scripture, with which Saint Denis's stained-glass windows are studded, in images and text. Directly inherited from Dionysian conceptions, medieval stained-glass windows perform a kind of meta-function between inside and outside, the inside appearing as the transfiguration by light, a divine figure of the materiality of an outside to which they confer a Christian intelligibility through the mediation of Scripture.

This contemporary reconfiguration of the building's relationship with its environment can also be thought of in terms of hospitality. In today's multicultural, even post-Christian societies, the design of Christian churches, whether inherited from the past or new, can no longer avoid taking into account what the empty church has to say outside the celebrations for which it was built and from which it was too exclusively conceived.

The case of Notre-Dame de Paris is obviously exceptional but in a way paradigmatic: With 12 million visitors before the fire, and probably even more after its reopening, how is it possible to integrate a design entirely dedicated to the celebration of the liturgy, which continues to be its raison d'être, with the multiple and often plural motivations of the visitors who stroll through the cathedral? These two approaches cannot be mutually exclusive, if only because the intelligibility of the building depends on the intelligibility of what it was designed for: liturgy. The teams in charge of this issue in the diocese of Paris are attempting to resolve the problem by resorting to the theological concept of initiation:[23] The aim is to accompany visitors along multiple, often sensitive paths, to the threshold of the Mystery, the same one that the liturgy actualizes at the heart of the cathedral. It is not a question of being hospitable to an idealized cosmos, free of the scars of its degradation, or even of the perpetrators of those scars, but of a broad, inclusive hospitality, open to the motley crowd that, for better or for worse, inhabits it in these times of the Anthropocene, which are also the times of globalization.

This hospitality must be broadly considered in its relationship to time and not just to space and those who inhabit it. The Christological principle, mediated by Scripture, prevented Maximus in his *Mystagogy* from thinking of the church not so much as a stranger to the sensible world at the heart of which it is planted and of which it is a part but as an openness to a kind of ideal back-world. In its Eucharistic dimension, the church refers both to the intimacy of the cenacle and the sacrifice of Calvary, the founding event, and to their heavenly fulfillment. This twofold anamnetic dimension is essential if we are to avoid understanding the eschatological dimension, essential to the design of our churches, as the creation of spaces apart, places made for a liturgy that is ultimately seen as an escape from human history or an anticipation of a fantasized hereafter.

In the church of Saint Sulpice in Paris, its inspirer, Jean-Jacques Olier, a great pastor and reader of the recently republished Pseudo-Denys, took care to include an impressive radiating dove at the top of the dome that joins the sanctuary and the nave. In his *Explication de la messe*, he explains: If the liturgy is indeed the manifestation of the eternal sacrifice accomplished by Christ before the Father – we are in a post-Tridentine world marked by the spirituality of Bérulle – the Spirit is the one who associates the very earthly body of Christ, that of the faithful in the nave, with a work whose shepherd never forgets that it is a work of *Christus totus* celebrated with and above all for his body, the sacraments being *sacramenta propter homines* according to the best scholastic tradition.

---

[23] Gilles Drouin, "Initier au mystère de et par la cathédrale," *Transversalités* 154 (2020): 49–64.

The Church's architectural tradition has multiplied the means of mediating the eschatological dimension of the celebration, in particular the Eucharist: The apse of Roman basilicas, then Romanesque, was the setting for the deployment of immense Pantocrators, and even, as at Sant'Apollinare in Classe, for the tearing open of a first heaven, paradisiacal, which opens onto the true heaven, in the midst of which a cross of glory blazes with a thousand gems – a cross of glory that is found in many contemporary creations as a sign of Easter eschatology. The dome played a similar role in the Byzantine tradition. In the Gothic world, the entire edifice opens up, elevating and condensing in a double diastole–systole movement a completely transfigured cosmos.

The Baroque tradition multiplied its devices, often theatrical, made up of altarpieces, trompe l'œils, and skillfully orchestrated escapes, to construct spaces that were sometimes entirely eschatological, in rupture with the profane world, the screen façade being the cipher of the passage from a world, that of the earth over which the Church was progressively losing its control, to that of a community henceforth envisaged as a perfect society. The buildings inherited from the Liturgical Movement, despite a greater sobriety of means, never abandoned this manifestation of a beyond in the sacramental economy. Jean Cosse even theorized about it with the notion of a space of glory.[24] Here one finds the necessary, structuring tension of Christian liturgical spaces between the Augustinian primacy of the assembly and the Chrysostomian openness to a beyond itself – to use François Cassingena-Trévedy's categories.

For the Christian liturgy and its celebration spaces, a habitable cosmos is not a space sheltered from the shocks of a battered, damaged world, but rather one that proposes spaces open simultaneously to this world and to the ultimate Kingdom. In this way, our liturgical spaces can contribute to making the world habitable, with the efficacy of sacramental realities. The concrete, architectural ways toward such a possible habitability are still largely to be imagined.

HOSPITABLE AND SYMBOLIC SPACES

The great basilicas of the Mediterranean tradition had three or five naves. As a theologian, I have sketched out a three-vessel plan for the contemporary church building. Like the ancient basilicas, each of the

---

[24] Jean Cosse, "Le créneau étroit d'une architecture pour notre temps," *Bulletins de l'Académie Royale de Belgique* 13.1–6 (2002): 53–84.

three naves has a different status. There are aisles and a nave. The first vessel, the church as epiphany of the Church, and the second, the church as sign of Christ's presence, are in fact, direct heirs to the tradition of the Liturgical Movement and that too at a time when a more synodal face of the Church is being sought, at least in Catholicism. These two vessels, the collaterals of our edifice, are in a state of permanent construction, lacking a sufficiently elaborate theology of the assembly, or a still very partial consideration of the rediscovery of Christian initiation or sacramentality in our celebration spaces. But the central vessel, the *cardo*, which dominates the whole plan, probably corresponds to what we tried to sketch out in section three of this chapter: A church that is hospitable both to the cosmos and to its inhabitants.

This idea of hospitality is probably a way of rearticulating the two tensions in the design of our Christian buildings, right down to a proper integration of their cosmic and eschatological dimensions: places of gathering and places of openness beyond time and space. Because it is open and hospitable to God made human, who takes the initiative of the encounter, the Christian church can and must be hospitable to the whole of creation, foremost among which is the human community, and to its history, which has once again become open and thinkable.

Another poet warns us that the house of prayer can be the place where one can relearn to read, and thus to inhabit, a Nature that is once again legible and thus livable:

> In Nature's temple, living columns rise,
> Which oftentimes give tongue to words subdued,
> And Man traverses this symbolic wood,
> Which looks at him with half familiar eyes.[25]

For Further Reading

Bouyer, Louis, *Architecture et liturgie* (Paris: Cerf, 2009).
Daelemans, Bert, *Spiritus Loci: A Theological Method for Contemporary Church Architecture* (Leiden: Brill, 2015).
Debuyst, Frédéric, *Le génie chrétien du lieu* (Paris: Cerf, 1997).
Drouin, Gilles (ed.), *L'espace liturgique, un espace d'initiation* (Paris: Cerf, 2019).

---

[25] Charles Baudelaire, "Echoes," in *The Flowers of Evil*, trans. Cyril Scott (London: Elkin Mathews, 1909).

Iogna-Prat, Dominique, *Cité de Dieu, cité des hommes: L'Eglise, l'architecture et la société* (Paris: Presses Universitaires de France, 2016).

Kieckhefer, Richard, *Theology in Stone: Church Architecture from Byzantium to Berkeley* (Oxford: Oxford University Press, 2004).

Seasoltz, R. Kevin, *A Sense of the Sacred: Theological Foundations of Christian Architecture and Art* (New York: Continuum, 2007).

13 Liturgy, Icons, and Images
NATALIE CARNES

If the Christian life is one of both ascent and descent, of drawing near God and the world, images and icons dramatize that movement together with one perpendicular to it, a coming in and going out. Images are, after all, ecclesial objects that draw from patterns, media, and sources outside the church. Once inside, they focus the faithful's attention on worship while also extending the liturgy beyond the walls of the church through processions, celebrations, and connections to private homes or other sites. In these movements out and in, images display the importance of materiality for Christian life while also pointing to the eventual transfiguration of such materiality, issuing the viewer an invitation into divine things and evoking the ascending and descending of Christ and the faithful. This chapter will elucidate these activities, transfers, and migrations by focusing on one image-adjacent object and four images, as it explores their complex histories and entanglements with a life of liturgy and worship. Images, it argues, are an important site of liturgy's dynamic relation with God and world.

THE RELIQUARY BOX

Before Christians venerated images, they venerated relics.[1] In important respects, the latter even funded the former. When in the second century the people of Smyrna celebrated the anniversary of Polycarp's martyrdom with bones they described as "more dear than precious stones,"[2] it was but a short step toward rendering that dearness visually

---

[1] The earliest evidence of image veneration dates to the fourth century, while veneration with relics is traceable to the second. Cynthia Hahn, *Strange Beauty: Issues in the Making and Meaning of Reliquaries, 400–circa 1204* (University Park, PA: Penn State University Press, 2013), 9.
[2] Ibid., 9. Quoting Eusebius, *Historia Ecclesiastica* 4.15.

available through reliquaries adorned with actual precious stones as well as images narrating and framing the value of the relics inside. In the fourth century, Gregory of Nyssa explicitly connects images with relics in a homily at the martyrion (a non-portable reliquary) of the Blessed Theodore: "The pictures located on the walls are eloquent by their silence and offer significant testimony ... These spectacles strike the senses and delight the eye by drawing us near to [the martyr's] tomb which we believe to be both a sanctification and blessing."[3] He goes on to describe the vividness of holding a relic, his rhetoric connecting the presentation of the martyr via the images of the martyrion and the presentation of that martyr in the relics it contains. As Gregory suggests, the reliquary box functions as an important and complex visual site in Christian liturgy: revealing while also concealing its objects as it participates in the horizontal movement of the liturgy – the going out and the coming in – by connecting personal and corporate worship as well as a holy place and martyr's life with church and home.

One of the earliest reliquaries we have today is a sixth- or seventh-century pilgrimage box found in the Vatican's *Sancta Sanctorum*. Filled with souvenirs from the Holy Land, it exemplifies the connections of relics and images.[4] On the exterior lid is a cross. On the interior are five scenes from the life of Christ, depicted to connect Jesus's earthly ministry to the pilgrim's memories of her own time in the Holy Land. The scene of the tomb, for example, includes the grille and dome of the church of the Holy Sepulcher. The reliquary box thus shows the value of its unassuming contents (stone, wood, cloth, earth), interpreting the relics as connected with the Holy Land and the body of Christ, which comes anew to the one holding the reliquary box. The images, as Charles Barber writes, "mark a continuation in the claims to material truth made by the relics themselves" and so display the way "visual representation can present the things it shows in a manner akin to the relics themselves."[5]

The visual presentation comes through the shape and materials of the reliquary as well as the pictures painted on it. The beautiful, jeweled staff raised in a liturgy; the colored bust of a saint; the miniature of a

---

[3] Gregory of Nyssa, "In Praise of the Blessed Theodore, the Great Martyr," trans. Richard (Casimir) McCambley. Available on *Lectio Divina* at bit.ly/3RNgWKw. Accessed March 17, 2022.

[4] Hahn and Barber both describe this particular reliquary. Charles Barber, *Figure and Likeness: On the Limits of Representation in Byzantine Iconoclasm* (Princeton, NJ: Princeton University Press, 2003), 15–16. Hahn, *Strange Beauty*, 19.

[5] Barber, *Figure and Likeness*, 17.

church; the *chasse* adorned with image and jewel – all of these different forms of reliquaries give relics a visual presence that authenticates their value.[6] Patricia Cox Miller writes of the importance of the imagination in transforming the relic from dust and bone to treasure of heaven.[7] Aesthetics, as Cynthia Hahn expands on in her work, is part of how a relic means, so that the "strange beauty" of the reliquary is part of "creating or constructing the saint and his or her spiritual meaning for (and by) the viewer."[8] Even when the transparent reliquary material of rock crystal rose to prominence after the year 1000 CE, reliquaries still visually mediated the significance of the relic. The tiny splinters of the cross, for example, are only visible *as* the cross when magnified and interpreted through the art of the reliquary holding them.

But reliquaries conceal as much as they reveal, particularly the ones created before transparent material made holding and revealing simultaneously possible. To return to the example of the ancient pilgrimage box: When the lid is down, what does the bearer of the reliquary see? It is only a box, with a cross on the front. The drama of revelation comes only with opening. And this concealment, too, is significant; the aesthetics of hiddenness was theologically interpreted in antiquity and the Middle Ages. Early relics were concealed in altars, connecting them to the ancient Jewish practice of keeping relics in the ark of the covenant and to another ancient practice of hiding God's word and the saints in one's heart.[9] The concealment in these ways speaks to treasure in heaven in a way different from and complementary to precious stones and magnificent beauty.

The value of the relics visually proclaimed by the reliquary is also affirmed in liturgical processions and other ecclesial practices of veneration. Hahn describes reliquaries as almost restless: They purportedly spoke to and elicited speech from the faithful; they were lifted up in ceremonies and "gestured with, carried in processions, opened, and closed."[10] In some cases, they leave the church to

---

[6] A sampling of this great variety of reliquaries can be found in Hahn's *Strange Beauty* and Martina Bagnoli's edited volume *Treasures of Heaven: Saints, Relics and Devotion in Medieval Europe* (Baltimore, MD: Walters Art Museum, 2010).

[7] Patricia Cox Miller, "'The Little Blue Flower is Red': Relics and the Poetizing of the Body," *Journal of Early Christian Studies* 8 (1997): 213–36.

[8] Hahn, *Strange Beauty*, 311.

[9] Both Paulinus of Nola (354–431) and Durandus of Mende (1230–1296) make statements drawing such connections as Hahn points out. Cynthia Hahn, "What Do Reliquaries Do for Relics?" *Numen* 57 (2010): 284–316, at 308.

[10] Hahn, *Strange Beauty*, 312.

process through a city or to a beach.[11] In this way, the relic, which comes into the church to authenticate and confirm the sacrality of the church, still today sometimes embedded in its very altar, which becomes a reliquary, can also create sacred places of worship outside the walls of the church, literally going out and coming in the church doors – even as the very existence of the relic acknowledges sacred sites outside the walls of the church. Sacredness is found in Christ, in the land Christ inhabited, and in the bodies of the ones conformed to Christ. And as the motions and processions of reliquaries affirm the sacredness of the relics of the church, they also speak obliquely to the value of privately held relics, suggesting the value of the reliquaries in homes of the faithful and so connecting the holiness the relic confers on the church to a holiness implicitly conferred on the home as well. In their dynamics of revelation and concealment, reliquaries are multifaceted visual objects both akin to images and funding image veneration, and in their multiple goings out and comings in, relics and reliquaries also suggest webs of sacredness spanning the world, in a manner, as we will see, also resonant with images and image veneration.

VIRGIN OF THE SIGN

In one ancient image of Mother and Child, Mary's arms are raised, palms up in prayer, as she stares out at the viewer. She wears her traditional red and blue, her hair veiled, head haloed. Sometimes cherubim hover just above her open palms. Always in the center is the Child, often encircled by a mandorla that looks like a medallion on Mary's chest. He is in her womb, invisible to the world, and yet revealed to the viewer through this mandorla that gives us a glimpse of the Child who is coming.

The icon is the *Virgin of the Sign*, an ancient and beloved image with roots that predate Christianity. It is an adaptation of the *Orant*, the praying woman of Greco-Roman art, and it enters Christian symbology as funerary art personifying the soul of the dead, suggesting in the figure's pose the cross of Christ and the hope of heaven. By the fourth century, the image is increasingly associated with Mary, and it is then

---

[11] Hahn describes one in which two figural Marys in a boat are processed together with an arm reliquary to a beach, where the boat is held above the water and the arm used by a bishop to bless the gathered crowd. Ibid., 145.

that the *Virgin of the Sign* pattern develops.[12] Mary in this image is the sign because of Isaiah 7:14, the prophecy of the virgin bearing a child as a sign of the Lord, and because the icon is associated with a miraculous military victory of Novgorod.[13] Over the years, this icon of Christ within the body of Mary has also been interpreted as a depiction of the Church in whom Christ is hidden and yet present.

In many ways the *Virgin of the Sign* anticipates and embodies the tensions of the Byzantine image controversy that erupts in the eighth and ninth centuries. It is structured by the dynamics of manifestation and hiddenness, of divine life revealed in flesh and yet arriving as a sign of an invisible God. Rowan Williams describes the Church depicted in the icon as "suspicious of idolatry" and "able to stay with the mysteriousness of Christ's presence rather than creating an accessible but false picture to hang on to."[14] In this way it internalizes the suspicion of the *iconomachs* (image-fighters), who were also preoccupied with idolatry and false images, worrying as they did that *iconodules* (those who venerated images) gave to images the adoration due God alone and that images of Christ were necessarily dangerous and false, expressions, as they insisted, of the heresies of Arianism, Nestorianism, or monophysitism.[15] The image expresses a version of this anxiety, and yet, by doing so as an image, it ultimately affirms the value of images in the face of the most biting Christian critique.

The theology expressed in the *Virgin of the Sign* did not immediately prevail. The *iconomachs* gained ascendancy through Leo III's 726 decree against images, and their theology was codified in the Council of 754 that anathematized images under Constantine V – until the iconodules in turn anathematized that council and vindicated images in the Second Council of Nicaea in 787, now also known as the Seventh Ecumenical Council.[16] The arguments of John of Damascus were important for the iconodules' victory. The Damascene points to

---

[12] Robin Jensen, *Understanding Early Christian Art* (London: Routledge, 2000), 36. Leonid Ouspensky and Vladimir Lossky, *The Meaning of Icons* (Crestwood, NY: St Vladimir's Seminary Press, 1999), 77.

[13] Jensen, *Understanding Early Christian Art*, 35–6.

[14] Rowan Williams, *Ponder These Things: Praying with Icons of the Virgin* (Franklin, WI: Sheed & Ward, 2002), 55.

[15] Natalie Carnes, *Image and Presence: A Christological Reflection on Iconoclasm and Iconophilia* (Stanford, CA: Stanford University Press, 2017), 59–62. Original documents found in Daniel J. Sahas, *Icon and Logos: Sources in Eighth Century Iconoclasm: An Annotated Translation of the Sixth Session of the Seventh Ecumenical Council* (Nicaea, 787) (Toronto: University of Toronto Press, 1986).

[16] Sahas, "Introduction," in *Icon and Logos*, 30.

continuities between worship with images and various forms of worship with materiality in the Old Testament; distinguishes between the worship due only to God (*latreia*) and the veneration given to images (*proskynesis*); and points to the Incarnation, in which God became visible in Christ. For this latter argument, the Damascene answered the charges of various Christological heresies and turned them into counteraccusations, arguing that while God, the Second Person of the Trinity, became visible in the human nature of Christ, the divine nature as such remains invisible.[17]

Iconoclasm broke out again in the ninth century, culminating in the Council of 813 (later repudiated) that condemned Nicaea II and renewed the ban on icons, but the *iconomachs'* victory was short. The Triumph of Orthodoxy is celebrated in memory of 843, when icons were vindicated and permanently incorporated into the worship life of the Church – in the East, at least. Key to this victory for the *iconodules* was the theology of Theodore of Stoudios, who extended the Damascene's theology through a sophisticated argument for how the icon presents the hypostasis of its subject and by underscoring that the worship given to the image passes through to the prototype.[18] Patriarch Nikephoros develops this theology through an emphasis on *kenosis*, in which he describes the way divine figures are inscribed but not circumscribed in the icon, the way they are both absent and present to the image, since they are not consubstantial with but only formally resemble what they present.[19]

Since the Triumph of Orthodoxy, the iconographic tradition has flourished in worship traditions in the Orthodox Church and been central to much of their worship life and theology. Patterns have proliferated for these icons, which have been incorporated into processions and prayed with in corporate and private worship. The low-chancel barrier between the nave and the sanctuary eventually expanded into the great *iconostasis*, the wall of images that invites the contemplation

---

[17] John of Damascus, *Three Treatises on Divine Images*, trans. Andrew Louth (Crestwood, NY: St Vladimir's Seminary Press, 2003). Robin Cormack, "Art and Iconoclasm," in *Oxford Handbook of Byzantine Studies*, ed. Robin Cormack, John F. Haldon, and Elizabeth Jeffreys (Oxford: Oxford University Press, 2008), 750–57.

[18] Theodore the Studite, *On the Holy Icons*, trans. Catharine P. Roth (Crestwood, NY: St Vladimir's Seminary Press, 1981). Dirk Krausmüller, "Christ and His Representation, One or Two? The Image Theologies of Theodore of Stoudios, Leo of Chalcedon and Eustratius of Nicaea," *Scrinium: Journal of Patrology and Critical Hagiography* 17 (2021): 356–71.

[19] Christoph Schönborn, *God's Human Face: The Christ-Icon*, trans. Lothar Krauth (San Francisco: Ignatius Press, 1994), 209–11.

and prayers of the gathered faithful.[20] By the twelfth century, images in the Orthodox Church were not just used in the liturgy; they reflected it, as in images of bishops carrying the scrolls with the Divine Liturgy on them and hymnographers gesturing as if to conduct a choir. Moreover, the liturgy at that time began to take cues from the images, as in portraits of female saints signaling the space for women in the church and those of hymnographers marking off the position of the choir.[21]

The tradition of flat perspective, egg tempura icons that flourished in the East was much less prominent in the West, which did not inherit the full theology of images developed in the East.[22] In the 790s, Charlemagne commissioned the *Libri Carolini*, a set of four books that refutes the Council of 787 and indicates he had received a poor translation of the Council's texts. The *Libri Carolini* becomes well-known when John Calvin references it in the Reformation as an argument against venerating images.[23] In the meantime, the Roman Catholic Church developed strong image traditions of altar paintings, statuary, and illuminated manuscripts. It was not until the twentieth century that the tradition of icons became more prominent in the Roman Catholic Church, as Orthodox theologians in exile from Russia begin writing about their traditions and theologies for Western theologians. Today there are schools of iconography in the United States and elsewhere, and images have become sites of religio-cultural exchange across churches and nationalities. Even some Protestant churches have incorporated the replica of Orthodox icons on church bulletins, worship projectors, and even sanctuary décor.

These cultural exchanges and migrations have led to an icon written by Protestant artist Mark Doox. It is a new pattern of the *Virgin of the Sign* that gained popularity through a Facebook post by Catholic priest Father James Martin in 2016 and is called *Our Lady of Ferguson and All Those Killed by Gun Violence*. Mary's hands are up in the orans position, which echoes the hands-up-don't-shoot position of the child in her womb. Like all *Sign* icons, the child is Christ, though he is shown only in silhouette, except for his sacred heart, which beats red and is

---

[20] Maria Vassilaki, "Icons," in *Oxford Handbook of Byzantine Studies*, ed. Robin Cormack, John F. Haldon, and Elizabeth Jeffreys (Oxford: Oxford University Press, 2008), 762.

[21] Nancy Sevcenko, XI: "Icons in the Liturgy," *Dumbarton Oaks Papers* 45 (1991): 45–57.

[22] Celia Chazelle, "Matter, Spirit, and Image in the *Libri Carolini*," *Recherches Augustiniennes* 20 (1986): 163–86.

[23] See John Calvin, *Institutes of the Christian Religion*, bk I, ch. 11, s. 14.

encircled by gold thorns. The Child is marked by the sight of a gun, which forms a cross on his body. The suffering and the prayers of Mary in *Our Lady of Ferguson* are identified with the mother of Michael Brown, who died at the hands of the police in 2014 in Ferguson, Missouri.

Since the beginnings of Christianity, patterns of migration, travel, and cultural encounter led to the movement and transformation of images and their liturgies. But new digital channels have accelerated and changed these patterns of going out and coming in. Centuries after the *Orant* entered Christian worship life, centuries after the *Virgin of the Sign* pattern developed, a new, very different image has gone out from the liturgy in the life of Catholics, Protestants, and even some of the Nones of the world – even while *Our Lady of Ferguson* has been incorporated into new liturgies of images. As the image moves in and out of the church, it transforms, suggesting new ways of binding humanity to God.

PASSION PLAYS AND LIVING STATIONS OF THE CROSS

"All that walk by way or street ... behold my head, my hand, and my feet."[24] The tortured Christ calls out to the audience in the late medieval York Corpus Christi plays and then invites them to contemplate his pain as the cross is elevated. He asks, in paraphrase: Does any suffering or grief equal my own? As an affective piety centered on the suffering of Christ was elaborated, recognized, and extended in the Middle Ages, no aspect of Christianity was more visually and liturgically represented than Christ's Passion. Churches were filled with crosses, crucifixes, and scenes from Holy Week. The Stations of the Cross found on the walls of Catholic churches today developed its definitive fourteen-image form during this time. But as the example of the York play suggests, the pictures of the Passion did not merely sit, silent and immobile, on church walls, windows, and altars. They also spoke and moved, through the church and into the streets.

The York plays were not the only plays about the Passion of Christ in Europe. One volume on theater describes the Passion of Christ as "probably the most frequently reenacted event of Western theatre and

---

[24] Sarah Beckwith, *Signifying God: Social Relation and Symbolic Act in the York Corpus Christi Plays* (Chicago: University of Chicago Press, 2001), 66. Quoting *The York Plays*, ed. Richard Beadle (London: Edward Arnold, 1982), 231. I modified it into modern English for ease of reading.

performance."²⁵ Throughout the fourteenth through sixteenth centuries, Passion Plays were popular throughout Europe, particularly in German-speaking towns, and most famously in Oberammergau, which began slightly later than some of the others (1634) and was revived in the twentieth century.²⁶ These Passion Plays developed out of the Good Friday gospel reading sung in parts assumed by different people, both generating and expressing an affective piety toward the cross. They were a living image of the Passion that solicited the viewer's emotional engagement and elicited further images related to the Passion.²⁷ But the iterative relationship these plays share with liturgy and other visual images can also spawn stranger fruit, some unexpected, some sinister. Regarding the sinister, it is hard not to see connections between the animosity expressed toward the Jews in the revival of the Oberammergau Passion Play – which Hitler praised in 1934 for portraying "the menace of the Jewry"²⁸ – confirmed and devastatingly repeated in the Holocaust, itself a type of repetition of violent medieval anti-Semitism. This is liturgy's going out and coming in in its most malevolent key.

Another iteration of Passion theater is found, paradoxically, in Protestant iconoclasm. Joseph Leo Koerner describes such theatrical iconoclasm, as in Hildesheim 1543, when a crowd dragged a statue of Christ into a drinking hall and ordered it to drink. "Playing off its nonresponse," Koerner writes, "they began to taunt the effigy with words like those spoken by Christ's tormentors in Passion plays of the time: 'Now how's he supposed to drink? Can't you see? He's been whipped, his blood is squirting out of him and he's holy and impotent, so he just can't do it.'"²⁹ Eamon Duffy titles his book chronicling changes in Reformation England *Stripping of the Altars*, the name referencing a liturgical act of Holy Thursday that also became an act of iconoclasm in the Reformation. Reformers and Protestant communities had different views on images – John Calvin was worried about

---

[25] Kenneth Pickering, *Key Concepts in Drama and Performance* (New York: Palgrave Macmillan, 2005), 38.

[26] There is an origin story for the play, though it has been disputed. James S. Shapiro, *Oberammergau: The Troubling Story of the World's Most Famous Passion Play* (New York: Vintage Books, 2000).

[27] Lynette R. Muir, *The Biblical Drama of Medieval Europe* (Cambridge: Cambridge University Press, 1995).

[28] Sonja E. Spear, "Claiming the Passion: American Fantasies of the Oberammergau Passion Play, 1923–1947," *Church History* 80.4 (December 2011): 832–62.

[29] Joseph Leo Koerner, *The Reformation of the Image* (Chicago: University of Chicago Press, 2004), 132.

the heart as a factory of idols, while Martin Luther did not defend images but expressed more worry about the disorderliness of image-breaking[30] – but in these acts of iconoclasm, Protestants used the scripts of Passion images and liturgies in order to express a commitment to a God who cannot be bound by the created order, human artifice, or human destruction. They appropriated the Passion script of a God uncontained by death despite all human effort, a God who is present to them even under signs of absence, or attempted erasure, to affirm a God whose presence is uncontained by material sites or human artifact and so may be claimed by performances of absence from those site and artifacts.[31]

One reason the Passion Plays initially declined and then died out was because of Protestant opposition. Yet they continue to birth new iterations of Passion images. Not only was the play at Oberammergau revived and not only do most Catholic churches have stations of the cross, but other forms developed or rose in popularity. Inspired by Oberammergau, a Black Catholic church in Chicago began performing a popular living stations of the cross, which assumed an important role in its community.[32] Similar living stations have gone on for decades in Latin American and Latin American-influenced churches in the United States.[33] Some of these are more like living tableaux, some like mimes, and others more like plays. Many Protestant churches began putting on Easter pageants, which similarly tell the story of Christ's suffering, death, and resurrection on or around Easter Sunday. In 2004, Mel Gibson released his movie *The Passion of the Christ*, structured by the fourteen stations of the cross.[34] Though the movie was not part of a church liturgy, it answered to and extended the liturgy in fascinating

---

[30] Carlos M. N. Eire, *War Against the Idols: The Reformation of Worship from Erasmus to Calvin* (Cambridge: Cambridge University Press, 1986), 3, 67.

[31] Carnes, *Image and Presence*. See especially the third chapter.

[32] Matthew J. Cressler, *Authentically Black and Truly Catholic: The Rise of Black Catholicism in the Great Migration* (New York: New York University Press, 2017). See especially the third chapter.

[33] Michelle Wibbelsman describes a particularly fascinating set of competing Mestizo and indigenous Living Stations in Ecuador. Wibbelsman, *Ritual Encounter: Otavalan Modern and Mythic Community* (Urbana, IL: University of Illinois Press, 2009), 142–43. Leonor Calvijo, "Living Stations of the Cross: An Hispanic Faith Tradition," *NC Catholic* (April 28, 2019), https://dioceseofraleigh.org/news/living-stations-cross-hispanic-faith-tradition.

[34] There have been other cinematic versions of the Passion since then, and Mirella Klomp describes such efforts in the Netherlands in her article, "Staging the Resurrection: The Public Theology of Dutch Production and Broadcasting Companies," *International Journal of Public Theology* 9 (2015): 446–64.

ways, as churches organized trips to go view the movie together, developed discussion groups around the movie, and saw the movie as an effort to evangelize an increasingly secular world. The marketing strategy for the movie centered on churches and evangelical pastors. At a time when most Easter pageants take place inside church doors and living stations remain close to church grounds, the movie was a twenty-first century version of the way the York plays took place throughout the streets of the city, demanding all to "behold my hands, my head, and my feet." The movie was not without controversy – including charges of re-iterating the old anti-Semitism[35] – and in this way and others it illustrates the iterative aspect of Passion images and the way liturgical images are part of a dynamic of constantly going out and coming in, transforming and yet also repeating what has come before.

REMBRANDT VAN RIJN'S *SACRIFICE OF ISAAC* (1655)

The scene is a familiar one. The angel has just arrived at Abraham's back, wings still raised from flight. One hand grips the patriarch's right hand, which covers the eyes of his beloved, would-be victim Isaac; the other stays his left, which raises the sword. It is as if the angel is embracing Abraham, as if, as one writer has pointed out, their figures are melding together.[36] Their faces are mere breaths apart, intensifying the contrast of the angel's gentle impassivity and Abraham's anguish, now pierced with a ray of relief. Perhaps in the next moment he will weep.

Interpreted as a foreshadowing of the cross, the story of Abraham's sacrifice of Isaac has been a popular subject of ecclesial art – in catacomb frescoes, ancient pyx, scenes in stained glass, basilica reliefs, and large paintings for church interiors. But Rembrandt von Rijn's 1655 etching is small, approximately six by five inches. He did larger versions as well, but this one is not meant for a crowd in a public space. It has no liturgical processions nor feast days associated with it – and yet neither is it entirely separate from the liturgy. It represents, instead, a way that the liturgy goes out into the home, to cultivate a personal and affective

---

[35] "Anti-Defamation League Statement on Mel Gibson's *The Passion*" (New York, NY: June 24, 2003), https://web.archive.org/web/20080723132238/http://adl.org/PresRele/Mise_00/4275_00.asp.

[36] David R. Smith, "Towards a Protestant Aesthetics: Rembrandt's 1655 *Sacrifice of Isaac*," *Art History* 8 (1985): 296–98. Also William A. Dyrness, *The Origins of Protestant Aesthetics in Early Modern Europe: Calvin's Reformation Poetics* (Cambridge: Cambridge University Press, 2019), 298–99.

engagement with the stories of faith. It exemplifies a shifting visual culture in Christianity, nurtured by Protestant image anxieties – but also hopes – for images.

The magisterial Reformers were not anti-image so much as they were against certain image attitudes and practices. Luther worried primarily about venerating images or attempting by them to secure favors from God, Calvin about the mediating function of sacramentals generally and what they do in a heart that is a factory of idols.[37] Even Henrich Bullinger, successor of the most iconoclastic Reformer Huldrych Zwingli, nevertheless endorsed the use of images in homes for exemplifying virtue, for decoration, and for teaching.[38] The consequence of the Reformation for Christian life was not the eradication of art but its transformation. As the last section explored how the very performance of iconoclasm reiterated the theatricality of the Passion Plays many Protestants objected to, so this one maintains that the iconoclasm of Protestants against images begets a new visuality. Mia Mochizuki's work shows how even the white-washed walls of Dutch churches – walls that themselves embody a visual aesthetic that insists on God's transcendence – nevertheless hold a type of image. Large, often Scriptural text-scripts are elaborately framed and installed at the church's visual focal point, just behind the altar, where a figural painting used to hang.[39] Figural images, moreover, did not disappear from Protestant worship life but migrated into homes and, at times, non-religious public spaces like town halls.[40] As religious art went out from the church and into domestic and secular spaces, it also connected

---

[37] Christiane Andersson, "Protestant Painting: Artworks by Lucas Cranach and His Workshop," in *Protestant Aesthetics and the Arts*, ed. Sarah Covington and Kathryn Reklis (London: Routledge, 2020), 41–54. Luther said at one point he wished "the whole Bible to be painted on houses, on the outside and inside, so that all can see it." Quoted in Ernest B. Gilman, *Iconoclasm and Poetry in the English Reformation* (Chicago: University of Chicago Press, 1986), 35, 41. Andrew Morall, "The Family at Table: Protestant Identity, Self-Representation and the Limits of the Visual in Seventeenth-Century Zurich," *Art History* 40 (April): 336–57, at 340.

[38] Dyrness, *The Origins of Protestant Aesthetics*, 173.

[39] Mia Mochizuki explores this phenomenon in *The Netherlandish Image after Iconoclasm, 1566–1672: Material Religion in the Dutch Golden Age* (Aldershot: Ashgate, 2008).

[40] Charles M. Rosenberg, *Rembrandt's Religious Prints: The Feddersen Collection at the Snite Museum of Art* (Bloomington: Indiana University Press, 2017), 23–24. And also Tara Hamling, *Decorating the "Godly" Household: Religious Art in Post-Reformation Britain* (New Haven, CT: Yale University Press, 2010). Hamling argues against a narrative of Protestant hostility to art by showing that many Protestant patrons commissioned traditional religious art to decorate their homes.

the liturgy to those spaces, insisting that all spaces are potential sites of religious devotion.

As images migrated out of the church, they also began to change. Artists made smaller images appropriate for personal piety in households. Etchings like Rembrandt's *The Sacrifice of Isaac* became more popular because of their size and price point.[41] The aesthetic sensibility of such art solicited a meditative, introspective response. In the case of Rembrandt, his artistic subject was often divine grace transforming the ordinary and the individual.[42] David R. Smith argues that where the Catholic devotional image emphasizes transporting the individual soul into the events of sacred history, the Protestant sensibility embodied in Rembrandt instead emphasizes the biblical story coming to an individual soul. Images like *The Sacrifice of Isaac* exalt Abraham, not as a divine type but as a model of faith for individuals to emulate, and encourage such emulation by affectively imparting to the viewer the psychological drama of sin and salvation.[43] In addition to this affective engagement, images also had a didactic purpose, and much Protestant art in the wake of the Reformation focused on biblical scenes, capitalizing in this way on a longstanding justification for Christian images as "bibles of the illiterate" and extending the possibilities for educating the laity.[44]

Through these smaller, cheaper, more Scripturally focused images, the Bible goes out from the church into the world, inviting individual conversion and affective transformation, often dramatizing the psychological aspects of divine transformation. What did it mean for Rembrandt to etch this scene, in which he appeared to use his son Titus as model for Isaac?[45] What kind of encounter was he trying to stage? For Smith, the clue is in Rembrandt diminishing the technique of

---

[41] Graham Howes, "Christianity and Visual Art," in *The Oxford Handbook on Religion and the Arts*, ed. Frank Burch Brown (Oxford: Oxford University Press, 2014), 295.

[42] Ibid., 295. Simon Schama also emphasizes transformation of the everyday throughout his magisterial book *Rembrandt's Eyes* (New York: Alfred A. Knopf, 1999).

[43] Smith, "Towards a Protestant Aesthetics: Rembrandt's 1655 *Sacrifice of Isaac*," 188–89.

[44] Rosenberg, *Rembrandt's Religious Prints*, 23. Andersson writes that Luther in particular "welcomed such narrative images as effective reminders of Christ's actions as recorded in the Bible" and "felt that images rather than words were more helpful to common people in understanding biblical stories." "Protestant Painting," 41, 42. And Rembrandt was a painter especially focused on biblical scenes. John I. Durham, *The Biblical Rembrandt: Human Painter in a Landscape of Faith* (Macon, GA: Mercer University Press, 2004), 55–57.

[45] Smith, "Towards a Protestant Aesthetics," 294.

contrapposto, a staging of oppositions, and enfolding the contrasts of angel and patriarch into embrace. As a theme that also plays out in Rembrandt's other late works like *Jacob Wrestling with the Angel* (1658) and *Return of the Prodigal Son* (1669), the play of "embrace and separation, unity and opposition ... echoes the Protestant understanding of Grace."[46] The going out of images into the world reflects for him the ubiquity and possibilities of divine grace at work, the sacred saturating the ordinary, in a way that both opens and closes possibilities for images' relationship to the liturgy.

VIRGIN OF GUADALUPE

On December 12, the *matachines*' feet hop and shuffle in intricate patterns to a heavy drumbeat. As the dancers move, their long beads swish and rattle. The beads are one part of the ceremonial dress, which often includes plumed headdresses and stylized bows and arrows. Sometimes the *matachines* wear red, white, and green for Mexico; sometimes blue for Mary; and sometimes bright colors meant to evoke the indigenous origins of the dance. Always the Virgin of Guadalupe image is near the dance. She is, after all, the center of *la danza guadalupana*, this kinetic celebration of her feast day in Mexico, among Latinx populations in the United States, and in many churches around the world.

The Virgin of Guadalupe is the only image in Christianity to have her own liturgical dance, but, then, she is unique among images in many ways: She is, since 1999, the only image to be named a patroness of two entire continents; her basilica is the most visited pilgrimage site in the Americas; and after Jesus of Nazareth, the Virgin of Guadalupe is the most reproduced sacred image in the Western hemisphere.[47] The story of this image is one of the most remarkable examples of an image going out from and into the church's liturgical life – generating or helping to generate liturgies, dances, prayers, sermons, image reproductions, image variations, political movements, national identity, and multiple theologies. Truly she is among the most revered and powerful images in Christianity.

The ubiquity and significance of Guadalupe for the church is undeniable, and yet her origin story is humble and decidedly local.

---

[46] Ibid., 299.
[47] Timothy Matovina, *Theologies of Guadalupe: From the Era of Conquest to Pope Francis* (New York: Oxford University Press, 2019), 4.

The traditional story is that in 1531, Mary appeared to an indigenous man named Juan Diego (Quauhtlatoatzin in his native language Nahuatl) at the hill of Tepeyac, just north of Mexico City. She appeared indigenous, like him, and told him she wanted a church built at that location, and on their fourth meeting, she gave him a sign he could use to persuade the bishop to build a church. Juan Diego saw the flowers unseasonably blooming and carried them in his *tilma* to the bishop. When he unfurled the mantle, a miraculous image of the Virgin of Guadalupe appeared, the sign Mary had promised him. The story is contested, as is the history of how and why the image rose in popularity.[48] But the origin story is also one that is often repeated and remembered together with the image. It narrates the Virgin of Guadalupe as an image that performs how God comes to us – in mercy, by embracing our humanity – and has generated multiple possibilities for the image's meanings, myriad reinterpretations, and perceived political–social possibilities.

The Virgin of Guadalupe goes toward and out from the church's liturgy. From the sacred site of the apparition (sacred even before Christianity arrived in Latin America), the Virgin of Guadalupe image literally went into a church, now the basilica of Guadalupe, which she herself founded and to which she has welcomed millions of pilgrims each year. From that basilica, she has gone out into thousands of churches in the Americas and around the world that have developed or adapted liturgies related to the image and her feast day – and to hundreds of non-ecclesial sites as well. The dissemination of the Virgin of Guadalupe is astonishing. She has inspired a play, *The Miracle at Tepeyac*, which protests the gentrification of housing that displaces Chicanx communities. She has been used by United Farm Workers in California and los comités Guadalupanos in New York City to criticize unjust political and economic arrangements.[49] She became a symbol of Mexican national identity and has been taken up

---

[48] David Brading covers this history in *Mexican Phoenix: Our Lady of Guadalupe: Image and Tradition Across Five Centuries* (Cambridge: Cambridge University Press, 2001). In a debate in print and in their books, Timothy Matovina defends the apparition tradition while Stafford Poole casts doubt on it. Timothy Matovina, "The Origins of the Guadalupe Tradition in Mexico," *The Catholic Historical Review* 100.2 (Spring 2014): 243–70. Stafford Poole, "A Response to Timothy Matovina," *The Catholic Historical Review* 100.2 (Spring 2014): 271–83. Stafford Poole, *Our Lady of Guadalupe: The Origins and Sources of a Mexican National Symbol, 1531–1797* (Tucson, AZ: University of Arizona Press, 1995). Matovina, *Theologies of Guadalupe*.

[49] Nichole Flores, *The Aesthetics of Solidarity: Our Lady of Guadalupe and American Democracy* (Washington, DC: Georgetown University Press, 2021), 3, 7, 38.

in the United States by pro-life groups on the right as well as pro-immigrant groups on the left. She is a popular tattoo, even among largely secular Latinx populations.[50] And from the Roman Catholic Church, she has gone into other churches as well, particularly Protestant churches with large Latinx populations.[51]

What exactly is this going out, and how might it suggest a new role for sacred images and their relationship to liturgy? Long have images processed out of churches and into the streets of cities; long have they been held up in wars and lent out for their miraculous properties. These are examples of a sacred image sacralizing, at least temporarily, a secular space. But when an image is reproduced and then identified with political, social, or national causes, does it still confer sacrality on the secular, or has the sacred image itself been secularized? This, it seems, is a different way that an image goes out into the world, where it goes out to develop new associations that may be only distantly related to liturgy and theology and yet are never entirely separated from them. These new associations remain tied to the liturgy and intense devotional piety as long as the faithful keep celebrating her, and, in their celebrations, the Guadalupe continues to invite the transformation of the world in multiple realms and keys.

CONCLUSION

The going out and in from the liturgy of the reliquary box, *Virgin of the Sign*, living stations of the cross, *Sacrifice of Isaac*, and the Virgin of Guadalupe evidence a liturgical life in which the faithful by their liturgical items transfigure the world, sacralizing it. And yet the liturgical items are also converted in this going out, taking on new iterations, forms, locations, and meanings. The transformation, in other words, runs in both directions. As long as images are part of this dynamic movement of change and exchange, they will continue to be an anxious,

---

[50] See, for example, Jacqueline Serrato, "Wearing Her Faith on Her Sleeve: Honoring Our Lady of Guadalupe outside the Church," *Chicago Tribune*. Accessed December 11, 2018, at bit.ly/4iPgimp. Or also Cedar Attanasio, "Our Lady of Guadalupe: How 'La Virgen' Inspires Tattoos, Death Threats, and Latina Power," *Latin Times* (12 December 2015), www.latintimes.com/our-lady-guadalupe-how-la-virgen-inspires-tattoos-death-threats-and-latina-power-358242. For more on the myriad images and media the Virgin of Guadalupe inspires, see María Del Socorro Castañeda-Liles, *Our Lady of Everyday Life: La Virgen de Guadalupe and the Catholic Imagination of Mexican Women in America* (Oxford: Oxford University Press, 2018).

[51] Maxwell E. Johnson, *The Virgin of Guadalupe: Theological Reflections of an Anglo-Lutheran Liturgist* (Lanham, MD: Rowman & Littlefield, 2002), 122–27.

vibrant, contested, and creative site of the church's life and liturgy, vital in world, church, and theological reflection.

For Further Reading

Carnes, Natalie, *Image and Presence: A Christological Reflection on Iconoclasm and Iconophilia* (Stanford, CA: Stanford University Press, 2017).

Covington, Sarah, and Kathryn Reklis (eds.), *Protestant Aesthetics and the Arts* (London: Routledge, 2020).

Dyrness, William A., *The Origins of Protestant Aesthetics in Early Modern Europe: Calvin's Reformation Poetics* (Cambridge: Cambridge University Press, 2019).

Eire, Carlos M. N., *War Against the Idols: The Reformation of Worship from Erasmus to Calvin* (Cambridge: Cambridge University Press, 1986).

Hahn, Cynthia, *Strange Beauty: Issues in the Making and Meaning of Reliquaries, 400–circa 1204* (University Park: Penn State University Press, 2013).

Ivanic, Suzanna, *Catholica: The Visual Culture of Catholicism* (London: Thames & Hudson, 2022).

Jensen, Robin M., *The Cross: History, Art, and Controversy* (Cambridge, MA: Harvard University Press, 2017).

Understanding Early Christian Art (London: Routledge, 2000).

Ouspensky, Leonid, and Vladimir Lossky, *The Meaning of Icons* (Crestwood, NY: St Vladimir's Seminary Press, 1999).

Part IV

Liturgy and the Life of the Churches

14 Liturgy, the Body, and the Senses
BRIDGET NICHOLS

INTRODUCTION

There is no liturgy without bodies. The liturgical assembly, as Gordon Lathrop eloquently describes, is a primary statement of this claim: a gathering of human beings with the common desire to offer their prayers and praises to God, as Christ's earthly body.[1] Yet this observation immediately invokes the complexity of symbol, metaphor, identity, theological and sacramental understanding, and liturgical formation that simple words conceal. The assembly is made up of many bodies, and not always the same bodies. Together, they constitute the Church, the body of Christ in a particular place. They are not only in spatial and intentional relationship to one another but also in relationship to God. They react to one another and to the space they occupy, and to the stimuli of audible and visible elements not only physically but also imaginatively. In addition, the places where they gather may draw them into relation with bodies no longer present, especially where a columbarium or a churchyard adjoining the church building houses the remains of the dead, or where a shrine connects the living to a prominent witness to the faith. If the gathering is a celebration of the Eucharist, the participants will receive the body of Christ in the ordinary substances of bread and wine.

None of this is contradicted by growing numbers of virtual liturgical communities emerging partly as a phenomenon of the Covid-19 pandemic. Even worshippers in isolation, meeting the assembly online, are bodies present in a certain place, at a specified time, and for a particular purpose. They occupy a position in relation to a screen or an audio

---

[1] Gordon Lathrop, *The Assembly: A Spirituality* (Minneapolis, MN: Fortress Press, 2022), 1–5.

device. Some light candles or bring bread and wine to consume in solidarity with a dispersed community. They might make the sign of the cross, close their eyes to pray, stand, or kneel.[2] The time may come when it is no longer sufficient to regard these forms as derivative of the physical assembly.

Lathrop's typology or *ordo* of book, bath, and meal provides a helpful outline of the basic actions in time and space that ensure the life, continuity, and development of the body that is the Church.[3] The reading and preaching of Scripture, baptism in response to proclamation, and the Eucharist as the ongoing celebration of the mystery of salvation thus become a paradigm. It is not, however, a paradigm that can be assumed. The Church as institution and its designated ministers might once have presided automatically over the body's journey through time, from birth to marriage to death, administering the water of baptism, laying hands on bodies and blessing them, anointing them for healing, uniting bodies in marriage, and preparing embodied individuals for death. That right is no longer a "given." Naming ceremonies, secular marriage and funeral or "thanksgiving for a life" ceremonies, and other improvised rituals now stand as alternatives and may appeal particularly to people who wish for a ritual but do not wish to attach it to a commitment of faith.[4]

This preamble indicates a number of themes for a discussion of liturgy, the body, and the senses: physical bodies; the worshipping assembly; the Church as body of Christ; the body as capable of movement, attention, and response; relationships across time and space; the Church as intimately involved in accompanying bodies through earthly existence. I propose to gather them in two large and sometimes overlapping fields of ideas: human bodies present in the liturgy, and the body of God. Beginning with preparation for gathering, the discussion traces the symbolic and formational aspects of what bodies "do" in worship, where they worship, and where problematic issues arise. The role of the physical senses is critical here, and it is extended to a short discussion of the spiritual senses.

---

[2] "Virtual Liturgy is Still Embodied Says This Yale Liturgist" (Interview with Teresa Berger), *US Catholic* 85.12 (2020): 16–20. Accessed February 18, 2023, at https://tinyurl.com/ynsybsjm.

[3] Gordon Lathrop, *Holy Things: A Liturgical Theology* (Minneapolis, MN: Fortress Press, 1993), 89, 100–1.

[4] Ronald L. Grimes, "Liturgical Supinity and Liturgical Erectitude: On the Embodiment of Ritual Authority," in *Studia Liturgica* 23 (1993): 51–69.

One miscellaneous category should be mentioned, although it cannot be treated here. It encompasses two kinds of bodies. The first might be termed "liminal" and covers events in which individuals move from one form of life to another or are connected to the gathered assembly in a detached way. The churching of women – now better described as thanksgiving after childbirth – formally receives mothers back into the community after they have given birth. The clothing of a religious marks the movement of a person out of the world, into an intentional life that exists for the sake of the world. Visiting the sick and bringing the Eucharistic elements maintain the bond with the body that housebound members cannot physically join. The second group might be termed "ecstatic" and finds individuals undergoing a sudden powerful experience within the context of the liturgy, which affects those witnessing it. Glossolalia and miraculous healing in response to prayer are obvious examples.

The body of God is discussed both in terms of its sacramental resonance – the body of Christ – and as a presence imagined in the poetic language of the liturgy through a rich array of anthropomorphizing metaphors with immense significance in the realm of affective participation. Although the language of "assembly" is used frequently, it does not imagine homogeneous gatherings of human beings. The discussion will touch briefly on new imperatives in the way worshippers see other bodies within the assembly, noting the responsibility that comes with acknowledging difference in the form of neurodiversity, ethnicity, gender, sexuality, and physical and intellectual limitations. Its counterpart is an urgent summons to the assembly to look in new ways at the world outside as global ecological crisis accelerates.

A short concluding note on "Liturgy, the Body, and Society" acknowledges that the Church is now one among several contenders for the oversight of the body. How it responds to this reality, balancing a measure of humility with proper confidence in what it has to offer to the wholly integrated flourishing of souls and bodies, is a direct challenge to its liturgy.

PREPARING THE BODY TO JOIN THE ASSEMBLY

Christian communities have prepared in a variety of ways to participate in the liturgical assembly. Of these, fasting is probably the most common. Frank Senn identifies two types: liturgical fasting before the celebration of the Eucharist and ascetical fasting, normally for a season (Lent especially), when the discipline is accompanied by prayer and almsgiving but intensified in the patterns of monastic life. Both types bear directly on the body, by controlling its desire for food in order to concentrate on the encounter with God. In communities where sexual abstinence is prescribed during Lent and before participating in the Eucharist, a further attempt to master the body's appetites emerges. Senn warns that liturgical fasting should avoid any element of "self-care or personal gain." Its purpose is to "[heighten] the experience of hearing the word of God and receiving the sacrament of Holy Communion."[5]

Other physical disciplines in addition to fasting have historically been associated with penance. An order of public penitents seems to have emerged in the fourth and fifth centuries, and their temporary exclusion from the Christian community was marked by sackcloth garments, imposition of ash on the head, and some limitations on practices of personal hygiene. The history of penance is immensely complicated and rich in regional difference, but it is worth noting the development of tariff penance, where "prices" – usually forms of discipline, whose severity matched the offence, or actions like pilgrimages – were attached to a catalogue of sins.[6] Modern provision for the reconciliation of penitents has a different pastoral emphasis, focusing on the restoration and reintegration of the individual. It is hardly necessary to add that fulfilling this noble aim depends on the skill of pastoral practitioners.

THE BODY PRESENT AND ACTIVE IN THE LITURGY

The sociologist and anthropologist Marcel Mauss concluded a lecture on "Techniques of the Body" (1934) thus: "I think that there are necessarily biological means of entering into 'communication with God'."[7] All Christian gatherings – from the most formal, solemn, and elaborate to the most relaxed and apparently casual – have their own rules or

---

[5] Frank C. Senn, *Introduction to Christian Liturgy* (Minneapolis, MN: Fortress Press, 2012), 106.
[6] The work of Cyrille Vogel is seminal in the history of penance. For a selection of essays see Cyrille Vogel, *En rémission des péchés: Recherches sur les systèmes pénitentiels dans l'Église latine*, ed. Alexandre Faivre (Brookfield, VT: Ashgate, 1994). See also Thomas O'Loughlin, "Penitentials and Pastoral Care," in *A History of Pastoral Care*, ed. G. R. Evans (London: Cassell, 2000), 93–111.
[7] Marcel Mauss, "Techniques of the Body," in *Sociology and Psychology*, trans. and ed. Ben Brewster (London: Routledge & Kegan Paul, 1979), 97–123, 122. See also Bridget Nichols, "Liturgical Participation and Techniques of the Body," in *Anaphora* 16 (2022): 1–14.

conventions governing the physical behavior of worshippers. Doing the same thing at the same time is itself a marker of common intention and of a desire to act as one body. The range of physical postures and gestures that seem indigenous to acts of worship is familiar: kneeling to pray and to confess one's sins; standing to acknowledge the entries and exits of ministers, to sing, and to hear the gospel reading at the Eucharist; bowing in reverence at the name of God or to acknowledge an action performed by another person; sitting for certain readings, for sermons, and sometimes to recite psalms and canticles. The hands are used in blessing, in exchanging a greeting of peace, and in receiving the Eucharistic elements.[8] Walking too, especially in processions, should be counted among the modes of bodily engagement in liturgy. In some contexts, dance plays a regular role, celebratory and interpretative, in the liturgy.[9]

Postures may be physically efficient. Standing to sing results in "better sound production and better spatial awareness."[10] This efficiency may also contribute to the beneficial value of activities that are inherently capable of producing what Dorothea Haspelmath-Finatti calls "prosocial behaviour."[11] Postures and gestures will, after a period of time, become habitual. The body remembers how to perform regularly repeated actions without the prompting of a conscious decision. Absence of familiarity with a practice marks out the newcomer in the assembly who does not know what to do, or the person who suffers from cognitive impairment. Loss of earlier familiarity is poignantly exposed in the confusion experienced by sufferers from dementia and Alzheimer's disease in liturgical settings.

Beyond this somewhat instrumental understanding of the body in liturgy lies a theological invitation. Here, Patrick Prétot's essay on the liturgy as embodied experience is indispensable.[12] Prétot sets out to investigate how the meaning of our liturgical participation is discovered in and through the body.[13] While God does not need human gestures and

---

[8] Jeremy Haselock, "Gestures," in *New SCM Dictionary of Liturgy and Worship*, ed. Paul F. Bradshaw (London: SCM, 2002), 227–30.
[9] See David Brown, *God and Grace of Body: Sacrament in Ordinary* (Oxford: Oxford University Press, 2007), 89–91. Brown laments that dance is not more widely practiced as a way of involving the body in liturgy.
[10] Cally Hammond, *The Sound of the Liturgy* (London: SPCK, 2015), 36.
[11] Dorothea Haspelmath-Finatti, "Sacramentality and Music," in *T&T Clark Handbook of Sacraments and Sacramentality*, eds. Martha Moore-Keish and James W. Farwell (London: T&T Clark, 2023), 112–25, at 113. See also Chapter 11.
[12] Patrick Prétot, "La Liturgie, une expérience corporelle: Jalons pour une grammaire du corps en liturgie," *La Maison-Dieu* 247 (2006): 7–36.
[13] Ibid., 7 (all translations from this article are mine).

ceremonies in order to confer grace, human beings need these things, and the sacraments, as signs of grace.[14] Prétot positions the body in liturgy at the horizon of sacramentality, the point where God comes to meet human beings. The liturgy functions here as a place of mediation, but not only, or even principally, that: "The body is less a means of expression than the very place where God joins humanity in order to save humanity."[15] Gestures are by no means unimportant in this account, and Prétot attends to the multivalent nature of actions and postures. Thus kneeling connotes penance as well as prayerfulness and adoration; the legs and feet can signal a respectful posture or a casual attitude (crossing the legs); the head bows in reverence, or penitence, or to acknowledge others. Movement changes the perspective of the individuals engaged in the liturgical action. The communion procession, for instance, is both movement to a destination in the place of worship and the pilgrim people of God walking toward the meeting with their Lord.[16]

All of this contributes, ideally, toward the building up of the body. Yet Prétot expresses concern over a current "deficit in formation," a loss of the know-how that used to be handed down through generations of worshippers. The task confronting the churches is to discern what is appropriate in societies that embody multiple forms of diversity and where nothing can be assumed about inherited practices of worship, in order to ensure that the bodies of those who participate may enter fully into the transformative and constantly transforming relationship between human beings and God. This is not a matter of individual choice and preference. Rather, it entails assent to the action that unites the whole community. An example is the recitation of the creed, in which the individual "becomes a believer with others, becomes the faithful one who proclaims his or her faith."[17] That this proclamation includes "the resurrection of the body" should summon worshippers to value the earthly body in the light of its unimaginably transformed continuation.

THE PHYSICAL SENSES

Up to this point, attention has rested on the physical body, its relationship to other bodies, its position in space, and its capacity for variation of posture when still, and for movement where this is demanded by the

---

[14] Ibid., 9.
[15] Ibid., 21.
[16] Ibid., 28.
[17] Ibid., 34.

liturgy. Insights from Patrick Prétot especially have assisted in tracing the formational implications of all these elements. Indivisible from all this, though much less frequently evoked in descriptions of rites and, importantly, in the rubrics that govern them, are the senses of sight, hearing, touch, taste, and smell. Contemporary worshippers must look back to the mystagogical teaching of the fourth century baptismal homilies for explicit invitations to a sensory response to liturgical participation. Ambrose, in his lectures to the newly baptized, reminds them of the fragrance of the oil of anointing, the feeling of the laying on of the bishop's hands, the sight of the church illuminated for the Easter liturgy, and the unexpected ordinariness of the bread and wine when they saw it for the first time on the altar.[18]

The same invitation is implicit in every gathering of the body of Christ. The senses that help human beings to navigate their world in general, in communicating and relating spatially and culturally to other people, following directions, enjoying food, appreciating beauty, and detecting what might harm them, are all marshalled within the liturgical assembly. Worshippers listen, speak, and sing. They experience their proximity to one another through touch and smell. They ought to find themselves entering aesthetically into the space where they meet through pleasing structures, stained glass, furnishings and images, flowers, and the ability to appreciate music. The use of incense, candles, textiles, and Eucharistic vessels should invite them to imagine the eternal worship offered in the nearer presence of God by "angels, archangels and all the company of heaven." "Ought" and "should" in this account underline its provisionality, for there remains a gap between official guidance on the aesthetics of the liturgical environment and its local implementation.[19] This is particularly the case where functionality has been the dominant consideration. Yet space can be flexible enough to allow different configurations of the assembly, or to facilitate those whose limited mobility requires certain adaptations, or to provide for the inclusion of infants and children, without loss of beauty.[20]

---

[18] Ambrose, *De Sacramentis* I–VI.10. I have used the translation provide by Edward Yarnold, S.J., *The Awe-Inspiring Rites of Initiation: The Origins of the R. C. I. A.*, 2nd ed. (Edinburgh: T&T Clark, 2001), 98–149.

[19] See *Sacrosanctum Concilium*, 122–30 on "Sacred Art and Furnishings."

[20] Ann Loades, "Children are Church," in *Lively Oracles of God: Perspectives on the Bible and Liturgy*, eds. Gordon Jeanes and Bridget Nichols (Collegeville, MN: Liturgical Press, 2022), 206–26.

On the other hand, adaptations that obstruct the full engagement of the body, such as platforms occupied by music groups, often dividing the nave and the chancel in a classic church design, can be both a visual impediment and a disincentive to participation in singing and variation of posture.[21]

Perhaps it is through a recovered understanding of the sacramental value of the ordinary things that play a part in our celebrations, even if in attenuated form – bread, water, wine, and oil, as well as wood, glass, and fabric – that a new movement might begin. Here, the churches of the Reformation arguably have most to learn. Unadorned buildings and a distinctive musical repertoire of hymns and metrical psalms have furnished a setting for concentrating on the Word, but this has not been a rich sensory experience. Over-privileging of the auditory senses results where worship consists mainly of reading and preaching or of music in which the assembly does not actively participate.

THE SPIRITUAL SENSES

The physical senses are not just devices for navigation, self-defense, and delighting in the world: They are also gateways to a kind of imaginative and even transcendent experience. In this way, it is possible to speak of "spiritual senses." Susan Ashbrook Harvey records the interest among Christian scholars of the fourth and fifth centuries in the power of sense perception to lead first to some apprehension of the "God who made [the physical world]" and then to perception beyond the boundaries of that world.[22] Joris Geldhof, who laments that a concept of the "spiritual senses" has all but vanished from the theological landscape, emphasizes that "they do not lead into a parallel or separate world, they are not opposed to the five natural senses."[23] Rather,

> they function *through* the natural senses as well as synaesthetically, in the sense that they operate via simultaneous combinations and an intriguing whirling of the senses. A person can hear what they see, although the source of the corresponding sound is invisible, they can

---

[21] See Kevin W. Irwin, *Context and Text: A Method for Liturgical Theology*, rev. ed., (Collegeville, MN: Liturgical Press, 2018), 469–98, esp. 491–98.

[22] Susan Ashbrook Harvey, *Scenting Salvation: Ancient Christianity and the Olfactory Imagination* (Berkeley: University of California Press, 2006), 113–14.

[23] Joris Geldhof, *Liturgical Theology as a Research Program* (Leiden: Brill, 2020), 110.

feel what they hear, taste what they see, smell what they feel, all in the absence of clearly identifiable causes.[24]

Geldhof argues "that the spiritual senses are particularly apt to disclose sacramentality, God's presence and Christ's saving operations in and beyond liturgical celebrations."[25] Some reflection on the language of Christian liturgies will suggest how the senses in their physical dimension might be gateways to the spiritual: Psalm 34.8 is an invitation to "taste and see how gracious the Lord is" as part of a thanksgiving for deliverance; Eucharistic congregations are called to "Behold the Lamb of God" before they receive consecrated bread and wine. They are invited to picture themselves joining the angels and archangels and the whole company of heaven in the words of the *Sanctus*. The scented oil of chrism at baptism and confirmation draws on the sensory associations of paradise. The water of baptism, the contrast between light and darkness (e.g., in the office of Tenebrae or in the Easter Vigil), the use of oil for anointing, ashes to mark those who begin the journey of Lent, and palms on Palm Sunday, and the tactile act of foot washing are more than dramatic devices. Participating simultaneously in the ordinary substance of the world and connecting worshippers to a worshipping tradition that has found inspiration in the vivid detail within the scriptural narrative, they become conduits leading into the mystery of salvation.

To this might be added an ethical footnote. The sensory–symbolic actions described entail a two-way reflection, which is ultimately a call to stewardship or service. As Anscar Chupungco writes,

> Liturgical symbols are often aligned with some human circumstances. Through symbols the liturgy grafts the heavenly reality on the earthly, the divine is encountered through the human, and the world is bathed in God's grace. Because of this, every time we break bread, that is, share food with our family, friends, and strangers, we are invited to remember the broken bread on the altar. On the other hand, the food on our table points to the food on the altar and acquires from it a fuller meaning. Liturgical symbols elevate the reality of our day-to-day lives to the higher plane of human existence.[26]

---

[24] Ibid., 110.
[25] Ibid., 111.
[26] Anscar Chupungco, *What, Then, Is Liturgy? Musings and a Memoir* (Collegeville, MN: Liturgical Press, 2010), 160.

THE BODY OF GOD IN LITURGY

All sensory stimuli in the liturgical environment should assist worshippers to picture themselves in the presence of God. Often taking the form of gifts of ordinary things for sacred use, they add depth and resonance to the Church's proclamation of God present in word and in sacrament. This gift of presence reaches its climax in the Eucharistic celebration, in which Christ's people feed on his body and are themselves constituted as his body on earth by "[sharing] in the one bread."[27] Enduring differences in theological understanding of *how* Christ is present remain a cause of division among the Christian churches and continue to be addressed in ecumenical dialogues. This chapter does not attempt to represent them.

In the meantime, the presence of God is recalled frequently via a range of metaphors, in the prayers and songs of the assembly. Human beings tend to speak of the first person of the Trinity particularly in anthropomorphic terms, despite doctrinal assertions like the first of the Thirty-Nine Articles of Religion of the Church of England (1562) – "Of Faith in the Holy Trinity":

> THERE is but one living and true God, ever-lasting, without body, parts, or passions; of infinite power, wisdom, and goodness; the Maker, and Preserver of all things both visible and invisible. And in unity of this Godhead there be three Persons, of one substance, power, and eternity; the Father, the Son, and the Holy Ghost.[28]

The Psalms attribute arms, hands, eyes, ears, and breath to God (Psalms 33:18–19, 63:8, 86:1, 98:1, 104:27–30, 119:132). The prayers of the Church, notably the collects, ask God to look on creation, to support the frail and weak, to receive their petitions with a merciful ear, to touch and heal the sick. These prayers are offered through the mediation of Christ, who shares our humanity and in his ascension carries it to (another physical metaphor) the right hand of God the Father, a title to which I shall return.

These ways of imagining God in liturgy allow worshippers to envision themselves as always in relation and as beneficiaries of love and

---

[27] Archbishops' Council of the Church of England, *Common Worship: Services and Prayers for the Church of England* (London: Church House Publishing, 2000), 180.
[28] Brian Cummings (ed.), *The Books of Common Prayer 1549, 1559, and 1662* (Oxford: Oxford University Press, 2011), 674.

protection, and, in general, never abandoned to "get on with things" on their own. The liturgy of the hours (daily offices) has continued the practice commended by John Cassian (*Conferences* X) of beginning with a verse from Psalm 70 – "O Lord, open my lips. And my mouth will proclaim your praise" – as if in expectation that God will empower individuals who desire to pray.[29] Eucharistic prayers, too, position the assembly in various ways, as examples from the Church of England illustrate. First, a prayer emphasizing the maternal aspect of God's care for human beings:

> How wonderful the work of your hands, O Lord.
> As a mother tenderly gathers her children,
> you embraced a people as your own.
> When they turned away and rebelled
> your love remained steadfast.[30]

A proper preface for use in Lent dramatizes the season as a time of pilgrimage, in which the faithful are accompanied by God, who seeks to bring a people formed through penitence and discipline back into close relationship:

> For in these forty days
> you lead us into the desert of repentance
> that through a pilgrimage of prayer and discipline
> we may grow in grace
> and learn to be your people once again.
> Through fasting, prayer and acts of service
> you bring us back to your generous heart.
> Through study of your holy word
> you open our eyes to your presence in the world
> and free our hands to welcome others
> into the radiant splendour of your love.[31]

Both compositions have a scriptural density woven out of arresting images. In the first example, Jesus' lament over Jerusalem, comparing himself to a mother hen gathering her chicks (Matthew 23:37), and Isaiah's assurance that, while a human mother might conceivably stop

---

[29] Boniface Ramsey, O.P. (tr.), *John Cassian: The Conferences* (New York: Paulist Press, 1997).

[30] Archbishops' Council of the Church of England, *Common Worship: Services and Prayers for the Church of England* (London: Church House Publishing, 2000), 201.

[31] Ibid., 309.

caring for her child, God is a parent who never abandons his people (Isaiah 49:15–17) are clear inspirations. The second captures the drama of disobedience and return that is thematically dominant in the Pentateuch, prophetic books, and chronicle history of the Hebrew Bible, aligning this with the Synoptic accounts of Jesus' forty days in the wilderness.

The Prayer of Humble Access, found in most prayer books of the Anglican Communion, performs a series of interesting maneuvers in depicting the proper attitude with which worshippers should approach the Eucharistic table:

> We do not presume to come to this thy Table, O merciful Lord, trusting in our own righteousness, but in thy manifold and great mercies. We are not worthy so much as to gather up the crumbs under thy Table. But thou art the same Lord, whose property is always to have mercy: Grant us therefore, gracious Lord, so to eat the Flesh of thy dear Son Jesus Christ, and to drink his blood, that our sinful bodies may be made clean by his Body, and our souls washed through his most precious blood, And that we may evermore dwell in him, and he in us. Amen.[32]

Here, God becomes the host, whose guests have no intrinsic right to be present at the table except as house dogs grateful for fallen crumbs. Drawing vividly on the encounter between Jesus and a Syro-Phoenician woman who asks him to heal her daughter (Matthew 15.21–28), it situates the worshippers in a paradox, unworthy to ask for anything, yet appealing in total dependence on God's mercy. By allowing them to consume Christ's body, his flesh and blood, God cleanses their own bodies and souls and makes possible a wholesome mutual indwelling. For some, this is a powerful assurance without which they do not feel their Eucharistic experience has been complete. For others, its emphasis on unworthiness seems to negate the force of the absolution, while its final vivid images of flesh and blood seem almost grotesque.

Sometimes a metaphor can be weakened. To the acclamation preceding the administration of communion, "Jesus is the Lamb of God. Blessed are those who are called to his supper," an English-speaking Roman Catholic congregation might respond, "Lord, I am not worthy that you should enter under my roof, but only say the word and my soul

---

[32] Cummings, *The Book of Common Prayer*, 402.

shall be healed." David Brown points out how some contemporary Anglican liturgies have both diluted this rich and allusive picture of the Johannine Word who comes to pitch his tent in mortal flesh and squandered the reference to the healing of the centurion's servant.[33] Modifying the response to "Lord, I am not worthy to receive you, but only say the word and I shall be healed," loses the astonishing notion that Jesus might enter the home of a stranger when he could simply issue a verbal command, and, by analogy, his astonishing act in taking human flesh for his own home.[34]

A note on gendered language for God closes this part of the exploration. To use "Father" and "Son" language is to open up the contested area of relational description in exclusively masculine terms, especially when it comes to imagining the life of the Trinity and the way in which that life touches the lives of human beings. A considerable literature now exists and includes some outstanding theological contributions, to name only two, Janet Martin Soskice's extended thinking on naming God and Elizabeth Johnson's powerful revisiting of trinitarian theology in *She Who Is*.[35] Soskice argues that it is legitimate to call God "Father," since the name gains its meaning from relationship to the "Son," and not by analogy with human parental and filial relationships. Johnson explores the use of "wisdom" language with its biblically feminine resonances in her consideration of the persons of the Trinity and how to refer to them. These proposals have not satisfied by any means all objections. Gail Ramshaw advocates a move away from using masculine language, most of it carrying resonances of hierarchy and power, altogether, and instead exploiting the rich sources in Scripture and Christian tradition for feminine and ungendered metaphors for God.[36]

---

[33] Matt 8:8.
[34] David Brown, *God and Mystery in Words: Experience through Metaphor and Drama* (Oxford: Oxford University Press, 2008), 58.
[35] Janet Martin Soskice, *Metaphor and Religious Language* (Oxford: Clarendon Press, 1985), esp. ch. 8; Janet Martin Soskice, "Calling God 'Father'," in *The Kindness of God* (Oxford: Oxford University Press, 2007), 66–83; Elizabeth A. Johnson, *She Who Is: The Mystery of God in Feminist Theological Discourse* (New York: Crossroad, 2007).
[36] Gail Ramshaw, *Reviving Sacred Speech: The Meaning of Liturgical Language* (Akron, OH: OSL Publications, 2000); *Under the Tree of Life: The Religion of a Feminist Christian*, new ed. (Akron, OH: OSL Publications, 2003); *Praying for the Whole World: A Handbook for Intercessors* (Minneapolis, MN: Augsburg Fortress, 2006); and *Pray, Praise and Give Thanks: A Collection of Litanies, Laments and Thanksgivings at the Font and Table* (Minneapolis, MN: Augsburg Fortress, 2017).

THE LITURGICAL BODY AS A FOCUS FOR NEW QUESTIONS

Seeing Other Bodies

Increasingly, communities gathered for worship find themselves required to respond consciously to forms of difference that were always there but not acknowledged as material to the life of the assembly. Of these, gender is probably the most obvious. Christian assemblies, realizing that bodies can be vulnerable to abuse and to the distorted desires of others, have taken steps to ensure propriety from early times: The First Letter to the Corinthians prescribes head covering for women;[37] other restrictions have been placed on women teaching.[38] Later assemblies would seat men and women separately. These measures no longer obtain in mainstream churches, and their discussion of gender is now more likely to be framed in terms of justice and equality, extending to the roles that individuals may perform liturgically. Most would acknowledge that there is still much work to do in this area to overcome persistent forms of discrimination and injustice.

Churches in societies that embrace wide cultural and ethnic diversity continue to learn how to honor these differences. When an ethnic majority offers a welcome to members of an ethnic minority, it is not enough to invite them to join in what the majority have always done. A reexamination of local custom and careful attention to the way language, especially figurative language, is used may result in liturgical practice in which no one is a guest or a spectator. Occasions in the calendar of a number of churches, such as Racial Justice Sunday, provide opportunities for honest discussion as well as liturgical response.

The assembly that meets for worship is now also called to acknowledge the differences in sexual orientation among those present, and to be sensitive to the gender identity of individuals. Such acknowledgment goes beyond welcome: It might engage communities in reexamining some of the language conventions of their worship, as well as in considering specific liturgical responses. Forms for blessing the civil unions of same-sex couples and revision of marriage rites to allow such unions to be celebrated within the life of the Church now form part of the life of some ecclesial bodies. Transgender people who seek to have their baptismal records adjusted to reflect their new identity present the churches with new questions.

---

[37] 1 Cor 11:4–12.
[38] 1 Tim 2:11–12.

Progress in accommodating the needs of individuals with limited mobility, visual impairment, and hearing loss has been a positive outcome of a growing response to differences in bodily capacity. This is reflected in adaptations to church buildings, like ramps for wheelchairs and sound systems compatible with hearing aids, or in the appointment of people trained in sign language. Not all difference is visible, however. Neurodiverse worshippers – affected in sometimes negative ways by close physical contact, eye contact, sound, and certain configurations of space – need carefully considered forms of assistance in order to be comfortable in the assembly. Léon van Ommen's pioneering work on the liturgical experience of people with autism in the liturgical assembly, and his proposals for creating environments in which they are able to participate in worship without anxiety or threat or sensory oppression, is required reading.[39]

Interacting with the World Outside

The world beyond the church building should be a principal concern of those who gather inside the building. Justin Martyr explains that once the deacons have distributed the bread of the Eucharist to the assembly, they take food to those who are absent.[40] This is not necessarily a ministry to the poor, but feeding the poor has been part of the life of Christian communities from the earliest times and continues in food banks, soup kitchens, and other forms of provision. In this way, the body present is extended beyond its gathering place. The gathering place itself can be part of a renewed and increasingly important bodily experience, as intercession for a global ecology in crisis motivates practical responses. Churchyards can be planted with species that attract insects and create a habitat for wildlife. Where there is hospitality, there is also a choice to be made between compostable paper cups or methods of washing ceramic cups that conserve water. Sourcing of tea and coffee matters if the churches are going to witness against the destruction of rainforests and exploitation of local farmers. Solar-powered heating systems and other deliberate choices to use renewable sources of energy embody a commitment to environmental renewal. All of these choices demand financial resources and, to some extent, that limits the choices

---

[39] See, for example, Armand Léon van Ommen and Topher Endress, "Reframing Liturgical Theology through the Lens of Autism: A Qualitative Study of Autistic Experiences of Worship," in *Studia Liturgica* 52 (2022): 219–34.

[40] Justin Martyr, *First Apology*, ch. 65. See Colin Buchanan, *Justin Martyr on Baptism and Eucharist: Texts in Translation with Introduction and Commentary* (Norwich: Canterbury Press, 2007).

of the poor. How do liturgical bodies also become grateful and responsible consumers and wise stewards and servants of the whole order of life on earth?[41]

Liturgy itself has a part to play. Celebrations outdoors remind worshippers of the environment as a holy place. The recovery of processions for agricultural festivals like Rogationtide reminds communities of the whole cycle from ploughing and planting to harvest and its vulnerability to climatic events. Cathriona Russell in an article on liturgy and urban ecology mentions the annual blessing of bicycles in St. John's Cathedral, New York – an event that celebrates an ecologically responsible form of transport, while also praying for the safety of those who cycle and commemorating cyclists who have died in road traffic accidents.[42]

LITURGY, THE BODY, AND SOCIETY

If the Church once accompanied the bodies of Christians through every stage of their lives, it now takes its place – certainly in prosperous and increasingly secular societies – alongside hospitals, hospices, funeral homes, crematoria, and civil celebrants or humanist organizations offering marriage services, naming ceremonies, and funerals. Two brief observations might be made. This does not mean that the Church has less and less to offer in comparison with other agencies, though it cannot be denied that churches find themselves striving to balance the desire to personalize these events with proper use of the rich resources within their own inherited and unfolding traditions. Contemporary developments have been catalysts for projects designed to encourage people to consider a church marriage, baptism, or funeral.[43] Reciprocally, it is noteworthy that civil and secular ceremonies tend to follow a liturgical shape and, though scriptural content and theistic expressions are avoided, material broadly classifiable as spiritual, including religious poetry, is popular. Ritual shape has found another expression in forms of public gathering that mark particular violations of human dignity and justice. The mass vigils for Black

---

[41] Kevin W. Irwin, "Sacramental Theology after *Laudato Si'*," in *Full of Your Glory: Liturgy, Cosmos, Creation*, ed. Teresa Berger (Collegeville, MN: Liturgical Press, 2019), 267–84.

[42] Cathriona Russell, "Liturgy and Urban Ecology," *Doctrine and Life* 72 (2022): 35–42, esp. 41–42.

[43] The Church of England is an example. See Sandra Millar, *Life Events: Mission and Ministry at Baptisms, Weddings and Funerals* (London: Church House Publishing, 2018).

victims of police violence in the United States, for murdered women, and for gay and transgender people murdered in "hate" crimes have drawn on the symbolic language of their ecclesiastical counterparts: lighted candles, lament, solemn procession, and dramatic silence.

David Brown, summing up the project of the last part of his five-volume systematics, *God and Mystery in Words: Experience through Metaphor and Drama*, says: "The Church has the greatest possible gift to offer the world in the God who became human for our sake and adopted a bodily identity that continues into his present existence. So it has rightly things to say about and through the body." But, he continues a little further on, "The danger is that, as the Church simplifies and seeks constantly to explain rather than to enjoy Christ's presence in its own right and with no further object in view, it will force people to find mystery in God at work everywhere else than in this, its greatest gift, the liturgy itself."[44] This is a serious call to action. Recovering the mystery of which Brown speaks is only partly a matter of liturgical language that notices the body: Beyond that, the full capacities of the human bodies meeting regularly to offer their worship must be alerted to taste and see how gracious the Lord is.

For Further Reading

Chauvet, Louis-Marie, and François Kabasele Lumbala (eds.), *Concilium 1995/3: Liturgy and the Body*.

Gavrilyuk, Paul, and Sarah Coakley (eds.), *Religion and the Body* (Cambridge: Cambridge University Press, 1997).

Kearney, Richard, *Touch: Recovering Our Most Vital Sense* (New York: Columbia University Press, 2021).

Larson-Miller, Lizette, *Sacramentality Renewed: Contemporary Conversations in Sacramental Theology* (Collegeville, MN: Liturgical Press, 2016).

O'Loughlin, Thomas (ed.), *Shaping the Assembly: How Our Buildings Form Us in Worship* (Dublin: Messenger, 2023).

Prétot, Patrick, "La Liturgie: Une Expérience Corporelle: Jalons pour une grammaire du corps en liturgie," *La Maison-Dieu* 247 (2006): 7–36.

Senn, Frank C., *Embodied Liturgy: Lessons in Christian Ritual* (Minneapolis, MN: Fortress Press, 2016).

US Conference of Catholic Bishops, *Built of Living Stones: Art, Architecture, and Worship – Guidelines of the National Conference of Catholic Bishops* (issued November 16, 2000, by NCCB/USCC [Now USCCB]), https://charlestondiocese.org/wp-content/uploads/2022/08/Built-of-Living-Stones.pdf.

---

[44] Brown, *God and Mystery in Words*, 268.

15 Liturgy, Spirituality, and Piety
JOB GETCHA

THE MYSTERY OF PIETY

The term "piety," coming from the Latin word *pietas* – meaning "devout" or "dutiful" – designated in Antiquity the feeling that makes one recognize and fulfill one's duties toward the gods, one's parents, and the fatherland. In ancient Greek, we find two distinct equivalent words. The first one, εὐσέβεια (eusebeia) – from εὐσεβής (eusebès), which is composed of εὖ (eu), meaning "well," and σέβας (sebas), meaning "reverence" – is itself formed from σέβ- (seb-), meaning "sacred awe and reverence," especially in actions. It means therefore "respectful, pious, faithful, dutiful." The term εὐσέβεια is abundantly used in Greek philosophy as well as in the New Testament, meaning to "perform the actions appropriate to the gods." Thus, it designates respect as love of God. The other word is ὁσιότης (hosiotès), coming from ὅσιος (hosios) and meaning "holy, pious, pure," which is applied to respect as holiness, virtue, or asceticism. Piety is therefore both respectful love for the things of religion and respect for the rules that are its pillars.[1]

Indeed, popular piety generally manifests a thirst for God. Expressions of piety may vary according to country and local tradition. Various religious celebrations and rites have contributed to forging the traditions peculiar to a community. Churches and religious families have developed many pious rites as a part of their worship, which helps incorporate faith into daily life. In the Bible, the term εὐσέβεια designates devotion toward God, or godliness.[2] Thus, the term may be applied to spirituality and to liturgy. Saint Paul also

---

[1] John Mikalson, *Honor Thy Gods: Popular Religion in Greek Tragedy* (Chapel Hill: University of North Carolina Press, 1991), 165–202.
[2] Cf., for example, 1 Tim 2:2, 4:8, 6:11; Titus 1:1; 2 Pet 1:3.

uses the term εὐσέβεια when he speaks about the mystery of salvation: "And without controversy great is the mystery of godliness (τὸ τῆς εὐσεβείας μυστήριον): God was manifest in the flesh, justified in the Spirit, seen of angels, preached unto the Gentiles, believed on in the world, received up into glory."[3] The term εὐσέβεια is thus connected with the mystery of the salvation of God, who became human. Therefore "piety" in liturgical theology should be distinguished from mere devotional actions or attitudes.

Since the primitive Church, the incarnation of God was related to the sanctification of the human being or their deification.[4] The notion of deification (θέωσις; theosis), which is central in Eastern Christianity, is connected with the sacraments of the Church as it was highlighted by Pseudo-Dionysius. The author of the *Ecclesiastical Hierarchy* asserts that salvation is possible through the sacraments of the Church.[5] Maximus the Confessor considered the Church and her sacraments the extension of the incarnation of God. Unable to remain eternally present on earth in his physical body, for such is not proper to human nature, Christ left on earth the Church as his Mystical Body to perform the sacraments that provide salvation to believers.[6] Maximus also underlined that the deification of human beings is accomplished in the Church through her sacraments.[7] This led the Byzantine mystic Nicolas Cabasilas to envisage the spiritual life of Christians as a "life in Christ" shaped by the sacraments of the Church.[8] The sacraments of the Church communicate life in Christ to believers since they are the extension and actualization of the unique mystery of salvation accomplished by Christ. This is precisely what the Second Vatican Council affirmed in its constitution on the liturgy:

> For the liturgy, "through which the work of our redemption is accomplished," most of all in the divine sacrifice of the Eucharist, is the outstanding means whereby the faithful may express in their lives, and manifest to others, the mystery of Christ and the real nature of the true Church.[9]

---

[3] 1 Tim 3:16.
[4] Cf. Irénée de Lyon, *Contre les hérésies*, III, 19, 1 (SC 211, 374); Athanase d'Alexandrie, *De l'Incarnation du Verbe*, 53 (SC 18, 312).
[5] Pseudo-Dionysius, *Ecclesiastical Hierarchy*, PG 3, 376 A and 373 B.
[6] Cf. Maximus the Confessor, *Ambiguorum liber*, PG 91, 1281A, 1365C.
[7] Maximus the Confessor, *Mystagogia*, I and XXIV, PG 91, 665C, and 704A.
[8] Nicolas Cabasilas, *La vie en Christ*, I, 18 (SC 355, 94).
[9] *Sacrosanctum Concilium*, 2.

The present chapter intends to illustrate the intimate link between liturgy, spirituality, and piety by focusing on Christian life as being initiated and nourished by the sacraments of the Church and, therefore, as communal, and definitely not individual, piety. It will show as well how liturgical services are intended to be a school of prayer of the ecclesial community. Finally, it will focus on how Christian spirituality is shaped by the succession of liturgical feasts and fasts.

THE SACRAMENTAL DIMENSION OF CHRISTIAN LIFE

The sacraments transform the life of the Christian, which becomes punctuated by the liturgy, by the rhythm of its feasts and its seasons, and by the rhythm of the different sacramental moments of life. Thomas Aquinas developed, by analogy with the different ages of bodily life, a theory of the different ages of spiritual life to which the sacraments should correspond, "For spiritual life has a certain conformity with the life of the body," he asserted. To the generation that inaugurates the existence and life of man, he corresponded the sacrament of Baptism as spiritual regeneration. With the growth that brings man to his perfect size and strength, he matched the Confirmation, where the believer receives the Holy Spirit to be strengthened. To the healing of corporal infirmity, he corresponded the healing of spiritual infirmity (sin) through Penance and Unction (sacrament of the sick). To the nutrition that keeps man alive, he made the Eucharist correspond. In regard to the whole community, humanity is perfected by the rule of the community, to which corresponds the sacrament of Order, and by natural propagation that is accomplished by Matrimony.[10]

According to Alexander Schmemann, the sanctification of life is the purpose of the sacraments.[11] For him, a sacrament is an action that transfigures, and transfiguration is precisely the goal of the Divine economy. As the Second Vatican Council stated, from the liturgy, "The sanctification of men in Christ and the glorification of God, to which all other activities of the Church are directed as toward their end, is achieved in the most efficacious possible way."[12] It is obvious from the point of view of Christian theology that there cannot be a Church

---

[10] Thomas Aquinas, *Summa Theologica*, Tertia Pars, Question 65, 1.
[11] Alexander Schmemann, *Liturgy and Life: Lectures and Essays in Christian Development through Liturgical Experience* (New York: DRE/OCA, 1974), 1.
[12] *Sacrosanctum Concilium*, 10.

without Baptism, since there cannot be members of the ecclesial body without them having received Baptism. This is why Baptism is a constitutive act of the Church. The incorporation of the believer into Christ and the Church takes place through Baptism. The rites of Christian initiation culminate in the Eucharist, in which the baptized commune with the Body and Blood of Christ and thus are intimately united with Him.[13]

For this reason, Schmemann once pointed out that "The Church, the sacrament of Christ, is not a 'religious' society of converts, an organization to satisfy the 'religious' needs of man. It is new life and redeems therefore the whole life, the total being of man."[14] Indeed, liturgical piety implies and engages the whole human person as body, mind, and soul. As a result, the language of the liturgy goes beyond the mere verbal language that is its basis. Its symbolic language is intended through the ritual for the whole man and not only for his intellect. It speaks to his heart, to his memory, to his body. The liturgy is expressed as much through architecture, iconography, and hymnography as through rituality. The body is involved in it through various gestures, actions, and postures. All the bodily senses are invited to participate in the liturgy: the sense of smell if only by breathing in the perfume of incense; hearing by listening to liturgical chant; sight by contemplating the beauty of iconography; taste when eating and drinking; touch if only by venerating the icons, exchanging the kiss of peace, and so on.

The twentieth century certainly emphasized the importance of understanding the meaning of the liturgy, but it sometimes devalued, or even despised, the symbolic language of rites or rituality in general. On the other hand, we must not forget that it was also, thanks to the works of Paul Ricœur and Louis-Marie Chauvet on the interpretation of the symbol and on symbolism, the century of the revalorization of the power of sign, which intimately unites the signifier and the signified.[15] The twentieth century also rediscovered the language of rituality

---

[13] Cf. Nicolas Cabasilas, *La vie en Christ*, I, 18 (SC 355, 94).
[14] Alexander Schmemann, "The Missionary Imperative," in *Church, World, Mission* (Crestwood, NY: St Vladimir's Seminary Press, 1979), 216.
[15] Paul Ricœur, "Le symbole donne à penser," *Esprit* 27 (1959): 60–76, and *La symbolique du mal* (Paris: Seuil, 1960); Louis-Marie Chauvet, *Du symbolique au symbole: Essai sur les sacrements* (Paris: Cerf, 1979), and *Symbol and Sacrament: A Sacramental Reinterpretation of Christian Existence* (Collegeville, MN: Liturgical Press, 1995).

thanks to the anthropological research of Arnold Van Gennep on rites of passage.[16]

The symbolic language of the liturgy cannot in any way be reduced to superficial symbolism. The symbol of the liturgy has a strong meaning. It unites two realities, one visible and the other invisible, which are both equally present and effective. Symbolism is not limited to the anamnesis by a representation of events of the past but implies an actualization, a representation of the mystery, which is a present reality and active in the present. It is also thanks to this symbolic language that the liturgy succeeds in bringing together the past of the history of salvation, the present of liturgical action, and the future of the eschaton.

Nicolas Cabasilas considered "life in Christ" both as a present experience and as a reality to come, in the *eschata*.[17] Following him, Schmemann also recalled and insisted on the eschatological dimension of liturgy. Liturgy is not simply the reminder or the memorial of the past but the revelation and manifestation of the Kingdom of God. In his view, the liturgy not only fulfills the Church but also reveals the Kingdom of God. He frequently used to ask participants to consider the Eucharist not only as the "sacrament of the Church" but also as the "sacrament of the Kingdom."[18] He stated, "The Eucharist constitutes the heart, the center of this eschatological experience."[19] It is in the light of this liturgical experience that we must undoubtedly understand the passage of the *Epistle to Diognetus*, where it is said that Christians "spend their lives on earth, but are citizens of heaven."[20] The same was affirmed by the Second Vatican Council in its constitution on the liturgy: "In the earthly liturgy we take part in a foretaste of that heavenly liturgy which is celebrated in the holy city of Jerusalem toward which we journey as pilgrims."[21]

Schmemann further suggested that the liturgy should be considered not only from the perspective of man's relationship with God but also from the perspective of man's relationship with the cosmos.

---

[16] Arnold Van Gennep, *The Rites of Passage* (Chicago, IL: University of Chicago Press, 1961).
[17] Nicolas Cabasilas, *La vie en Christ*, I, 1, 3, 4 (SC 355, 79).
[18] Alexander Schmemann, *The Eucharist: Sacrament of the Kingdom* (Crestwood, NY: St Vladimir's Seminary Press, 1987).
[19] Alexandre Schmemann, "Théologie liturgique. Remarques méthodologiques," in *La liturgie: son sens, son esprit, sa méthode (Liturgie et théologie). Conférences Saint-Serge. XXVIIIe Semaine d'études liturgiques* (BELS 27) (Rome, 1982), 301–2.
[20] *Epistle to Diognetus* V, 9 (SC 33bis, 62–64).
[21] *Sacrosanctum Concilium*, 8.

He willingly spoke of the sacramentality of man and of the world. According to him, liturgical rites must permeate and give rhythm to the daily life of man and the world. He underlined the need to rediscover the true meaning of worship in its cosmic, ecclesiastical, and eschatological dimensions.[22]

With such an approach, baptism ought not to be understood only as a personal initiation into a community but also as the recreation of humanity and the world in the light of Christ. Confirmation is not just a personal invitation to discern Christ but a call to recognize the face of God on the face of each person and on the face of the world. The Eucharist is not only the spiritual food of the Christian but it also invites him to develop a Eucharistic attitude, that is, to be grateful to God for everything. Confession is not just an opportunity to express personal remorse, dispel guilt, and secure forgiveness but an opportunity to reconcile with God and the rest of creation. Marriage is not just a social contract and the union of two persons but the expression of the deep unity that exists between the Creator and creation. The Sacrament of the Sick cannot be understood only as what brings about physical healing but as the sacrament that heals the brokenness between body and soul and reconciles creation with God. The Sacrament of Holy Orders is not merely the granting of authority to clerics but the means by which creation is transfigured for the Kingdom of God.

A COMMUNAL PIETY

Liturgical piety, as a manifestation of the Church and the Kingdom of God, thus cannot be reduced to individual piety. On the contrary, it should always be understood as a community experience. The Church is an assembly: an assembly of the people of God around Christ. It is the mystical body of Christ, of which the baptized are the members. Through the celebration of the Eucharist, the liturgical assembly already participates in the Kingdom to come through the new life that Christ offers them through the sacraments in the Holy Spirit.

The father of Eucharistic ecclesiology, Nicolas Afanassieff, underlined that the Eucharist is not simply one of the seven sacraments of the

---

[22] Alexander Schmemann, *For the Life of the World: Sacraments and Orthodoxy* (Crestwood, NY: St Vladimir's Seminary Press, 1973), and *The World as Sacrament* (London: Darton, Longman & Todd, 1966).

Church but the sacrament of the Church par excellence.[23] Schmemann underlined the ecclesial dimension of the Baptismal Rites as the sacrament of the entry into the Church and therefore argued for their reintegration into the framework of the Eucharistic assembly.[24]

For this reason, in the ancient Church, baptism was not only celebrated but also prepared in connection with the liturgy of the Christian community. Indeed, the period of preparation of catechumens for baptism coincided with Great Lent, since baptism was celebrated during the Easter Vigil. The catechumenate therefore did not consist of a private catechism lesson but was performed in a liturgical framework between the third and sixth hour of the day. During this service of the hours, prayers of exorcism were read over the catechumens, who then heard the biblical reading and listened to the catechetical homily, as evidenced by the catechetical homilies of Cyril of Jerusalem. And during eight days following their baptism, the neophytes remained in the church to attend liturgical services during the Easter week and listen to the mystagogical homilies, which explained the meaning of the sacred rites of the sacraments.[25]

THE SCHOOL OF PRAYER

Liturgy is not the place for the personal devotions of individuals who would come to derive individual spiritual benefit. Any liturgical assembly is an ecclesial assembly. It is therefore appropriate to distinguish between personal prayer and common prayer; prayer in the cell or at the house and prayer in the church. The common prayer is performed by the entire Church community. The Church gathers for common prayer at hours specially established by the tradition and enclosed in the liturgical cycle. It is performed with the participation of the clergy on behalf of the worshipers. The common liturgical prayer structures and shapes personal prayer, which is a necessary complement to common prayer. As *Sacrosanctum Concilium* states, "The spiritual life ... is not limited solely to participation in the liturgy. The

---

[23] Cf. Nicolas Afanassieff, Трапеза Господня (Paris, 1952) [= *Le Repas du Seigneur* in *Contacts* 256 (2016), p. 445–571], and *L'Église du Saint-Esprit*, Cogitatio Fidei vol. 83 (Paris: Cerf, 1975) [= *The Church of the Holy Spirit* (Notre Dame, IN: University of Notre Dame Press, 2007)].
[24] Alexandre Schmemann, *D'eau et d'Esprit* (Paris: DDB, 1987), 202–3.
[25] Cf. Egeria, *Itinerarium*, 45 (SC 296, 304–16).

Christian is indeed called to pray with his brethren, but he must also enter into his chamber to pray to the Father, in secret."[26]

In the second half of the second century, Clement of Alexandria attests that Christians gathered for prayers and praises, reading the Scriptures and psalms, and singing hymns at the third, sixth, and ninth hours, before sunset, and even during the night, before sunrise.[27] He points out as well that the perfect Christian should pray without ceasing, according to Paul's exhortation to "pray without ceasing," as opposed to the practice of the people of Israel to pray seven times a day.[28] It is generally agreed that Christians prayed three times a day – in the morning, in the middle of the day, and in the evening, or at the third, sixth, and ninth hours, following the Jewish tradition.[29] In this sense, the number seven mentioned in the Psalm should probably not be taken literally but figuratively, as in "many times" and therefore "constantly."[30] In the third century, Origen compared the life of the saints as a long uninterrupted prayer and mentions the necessity to pray three times a day, following the example of Daniel (Dn 6:10).[31] It is not always easy to distinguish in these texts private prayer from common liturgical prayer, on which the former is shaped. According to the opinion of Robert Taft, Clement and Origen did not describe the Liturgy of the Hours but rather made an allegorical commentary on prayer at any time of the day.[32]

Nonetheless, by the end of the fourth century, the *Apostolic Constitutions* prescribed that Christians pray in the morning, at the third, sixth, and ninth hours of the day, in the evening, and at cockcrow, and that if it was impossible for them to go to church, they had to meet at home, and that if even that was impossible, "let each sing, read and pray at home, or else in twos or threes together." This document also directs the bishop to "assemble the Church" each evening and morning

---

[26] *Sacrosanctum Concilium*, 12.
[27] Clement of Alexandria, *Stromates* VII, 7, 40 and 49 (SC 428, 142–44.166).
[28] 1 Thess 5:16 as opposed to Ps 119:164. See Clement of Alexandria, *Stromates* VII, 35 (SC 428, 128–30).
[29] J. Jeremias, "La prière quotidienne dans la vie du Seigneur et dans l'Église primitive," *La prière des heures*, ed. Mgr. Cassien and B. Botte (Paris: Cerf, 1963), 43–58; K. Hruby, "Les heures de prière dans le judaïsme à l'époque de Jésus," *La prière des heures*, 59–84; Gilles Dorival, "Les heures de la prière (à propos du psaume 118, 164)," *Annales de Bretagne et des pays de l'Ouest* 83 (1976): 281–301.
[30] Dorival, "Les heures de la prière (à propos du psaume 118, 164)," 283.
[31] Origen, *On Prayer*, 12.
[32] Robert Taft, *The Liturgy of the Hours in East and West* (Collegeville, MN: Liturgical Press, 1985), 14–17.

for a service consisting of appropriate psalms and prayers.[33] At the same time, a Western pilgrim by the name of Egeria bears witness to a daily Liturgy of the Hours at the Anastasis (Holy Sepulcher) in Jerusalem that was provided by deacons, priests, and the bishop, and in which participated monks, virgins, and laity, men and women. It began each morning before cockcrow, continued in the morning, then began again at the sixth and ninth hours of the day. At the tenth hour of the day, evening service took place, during which torches and candles were lit, and which ended at dusk. These offices were composed of psalms, antiphons, hymns, and prayers, and on feast days the Scriptures were read.[34]

In addition to these testimonies to prayer of the hours in secular churches, the prayer of the hours has also developed in the monastic setting. The Life of Saint Saba the Sanctified recounts that he required novices who entered the monastery he had founded near Jerusalem to learn the Psalter and to know the "canon of psalmody" by heart, that is to say the offices of the hours.[35] The divine office punctuated the continual prayer of the monks at different times of the day and night, which is also witnessed by the Hesychast tradition transmitted through the *Philokalia* of the Neptic Fathers. It is through the recitation of the liturgical offices of the prayer of the hours that Christians, monks, and lay people were formed in prayer.[36]

Concerning the Liturgy of the Hours, Schmemann spoke of "sanctification of time." Being aware that the Church, although not "of this world," abides in this world for its salvation, as the "mystery of the Lord's day" and the "mystery of the new age," he considered that while being confronted with time, she fills it with the "eschaton," and, in doing this, proceeds in the "sanctification of time."[37] The Second Vatican Council encouraged the renewal of the prayer of the hours in parish circles, specifying: "Because the purpose of the office is to sanctify the day, the traditional sequence of the hours is to be restored so that once again they may be genuinely related to the time of the day when they are prayed."[38]

---

[33] *Apostolic Constitutions* VIII, 34 (SC 336, 242–44).
[34] Egeria, *Itinerarium*, 24–25 (SC 296, 234–50).
[35] Cyrille de Scythopolis, *Vie de saint Sabas*, 28 [113, 9] (A. J. Festugière, *Les moines d'Orient*, III/2, Paris, 1962, p. 39).
[36] Kallistos and Ignatios Xanthopouloi, "Centurie spirituelle," 25–27, 37, *La Philocalie* (trad. J. Touraille), vol. 2, (Paris, 1995), 572–75, 584–85.
[37] Alexander Schmemann, *Introduction to Liturgical Theology* (Crestwood, NY: St Vladimir's Seminary Press, 1986), ch. 2.
[38] *Sacrosanctum Concilium*, 88.

THE CHRISTIAN LIFE AS A SACRED FEAST

This sanctification of time occurs as well through the celebration of liturgical feasts throughout the year. As the constitution on the liturgy of Vatican II says, "Within the cycle of a year, moreover, [the Church] unfolds the whole mystery of Christ, from the incarnation and birth until the ascension, the day of Pentecost, and the expectation of blessed hope and of the coming of the Lord."[39] Certainly, liturgy makes the believer relive important events of the history of salvation. But liturgy is not just a simple memorial or an actualization of the past. Liturgical celebrations, by gathering believers in the risen Christ, unite past, present, and future. Each liturgical commemoration transforms the faithful into witnesses of the events of the past and also transports them to the future by making them communicate with the Kingdom of God.[40]

In the liturgy, celebrated here and now, the past, present, and future are linked in mystery. This is why the liturgical hymns as well as the patristic homilies describe the events of the mystery of salvation in the eternal present of God, as do in particular the hymns of the Byzantine tradition, which proclaim, for instance, "Today the Virgin brings to world the Eternal ..."; "Today hangs on a tree He who keeps creation in his hand ..."; "Today the Master has defeated Hades ...."

Already in the second half of the second century, Clement of Alexandria spoke of Christian life as a "sacred feast."[41] Liturgy fixed an order in the celebration of the mystery of salvation in a liturgical calendar. Liturgical feasts were an opportunity for Christians to celebrate decisive events of the past with not only universal but also eternal repercussions. The institution of Christian feasts was not a new phenomenon. Humanity has always needed feasts to structure its life. Whether in pagan civilizations or in ancient Judaism, festivals punctuated daily life. Already in the book of Genesis, we find the model and the reason for the weekly rest in the Sabbath of God when God blesses and sanctifies the seventh day and rests after his work of creation.[42] On the basis of God's rest on the seventh day, according to the first narrative of creation, the celebration of the Sabbath was instituted by the Decalogue.[43]

---

[39] Ibid., 102.
[40] Thomas J. Talley, *The Origins of the Liturgical Year* (New York: Pueblo, 1986).
[41] Clement of Alexandria, *Stromates* VII, 49, 3 (SC 428, 166).
[42] Gen 2:1–3.
[43] Exod 20:8–10.

It is remarkable that even in the fulfillment of the mystery of salvation, Christ kept the Sabbath by remaining in the tomb on the Great Sabbath (Holy Saturday) and rising from the dead on the first day of the week. Thus, the first day of the week became the first and greatest Christian holiday, celebrating the resurrection of Christ, and would ultimately receive the name "Lord's day."[44]

The *Apostolic Constitutions* provide that Christians work five days during the week but rest on the Sabbath and on Sundays, when they are required to attend Church services for the teaching of the faith, noting that "Saturday has its justification in creation and Sunday in the resurrection."[45] In the ancient Church and the Byzantine tradition, Saturday remained a holiday that remembered not only Christ's repose in the tomb but also all the deceased who "have fallen asleep" in the Lord. From the point of view of the Church Fathers, Sunday is both the first day and the eighth of the week because the resurrection of Christ completes the first creation of man and inaugurates the age to come – the Kingdom of God, regarded as the new creation.[46]

The invention of holy places and the construction of churches under the impulse of the emperors Constantine and Helen in the fourth century contributed not only to the development of a liturgical calendar wishing to celebrate the mystery of salvation in time but also to the constitution of a real sacred topography aimed at reviving the divine economy in space. As attested by the Pilgrim from Bordeaux who visited the Holy Land in the year 333, it was Emperor Constantine who took the initiative to build three large basilicas, which were to be important poles in this nascent liturgy in what would become "the Holy City": the Basilica of the Nativity in Bethlehem, the Martyrium in Jerusalem, and the Eleona on the Mount of Olives.[47] We can also compare these fundamental places in the history of salvation with the events mentioned in the Nicene Creed: the incarnation, the passion–resurrection, and the ascension.

---

[44] Samuele Bacchiocchi, *From Sabbath to Sunday: A Historical Investigation of the Rise of Sunday Observance in Early Christianity* (Rome: Pontifical Gregorian University Press, 1977); D. A. Carson (ed.), *From Sabbath to Lord's Day: A Biblical, Historical and Theological Investigation* (Grand Rapids, MI: Zondervan, 1982).

[45] Apostolic Constitutions VIII, 33 (SC 336, 240–42).

[46] Gregory of Nazianzus, *Discourse* 41, 2 (SC 358, 317–19).

[47] *Itinerarium Burdigalense*, ed. P. Geyer et O. Cuntz, CCL 175 (Turnhout: Brepols, 1965), 594 and 598 (Pierre Maraval, *Récits des premiers pèlerins chrétiens au Proche-Orient [IVe–VIIe siècle]*, Sagesses chrétiennes (Paris: Cerf, 1996), 32, 33, and 35).

However, although the pilgrims were attracted to the holy places following the Constantinian constructions that aimed to relive the different events of the mystery of salvation *in situ*, the Church, in its liturgical celebration, retained a global, not fragmentary, conception of the economy of salvation. For example, Hesychius of Jerusalem, in homilies preached in the fifth century, constantly emphasizes that the Incarnation is never separated from the Cross and the Resurrection, nor from eschatology. Each feast certainly commemorated a particular event of the history of salvation, situated in time and space, but above all commemorated the entire mystery of salvation, realized through the incarnation, death, resurrection, and ascension of Jesus Christ, whose return the Church never ceased to await. As a result, each feast day, celebrated on a specific date and in a given place in Jerusalem, most often consistent with history, was certainly a memorial of an event in the history of salvation accomplished by Christ in time and space, but it sought, beyond that, to encourage each Christian to relive this mystery of salvation by the celebration of his own salvation in the perspective of the second and glorious coming of the Lord.

Admittedly, the constitution of the liturgical calendar of the Church of Jerusalem in the Constantinian era was necessarily influenced by the proximity of the holy places and the basilicas that were built there, but it also reflected the defense of the Nicene faith in the midst of theological controversies and underlined the unicity of the mystery of salvation, since "indivisible is piety (ἀμέριστος γάρ ἐστιν εὐσέβεια)," as Cyril of Jerusalem once affirmed.[48] Thus, from the end of the fourth century, Christian feasts spread in Christendom. The *Apostolic Constitutions* already mention, in addition to Easter, the feasts of Ascension, Pentecost, Nativity, and Epiphany; the days of the apostles; and the feasts of the first martyr Stephen and of the other holy martyrs.[49] The number of feasts continued to grow in subsequent centuries. Thus, Christian feasts served as a means for believers to relive throughout the liturgical year the main moments of the mystery of salvation.

THE ASCETIC ETHOS

The liturgical year was not only a succession of feasts in the Ancient Church but also a succession of fasting days. Even today, Orthodox

---

[48] Cyril of Jerusalem, *Baptismal catechesis* XVI, 4. PG 33, 924A.
[49] *Apostolic Constitutions* VIII, 33 (SC 336, 240–42).

Christians fast more than half of the year. From the time of the Early Church, Christians renounced food in order to pay tribute to God's power, to acknowledge their sinfulness, and to practice asceticism. They gave to the poor and sick the food they denied themselves. Food is actually a powerful symbol in Christianity, since Christians in the bread and wine of the Eucharist partake of the Body and Blood of Christ. For this reason, they also fasted before receiving communion. Thus eating and not eating are powerful symbols in Christian spirituality.[50]

Since the apostolic era, Wednesdays and Fridays have been fasting days, as attested by the Didachè.[51] This ancient Christian practice of fasting twice a week was inspired by Judaism, which observed the fast on Monday and Thursday.[52] According to Basil of Caesarea the practice of fasting is as old as mankind and of divine institution. He indeed sees its origin in the commandment given by God to Adam in Paradise not to eat of the fruit of the tree of the knowledge of good and evil,[53] which he interprets as the law of fasting and abstinence. According to him, fasting reflects the heavenly life when humans lived like angels with few or no needs. He believes that it was through contempt of fasting that man was driven out of paradise.[54]

There are several ways to fast. Fasting can be a voluntary deprivation of all food, following the examples of Moses and Christ, who each fasted for forty days.[55] Such a practice is difficult, and not everyone has the strength to observe it. Already at the end of the fourth century, Egeria observed various observances of such a fast in Jerusalem: those who would fast throughout the week and eat only on Saturday and Sunday; those who had dinner in the middle of the week, on Thursday; those who had meals every other day; and finally, the weakest, who fasted all day and allowed themselves a meal in the evening.[56] But fasting can also be abstinence from certain types of foods. The Byzantine monastic *typika* (rules), still observed in the Orthodox Church, describe different levels of fasting consisting of abstinence from

---

[50] Caroline Walker Bynum, *Holy Feast and Holy Fast: The Religious Significance of Food to Medieval Women* (Berkeley: University of California Press, 1987), 31–70.
[51] *Didachè* 8, 1 (SC 248, 173).
[52] As mentioned in the parable of the Publican and the Pharisee, cf. Luke 18:12.
[53] Gen 2:16–17.
[54] Basil of Caesarea, *On Fasting* 1, 3. PG 31, 168A.
[55] Cf. Exod 34:28; Matt 4:1–2.
[56] Egeria, *Itinerarium* 27.9 and 28.3 (SC 296, 265–67).

meat, eggs, and dairy products, and even on some days from fish, wine, and oil.[57]

To the practice of fasting twice a week was added a fast of forty days, "Great Lent," which preceded the feast of Easter and was modeled on the forty days of fasting by Christ in the desert.[58] Dorotheus of Gaza also sees in these forty days a tithe for the whole year and thus develops an interesting idea that fasting is an offering or a consecration of a period of the year to God.[59] The fact of devoting a part of the year to God to give thanks to him reflects a "Eucharistic attitude" and teaches moderation. In addition to Lent, which prepares for Easter, the Christian East also knows, by analogy, another period of fasting, one that precedes Christmas and is equivalent to Western Advent. Easter and Christmas were in fact the two great festivals of the ancient Christian calendar, since the mystery of the incarnation is inseparable from the Paschal Mystery.

The Byzantine liturgical tradition has a third period of fasting in the year called the Apostles' Fast. This originally lasted only one week, after the octave of Pentecost, and marked, after the abolition of fasting throughout the festive period of the fifty days after Easter, the resumption of ordinary time.[60] This week was then extended until the feast of the holy apostles Peter and Paul (June 29). In the fourteenth century in Byzantium was then added a fourth period of fasting that precedes the feast of the Dormition (Assumption) of the Mother of God on August 15.[61]

In the Christian East, fasting is a liturgical practice. Not only does it prepare the faithful for the celebration of major feasts but it also marks the liturgical season by the content of the prayers and the hymnography. Fasting is not merely an individual practice of piety. It has a communal and ecclesial character. Christians cannot be attributed any personal merit, for they fast with the Church by following ecclesial prescriptions. One does not choose when he will fast and for how long, nor what he will eat and what he will abstain from. He fasts during the established periods by following the rules that the Church provides him. This is how fasting as a communal practice shapes the ecclesial identity.

---

[57] Job Getcha, "La pratique du jeûne pendant la quarantaine pascale d'après le Triode byzantin," in *Thusia aineseôs. Mélanges liturgiques offerts à la mémoire de l'archevêque Georges Wagner (1930–1993)*, ed. Job Getcha and André Lossky (Paris: Presses Saint Serge, 2005), 95–112.

[58] Matt 4:1–2.

[59] Dorotheus of Gaza, *Spiritual Works*, XV, 159 (SC 92, 446).

[60] *Apostolic Constitutions* V, 20, 14 (SC 329, 382).

[61] Job Getcha, *The Typikon Decoded: An Explanation of Byzantine Liturgical Practice*, trans. P. Meyendorff (Crestwood, NY: St Vladimir's Seminary Press, 2012), 129, 283–85.

Although fasting has fallen into disuse in the West, the Second Vatican Council reiterated the importance of pre-paschal fasting by stating, "Let the paschal fast be kept sacred. Let it be celebrated everywhere on Good Friday and, where possible, prolonged throughout Holy Saturday, so that the joys of the Sunday of the resurrection may be attained with uplifted and clear mind."[62] The practice of fasting and abstinence has an ascetic aspect. Asceticism and spiritual struggle are endless in the present life. All are called to respond according to their own strength. The spiritual warfare of fasting makes it possible to progress in the spiritual life.

This chapter has illustrated how piety, spirituality, and liturgy are interconnected. Spiritual life is initiated by the sacraments of Christian initiation and is nourished by the Eucharist. It is structured by the sacraments of the Church. Therefore, genuine Christian piety is not individual but communal, or more exactly ecclesial. Prayer is the fruit of baptism. The prayer life of the Christian is punctuated by the Liturgy of the Hours. Christian feasts and days or longer periods of fasting shape the life of the Christian, whose purpose is to be a life in Christ and a life in communion with the Holy Spirit, in the perspective of deification.

For Further Reading

Afanassieff, Nicolas, *The Church of the Holy Spirit* (Notre Dame, IN: University of Notre Dame Press, 2007).
Bacchiocchi, Samuele, *From Sabbath to Sunday: A Historical Investigation of the Rise of Sunday Observance in Early Christianity* (Rome: Pontifical Gregorian University Press, 1977).
Botte, Bernard, and Mgr Cassien (eds.), *La prière des heures* (Paris: Cerf, 1963).
Bynum, Caroline Walker, *Holy Feast and Holy Fast: The Religious Significance of Food to Medieval Women* (Berkeley: University of California Press, 1987).
Getcha, Job, *Participants de la nature divine: La spiritualité orthodoxe à l'âge de la sécularisation* (Paris: Apostolia, 2020).
Lossky, Vladimir, *À l'image et à la ressemblance de Dieu* (Paris: Cerf, 1967).
Mikalson, John, *Honor Thy Gods: Popular Religion in Greek Tragedy* (Chapel Hill, NC: University of North Carolina Press, 1991).
Schmemann, Alexander, *The Eucharist: Sacrament of the Kingdom*, trans. Paul Kachur (Crestwood, NY: St Vladimir's Seminary Press, 1988).
 For the Life of the World: Sacraments and Orthodoxy (Crestwood, NY: St Vladimir's Seminary Press, 1973).
Taft, Robert, *The Liturgy of the Hours in East and West* (Collegeville, MN: Liturgical Press, 1985).

---

[62] *Sacrosanctum Concilium*, 110.

16 Liturgy and Pastoral Ministry

SAMUEL GOYVAERTS

The purpose of this contribution is to elucidate the relationship between the celebration of the liturgy and the other ministries that are part of the Church's mission and work in this world. Since about the middle of the last century, it has become commonplace to speak about the work and mission of the Church from the threefold office (*tria munera*) of Christ as priest, prophet, and king. Through baptism, all share in these offices, and, parallel with this, the pastoral ministry of the Church is described as proclamation, liturgy, and charity. These three offices form the Church as a community, *koinonia*. When considering liturgy and pastoral ministry from not only a systematic but also a practical point of view, the mutual relationship between the liturgy and the other "foundational functions" of the Church comes to the fore.

This chapter starts with some brief historical remarks on the rise and recent evolutions regarding liturgy and pastoral practice. This will organically grow into a reflection on the double claim of the Second Vatican Council, whose influence extended far beyond the borders of the Roman Catholic Church: Liturgy is designated as source and summit of the life of the Church,[1] and at the same time liturgy does not exhaust the entire activity of the Church and is firmly connected with the proclamation of faith and doing works of charity.[2] This double claim will be explored and unfolded throughout the entire article, exploring how liturgy connects to the life of the Church understood as charity, proclamation, and community.[3]

---

[1] *Sacrosanctum Concilium*, 10.
[2] Ibid., 9.
[3] In this respect, my perspective is broader than that of pastoral liturgy as used by Léon van Ommen, for example, in a highly informative publication. He limits his scope to those regular liturgies that involve "worshiping God and caring for the people at the same time," which is also the focus of Mark Eary and others, who write on the topic of "liturgy" and "pastoral." See Léon van Ommen, "Liturgy and Pastoral Care: Pastoral Worship and Priestly Counseling," in *Studia Liturgica* 46 (2016): 208–21; Mark Eary,

HISTORICAL EVOLUTIONS: LITURGY AS SOURCE AND SUMMIT OF THE LIFE OF THE CHURCH

For a general overview and introduction into the history, subject, and methods of pastoral ministry, other sources are available.[4] In this introduction, I will very briefly sketch the evolution of the relation between the different offices of pastoral ministry, seen from the perspective of the liturgy. There has always been an obvious relation between worship, proclamation, and charity. Foundational is the gospel and the person of Jesus Christ Himself, who prayed and worshipped, proclaimed the Kingdom of God, and had unusual care and love for the poor and the outcast. We also have scriptural information on the "pastoral" activities of the first Christian communities:

> All who believed were together and had all things in common; they would sell their possessions and goods and distribute the proceeds to all, as any had need. Day by day, as they spent much time together in the temple, they broke bread at home and ate their food with glad and generous hearts, praising God and having the goodwill of all the people. And day by day the Lord added to their number those who were being saved.[5]

Consequently, the proclamation of the gospel (*kerygma*), the care for one another (*diakonia*), and liturgical prayer (*leitourgia*) have been the ways in which the community of faith (*koinonia*) has realized itself throughout the centuries.[6]

Augustine makes it very clear how all Christians share in this threefold ministry of Prophet (proclaiming), King (caring), and Priest (celebrating) of Christ.[7] Nevertheless, this triad disappears into the

---

Worship That Cares: An Introduction to Pastoral Liturgy (London: Hymns Ancient & Modern Ltd, 2012).

[4] See, among others, Gerben Heitink and Reinder Bruinsma, *Practical Theology: History, Theory, Action Domains. Manual for Practical Theology*, trans. Reinder Bruinsma (Grand Rapids, MI: Eerdmans, 1999); Annemie Dillen and Stefan Gärtner, *Discovering Practical Theology: Exploring Boundaries* (Leuven: Peeters, 2020).

[5] Acts 2:44–47, NRSV.

[6] In view of the given limitations, I will not enter into a discussion of *kerygma/martyria* or *diakonia/caritas* and will instead opt for the broadest sense in which to use the terms just mentioned. Also see the Faith and Order document on the Church, which uses the same terminology: WCC, *Nature and Mission of the Church: A Stage on the Way to a Common Statement*, "Faith and Order Paper 198," 2005, www.oikoumene.org/sites/default/files/Document/FO2005_198_en.pdf, in particular §36.

[7] Cf. Michael Schmaus, "Ämter Christi," *Lexikon für Theologie und Kirche*, no. 1 (1957): 457–59.

background during the Middle Ages. Thomas Aquinas only mentions Christ's priestly and judicial power.[8] When it comes to the Church, for Aquinas mainly the priestly, sacramental ministry comes to the fore; a systematic reflection on the threefold office is not found in the *Summa*. During the Reformation and in particular thanks to Calvin, the idea of the *tria munera* is rediscovered. Eventually in the eighteenth and especially the nineteenth centuries, the threefold office of Christ becomes a more widespread schema for thinking about pastoral ministry.[9] Noteworthy for this period, from a liturgical perspective, is the position of Johann Sebastian von Drey (1777–1853) and his fellow theologians of the Catholic Tübingen School.[10] For Drey, doctrine, cult, and polity (in which also charity is situated) are the three essential elements that enable the Church to fulfill its purpose.[11] That purpose is, above all, relating humankind to God. According to Drey, however, the liturgy is especially crucial in achieving this goal, and the Eucharist is at the center of it. In his theological system, the liturgy is the bearer of tradition, the concrete expression of doctrine, and it transforms people and the whole Church community.[12]

Eventually, especially in the twentieth-century Liturgical Movement and its *ressourcement*, the relationship between the liturgy and pastoral ministry really came to the fore, and the concept of pastoral liturgy emerged.[13] First of all, Athanasius Wintersig's (1900–1942) name should be mentioned. He is one of the first to describe pastoral liturgy as a separate branch of liturgical studies. In this context, even more strongly

---

[8] See *Summa Theologiae* III, q. 22 and q. 59.
[9] Cf. Lothar Ullrich, "Ämter Christi," *Lexikon für Theologie und Kirche*, no. 1 (1993): 561–62.
[10] See Samuel Goyvaerts, "The Incarnation as the Fundamental Mystery for Sacramentality in the Catholic Tübingen School," *Studia liturgica* 50 (2020): 176–87.
[11] Johann Sebastian von Drey, *Brief Introduction to the Study of Theology: With Reference to the Scientific Standpoint and the Catholic System*, trans. Michael J. Himes, vol. 1, Notre Dame Studies in Theology (Notre Dame, IN: University of Notre Dame Press, 1994), 126ff.
[12] See Samuel Goyvaerts, "A Romantic Theology of the Eucharist: The Catholic Tübingen School and the Communal Celebration of the Liturgy," *Ephemerides Liturgicae* CXXVII.1 (2013): 60–84.
[13] See Domenico Sartore, "Pastoral Liturgy," in *Handbook for Liturgical Studies, vol. 2: Fundamentel Liturgy*, ed. Anscar J. Chupungco (Collegeville, MN: Liturgical Press, 1998), 65–95; Samuel Goyvaerts, "Moving between Liturgical Theology and Liturgical Pastoral: On Theology, Liturgy, and Christian Life," *Questions Liturgiques* 100 (2020): 294–312.

than Drey, he assigns a principal place to the liturgy in the whole of the Church's life:

> The value of pastoral liturgy is derived from the value of the liturgy itself. Christ's mission is that of a priest-king who as such is also prophet and teacher. His offices and dignities are enclosed in this character of priest-king. The liturgy, as the high priestly perpetuation of Christ in the Church, the sacred mystery, is therefore the true centre of the religious life of the community of the faithful.[14]

Similar thoughts can also be found later during the Liturgical Movement, for example, in the work of the famous Jesuit scholar Joseph Andreas Jungmann (1889-1975). In his work *Pastoral Liturgy*, he describes the relation between the liturgy and pastoral ministry in a very concrete way:

> [I]t means rather that all catechesis and all preaching, all child-welfare and youth work, all charity and all care of particular classes and conditions of people, all work for Catholic education and all religious journalism, can only be seen as a preparation which will lead the faithful to that outlook on life, that disposition of faith, hope and love, that attitude of thankfulness to the revealing and redeeming God, which breaks forth on Sunday like a mighty stream in the corporate celebration of the Eucharist, and presents to God "all honor and glory."[15]

For the theologians of the Liturgical Movement the liturgy is really the center around which all pastoral activities revolve. It must be noted that this often is a more bipolar idea of the relation between liturgy and Church ministry, not so much using the tripod of the threefold office. The influence of theologians such as Wintersig and Jungmann, and the liturgical position they represent, is evident in the concept of the liturgy as *fons et culmen*, as articulated by the Second Vatican Council.[16] First of all, in no. 9 the council fathers state, "The sacred liturgy does not exhaust the entire activity of the Church. Before men can come to the liturgy they must be called to faith and to conversion." Therefore, the

---

[14] Athanasius Wintersig, "Pastoralliturgik," *Jahrbuch für Liturgiewissenschaft* 4 (1924): 166. My translation.

[15] Josef Andreas Jungmann, *Pastoral Liturgy* (Notre Dame, IN: Christian Classics, 2014), 386.

[16] See the Constitution on the Sacred Liturgy *Sacrosanctum Concilium*.

Church must teach and proclaim the gospel but also invite to works of charity. Then in the next paragraph the constitution on the liturgy reads,

> Nevertheless the liturgy is the summit toward which the activity of the Church is directed; at the same time it is the font from which all her power flows. For the aim and object of apostolic works is that all who are made sons of God by faith and baptism should come together to praise God in the midst of His Church, to take part in the sacrifice, and to eat the Lord's supper.
>
> The liturgy in its turn moves the faithful, filled with "the paschal sacraments," to be "one in holiness"; it prays that "they may hold fast in their lives to what they have grasped by their faith"; the renewal in the Eucharist of the covenant between the Lord and man draws the faithful into the compelling love of Christ and sets them on fire. From the liturgy, therefore, and especially from the Eucharist, as from a font, grace is poured forth upon us; and the sanctification of men in Christ and the glorification of God, to which all other activities of the Church are directed as toward their end, is achieved in the most efficacious possible way.[17]

This paragraph of the constitution clearly places liturgy at the heart of Church life and its ministry. Both proclamation and charity not only have the liturgy, which is sanctification of humankind and glorification of God, as their goal, but they also flow from it. The encounter with Christ in the liturgy sets the faithful and the Church in motion to build the Kingdom of God in word and deed.[18]

From here, the influential liturgist and theologian Cipriano Vagaggini (1909–1999) formulates his description of what *pastorale liturgica* actually is: "The general way of conceiving and putting pastoral into practice by consciously centering it in the liturgy."[19] Vagaggini mentions different important aspects of liturgical pastoral work, namely, participatory, active, communitarian, hierarchically structured, public, and convergent to the local Church. In discussing

---

[17] Ibid., 10.
[18] Peter Phan correctly notices that the other paragraphs before and after no. 10 should also be considered. See Peter Phan, "Liturgy of Life as the 'Summit and Source' of the Eucharistic Liturgy: Church Worship as Symbolization of the Liturgy of Life?," in *Incongruities: Who We Are and How We Pray*, ed. Timothy Fitzgerald and David A. Lysik (Chicago, IL: Liturgy Training Publications, 2000), 5–33, at 6–7.
[19] Cipriano Vagaggini, *Theological Dimensions of the Liturgy: A General Treatise on the Theology of the Liturgy* (Collegeville, MN: Liturgical Press, 1976), 838.

these themes, he constantly moves back and forth between liturgy and Church life. In these liturgical pastoral reflections, ecclesiology comes to the fore, but so does the individual human being. For example, active participation is not exclusively about the participation in the liturgy but also about the participation of the inner self of people in Christ. Here we encounter an important dynamic, which not all liturgists always clearly articulate: The dynamic between liturgy and Church life must go both ways. The metaphor of source and summit, and the strong focus on the liturgy, risks leading to a one-way movement or perspective: from the liturgy to all other domains of Christian life. Although not intended that way by the council, if one carefully reads paragraphs 9 and 10 of the constitution, this is certainly a pitfall of this metaphor.[20]

At the same time, this metaphor and the renewed attention to liturgy and its relation to pastoral ministry that followed the Second Vatican Council also inspired modern theologians, such as Mark Searle (1941-1992) in the 1980s, who tried to develop a new, interdisciplinary program for pastoral liturgics.[21] More recently, mention can be made, among others, of Birgit Jeggle-Merz.[22] She emphasizes in her work that Christian praxis is not merely an area of theological application but an independent *locus theologicus*. Not just texts and Church documents, but the concrete form of the liturgy itself and Christian practice can be regarded as a normative source and starting point of theological reflection.

However, one observes that in recent decades there has been little movement in the field of pastoral liturgy. One cause is the separation between the disciplines of pastoral theology on the one hand and liturgical science on the other, which hampers a common starting point for pastoral liturgy. At the same time, there have been many other evolutions in the field of liturgical studies since the Second Vatican Council, including, for example, the rise of ritual studies and developments in liturgical theology. Simultaneously there are evolutions in view of pastoral ministry and the larger context in which the Church seeks to carry out its mission. Empirical and other research also shows that, at least in Europe, not only is participation in liturgical celebrations

---

[20] See Phan, "Liturgy of Life," 11-16.
[21] See Mark Searle, "New Tasks, New Methods: The Emergence of Pastoral Liturgical Studies," *Worship* 57 (1983): 291.
[22] See, among others, Birgit Jeggle-Merz, "Liturgiewissenschaft als theologia experimentalis: Zu Vision und Mission des praktisch-theologischen Zweiges der Liturgiewissenschaft," in *Im Aufbruch: Liturgie und Liturgiewissenschaft vor neuen Herausforderungen*, ed. Benedikt Kranemann and Stephan Winter (Münster: Aschendorff, 2022), 195-208.

declining but also, for many people who do participate in the liturgy, this does not really function as the source of their Christian faith and practice.[23]

Can we, in this contemporary context, revisit the idea of source and summit and still talk about the "liturgical pastoral" as envisaged by Vagaggini and others? It remains the Church's mission to be near others, especially the poor (*diakonia*), to proclaim the gospel (*kerygma*), to form a community of salvation (*koinonia*), and, as Drey said, to perpetuate and foster in all this the relationship between God and humans. What place, then, does liturgy have in view of pastoral ministry? To answer this question, the next three paragraphs position the different classical areas of pastoral ministry just mentioned in their relation to the liturgy.

LITURGY AND *DIAKONIA*: THE LITURGICAL AND TRANSFORMATIVE SERVICE

Fundamental regarding the relationship between liturgy and charity or *diakonia* is the theology of Orthodox theologian Alexander Schmemann (1921–1983) and the way he inextricably linked liturgy with the "life of the world."[24] For Schmemann, the liturgy, and in particular the Eucharist, reveals the true nature and purpose of all creation. The liturgy is an invitation to participate in God's work of restoring and renewing the world not only through prayer and worship but also through acts of charity and by living a liturgical life. Elaborating on this in more recent times, the French sacramental theologian Louis-Marie Chauvet adds an important dimension to the debate on liturgy and ethics, the latter being related to charity. He points to the fundamental relationship between Scripture, sacraments, and ethics and emphasizes the fundamental bodily aspect of the liturgy.[25] Celebrating liturgy and

---

[23] See, for example, the data present in the European Values Studies on religion and, among others, church attendance: "Religion: Church Attendance – Confidence in the Church – Importance of God – Traditional Beliefs," *The European Values Studies*. Accessed June 5, 2023, at https://europeanvaluesstudy.eu/about-evs/research-topics/religion/. For interpretation, see, for example, Michael J. Breen and Ross Macmillan, "Saints, Scholars, Sceptics and Secularists: The Changing Faith of Religious Practice in Ireland, 1981–2020," in *Reflections on European Values: Honouring Loek Halman's Contribution to the European Values Study*, ed. R. Luijkx, T. Reeskens, and I. Sieben (Tilburg: Open Press TiU, 2022).

[24] See Alexander Schmemann, *For the Life of the World: Sacraments and Orthodoxy* (Yonkers, NY: St Vladimir's Seminary Press, 2018).

[25] See Louis-Marie Chauvet, *The Sacraments: The Word of God at the Mercy of the Body* (Collegeville, MN: Liturgical Press, 2001).

sacraments involves the whole person, including our bodies, emotions, and intellect, and is therefore deeply connected to our ethical behavior. In other words, Chauvet made clear that the way we worship shapes the way we live our lives. Through the symbols, gestures, and words of the liturgy, we are invited to see the world in a new way and to live in greater solidarity with others, particularly those who are marginalized or oppressed. In doing so, Chauvet places the transformative power of liturgy in relation to Christian action in the world at the forefront.

This is also the starting point of Bruce Morrill's recent work on liturgy and ethics. The key to this relationship is the idea of sanctification.[26] Morrill shows how time and again the liturgy in all its pluriformity sanctifies and draws the faithful into the Paschal Mystery, which leads to the transformation of everyday life and the entire world: "The work of the church's liturgical worship is thereby at once sacramental and prophetic: sacramental because symbolically revealing God's saving presence and action in embodied lives, and prophetic because Christians continuously need their thoughts and actions (re)oriented to the divine imagination for the world."[27] Morrill not only interprets the transformative power of the liturgy from the liturgical theological tradition, in the footsteps of Schmemann and Chauvet, but also reinforces it with insights from ritual studies.[28] From there, he emphasizes the bodily aspect of the liturgy and points to the importance of ritualization for forming identity and moral action. In so doing, Morrill also places great emphasis on the community aspect of the liturgy.

Of course, the diaconal dimension of the liturgy and the link between *diakonia* and *leitourgia* become evident through processes such as sanctification and transformation, which lead to a more ethical and charitable life. In addition, in the liturgy itself, *diakonia* becomes present. Think, for example, of the liturgical intercessory prayer, of the preparation of the gifts and accompanying collection, or in some Christian Churches of the liturgical washing of feet on Maundy Thursday. But even outside of the Eucharist, much liturgy is inherently diaconal. Blessing and praying over people in particular circumstances, anointing the sick, offering forgiveness to those who have sinned, and accompanying the dead and grieving are all liturgical–diaconal

---

[26] Bruce Morrill, *Practical Sacramental Theology: At the Intersection of Liturgy and Ethics* (Eugene, OR: Cascade Books, 2021).
[27] Ibid., ix.
[28] See in this context Chapter 21, Kimberly Belcher's "Liturgy as Ritual and Prayer."

moments in the life of the Church and exercises of the pastoral ministry of the Church.

When discussing liturgy and *diakonia*, the transformative power of liturgical worship is apparent. The liturgical service calls for and leads to Christian service and transformation of the world. Through the liturgical celebration, we are transformed by God's grace, and, through acts of charity, we can share that transformation with others. However, one aspect often overlooked in the dynamic between liturgy and charity is whether our acts of caring in the world also transform our liturgies. Liturgical prayer can indeed address the concerns and suffering of "the other" and the world and establish this relation, but we also critically need to ask ourselves if, when, and how liturgical celebrations perpetuate mechanisms of exclusion, oppression, inequality, and injustice.[29] It is essential that pastoral ministry is critical of liturgies and examines where and when they may be perpetuating or even installing these issues of injustice. Although offering and sharing our gifts around the liturgical table has a logical and practical connection to sharing with those who are in need, we must continue to ask how our liturgical celebrations can be more inclusive and transformative. Indeed, the dynamic between liturgy and charity must go both ways. Letting ourselves be transformed by God's grace to transform the world and at the same time also critically examining our liturgical practices from a diaconal perspective are both paramount in creating a more just and equal world.

LITURGY AND *KERYGMA*: ON LITURGICAL FORMATION

The proclamation of the gospel and the celebration of the mysteries of faith are easily connected to the teaching office of the Church and its *kerygmatical* apostolate. However, since proclamation is already studied in another contribution of this volume,[30] the focus here will be on liturgical formation. Leading people into the mysteries celebrated also requires a strong liturgical formation, certainly in an age and in cultures where Christian symbolic thinking is not default.

---

[29] On this, see Benjamin Durheim, "Bridging the Divide: Connecting Liturgy and Ethics in an Era of Polarization," *Worship* 91 (2017): 435–49; Leon van Ommen, "Liturgy and Pastoral Care," 220.

[30] See Chapter 17, Cas Wepener's "Liturgy and the Proclamation of the Word."

In his historical overview on liturgical formation, Patrick Prétot points out how, in the first centuries of Christianity, there was a kind of natural and automatic merging of liturgy and catechesis.[31] The liturgy was the place where the Christian faith was "taught," both in terms of the "savoir faire" and the content of faith. This is the period when Prosper of Aquitaine (fifth century) formulated the ancient wisdom of the *lex orandi legem statuat credendi*. Prétot then describes how this natural relationship slowly grew apart in the Middle Ages. Liturgy became increasingly reduced to ritual performance, and liturgical formation became the imparting of knowledge *about* the liturgy. Increasingly, liturgical formation exclusively became teaching the correct technical performance of the liturgy for the priest. For the faithful, liturgical formation was limited to some questions and highly theoretical answers in classical catechism teaching on the necessity and effects of the sacraments.

This only changes at the end of the nineteenth century and especially during and thanks to the Liturgical Movement in the twentieth. Prétot: "The liturgy gradually recovered its place not only as a science, but also as a form of ecclesial life."[32] Liturgical formation was extremely high on the agendas of pioneers such as Lambert Beauduin (1873–1960), the already mentioned Jungmann, Romano Guardini (1885–1968), Pius Parsch (1884–1954), Joseph Gelineau (1920–2008), and many others. Inspired by Pope Pius X, the aim of the Liturgical Movement from its beginning onward was to move the people closer to the liturgy and to deepen liturgical prayer and active participation, through training and formation of pastors and faithful. Only later in the Liturgical Movement did this become a double aim: moving the people closer to the liturgy, but also moving the liturgy closer to the people and reforming it to that end.

Liturgical formation during the first half of the twentieth century was worked on through both scientific and popular publications, liturgical formation weeks for both priests and lay people, "new" media like radio and television, meeting groups, the establishment of institutes for liturgical formation, and so on. At the same time, the gap between secular culture and the Christian religion was widening, and, in view of our time, Prétot admits "that it [the liturgy] has become inaccessible,

---

[31] Patrick Prétot, "Benchmarks for a History of Liturgical Formation," *Studia Liturgica* 46 (2016): 14–38.
[32] Ibid., 37.

at least in part, to a large number of our contemporaries."[33] For many pastors, the Liturgical Movement's goal of bringing the liturgy closer to the people and the people closer to the liturgy seems to have been achieved with the Second Vatican Council and the post-conciliar liturgical reform. Sadly, nothing could be further from the truth: When the (new) form of the liturgy was completed, formation in the liturgy should really have begun. However, basic literature and practical material for liturgical formation seems to be almost completely absent, as the editors of a recent book on liturgical pedagogics state.[34] The changed place of the Church and Christian life in Western societies poses great challenges to contemporary liturgical formation, and there is still a long way to go for both initiation and a deeper mystagogical formation in the liturgy.

According to James Pauly, who writes on liturgical catechesis for the twenty-first century, one of the greatest challenges for contemporary liturgical formation is that people are "accustomed to approaching God collectively," specifically in the liturgy. He pleads for a more personal approach, starting from the language of a personal relationship with God, not unlike Drey and some of his contemporaries in the German Romantic period.[35] In addition, while many have received sacramental initiation, this does not mean they are aligning their lives with Christ: "[B]eing sacramentalized may not yet mean we have been evangelized."[36] Pauly still sees many opportunities for formation and growth here and, to this end, advocates a model of "apprenticeship." This model, which is of course one among many, focuses on a personal approach and guidance but also seeks to strengthen the mutual dynamic between liturgy and catechesis, always starting from the idea of liturgy as the "transformative divine encounter *par excellence*."[37] Alternative models, such as Sartore's, adopt a more traditional catechetical approach, prioritizing instruction and the transmission of tradition.[38] At the other end of the spectrum, certain liturgical–catechetical models

---

[33] Ibid., 37.
[34] Michael Langer, Andreas Redtenbacher, and Clauss Peter Sajak (eds.), *Unterwegs Zum Geheimnis: Handbuch Der Liturgiepädagogik*, Schriften des Pius-Parsch-Instituts Klosterneuberg, Band 9 (München: Herder Verlag, 2022), 9.
[35] James C. Pauly, *Liturgical Catechesis in the 21st Century: A School of Discipleship* (Chicago, IL: Liturgy Training Publications, 2017), 67.
[36] Ibid., 67.
[37] Ibid., 81–82.
[38] Domenico Sartore, "Catechesis and Liturgy," *Handbook for Liturgical Studies*, vol. 2: *Fundamental Liturgy*, ed. Anscar J. Chupungco (Collegeville, MN: Liturgical Press, 1998), 97–111.

take postmodern culture as a starting point, drawing upon significant insights from anthropology and ritual studies. Marcel Barnard's model for liturgical catechesis in a network culture serves as a valuable exemplar in this regard.[39]

Pauly's model of liturgical catechesis is shaped from and focused on developing three skills, all of which are at the intersection between proclamation and catechesis: attuning ourselves to God, uniting ourselves to God, and cooperating with the grace of God.[40] These skills are taught and discussed in catechesis and at the same time "trained" or practiced in the liturgy. They strengthen active participation and seek to bring believers closer to God both inside and outside of the liturgy, which, as mentioned earlier, is the goal of pastoral ministry. Pauly also stresses that liturgical catechesis is not just something for those preparing for the sacraments, although it is approached and practiced in many churches almost exclusively in this context. On the contrary, liturgical catechesis specifically belongs to the field of mystagogical catechesis, which also historically only starts after baptism.

In the early Church, mystagogy was the form of catechesis for the neophytes, given by the bishops in the period right after Easter, when they were baptized. From a certain perspective and definitely with the contemporary situation in mind, one could say that this phase has never actually been completed, as was already stated decades ago, chiefly by Karl Rahner.[41] This brings us to a final, interesting development of recent decades when it comes to catechesis and liturgy, namely the *Rite of Christian Initiation of Adults* (RCIA), 1972.

This model of adult catechesis – a practice that is not exclusively present in the Roman Catholic Church – provides not only liturgical but also catechetical forms.[42] In the RCIA, meanwhile the OCIA (2024), there is a strong mutual dynamic between major and minor liturgical rites of passage of the adult initiation and the catechetical and pastoral formation that leads to and flows from the liturgical celebration. Moreover,

---

[39] Marcel Barnard, "Liturgical Formation in the Network Culture," *Studia Liturgica* 46 (2016): 180–94.

[40] Pauly, *Liturgical Catechesis*, 120–39.

[41] See, for example, Karl Rahner, "Mystical Experience and Mystagogical Catechesis," *Theological Investigations* 6 (1969): 237–55; Anthony Mellor *Karl Rahner, Culture and Evangelisation: New Approaches in an Australian Setting*, Theology and Mission in World Christianity, vol. 13 (Leiden: Brill, 2019).

[42] See on the RCIA, among others: Thomas Morris, *The RCIA. Transforming the Church: A Resource for Pastoral Implementation* (Mahwah, NJ: Paulist Press, 1997); Peter McGrail, *The Rite of Christian Initiation and Roman Catholic Ecclesiology* (Abingdon: Routledge, 2016).

according to Rita Ferrone, among many others, various novel approaches regarding catechesis and religious formation are also integrated into the liturgy itself. In this model it is the whole community that initiates. Ferrone also argues that in the RCIA it becomes clear how "discipleship and mission flow from the liturgy and lead back to its celebration; discernment and mystagogical reflection based upon the liturgy are fundamental practices of the Christian life. Furthermore, the interplay of all these elements in initiation 'teach' one how to be church."[43] This makes the RCIA an example of how the liturgy is not just the source and summit that directs all pastoral ministry, but how insights from catechesis and proclamation can be integrated into liturgical practice, creating a real dynamic and fostering Church community, which brings us to the last of the four dimensions.

LITURGY AND *KOINONIA*: LITURGICAL ECCLESIOLOGY

In describing the connection between liturgy and *diakonia* and liturgy and *kerygma*, community also emerged each time as an important dimension. Discussing liturgy and pastoral ministry, I started from the triple office of Christ: priest, king, and prophet. However, in the Christian tradition, besides *leitourgia*, *diakonia*, and *kerygma*, *koinonia* is also considered one of the four essential functions or characteristics of the Church.

There is a clear link between the liturgy and *koinonia*, or the ecclesial community, one that goes far beyond the scope of this contribution.[44] Excellent synthesizing work on the many existing ideas and theologies related to the topic of liturgy and Church was done by Mattijs Ploeger.[45] Drawing on the reflections of theologians throughout Christian traditions of the past century, this Old-Catholic priest arrives at what he himself calls a "liturgical koinonia ecclesiology in ecumenical perspective."[46] The starting point for this liturgical ecclesiology is a

---

[43] Rita Ferrone, "Reciprocity in Liturgical Formation," *Studia Liturgica* 46 (2016): 144–56, 153–55.

[44] See, for example, the seminal work on this topic of Gordon W. Lathrop, in particular *Holy People: A Liturgical Ecclesiology* (Minneapolis, MN: Fortress Press, 1999).

[45] Mattijs Ploeger, *Celebrating Church: Ecumenical Contributions to a Liturgical Ecclesiology*, in Netherlands Studies in Ritual and Liturgy, vol. 7 (Groningen/Tilburg: Instituut voor Liturgiewetenschap/Liturgisch Instituut, 2008).

[46] Ploeger discusses the thought of N. Afanasiev, J. Ratzinger, L. Boff, A. Rinkel, G. Dix, P. Avis, C. Pickstock, G. Wainwright, and G. Lathrop, to name just a few.

pneumatological, eschatological, and sacramental vision of Christ, and the initiation to the *koinonia* with Christ in baptism. Throughout the ages and in all Christian churches one can find the idea that the liturgy, the sacraments – and in particular the Eucharist – are indispensable for the strengthening and broadening of the ecclesial community. The basis of a liturgical ecclesiology is the conviction that the liturgy is the communal celebration and participation of the Church community in God, whose being is the communion of Father, Son, and Holy Spirit. This is not a purely inward movement or concentration because it is the mission and pastoral ministry of the Church to expand this community and to reunite all people and the entire world with God.

Many ideas and topics dealing with the Church can be derived from the liturgy, as a heuristic starting point. Ploeger points, for example, to ideas on the Church as Eucharistic and liturgical community, the importance of the local church where the liturgical celebration takes place, and ideas on the (baptismal) priesthood and ministry. In and from the liturgy and in particular through baptism, all bear a ministerial responsibility to build up the Christian community. Certainly, in more priestly or hierarchically structured Churches, this liturgical insight is not prevalent and needs to be more strongly embedded in the theology and practice of pastoral ministry.[47]

Ploeger emphasizes the centrifugality of the liturgical ecclesiology that he derived from his ecumenical analysis. He makes clear that it is not a depreciation of the margin to designate liturgy as the center, or as source and summit, but rather an invitation to a serving and missionary pastoral ministry. Putting the liturgy at the center of these activities is putting the relation with God in the center. At the same time, Ploeger also recognizes that the majority of people living in a post-Christian society do not experience the liturgy as the center of their lives, and even for many believers this is the case.

This observation is confirmed by Alexander Saberschinsky and was even reinforced during the Covid-19 pandemic.[48] During this period,

---

[47] A good example of this from an ecclesiological perspective is the liturgical theology of the assembly, as developed by Susan Wood. See Susan Wood, "Liturgical Ecclesiology," in *A Church with Open Doors: Catholic Ecclesiology for the Third Millennium*, ed. Richard R. Gaillardetz and Edward P. Hahnenberg (Collegeville, MN: Liturgical Press, 2014): 138–58.

[48] Alexander Saberschinsky,"Kirchenentwikclung aus der Liturgie unter heutigen Bedingungen," in *Ecclesia de Liturgia: Zur Bedeutung des Gottesdienstes für Kirche und Gesellschaft*, eds. Jürgen Bärsh, Stefan Kopp, and Christian Rentsch (Regensburg: Friedrich Pustet, 2020), 33–46.

liturgy and Church were compelled to transition to digital platforms and/or be restricted to domestic settings. This particular circumstance prompted significant theological and practical inquiries regarding the development of *koinonia* from the liturgy. Saberschinsky regards the practice of the catechumenate, again, as an exemplary model for contemplating the interplay between liturgy and community. Within this framework, the focal point revolves around the personal relationship with Christ, which is established, sustained, and celebrated in the communal liturgy, as well as manifested in the acts of proclamation and charity. Simultaneously, Saberschinsky advocates for an expansion of thinking concerning Church development from the liturgy. This entails exploring and examining which and how both traditional and new liturgical and sacramental forms provide answers to contemporary societal challenges. The diverse nature of contemporary liturgical practices proves to be invaluable in this regard, particularly if we genuinely embrace the sacramental breadth and theological diversity inherent in God's continuous revelation and salvation within individuals' lives and the world. Following Saberschinsky, the notion of *koinonia* developing from the liturgy should be perceived not just as a centrifugal movement but also as centripetal learning. It is a search for "new liturgical spaces" from which community and Church develop, and which should be theologically and pastorally appreciated.

CONCLUSION

The relationship between liturgy and pastoral ministry is fundamental, obvious, and necessary but also exceedingly complex, as the theologians of the Liturgical Movement showed. Their role in bringing these different poles of the life of the Church back together cannot be underestimated. Since the twentieth century, but having ancient roots, the relation between liturgy and pastoral ministry is situated in the framework of the fundamental functions of the Church: liturgy, charity, proclamation, and community building. However, it is evident that liturgy holds a distinct position within this framework and has a special relation to each of these functions. The primary task of the Church is to bring people into relationship with God, and this is manifested in a special and inimitable way when the community comes together to celebrate liturgy. As the source and summit of Christian life, it is imperative to connect all pastoral activities with the spirit of the liturgy, because this means that they start from and lead to the relationship with the trinitarian God.

Nonetheless, in recognizing the pastoral centrality of the liturgy, it is crucial to acknowledge that this relationship is dynamic and mutually enriching. Unfortunately, within both theological contemplation and practical pastoral work, liturgy and other domains of pastoral ministry are often treated as isolated entities or only in a unidirectional manner. Simultaneously, the current situation of the Christian faith, especially in a secularized context, creates specific challenges. Nevertheless, it is precisely in this context that a strong connection between liturgy and pastoral ministry is invaluable. Participation in the liturgy leads to the transformation of everyday life and the entire world. A mystagogical and personal approach in view of liturgical formation can bring people closer to themselves and to God. In particular the practice of the RCIA shows how potent the connection between liturgy and pastoral ministry can be and challenges theologians and pastoral ministers alike to endeavor to find new ways of liturgical life and community.

For Further Reading

Eary, Mark, *Worship That Cares: An Introduction to Pastoral Liturgy* (London: Hymns Ancient & Modern Ltd, 2012).

Gelineau, Joseph, *Dans vos assemblées: Manuel de pastorale liturgique* (Paris: Desclée, 1989).

Goyvaerts, Samuel, "Moving between Liturgical Theology and Liturgical Pastoral: On Theology, Liturgy, and Christian Life," *Questions Liturgiques* 100 (2020): 294–312.

Jungmann, Joseph A., *Pastoral Liturgy* (Notre Dame, IN: Christian Classics, 2014).

Koester, Anne Y., and Barbara Searle, *Vision: The Scholarly Contributions of Mark Searle to Liturgical Renewal* (Collegeville, MN: Liturgical Press, 2004).

Morrill, Bruce T., *Practical Sacramental Theology: At the Intersection of Liturgy and Ethics* (Eugene, OR: Cascade Books, 2021).

Pauly, James C., *Liturgical Catechesis in the 21st Century: A School of Discipleship* (Chicago, IL: Liturgy Training Publications, 2017).

Ploeger, Mathijs, *Celebrating Church: Ecumenical Contributions to a Liturgical Ecclesiology*, in Netherlands Studies in Ritual and Liturgy, vol. 7 (Groningen/Tilburg: Instituut voor Liturgiewetenschap/Liturgisch Instituut, 2008).

17 Liturgy and the Proclamation of the Word

CAS WEPENER

INTRODUCTION

Practices related to the proclamation of the Word in the liturgy are not restricted to the celebration of liturgy on, for example, a Sunday. They extend backward and forward into the life of the worshipping community during the preceding and succeeding Monday to Saturday. The homiletical and liturgical process of sermon preparation culminates in the event of preaching during the liturgy, which spills over into the living of the proclaimed Word by the hearers in the liturgy of life, the formation of their faith, and the formation of the community of believers. When Karl Barth deals with "The Word of God in Its Threefold Form" in his *Church Dogmatics*, he emphasizes that preaching is attestation: "To point in a definite direction beyond oneself to something else."[1] As illustration he refers to the figure of John the Baptist in Matthias Grünewald's Isenheim Altarpiece. In this painting John the Baptist holds a Bible in his left hand and with the very long index finger of his right hand points toward the crucified Christ. Several homiliticians have followed Barth in using this painting as an illustration to describe both the event of preaching and a particular theology of the Word of God.[2]

In this chapter the witnessing character of the proclamation of the Word[3] is appreciated, specifically also the event of preaching as a

---

[1] Karl Barth, *Church Dogmatics. First Half-Volume: The Doctrine of the Word of God*, trans. G. T. Thomson (Edinburgh: T & T Clark, 1956), 125–26.

[2] Leanne Van Dyk, "Proclamation: Revelation, Christology," in *A More Profound Alleluia: Theology and Worship in Harmon*, ed. L. van Dyk (Grand Rapids, MI: Eerdmans, 2005), 55–82.

[3] Thomas Long, *The Witness of Preaching*, 3rd ed. (Louisville, KY: Westminster John Knox Press, 2016); Jean-Jacques Von Allmen, *Preaching and Congregation*,

liturgical practice. However, there is more to see in the altarpiece by Grünewald than fingers pointing to Jesus Christ encapsulating the event of preaching as an act of attestation. There are also signs of poverty in the clothing of John the Baptist, wounds on Christ's body, the sorrow of a mother and comfort offered by a friend, prayer-like postures suggesting lament, and blood dripping onto the earth. In the painting three expressions of the Word of God – namely the Bible, preaching, and Jesus Christ as incarnated Word of God – can be seen. All three of these forms of God's Word, these "texts," are, however, attested to within a very specific challenging first-century context, and the attestation thus includes contextual realities.

With regard to the context within which liturgy is celebrated Claudio Carvalhaes argues that the liturgical adage *lex orandi lex credendi lex vivendi* should not be viewed in a strictly linear way as always starting with the law of prayer (*lex orandi*).[4] The starting point can rather be *lex vivendi*, the daily reality and lived experience, and only from there move to *lex orandi*. Carvalhaes advocates a postcolonial approach to liturgy, which for him entails liturgy that is performed in "with-ness" with the pain of the world. Consequently, there should be a kind of simultaneity of *lex-orandi-credendi-vivendi*. Carvalhaes writes, "That is why praying is such a troubling act: because we act and are acted upon, word and performance giving shape to my soul, marking my body, disturbing my mind, moving my emotions, challenging my allegiances, changing my faith, reinventing my life."[5]

Proclamation as part of liturgy that seeks to be proclamation that impacts on the lives of the hearers and faith communities, contributing to their individual and communal formation and forging a close connection between liturgy and life, is proclamation as attestation. But this is attestation that takes the lived reality within which the Word is interpreted and proclaimed seriously, thus attesting to the Word within the lived reality in which it is proclaimed. This chapter focuses on the proclamation of the Word, the ways in which it matters in the lives of individuals and communities, and sees preaching as a word/Word event in which a reciprocal relationship between the gospel of God's revelation in Jesus Christ and the lives of the hearers is established through

---

Ecumenical Studies in Worship 10, trans. B. L. Nicholas (Louisville, KY: John Knox Press, 1962), 7; Nicholas Wolterstorff, *The God We Worship: An Exploration of Liturgical Theology* (Grand Rapids, MI: Eerdmans, 2015), 133.

[4] Claudio Carvalhaes, *Praying with Every Heart: Orienting Our Lives to the Wholeness of the World* (Eugene, OR: Cascade Books, 2021), 5.

[5] Ibid., 21.

the power of the Holy Spirit. Both older views in line with a *kerygmatic* approach to preaching and newer developments regarding the turn to the hearer are integrated as meaningful in what is referred to in this chapter as the event of preaching.

To explore proclamation as part of liturgy and its role in the formation of the hearers, the event of preaching is firstly set against a brief liturgical-historical backdrop regarding the liturgy of the Word in Jewish worship and examples of forms in which it finds expression liturgically in our own day. This will be followed by a discussion of a selection of approaches to proclamation. An account of preaching as a Christian practice that is part of liturgy and the relationship between liturgy and preaching will form the last section of the chapter. The chapter shows how the liturgy of the Word and proclamation are, in the words of Jean-Jacques Von Allmen, "an essential constituent of Christian worship. Without it, the cult would not be a living encounter," and as such proclamation is an irreplaceable Christian practice, specifically also with regard to the formation of individuals and communities.[6]

HISTORICAL AND CONTEMPORARY EXPRESSIONS OF PROCLAMATION

The reading of Scriptures, as well as preaching and teaching, were elements of the service of the Temple in Old Israel. As part of their Temple ministry the prophets proclaimed the Word, and priests had a ministry of both altar and Word.[7] During the Babylonian exile the study of Scripture gained prominence, and the reading of the Scriptures and preaching became primary elements of worship.[8] Boon and Old show how the core liturgical elements related to the reading and preaching of Scripture are described in Nehemiah 8, and that it was this rite that was adopted by the synagogue. The service of the synagogue was celebrated alongside the Temple service until the destruction of the Temple in Jerusalem in 70 CE, after which the synagogue service replaced the Temple service, also in the thoughts and lives of the Jewish people.[9] When Christians were expelled from synagogues by the middle of the

---

[6] Von Allmen, *Preaching and Congregation*, 130.
[7] Hughes Oliphant Old, *Worship: Reformed according to Scripture*, rev. and expanded ed. (Louisville, KY: Westminster John Knox Press, 2002), 59–60.
[8] See, Rudolf Boon, *De Joodse Wortels van de Christelijke Eredienst* (Amsterdam: Prof. Dr. G. van der Leeuw-Stichting, 1973), 8, 128. Cf. Old, *Worship*, 60.
[9] Attie Barnard, *Die Erediens* (Pretoria: N. G. Kerk Boekhandel Transvaal, 1981), 87–88.

second century CE, elements of the Word-based synagogue service, as well as elements of Jewish liturgies celebrated at home, fused with other elements, such as the sharing of the meal.[10]

During the Babylonian exile and after the destruction of the Temple in 70 CE and the succeeding diaspora, the strongly Word-based synagogue service played and still plays a critical role in the survival of the Jewish people. Already in the Temple worship, but also in the synagogue service, the ministry of the Word was closely connected to the formation of the identity of people struggling to survive. According to James F. White, the synagogue service was Israel's answer to the question, "How could we sing the lord's song in a foreign land?"[11] The power of remembering as it is connected to identity formation is inherent in the word-based synagogue service and also underlies the Christian service of the Word: "As past events were recited, they became present reality through which God's power to save could be experienced again and again."[12] Reading and proclamation are closely connected to the Hebrew concept of *zakar*; this is because in and through the reading and proclamation of Scripture God's words and deeds are commemorated in liturgical practices of the Word that simultaneously call upon and invoke God's presence, and hence commemoration becomes witnessing and proclamation of God's covenantal faithfulness.[13] Von Allmen sees the reading of Scripture as also being proclamation and that nothing essentially different happens in reading and in preaching, as in both "the Word which has been in chains, imprisoned by the letters of the alphabet, comes alive."[14] Knowledge of Scripture was especially spread through the readings in the synagogue and the content appropriated during many years of hearing the readings and listening to their explication.[15] The Jewish roots of

---

[10] Francois Wessels, "Ontdek die Joodse wortels van die erediens," in *Ontdekkings in die erediens*, ed. Cas Wepener and J. Van der Merwe (Wellington: Lux Verbi.BM, 2009), 31–33.

[11] James F. White, *Introduction to Christian Worship* (Nashville, TN: Abingdon Press, 2000) 152. Cf. Boon, *De Joodse Wortels*, 8.

[12] White, *Introduction*, 152–53.

[13] Boon, *De joodse wortels*, 30–32. This anamnetic structure in which God's presence in worship is related to God's past action, which is remembered in the present celebration in and through which the future is reframed, has been inherent in both Jewish and Christian liturgy.

[14] Von Allmen, *Worship: Its Theology and Practice*, 132.

[15] Boon, *De Joodse Wortels van de Christelijke Eredienst*, 136. That Christian Churches followed the synagogue in the liturgical reading of the Scriptures is already apparent in Justin's First Apology and his reference to texts that were read during worship. The prominence and importance of the liturgy of the Word and proclamation as part of the

the liturgy of the Word in Christian liturgy, its emphasis on remembering as a form of attestation impacting spiritual formation, will now be juxtaposed with present-day examples of proclamation in different parts of the world.[16]

March 2022, Sunday morning, Khayelitsha, South Africa. We are in a dwelling made of corrugated iron. The structure and flow are those of classic Pentecostal liturgy – praise and worship, witnessing, Scripture reading, preaching, an altar call, extemporaneous praying, offerings, and a benediction, all bound together with large amounts of loud unaccompanied singing and hand clapping. Before the preaching, an epiclesis prayer and one Bible verse (Acts 1:14) are read by a member. After that the pastor preaches for more than an hour. Throughout her preaching there is lively interaction by the congregation. An altar call, directly related to the content of the sermon, follows. The epiclesis, the Scripture reading, and the preaching are obviously part of the liturgy of the Word and proclamation; however, the free prayer and altar call are every bit as much part of the liturgy of the Word. The proclamation in this liturgy cannot be separated from elements that succeeded it, and even from the witnessing that preceded the epiclesis. The whole liturgy of this congregation can be designated as liturgy of the Word with a theological emphasis on conversion of individuals and the building up of the faith community.

June 2022, Sunday morning, Castle Church, Wittenberg, Germany. The liturgy flows from gathering, Word, and table to sending. I am the invited preacher. The liturgy of the Word is distinguishable as epiclesis, the reading of four lectionary texts, and preaching from the pulpit. Thematically, the lectionary readings and sermon relate to all the other parts of the liturgy. The preacher is a stranger from South Africa, his message about the identity of Christians as strangers and sojourners (as guests) is addressed to a few members, but mostly tourists and students. The liturgy and typed sermon text are afterward uploaded onto the congregation's website where they can be read. The proclamation thus does not end in the liturgical space of the Castle Church but continues in cyberspace. The potential formation inherent in the Word event,

---

liturgy, however, varied throughout the history of the Christian liturgy. What is lacking to date, for example, are descriptions of recent developments in the global South.

[16] The descriptions are all based on my experiences and observations over the course of one year (2022).

regarding both content and form, is related to the identity of Christians within the flows of globalization and a network culture.

August 2022, Sunday morning in Stellenbosch, South Africa, and early evening in Melbourne, Australia. The South Yarra Community Baptist Church in Melbourne started a Zoom worship service during the Covid-19 pandemic and decided to continue with online worship after it was no longer necessary to do so. The liturgy is online and interactive with synchronic active participation by all worshippers throughout the entire Baptist liturgy (which includes celebration of the Eucharist). Page fourteen of the PDF-formatted liturgy has the heading "The Liturgy of the Word." It includes readings (Deut 8:3; Matt 4:4), a sung response, lectionary readings with responses, ten minutes of silence before the preaching, a sermon, the creed, the prayers of the people, and a sung Lord's Prayer. After the benediction at the end of the liturgy, worshippers join online break-out rooms that include reflections and questions by worshippers regarding the sermon. I am the preacher, and many members tell me they attend this online service but augment it with other liturgies. They are thus hearers of proclamation from a variety of denominations and in both online and offline formats. The sermon is also recorded and uploaded onto the congregation's website.

November 2022, Sunday morning, St. John the Baptist Roman Catholic parish, Leuven, Belgium. The liturgy is a "Word and Communion service." During the Word service thirty children who are to be confirmed in a few months are called forward; 1 Samuel 3 is read; a female pastor ministers the Word by means of an informal intergenerational dialogue on biblical topics (*leerhuisgesprek*)[17] and an informal intergenerational dialogue based on the text of 1 Samuel 3. The content of the proclamation is explicitly aimed at the formation of baptized children preparing for confirmation; however, their parents and other members are also involved in the conversational format of the proclamation, which is explicitly intended not to be one directional. Proclamation is thus not a monologue and not hierarchical, as the flow of information is reciprocal between preacher and hearers, and concomitantly the possibility of formation includes the preacher (who is also a presider), who is thus also a hearer.

---

[17] In personal communication with the preacher, she described the proclamation as "a biblical learning dialogue, based on the Jewish tradition of discussing the Talmud. It is a mixture of an informal introduction by the one presiding the liturgy; some questions for the audience and then everyone can freely respond."

The above examples can be described in terms of concepts such as liquidity, flow, liminality, bricolage, ancient–future, disruption, and interruption, as solid, unyielding concepts are not sufficient for designating the actual liturgical praxis regarding proclamation in our own day. This is true not only of late-modern worship in the West but also of worship in (postcolonial) contexts of the global South, where Christianity is growing rapidly. With reference to Christianity in the global South, Philip Jenkins argues that it is no longer possible to assert "what Christians uniformly believe," alluding to a shrinking remnant of Christians in the West. His insight is also applicable to the way that Christians worship.[18]

The tension between being rooted in local contexts and traditions and connection to global influences is discernible in the above descriptions. A congregation in Khayelitsha is rooted in the Pentecostal tradition and African culture and simultaneously connected to global expressions of worship via the media and the internet. A Baptist congregation in Melbourne synchronously includes a presider and worshippers in Australia and a South African preacher in worship online.[19] A liturgy in Wittenberg, Germany, is simultaneously rooted in the Lutheran tradition and Liturgical Movement, whilst a continuous flow of (Lutheran) pilgrims and tourists from across the globe and a polyphony of Christian and non-Christian traditions (as I found whilst greeting worshippers after the service) appropriate the worship and proclamation in their idiosyncratic ways. People attend liturgy in a variety of modes (on- and offline) and liturgical traditions and in our late-modern age use what Martin Stringer, following Gerd Baumann, calls a dual discursive competence as they combine liturgical experiences in ways that they appropriate as meaningful with the concomitant spiritual formation such dual discursive competence and practice potentially entail.[20] In Leuven the structure of the traditional Roman Catholic liturgy is discernible in the overarching form and flow of the service; however, the

---

[18] Phillip Jenkins, *The Next Christendom: The Coming of Global Christianity*, 3rd ed. (Oxford: Oxford University Press, 2011), 3.

[19] According to Post, online ritual is ritual that is only available online, for example, the Zoom liturgy described above, whereas an example of ritual online is streamed worship services that can be followed online, for example, the recorded sermon from the same liturgy, which was uploaded after the service to the congregation's website, *Rituelen. Theorie en Praktijk in Kort Bestek*, 105.

[20] Martin Stringer, *Sociological History of Christian Worship* (Cambridge: Cambridge University Press, 2005), 150–51.

presiders and preacher are bricoleurs who have shaped the liturgy into a new format, tapping into ancient roots whilst keeping contemporary hearers in mind; on an epistemological level they have interrupted the traditional monological flow of information, and thus also of power, by means of eliciting the active involvement of the hearers in the communication process.[21]

In *Worship in a Network Culture* it is asserted that

> Late modernity and late-modern worship seems to be driven by the ambivalent forces of globalization and particularization, connectedness and rootedness. The ambivalence is central to the network society. De-boarding and drawing boundaries go hand in hand; networking and emphasizing the particular, "the space of flows" and local space, "timeless time" and local time, dislocation and relocation go together.[22]

Regarding proclamation in worship, this entails ongoing and renewed attention to both the kind of attestation that happens in and through proclamation and the layered context(s) in which hearers live, since the event of preaching as formative practice occurs as attestation in context. Worship leaders become bricoleurs, and worshippers develop their double discursive competence, while traditional liturgical authorities are challenged.

From a postcolonial perspective this development is commendable, as it does not uncritically accept power structures inherent in existing liturgies. However, as Von Allmen advised many decades ago regarding the role of preaching in the formation of faith communities, it is necessary to "ensure that the building up of parishes is not at the mercy of the convictions, uncertainties and whim of their pastors."[23] This was a challenge at the time Von Allmen wrote and will remain, albeit in new ways, a challenge in our own day. Stringer critically observes about worship in the twenty-first century:

---

[21] The active involvement of hearers can be a facet of the sermon preparation as McClure (1995) proposes, but this view is not without criticism (Von Allmen, 1962, 52–53). Cf. Cas Wepener, "Participation and Power: Opportunities for Method and Theory in Liturgical Research from a Changing (Dutch Reformed) South African Liturgical Landscape," *Yearbook for Ritual-Liturgical Studies* 22 (2006): 49–66.

[22] Marcel Barnard, Johan Cilliers, and Cas Wepener, *Worship in a Network Culture: Liturgical Ritual Studies. Fields and Methods, Concepts and Metaphors*, Liturgia Condenda 28 (Leuven: Peeters, 2014).

[23] Von Allmen, *Preaching and Congregation*, 46.

I have noticed ... an increasing sense of comfortableness and intimacy in contemporary worship that stretches across the traditions: carpets on the floor, a crèche for the children, PowerPoint technology providing reassuring images, language that does not offend, and music aimed to speak to our emotions and calm us down. This clearly reflects contemporary, global society and the discourses of consumerism and individual well-being that dominate it, but is this truly Christian?[24]

Liturgy and proclamation have a potential impact on spiritual formation, a process that should continuously be critically scrutinized.

RECENT APPROACHES TO PROCLAMATION AND FORMATION IN HOMILETICS

Starting in the 1960s and continuing through the 1980s and into our own day is a movement in Homiletics called the New Homiletic (in the North American context), which is grounded in the New Hermeneutic.[25] Insights into the performative power of language and communication influenced how preaching came to be viewed, namely, as more than just a set of propositional truths that a preacher conveys to listeners, but as communication by means of language and as such as an *event* in which the preacher and the hearers cocreate meaning through the experience of the performance.[26] The origin of the New Homiletic is often linked to Fred Craddock and his so-called inductive approach. Thomas Long explains how Craddock realized that in many cases preachers experience exciting journeys of discovery whilst doing exegesis in preparation for preaching, but when the preacher starts to develop the sermon the exciting inductive discovery process is replaced by deductive exhortation.[27] His solution was that the inductive experience whilst doing exegesis should be recreated for listeners in the preaching event. According to Gerrit Immink, whereas older theologians such as Barth looked at preaching especially as "an encounter

---

[24] Stringer, *Sociological History of Christian Worship*, 239.
[25] Gerrit Immink, "Homiletics: The Current Debate," *International Journal of Practical Theology* 8 (2004): 89–121. Immink (96–100) shows how developments in Europe, even though they have different nuances, have significant similarities with the New Homiletic.
[26] Ibid., 96–100; McClure, *Preaching Words*, 94–96.
[27] Long, *The Witness of Preaching*, 102; Cf. Barbara K. Lundblad, "Narrative Theory," in *The New Interpreter's Handbook of Preaching*, ed. Paul Scott Wilson et al. (Nashville, TN: Abingdon Press, 2008), 203.

with God's redemptive presence," the new homileticians "are turning to the process of understanding."²⁸ In the wake of the New Homiletics, in which hearers are seen as actively participating in the preaching event, a variety of approaches has developed, a few of which are discussed in exemplary fashion.

From the introduction to Eugene Lowry's *The Homiletical Plot* it is clear that his narrative approach fits well within the New Homiletic. "Truth is ... a sermon is not a doctrinal lecture. It is an *event-in-time*, a narrative art form more akin to play and novel in shape than to a book."²⁹ John McClure defines narrative preaching as a kind of preaching "in which some aspect of narrative exerts a controlling influence on the sermon" and shows how the form of the sermon is important, but that narrative preaching involves more than form and includes aspects such as a narrative hermeneutic.³⁰ Barbara K. Lundblad states that "Narrative theory suggests a different way of knowing, a different way of interpreting texts, and a different way of preaching."³¹ The aim of this kind of preaching is often to create within the event of preaching the possibility that the story of God and the story of the hearers intersect, allowing hearers to look in a new way at their own stories. When the listeners experience biblical narratives as they are retold in preaching in ways that make it possible for them to forge connections between the stories and their own lives, then there is a possibility that these narratives can form the listeners and the community of faith: "By weaving the stories of human experience into the biblical narrative, and by naming the theological dimension of those experiences, the storyteller/poet announces: 'Today this Scripture has been fulfilled in your hearing'" (Long, 2016, 43). Narrative preaching has been a fertile field for many homileticians who have gained much wisdom from fiction, such as Alyce M. McKenzie's *Novel Preaching* and *Making a Scene in the Pulpit* (2010, 2018), and is akin to the way that some homileticians view the aesthetic approach to preaching, another contribution of the New Homiletic.

The aesthetic approach is closely linked to the art of reframing reality so that hearers can see in new ways. One of Walter

---

²⁸ Immink, "Homiletics: The Current Debate," 89.
²⁹ Eugene Lowry, *The Homiletical Plot: The Sermon as Narrative Art Form* (Louisville, KY: Westminster John Knox Press, 2001), xx. Von Allmen (*Preaching and Congregation*, 21) had already written decades ago: "In preaching the Gospel we enroll our parishioners in a story; we do not explain an idea to them."
³⁰ McClure, *Preaching Words*, 90.
³¹ Lundblad, "Narrative Theory," 203.

Brueggemann's theses on "Preaching as Reimagination" describes preaching as "an act of imagination, that is, an offer of an image through which perception, experience, and finally faith can be reorganized in alternative ways."[32] Brueggemann's insight is critical in understanding the potential of preaching to stimulate the senses of the hearers to approach the world that they inhabit in new ways. Johan Cilliers sees a sermon as a work of art that frames and reframes reality and as such the perspective of the listeners.[33] In this regard, he follows in the footsteps of one of his promotors (Bohren); he moves beyond a reductionist view of preaching as a practice that involves only the auditory sense and argues that all the senses are involved in preaching, but especially seeing as related to reframing. Akin to the image of a preacher in Long (2005) as a witness who witnessed, and on that basis can bear witness,[34] Cilliers argues that the preacher can say something after he has seen something.[35] And a preacher who has seen can assist the hearers to also see.

Reframing can happen through preaching in three ways. Firstly, reframing can be understood as renaming and, especially for Cilliers in continuity with Calvin, as a reframing of reality through the spectacles of Scripture. Secondly, reframing can also be understood as a reconfiguration in which reality is, when necessary, disrupted so that it can be reconfigured. Lastly, reframing can occur as reimagination, especially as continuous reimagination of Christ is proclaimed over and against accepted Christ images.[36] Cilliers writes, "Preaching as reframing observes and re-names; it disrupts and upsets. However, it also points towards new realities and possibilities."[37] Together with Charles L. Campbell, Cilliers coauthored *Preaching Fools* in which they engage the metaphor of the preacher as clown or jester confronting the powers. The preacher as fool interrupts and disrupts with the aim of reframing reality in the light of Scripture. *Preaching Fools* is aligned with both the aesthetic approach and the tradition of prophetic preaching.

Prophetic preaching is often misunderstood as proclamation that either challenges oppressive power structures or foretells future events.

---

[32] Walter Brueggemann, *Cadences of Home: Preaching among Exiles* (Louisville, KY: Westminster John Knox Press, 1997), 32.
[33] Johan Cilliers, "Die optiek van homiletiek: Prediking as om-raming van perspektief," *Stellenbosch Theological Journal* 53 (2012): 52–69.
[34] Cf. Von Allmen, *Preaching and Congregation* 7.
[35] Cilliers, "Die optiek van homiletiek," 57.
[36] Ibid., 60–68.
[37] Ibid., 69.

However, prophetic preaching is rooted in the prophetic tradition of Scripture and as such works with "the distinctive power of language" through which newness can come.[38] Many homiliticians have over recent decades followed Brueggemann in his understanding of the prophetic ministry and applied it to preaching. According to Brueggemann, *"The task of prophetic ministry is to nurture, nourish, and evoke a consciousness and perception alternative to the consciousness and perception of the dominant culture around us"* (italics in original).[39] Two aspects are thus simultaneously at stake in prophetic preaching and should be held together in a dialectic, namely criticism of a dominant consciousness and a promissory energizing. Mary D. Turner argues that prophets had to assist communities to make connections between their past, their present, and their future.[40] Undergirding the possibility of prophetic preaching is a God who is free – "free from and even against the regime, free to hear and even answer slave cries, free from all proper goodness as defined by the empire," as religion is never disinterested.[41]

Instead of providing a definition of prophetic preaching, Leonora Tubbs Tisdale describes seven hallmarks of this kind of preaching, which include being rooted in the biblical witness; being countercultural and challenging the status quo; being interested in corporate and public issues; entailing a dialectic between criticizing and energizing; offering hope and liberation; inciting to courage and empowerment toward change; "and [having] a heart that breaks with things that break God's heart," which assumes a pastoral and spiritual approach toward the task.[42] Drawing on postcolonial theory and working from a South African contextual perspective, Wessel Wessels explores both prophetic preaching and aesthetic homiletics.[43] The former he critiques as a middle-class endeavor: "Prophetic preaching only becomes the focal point for homiletical thought once the White middle-class person's livelihood is in jeopardy."[44] The latter's contribution he appreciates in

---

[38] Walter Brueggemann, *The Prophetic Imagination*, 40th anniversary ed. (Minneapolis, MN: Fortress Press, 2013 [1973]): 2-3; Leonora Tubbs Tisdale, *Prophetic Preaching: A Pastoral Approach* (Louisville, KY: Westminster John Knox Press, 2010): 6-7.
[39] Brueggemann, *The Prophetic Imagination*, 3.
[40] Mary Donovan Turner, "Prophetic Preaching," in *The New Interpreter's Handbook of Preaching*, ed. P. S. Wilson et al. (Nashville, TN: Abingdon Press, 2008), 101.
[41] Brueggemann, *The Prophetic Imagination*, 8, 23.
[42] Tisdale, *Prophetic Preaching: A Pastoral Approach*, 9-10.
[43] Wessel Wessels, "On Justice and Beauty in Recent South African Homiletics: A Post-Colonial Reflection," *Acta Theologica Supp* 29 (2020): 176-94.
[44] Ibid., 182.

its contribution to a broader understanding of justice and concludes that "aesthetic homiletics has strong postcolonial imagination."[45]

Postcolonial preaching challenges myths of binarity and heteronormativity to interrupt dominant discourses and make new imagination possible.[46] In that sense it is related to an aesthetic approach to preaching, as Wessels also pointed out in his doctoral work on postcolonial preaching. Preachers can potentially perpetuate or challenge oppressive systems, which puts them in powerful positions as they can conceivably become part of the dominant discourse in society.[47] This happened in, for example, apartheid South Africa. Martin Laubscher explores the role of whiteness in the pulpit and how it can affect the kind of formation that is effected by preaching.[48] Preachers preach who they are, and some preachers perpetuate whiteness, which is much more than only a racial issue and is, in fact, a metaphor for privilege.[49] Postcolonial preaching, like the other approaches to preaching that have been discussed, includes the way in which preachers do exegesis and interpret texts and their contexts. Kwok Pui-lan defines postcolonial preaching as "a locally rooted and globally conscious performance that seeks to create Third Space so that the faith community can imagine new ways of being in the world and encounter God's salvific action for the oppressed and marginalized."[50] Preachers should thus prepare sermons critically in the light of notions such as empire and power. Sarah Travis defines preaching as "a theological act that names, out loud, the world as it is and as it may become."[51] This naming is a kind of attestation in proclamation.

Travis (2014, 52–54) argues that the good news in postcolonial preaching may sound like bad news to listeners benefiting from empire.

---

[45] Ibid., 189.
[46] Kwok Pui-lan, "Postcolonial Preaching in Intercultural Contexts," *Homiletic* 40 (2015): 9.
[47] Wessel Wessels, "Prophetic Preaching's Deadly Sins: Reflections on Preaching Black Theology of Liberation," *Stellenbosch Theological Journal* 8/2 (2022): 1–22. Dominant discourses shift, and Wessels warns against the possibility that the power critiqued by a preacher can also be power that is desired.
[48] Martin Laubscher, "Oor prediking, geloofsvorming, en witheid in Suid-Afrika vandag," in *Om te word wie ons is: oor geloofsvorming in en deur gemeentes*, ed. Coenie Burger, Marnus Havenga, Jana van den Munckhof, and Cas Wepener (Wellington: Bible Media, 2023).
[49] Willie James Jennings, *After Whiteness: An Education in Belonging* (Grand Rapids, MI: Eerdmans, 2020).
[50] Pui-lan, "Postcolonial Preaching in Intercultural Contexts," 10.
[51] Sarah Travis, *Decolonizing Preaching: The Pulpit as Postcolonial Space* (Eugene, OR: Cascade Books, 2014), 2.

This good news sounding like bad news is the good news of freedom from the bondage of oppressive systems, which is ultimately good news for both the oppressed and those benefiting from the oppression. Postcolonial forms of preaching interrupt and disrupt some of the existing ways in which preaching is performed and as a practice forming the faith of the listeners and their community.

This section made a distinction between various approaches to preaching, specifically narrative, aesthetic, prophetic, and postcolonial. However, such neat categorization does not do justice to recent developments in Homiletics. To a large extent all these approaches are attempts, like liturgy in general, to invite worshippers into preaching as an event in which God acts; the reality of the listeners is reframed in the light of God's reality, and they are reminded of God's ongoing story with creation and their place in it, and as such are formed as God's people. It is thus important to also consider the relation between liturgy and proclamation.

PROCLAMATION AS A LITURGICAL–RITUAL PRACTICE EMBEDDED IN LITURGY

From a practical theological perspective "religion is also something people do."[52] It involves people engaging in practices such as liturgy and proclamation. Proclamation as part of liturgy can be viewed as liturgical ritual: "Worship continuously moves between context and the Lord who is signified in it, between religious language about God and the 'Word of God,' human interpretation and divine truth, human acting and the coming of the Lord. Consequently, the study of worship moves between anthropology and theology."[53] The dynamics involved in liturgical rituals are thus also part of the practice of proclamation in liturgy, albeit regarding proclamation as a distinctly word-event. Preaching is an event in which both humans and God engage. The emphasis in human participation is often on the auditory; however, in the practice of the liturgical ritual called preaching, both preacher and listeners are involved with their whole body, which includes all five senses.

Theodore Jr. Jennings (1996) sheds lights on the importance of a bodily based epistemology of ritual and of the human body as a site of

---

[52] Birgit Weyel, Wilhelm Gräb, Immanuel Lartey, and Cas Wepener (eds.), *International Handbook of Practical Theology* (Berlin: De Gruyter, 2022), 5.
[53] Barnard, Cilliers, and Wepener, *Worship in a Network Culture*, 1.

knowledge production.[54] This knowledge is knowledge gained from engaging in practices such as liturgical rituals. And liturgical ritual, even within the same religious or denominational tradition, differs from week to week and from congregation to congregation. Proclamation also differs depending on many variables (choice of text, theology and identity of the preacher, context); however, the way that the sermons of various preachers differ, in combination with the varied ways in which the hearers of the same sermon appropriate and understand the message, reveals how preaching as a practice is, like ritual and liturgy, a bodily mode of discovery and inquiry.[55] Preaching as liturgical ritual is thus, like ritual in general, a noetic quest, "an exploration which seeks to discover the right action or sequence of actions."[56] Between the opening and closing of a sermon, hearers enter a kind of liminality in which they are involved with their whole bodies, not only their ears. As such, preaching, like ritual and liturgy, is corporeal, active, and transformative.[57] "Ritual action is gained through a bodily action which alters the world or the place of the ritual participant in the world."[58] These insights from Ritual Studies shed light on the close link between liturgy and proclamation and show that preaching is a liturgical ritual. From a theological perspective, a close unity between liturgy and proclamation can also be discerned.

The Dutch theologian Arnold Van Ruler (1973) coined the term "theonomic reciprocity" in a discussion on pneumatology, specifically the work of the Holy Spirit in salvation, in which there is a reciprocal relationship between God and humans.[59] This relation is theonomic, meaning that God's actions have primacy over the actions of humans. Akin to Van Ruler's discussion, Immink calls preaching "a corporate action that links speaking and listening."[60] Regarding the work of the Spirit in the practice of preaching he writes, "The Spirit works in two ways, not only opening the Bible through the preacher, but also illuminating the hearts of the listeners."[61] The link between preacher and hearer in the w/Word event of preaching, in which a theonomic

---

[54] Theodore Jr. Jennings, "On Ritual Knowledge," in *Readings in Ritual Studies*, ed. Ronald L. Grimes (Upper Saddle River, NJ: Prentice Hall, 1996), 324–34.
[55] Cf. ibid., 326.
[56] Ibid., 326.
[57] Ibid., 327.
[58] Ibid., 327.
[59] Arnold Van Ruler, *Theologisch Werk Deel IV* (Nijkerk: Callenbach, 1973).
[60] Immink, "Homiletics: The Current Debate," 105.
[61] Ibid., 105.

reciprocal relationship between the gospel of God's revelation in Jesus Christ and the lives of the hearers is established, is the Spirit. This discussion leans toward the work of Calvin and his emphasis on the Spirit in preaching.[62] There is an intersubjectivity between the work of the Spirit and the work of the hearers that becomes possible in and through the event of preaching. In this chapter, I call this reciprocal working "pneumapraxis." In his Practical Theology study entitled *Christopraxis*, Andrew Root argues that, along with the actions of humans, there should be a greater emphasis on the actions of God.[63] In this regard he uses the word "ministerial" because the event of God's being in coming to humanity is an ontological encounter between the divine and human in which time is infused with eternity, where God gives or ministers Godself for humanity. Proclamation is a form of both christopraxis and pneumapraxis, but from a trinitarian perspective it is also a trinipraxis. However, I would reserve the designation "trinipraxis" for liturgy in general and here emphasize the distinctly pneumatological nature of proclamation, and as such it is pneumapraxis in which proclamation is in practice preceded by epiclesis. Preaching cannot and should not be divorced from liturgy as encompassing trinipraxis.

Despite the close correspondence between liturgy and preaching, the tension between the two should be respected. Von Allmen describes liturgy as "an echo of incarnation in that it includes, like the ministry of Jesus, what one could call a 'Galilean' moment – centred on the sermon – and a 'Jerusalemite' moment – centred on the eucharist."[64] Von Allmen (1962, 40) writes that the Word of God is given in two forms – preached and signified, and this in turn links preaching to *theologia crucis* and the Eucharist to *theologia gloriae*.[65] In eschatological terms the Galilean preaching is linked to *theologia crucis*, which is attestation to the "not yet" and the Jerusalemite *theologia gloriae* Eucharist attestation to the "already." The tension between liturgy (Eucharist) and preaching is critical for the formation of people who are simultaneously citizens of the kingdom of God and strangers and sojourners on earth: "It is only in so far as the *theologia crucis* and the *theologia gloriae* balance one another in the tension of a

---

[62] Ibid., 106.
[63] Andrew Root, *Christopraxis: A Practical Theology of the Cross* (Minneapolis, MN: Fortress Press, 2014), 94.
[64] Von Allmen, *Preaching and Congregation*, 32.
[65] Ibid., 40.

theologia viatorum, of pilgrims, that the church can be said to be in good health."[66]

Pui-lan writes from a postcolonial perspective and emphasizes that preaching takes place within the matrix of Christian worship. She asks for a critical scrutiny of all aspects of worship.[67] A sermon preached from a high pulpit can, for example, reinforce a certain power discourse of the authority of the preacher, a separation of clergy and laity, and is "monological and, as such, does not create a plurivocal and dialogical community."[68] The liturgist Elsabe Kloppers (2003) describes liturgy as a *Gesamtkunstwerk*.[69] This was a term Wagner used to emphasize that all the various elements of an opera fit together to form an integrated creation. In the *Gesamtkunstwerk* of liturgy the liturgical ritual of preaching should be viewed as one part of a bigger whole. Liturgy is a collection of rituals and symbols, and, within that collection, proclamation is a symbol and liturgical ritual, which acquires its full meaning only in relation to the rest of the symbols and liturgical rituals of liturgy.[70] In answer to the question of whether liturgy must be determined by the sermon or the sermon by the liturgy, Von Allmen responds that they should be complementary, that the sermon should not overshadow the Eucharist; however, the sermon will strongly influence the "Galilean" parts of the service such as the prayers and hymns.[71] The cases above reveal the risk that a worship service can become merely a preaching service in which not much room is left for any other liturgical ritual.

CONCLUSION

Proclamation is attestation within specific contexts. Like liturgy, proclamation in all its forms is an anamnetic event in which the past is remembered in the present that reframes the future. With reference to proclamation, Von Allmen writes that the Word of God "makes that

---

[66] Ibid., 45.
[67] Pui-lan, "Postcolonial Preaching in Intercultural Contexts," 12.
[68] Ibid., 13.
[69] Elsabe Kloppers, "Die Erediens as Omvattende Kunswerk," *Nederduitse Gereformeerde Teologiese Tydskrif* 44 (2003): 80–88.
[70] Marcel Barnard, Johan Cilliers, and Cas Wepener, "Rituals/Conducting Liturgies/Performances," in *International Handbook of Practical Theology*, eds. Birgit Weyel, Wilhelm Gräb, Immanuel Lartey, and Cas Wepener (Berlin: De Gruyter, 2022), 148.
[71] Von Allmen, *Preaching and Congregation*, 33–34. Cf. Von Allmen, *Worship: Its Theology and Practice*, 130.

illic et tunc newly operative in the *hic et nunc*," and hence hearers can participate in this Word event within the broader horizons of the complete liturgy of both Word and sacrament.[72] In this way their lives are continuously disoriented and reoriented, and framed and reframed, along the liturgical road that runs between Galilee and Jerusalem.

For Further Reading

Allmen, Jean-Jacques von, *Preaching and Congregation*, Ecumenical Studies in Worship 10, trans. B. L. Nicholas (Louisville, KY: John Knox Press, 1962).

Barnard, Marcel, Johan Cilliers, and Cas Wepener, *Worship in a Network Culture: Liturgical Ritual Studies. Fields and Methods, Concepts and Metaphors*, Liturgia Condenda 28 (Leuven: Peeters, 2014).

Brueggeman, Walter, *The Prophetic Imagination*, 40th anniversary ed. (Minneapolis, MN: Fortress Press, 2013).

Carvalhaes, Claudio, *Praying with Every Heart: Orienting Our Lives to the Wholeness of the World* (Eugene, OR: Cascade Books, 2021).

Pui-lan, Kwok, "Postcolonial Preaching in Intercultural Contexts," *Homiletic* 40 (2015): 8–21.

Travis, Sarah, *Decolonizing Preaching: The Pulpit as Postcolonial Space* (Eugene, OR: Cascade Books, 2014).

White, James F., *Introduction to Christian Worship* (Nashville, TN: Abingdon Press, 2000).

Wilson, Paul Scott et al., *The New Interpreter's Handbook of Preaching* (Nashville, TN: Abingdon Press, 2008).

---

[72] Von Allmen, *Worship: Its Theology and Practice*, 143.

18 Liturgy and Ecumenism
THOMAS POTT

> So then, my brothers and sisters, when you come together to eat, wait for one another.... About the other things I will give instructions when I come.[1]

INTRODUCTION

St. Paul, in his Letter to the Corinthians, exhorts the members of the local Church to live in harmony and communion. The Lord's Supper is not a symbol of unity and communion but rather of division. The Corinthians apparently do not recognize the Body they constitute by celebrating the memorial of the Lord's Supper. Aware of the internal tensions of the Church at Corinth, St. Paul is adamant to restore order to the celebration of the Lord's Supper, which consists in waiting for one another to eat together. For it is here, in the enactment of the Lord's Supper, that Christians manifest who they are as members of the Body of Christ.

The unity of the Body is thus an essential quality of the community, manifested above all through genuine communion. This communion is physical, in that all eat from the same bread and drink from the same cup, and spiritual, as it expresses communion between the members. A traditional liturgical expression of this reality is the idea of "the communion of saints," as reflected in the ancient invitation to communion in the Byzantine Divine liturgy: "The saints [i.e., the holy gifts] for the saints" ("*ta hagia tois hagiois*").[2] Exclusion from communion, that is, not sharing the meal, whether of one's own free will or as imposed by

---

[1] 1 Cor 11, 33–34.
[2] Robert F. Taft, *A History of the Liturgy of St. John Chrysostom*, vol. V (*The Precommunion Rites*, Orientalia Christiana Analecta 261 (Rome: Pontificio Istituto Orientale, 200), 230–40.

"the saints," expresses that one is not counted as a member of the Body of Christ. Hence, the liturgical celebration contains the expression *par excellence* of the unity of the Church and the constitutive relationship between its members: communion.

In the logic of St. Paul's Letter to the Corinthians, when communion is broken, unity is lost. Now, the history of the Church is punctuated with ruptures of communion between individuals or groups, often reciprocal, producing the constitution of ecclesial realities, each of which claims to be the authentic continuation of the one Body of Christ and, thus, to represent the original unity of the Church. These ruptures have taken place both within local Churches (or "particular Churches," according to the more recent expression of the Code of Canon Law of the Roman Catholic Church)[3] and between groups of local Churches, suspending the existence of unity and communion. But the "solemn" and symbolic manifestation of separation is liturgical because it consists in the rupture of Eucharistic communion and the cessation of all common prayer. After some time, some form of common prayer may be reestablished. But the "restoration of communion," the sharing of the Lord's bread and cup, is generally seen to precede the resolution of all the tensions that may have caused the schism, as well as all the contentions that arose afterward. In this sense, efforts to restore unity and communion are not in line with St. Paul's instruction to the Corinthians and, consequently, do not put the liturgical manifestation of unity at the center of the path toward reconciliation. Indeed, "noncommunion with the others" has become part of the identity of many Churches, divided among themselves.

In what follows, I will suggest how liturgy is a genuine instrument for growing toward Christian unity, not by pretending that Eucharistic communion alone can heal the wounds of history[4] but by arguing that unity in the Body of Christ is already authentically lived in the real relationships and the existential faith in God of many divided Christians. In this sense, communion is restored in a personal and ecclesial acknowledgment of the authenticity of the other in their faith in God and inclusion in the Body of Christ. The respectful recognition of this authenticity of life expressed in the liturgy of "the others" is the

---

[3] Leon Siwecki, "Relationship between the Universal Church and the Local Churches," *Roczniki Teologiczne* 45 (2018): 101–17, at 101, n. 1, and the bibliography at 116–17.
[4] Although I would not contest that it might be helpful, see Thomas O'Loughlin, *Eating Together, Becoming One: Taking Up Pope Francis's Call to Theologians* (Collegeville, MN: Liturgical Press, 2020).

first step toward the discovery of unity and authentic communion. A prerequisite for such a recognition is the appraisal of how other Churches theologically value their liturgical tradition and their concept of unity in Christ. Ecumenism consists not in restoring communion alone but in the faithful commitment of Christians to work for the achievement of reconciliation and unity, and out of faith that true reconciliation is possible and that unity in Christ is the divine gift *par excellence* to humanity.

In this chapter, I focus on the challenges that ecumenism encounters in the realm of liturgy, especially where the theology and the celebration of sacraments are concerned. This does not mean that the Liturgy of the Hours or other congregational liturgical worship is not relevant to the ecumenical approach. Indeed, "non-Eucharistic" liturgical services, in which Christians from other Churches are welcomed to join, often prove to be intense moments of spiritual encounter and of learning from the praying heart of a Church. Moreover, to understand the liturgy in depth, it must be perceived as entirely sacramental,[5] that is, it is always the mystery (*mustèrion*) of God's saving presence among his people. However, the celebration of sacraments and sacramental theology are specific in that they manifest the constitution of the Church as the unity of those who share in the symbols that attest to their full insertion into the Body of Christ. For ecumenism, sacramental liturgy represents a particular challenge, as it relates not simply to the official liturgical prayer of the Churches but to the way in which these Churches understand themselves, as revealed by their sacramental discipline and ritual tradition.

THE INTERCONNECTION OF UNITY AND CHURCH

Numerous doctrinal texts from many Churches emphasize the essential link between liturgy and Church and explain how this link is articulated theologically in the liturgical celebration. In various ways, these texts take up the thread of patristic theology that concerns the constitution of the Church.[6] It is one of the achievements of the Liturgical Movement

---

[5] Alexander Schmemann, *For the Life of the World* (Crestwood, NY: St Vladimir's Seminary Press, 2018).

[6] Pantelis Kalaitzidis, "From the 'Return to the Fathers' to the Need for a Modern Orthodox Theology," *St Vladimir's Theological Quarterly* 54 (2010): 5–36; Pantelis Kalaitzidis, "Theological, Historical, and Cultural Reasons for Anti-Ecumenical Movements in Eastern Orthodoxy," in *Orthodox Handbook on Ecumenism: Resources for Theological Education*, ed. Pantelis Kalaitzidis et al. (Minneapolis,

of the early twentieth century in the Christian West to have rediscovered the profound ecclesial and soteriological meaning of liturgy,[7] overcoming the more pietistic and individualizing understandings typical of modernity. This new awareness is amply reflected in the Second Vatican Council's constitution on the liturgy, *Sacrosanctum Concilium*. For a large number of Churches, this document represents a point for reflection on how liturgy constitutes the Church as a unity in the Mystical Body of Christ.[8]

The relation between liturgy and the unity of the Church is further articulated by the Decree on Ecumenism from the same council, *Unitatis Redintegratio*. According to this document, the Church is called by Christ to a "continual reformation,"[9] which is "grounded in an increase of fidelity to her own calling." This reformation takes place in the various aspects of the Church's life, such as the Biblical and Liturgical Movements. Hence, by the Liturgical Movement – that is, by the thorough preparation for the reform of the liturgy – the Church increases fidelity to her calling. This is said to be a pledge and sign "of the future progress of Ecumenism." In that way, as much as liturgy is related to the unity of the Church, liturgical reform is related to ecumenism – the effort for reconciliation among divided Christians.

However, the concept of unity and the purpose of ecumenism are understood in different ways within different confessional traditions and theological approaches. In bilateral theological dialogues between divided Churches, the concept of unity is a theme frequently addressed, explicitly or implicitly, because the desire to restore lost unity is ultimately what drives theologians and Church pastors to meet. In this sense, ecclesiological dialogue has often been considered the ecumenical dialogue *par excellence*, by having as its ultimate goal the restoration of ecclesiological unity: Church unity, founded in a common theological understanding of communion. Yet, even if common participation at the Lord's Table – Eucharistic communion – is not denied as the ideal goal,

---

MN: Fortress Press, 2014), 134–52, at 146–49, subsequently referred to as *Orthodox Handbook*.

[7] In this context, see Katharine Harmon, Chapter 6.

[8] Cf. Richard Gaillardetz and Edward Hahnenberg, *A Church with Open Doors: Catholic Ecclesiology for the Third Millennium* (Collegeville, MN: Liturgical Press, 2015); cf. Gordon W. Lathrop, *Holy People: A Liturgical Ecclesiology* (Minneapolis, MN: Fortress Press, 1999); cf. Gordon W. Lathrop, "The Gift and Challenge of Liturgical Ecclesiology," in *Ecclesiologica & alia: Studia in Honorem Sven-Erik Brodd*, ed. Erik Berggren and Maria Eckerdal (Skellefteå: Artos, 2015), 337–47.

[9] *Unitatis Redintegratio*, 6.

in many dialogues the quest for unity is not really considered in its liturgical key but rather as an effort to come closer together in the realm of theology, anthropology, morals, and humanitarian collaborations. Alliances between Churches that have been sealed in a restoration of Eucharistic communion are rather rare.[10]

Pursued as an ecclesiological agreement, the question of unity shows how the Churches define themselves and how they claim to represent the "original unity." In bilateral dialogues, liturgy has an important place, as it reveals the being of the Church.[11] The argumentation usually refers to a deposit of doctrine in dogmatic and canonical matters that the liturgy is believed to express. Above all, the sacramental theology and discipline of a Church, as expressed in official doctrinal texts and in the liturgical books that contain the euchological and ritual legacy, are the points of reference to which the Churches formally refer to discern the degree of closeness – or, indeed, distance – in faith from the dialogue partner Church. However, liturgy plays a peculiar role here, in that it functions as a kind of "identity certificate" of a Church, without taking into account its true value as the celebrating and enacting witness to faith and communion in Christ.

In this context, we may think of "Eucharistic hospitality" (the fact of being admitted, more or less formally, to communion in a Church with which one's own Church lives in a situation of schism or "rupture of communion"), "mixed marriage," and other sorts of sacramental or non-sacramental shared worship. Generally, these are exceptional occasions, for pastoral reasons,[12] and do not represent any reform of sacramental discipline to restore Christian unity. However, the meaning of communion and liturgy might be reduced to an expression of personal religiosity, with no real ecclesial significance, if one considers the permission to participate at the Lord's Table as a pastorally justified exception to be applied individually and punctually. Yet it is important not to underestimate any form of concrete rapprochement for baptized

---

[10] The Bonn Agreement between Anglicans and Old-Catholics is one such example of this rare occurrence (www.utrechter-union.org/page/146/declaration_of_the_ibc_on_the_pa). See also the Porvoo Agreement (1994) between Anglicans and Lutherans (https://porvoocommunion.org/porvoo_communion/statement/) and the Common Christological Declaration between the Catholic Church and the Assyrian Church of the East (1994).

[11] John Zizioulas, *L'Eucharistie, l'Évêque et l'Église* (Paris: DDB, 1994); Paul McPartlan, *The Eucharist Makes the Church: Henri de Lubac and John Zizioulas in Dialogue* (Edinburgh: T&T Clark, 1993).

[12] See note 21.

Christians when liturgical worship is a witness to it or even an operational dynamic of it. For, if at the level of official theological dialogues between divided Churches, progress sometimes stagnates, liturgy lived and shared, at any level, remains a witness to the fact that, in spite of all separations, the One Mystical Body of Christ is indivisible.

To summarize, liturgy and ecumenism are essentially linked, since liturgy reveals the Church as unity in Christ, while ecumenism is the quest for the restoration of unity between divided Christians. The rapprochement between Churches is hindered by how these Churches understand their liturgical identity as an expression of unity in Christ, in a self-sufficient and self-referential way, traditionally led by dogmatic theology and canon law, rather than by the liturgical texts and rites.

Hence, the unity of the Church is often seen as a matter of ecclesial government and jurisdiction, prioritizing the "balance of power" between the members of the Church over the spiritual bonds of fellowship, which, even if hierarchical, flow from Eucharistic communion. The concept of communion tends to lose its immanently Eucharistic and celebrative dimension and instead incorporates members of the Church into a canonically established and dogmatically defined institution. Ideologies that promote the idea of national or ethnic belonging reinforce the consciousness of unity as the exclusive property of a particular group. In this context, liturgy is in danger of being hijacked by dynamics that go against its own nature. One of the tasks of ecumenism, then, should be to gather the energies of divided Christians in order to strive for the preservation of liturgy as the common language of the whole Body of Christ, even if all the obstacles to the restoration of communion have not yet been resolved.

THE MANIFESTATION OF UNITY THROUGH LITURGY

The Nicene–Constantinopolitan Creed is a symbol of faith that holds a prominent place in many liturgical traditions. It declares faith in "the One, Holy, Catholic and Apostolic Church." It is a witness not only to the time when there was communion among various Churches that adhered to this symbol but also to the time when some Churches were dropping out from communion with the others. This symbol remained in use in the Churches that adhered to it, even after they had separated from each other over the centuries. The faith in the "One, Holy, Catholic and Apostolic Church," however, is not understood to refer to the undivided Church of the time of the first ecumenical councils (even if "unity" was then already a relative term) but to the unity, holiness, catholicity, and apostolicity that each of the divided Churches professed to embody.

The "Ravenna Document" of the Joint International Commission for the Theological Dialogue between the Roman Catholic Church and the Orthodox Church (2007)[13] states that "Unity and multiplicity, the relationship between the one Church and the many local Churches, that constitutive relationship of the Church, also poses the question of the relationship between the authority inherent in every ecclesial institution and the conciliarity which flows from the mystery of the Church as communion."[14] In response to the question of how the Church as communion is shaped in the world, the document distinguishes between "three levels of ecclesial institutions: that of the local Church around its bishop; that of a region taking in several neighboring local Churches; and that of the whole inhabited earth (*oikoumene*) which embraces all the local Churches." This distinction offers a "model of Unity and Catholicity" in which the Byzantine Orthodox and Catholic Churches, divided since the Great Schism of 1054,[15] should be able to rebuild their canonical unity in harmony without sacrificing their centuries-old and autonomous ecclesiastical identity.

Although historically justified and open to a reconciled future, this "ecumenical" and irenic model risks coming up against the traditional self-understanding of unity and catholicity of each Church and the specific liturgical way in which it is expressed. It is also typically a product of bilateral dialogue – here between the Roman Catholic and the Byzantine Orthodox Churches – which does not take into account how other Churches may find a satisfactory place in this model. While the Catholic and Orthodox Churches find it challenging to have unity at a universal level, other Churches (especially those originating from

---

[13] "Ecclesiological and Canonical Consequences of the Sacramental Nature of the Church: Ecclesial Communion, Conciliarity and Authority," Ravenna, October 13, 2007. Accessed July 21, 2023, at www.christianunity.va/content/unitacristiani/en/dialoghi/sezione-orientale/chiese-ortodosse-di-tradizione-bizantina/commissione-mista-internazionale-per-il-dialogo-teologico-tra-la/documenti-di-dialogo/testo-in-inglese.html.

[14] Ibid., 4.

[15] "The so-called Great Schism of 1054 was one of a series of minor, temporary separations between the Byzantine and Latin churches: and was not the great divide later text books have often made of it. The real alienation of the churches came a few centuries later, and it has not been healed to this day although ecumenical relations from the early twentieth century onward between Orthodox and Roman Catholics have been greatly improved." John McGuckin, "The Role of Orthodoxy in World Christianity Today – Historical, Demographic and Theological Perspectives: An Introduction," in *Orthodox Handbook*, 3–8, at 5.

Reformation in the West) find it problematic even at the local and regional levels.

In this sense, the "theological unity" of ecumenical dialogues is not the unity lived and fostered in the liturgy. Liturgical identity constitutes the binding force of the assembly of believers, which no theological stratagem can replace. From the point of view of liturgy, therefore, the model presented by the Ravenna Document is problematic, as it claims an understanding of the unity of the Church that goes beyond the confessional barriers of the Orthodox Churches and for which there is no unequivocal connection at the level of liturgical tradition. Although there should not be a real obstacle for an honest endeavor to restore communion, part of the problem is what Sigmund Freud, in a quote by Rowan Williams, called "the narcissism of small differences."[16] Without a real reform of liturgical and theological mentalities all ecumenical rapprochements, as thorough and well-intended as they may be, are doomed to fail.

The Dogmatic Constitution on the Church of Vatican II, *Lumen Gentium*, famously introduces the concept of "subsistit in,"[17] testifying to the Roman Catholic Church's new openness to the ecclesial and sacramental authenticity of other Churches and ecclesial communities. But the same principle risks supporting a centralist way of understanding the Church, in which recognition of the ecclesiality of other Churches automatically gives these Churches a place within the categories of Latin Catholic ecclesiology. Furthermore, a certain separation between the communion in the holy gifts (the Eucharistic gifts, in which the Orthodox faithful are admitted to participate) and the communion of saints (the Eucharistic community, of which they are not fully a part) is incoherent with a sacramental theology wherein communion at the Table of the Lord is celebrated worship of the Church.[18]

---

[16] Michael Collins, "Rowan Williams in Conversation," www.linkedin.com/pulse/rowan-williams-conversation-michael-collins (first published in *The Catholic Times*, February 6, 2019).

[17] *Lumen Gentium*, 8.

[18] Cf. Thomas Pott, "A partire dalla liturgia: fra tradizione orientale e occidentale," in *Liturgia ed ecumenismo*, ed. Goffredo Boselli (Roma: Edizioni Liturgiche, 2009), 67–89; cf. Grigorios Papathomas, "Methods of Teaching about and with Other Christian Denominations in Ecumenical Theological Education of Orthodox Institutions," in *Orthodox Handbook*, 898–905, at 903–4.

LITURGICAL FORMS OF THE MANIFESTATION OF UNITY

Liturgy presents a paradigm of unity in the Body of Christ that consists in the concelebration of all the members of the Church, each at their own level, and in the communion of all at the same Table of the Lord. This communion encompasses not only the assembly of those actually present but all the members of the local Church and, indeed, "the whole Church" – that is, all the local Churches with which one is in communion. All the liturgical and theological vocabulary around Eucharistic communion subtends that there exists a "universal communion" that is enacted in each Eucharist. This communion between local Churches is expressed in several ways described briefly below.

Diptychs

Both in the West and in the East, this communion that goes beyond the locally assembled community is expressed in the "diptychs,"[19] a formula of invocation that manifests the ecclesial hierarchy with whom one is "in communion." When a priest celebrates, he will mention his own bishop and the head of the Church (the pope, a patriarch, a metropolitan, or an archbishop). During celebration, a bishop mentions the head of the Church with whom he is in communion. In the Byzantine Orthodox Churches, a head of the Church mentions all the other heads of local Churches with whom he is in communion. This invocation has its fixed place during the Eucharistic prayer. For the head of a local Church, removing someone from the diptychs is the liturgical act that expresses the breaking of communion with another local Church.

While the Diptychs show how the communion between local Churches is rooted in the local celebration of the Eucharist, it also heavily accentuates the hierarchical organization of the Church as a condition for unity in the Body of Christ. As a consequence, human conflicts between hierarchs can easily affect the bonds of communion between the faithful, who constitute the "flock," while their pastors are expected to guarantee their unity in One, Holy, Catholic and Apostolic body.

---

[19] Stefano Parenti, "The Liturgical τοποι of Ecclesiastical Communion: Diptychs, Commemorations, and Acclamations," in *Autocephaly, Coming of Age in Communion: Historical, Canonical, Liturgical and Theological Studies*, ed. Edward G. Farrugia and Zeljko Pasa, Orientalia Christiana Analecta 314-15 (Rome: Pontifio Istituto Orientale, 2023), 865–901.

Paradoxically, ecumenical contacts often seem easier to maintain than relations within one's own "communion" of local Churches, especially when communion is under threat. The task of people engaged in ecumenism should be to show comprehension for the internal sufferings of Churches with whom one is not in communion. Praying for each other is a pledge and a sign (cf. *Unitatis Redintegratio* 6) that the unity in the Body of Christ is stronger than all our divisions.

Eucharistic Hospitality

According to the Ravenna document, "Eucharistic hospitality"[20] means to welcome other local Churches that are in communion with each other into a local Church of members.[21] In contemporary practice, however, the term "Eucharistic hospitality" refers to the concrete situation of the faithful of divided Churches meeting in a liturgical or Eucharistic setting. In relation to the sacramental discipline of the Catholic Church, Eucharistic hospitality is formally regulated within the broader framework of "communicatio in sacris."[22] Applying the idea of "subsistit in," the faithful of Churches whose sacraments are recognized by the Catholic Church are permitted to receive the "Catholic sacraments." Orthodox Churches generally admit non-Orthodox faithful to receive sacraments only through the principle of Economy,[23] whereby strict rules are momentarily alleviated. For many Churches of the Protestant Reformation, the invitation to the Lord's Table is extended to all present, leaving participation in communion to the discernment of each individual.

[20] On the concept of Eucharistic hospitality, see Thomas Pott, "'L'hospitalité eucharistique': réflexions théologiques et pastorales," in *Rites de communion, 55ᵉ Semaine Liturgique Saint-Serge, Paris 2008*, ed. André Lossky and Manlio Sodi (Roma: Libreria Editrice Vaticana, 2010).

[21] Cf. Document of Ravenna (note 13), 23.

[22] Can. CIC 844. Cf. Alphonse Boras, "L'Église catholique et la 'communicatio in sacris' appliquée à l'eucharistie," *Irénikon* 72 (1999): 365–434; André Birmelé, "Communion ecclésiale et *communicatio in sacris* appliquées à l'eucharistie. Une approche luthérienne," *Irénikon* 72 (1999): 562–85; Emmanuel Lanne, "Quelques questions posées à l'Église orthodoxe concernant la *communicatio in sacris* dans l'eucharistie," in *Irénikon* 72 (1999): 435–52. See also the fundamental work of Georges-Henri Ruyssen, *Eucharistie et œcuménisme. Évolution de la normativité universelle et comparaison avec certaines normes particulières* (Paris: Cerf, 2008).

[23] Cf. Georges Florovsky, "The Boundaries of the Church," in Georges Florovsky, *Ecumenism I: A Doctrinal Approach* (Vaduz: Buchervertriebsanstalt, 1989), 36–45, quoted in Stylianos Tsompanidis, "Orthodox Participation in the Ecumenical Movement – A Detailed Historical Survey," in *Orthodox Handbook*, 104–15, at 110; see also Emmanuel Clapsis, "Theology of Religions as Concern for Ecumenical Dialogue of Orthodox Theologians," in *Orthodox Handbook*, 706–13, here 707–8.

In this regard, the understanding of the other and respect for a Church's application of its theological perspectives must precede the possible questioning of what is difficult to understand, or even what gives rise to indignation. Therefore, a concrete question concerns the mutual recognition between Churches of the sacraments of initiation.[24] While the recognition by many Churches of baptism administered outside their own canonical structures is based on the formal and objective fact that baptism was celebrated with true water and the Trinitarian formula, for other Churches it is inconceivable that a true sacrament could exist outside the sacramental economy of one's own Church. A further problem may be the precise way in which the ritual of baptism or chrismation/confirmation is administered.

It is essential to contextualize theologically, historically, and culturally both the rigor with which some Churches adhere to their rules and the tolerance that other Churches show. The principle of "subsistit in" enables the Catholic Church to recognize as "valid" whatever it discerns as "forces impelling toward Catholic unity."[25] Even if this is a principle of "ecumenical" openness, this recognition still refers to a somewhat self-referential ecclesiological dynamic that other Churches would not easily accommodate. The Roman Catholic Church's uncompromising non-recognition of Anglican orders, following Pope Leo XIII's bull *Apostolicae Curae* (1896),[26] is an example of how the recognition of the existence of an obvious sacramental economy in one Church can be subject to a rigorous scrutiny from another, relying more on a fixed and time-stamped system of theological categories[27] than on what the liturgy manifests today of the Church's faith.

---

[24] Cf. Michel Stavrou, "Relations œcuméniques et reconnaissance du baptême des autres Eglises," *Contacts* 243 (2013): 519–33; Theresia Hainthaler, "Christological Declarations with Oriental Orthodox," in *Christians Shaping Identity from the Roman Empire to Byzantium: Studies Inspired by Pauline Allen*, ed. Geoffrey D. Dunn and Wendy Mayer (Leiden: Brill, 2015), 426–53.

[25] *Lumen Gentium* 8.

[26] Cf. Thomas O'Loughlin, "Locating Contemporary Catholicism in Relation to *Apostolicae Curae*: What It Can Tell Catholics About Themselves," Bolletino E-book, n. 101/Primavera 2022, Centro Pro-Unione, Rome, www.prounione.it/bulletin/it/web-n101-spring2022/, 30–40.

[27] See the document *Sorores in Spe* of the Malines Conversations Group: "Sisters in Hope of the Resurrection: A Fresh Response to the Condemnation of Anglican Orders (1896)," 2021, www.malinesconversations.org/sorores-in-spe/.

Bishop's Consecration

The prescriptions for the election and consecration of a new bishop for a local Church, as attested by a longstanding tradition since the first Council of Nicaea,[28] were expressly intended to signify and reinforce the awareness of sharing the same apostolic faith and the same ecclesial structure: "A bishop ought to be chosen by all the bishops of his province, but if that is impossible because of some urgent necessity, or because of the length of the journey, let three bishops at least assemble and proceed to the consecration, having the written permission of the absent" (Nicaea I, can. 4).[29] The co-consecrating bishops, having themselves received their ministry through the Holy Spirit and the imposition of hands by bishops in the apostolic succession, act in the name of the episcopal body and the people of God. According to the Ravenna Document, "When this is accomplished in conformity with the canons, communion among Churches in the true faith, sacraments and ecclesial life is ensured, as well as living communion with previous generations."[30]

However, communion is understood as a parameter of canonicity, attesting to the unity of the Church as "communion" in the apostolic faith and the same ecclesiastical structure. The liturgical ritual of co-consecration is a very significant symbol of this. This is justified by the fact that the faith of the believers is the faith of the Church, guaranteed and authenticated by the bishops. However, as a manifestation of the unity between local Churches that are in communion with each other and, therefore, as a witness to a certain ecclesiological self-referentiality of the Churches concerned, the tradition of the co-consecration of bishops does not pose a real challenge to ecumenism.

An application of this tradition is witnessed in the Anglican liturgy of episcopal consecration through the so-called Dutch touch. This originated in the 1930s when the Church of England invited Old-Catholic Dutch bishops to participate in the consecration of new Anglican bishops.[31] Since Old-Catholic ordinations have never been formally questioned in terms of their validity by the magisterium of

---

[28] Paul F. Bradshaw, *Rites of Ordination: Their History and Theology* (Collegeville, MN: Liturgical Press, 2013), 51–52.

[29] Cyril Hovorun, "Ecclesiological Foundation for Ecumenism," in *Orthodox Handbook*, 77–85, at 83–84.

[30] The Ravenna Document (note 14), n. 22.

[31] Brian Taylor, *Accipe Spiritum Sanctum: Historical Essays on the Agreements of Bonn and Meissen* (Guildford: St Thomas's Trust, 1995); Charlotte Methuen, "The Bonn Agreement and the Catholicization of Anglicanism: Anglicans and Old Catholics in

the Roman Catholic Church, the "Dutch touch" was thought to provide a kind of "infusion" of validity, whereby the deficiencies of Anglican orders would be resolved and remedied. It should be noted, however, that Anglican bishops in no way wished to question their own orders, for which a kind of *sanatio in radice* would have been necessary. Instead they intended to make the Anglican orders more acceptable to Rome in the event that a restoration of communion became conceivable.

From an ecumenical point of view, this particular usage is an inappropriate – although in some way comprehensible – response to a negative assessment by one Church of the ecclesiality of another. The response is inappropriate because the attempt to conform to the theological paradigm of the other, without a genuine attempt to know the other Church in its authenticity as communion in Christ – as experienced in the liturgical assembly[32] – means making a sacrifice, in the eyes of the other, of one's own sacramental self-understanding. Furthermore, the apostolic succession as a mechanical transmission of sacramental grace represents the line of continuity from the apostles to the bishops of today as a guarantee of the Church's communion in faith and life from its origin and an impoverishment of the conception of apostolicity as a succession in the gifts and ministries, given to the whole Church by the Holy Spirit.[33]

Holy Chrism

Holy chrism and the rituals in which it is used have greater impact on ecumenism. Consecrated and administered by the bishop from the earliest textual evidence, anointing with holy chrism completes the ritual of baptism. By its reservation to the bishop – or, in the case of the Byzantine Orthodox Churches, to the head of the autocephalous Church – the consecration of the chrism is another symbol of communion and the unity of the Church. Canon 48 of the Council of Laodicea (364) makes the anointing with chrism obligatory as a post-baptismal anointing.[34] The Council of Constantinople (380) in its ninth canon prescribes this anointing as obligatory for converts who had not

---

the Lang Papers and the Douglas Papers 1920–1939," *Internationale kirchliche Zeitschrift: Neue Folge der Revue internationale de théologie* 79 (2007): 1–22.

[32] Gordon Lathrop, *The Assembly: A Spirituality* (Minneapolis, MN: Fortress Press, 2022).

[33] Cf. *Sorores in Spe* (note 27), n. 8. Cf. also Hovorun, "Ecclesial Foundation," 85.

[34] Cf. Thomas Pott, "La Chrismation comme rite d'admission ou de réconciliation de 'frères séparés.' Implications sacramentelles et ecclésiologiques," in *Chrismation et confirmation: Questions autour d'un rite post-baptismal*, ed. Carlo Braga (Roma: Edizioni Liturgiche, 2009), 199–210.

received it in their original Church. The anointing with holy chrism, or chrismation, "Seal of the gift of the Holy Spirit," during the rite of baptism, marks the insertion into the communion of the Church, completing in a way what was missing in their baptism. In this case, chrismation did not represent a negation or repetition of the baptism received in "another community"; rather it was intended to complete the prescribed liturgical rite and to insert the faithful into the communion of the Church. This changed toward the end of the first millennium, when, according to the "Diataxis of Patriarch Methodius for the Reconciliation of Apostates,"[35] chrismation was to be administered during the ritual of reception into the Church of those who were separated from it, whether they had already received it or not.

To administer the rites of Christian initiation to one from another Church calls into question the prior insertion of this person into the Body of Christ and, therefore, the full ecclesiality of their Church of origin. Different Churches differ from each other in terms of customs and underlying theologies. However, the act of reiterating non-repeatable sacraments encloses these same sacraments in a framework where questions of validity and canonicity take precedence over what the liturgy of each Church says about itself.

Following the prescriptions of the Synod of Constantinople of 1484 and the Synod of Moscow of 1667, the Agreed Statement of the North American Orthodox–Catholic Consultation on Baptism and Sacramental Economy (St. Vladimir's Orthodox Seminary, Crestwood, New York, June 3, 1999)[36] recommends that the Orthodox practice of chrismation of Catholic converts should be explicitly affirmed not as a repetition of part of the Catholic Christian initiation but as having a penitential character. This is a way of theologically reinterpreting a rite without having to change the liturgy. The recommendation, while explicitly working just for the minimum achievable, nevertheless represents an important step in that it calls on the Churches to assess the fittingness of their liturgical traditions.

Another instance of the reiteration of the anointing with holy chrism is the anointing of an emperor or king. First attested at the

---

[35] Miguel Arranz, "La 'Diataxis' du patriarche Méthode pour la réconciliation des apostats," *Orientalia christiana periodica* 56 (1990): 283–322.

[36] "Agreed Statement on Baptism and 'Sacramental Economy' Issued by North American Orthodox–Catholic Consultation," *United States Conference of Catholic Bishops*, June 8, 1999. Accessed July 21, 2023, at www.usccb.org/news/1999/agreed-statement-baptism-and-sacramental-economy-issued-north-american-orthodox-catholic.

coronation of Pepin the Short (Reims, 754), this practice spread widely in the West. In the East, the anointing of the sovereign only came into use after the departure of the Crusaders from Constantinople (1204-1261). In Russia, Fëdor I Ivanovič (1584) was the first tsar enthroned without anointing. The coronation of Charles III on May 6, 2023, in Westminster Abbey provided a significant ecumenical gesture but also raised some sacramentological questions. As Archbishop Justin Welby of Canterbury said, "Since beginning the planning for the coronation, my desire has been for a new coronation oil to be produced using olive oil from the Mount of Olives. This demonstrates the deep historic link between the coronation, the Bible and the Holy Land (March 6, 2023, WAFA)." The Patriarch of Jerusalem, Theophilos III, was willing to consecrate this oil according to the ritual used to make holy chrism, as the Anglican Archbishop of Jerusalem attended the ceremony. Rooted in the sacramental reality of the Orthodox Church of Jerusalem, the profound links thus created what *Unitatis Redintegratio* would call "a pledge and sign of the future progress of Ecumenism." Nevertheless, the fact that this holy chrism was created specifically for the coronation of King Charles and was therefore not the holy chrism that the Church of Jerusalem also uses in its own baptismal liturgy diminishes its power as a gesture of communion. However, such an initiative points to an important way ahead for the future of ecumenism.

LITURGY AS A TOOL TOWARD RESTORING UNITY

The Ecumenical Movement is special, as it endorses the awareness that the search for unity must itself be a common journey: A fruitful and truthful rapprochement must set all parties involved in motion toward each other. This implies that mutual respect for the tradition of each Church is an invaluable asset of the Ecumenical Movement. The temptation to level out differences and to create a kind of "Super Church,"[37] as some Churches fear, betrays the very roots of the Ecumenical Movement. For at the root of the contemporary search for unity is the discovery of liturgy as the key to unity in the Church as the Body of

---

[37] Daniel Buda, "On the Critical Role of Orthodox Churches in the Ecumenical Movement," in *Orthodox Handbook*, 127 (quoting the letter by the Russian Orthodox Church to the WCC Central Committee moderator, in reaction to the fifth WCC assembly in Nairobi, 1975).

Christ. In this discovery, liturgy appears as a living reality, a common expression of faith and celebration of the Church.[38]

Models of unity based on an institutional or doctrinal understanding of the Church gave liturgy a subsidiary rather than a substantial place. The Church was seen as "owning a rite," rather than being constituted in substance by its liturgy. This understanding gave rise to phenomena such as "Uniatism," which refers to the unification of one Church, in whole or in part, while continuing its own liturgical tradition.[39] However, the resourcing of ecclesiology in patristic theology in the second half of the nineteenth century led to a rediscovery of the Church as a *mustèrion*, as a sacrament, as the mystery of Christ's presence in the world through the power of the Holy Spirit who dwells in the faithful gathered in his Name.

Within this theological context, liturgy becomes the lens through which the Church is most authentically viewed. This is also the life story of a visionary of Church unity like Dom Lambert Beauduin (1873–1960), initiator of the Liturgical Movement in Belgium and founder of the Benedictine monastery of Amay-Chevetogne (1925).[40] His journey appears as the discovery of the mystery of the Church in consecutive and complementary stages, going from the Social Movement to the Ecumenical Movement, passing by monastic renewal and the Liturgical Movement. The monastic reform that the foundation of Amay represented, in a way, as the "Œuvre monastique pour l'unité des chrétiens," with all its ecumenical aspirations, was rooted in and nourished by the Liturgical Movement.[41]

Liturgy played a pivotal role in the Ecumenical Movement. One example of this is how the community of the monastery of Amay-Chevetogne prayed the Liturgy of the Hours simultaneously in the

---

[38] On this theme see Kallistos Ware, "Sobornost and Eucharistic Ecclesiology: Aleksei Khomiakov and His Successors," *International Journal for the Study of the Christian Church* 11 (2011): 216–35.

[39] Vittorio Peri, "Uniatism and Its Origins," *Journal of Early Christian Studies* 49 (1997): 23–46; on the phenomenon of uniatism and the issues at stake today, Hyacinthe Destivelle, "De l'unionisme à l'œcuménisme. L'Église catholique et l'unité des chrétiens durant la première moitié du XXe siècle," in *Conduis-la vers l'unité parfaite: Œcuménisme et synodalité*, ed. Hyacinthe Destivelle (Paris: Cerf, 2018): 19–34.

[40] Raymond Loonbeek and Jacques Mortiau, *Un pionnier, Dom Lambert Beauduin (1873–1960). Liturgie et Unité des chrétiens*, 2 vols. (Louvain-la-Neuve, Collège Érasme: Éditions de Chevetogne, 2001).

[41] Thomas Pott, "Quelle réforme liturgique? Réflexions sur son objet et son sujet," *Irénikon* 74 (2001): 379–99.

Byzantine and Latin rites, thus offering the much needed spiritual rapprochement. However, more than 100 years after the beginning of the Liturgical Movement, the canonical structures of the Churches and a certain measure of ecclesiological self-referentiality have not been able to face up to the challenges posed by the Biblical, Patristic, and Liturgical Movements of the early twentieth century. Other religious communities or associations of faithful, dedicated in a particular way to Christian unity, have since emerged, often with a strong emphasis on liturgical life.[42] These communities, thanks to their culture of fraternal open-mindedness, have become eminent places of ecumenical encounter and rapprochement. But liturgy, as theological breeding ground *par excellence* for the reconstitution of unity, plays a less substantial role.

The pivotal function of liturgy in bringing divided Churches together is also reflected in the comparative method of liturgical studies ("Liturgie comparée") initiated by the German philologist and orientalist Anton Baumstark (1872–1948). Interestingly, Baumstark gave his first presentation of the method of comparative liturgy in 1932 to the monks of Amay.[43] Revised many times in its principles,[44] the method contains an important insight for the relationship between liturgy and ecumenism, albeit in a more intellectual way. On the one hand, liturgical research knows no confessional barriers; on the other hand, liturgical research shows that Christians of all times are united by having been confronted with the challenges of transmitting Tradition.

CONCLUSION

On several occasions rather than unity and communion, liturgy becomes the context in which separation and division are generated. Liturgy sometimes becomes a shielded environment where people celebrate the faith and convictions they share with a group but which they protect against others. When liturgy becomes a symbol of division and an instrument of excommunication, it clearly misses its purpose and should no longer be considered a true Christian liturgy. This is not yet about ecumenism, but about the essence of liturgy as the celebration of

---

[42] For example, Taizé, Bose, Community of Jerusalem, Sant'Egidio, Community of Iona.
[43] Anton Baumstark, *Liturgie comparée: principes et méthodes pour l'étude historique des liturgies chrétiennes*, 3rd ed. (Chevetogne: Éd. de Chevetogne, 1953).
[44] Robert F. Taft and Gabriele Winkler (eds.), *Acts of the International Congress: Comparative Liturgy Fifty Years after Anton Baumstark (1872–1948)* (Paris: Institut Français d'Études Byzantines, 2003); see also Destivelle, *Conduis-la vers l'unité parfaite*, 202.

the mystery of God's presence amidst his people. Each Church has its own responsibility in this respect. This is what the Second Vatican Council's decree on ecumenism, *Unitatis Redintegratio*, expresses when it says: "Christ summons the Church to continual reformation as she sojourns here on earth."[45] Unfolding the renewal of liturgy in a unique way, the renewal of the Church passes through the conversion of hearts. Likewise, liturgical reform[46] is not about possible changes to the rites or liturgical texts: This is only the stereotypical understanding of the idea of reform. On the contrary, liturgical reform is first and foremost a journey of faith, a movement of conversion, in which the Church seeks to restore the liturgy to its primordial meaning as the mystery of the presence in the world of a God who saves, through the incarnation of his Son and the power of the Holy Spirit.

If ecumenism, in its primary sense of searching for lost unity, intends to go beyond mere politeness, it will have to reorient itself to that instant of the Church's life where it constitutes faith lived and shared, where it reaches the reality of life and the truth of faith. This is where liturgy subsists as an experience of life as the living Body of Christ in the world. This Body, signified and strengthened by the meal eaten together by those who labor in Him within God's creation, may not entirely coincide with the ritual structures of the Church, but it is the basis on which liturgy is built. Far from being a fixed reality of customs, gestures, and doctrines, liturgy and ecumenism are dynamics and movements. They should mutually stimulate each other in order to rediscover themselves as dynamics and, from that dynamic, reshape their manifestation in the world.

For Further Reading

Kalaitzidis, Pantelis et al. (eds.), *Orthodox Handbook on Ecumenism: Resources for Theological Education* (Minneapolis, MN: Fortress Press, 2014).

Lathrop, Gordon, *Holy People: A Liturgical Ecclesiology* (Minneapolis, MN: Fortress Press, 1999).

O'Loughlin, Thomas, *Eating Together, Becoming One: Taking Up Pope Francis's Call to Theologians* (Collegeville, MN: Liturgical Press, 2020).

Pott, Thomas, James Hawkey, and Keith F. Pecklers (eds.), *Malines: Continuing the Conversations* (London: SPCK, 2023).

Zizioulas, John, *L'Eucharistie, l'Évêque et l'Église* (Paris: DDB, 1994).

---

[45] *Unitatis Redintegratio* 6; cf. note 9.

[46] On the idea of reform, see Thomas Pott, *Byzantine Liturgical Reform: A Study of Liturgical Change in the Byzantine Tradition* (Crestwood, NY: St Vladimir's Seminary Press, 2010), 28–30 and passim.

19 Liturgy and the Religions of the World

MARIANNE MOYAERT

Starting from the 1960s–1970s, the Roman Catholic Church set in motion a turn to dialogue.[1] The ecclesial support for interreligious dialogue gave impetus not only to new interfaith initiatives but also to theological reflection about religious diversity.[2] Theologians of religions approach the challenge of religious diversity mainly in terms of doctrine; far less attention goes to the experiential and more specifically the ritual and/or liturgical dimension of interreligious encounters.[3] It is as if the dialogical turn has no bearing on the way Christians pray, worship, and celebrate; as if theological questions about religious diversity may be settled exclusively by discussing doctrine; and as if interrituality is merely a performative expression of already formulated

---

[1] I approach the topic of this chapter as a Roman Catholic theologian with a specific interest in liturgical theology. However, the dialogical turn is also supported by the World Council of Churches, and many of the questions that I address in this chapter are also picked up by Protestant theologians working in the fields of theologies of religions, comparative theology, liturgical theology, and theologies of interreligious dialogue. Several of the authors whom I reference in this chapter and who share my interest in the ritual dimension of interreligious encounters belong to other Christian confessions. Approaching theological questions related to religious diversity from a particular confessional tradition translates into diverging sensitivities, concerns, and insights. On the other hand, it is also true that diversity-related issues have been dealt with *across* Christian confessional lines, resulting in Protestant and Catholic theologians learning from one another. Finally, it should also be noted that many of the issues discussed in this chapter are also increasingly dealt with in interfaith circles, resulting in practices of theology that are profoundly *comparative* and/or interfaith.

[2] See Jacques Dupuis, *Toward a Christian Theology of Religious Pluralism* (Maryknoll: Orbis Books, 1997); John Hick and Paul Knitter (eds.), *The Myth of Christian Uniqueness* (London: SCM, 1988); Elizabeth J. Harris (ed.), *Twenty-First Century Theologies of Religions: Retrospection and Future Prospects* (Leiden: Brill, 2016).

[3] For an in-depth analysis of this disinterest, see Marianne Moyaert, "Towards a Ritual Turn in Comparative Theology: Opportunities, Challenges, and Problems," *The Harvard Theological Review* 111 (2018): 1–23.

theologies of religions rather than itself a site productive of theological discernment.[4] Thus, many of the prevailing assumptions about the "limited" theological significance of worship also impact the way theologians of religions and/or dialogue approach the topic of religious diversity.

Fully in keeping with the field of liturgical theology, this chapter starts from the assumption that how we pray and celebrate *does* inform what we believe and vice versa. This is no different in a context of plurality. I suggest shifting attention from interreligious theological *dialogue* to the way interreligious encounters are concretized and materialized through ritual practices.[5] Looking at interreligious encounters through the prism of ritual does more justice to the nature of religion as a lived reality, which revolves around a wide variety of bodily practices; centering ritual will also offer a richer understanding of the "dialogical turn" and how it has become an integral aspect of what it means to be a church today.

THE ROMAN CATHOLIC CHURCH AND *THE DIALOGICAL TURN*

For most of its history, the Roman Catholic Church assumed a binary system to distinguish between *Christians* on the one hand and Jews, pagans, and Muslims on the other. "Non-Christians" were imagined in terms of their *lack* of faith or even as enemies of true religion.[6] In polemical literature, their bodies, symbols, and sacred places were depicted as filthy, their rituals as legalistic or idolatrous. Church policies were put in place to restrict social, sexual, and marital relations

---

[4] See Joris Geldhof, "Liturgy as Theological Norm: Getting Acquainted with 'Liturgical Theology'," *Neue Zeitschrift für systematische Theologie und Religionsphilosophie* 52 (2010): 155–76.

[5] Elsewhere, I and others have suggested the term "inter-rituality" to that end. Marianne Moyaert, "Ritualizing Interreligious Encounters: Mapping the Field of Interrituality," *Interreligious Studies and Intercultural Theology* 1.2 (2017): 164–86; Marianne Moyaert, *Interreligious Relations and the Negotiation of Ritual Boundaries: Explorations in Interrituality* (Cham: Springer International Publishing, 2019); Jens Kreinath, "Interrituality," in *The Sage Encyclopedia of the Sociology of Religion*, ed. Adam Possamai and Anthony Joseph Blasi (Thousand Oaks, CA: Sage Publications, 2020), 398–99.

[6] Sara Lipton, "Christianity and Its Others: Jews, Muslims, and Pagans," in *The Oxford Handbook of Medieval Christianity*, ed. John H. Arnold (Oxford: Oxford University Press, 2014), 413–35.

between Christians, Jews, Muslims, and pagans.[7] Practices of separation and rituals of purgation helped establish boundaries between these social groups. This radically changed during the Second Vatican Council. Documents like *Dei Verbum* and *Lumen Gentium*, as well as *Ad Gentes*, projected dialogue as intrinsic to God's dealings with humans and encouraged all Christians to enter into positive and constructive dialogue with "people of other faiths." The encyclical *Ecclesiam Suam* (1964) even suggests that to be disciples of Christ one must be dialogical, and the conciliar declaration *Nostra Aetate* (1965) states that

> The Catholic Church rejects nothing that is true and holy in these religions. She regards with sincere reverence those ways of conduct and of life, those precepts and teachings which, though differing in many aspects from the ones she holds and sets forth, nonetheless often reflect a ray of that Truth which enlightens all men.[8]

Nostra Aetate calls upon Christians to promote dialogue with those of other faiths. Following this dialogical vision, Christian self-understanding had to be remade as dialogical. When considering such a dramatic change in Church teaching, liturgical theologians ask: How do you go from animosity to fellowship; from polemics to dialogue; from separation to embrace? How is this theology of dialogue realized?

The importance of these questions is underscored by Claudio Carvalhaes, a liturgical theologian of Brazilian descent who, according to his own admission, was "taught to evangelize ... the practitioners of African religion [Candomblé] and cast away their demons." He writes about his personal transformation from wanting to save these people to wanting to learn from them. At a certain moment, he attended a Candomblé worship service and noticed, beyond his will, how his body froze:

> I realized that while my mind had made the journey from wanting to save this group to desiring to learn ... from them, my body was still dominated by a narrative of fear.... My body was telling me, "I am not going to expose us to this danger!" This experience changed my life, my scholarship, and my way of thinking about interreligious dialogue. From that day on, I have been challenged

---

[7] See Marianne Moyaert, *Christian Imaginations of the Religious Other: A History of Religionization* (Hoboken, NJ: Wiley-Blackwell, 2024).
[8] *Nostra Aetate*, 2.

to think about interreligious dialogue from the perspective of religious rituals.⁹

Transformation of the mind implies transformation of the body, on an individual, collective, and ecclesial level.

RITUALIZING THE DIALOGICAL TURN

We are shaped as Christian disciples in how we pray, worship, and celebrate; if our understanding of discipleship is refigured in terms of the dialogical, our ritual life ought to change too; new habits have to be acquired and learned, through imitation and practice.¹⁰ To that end, new ritual practices, expressing respect, appreciation, hospitality, and fellowship, have to be invented.

Ritual Performance of Ecumenical Hope

A first symbolic action to consider is the handshake between Pope Paul VI and Ecumenical Patriarch Athenagoras. True, this is an *ecumenical* rather than an *interreligious* gesture, but this gesture did take place in the midst of the dialogical turn and was later imitated in various interreligious settings. From an anthropological vantage point, to reach out one's hand to another person is a risky endeavor; the offering of an open hand can be rejected, and the intentions of the other might not be peaceful at all. Will the other open his hand or reach for a weapon? If the hand is accepted, the imaginary other who was previously *gazed at* (and held at a distance) is now touched – flesh to flesh – and recognized as a fellow human being. The handshake (or another kind of embrace) enables one "to feel with others"¹¹ – to *sym*-pathize.

Significantly, this specific gesture was also projected as an act of Christian discipleship. After all, the meeting between Pope Paul VI and Patriarch Athenagoras took place in January 1964 on the Mount of Olives, a site of Christian worship since ancient times and of pilgrimage for Orthodox, Catholic, and Protestant Christians. Here Jesus "addressed His Father on the night of His betrayal for the unity of His

---

⁹ Claudio Carvalhaes, "Praying Each Other's Prayers," in *Postcolonial Practice of Ministry: Leadership, Liturgy, and Interfaith Engagement*, ed. Kwok Pui-lan and Stephen Burns (Lanham, MD: Lexington Books, 2016), 144.
¹⁰ James K. A. Smith, *You Are What You Love: The Spiritual Power of Habit* (Grand Rapids, MI: Brazos Press, 2016).
¹¹ Richard Kearney, "What Is Carnal Hermeneutics?" *New Literary History* 46 (2015): 105.

followers, boldly and passionately praying that His disciples may be one, *ut unum sint* (John 17:21)."[12] After centuries of silence, this simple gesture between two Church leaders, representing two ecclesial bodies that had been ripped apart, was a symbolic performance of the ecumenical hope that had been growing in the decades prior to the council and that would only months later be expressed in the document *Unitatis redintegratio* (November 1964).[13]

Perhaps, this sign of peace also evokes or even mimics the liturgical sign of peace performed before approaching the Eucharistic table and thus anticipates the moment when Catholics and Orthodox might be in full communion. In any case, this handshake between leaders brave enough to take a risk epitomized a great breakthrough in Christian history: It was a ritualized enactment of an ecumenical hope that has yet to be fully realized.

Sending Greetings: Ritualized Expressions of Interreligious Recognition

In 1967, for the first time, Vatican radio broadcast a message of good wishes to Muslims on the occasion of *Eid al-Fitr*, the feast marking the end of Ramadan. Since then, the Dicastery has sent an annual greeting on this occasion, and sometimes the pope sends a personal greeting. This practice was later extended to include the major world religions on their important holidays. While the content of these messages matters, the repeated gesture itself is as important.

We are dealing with a ritualized expression of recognition; by sending these greetings, the Church says: "We know this is an important time for you, and we share in your joy at the occasion of your holy day."[14] In addition, a posture of curiosity is demonstrated: To utter a greeting requires one to have taken an interest in and learned about other traditions. Thus, these greetings demonstrate to Christians what it means to relate to religious others: You do not remain indifferent, but you learn about the particularities of the feasts of those of other faiths. These blessings also showcase how the Church combines dialogical

---

[12] John Chryssavgis, "Pilgrimage toward Unity: Ecumenical Patriarch Athenagoras and Pope Paul VI in Jerusalem Based on Correspondence and Archives," in *Dialogue of Love: Breaking the Silence of Centuries*, ed. John Chryssavgis (New York: Fordham University Press, 2014), 1–26, at 3–4.

[13] Ibid.

[14] Jutta Sperber, *Anthropological Aspects in the Christian–Muslim Dialogues of the Vatican* (Berlin: De Gruyter, 2019), 235.

outreach with an element of Christian witness. One fitting example is a greeting once sent on the occasion of the Feast of Vesakh, which not only commemorated the birth, enlightenment, and death of the Buddha but also included a word of wisdom of the Buddha himself about how to overcome resentment by kindness, while drawing a parallel between Christian and Buddhist teachings. Clearly, the Church has come a long way from considering others as pagans and idolators. Now, the Church expresses the desire to share the joy, hope, and sorrows of all children of God by attending to their religious particularities.

It is interesting to compare these blessings with the discussions that occur nowadays in many secularized Western European countries, where, in an effort to treat all religions equally while maintaining a neutral public sphere, inclusive religious feasts and blessings – like "Happy Holidays" and Winter feasts (rather than Hanukkah and Christmas) – are being set up. Perhaps these ritualized practices project an alternative vision of what it might mean not only to be a Christian but also to be human in the context of diversity.

A Ritual Transformation of Jewish-Christian Relations

For most of Christian history, a supersessionist account of God's plan of salvation prevailed. The Jewish people, because they did not accept Christ Jesus as Messiah, were no longer God's beloved people, and all the blessings and promises that God had once bestowed upon Israel were now passed onto the Church. This was rendered artistically in the contrast between *Ecclesia*, who stood proud with chalice, crown, and staff, and *Synagoga*, with a broken staff, a blindfold, and the tablets slipping from her hand. *Synagoga* personified powerlessness and subordination in a theological triumphalist ecclesial storyline that was not hers.

"Nostra Aetate" §4, in an effort to bring about reconciliation, states that "[t]he Church cannot forget that she received the revelation of the Old Testament through the people with whom God in His inexpressible mercy concluded the Ancient Covenant. Nor can she forget that she draws sustenance from the root of that well-cultivated olive tree onto which have been grafted the wild shoots, the Gentiles."[15] God "does not repent of the gifts He makes or of the calls He issues." Several ecclesial documents have since been produced, which further elaborate a

---

[15] Rom 11:17–24.

non-supersessionist theology of Judaism and what this means for how Christians read the Bible, pray, and celebrate.[16]

The Good Friday Prayer: Transformation, Negotiation, and Contestation

When the Church came to refigure its relation to Israel in terms of continuity rather than discontinuity, this had repercussions for its prayerful life. For centuries, following the supersessionist logic, the Jews were called perfidious. This was also the case in the prayer for the Jews during the intercessions on Good Friday. In 1959, Pope John XXIII, eager to change Christian–Jewish relations in the aftermath of the Shoah, deleted the term *perfidi* from the prayer for the Jews. This prayerful change anticipated conciliar changes, as made explicit in "Nostra Aetate" §4. In 1970, following the liturgical renewal that was initiated at the Second Vatican Council and the explicit commitment of the Church to seek reconciliation with the Jewish people, the Good Friday prayer underwent an even more profound change.

Good Friday Prayer 1948	**Good Friday Prayer 1970**
Let us pray also for the **perfidious Jews** that Almighty God may remove **the veil from their hearts**; so that they too may acknowledge Jesus Christ our Lord.	Let us pray for **the Jewish people, the first to hear the word of God**, that they may continue **to grow in the love of his name and in faithfulness to his covenant**.
Almighty and eternal God, who dost not exclude from thy mercy even Jewish faithlessness: hear our prayers, which we offer for the **blindness of that people**; that acknowledging the **light of thy Truth, which is Christ, they may be delivered from their darkness**.	Almighty and eternal God, long ago you gave your promise to Abraham and his posterity. Listen to your Church as we pray **that the people you first made your own may arrive at the fullness of redemption**.
Through the same Lord Jesus Christ, who lives and reigns with thee in the unity of the Holy Spirit, God, for ever and ever. Amen.	We ask this through Christ our Lord. Amen

The 1970 missal recognizes the soteriological priority of the Jewish people in God's salvific plan. God approached Israel first. Israel is the chosen people that "God elevates in love for God's name." In this new version of the Good Friday prayer, the Church no longer prays for the

---

[16] Gavin D'Costa, *Catholic Doctrines on the Jewish People after Vatican II* (Oxford: Oxford University Press, 2019).

conversion of the Jews to Christianity. Moreover, the 1970 prayer for the Jews mirrors the prayer of the Church for itself. Thus, the Church indicates that it has not yet arrived at complete salvation itself. With this, the Church recognizes that not the Church but only God determines the how and when of salvation. The completion of salvation is placed in an explicitly eschatological perspective, and the Jews are liturgically recognized as God's beloved people. The refigured understanding of the Jewish people also goes together with a refiguration of the Church's self-understanding: We are no longer dealing with *Ecclesia triumphans* but rather with a Church that accepts that it is also longing for the fullness of redemption.

The 1970 changes are not the end of the story. In 2007, Pope Benedict XVI rehabilitated the old Ordo Missae through the motu proprio *Summorum Pontificum* as an extraordinary form of the Latin Rite. The 1970 Roman Missal (the new Ordo Missae) would remain the ordinary form or expression. This papal initiative ignited concern among Jews and Catholics engaged in Jewish–Christian dialogue, who feared a reintroduction of the Good Friday prayer of 1948. In reaction, on January 28, 2008, Pope Benedict made it known that he intended to write a new prayer that would take into account the sensitivities on the Jewish side, rather than inserting the 1970 version into the old *Ordo Missae*. This new prayer reads:

> Let us pray also for the Jews. That our Lord and God may enlighten their hearts, that they may acknowledge Jesus Christ as the savior of all men. Almighty ... who wills that all men would be saved ... grant that all Israel may be saved when the fullness of the nations enter into Your Church. Through Christ Our Lord. Amen.

For several reasons, this prayerful change did not lift concerns. The notion of enlightenment in this new prayer gives the impression that the Jewish people still find themselves in darkness. The prayer also appeals to the conversion of the Jews to Christ and was conceived as a return to the ecclesiological and soteriological triumphalism associated with pre-Vatican II Christian–Jewish relations. Both Jews and Catholics engaged in dialogue expressed their concern, and relations between Church and Synagogue took a serious blow.

This controversy shows how the dialogical turn sets in motion a process of theological contestation as to the precise relationship between Church and Israel in God's plan for salvation; how theological refiguration impacts ritual and vice versa; how lack of clarity about what we believe translates to lack of clarity in how to pray and in the

power of dialogue: The criticisms expressed by Jews were heard and taken into account, to the extent that a new prayer was written. While this new prayer was in the end not reassuring, the discussion makes clear that a Church that claims to be dialogical needs to reflect this in the way it prays, preaches, and worships and has to take seriously the voices of non-Christians. In July 2021, Pope Francis abrogated *Summorum Pontificum* issued by Pope Benedict XVI with the *motu proprio Traditionis custodes*.

The Pope Visits the Synagogue of Rome: An Act of Inter-Ritual Hospitality

On April 13, 1986, Pope John Paul II made the first ever official papal visit to the Great Synagogue in Rome: A Catholic body – in fact a body which represents the Roman Catholic Church – moved into a sacred Jewish space. In the literature, this is called an act of inter-ritual hospitality. Before the eyes of the entire world, the Italian capital's chief rabbi, Elio Toaff, and the pope embraced one another before entering the synagogue.

Entering the sacred space of another means accepting the ceremonial authority of the host community. While hospitality is an act of welcome of making space for the other, we are not dealing with a relationship of symmetrical relationality. The host is at home, and, while it is their task to make the guest feel at home, the latter crosses a boundary (a threshold) and is out of their comfort zone. This asymmetry between guest and host continues in the ritual performances. Though (minor) adjustments may be made because of the presence of guests, usually the liturgical standards of the home tradition will be followed.[17]

In light of the violent history of Christian–Jewish relations, when Christians denied the vitality of Jewish traditions, rejected Jewish law as superseded, and imagined the Church as having replaced the Synagogue, this ritual reversal of positionality was important. The pope accepted a position of *vulnerability* as the guest of the rabbi. This is a significantly different ritual act than that of inviting the chief rabbi of Rome to the Vatican as a guest in a Christian ceremony, which had happened before more than once. Alana Vincent observes:

> The 1986 visit represented a symbolic ceding of power on the part of the Catholic Church, in which the Pope relinquished the

---

[17] Catherine Cornille, "Interreligious Hospitality and Its Limit," in *Hosting the Stranger Between Religions*, ed. Richard Kearney and James Taylor (London: Continuum, 2011), 35–44.

ceremonial authority derived from ownership of the space of encounter – a gesture that has yet to be replicated in any official document of dialogue ... Gesture thus opens up a world of significance that verbal discourse cannot entertain.[18]

During the ceremony, the pope and the chief rabbi sat side by side on the same level on identical thrones while taking turns reading from the Psalms, acknowledging "co-ownership of the shared scriptural tradition." Compare this to the idea that the Jewish people were blind to the deeper meaning of their own scriptures or had lost any role of significance in God's plan of salvation. This is a ritual performance of a co-covenanted relation. Rather than *Synagoga* being a *superseded* storyline in a Christian theological frame that projects *Ecclesia* as God's people, the supersessionist logic is reversed, and *Ecclesia* (represented by the pope) acknowledges its place as a guest in the story line begun between God and Israel.[19]

The ceremonial exchange of gifts that took place between the two religious leaders helped to restore the bond between both communities. The pope was offered the Menorah, which is a symbol of the divine "light" of Torah and of the responsibility of the Jewish People to follow its laws, and the pope returned a copy of a Torah from the Vatican Museum to its rightful owners. That in the past gifts offered by the Jewish people to the pope (for example on the occasion of the papal coronation) were ritually rejected by the pope to underscore the subordination of Israel to the Church reinforces the liturgical and theological importance of this exchange of gifts.

Pope John Paul II, in doing what no pope had done before him, paved the way for the next popes, Pope Benedict XVI and Pope Francis I, who likewise visited the Synagogue of Rome. When the latter visited the Synagogue, the rabbi welcomed him, saying that "according to rabbinic tradition, an act that is repeated three times – in this case, the papal visits to the Great Synagogue of Popes John Paul II, Benedict XVI, and now Francis –becomes a chazaqà, a set habit."[20]

---

[18] Alana M. Vincent, "Rituals of Reconciliation? How Consideration of Ritual Can Inform Readings of Catholic-Jewish Dialogue after the Holocaust," in *Interreligious Relations and the Negotiation of Ritual Boundaries: Explorations in Interrituality*, ed. Marianne Moyaert, Interreligious Studies in Theory and Practice (London: Palgrave Macmillan, 2019), 186.

[19] Willie James Jennings, *The Christian Imagination: Theology and the Origins of Race* (New Haven, CT: Yale University Press, 2010).

[20] Fredric Brandfon, *Intimate Strangers: A History of Jews and Catholics in the City of Rome* (Philadelphia, PA: Jewish Publication Society; Lincoln, NE University of Nebraska Press, 2023), 273.

The Prayer for Peace in Assisi

On October 27, 1986, religious leaders from various traditions came together to pray in Assisi. At the time, this was a groundbreaking gesture. If in the past Christian sanctuaries had to be purged of the contaminating presence of non-Christians, now the latter were hospitably received in the hometown of Saint Francis (1182–1226). The pope also welcomed the prayers of these religious leaders, hoping that they would invoke from God "the gift of peace." He proclaimed, "To build the peace of order, justice and freedom requires, therefore, *a priority commitment to prayer*, which is openness, listening, dialogue and finally union with God, the prime wellspring of true peace."[21]

After an opening event, all participants went their separate ways to various locations in the city of Assisi, where they prayed for peace according to their own rites, albeit simultaneously and all of them in churches and monasteries. Afterward, they walked silently to the lower piazza of the church of St. Francis, where they reconvened. There, the religious leaders committed themselves in silent meditation to help bring about peace.

Critics accused the pope of syncretism and indifferentism; they were concerned that Catholics could come to the wrong conclusion that all religions are equally true. The Assisi imagery indeed gave rise to such an interpretation: the pope standing in a half circle surrounded by representatives of different traditions, like a *primus inter pares*. The ritual performance suggested a pluralistic theology, which contradicted the inclusivist theology that the Church since *Nostra Aetate* seemed to favor but that had not yet been fully developed.

Even before the actual day of prayer, Pope John Paul II went to great lengths to clearly delineate its theological significance. To that end, he established a ritual distinction between a multireligious and an interreligious prayer, which has since become widely accepted. Thus the pope remarks,

> What is going to happen in Assisi will not be some kind of religious syncretism, but a sincere attitude of prayer to God in mutual respect. This is why the motto chosen for the Assisi gathering is: "being together to pray." ... [I]n this manner we manifest our respect for the prayer of the others and for the stance of the others

---

[21] John Paul II, "Address of His Holiness Pope John Paul II to the Representatives of the World Religions," Assisi, January 24, 2002 (emphasis in original), https://bit.ly/438x26O.

toward the divinity: at the same time, we offer them the humble and sincere testimony of our faith in Christ, Lord of the Universe.[22]

What is lacking in the multireligious prayer is key in interreligious prayer: co-intentionality.[23] Since people who belong to different religious traditions do not share faith, they cannot pray together. *Lex orandi, lex credendi* supposedly excludes the possibility of interreligious prayer: If prayer is an expression of faith, we cannot pray together when we do not share one faith. In the case of multireligious prayer, however, one prays in the presence of one another (simultaneously or subsequently), but one does not speak the same words. It is not assumed that those who engage in a multireligious prayer share the same beliefs or direct their prayers to the same Ultimate Reality. Neither is it assumed that all participants interpret the event in the same way.

> There is no intermingling of principal prayer actions; the full integrity of religious identity and the authenticity of specific actions are maintained. As at Assisi, it might be by way of being held within a unifying time and place: the same town on the same day, and including an opening and closing shared action.[24]

According to Pope John Paul II, this prayerful event ritually expressed the divine "mystery of unity": All human beings are created in God's image and all are incorporated in God's single plan for salvation, even though not all present will agree on this or are even conscious of this. The pope also saw the Spirit at work in this religious gathering; not only in bringing these leaders together, but also in their prayers. In an address to the Roman Curia, in which the pope defended the Assisi event, he even stated, "We maintain that any authentic prayer is raised up by the Holy Spirit, who is mysteriously present in the heart of every human being." Later, the pope, who gave much thought to pneumatology, further elaborated on the work of the Spirit in his encyclical *Redemptoris Missio* (December 7, 1990):

> The Spirit manifests himself in *Redemptoris Missio* and in her members. Nevertheless his presence and activity are universal,

---

[22] Pontifical Commission, "Justitita et Pax," *Assise: Journée mondiale de prière pour la paix* (October 27, 1986): 25–26.

[23] D'Costa, Gavin. "Interreligious Prayer Between Christians and Muslims," *Islam & Christian Muslim Relations* 24 (2013): 1–14.

[24] Douglas Pratt, "Religion Is as Religion Does: Interfaith Prayer as a Form of Ritual Participation," in *Ritual Participation and Interreligious Dialogue: Boundaries, Transgressions and Innovations*, eds. Marianne Moyaert and Joris Geldhof (London: Bloomsbury Academic, 2015), 53–66, at 57.

limited by neither space nor time. ... The Spirit's presence and activity affect not only individuals but also society and history, peoples, cultures and religions. Indeed, the Spirit is at the origin of the noble ideals and undertakings which benefit humanity on its journey through history ... Again, it is the Spirit who sows "the seeds of the Word" present in various customs and cultures, preparing them for full maturity in Christ.[25]

Authentic prayer, according to the pope, is always the fruit of the Spirit, even when it comes from those of other faiths, and it is part of the dialogical calling of the Church to listen attentively to the fruits of the Spirit in other traditions, without, however, somehow claiming that other religions are independent paths of salvation. While continuing the inter-ritual tradition initiated by his predecessor, Pope Benedict XVI later changed its scope by explicitly including secular, humanist, and atheist voices. In so doing, he tried to diminish the *spiritual* nature of Assisi, by emphasizing especially the anthropological scope of the event: What brought the religious leaders together was their common commitment to peace and to showing that the true face of religion is not violent. One should avoid giving the impression that this event assumes some kind of shared (pluralist) belief. The ritual change initiated by Pope Benedict XVI followed the same lead as the *Dominus Iesus* document, which was promulgated under his authority as head of the *Congregation for the Doctrine of Faith* in 2001: Avoid relativism and pluralism, which seek to place Christian religion on par with other religions.

INTERRELIGIOUS ENCOUNTERS AND THE NEED FOR A COMPARATIVE LITURGICAL THEOLOGY

The dialogical turn impacted how *Christians pray and worship* and vice versa. New rituals, which emerged in the aftermath of the dialogical turn, yielded new experiences, which provoked further theological discussion, which sometimes led to ritual adaptations.

The Assisi event is a case in point. For some theologians the whole event was nothing short of syncretism. Others state that Assisi symbolized that ecclesial calls for interreligious dialogue had taken a

---

[25] Joannes Paulus PP. II, "Redemptoris Missio: On the Permanent Validity of the Church's Missionary Mandate," 28. Accessed June 9, 2023, www.vatican.va/content/john-paul-ii/en/encyclicals/documents/hf_jp-ii_enc_07121990_redemptoris-missio.html.

dangerous turn toward relativism. Other theologians were of a different opinion and saw Assisi as an important step in the direction of pluralism. The Assisi prayer reawakened theological reflection on the workings of the Spirit in other traditions and in Catholic theology provoked a shift from a Christocentric and ecclesiocentric theology of religions to a Trinitarian approach to religious diversity. This peaceful gathering also challenged theologians to further question whether interreligious prayer is possible and under which (theological) conditions. Is it possible for Jews and Christians to pray together? Do they pray to the same God, even if they do not share Trinitarian beliefs? If we say that Jews and Christians worship the same God, could this also hold true for Muslims, who base their faith on the God of Abraham but who like Jews reject Christian Trinitarian beliefs? Some also extended these questions to adherents of Buddhist, Hindu, and other traditions. If we say that shared faith is the condition for shared prayer, what does it mean to share faith; what does it mean to worship the same God? What is the same and what is different in this setting?

Here, I am not interested so much in answering whether Muslims, Jews, and Christian believe in the same God and if they can pray to the same God. Or if Christians can pray together with Buddhists. I do want to ask what kind of theology we need to explore such questions. Following some of the recent developments in the field, I argue for an approach that combines comparative theology of religions with liturgical theology. Before the dialogical turn, religious others functioned mainly as rhetorical figures, which taught little about their proper beliefs, practices, hopes, and fears. Generalization and essentialization were *legio*, and pejorative claims about non-Christians prevailed. Today comparative theologians are increasingly considering other religious traditions as possible resources for constructive theological reflection. Rather than theologizing about non-Christians, they suggest studying their traditions in depth and with an eye for detail and nuance. Before making a priori theological judgments about others and their faith tradition, comparative theologians suggest doing theology after comparison. The ultimate aim is a deep learning across traditions.[26] Typically, comparative theologians uphold strong commitments to their home tradition "but ... also take seriously the normative claims

---

[26] Catherine Cornille (ed.), *Meaning and Method in Comparative Theology* (Hoboken, NJ: Wiley, 2020); Francis X. Clooney, *Comparative Theology: Deep Learning across Religious Borders* (Malden, MA: Wiley-Blackwell, 2010).

of at least one other religious tradition."²⁷ Nuanced knowledge of the Christian tradition is matched with nuanced knowledge of the other tradition. Some also call comparative theology interreligious theology because it revolves around a rereading of the home theological tradition in light of another's tradition and vice versa.

Until recently, comparative theologians focused primarily on their creed, that is, their core beliefs as they are mediated through their scriptures and traditions. The belief-centeredness and textual fixation of systematic theology as classically understood were thus perpetuated in their theological work. Comparing texts – sacred texts, theological commentaries, mystical treatises, or philosophical tractates – from various traditions is at the heart of their work. When dealing with the question mentioned above – can Jews, Muslims, and Christians pray together? – comparative theologians approached this question by studying and comparing particular theologies from these respective traditions – what did Thomas Aquinas argue and how does this compare to Maimonides or Al-Ghazali? The liturgical dimension, however, did not figure into this line of reasoning. Recently, however, comparative theologians have begun to take seriously some of the key aspects of liturgical theology, and some even suggest that we cannot answer the question of whether Jews, Christians, and Muslims can pray together without also taking into consideration the encounter with the others' practices – in particular, their (prayer) rituals.

Comparative theologians who engage liturgical theology focus on religion as a lived embodied practice: To be religious cannot be reduced to belief but rather revolves around concrete ritual practices, which shape both mind and body and are aimed at bringing about transformation. The primary language of religion, that is, the religious language people first learn, is acquired by means of tangible symbols and symbolic practices.²⁸ People learn to master this language through practice: They are introduced into a temporo-spatial continuum of concrete religious objects, festivities, ritual gestures, religious formulae, customs, and values central to tradition. In this learning process, believers are guided by masters who set the example and demonstrate their knowledge. Acquiring religious literacy relies on illustration, imitation,

[27] Christian T. Collins and Martha Moore Keish, "Introduction," in *Karl Barth and Comparative Theology*, ed. Martha Moore Keish and Christian T. Collins (New York: Fordham University Press, 2019), 2.
[28] Marianne Moyaert, "Inappropriate Behavior? On the Ritual Core of Religion and Its Challenges to Interreligious Hospitality," *Journal for the Academic Study of Religion* 27 (2014): 1–21.

repetition, and rehearsal. Throughout this process of inculcation, certain ways of thinking, feeling, and behaving become interiorized. The knowledge that results from this socialization process is not explicit but tacit. It is a knowledge that goes deeply into the bone. At this embodied level, religious people know and understand what it means to worship, who they worship, and how they ought to worship. This knowledge is experiential, performative, and enfleshed, and it is not accessible in the same way via textual resources.

Returning to the question of whether Jews, Muslims, and Christians can pray together or if Buddhists and Christians can participate in one another's ritual practices, the truth may very well be that one cannot decide this apart from a deep engagement across ritual traditions. While such comparative liturgical theology would include textual engagement across traditions – comparing ritual scripts from the different traditions involved as well as theological commentaries on the life of prayer in these respective traditions – some kind of interreligious engagement with the lived reality of ritual would also be called for. Comparative liturgical theologian James Farwell suggests precisely this:

> If religions are performances in this way, then the question of whether one can participate in another religion cannot be answered without at least some performative engagement of the world in and through it; otherwise, one does not know what one is saying "yes" or "no" to participating in. Certainly, there are some conditions: the initial decision to practice another tradition requires some basic literacy about the other tradition as well as your own. It also depends on the welcome extended by the other tradition; one does not enter into practices understood to be inappropriate to those not committed formally to the aspirations they encode. Otherwise, one risks insult, or sacrilege, and some other form of irreverence. In my case, I knew enough about Soto Zen Buddhism – particularly about the complex way in which the Buddha is understood as both object of veneration and, at the same time, as the last form of attachment to be let go – that, when confronted with that awkward moment that my presence would have created had I sat in the small zendo as a non-participant, I knew that I would be welcomed to participate. But I could not have determined *finally* whether it was appropriate for me to sustain Buddhist practice, *except by practice*. This paradox will scandalize some who question inter-religious practice to begin with; but given the nature of ritualization, it must be reckoned with, within the

conditions of respect for the religious other that might prevent some types of participation, or even any participation at all in some traditions.[29]

From this perspective the path ahead for those seeking to explore complex theological questions that deal with the life of prayer and worship would be to attend to "the messy particularity" of the ritual practices of different traditions.[30]

CONCLUSION

The Second Vatican Council set in motion a time of ritual creativity and dialogical exploration. Theologians were challenged to reflect on Christian self-understanding in light of the reality and vitality of religious diversity and vice versa. They did so, both in a context of dialogue and a context of ritual. Three remarks are important in conclusion. First, the ritualization of dialogue was a creative undertaking. There were no officialized ritual traditions shaping Christian identity in terms of the dialogical, and many of the ritual actions initiated in the aftermath of Vatican II, which "remain as icons speaking to people's mind and heart," were possible only because there was room to get theologically creative and to experiment ritually.[31] Furthermore, while at some level this ritualization is an expression of the dialogical turn, I have suggested that inter-rituality may also be seen as a locus of theological creativity. Since, the doctrinal contours of the dialogical turn were not yet crystal clear – theologians of religions were, as I said, exploring the frontiers – ritualized encounters evoked profound questions, which called for further theological reflection. In this sense, inter-ritual encounters were not merely expressive but also productive of theology, and ritual practices shape and complicate beliefs and vice versa. Third, while some Christians based on their dialogical and ritual experiences were seeking to push theological boundaries, others were more

---

[29] James Farwell, "On Whether Christians Should Participate in Buddhist Practice: A Critical Autobiographical Reflection," *Interreligious Studies and Intercultural Theology* 1 (2017): 242–56, at 248.
[30] Martha Moore-Keish, "Interreligious Ritual Participation: Insights from Inter-Christian Ritual Participation," in *Ritual Participation and Interreligious Dialogue: Boundaries, Transgressions and Innovations*, ed. Marianne Moyaert and Joris Geldhof (London: Bloomsbury Academic, 2015), pp. 67–77.
[31] Roberto Catalano, "Pope Francis' Culture of Dialogue as Pathway to Interfaith Encounter: A Special Focus on Islam," *Religions* 13.4 (2022): 279, https://doi.org/10.3390/rel13040279.

concerned about maintaining tradition and containing theological creativity, and some novel inter-ritual practices became sites of controversy and ritual and theological negotiation.

For Further Reading

Carvalhaes, Cláudio, *Eucharist and Globalization: Redrawing the Borders of Eucharistic Hospitality* (Eugene, OR: Pickwick Publications, 2013).

Cheetham, David, "Ritualising the Secular? Inter-Religious Meetings in the 'Immanent Frame'," *Heythrop Journal* 60 (2019): 383–96.

D'Costa, Gavin, "Interreligious Prayer between Christians and Muslims," *Islam & Christian Muslim–Relations* 24 (2013): 1–14.

Kreinath, Jens, "Infrastructures of Interrituality and the Aesthetics of Saint Veneration Rituals among Orthodox Christians and Arab Alawites in Hatay," in *The Palgrave Handbook of Anthropological Ritual Studies*, ed. Pamela J. Stewart and Andrew J. Strathern (Cham: Palgrave Macmillan, 2021), 345–71.

Meyer, Barbara U., "Not Just the Time of the Other – What Does It Mean for Christians Today to Remember Shabbat and Keep It Holy?," *Religions* 13 (2022): 736.

Moyaert, Marianne, *Interreligious Relations and the Negotiation of Ritual Boundaries: Explorations in Interrituality* (Cham: Springer International Publishing, 2019).

Moyaert, Marianne, and Joris Geldhof (eds.), *Ritual Participation and Interreligious Dialogue: Boundaries, Transgressions and Innovations* (London: Bloomsbury Academic, 2015).

O'Donnell, Emma, *Remembering the Future: The Experience of Time in Jewish and Christian Liturgy* (Collegeville, MN: Liturgical Press, 2015).

Poorthuis, Marcel, *Rituals in Interreligious Dialogue: Bridge or Barrier?* (Cambridge: Cambridge Scholars Publishing: 2020).

Part V

The Study of Liturgy

20 Liturgical Texts
JULIETTE J. DAY

The liturgical text is a foundational element of Christian worship, providing structure, content, and meaning, even if worshippers overlook the way in which their relationship to God is facilitated by these texts. Private and communal prayer is constructed from texts, from something as simple as reciting the Lord's Prayer to the more complex liturgies of Easter in Catholic and Orthodox churches. The texts are preserved and transmitted in material form, that is, they are inscribed on parchment, printed on paper, and in recent decades accessible through the internet. This creates more than one paradox – inscribing the texts gives them permanence, just as the material in which they are inscribed is ephemeral; and the performed content of the texts establishes the present reality of divine–human communication, just as it preserves the tradition of such communication within a worshipping community. Additionally, there is the linguistic problem of "liturgical text" being applied more generally and imprecisely to the verbal and inscribed content of worship, as well as to individual prayers and to the material object in which they are inscribed. This investigation into liturgical texts will open up some of these issues by first considering what a liturgical "text" is and then investigating how worshippers-as-readers use their experience of textual interpretation when praying with the texts.[1]

WHAT IS A LITURGICAL "TEXT"?

"Text" comes from the Latin word *textus*, something which is woven together. This suggests that a text is the product of an intentional construction and that it is composed of preexisting elements brought

---

[1] A much fuller discussion of liturgical textuality can be found in my *Reading the Liturgy: An Exploration of Texts in Christian Worship* (London: Bloomsbury, 2014).

together to create something new. The product, words connected together to create meaningful units, is produced by symbols and letters inscribed on a page. It is this act that transforms speech and thought into an object that preserves it after the moment, enabling recall and repetition. However, once the text is produced it has a life of its own among other texts and speech/thought events. It is no longer tied to the original moment of composition for its interpretation and use, and so, although the act of writing fixes the form of the words, it cannot fix the meaning, as the producer is no longer able to control the context of use nor the interpretative strategies of the readers.

Unlike speech, where the participants are able to correct and explain themselves, texts stand alone in the world and may rely on other texts for their interpretation. Paul Ricoeur clearly separated speech from writing: "What is fixed by writing is a discourse which could be said but it is written precisely because it is not said."[2] The discourse, what is to be said or the message, is intentionally written to be preserved and transmitted, unlike speech, which disappears. Walter Ong remarked that in literate cultures, people's thoughts and speech are so conditioned to the text that they are able to separate the inscribed form of the words from the sounds they represent. Print, he argued, further removes the word from speech by locking the symbols into space in an ordered and conventionally regulated way so that, sensorially, reading has become a visual and tactile experience, and the words no longer need to be heard.[3]

Liturgical texts are similar but with certain peculiarities. In worship the liturgical texts reveal God, enact the sacraments, and establish divine–human relationships; however, as inscribed symbols on a page, liturgical texts look very much like other texts, follow the same conventions, and require the same strategies for their use. Thus they require a specific context to be meaningful: Studying the Eucharistic prayer in the classroom is not at all the same as hearing it at Mass. Additionally, liturgical texts do not function in quite the way that Ricoeur suggested for other texts because the text does not replace speech but facilitates it where no speech to/with God may be possible. It is often the liturgical texts that provide the content and formulae of spontaneous private prayer, and thus, conversely, the text precedes

---

[2] Paul Ricoeur, "What Is a Text?" in Paul Ricoeur, *From Text to Action: Essays in Hermeneutics II*, trans. Kathleen Blamey and John Thompson (London: Athlone Press, 1991), p. 106.

[3] Ong, *Orality and Literacy*, 74.

speech. And individual texts can function as visual signs of prayer or of worship, when in certain Protestant churches the texts of the Lord's Prayer or the Creed were inscribed on church walls to replace the images of the saints. This orality/text paradox extends to the worship event itself when there is a ritual call to attentiveness to an oral activity the content of which is provided by an authorized text.

Some traditions rejected the authority of the liturgical text but ironically only to replace it with other text. The 1644 *Directory of Public Worship* critiqued the set forms of Anglican worship and urged the minister to exercise his ministry of prayer; nevertheless, the directory provided written models of what words were suitable. In contemporary liturgical books rubrics allowing the minister to use her own words rather than the printed ones are common; however, experience shows that the option is almost never taken. Even within churches with seemingly more spontaneous forms of public prayer, fixed formulae are common, as Daniel E. Albrecht showed for Pentecostal/charismatic worship.[4]

The liturgical text provides a temporal constraint upon the biblical injunction to "pray without ceasing,"[5] through the formal beginning with the Introductory Rites and conclusion with a Dismissal. Liturgical speech, even when facilitated by the text, retains the impermance of speech more generally, which Ong highlighted.[6] We could say that it is the discourse of praise that endures after the event. Sara Irwin suggested that liturgical texts should be placed between speech and writing, as a third genre:

> [Liturgical] speech that is spoken is tied not to the speaker, but to the community, to those who went before and those who will come after. Speech that is spoken liturgically "belongs" to no one, is directed to God; the assembled body speaks, in a sense, but is also spoken as they open themselves to God's purpose. Neither the permanence of writing nor the ephemeral nature of speech can account for how things are done with words and bodies in the liturgy.[7]

---

[4] Daniel E. Albrect, *Rites in the Spirit: A Ritual Approach to Pentecostal/Charismatic Spirituality* (Sheffield: Sheffield Academic Press, 1999).
[5] 1 Thess 5:17.
[6] Walter Ong, *Orality and Literacy: The Technologizing of the Word* (London: Routledge, 2002), 32.
[7] Sara H. Irwin, "The Religiophenome: Liturgy and Some Uses of Deconstruction," *Worship* 80 (2006): 243.

Irwin's observation is useful in moving us on from the speech/text dichotomy.

The text has become increasingly central to the worship of the liturgical churches in recent decades. Liturgical reform in Anglican, Lutheran, and Methodist Churches has been dominated by rewriting the liturgical texts rather than by any ritual innovation or renewal. In the Roman Catholic Church, debates about the use of Latin or the vernacular, and about the translation of the *editio typica*, again focus attention on the text as the object and discourse. Cheap printing and the internet have enabled the production of ever more authorized liturgical texts, as the library of the Church of England's *Common Worship* project attests, in contrast to Thomas Cranmer's desire for there to be only one book.

Thomas Cranmer was certainly aware of how the book might cause a shift in the way worship was done when worshippers' attention was brought back to the book and the printed text:

> And where heretofore, there hath been great diversitie in saying and synging in churches within this realme: ... Now from hencefurth, all the whole realme shall have but one use. And if any would judge this waye more painfull, because that all thynges must be read upon the boke, whereas before, by the reason of so often repeticion, they could saye many thinges by heart: if those men will waye their labor, with the profite in knowlege, whiche dayely they shal obtein by readyng upon the boke, they will not refuse the payn, in consideracion of the greate profite that shall ensue therof.[8]

There was a risk that worshippers would become readers, and that indeed is what has happened.

Participation in much worship requires a good level of literacy and familiarity with the conventions of printed books. Competent participation in worship requires the ability to locate and then read the required texts. This shifts the dominant sensory mode from aural to visual and tactile. Walter Ong reflected on the interiority of sound, which comes into us from outside, and sight, which goes out from us, as what we see and read is always external to us. He remarks:

> When a speaker is addressing an audience, the members of the audience normally become a unity, with themselves and with the speaker. If the speaker asks the audience to read a handout provided for them, as each reader enters into his or her own private reading

---

[8] Thomas Cranmer, "Preface to the Book of Common Prayer," 1549.

world, the unity of the audience is shattered, to be re-established only when oral speech begins again. Writing and print isolate.[9]

So if speech exteriorizes and writing interiorizes the discourse, worshippers need to navigate between them in order to find an appropriate level of participation that balances individual and communal worship.

Independent of the worship event, the possession and use of liturgical texts have other signifiers in the Churches: authority and identity. First, we can investigate them in terms of power in the community, which is revealed by reserving the use of certain texts to particular people depending on their place in the hierarchy. The book then symbolizes the status of the user. Power is also embedded in the texts, when rules to govern the use and misuse of the texts are set out and may even have the force of law, as was the case for Anglicans in England and Wales until the twentieth century. The liturgical texts used in worship, together with the rituals and the ritual context, form each congregation into the people of God; they shape attitudes to God and each other, and to the world. They contain the potential to transform individuals and the community. So liturgical texts are very much bound up with questions of identity – the use of one text instead of another distinguishes communities and ecclesial groups.

Organizations such as the Latin Mass Society or the Prayer Book Society promote certain liturgical texts as the essence of their church's identity against more contemporary authorized texts. Related to this is the way in which large national and pan-national churches consider the authorized liturgical forms as an instrument and sign of unity. For example, the 1559 Act of Uniformity printed at the beginning of the restored Book of Common Prayer under Elizabeth I insisted that only this book was to be used in the realm. The translation principles set forth in recent Roman Catholic documents are intended to ensure that the vernacular Mass is as close to the *editio typica* as possible regardless of the language into which it is translated. The text ensures unity of worship and thereby the unity of the church.

LITURGICAL BOOKS

Most Christian worship is facilitated by a text object. In keeping with late antique synagogue worship, early Christian communities devoted much of their worship time to the reading of Scripture, which

---

[9] Ong, *Orality and Literacy*, 73.

necessitated some form of scroll or codex, but for the other parts of worship there is less evidence of scripts until the fourth century. As the account in Justin Martyr suggests, worship involved both authoritative texts and improvisation:

> And on the day called Sunday, all who live in cities or in the country gather together to one place, and the memoirs of the apostles or the writings of the prophets are read, as long as time permits; then, when the reader has ceased, the president verbally instructs, and exhorts to the imitation of these good things. Then we all rise together and pray, and, as we before said, when our prayer is ended, bread and wine and water are brought, and the president in like manner offers prayers and thanksgivings, according to his ability, and the people assent, saying Amen.[10]

But that does not necessarily mean that the presider/bishop created the words and structure of worship afresh every time; this is most unlikely and is in any case refuted by what seems to be liturgical formulae in the New Testament (the Lords' Prayer in the Gospels, an institution narrative 1 Cor 11), as well as ritual structures presented as normative in the third century *Didascalia Apostolorum*.

The Didachè is unusual in this regard, as in many others, in that it permits improvisation to prophets but not to bishops, but improvisation clearly did remain after the demise of the prophetic ministry. Improvisation does not mean a fresh, innovative creation at every liturgy but, as the research on oral poetry by Albert Lord indicated, the retelling of the formulae according to known and communally accepted structures and content.[11] As bishops were from the literate classes, and both Latin and Greek education was geared toward rhetorical skills, delivering a known prayer formula without a text would not have posed any great challenge. This does not mean that some text object did not lie behind the oral performance of prayer, rather that the "text" of the liturgy was constituted by the structures and themes and not a script.

The scant evidence of liturgical formulae prior to the fifth century is found as incidental references in sources whose main theme is rarely liturgical – for example, church orders, sermons, catechetical

---

[10] Justin Martyr, *Apology* I, 67 (ANF, vol. 1, 186).
[11] Albert B. Lord, *The Singer of Tales*, 2nd ed. revised by S. Mitchell and G. Nagy (Cambridge, MA: Harvard University Press, 2001). The first edition was published in 1960.

instructions, theological treatises, hagiography, historiography, and so forth.[12] Although some of these references may have been from memory, others do appear to quote from fixed prayer formulae, which suggests a text object behind it (the mystagogy of Jerusalem and Milan, for instance). Various factors influenced the need for such text objects. It has been suggested that the concerns over theological orthodoxy in the late fourth and fifth century caused prayer formulae to become longer as additional biblical, credal, and anamnetic material was added. Presbyters, who took charge of the increasing numbers of churches and congregations, needed greater guidance to ensure their liturgical formulae were in accordance with their bishop's. The multiplication of liturgical events and their elaboration in the large basilicas with their baptisteries, as well as at shrines and in the streets, resulted in liturgies too complex to be directed by the improvised prayers of one man alone. The increased number of commemorations of biblical and martyr feasts necessitated an organized calendar with assigned biblical readings and even particular rituals, and thus the lectionary seems to predate any collection of prayer formulae. Hymns and chants for communal singing did require some text, even if only for the cantor. For these reasons writing down and circulating prayer formulae and instructions was necessary and inevitable.

The earliest liturgical textual objects appear to be aide-mémoires for the formulae required by the bishop. These are referred to as *libelli*. They may be just one prayer but more often a booklet of prayers for a church or a particular liturgy. Eric Palazzo referred to them as "the intermediary link in the evolution between the period of improvisation to the liturgical book properly so called."[13] The so-called Sacramentary of Serapion, Bishop of Thmuis in Egypt (early fourth century), is just such a collection of prayers, including the anaphora, consecration of oils, and so on; there are no rubrics or texts for other ministers, and it does not form a complete script for the actual rites of Thmuis.[14] The evolution was slow and gradual: In the late fifth century in Gaul, Sidonius Apollinaris, Bishop of Clermont Ferrand (d. c. 487), was still able to improvise, as Gregory of Tours (538–94) recorded with approval:

[12] See Basil Studer, "Liturgical Documents of the First Four Centuries," in *Handbook for Liturgical Studies*: vol. 1: *Introduction to the Liturgy*, ed. Anscar J. Chupungco (Collegeville, MN: Liturgical Press, 1997), 199–224.
[13] Eric Palazzo, *A History of Liturgical Books from the Beginning to the Thirteenth Century* (Collegeville, MN: Liturgical Press, 1998), 37.
[14] See Maxwell E. Johnson, *The Prayers of Sarapion of Thmuis: A Literary, Liturgical, and Theological Analysis* (Rome: Pontificio Istituto Orientale, 1995).

> The holy Sidonius was so eloquent that he generally improvised what he wished to say without any hesitation and in the clearest manner. And it happened one day that he went by invitation to a fête at the church of the monastery which we have mentioned before, and when his book, by which he had been wont to celebrate the holy services, was maliciously taken away, he went through the whole service of the fête improvising with such readiness that he was admired by all, and it was believed by the bystanders that it was not a man who had spoken there but an angel.[15]

Such *libelli* must have been very commonplace but are not preserved, except, it seems, in the Lateran library, where the *libelli* of a number of popes were collected in the sixth century into what is now called the Verona Sacramentary, also known as the Leonine Sacramentary. The compilers of the Verona used material that has been attributed to various authors – Popes Leo the Great, Gelasius, and Vigilius have been identified – and material collated for the sanctorale and for the sacraments from probably two earlier compilations, which were organized according to the months of the year.[16] It was not intended for use in the liturgical event, unlike the seventh-century Gelasian Sacramentary, which organized the prayer formulae for the temporale, the sanctorale, ordination, baptism, and consecrations, as well as for Masses for different occasions, such that it could have been used by a presbyter in a titular church in Rome.

Once text-based liturgy becomes the norm, there follows an increase in the type of books in which it is contained: antiphonaries and psalters for choirs, gospel books for deacons, office books for monks, sacramentaries for priests, and pontificals for bishops. Even the laity were not immune from textualization, as richly decorated Books of Hours indicate, in which the textual nature of worship was emphasized by the owner of the book being depicted at prayer with the book in her hands as a frontispiece. The Protestant Reformations challenged the theological and hierarchical aspects of worship, and for many the liturgical text was a touchstone. Calvinists rejected the text completely in favor of improvised worship, whereas in England, Cranmer's single short book might be considered a rather radical and democratizing move.

---

[15] Gregory of Tours, *History of the Franks* 2.22, English trans. in Ernest Brehaut, *Gregory of Tours: History of the Franks* (New York: Norton, 1969), n. p.

[16] See Palazzo, *A History of Liturgical Books*, 37–42.

Printing clearly had a huge impact on worship and its texts. It enabled the more widespread dissemination of liturgical material and removed the imprecision of manuscript copying. Liturgical texts would henceforth have a uniformity that was not possible in earlier centuries. The text becomes truly fixed. It is also notable that printed liturgical books, in their external appearance, follow the publishing conventions of their age in terms of typeface, frontispieces and title pages, chapter headings, page numbers, tables of contents, and in the modern era even indices.[17] Although the intended context of use distinguishes liturgical texts from other literary forms, there are a number of themes in textual interpretation that throw light upon the construction, use, and interpretation of liturgical texts. Our focus here will be on authorship and genre.

THE AUTHORSHIP OF LITURGICAL TEXTS

It is yet another paradox that liturgical historians expend much energy determining the authors of historical liturgical texts, but there is barely any concern with the authorship of modern texts. Worshippers, too, rarely question the authorship of their texts, particularly when they are authorized by national and international churches. Authorship is related to both the production of the text and to its interpretation. In terms of the latter, the assignment of a named author provides a concrete context in which the meaning of the text can be revealed and thus acts as a constraint upon its use and interpretation outside that context. We could cite numerous studies of the Sacramentary of Serapion, where the identity of the early fourth-century bishop of Thmuis provides a context for understanding the content and use of the prayers. Or we could also investigate what the contribution of John Chrysostom was to the liturgy that bears his name. Geoffrey Cuming's three categories of authorial attribution remain useful: pseudonymous attribution, where a text is attributed to an apostle or saint to lend authority to the text; authentic attribution, where the balance of probabilities is that the named author had some involvement in its creation; and a mid-point, where the historical context appears right but the name attached to it may not be.[18] All these attitudes to authorship

---

[17] See my *Reading the Liturgy*, ch. 7: "Paratexts."
[18] G. J. Cuming, "Pseudonymity and Authenticity, with Special Reference to the Liturgy of St John Chrysostom," *Studia Patristica* 15 (1984): 532.

imply a single author who created liturgical formulae anew, but the reality is that "new" texts reuse other texts, the Bible especially; repeat formulae; and follow established prayer genres. What is needed is not to discard the notion of authorship but to consider authorship in a new way. Even in 1930, the liturgist F. E. Brightman warned against individual authorship: "The greater part of any fully developed liturgy is likely to be common form, and marks of individual authorship are only to be looked for in occasional features, whether dogmatic statement or of characteristic or favourite phraseology."[19]

Harold Love provided a model that promoted authorship as a collaborative process with four linked but separate activities: precursory authorship, where material is borrowed or reused; executive authorship, the compilation of the final text; declarative authorship, the named author; revisionary authorship, the process of editing or revising the text.[20] Both historic and contemporary liturgical texts readily display such characteristics and indicate that the production of the text is a process involving many points of origin, rather than a single one. The Church of England's complete revision of its liturgy published from the year 2000 onwards under the overall title of *Common Worship* displays collaborative authorship. The work of preparing the texts was assigned to the Liturgical Commission and its subcommittees, but names are not attached to the compositions; the texts were reviewed and revised in the commission and in General Synod, but in the end the declared author, according to the copyright information, is the Archbishop's Council.

Notions of authorship are directly tied to the considerations of the meaning and interpretation of the text: The meaning is solely what the author intends; the meaning lies in the text alone; meaning is a result of collaboration between the author's intentions and the interpreter's own context. In the absence of a named author to provide an authoritative interpretation, liturgical texts are often surrounded by "para-liturgical texts" such as rubrics, general instructions, and the like, which carry the same authorizing force as the liturgical text itself, and as such they differ from commentaries and manuals. For much liturgical material it is almost impossible to assign a single author who controls the meaning and interpretation of the text, particularly when the meaning is revealed fully only in the ritual performance of the text in many different contexts. Although authorized liturgical texts have been composed

---

[19] F. E. Brightman, "The Anaphora of Theodore," *Journal of Theological Studies* 3 (1930): 161.
[20] Harold Love, *Attributing Authorship* (Cambridge: Cambridge University Press, 2002).

(collaboratively) to convey theologies consistent with the traditions of the denomination, the interpretation is a collaboration between the text and worshippers in their own context. The liturgical text has clearly been composed with certain intentions, and these cannot be ignored, but the authors' ability to direct the interpretation – theologically and ritually – is relatively limited.

Genre and Liturgical Texts

The genre of texts operates at a number of different levels. For an author, genre allows for the structuring of the content into recognizable patterns. For the reader/user, it enables a classification system to distinguish one text from another and to distinguish between different types of texts. Familiarity with a particular genre enables a reader or listener to anticipate the content and how it is organized, and this aids comprehension. Experienced authors, readers, and listeners are alert to the genre indicators that were usefully and concisely summarized by John Frow:[21]

(1) Formal organization: the way in which the material is structured, its language and style, and how it looks on the page;
(2) Rhetorical structure: the mode of address between author and reader/listener, as well as mood and tone;
(3) Thematic content: actions, actors, topic, argument, and so on.

These indicators were established for literary texts, but they are equally applicable to liturgical texts. Formal organization is evident when distinguishing prose texts from poetry (hymnody, psalms), as well as according to function (a lectionary is different from a sacramentary). Rhetorical structure is evident when we consider who is the intended and indirect addressee of the text. Thematic content (praise or penitence) is easier to detect, even though in reality this is a weak consideration when discussing liturgical genres. Genre identification depends on a variable combination of these factors, and the experienced author, reader, or listener is most likely to use them instinctively.

Discussing genre in relation to prayer texts is not new. Origen in his treatise *On Prayer* (c. 230) recommends a structure for prayer that he finds in Scripture: address glorifying God through Christ; thanksgivings; repentance; requests; and the conclusion in which "one should bring prayer to an end ascribing glory to God through Jesus Christ in the Holy

---

[21] John Frow, *Genre* (London: Routledge, 2006), 74–76.

Spirit."[22] Louis Duchesne in his *Origines du Culte Chrétien* (1889, published in English in 1912 as *Christian Worship: Its Origin and Evolution*) identified three genres of common prayer – litany prayers, collective prayers, and Eucharistic prayers – on the basis of the rhetorical address between priest and people, as well as the use of set formulae. He did not consider theme a differentiating characteristic.[23] Kathleen Hughes similarly identified rhetorical structure as the key to classifying prayer types.[24]

These attempts at classification only considered purely euchological material, but a worship event consists of much more than that. I suggest that any definition or taxonomy of liturgical genres should encompass all the text that may be encountered. Thus at the basic level there are three principal genres, which can be subdivided into subgenres:

(1) prose texts: scripture readings, introductory prefaces;
(2) poetry: psalmody, hymns, choruses, anthems, and so on;
(3) prayer: collects, anaphoral-type prayers, blessings, litanies, intercessions.

These genres and subgenres rely upon different combinations of John Frow's genre indicators, what we might call strong and weak indicators. His first indicator is formal organization, a strong indicator: The texts presented in liturgical books distinguish genres by their presentation on the page, which also gives performance indications. Gospel books, lectionaries, hymnbooks, and psalters collect together texts of a similar genre. We have already noted how rhetorical structure, Frow's second characteristic, has been considered important, especially in my genre of prayer; for the other genres this is a weak indicator. Addressivity is particularly important in the subgenres: Prayer is always addressed to God and never to people, whereas prose and poetry are not obliged to do so. The subgenres of prayer may be further distinguished by thematic content. Although this may be more immediately apprehended by the reader/listener, the subgenres should be more accurately distinguished by their structure, that is, their formal organization.

---

[22] Origen, *On Prayer*, 20.
[23] Louis Duchesne, *Christian Worship: Its Origin and Evolution*, trans. M. L. McClure, 5th ed. (London: SPCK, 1923), 106.
[24] Kathleen Hughes, "Prayer, Types of, in the Liturgy," in *The New Dictionary of Sacramental Theology*, ed. Peter E. Fink (Collegeville, MN: Liturgical Press, 1990), 959–67.

The text with the strongest and most enduring genre indicators is the collect. Its distinctive formal organization and rhetorical structure enable the presentation of a wide range of themes. The stable structure of a collect is as follows:

Invitation to prayer addressed to people by minister
Silence
Address to God
Relative clause naming a divine attribute or action
Petition
Justification for the petition
Doxology
Amen, from the congregation.

This structure remains the same regardless of the content of the collect or even the period in which it was composed. Collects in the Verona Sacramentary have the same structure as those in the Book of Common Prayer and in modern liturgical books. For the experienced worshipper, hearing the words "Let us pray" alerts them to the type of prayer that is to come and the way in which the information/narrative will be revealed, even if it does not alert them to the specific content. The correct identification of the genre enhances participation in the liturgical act, as the worshipper instinctively prepares their posture, attitude, and response. Note that this is not a result of the thematic content, which they are yet to hear, but it is a response to the genre indicator.

CONCLUSION

Liturgical texts can be investigated using many other literary theories relating to narrative and intertextuality. It is also possible to identify the distinctive conventions by which liturgical texts are presented in liturgical books. These topics, as well as the ones discussed so far, were considered more closely in my 2018 *Reading the Liturgy*. It remains here to consider the way in which the text functions in the worship event. The text is ever present in the worship event, and textual competency is often required to successfully participate. However, unlike a good novel, liturgical texts do not present information in a clear and straightforward way. Wade Wheelock remarked on the "choppiness of liturgical texts" and noted that liturgies "lack ... cohesiveness" because of the ritual event. It seems obvious that, for the experienced worshipper, it is her prior knowledge of the biblical narrative of salvation that enables her to create coherence from the disparate liturgical elements – the juxtaposition of different genres, non-standard speech patterns, culturally incongruous allusions, and disconnected ritual actions.

The ritual context – with movement, gesture, music, and the space – combines with the text to support or enhance its meaning (or in some infelicitous cases to do the exact opposite). As Wheelock noted, "Each utterance is seen as presenting or bringing into being some element of the predetermined situation that the ritual re-enacts."[25] It is possible for worshippers to create and appropriate new meanings for themselves at each worship event, even if the text itself does not change. Every repetition of the text brings about a new event. The liturgical text's function is not to convey information but to serve and structure participation in the ritual and thereby in salvation history.

For Further Reading

Bradshaw, Paul F., "Liturgy and 'Living Literature'," in *Liturgy in Dialogue: Essays in Memory of Ronald Jasper*, ed. Paul F. Bradshaw and Bryan Spinks (London: SPCK, 1994), 138–53.

Day, Juliette, *Reading the Liturgy: An Exploration of Texts in Christian Worship* (London: Bloomsbury, 2014).

De Zan, Renato, "Criticism and Interpretation of Liturgical Texts," in *Handbook for Liturgical Studies, vol. 1: Introduction to the Liturgy*, ed. Anscar J. Chupungco (Collegeville, MN: Liturgical Press, 1997), 331–65.

McCarthy, Daniel, and James Leachman (eds.), *Appreciating the Collect: An Irenic Methodology* (Farnborough: St Michael's Abbey Press, 2008).

Nichols, Bridget (ed.), *The Collect in the Churches of the Reformation* (London: SCM Press, 2010).

Palazzo, Eric, *A History of Liturgical Books from the Beginning to the Thirteenth Century* (Collegeville, MN: Liturgical Press, 1998).

Zimmerman, Joyce Ann, *Liturgy and Hermeneutics* (Collegeville, MN: Liturgical Press, 1999).

---

[25] Wade T. Wheelock, "The Problem of Ritual Language: From Information to Situation," *Journal of the American Academy of Religion* 50 (1982): 50.

21 Liturgy as Ritual (and Prayer)

KIMBERLY HOPE BELCHER

Seeing liturgy (or better, liturgies) as ritual means understanding it as a specific type of human behavior, one marked by rhythms and repetitions, symbolically linked to central anchors of a culture, and capable of sustaining personal and social continuity and change. Ritual studies tools prevent overgeneralization and romanticization about what assemblies do. They use comparisons with non-Christian religious practice to clarify how Christian liturgy forms persons and cultures. They use methods from anthropology, sociology, psychology, religious studies, and other disciplines to describe and analyze liturgical action.

There is no conflict between viewing the liturgy as a genuine locus of divine action and using the methods of the social sciences to understand it better. Social science perspectives and methods need not reduce the liturgical action to sociological function. Sociologists and anthropologists studying Christianity present the workings of God, saints, and sacraments as they are described by Christian practitioners, even when the author has a different cosmology. Social scientists and liturgists have studied and published together now for decades, as this chapter will show.

Liturgy is anabatic and katabatic, and ritual studies examines its anabatic side. As anabatic, the liturgy responds to God's prior deeds on our behalf: On the cosmic scale, it is a response to the katabatic fact of salvation history, and, on the individual scale, it is a response to the katabatic covenant reality of being called by God into a relationship of filial love. The visible, anabatic action of the liturgy is the work of an assembly convoked precisely in order to articulate a human and cosmic response to divine love. Having been gathered, a Christian or Jewish assembly is called to *remember*.[1]

---

[1] For a Jewish example, see Sonja Keren Pilz, "Holocaust Remembrance in German and North American Jewish Memorial Prayers: A Window onto Two Jewish Identities and Theologies," *Worship* 92 (2018): 436–55.

The anabatic dimension of liturgy is a human, ritualized action, subject to all the same capacities, modes, and limitations as any non-Christian human ritual. Nonetheless it is not *merely* human: As the human prayer of the body of Christ, it has been assumed into the risen Lord's life of prayer, is infused with his Holy Spirit, and participates in his filial relationship with the Father. When we study the liturgical rites, then, as ritual and prayer, we learn about the way the prayer of the head is manifest in the body of the church.

Of course, being a human activity, the church's ritual is subject to distortion and misuse that prevents it from being as fully the prayer of Christ as it ought to be. For example, Christian prayer may be anti-Semitic, xenophobic, or anti-ecumenical. Ritual studies allows scholars to critique these issues in the multisensory experience, personal interpretation, or social function of liturgy. Better still, ritual studies can suggest other modes of celebration that better represent the healing brought for all creation by the King of the Jews. This type of ritual repair is a way of being more genuinely open to the working of the Holy Spirit and theologically prepares us to participate more fully, by means of our baptism, in the always-complete prayer of Christ.[2]

In liturgical theology, the visible anabatic action of the liturgy reflects the katabatic action of grace bestowed by God alone in and through the liturgy.[3] We can make a distinction between the order of knowledge, in which it appears that the katabatic graces received in the sacraments are a response to the manifest anabatic worship of human beings, and the order of being, in which we know that God's gracious disposition toward human beings precedes and is the cause of our desire to worship God. What we know of God's grace is, then, often known by means of the symbols of our worship, which appears primary to us even though it is actually a visible reflection of God's eternal love. In short, we learn much about the katabatic action of God in the world by means of even the anabatic ritual symbols of Christian liturgy because those symbols are (when not distorted by personal and structural sin) a communication of the Trinitarian grace into the world.

This theological model suggests a two-part approach to incorporating ritual studies into liturgical theology. On the one hand, the

---

[2] This Trinitarian picture is of course specific to Christian liturgy. Jewish liturgical theologians such as Lawrence Hoffman and Pilz have integrated ritual studies into their theology through reflection on covenant and memory.

[3] Different Christian churches understand the relationship between the anabatic (worship) and the katabatic (grace) variously, but in all traditions God engages in liturgical worship as an active participant.

methods of ritual studies can be used to describe and analyze the anabatic mode of liturgical practice. This phase can also be assisted by ethnographies of Christian practice that are written by other social scientists or humanities scholars, as well as by theoretical models produced in the study of non-Christian ritual. On the other hand, a liturgical scholar poses theological questions about the images of God, church, humanity, and creation projected by the immersive environment of a liturgy in its cultural context. This may result in a greater understanding of how God reveals Godself in the church's liturgy or of potential modes of repair to clarify the way the liturgy reflects the God revealed in Scripture.

In the following sections, I will (1) explain the different available definitions of ritual and their advantages and drawbacks for studying liturgy, (2) describe the ritual theories that have had the strongest influence and the most promise in interpreting the anabatic character of Christian liturgy, and (3) outline ethnographic approaches to studying Christian liturgy. Ritual theory was adapted into liturgical studies earlier and is used to better understand why and how liturgy is used and adapted. Ethnographic methods have been adopted more recently and are especially useful in describing the multimodal practice of specific communities.

WHAT IS RITUAL?

While there are a range of definitions of ritual in ritual studies, the characteristics of ritual are widely agreed on. Ritual involves the whole body in a set of stylized actions (including words and sounds) that are often perceived as traditional and deeply meaningful. "Stylized" means actions are physically precise and abstracted from merely utilitarian considerations: For example, imagine me putting a book on a high shelf, and then imagine a mime or ballet dancer performing the stylized act of setting an object on a high shelf. The ability to perform stylized gestures, postures, musical pieces, or verbal recitations depends on physical mastery ("muscle memory"[4]), which in turn requires repetitive practice. Performances can be repeated; ritual repetitions can even be rhythmic. The resulting ritual event is generally multisensory and

---

[4] Ronald L. Grimes, *The Craft of Ritual Studies* (Oxford: Oxford University Press, 2013), 314.

Table 21.1 *Adapted from the List of Ritual Characteristics in Grimes, Ritual Criticism, 10–11*

Ritual Characteristics	Anti-Ritual Characteristics
performed, embodied, enacted, gestural (immersive, multisensory)	merely thought or said
formalized, elevated, stylized, differentiated	ordinary, unadorned, or undifferentiated
repetitive, redundant, rhythmic	singular or once-for-all
collective, institutionalized, consensual	personal or private
patterned, invariant, standardized, stereotyped, ordered, rehearsed	improvised, idiosyncratic, or spontaneous
traditional, archaic, primordial	invented or recent
valued highly or ultimately, deeply felt, sentiment-laden, meaningful, serious	trivial or shallow
condensed, multilayered	obvious
symbolic, referential	merely technological or primarily means–end oriented
perfected, idealized, pure, ideal	conflictive or subject to criticism or failure
dramatic, ludic (i.e., play-like)	primarily discursive or explanatory
paradigmatic	ineffectual in modeling either/ other rites or non-ritualized action
mystical, transcendent, religious, cosmic	secular or merely empirical
adaptive, functional	obsessive, neurotic, dysfunctional
conscious, deliberate	unconscious or preconscious

immersive ("performative"), laden with symbols that connect to the symbolic system of the surrounding culture in many ways.[5]

Clearly, a number of activities that are not generally understood as ritual, including musical and athletic performances, fit this description.[6] Music and sports *are* ritual in many traditional societies. Because of this permeability of ritual boundaries, Catherine Bell and Ron Grimes, among others, allow for activities to exist on a spectrum from most to least ritualized (see Table 21.1). Grimes produces an extensive list of ritual "family characteristics," which, like inheritable

---

[5] See characteristics in Catherine M. Bell, *Ritual: Perspectives and Dimensions* (New York: Oxford University Press, 1997), ch. 5; Grimes, *Ritual Criticism: Case Studies in Its Practice, Essays on Its Theory* (Waterloo, ON: Ritual Studies International, 2010), 10–11 (adapted in Table 21.1).

[6] See, for example, "Art in Ritual Context," special issue of the *Journal of Ritual Studies* 6 (1992); Ronald Grimes (ed.), *Ritual, Media, and Conflict*, Oxford Ritual Studies (New York: Oxford University Press, 2011).

physical features, demonstrate why some activities may be very clearly recognized as ritual (they have numerous characteristics of ritual), be more ambiguously ritualistic (they have both ritualistic and anti-ritualistic traits), or be very clearly non-ritual. Ambiguous activities are sometimes called "ritualized" or "ritual-like."

Bell suggests "ritualization" distinguishes from utilitarian activity. The mass, developing out of Late Antique meal practices, became differentiated from meal practice, as its food and drink became fixed, scant, and deeply significant. This made the Eucharist a stronger symbolic paradigm for food practices but also insulated it from the meaningful experience of ordinary dining. Ordinary practice, in becoming ritualized, becomes more independent from changing norms in ordinary life, even as it influences the whole symbolic system.[7]

For Bell, the ritualization of condensed symbols in a cultural system allows social groups to negotiate interpersonal and social conflicts. Something that is really a conflict about power and its exercise in the community can be reframed as a conflict over the interpretation of primary symbols. At that point, the conflict can be negotiated as a dispute over practice or symbols. One thinks – though Bell does not use this example – of the ways disputes over political primacy (like papal jurisdiction) in Christian history were transmuted into disputes about the inclusion or exclusion of particular liturgical practices (such as the *filioque*). Bell believes that it is essential for this process of negotiation that community members do not consciously know how the symbolic system represents a power struggle.[8] Whether essential or not, this idea suggests that worshippers need not explicitly understand a symbol's representation to use it meaningfully.

Adam Seligman et al. contrast ritual as highly scripted behavior with more improvisatory forms of behavior. The authors argue that Westernized cultures since the Enlightenment have privileged sincerity, which is associated with personal, extempore expressions, over rote ritualizations. They argue that ritual is on the one hand a force for cultural bonding, something imperiled by a unilateral emphasis on personal sincerity, and on the other hand a preparation for improvisatory symbolic behavior – a category that goes far beyond worship for

---

[7] Bell, "The Ritual Body and the Dynamics of Ritual Power," *Journal of Ritual Studies* 4 (1990): 299–313; on modern liturgical reforms, see Bell, "Ritual, Change, and Changing Rituals," *Worship* 63 (1989): 31–41.

[8] Bell, "The Ritual Body and the Dynamics of Ritual Power," 299–313.

them. One particularly notable example in chapter 2 treats the nighttime book-reading routine of a parent and child as an interesting middle of the ritualization spectrum, in which the child is formed by the repeated experience of a nighttime routine but also capable of negotiation and gradual assumption of authority over the routine.[9]

Rather than a contrast between a category (ritual behavior) and its opposite (improvisatory, sincere behavior), it might be more productive to consider a spectrum between more-ritual and less-ritual behavior. Less-ritual behavior might be in tension with ritual or resemble ritual: Either way, ritual studies can be a helpful tool. On the other hand, a less bounded model for ritual runs the risk of creating specious or misleading parallels between ritual and ritual-like behavior. In short, while it is possible to analyze toothbrushing using ritual theory, one ought also to be able to distinguish toothbrushing from the Liturgy of the Hours.

Roy Rappaport exemplifies theorists who are able to make this distinction. For Rappaport, "liturgical orders" constitute a system of interconnected ritual actions, social roles, and central symbols that together have the potential to undergird a cosmology. Liturgical rituals, then, might be distinguished from less ritualized behaviors not as somehow "more ritual" in a mathematical sense (counting more on the left than the right of Grimes's table) but because they structure an interconnected world of ritualized symbolic actions that have enough scope to speak to the whole of lived experience. A ritual action within a liturgical order has a greater pull on the social–symbolic system than a ritual that is emergent or otherwise less connected. Rappaport distinguishes between low-order meanings based on contrast, middle-order meanings based on similarity, and high-order meanings that promote radical unity in difference.[10] Despite disputes over the definition of ritual, theorists have examined a wide range of human behavior. Similarly, in liturgical studies, choosing a definition of ritual that brings the research question into sharp focus is a practical matter.

RITUAL–THEORETICAL METHODS

Liturgical ritual studies began with scholarship receiving ethnographic treatments of (generally) non-Christian ritual and using the resulting

---

[9] Adam Seligman et al., *Ritual and Its Consequences: An Essay on the Limits of Sincerity* (New York: Oxford University Press, 2008).

[10] Roy Rappaport, *Ritual and Religion in the Making of Humanity* (New York: Cambridge University Press, 1999).

theory to understand Christian liturgy. The works of early anthropologists, especially Bronisław Malinowski, Mircea Eliade, and Claude Lévi-Strauss, influenced how some Christian liturgists thought about liturgical symbols. A new generation of cultural anthropologists, including Mary Douglas, Victor Turner, and Edith Turner, bridged study of tribal rites in present-day Africa with the treatment of Catholic liturgical and para-liturgical practices, demonstrating in a new way how cultural anthropology could be brought to bear on Christian liturgy. With the development of ritual studies as a recognized subfield in the 1980s, religious studies scholars like Bell, Grimes, Robert Orsi, and Richard Schechner collaborated closely with Christian liturgical scholars such as Marcel Barnard, Margaret Mary Kelleher, Gerard Lukken, Paul Post, and Mark Searle. From the outset, ritual studies promoted global and gendered diversity of both topics and authors in liturgical studies: Rites from the global South, inculturated Christian ritual practice, women's liturgies, and LGBTQ+ rituals were featured prominently, for instance, in the first twelve years of the *Journal for Ritual Studies* (1987–1998).

Liturgists using ritual studies argued that Christian liturgy was shaped by anthropological factors and shared features with non-Christian ritual practice. Ritual studies permitted paying attention to what people gathered for liturgy actually did rather than what was prescribed by experts; it integrated consideration of the historical and cultural context of a liturgical practice, and it made it possible to study whether and how liturgical practice was actually formative. At the same time, it highlighted how Christian liturgies, like practices in other religions, were shaped by hierarchies and prohibitions that might not be functional or fair. In short, ritual studies scholarship takes seriously the truly human or anabatic character of Christian worship.

Ritual studies treatments that rely on ritual theory begin with a Christian practice and then introduce an understanding of human ritual drawn from an analogous practice. Concepts developed in social science analyses of the analogous practice are then applied to the Christian practice. For example, concepts drawn from adolescent men's adulthood initiations influenced the implementation of the adult catechumenate in the second half of the twentieth century.[11] "Rites of passage" theory suggested that initiation processes are engaged in by a cohort who experience a "liminal" period "betwixt and between" various statuses

---

[11] See, for example, Leonel L. Mitchell, "Christian Initiation, Rites of Passage, and Confirmation," in *Confirmation Re-Examined*, ed. Kendig Brubaker Kelly (Wilton, CT: Morehouse-Barlow, 1982), 81–92.

and roles in society, in which the normal restrictions and rules of social life are lifted, and thus who develop a profound bond (*communitas*) that relativizes and contextualizes hierarchical relationships.[12] This theory influenced and continues to influence the way that the catechumenal rites are interpreted and implemented, seeing the catechumenal ritual process as a way of allowing catechumens to develop a communal identity with the body of Christ by means of liminal experiences.

Treatments of Christian liturgy can also be used to critique ritual theories, to further specify their criteria for applicability, or to nuance them. In fact, this should be a much more pronounced aspect of liturgical ritual studies. Caroline Walker Bynum calls attention to the fact that Turner's theories of liminality and *communitas* were developed from Ndembu men's initiation rites, and that, in Christian medieval narratives, "Turner's ideas describe the stories and symbols of men better than those of women."[13] Perhaps liturgists have relied uncritically on Turner's least-nuanced descriptions of liminality.[14]

Liminality originated from observation of rituals for adolescent boys. They were not only gender segregated; they were also initiated as an age cohort into adulthood in the same basic social group. Contemporary adult Christian initiation consists of a self-selected group who are entering a new social body in a pluralistic culture, while at a variety of ages and social stages. Under what conditions will such a group develop a sense of *communitas*? The art of choosing the proper theory for understanding Christian liturgy, as this suggests, is probably the most difficult part of liturgical ritual studies. The fit between liturgy and theory comes from the liturgist's ability to conceptualize the similarities and distinctions between the whole social environment of the liturgy being studied and the theory's source culture. Finding this fit might require a great deal of theoretical reflection, conversations with experts in different theories, or good luck.

---

[12] Arnold van Gennep, *The Rites of Passage* (Chicago, IL: University of Chicago Press, 1960); Victor Turner, *The Ritual Process* (Chicago, IL: Aldine, 1969); Victor Turner and Edith Turner, *Image and Pilgrimage in Christian Culture* (New York: Columbia University Press, 1978); Edith Turner, *Among the Healers: Stories of Spiritual and Ritual Healing Around the World* (London: Bloomsbury, 2006).

[13] Caroline Walker Bynum, *Fragmentation and Redemption: Essays on Gender and the Human Body in Medieval Religion* (New York: Zone Books, 1991), 32.

[14] Other fields are not immune to this critique. See Don Handelman's bracing review essay: "Is Victor Turner Receiving His Intellectual Due?," *Journal of Ritual Studies* 7 (1993): 117–24.

Liminality has probably had the largest impact on liturgical ritual theory, followed by semiotics and embodiment. Though these overlap, distinguishing these concepts allows for a more streamlined exposition of the primary works. Liminality focuses on community formation and social change and has been used to understand practices of Christian initiation, the Christian year, and the more general way that liturgical experience can lead to close bonding. Despite my critique above, the theory of liminality has ameliorated an earlier anthropological emphasis on ritual as scripted and unchanging. The liminal effect highlights personal meaning, social transformation, moral impact, and the ludic, celebratory, or effervescent quality of liturgy. These dimensions are especially important for understanding the eschatological importance of Christian worship.[15]

Early uses of semiotics related the immersive, communicative aspect of Christian liturgy to theories of signification by Charles Pierce and Algirdas Julien Greimas, among others.[16] Lukken used these theories to contextualize liturgy as one of numerous postmodern ways Christians ritualize, calling into question the idea that Western culture today relies less on ritual than societies did in the past.[17] With Searle, he also examined architecture as a ritual environment, not merely a static art form.[18] In North America, ritual studies complemented and fused with existing feminist approaches to liturgy. Mary Collins developed the concept of the ambiguity of liturgical symbol, within which participants could experience the primary symbols in a variety of ways, and emphasized the contemplative action of the liturgical practitioner as a key meaning-maker of the rite.[19] Mary Margaret Kelleher developed a Lonerganian account of the communicative and hermeneutic quality of liturgy[20] and also wrote some of the earliest guides to liturgical

---

[15] Robert Hovda, "Liturgy as Kingdom Play," *Worship* 56 (1982): 261–63.
[16] Gerard Lukken, "Semiotics and the Study of Liturgy," *Studia Liturgica* 17 (1987): 108–17.
[17] Lukken, *Rituals in Abundance: Critical Reflections on the Place, Form, and Identity of Christian Ritual in Our Culture*, Liturgia Condenda 17 (Leuven: Peeters, 2005).
[18] Lukken and Mark Searle, *Semiotics and Church Architecture: Applying the Semiotics of A. J. Greimas and the Paris School to the Analysis of Church Buildings* (Netherlands: Kok Pharos, 1993); Searle, "The Emergence of Pastoral Liturgical Studies," *Worship* 57 (1983): 291–308; Searle, *Called to Participate: Theological, Ritual, and Social Perspectives* (Collegeville, MN: Liturgical Press, 2006).
[19] Mary Collins, *Worship: Renewal to Practice* (Washington, DC: Pastoral Press, 1987).
[20] Margaret Mary Kelleher, "Liturgy: An Ecclesial Act of Meaning," *Worship* 59 (1985): 482–97.

ethnography.[21] Janet Walton, likewise, combined attention to ritual and feminist theory with methodological reflection.[22] Teresa Berger has relied on ritual theory in her work on women's worship and, more recently, on liturgy in cyberspace.[23] Graham Hughes created an especially powerful liturgical application of Pierce's semiotics in *Worship as Meaning* and later developed an accessible postcolonial model with Steffen Lösel in *Reformed Sacramentality*.[24]

"Embodiment" is a conceptual framework that extends the scholar's gaze beyond verbal formulas and abstract actions to the specific gestures and multisensory modes of embodied liturgy. This understanding has influenced historical inquiries where multimodal evidence is scarce; in more modern contexts, it is an expectation. Douglas's work demonstrates that the physical treatment of individual bodies, especially in fasting and eating, represents and works on the social body, an insight that remains very important for liturgical ecclesiology.[25] Lawrence Hoffman extended this work to Jewish liturgy and argued that both historical and contemporary studies of liturgical action needed to examine performance and draw on anthropological models to fully understand what a ritual text meant either to its original community or to practitioners today.[26] Grimes was particularly attentive to the likeness between ritual and ordinary action. As a result, he developed an understanding of ritualization or emerging ritual – the incipient stylization and symbolic character of actions that are not

---

[21] Kelleher, "The Communion Rite: A Study of Roman Catholic Liturgical Performance," *Journal of Ritual Studies* 5 (1991): 99–122; Kelleher, "Hermeneutics in the Study of Liturgical Performance," *Worship* 67 (1993): 292–318.

[22] For example, Janet B. Walton et al., "Navigating Intersecting Roads in a Mixed Methods Case Study: A Dissertation Journey," *Journal of Mixed Methods Research* 14 (2020): 436–55.

[23] For example, Teresa Berger, *Women's Ways of Worship: Gender Analysis and Liturgical History* (Collegeville, MN: Liturgical Press, 1999); Berger, *Liturgy in Migration: From the Upper Room to Cyberspace* (Collegeville, MN: Liturgical Press, 2012); Berger, *@worship: Liturgical Practices in Digital Worlds*, Liturgy, Worship, and Society (London: Routledge, 2018).

[24] Graham Hughes, *Worship as Meaning: A Liturgical Theology for Late Modernity* (Cambridge: Cambridge University Press, 2003); Hughes and Steffen Lösel, *Reformed Sacramentality* (Collegeville, MN: Liturgical Press, 2017).

[25] Mary Douglas, *Natural Symbols; Explorations in Cosmology* (New York: Pantheon Books, 1970); Douglas, *Purity and Danger: An Analysis of the Concepts of Pollution and Taboo* (London: Routledge, 1978); Frank C. Senn, *Eucharistic Body* (Minneapolis, MN: Fortress Press, 2017). Douglas's later work, especially, still has the potential for more direct applications to liturgical studies.

[26] Lawrence A. Hoffman, *Beyond the Text: A Holistic Approach to Liturgy*, Jewish Literature and Culture (Bloomington, IN: Indiana University Press, 1987).

considered traditional or highly scripted.²⁷ With Paul Post and other scholars, this work was developed into the study of improvised ritual responses to disasters.²⁸

One reason a focus on embodiment has been so generative is that outside of Enlightenment-influenced Christianity, embodied ritual is an important way of knowing. Talal Asad's study of medieval Christianity and Islam portrays liturgy as a disciplinary program for developing bodily techniques related to *habitus,* or a culturally specified set of physical and verbal skills. *Genealogies of Religion* treats the relationship of medieval monastic preaching and the Liturgy of the Hours, for instance, to the development of the virtue of Christian humility.²⁹ Nathan Mitchell used this theory to deepen the formative function of liturgy beyond conscious thought into the physical and emotional capacities of worshippers.³⁰ My work continues these lines of thought, relating the embodied action of liturgy to the formation of persons in community and to the way liturgical symbols function in complex systems of embodied meaning.³¹ Since ritual theory authorizes alternate ways of knowing and the practices of ordinary people, it has influenced postcolonial, decolonial, and queer liturgical theologians, who embrace ritual as a way of looking at unscripted, unauthorized, or experimental religious practices. Claudio Carvalhaes, Kristine Suna-Koro, Layla Karst, Lis Valle-Ruiz, Becca Whitla, and other scholars have used ritual theory to explore experiences that have been critical for subaltern communities.³²

---

[27] Grimes, "Emerging Ritual," *Proceedings of the North American Academy of Liturgy* (1990): 15–31; Grimes, "Reinventing Ritual," *Soundings: An Interdisciplinary Journal* 75 (1992): 21–41; Grimes, "Modes of Ritual Sensibility," in *Beginnings in Ritual Studies* (Waterloo, ON: Ritual Studies International, 2010), 33–48; Grimes, *Deeply into the Bone: Re-Inventing Rites of Passage* (Berkeley, CA: University of California, 2002).

[28] Paul Post et al., *Disaster Ritual: Explorations of an Emerging Ritual Repertoire,* Liturgia Condenda 15 (Leuven: Peeters, 2003); Martin J. M. Hoondert et al., *Handbook of Disaster Ritual: Multidisciplinary Perspectives, Cases and Themes,* Liturgia Condenda 32 (Leuven: Peeters, 2021).

[29] Talal Asad, *Genealogies of Religion: Discipline and Reasons of Power in Christianity and Islam* (Baltimore, MD: Johns Hopkins University Press, 1993).

[30] Nathan Mitchell, *Liturgy and the Social Sciences* (Collegeville, MN: Liturgical Press, 1999).

[31] Kimberly Hope Belcher, *Efficacious Engagement: Sacramental Participation in the Trinitarian Mystery* (Collegeville, MN: Liturgical Press, 2011); Belcher, "Ritual Systems, Ritualized Bodies, and the Laws of Liturgical Development," *Studia Liturgica* 49 (2019): 89–110; Belcher, "Ritual Systems: Prostration, Self, and Community in the *Rule of Benedict,*" *Ecclesia Orans* 37 (2020): 321–56.

[32] See, for instance, Antonio Eduardo Alonso, *Commodified Communion: Eucharist, Consumer Culture, and the Practice of Everyday Life* (New York: Fordham University

There are still new opportunities to apply ritual theory to liturgical studies. Bell's work on the strategy of ritual action, Jean Comaroff's work on ritual resistance to colonialism, and Saba Mahmood's study of the agency of women adopting traditional piety could completely reshape our understanding of lay participation in prescribed ritual, both historical and contemporary.[33] Don Handelman's work on the ambivalent character of ritual as public spectacle, as well as its consequent flexibility of interpretation, could impel liturgists to a higher honesty about the fragility of liturgical ritual and its misuse, as well as its likeness to protest and other public performances.[34] Lindsay Jones's two-volume theory on the ritual character of public architecture draws on Jewish and Christian examples as well as pre-Columbian Native American spaces to describe numerous ways architectural space can be used in ritual events.[35]

ETHNOGRAPHIC METHODS

One mode of incorporating ritual studies into liturgical studies is by ethnography. A liturgist may be embedded into a worshipping

---

Press, 2021); Cláudio Carvalhaes, *Ritual at World's End* (York: Barber's Son Press, 2021); Carvalhaes (ed.), *Liturgy in Postcolonial Perspectives: Only One Is Holy*, Postcolonialism and Religions (New York: Palgrave Macmillan, 2015); Kristine Suna-Koro, *In Counterpoint: Diaspora, Postcoloniality, and Sacramental Theology* (Eugene, OR: Pickwick Publications, 2017); Lis Valle-Ruiz, "Performing Cultural Memory through Preaching," *Liturgy (Washington)* 35 (2020): 3–9; Layla Karst, "Itineraries," in *Practical Matters* 9 (2016) 1–4; E. Elochukwu Uzukwu, *Worship as Body Language: Introduction to Christian Worship: An African Orientation* (Collegeville, MN: Liturgical Press, 1997); Lis Valle-Ruiz and Andrew Wymer, *Unmasking White Preaching: Racial Hegemony, Resistance, and Possibilities in Homiletics*, Postcolonial and Decolonial Studies in Religion and Theology (Lanham, MD: Lexington Books, 2022); Becca Whitla, *Liberation, (De)Coloniality, and Liturgical Practices: Flipping the Song Bird*, New Approaches to Religion and Power (Cham: Springer, 2020); and the essays in Swee Hong Lim (ed.), "Global and Local Issues in Liturgy," a special issue of *Liturgy* 37:1 (2022).

[33] Bell, *Ritual Theory, Ritual Practice* (New York: Oxford University Press, 1992); Jean Comaroff, *Body of Power, Spirit of Resistance: The Culture and History of a South African People* (Chicago, IL: University of Chicago Press, 1985); Saba Mahmood, *Politics of Piety: The Islamic Revival and the Feminist Subject* (Princeton, NJ: Princeton University Press, 2012).

[34] Handelman, *Models and Mirrors: Towards an Anthropology of Public Events* (New York: Berghahn Books, 1998); Handelman, "Introduction: Why Ritual in Its Own Right? How So?," in *Ritual in Its Own Right*, ed. Galina Lindquist and Handelman (New York: Berghahn, 2004), 1–32.

[35] Lindsay Jones, *The Hermeneutics of Sacred Architecture: Experience, Interpretation, Comparison*, Religions of the World (Cambridge, MA: Harvard University Press, 2000).

community and describe, transcribe, or record their liturgical practices. The ethnographic methods of liturgical studies originate from anthropology, sociology, and religious studies, but liturgical ethnography is more likely to be done by "insider–outsiders," that is, those who already had an established connection with the community before their ethnographic training, than by social science ethnographers. Liturgical studies works are also more likely to be "activist ethnography," that is, ethnography intended to make a difference in practice, whether by recording practices of small, endangered communities (sometimes known as "salvage ethnography"), by spreading especially good practices, or by critiquing existing practice.[36]

The process of producing ethnographic liturgical ritual studies can be divided into data collection phases, analytical techniques, evaluation or comparison, and dissemination. The basic methods of liturgical data collection include participant observation, interview studies, documentary filmmaking, audio recording, and surveys. Participant observation has been used in the field most broadly and longest and relies on the expertise of the observer, whereas surveys and interview studies make it possible to find out what, how, and why liturgy means for non-experts. Analytical techniques include both coding the data (generally using software support) and employing theoretical tools (such as those listed in the previous section).

Liturgical researchers might evaluate the effectiveness of practices or compare them either synchronically or diachronically with the practices of other groups. Here is where the activist character of liturgical ethnography becomes important: Whereas it is disputed within anthropology whether a scholar ought to evaluate whether the practices they study are good or bad,[37] it is practically assumed that a liturgist engages in ritual studies to evaluate the moral and practical good and evil of liturgical practice and to improve it if possible. Siobhán Garrigan's *The Real Peace Process*, for example, explicitly sets out to improve liturgy as a tool in the Irish peace process: "The worship practices of many communities, contrary to the conscious peace-commitments of their members, allow congregations to engage in a

---

[36] On activist ethnography in anthropology, see Sharad Chari and Henrike Donner, "Ethnographies of Activism: A Critical Introduction," *Cultural Dynamics* 22 (July 1, 2010): 75–85.

[37] Robert Orsi, for instance, reflects on challenges to the ethnographic study of religion by practitioners, fellow scholars, and liturgical activists in *Between Heaven and Earth: The Religious Worlds People Make and the Scholars Who Study Them* (Princeton, NJ: Princeton University Press, 2007), ch. 5.

series of verbal and non-verbal interactions which play out (and thereby reinforce) division and express biases and stereotypes, which produce prejudice."[38] Each chapter contains suggestions of how the peace process can be furthered by alterations in Irish liturgical practice. Liturgical ethnographers, then, speak and write not only for one another and for other scholars of religion but also for churches, ministers, and those developing new rituals. This means that the liturgical ethnography dissemination phase might well involve publications or media productions aimed at practitioners as well as at other scholars. Sociologists and anthropologists studying ritual might also have practical aims, but they are less expected and embedded in the field than in liturgical ritual studies.[39]

The dissemination of liturgical ethnography is usually through written material, though it might also include photography, graphs and tables, and video or audio recordings. The written style of ethnography is sometimes called thick description.[40] A thick description ought not to rely on shared insider jargon of ritual experts, but it also does not describe a rite as it seems on the surface, as if seen by an alien.[41] Rather, it describes the multisensory and dynamic experience of a ritual in such a way that it also introduces some of the cultural embedding that would be known by most of the participants in a rite. In essence, it is a way to convey as responsibly as possible the ethnographer's experience of the ritual. A thick description is not necessarily limited to one participant observation; rather, good thick description permits the incorporation of data and perspectives known by interviews and analysis. In this way it exceeds one's field notes, though it may quote them, be adapted from them, or even be stylistically written "as if" field notes. Thick descriptions should induce in the reader a sense of secondary immersion into the cultural environment they study. Sarah Kathleen Johnson's ecumenical ethnography of online worship during the Covid-19 pandemic provides a brief example of good thick description: She locates herself in space, represents the backchannel chat function of online worship in an

---

[38] Garrigan, *The Real Peace Process*, 1.

[39] Todd Whitmore has developed a theology of theological ethnography based on imitation of Christ by the discipline of sustained attention in *Imitating Christ in Magwi: An Anthropological Theology* (London: Bloomsbury, 2019).

[40] Clifford Geertz, *The Interpretation of Cultures: Selected Essays* (New York: Basic, 1973), ch. 1.

[41] Grimes, "Ritual Criticism of a Catholic Liturgical Evaluation," in *Ritual Criticism: Case Studies in Its Practice, Essays on Its Theory* (Waterloo, ON: Ritual Studies International, 2010), 25–50.

innovative way, and describes varied cultural embeddings with sympathetic sophistication.[42]

Liturgical ethnography is especially important for studying liturgical practice "beyond the text."[43] This includes describing and analyzing practices that are not in official books, identifying adaptations and departures from prescribed rites, noting nonverbal embodied and sensory practices, and learning from communities that do not rely on written books at all. Music is certainly one aspect of liturgy imperfectly represented by books. Liturgical ethnomusicologists like Phil Bohlman, Jeffers L. Engelhardt, Margot Fassler, Michael C. Hawn, Monique Ingalls, Peter Jeffery, Kay Kaufman Shelemay, and Braxton Shelley explore the historical and contemporary cultural and ritual context of performances of liturgical music.[44] It is past time for liturgical ritual studies to supplement ethnographic writing with recordings of the soundscape and multimodal experience of liturgical ritual, as ethnomusicology does.

The inculturated worship of many ethnic communities in mainline, Catholic and Orthodox Churches, as well as the free church traditions in their entirety, are not easily represented by liturgical books. Ethnographic studies like Mary McGann's study of African American Catholic music[45] and Virgilio Elizondo and Timothy Matovina's work on the San Fernando Cathedral[46] give the lie to the notion that Roman Catholics in the United States have one liturgy. Ethnography has been even more important in studying free church and charismatic worship. Melanie Ross has illuminated the diversity of free church traditions that embrace the moniker "evangelical" and also weighed

---

[42] Sarah Kathleen Johnson, "Online Communion, Christian Community, and Receptive Ecumenism: A Holy Week Ethnography during Covid-19," *Studia Liturgica* 50 (2020): 188–210. The techniques of writing thick description require reflection on the relationship between ethnographer, observed communities, and prospective audience, often called "reflexivity and positionality."

[43] Hoffman, *Beyond the Text*.

[44] For an introduction to congregational music studies, see Andrew Mall, Jeffers Engelhardt, and Monique M. Ingalls, *Studying Congregational Music: Key Issues, Methods, and Theoretical Perspectives* (Milton: Taylor & Francis, 2021). "Salvage ethnography" on liturgical chant is represented, for example, by Kay Kaufman Shelemay and Peter Jeffery, *Ethiopian Christian Liturgical Chant: An Anthology*, 3 vols. (Middleton, WI: A-R Editions, Inc., 1993).

[45] Mary E. McGann, *A Precious Fountain: Music in the Worship of an African American Catholic Community* (Collegeville, MN: Liturgical Press, 2015).

[46] Virgilio P. Elizondo and Timothy Matovina, *San Fernando Cathedral: Soul of the City* (Maryknoll, NY: Books, 1998).

in on the relationship between ethnography and liturgical theology.[47] Anthropologist Thomas Csordas's extended and insightful studies of charismatic healing practices manifest the potential of a phenomenological approach to ethnography as well as providing powerful theoretical accounts of effective healing practices.[48] Tanya Riches's work situates contemporary Pentecostal worship within feminist, postcolonial, global, and disability conversations.[49] Such multifaceted conversations are increasingly common in free church and worship studies scholarship.[50]

Ethnography is used to study the rapid adaptation of liturgy in the tension between secularism and immigration in northern Europe. On the one hand, ethnographers like Post, Marcel Barnard, Mirella Klomp, Thomas Quartier, and their partners study the cultural role played by Christian-origin rituals such as funerals, candlelight vigils, and Advent and Holy Week spectacles.[51] On the other hand, they also study the evolving ritual practices of religious immigrant communities to northern Europe.[52] In addition to the qualitative ethnographic methods used by many of these scholars, Quartier has introduced

---

[47] Melanie C. Ross, *Evangelical versus Liturgical?: Defying a Dichotomy* (Grand Rapids, MI: Eerdmans, 2014); Ross, *Evangelical Worship: An American Mosaic* (New York: Oxford University Press, 2021).

[48] Thomas J. Csordas, *The Sacred Self: A Cultural Phenomenology of Charismatic Healing* (Berkeley: University of California, 1997); Csordas, *Language, Charisma, and Creativity: Ritual Life in the Catholic Charismatic Renewal*, 2nd ed. (New York: Palgrave Macmillan, 2002).

[49] See, for example, Tanya Riches, *Worship and Social Engagement in Urban Aboriginal-Led Australian Pentecostal Congregations*, illustrated ed. (Leiden: Brill, 2019).

[50] See, for example, Sarah Kathleen Johnson and Andrew Wymer (eds.), *Worship and Power: Liturgical Authority in Free Church Traditions* (Eugene, OR: Wipf & Stock, 2023); Adam A. Perez, "'It's Your Breath in Our Lungs': Sean Feucht's Praise and Worship Music Protests and the Theological Problem of Pandemic Response in the U.S.," *Religions* 13 (January 2022): 47; Shannan Baker and Monique Ingalls, "The Musical Rhetoric of Charismatic Revival: Continuity and Change in the Songs of the Toronto Blessing and Bethel Church," *Journal of the European Pentecostal Theological Association* 42 (2022): 17–32.

[51] Mirella Klomp, *Playing On: Re-Staging the Passion after the Death of God* (Leiden: Brill, 2020); Heleen Zorgdrager, "Epiphany between the Barricades: The Ukrainian Maidan as a Sacred Space," *Yearbook for Ritual and Liturgical Studies* 32 (2016): 167–85.

[52] Post and Arie L. Molendijk (eds.), *Holy Ground: Re-Inventing Ritual Space in Modern Western Culture*, Liturgia Condenda 24 (Leuven: Peeters, 2010); Klomp, *The Sound of Worship: Liturgical Performance by Surinamese Lutherans and Ghanaian Methodists* (Leuven: Peeters, 2011); Barnard, Johan Cilliers, and Cas Wepener, *Worship in the Network Culture: Liturgical Ritual Studies. Fields and Methods, Concepts and Metaphors*, Liturgia Condenda 28 (Leuven: Peeters, 2014); Paul Post and Suzanne

quantitative analysis to liturgical studies. These works and those of Cas Wepener in South Africa are also theoretically innovative, understanding liturgical liminality and embodiment in new and compelling ways.

Social processes of peace and division have been studied ethnographically as well. Wepener and partners' work on the ritual practices of African indigenous churches highlights the role of ritual practice in social reconciliation, race and emotion, and social bonding for more equitable development in South Africa.[53] Ritual in fraught political contexts may radicalize or reconcile, and the potential for ritual practice to create tight networks of mutual care has important ramifications for international development. Wepener and his partners demonstrate how ritual practice both expresses and alters fundamental ideas about mutual belonging, thereby creating political shifts by means of symbolic practice. Liturgical ethnographic study has also been used to evaluate and promote peacemaking by Garrigan in Ireland and Northern Ireland.[54] In North America, many liturgical scholars have been working on racial solidarity and other justice issues.[55] Recent studies on disaster ritual examine similarly creative ritualizing on an even more global scale, with short case studies on topics ranging from airline crashes to school shootings.[56]

Ethnography is becoming a significant way of studying the liturgical experience of worshippers with disabilities. Rebecca Spurrier's richly

---

van der Beek, *Doing Ritual Criticism in a Network Society: Online and Offline Explorations into Pilgrimage and Sacred Place* (Leuven: Peeters, 2016).

[53] Wepener, *From Fast to Feast: A Ritual-Liturgical Exploration of Reconciliation in South African Cultural Contexts*, Liturgia Condenda 19 (Leuven: Peeters, 2009); Ian Nell, "Transforming Congregational Culture: Suburban Leadership Perspectives within a Circuit of the DRC," *Scriptura* 114 (2015): 1-18; Wepener et al., *Bonding in Worship: A Ritual Lens on Social Capital in African Independent Churches in South Africa* (Leuven: Peeters, 2019).

[54] Garrigan, *The Real Peace Process*.

[55] Sarah Kathleen Johnson, "On Our Knees: Christian Ritual in Residential Schools and the Truth and Reconciliation Commission of Canada," *Studies in Religion* 47 (2018): 3-24; Kristen Daley Mosier et al., "'Water Brought Us Together': A Baptismal Ethic from Flint," *Religions* 13 (August 2022): 716; Lis Valle-Ruiz and Andrew Wymer (eds.), *Unmasking White Preaching: Racial Hegemony, Resistance, and Possibilities in Homiletics* (Lanham, MD: Lexington Books, 2022); Susan Bigelow Reynolds, *People Get Ready: Ritual, Solidarity, and Lived Ecclesiology in Catholic Roxbury* (New York: Fordham University Press, 2023); Stephanie A. Budwey, *Religion and Intersex: Perspectives from Science, Law, Culture, and Theology* (New York: Routledge, 2023).

[56] Post et al., *Disaster Ritual: Explorations of an Emerging Ritual Repertoire*, Liturgia Condenda 15 (Leuven: Peeters, 2003); Martin Hoondert et al., *Handbook of Disaster Ritual: Multidisciplinary Perspectives, Cases and Themes*, Liturgia Condenda 32 (Leuven: Peeters, 2021).

textured *The Disabled Church* investigates the disabilities-informed arts ministry of an Episcopal church in Atlanta as worship and construes the reflections of people with disabilities on their own desires and social embeddings as liturgical theology.[57] Léon van Ommen's ethnographic and liturgical–theological study of the experience of autistic people in Christian worship critiques the idolatry of the concept of normal and advocates for a kenotic theology of liturgical availability, to benefit not only neurodiverse but also neurotypical liturgical participants.[58] Ritual studies work allows liturgical scholars to differentiate various types and experiences of disability and neurodiversity, as well as to do justice to the variety of experiences of liturgy by people with the same type of disability.

Liturgical ethnography has benefitted from collaboration with cognate fields like congregational studies, ethnography and ecclesiology, ethnographic political theology, parts of practical theology and peace studies, and the anthropology of Christianity. Using qualitative (and occasionally quantitative) methods, liturgical ethnography and these closely related fields attempt to do justice to the diversity of lived Christian liturgy.

INTEGRATION WITH RITUAL TEXTS AND LITURGICAL THEOLOGY

In the introduction, I suggested that ritual studies can be used to describe and analyze the anabatic aspect of liturgy, which is the properly human performance of religious ritual but is also assumed into the humanity of Christ to become his own filial prayer. Both the ritual–theoretical analysis of Christian liturgy (especially as it is infused with systems of oppressive power) and the ethnographic description of particular community rites (which may be aberrant) may seem to destabilize confidence in this theological understanding of the liturgy. Liturgies, however, are embedded in the human condition, of which failure is a fundamental part. Although liturgies do convey glimpses of the eschatological end of humanity and of the cosmos, they also reflect the sin of the human condition and the brokenness of the world we know. That is, it is not only that liturgical worshippers are imperfect: Liturgical

---

[57] Rebecca F. Spurrier, *The Disabled Church: Human Difference and the Art of Communal Worship* (New York: Fordham University Press, 2019).

[58] Armand Léon van Ommen, *Autism in/out of Worship: A Liturgical Theology of Availability* (Waco, TX: Baylor University Press, 2023).

celebrations themselves are always imperfect. In the revelation of liturgical failure, ritual studies might distinguish shortfalls stemming from finitude or multiplicity (such as morally neutral differences in practice and participation) from those stemming from sin (such as liturgical oppression based in power, gender, class, or race).

In its evaluative mode, ritual studies (both theoretical and ethnographic modes) can not only critique but also improve liturgical practice. Fundamentally, Christian liturgy is the commemoration throughout the arc of history of the covenant established by Jesus Christ, and ritual analyses of the communicative quality of liturgy within its proper historical and cultural setting can aid communities in discerning how their own liturgy may be both more honest and more just. This usually requires that liturgical ritual scholarship be done in close connection with, and ideally by, an esteemed member of the community whose liturgy requires repair. At the same time, sympathetic outsiders, allies, or advocates who have a well-developed humility about their own position have often played an important role in mediating between communities of nonverbal or nonbookish persons and the academic world of liturgical studies.

Both in analysis and in repair, liturgical ritual studies offers tools for seeing liturgies differently. Combined with liturgical history, it instills in liturgists a salutary caution that the most important aspects of liturgy are not necessarily those that spring first even to the well-trained mind. It replaces a romantic wonder at the timelessness of liturgical worship with a more well-founded wonder at the multitudinous glory of God's plan of salvation as reflected in human cultural performance. Most importantly, it lifts up instantiations in real communities of the abstract principles of liturgical theology.

For Further Reading

Asad, Talal, *Genealogies of Religion: Discipline and Reasons of Power in Christianity and Islam* (Baltimore, MD: Johns Hopkins University Press, 1993).

Barnard, Marcel, Johan Cilliers, and Cas Wepener (eds.), *Worship in the Network Culture: Liturgical Ritual Studies. Fields and Methods, Concepts and Metaphors*, Liturgia Condenda 28 (Leuven: Peeters, 2014).

Belcher, Kimberly Hope, "Ritual Systems: Prostration, Self, and Community in the Rule of Benedict," *Ecclesia Orans* 37 (2020): 321–56.

Bell, Catherine M., *Ritual: Perspectives and Dimensions* (New York: Oxford University Press, 1997).

Hoffman, Lawrence A., *Beyond the Text: A Holistic Approach to Liturgy. Jewish Literature and Culture* (Bloomington, IN: Indiana University Press, 1995).

Mitchell, Nathan, *Liturgy and the Social Sciences* (Collegeville, MN: Liturgical Press, 1999).
Moschella, Mary Clark, *Ethnography as a Pastoral Practice: An Introduction*, 2nd rev. ed. (Cleveland, OH: Tpp, 2023).
Ross, Melanie C., *Evangelical Worship: An American Mosaic* (New York: Oxford University Press, 2021).
Spurrier, Rebecca F., *The Disabled Church: Human Difference and the Art of Communal Worship* (New York: Fordham University Press, 2019).

22 Liturgical Theology

NATHAN G. JENNINGS

Liturgical theology as a field was developed to draw out theological and doctrinal corollaries to the discoveries and goals of liturgical renewal in the twentieth century. Although arising out of the study of liturgy, which, at the time was primarily historiographic and philological in nature, the intended audience of liturgical theology was not primarily historians of liturgy but theologians, especially systematic theologians. Not just historical but also anthropological, ethnographic, phenomenological, and hermeneutical insights and discoveries, together with attempts at the retrieval of earlier expressions of Christian ritual, have paved the way for liturgical theologians to challenge systematic approaches to the study of Christian teaching and theology, especially with regard to the modern theological problem of sources and methods. The main criticisms of liturgical theology, despite its being targeted toward systematicians, have come from liturgical historians who challenged some of the most important commitments of liturgical theology. Liturgical theology as a post-critical retrieval of mystagogy can move forward, appreciating the criticism of the historians while more deeply advancing its engagement with systematic and dogmatic theologians.

To argue that liturgical theology represents a post-critical turn, this chapter first addresses the issue of sources and methods in theology and how post-critical approaches reframe and eschew these problems. The chapter then follows a roughly historical path through the development of liturgical theology as a discipline. Furthermore, this chapter looks at the birth of liturgical theology in the scholarship of Alexander Schmemann, an Orthodox theologian. Then the chapter moves to the reception of this new approach, in the West, by the Roman Catholics Aidan Kavanagh and David Fagerberg and the Lutheran Gordon Lathrop, and by some non-liturgical Christian traditions. Additionally, the chapter first describes the concerns brought to attention by liturgical historians about this new field and then goes on to answer them by understanding liturgical theology to represent a post-critical hermeneutic and phenomenology. It concludes with a proposal to take the post-critical turn of liturgical theology forward as a retrieval of the ancient church's practice of mystagogy.

SOURCES AND METHODS IN THEOLOGY AND POST-CRITICAL APPROACHES

The intended audience of liturgical theology has been, whatever is considered theology "proper," of the tradition of the liturgical theologian. In the West, this has meant systematic theologians and the like. The liturgical theologian offers liturgy itself as an alternative starting point for a post-critical end-run around perennial issues of "methods and sources" in modern theology. Liturgical theologians use the word "liturgy" to refer to a logically discernable structure in Christian ritual shared among most of the Christian liturgical traditions, broadly consisting of four things: rites of initiation, the Holy Eucharist and its related rites, the observances of the Christian year and day, and pastoral rites.[1] Liturgical theologians refer to the entire structure as *ordo*. Central to these four is the structurally discernable shape of the Holy Eucharist as the central act of Christian worship, referred to with the definite article, as in *the* Liturgy or *the ordo*.

The modern assumption of a fundamental divide between subject and object demands methods for gaining knowledge of the object behind subjective phenomena. The central approach of most modern methodology is "criticism." "Scientific" academic modes of theology in the West come under many names: systematic, dogmatic, constructive theology. They share the need to prove that their work counts as legitimate fields of study in the modern academy. Under conditions of modern academic reasoning, the traditional practice and discipline of theology undergoes a kind of crisis. What is the object behind the phenomenon? How is theology, therefore, not completely subjective? What could count as legitimate sources of theological knowledge, and what methods could grant us objectivity in their study?

Liturgical theology represents another post-critical turn in this discussion. The post-critical turn grows from a cultural anthropological discovery that criticism itself was constituted as a Western project.

---

[1] Alexander Schmemann, *Introduction to Liturgical Theology* (Portland, ME: American Orthodox Press, 1966), 25–27.

Post-critical approaches are open to "emic"[2] accounts of a given group's own culture and, therefore, religion because "etic" models are ethnocentric, assuming a Western intellectual culture of criticism. Extending openness to the "other," conversely, allows emic readings of what is "other" in the West's own premodern inheritance, such as traditional theology and received doctrinal formulations. Anthropological, ethnographic, phenomenological, and hermeneutical insights and discoveries, together with attempts at the retrieval of earlier expressions of Christian ritual, have paved the way for liturgical theologians to challenge systematic approaches to the study of Christian teaching and theology. Post-critical approaches, therefore, turn away from epistemic models of objective knowledge to hermeneutical approaches of interpretation, and away from objective sources to phenomenologies of encounter.

SCHMEMANN'S *LITURGICAL THEOLOGY*

Alexander Schmemann was trained as a liturgical historian. His publication *Introduction to Liturgical Theology*,[3] which gave this new field its name, reads more like a history of the development of the Byzantine Rite than like a theological monograph. But this seminal book sets the trajectory for his own works and almost all the literature to go by the name "liturgical theology." These themes would develop into the more obviously theological works such as *Eucharist: Sacrament of the Kingdom*,[4] *For the Life of the World*,[5] and Schmemann's other seminal texts.[6]

One of Schmemann's key worries was what he considered a kind of "Westernification" of theology in the Eastern churches. He called this "scholasticism" and described its influence on the East as "scholasticising" tendencies:

---

[2] Cultural anthropology contrasts "emic," or indigenous, to "etic," or extrinsic, approaches to the study of human culture. I apply this terminology to the Christian "culture" of liturgy and ritual.
[3] Schmemann, *Introduction to Liturgical Theology*.
[4] Alexander Schmemann, *The Eucharist: Sacrament of the Kingdom*, trans. Paul Kachur (Crestwood, NY: St Vladimir's Seminary Press, 1988).
[5] Alexander Schmemann, *For the Life of the World: Sacraments and Orthodoxy*, 2nd rev. and expanded ed. (Crestwood, NY: St Vladimir's Seminary Press, 1982).
[6] Aleksander Schmemann, *Great Lent* (Crestwood, NY: St Vladimir's Seminary Press, 1974); Alexander Schmemann, *Of Water and the Spirit: A Liturgical Study of Baptism* (London: SPCK, 1976); Alexander Schmemann, *Liturgy and Tradition*, ed. Thomas Fisch (Crestwood, NY: St Vladimir's Seminary Press, 1990).

The neglect of liturgics, its acceptance as an applied science of interest for the most part to the clergy, but not to theologians, has been hardly accidental. It corresponded perfectly to that form of theology which is now called "school" theology, which in fact the Orthodox Church borrowed from the West .... [O]ur theology has for a long time been cut off from one of its most vital, most natural roots – from the liturgical tradition.[7]

Schmemann's concern was the way in which many theologians of the Eastern Churches were writing in a Western tone. His attempt to launch this field of liturgical theology was in one sense launching something new. But in another sense, he understood himself to be retrieving a more ancient mode of theological discourse that was more in accord with the spirit, the tone, and the traditional inheritance of the Eastern Churches.

Schmemann enters the debate concerning sources and methods of theology, eschewing the question altogether, through what could be described as a post-critical turn, something future liturgical theologians would clarify. In "Theology and Liturgical Tradition,"[8] Schmemann says that the liturgy,

> ... is not an "authority" or a *locus theologicus*, it is the ontological condition of theology, of the proper understanding of kerygma, of the Word of God, because it is in the church of which the *leitourgia* is the expression in life that the sources of theology are functioning precisely as sources.[9]

It is not so much that liturgy is one authoritative resource among others, such as the conciliar documents, creeds, and confessions, nor is it that liturgy is one focal point among many for spiritual and academic theological reflection ("theology of worship"). Rather, liturgy is the very point of contact with God and the divine economy for the body of Christ on earth – the ontological condition of anything Christian and, therefore, Christian discourse and theology. Schmemann intends a sacramental and liturgical realism when he says that liturgy is the "ontological condition of theology."

The liturgy is therefore, quite literally, the proper context of the proclamation of the Word of God. Thus, careful discursive reflection on the liturgy is the proper context for careful discursive reflection on

---

[7] Schmemann, *Introduction to Liturgical Theology*, 9–10.
[8] Alexander Schmemann, "Theology and Liturgical Tradition," in *Worship in Scripture and Tradition*, ed. Massey Shepherd (Oxford: Basil Blackwell, 1962).
[9] Ibid., 175.

Scripture. Because the liturgy, as ritual enactment of the Christian mystery, is the ground of the shared Christian life, it is the location and life of what systematic theologians would call the "sources" of theology. The liturgy sources theology as a dynamic enactment, not a phenomenon to get behind or under in order to discover a hidden object separate from the liturgy.

The "scholastic" approach to theology separated the rigorous discourse of the Church from the lived experience of the everyday Christian believer in a way that betrayed the depth of connection between Christian behavior and discourse. In *Eucharist: Sacrament of the Kingdom*, Schmemann asserts that "from the very beginning, we can see an obvious undoubted triunity of the *assembly*, the *eucharist* and the *Church* ... the fundamental task of liturgical theology consists therefore in uncovering the meaning and essence of this unity."[10] If the liturgy assembles the Church and makes a local body the corporate body of Christ, then reflection upon and contemplation of the liturgy itself is also a contemplation of the body of Christ.[11]

To reflect on the liturgy then, Schmemann would turn to recent liturgical historical reconstructions of what would come to be called the *ordo* – a discovered "shape" of Christian liturgy. Liturgical historians at that time believed they had discovered that Christian liturgy had some fundamental shapes shared across many different liturgical traditions, the *ordo* – potentially pointing to shared genetic origins of Christian liturgy.[12] The relative historical veracity of such reconstructions notwithstanding, the real brilliance of discerning a shape to liturgy as a form of human ritual behavior was that one could not just study the inherited verbal traditions of the liturgy or, say, inherited practices, such as what vestment you might wear or when you might pour the water into the wine at the Eucharist, but also see fundamental overarching shapes to the ritual action. One could therefore study the Christian liturgy the way that an anthropologist might study the ritual behavior of indigenous people and see in those shapes archetypal meaning just as significant if not more so than the surface-level concrete words used to achieve the liturgical action.

---

[10] Schmemann, *The Eucharist*, 11–12.
[11] Schmemann's views were clearly formed by *ressourcement*, especially Henri de Lubac. In his work, *Corpus Mysticum*, de Lubac uncovered the true body of Christ as the assembled gathering of Christians' Christ Corporate Body. Henri de Lubac, *Corpus Mysticum: The Eucharist and the Church in the Middle Ages: Historical Survey*, (Notre Dame, IN: University of Notre Dame, 2007).
[12] Dom Gregory Dix, *The Shape of the Liturgy* (London: T & T Clark, 2015).

When the Christian liturgy forms the local Christian body into the body of Christ on earth, and the liturgy has a shape that is shared across traditions deeper than any set of surface-level denotations of words, then the theologian can meditate on that shape to discern the shape of the body of Christ. Reflection on the shape of the ritual behavior allows a return to reflection on the words of a given tradition and to elucidation of them as speech acts within a ritual context. For Schmemann, the liturgy does not point beyond itself. Instead, it enacts transcendent and, importantly, eschatological realities.

When the church no longer has a living encounter with the manifestation of God and the divine economy through the ritual mysteries of the church, then it is easy for the church to fall into a stiff or rigid historicism, understanding doctrine to be a set of inherited propositions that must be passed on. In his criticism of these Westernizing tendencies in the Eastern Church, Schmemann of course is also criticizing Western theology. Whether or not his critique of Western theology is entirely fair is a separate question. What is certainly the case is that Western liturgical scholars, influenced by Schmemann, began to have similar insights as they received his criticism of their own recently inherited theological approaches.

THE WESTERN RECEPTION OF LITURGICAL THEOLOGY

Just as Schmemann tried to purge what he considered Westernizing, or scholasticizing, tendencies from being the predominant mode of theological discourse in the East, liturgical theologians in the West try not so much to replace as to provide a corrective to systematic theology as the predominant and assumed proper mode of theology in the West. Thus, Western liturgical theologians are critiquing the modern theological reception of their own inherited theological tradition.

Aidan Kavanagh's *On Liturgical Theology*

In his seminal work, *On Liturgical Theology*, Aidan Kavanagh would coin the phrase, *theologia prima*. Kavanagh argues that,

> The theology which we most readily recognize in practice is in fact neither primary nor seminal, but secondary and derivative, *theologia secunda*. Doing liturgical theology comes closer to doing *theologia prima* than *theologia secunda* or a theology of the liturgy. And doing primary theology places a whole set of

requirements on the theologian, which are not quite the same as those placed on a theologian who does only secondary theology.[13]

Kavanagh here contrasts secondary to primary theology, derivative theology to the actual source of theology, which is the living enactment of the mysteries of faith in the inherited liturgy of the Church. As a Roman Catholic, Kavanagh had a different relationship to what Schmemann called scholastic theology and its place within the Western tradition. Kavanagh instead made the distinction between primary and secondary theology.

A liturgical act is a theological act. The truism "actions speak louder than words" applies just as well to ritual behavior and liturgy. Look at what the assembled community is doing, rather than what it is saying, at least at first. The consistent ritual pattern provides the context for making sense of what the liturgical assembly is doing, and that, then, provides depth of context to any words they are saying as part of that ritual action.

To make his point, Kavanagh would come up with a metaphor. He named her *Mrs. Murphy*. When Kavanagh makes the distinction between *theologia secunda* and *theologia prima*, he talks about the difference between what an academically trained theologian might say in an academic scholarly paper compared to what Mrs. Murphy was encountering, simply by being a faithful member of her congregation.[14] His point is that the primary action of theology for Christians is a full participation in the liturgical assembly.[15] Secondary theology, rigorous academic intellectual discussion, flows from the encounter with God granted through the liturgy and is also in service to the liturgy and the faith community.[16]

David Faberberg's *What Is Liturgical Theology?*

Also Roman Catholic, David Fagerberg in his work *What Is Liturgical Theology?*[17] carries Kavanagh's insights forward. Agreeing with

---

[13] Aidan Kavanagh, *On Liturgical Theology* (Collegeville, MN: Pueblo, 1992), 75.
[14] Mrs. Murphy becomes the hypothetical example of theology beginning from the full liturgical participation of the faithful, the goal of liturgical renewal, especially for the Roman Catholic Church.
[15] Some worry, is Mrs. Murphy only bourgeois? Perhaps, but not necessarily. Kavanagh's more fundamental point is that we are to look at the ordinary faithful of any local Christian gathering and ask for their encounter. Mrs. Murphy can become anyone and thus move beyond social and geographic location as a tool for asking immediately germane questions.
[16] The contrast between *theologia prima* and *theologia secunda* is similar to Lindbeck's famous analogy of theology – or, better, doctrine – to language as a kind of grammar of faith.
[17] David W. Fagerberg, *What Is Liturgical Theology? A Study in Methodology* (Collegeville, MN: Liturgical Press, 1992).

Kavanagh about the distinction between *theologia prima* and *theologia secunda*, and also taking up the anecdote of Mrs. Murphy, Fagerberg presses the point that liturgical theology is not merely a theology of worship, a systematic theological exposition of what worship or liturgy is or ought to be, nor is it merely pious reflection on a given liturgy. Rather, given the nature of the inherent shape of the liturgy, the very performance of liturgical action *is* theology.

Fagerberg's point is that every enactment of the Christian liturgy is itself an act of Christian theology. In fact, it is the primary act of Christian theology. Fagerberg also draws out a phrase that will become important to the ongoing task of the church called theology: *lex orandi, lex credendi*, which is sometimes loosely translated from the Latin as "the law of prayer is the law of faith" or "the rule of prayer is the rule of belief."[18] This is a shortening or abbreviation of a longer phrase found in the writings of the church father Prosper of Aquitaine, who said, *legem credendi lex statuat supplicandi*, or "let the law of prayer establish the law of belief":[19]

> Liturgical action is theological. This is already real theology even though it is performed communally by people who do not speak the language of the scholar's guild. In the Church's *lex orandi* theology happens, and that makes it the ontological basis for the Church's expression of herself in *lex credendi*.[20]

As interpreted by Fagerberg, Prosper's phrase places an emphasis on the way in which the ritual action of the liturgy is a ritual behavioral pattern that precedes discursive articulation of Christian belief. This is understood to be, or used as a Christian way of saying, what cultural anthropologists intend by the phrase *creed follows cult*.[21] Human behavior precedes discursive accounts of behavior, especially when it

---

[18] Drawing from the Methodist liturgical scholar and liturgical theologian Geoffrey Wainwright and others. Geoffrey Wainwright, *Doxology: The Praise of God in Worship, Doctrine, and Life: A Systematic Theology* (Oxford: Oxford University Press, 1980).

[19] Since this writing, Maxwell Johnson's important recontextualization of this quotation radically relativizes the use of the phrase. Maxwell E. Johnson, "Liturgy and Theology," in *Liturgy in Dialogue: Essays in Memory of Ronald Jasper*, ed. Paul F. Bradshaw and Bryan D. Spinks (Collegeville, MN: Liturgical Press, 1993), 203–7. See Paul De Clerck, "'Lex orandi, lex credendi': The Original Sense and Historical Avatars of an Equivocal Adage," *Studia Liturgica*, 24 (1994): 178–200.

[20] Fagerberg, *What Is Liturgical Theology?*, 45.

[21] Leonel L. Mitchell, *Praying Shapes Believing: A Theological Commentary on the Book of Common Prayer*, 2nd ed. (Harrisburg, PA: Morehouse, 1991).

comes to things deep within the culture, such as a ritual. Ritual behavior precedes the discursive account of the ritual behavior. Many cultural anthropologists and anthropological historians point out that the ritual behavior of a group of people precedes the myths that are understood to correspond to those behaviors.[22] *Lex orandi, lex credendi*, the practice and *ordo* of the gathered Christian assembly precedes formal articulations of Christian belief.

Here we see a way in which liturgical theology is another example of the post-critical turn. The modern, critical theologian attempts to achieve objectivity in theology by taking concrete, especially dogmatic, statements of the church as factual data points and adopting the correct methodology to derive objectivity according to the goals of the criteria of truth defined by modernity. The post-critical liturgical theologian instead turns to the gathered assembly and their enactment of a ritual mystery as something that eschews the need for methodology altogether, where participation in the corporate body and its ritual behavior places us in contact with Christian realities. Ontological participation displaces a need to overcome the divide between subject and object. In these ways, Kavanagh and Fagerberg take a more deeply post-critical turn than Schmemann, extending and amplifying his work.

Gordon Lathrop's Juxtaposition

Gordon Lathrop, a Lutheran, is a key figure in the adoption of liturgical theology by Protestants. Just as Kavanagh and Fagerberg developed the language of *theologia prima* and a focus on Mrs. Murphy and *lex orandi, lex credendi*, so too Lathrop has contributed to the field of liturgical theology the important approach of noting what he calls "juxtaposition" in Christian ritual behavior.[23] By "juxtaposition," Lathrop calls attention to contrasts found within the Christian liturgy:

> Start with the simple things, the common human materials, then see how communal meaning occurs as these things are juxtaposed to each other and gathered together with speech about the promise of God. In this way, the assembly and the materials it uses become a rich locus of meaning, casting light on all common life and summed

---

[22] Walter Burkert, *Greek Religion* (Cambridge, MA: Harvard University Press, 1985).
[23] Gordon Lathrop, *Holy Things: A Liturgical Theology* (Minneapolis, MN: Fortress Press, 1993). Developed into a trilogy of books, including *Holy People: A Liturgical Ecclesiology* and *Holy Ground: A Liturgical Cosmology*.

up in the shorthand of such technical words as "baptism" and "eucharist."[24]

When we find a deep and seemingly mutually conflicting or contradictory thing within the ritual enactment of the liturgy, we find a flashpoint at which we are able to discern liturgical theology. For example, Christians gather to celebrate "communion." What the congregations present on the table are bread and wine, everyday food. But the minister who delivers them to the faithful says these odd words: "This is the body of Christ; this is the blood of Christ." Thus ordinary food is placed in juxtaposition with extraordinary words. In this juxtaposition of seemingly ordinary things with divine things, we have a divine encounter through the liturgy.

Juxtaposition extends further to the *ordo* as a whole and back to particulars, again, in a kind of liturgical hermeneutic circle. In reflecting on these juxtapositions, we are able to develop a liturgical theology – in this case, a liturgical theology within a Protestant,[25] and especially Lutheran, context.[26] Lathrop's hermeneutic of juxtaposition furthers the post-critical turn of liturgical theology away from supposed theological objectivity toward a phenomenology of liturgical encounter.

Non-Liturgical Traditions and Liturgical Theology

One question concerns liturgical theology for non-liturgical Christian traditions, especially those Protestant traditions that historically have deliberately rejected formal liturgy.[27] It is the case that there is a difference between liturgical and non-liturgical Christian traditions, and that difference implies that there are certain things in common among liturgical Christians that are not shared with non-liturgical Christians. Liturgical theology, or some core aspects of it, may be one of those things.

Most Protestant and non-liturgical Protestant traditions have a "theology of worship," and in sacramental Protestant traditions sacramental theology. But the approach of liturgical theology is not obvious

---

[24] Lathrop, *Holy Things*, 11.
[25] It is important to note that, alongside Lutheran receptions of liturgical theology, the Anglican tradition is another deliberately liturgical Protestant tradition, with theologians such as Louis Weil and Lionel Mitchell adopting liturgical theology. Methodism also retains liturgical expression, with theologians such as Don Saliers adopting liturgical theology.
[26] Juxtapositioning as an approach to liturgical theology forms a neat analogue to the Lutheran hermeneutic of law–gospel contrast in biblical interpretation.
[27] Cf. Melanie C. Ross's discussion in Chapter 4.

in Protestant, and especially non-liturgical Protestant, traditions. In Protestantism, the Bible is the sole source of theological authority. Because of this, worship usually remains a practical consideration, something that is developed as a result of reflections on biblical texts and thus comes after theological work. Worship is subordinate to theology when construed in these ways. It is difficult for such traditions to move to worship as a post-critical context for theology and biblical interpretation.

There are many non-liturgical traditions that have taken on the insight of liturgical theology that the gathering of the corporate body of Christ and its formal, shared active worship are the inherent grounds of theology. There has been a move among some non-liturgical theologians to adopt some of the features of liturgical theology and bring it to their own acts of corporate and formal worship. They adopt these features not simply as a locus for theological reflection but rather as a source and context for the so-called methods and sources of theology to work at all.

These non-liturgical Protestant theologians have adopted and adapted liturgical theology within their own contexts, placing the ground and context for theological reflection within the formal gathering of worship. For example, in *Liturgical Theology: The Church as Worshiping Community*,[28] Simon Chan critiques his own non-liturgical tradition from a liturgical theological stance, inviting his coreligionists to reconsider the role and place of liturgy in their own formal, corporate acts of worship.[29]

HISTORIANS' CRITICISMS OF LITURGICAL THEOLOGY

Although derived from liturgical historiography, liturgical theology as it developed, especially after Schmemann, quickly came under fire from liturgical historians. Historians of liturgy[30] became concerned, first, that liturgical theology as a discipline was growing increasingly

---

[28] Simon Chan, *Liturgical Theology: The Church as Worshiping Community* (Downers Grove, IL: IVP Academic, 2006).

[29] Other liturgical theologians of note from non-liturgical traditions include Melanie Ross, *Evangelical versus Liturgical?: Defying a Dichotomy* (Grand Rapids, MI: Eerdmans, 2014); Christopher J. Ellis, *Gathering: A Spirituality and Theology of Worship in Free Church Tradition* (London: SCM Press, 2004).

[30] A key example would be M. B. Aune, "The Current State of Liturgical Theology: A Plurality of Particularities," in *St Vladimir's Theological Quarterly* 53 (2009): 48. See also Maxwell Johnson and Paul Bradshaw's works, respectively.

groundless because it was becoming too distant from its historiographical moorings. To give one example, historians worried that the phrase *lex orandi, lex credendi* is applied in a misleading way, asking, does prayer really precede belief in the historical record? Historically, it is clearly not always and perhaps not often the case. Historians can easily show concrete cases where the development of belief in any tradition, especially in the Christian tradition, led to changes in worship.

At the core of these historical concerns is the apprehension that liturgical theology cuts itself off from concrete historical liturgies. Focus on the *ordo* keeps the "liturgy" a pure abstraction, never connecting with any historical instance or tradition. Related to the historical concern, there is also an anthropological concern that focusing on an abstraction ignores actual ritual enactments of a local Christian gathering. They worried about the extent of the validity of theological reflection on an *ordo* wide enough to embrace the anaphora of Addai and Mari, the Roman Mass, and the Methodist Book of Worship. In short, the worry is that liturgical theology is so abstract that it never connects with any lived encounter or concrete liturgical tradition. If this were true, it would, of course, be disastrous for liturgical theology and would undermine the discipline itself.

Another theological concern is that liturgical theology reduces Jesus and the incarnation to the gathered community, and God's action to ritual action. This immanentizing of the divine would take away the utter transcendence of God, reducing our contact with God to something that can easily be manipulated or performed as human beings through ritual behavior. The reduction of the divine and the transcendent to something immanent and human would be an idolatrous mistake in the context of Christian theology. The discipline of liturgical theology must strictly avoid both problems.

LITURGICAL REALISM AS POST-CRITICAL TURN

Under conditions of post-criticism, we cannot assume there is no transcendence and no contact with transcendence as described in indigenous, and even traditional Western, cultures.[31] The liturgical traditions received by the various liturgical churches can become for us a way through which human behavior shares in and participates in God. This

---

[31] Gavin Flood's work provides an excellent example of the extension of the post-critical turn into religious studies in general. Gavin D. Flood, *The Ascetic Self: Subjectivity, Memory, and Tradition* (Cambridge: Cambridge University Press, 2004).

is what is meant by *theologia prima*: The enactment of the ritual *ordo* is itself the primary example of the Christian body, in this case the corporate Christian body, contemplating God.

Liturgical theology assumes a sacramental or liturgical realism. Most modern historiography assumes a background metaphysical commitment to nominalism, holding that concrete particulars count as the only real thing. In the case of a liturgical realism, the difference between the shape or *ordo* of the liturgy and any given historic or local instance of liturgical action is that of archetype to manifestation rather than that of mere human abstraction to concrete particular. When the local and the historical instance is understood as a concrete manifestation of an archetype or shape, then the historical and the local can be taken seriously without losing the insights gained from placing weight on the *ordo*. The *ordo* is a logical, not chronological, reality – a ritual logic, not an historical event. Studying the structure of Christian liturgical action, phenomenologically and hermeneutically, is not separate from historical knowledge, but its goals differ from the goals of critical historiography.

The concerns to which recent historians have drawn attention regarding liturgical theology are vital in making sure that reflection on liturgy does not float free from the lived experience of a local gathered community – especially if this living experience is outside the bounds of the privileged class. It is essential that all liturgical theology as a scholarly field attend to the lived experience of the Christian faithful regardless of class or privilege. In turn, liturgical realism can help save historiography from the kind of particularism that may lead to washing out any unifying theme that defines a single thing called liturgy, both as a field of study and as the lived encounter with God through shared ritual action on the part of the faithful.

If any concrete human enactment of the liturgy is the manifestation of and a participation in a transcendent or heavenly and eschatological reality, then the liturgical theologian is not making the mistake of assuming that a human action can capture God. Rather, the theologian accepts the mystery that human actions – such as the ritual worship of the living God – become opportunities for participating in the life of the living God and God's actions within the created order. God in Christ is the agent of Christian ritual mysteries, not the gathering as merely human per se.

Assuming a strong sacramental realism, liturgical theology asserts the grounds of the possibility for sources and methods of theology, of knowledge of God, in this world to be possible for us at all. The adoption of a thoroughgoing metaphysical realism may not prove necessary, but a sacramental realism is certainly necessary for liturgical theology to function as such. Any commitment to sacramental or liturgical realism demands for its study and application the approach and work that liturgical theology brings.

LITURGICAL THEOLOGY AS RETRIEVAL OF MYSTAGOGY

Liturgical theology can be understood as a post-critical retrieval of what the ancients called "mystagogy." Mystagogy is the initiation into the Christian faith through the ritual mysteries, especially the ritual mysteries of Baptism and the Holy Eucharist. In the early Church, we find numerous attestations throughout the Mediterranean Christian world that, immediately after the culmination of catechesis and the ritual initiation of the faithful through Baptism, the continued instruction of the faithful would follow in catechetical mystagogy.[32] Catechetical mystagogy forms the discursive counterpart to the ritual initiation of mystagogy, proper, when the bishop or pastor led the faithful into a more discursive and mental understanding of the ontological realities they had encountered through ritual initiation.

Mystagogy as manifestation of God and participation of the initiate in the divine action of Christ corresponds to Kavanagh's and Fagerberg's *theologia prima*. Mystagogical catechesis as the extension of initiation into discursive teaching corresponds to liturgical theology as a field of theological reflection. Understanding liturgical theology as a post-critical retrieval of mystagogy, we find a trajectory in more recent liturgical theological scholarship of identifying theology with *ressourcement*'s tripartite definition of theology as (the doctrine of) the Trinity, contemplation, and exegesis;[33] that is to say, theology is the contemplation of the triune God in Scripture.

Fagerberg has moved into areas of liturgical theology that explore the relationship of liturgy to dogmatic theology, offering a *Liturgical Dogmatics*.[34] The liturgy itself is a ritual enactment and ritual

---

[32] Enrico Mazza is an important figure in the retrieval of mystagogy as liturgical theology. Enrico Mazza, *Mystagogy: A Theology of Liturgy in the Patristic Age* (New York: Pueblo, 1989).

[33] This tripartite definition of the nature of Christian theology is most clearly articulated in the works of Henri de Lubac, especially *The Mystery of the Supernatural*, *Medieval Exegesis*, and *Corpus Mysticum*.

[34] David W. Fagerberg, *Liturgical Dogmatics: How Catholic Beliefs Flow from Liturgical Prayer* (San Francisco, CA: Ignatius Press, 2021).

initiation into the life of the triune God. It also provides the behavioral and ritual context for sound discursive reflection on Christian doctrine. In liturgical worship Christians encounter a triune God praying to the Father through the Son by the gift of the Spirit.

Fagerberg has also moved in the direction of contemplative theology and the way that liturgy forms and tunes up corporate bodies (and, correspondingly, asceticism forms and tunes up corporal, individual, Christian bodies) to participate fully in, and therefore understand, God and God's creation.[35] The liturgy is one of the chief forms of Christian contemplation. In turn, contemplation of the liturgy, as such, guides our discursive theology. To put it in Schmemann's terms, the liturgy provides the condition of the possibility for the sources and methods of theology to function at all.

Lathrop, who gave us "juxtaposition," has also returned to his own formal training in historical critical biblical scholarship and has given us modes and approaches to a liturgical exegesis, a liturgical reading of holy scripture.[36] Liturgy is itself the chief Christian interpretation of Scripture, and simultaneously it provides the central context of an ecclesial and therefore authoritative interpretation of scripture for the faithful. Catechetical mystagogy is a sacramental realist exegesis of Scripture, where the catechist guides the faithful to understand their ritual initiation as initiation into the realities described in Scripture.

These three approaches – the doctrine of the Trinity and its dogmatic exposition, contemplation and asceticism, exegesis and the interpretation of Scripture – represent at least three of the ways in which liturgical theology continues to speak to academic theology as a post-critical retrieval of mystagogy. Christianity is a religion of ritual initiation into mysteries. Liturgical theology can move forward through a post-critical retrieval of mystagogy, addressing historical criticisms and advancing its engagement with systematic and dogmatic theology.

For Further Reading

Carvalhaes, Cláudio, *Liturgy in Postcolonial Perspectives: Only One is Holy* (Basingstoke: Palgrave Macmillan, 2015).

Chan, Simon, *Liturgical Theology: The Church as Worshiping Community* (Downers Grove, IL: IVP Academic, 2006).

---

[35] David W. Fagerberg, *On Liturgical Asceticism* (Washington, DC: Catholic University of America Press, 2013).

[36] Gordon W. Lathrop, *Saving Images: The Presence of the Bible in Christian Liturgy* (Minneapolis, MN: Fortress Press, 2017).

Fagerberg, David W., *What Is Liturgical Theology?: A Study in Methodology* (Collegeville, MN: Liturgical Press, 1992).

Fennema, Sharon R., W. Scott Haldeman, and Stephen Burns, *Queering Christian Worship: Reconstructing Liturgical Theology* (New York: Seabury Books, 2023).

Geldhof, Joris, *Liturgical Theology as a Research Program* (Leiden: Brill, 2020).

Jennings, Nathan G., *Liturgy and Theology: Economy and Reality* (Eugene, OR: Cascade Books, 2017).

Kavanagh, Aidan, *On Liturgical Theology: The Hale Memorial Lectures of Seabury-Western Theological Seminary, 1981* (Collegeville, MN: Pueblo, 1984).

Lathrop, Gordon W., *Holy Things: A Liturgical Theology* (Minneapolis, MN: Fortress Press, 1993).

Mazza, Enrico, *Mystagogy: A Theology of Liturgy in the Patristic Age* (New York: Pueblo, 1989).

Schmemann, Aleksander, *The Eucharist: Sacrament of the Kingdom*. Trans. Paul Kachur. Crestwood, NY: St Vladimir's Seminary Press, 1988.

Introduction to Liturgical Theology (Portland, ME: American Orthodox Press, 1966).

Vogel, Dwight W., (ed.), *Primary Sources of Liturgical Theology: A Reader* (Collegeville, MN: Liturgical Press, 2000).

Bibliography

Adam, Adolf, *The Liturgical Year: Its History and Its Meaning after the Reform of the Liturgy*, trans. Matthew J. O'Connell (New York: Pueblo, 1981).
Afanassieff, Nicolas, *The Church of the Holy Spirit* (Notre Dame, IN: University of Notre Dame Press, 2007).
Alexopoulos, Stefanos, and Maxwell E. Johnson, *Introduction to Eastern Christian Liturgies* (Collegeville, MN: Liturgical Press, 2022).
Allmen, Jean-Jacques von, *Preaching and Congregation*, Ecumenical Studies in Worship 10, trans. B. L. Nicholas (Louisville, KY: John Knox Press, 1962).
Asad, Talal, *Genealogies of Religion: Discipline and Reasons of Power in Christianity and Islam* (Baltimore, MD: Johns Hopkins University Press, 1993).
Bacchiocchi, Samuele, *From Sabbath to Sunday: A Historical Investigation of the Rise of Sunday Observance in Early Christianity* (Rome: Pontifical Gregorian University Press, 1977).
Bainton, Roland H., *Women of the Reformation, from Spain to Scandinavia* (Minneapolis, MN: Augsburg Publishing House, 1977).
   Women of the Reformation in France and England (Minneapolis, MN: Augsburg Publishing House, 1973).
   Women of the Reformation in Germany and Italy (Minneapolis, MN: Augsburg Publishing House, 1971).
Barnard, Marcel, Johan Cilliers, and Cas Wepener (eds.), *Worship in the Network Culture: Liturgical Ritual Studies. Fields and Methods, Concepts and Metaphors*, Liturgia Condenda 28 (Leuven: Peeters, 2014).
Bärsch, Jürgen, and Kranemann, Benedikt (eds.), *Geschichte der Liturgie in den Kirchen des Westens. Rituelle Entwicklungen, theologische Konzepte und kulturelle Kontexte*, 2 vols. (Münster: Aschendorff, 2018).
Belcher, Kimberly Hope, "Ritual Systems: Prostration, Self, and Community in the Rule of Benedict," *Ecclesia Orans* 37 (2020): 321–56.
Bell, Catherine M., *Ritual: Perspectives and Dimensions* (New York: Oxford University Press, 1997).
Berger, Teresa, *Liturgie und Frauenseele: Die liturgische Bewegung aus der Sicht der Frauenforschung* (Stuttgart: Verlag W. Kohlhammer, 1993).
Bonaccorso, Giorgio, *L'estetica del rito: Sentire Dio nell'arte* (Cinisello Balsamo: Edizioni San Paolo: 2013).
Botte, Bernard, *From Silence to Participation: An Insider's View of Liturgical Renewal*, trans. John Sullivan (Washington, DC: The Pastoral Press, 1988).

Botte, Bernard, and Mgr Cassien (eds.), *La prière des heures* (Paris: Cerf, 1963).
Bouyer, Louis, *Architecture et liturgie* (Paris: Cerf, 2009).
Eucharist: Theology and Spirituality of the Eucharistic Prayer, trans. Charles U. Quinn (Notre Dame, IN: University of Notre Dame Press, 2006).
Bradshaw, Paul F., *Daily Prayer in the Early Church: A Study of the Origin and Early Development of the Divine Office* (Eugene, OR: Wipf & Stock, 2008).
"Liturgy and 'Living Literature'," in *Liturgy in Dialogue: Essays in Memory of Ronald Jasper*, ed. Bradshaw Paul F. and Bryan Spinks (London: SPCK, 1994), 138–53.
The Search for the Origins of Christian Worship: Sources and Methods for the Study of Early Liturgy (London: SPCK, 2002).
Bradshaw, Paul F., and Maxwell E. Johnson, *The Origins of Feasts, Fasts and Seasons in Early Christianity* (London and Collegeville, MN: SPCK and Liturgical Press, 2011).
Bricout, Hélène, and Martin Klöckener (dir.), *Liturgie, pensée théologique et mentalités religieuses au haut Moyen Âge: Le témoignage des sources liturgiques*, LQF 106 (Münster: Aschendorff, 2016).
Brovelli, Franco, *Ritorno alla liturgia: Saggi di studio sul movimento liturgico* (Rome: Edizioni Liturgiche, 1989).
Brueggeman, Walter, *The Prophetic Imagination*, 40th anniversary ed. (Minneapolis, MN: Fortress Press, 2013).
Buchinger, Harald, "Liturgiegeschichte im Umbruch: Fallbeispiele aus der Alten Kirche," in *Dynamik und Diversität des Gottesdienstes. Liturgiegeschichte in neuem Licht*, ed. Albert Gerhards and Benedikt Kranemann (Freiburg: Herder, 2018), 152–84.
Budde, Achim, *Gemeinsame Tagzeiten: Motivation – Organisation – Gestaltung*: Praktische Theologie heute 96 (Stuttgart: Kohlhammer, 2013).
Bugnini, Annibale, *The Reform of the Liturgy 1948–1975*, trans. Matthew J. O'Connell (Collegeville, MN: Liturgical Press, 1990).
Bukovec, Predrag, *Die frühchristliche Eucharistie* (Tübingen: Mohr Siebeck, 2023).
Bynum, Caroline Walker, *Holy Feast and Holy Fast: The Religious Significance of Food to Medieval Women* (Berkeley, CA: University of California Press, 1987).
Campbell, Stanislaus, *From Breviary to Liturgy of the Hours: The Structural Reform of the Roman Office, 1964–1971* (Collegeville, MN: Liturgical Press, 1995).
Carnes, Natalie, *Image and Presence: A Christological Reflection on Iconoclasm and Iconophilia* (Stanford, CA: Stanford University Press, 2017).
Carvalhaes, Cláudio, *Eucharist and Globalization: Redrawing the Borders of Eucharistic Hospitality* (Eugene, OR: Pickwick Publications, 2013).
Liturgy in Postcolonial Perspectives: Only One Is Holy (Basingstoke: Palgrave Macmillan, 2015).
Praying with Every Heart: Orienting Our Lives to the Wholeness of the World (Eugene, OR: Cascade Books, 2021).
Chan, Simon, *Liturgical Theology: The Church as Worshiping Community* (Downers Grove, IL: IVP Academic, 2006).

Chauvet, Louis-Marie, *Symbol and Sacrament: Sacramental Reinterpretation of Christian Existence*, trans. Madeleine Beaumont (Collegeville, MN: Liturgical Press, 1994).

Chauvet, Louis-Marie, and François Kabasele Lumbala (eds.), *Concilium 1995/3: Liturgy and the Body*.

Cheetham, David, "Ritualising the Secular? Inter-Religious Meetings in the 'Immanent Frame'," *Heythrop Journal* 60 (2019): 383–96.

Chupungco, Anscar J., "The Liturgical Year: The Gospel Encountering Culture," *Studia Liturgica* 40 (2010): 46–64.

  What, Then, Is Liturgy? Musings and Memoir (Collegeville, MN: Liturgical Press, 2010).

Cooke, Bernard, *Sacraments and Sacramentality* (Mystic, CT: Twenty-Third, 1994/2004).

Covington, Sarah, and Kathryn Reklis (eds.), *Protestant Aesthetics and the Arts* (London: Routledge, 2020).

Daelemans, Bert, *Spiritus Loci: A Theological Method for Contemporary Church Architecture* (Leiden: Brill, 2015).

Dahill, Lisa E., Jim B. Martin-Schramm, and Bill McKibben, *Eco-Reformation: Grace and Hope for a Planet in Peril* (Eugene, OR: Wipf & Stock, 2016).

Dandelion, Pink, *The Liturgies of Quakerism* (Aldershot: Ashgate, 2005).

Day, Juliette, *Reading the Liturgy: An Exploration of Texts in Christian Worship* (London: Bloomsbury, 2014).

D'Costa, Gavin. "Interreligious Prayer between Christians and Muslims," *Islam & Christian–Muslim Relations* 24 (2013): 1–14.

Debuyst, Frédéric, *Le génie chrétien du lieu* (Paris: Cerf, 1997).

Depoortere, Kristiaan, "From Sacramentality to Sacraments and Vice Versa," in *Contemporary Sacramental Contours of a God Incarnate*, ed. Lieven Boeve and Lambert Leijssen (Leuven: Peeters, 2001).

De Zan, Renato, "Criticism and Interpretation of Liturgical Texts," in *Handbook for Liturgical Studies, vol. 1: Introduction to the Liturgy*, ed. Anscar J. Chupungco (Collegeville, MN: Liturgical Press, 1997), 331–65.

Drouin, Gilles (ed.), *L'espace liturgique, un espace d'initiation* (Paris: Cerf, 2019).

Dyrness, William A., *The Origins of Protestant Aesthetics in Early Modern Europe: Calvin's Reformation Poetics* (Cambridge: Cambridge University Press, 2019).

Eary, Mark, *Worship That Cares: An Introduction to Pastoral Liturgy* (London: Hymns Ancient & Modern Ltd, 2012).

Eire, Carlos M. N., *War Against the Idols: The Reformation of Worship from Erasmus to Calvin* (Cambridge: Cambridge University Press, 1986).

Ellis, Christopher J., *Gathering: A Theology and Spirituality of Worship in Free Church Tradition* (London: SCM Press, 2004).

Fagerberg, David W., *Liturgical Mysticism* (Steubenville, OH: Emmaus Academic, 2019).

  On Liturgical Asceticism (Washington, DC: The Catholic University of America Press, 2013).

  Theologia Prima: What Is Liturgical Theology? (Chicago: Hillenbrand Books, 2004).

Fennema, Sharon R., W. Scott Haldeman, and Stephen Burns, *Queering Christian Worship: Reconstructing Liturgical Theology* (New York: Seabury Books, 2023).
Ferguson, Everett, *Baptism in the Early Church: History, Theology, and Liturgy in the First Five Centuries* (Grand Rapids, MI: Eerdmans, 2009).
Foley, Edward, John F. Baldovin, Mary Collins, and Joanne M. Pierce (eds.), *A Commentary on the Order of Mass of The Roman Missal* (Collegeville, MN: Liturgical Press, 2011).
Foley, Edward, Nathan D. Mitchell, and Joanne M. Pierce (eds.), *A Commentary on the General Instruction of The Roman Missal* (Collegeville, MN: Liturgical Press, 2007).
Frank, Georgia, *The Memory of the Eyes: Pilgrims to Living Saints in Christian Antiquity* (Berkeley, CA: University of California Press, 2000).
Gavrilyuk, Paul, and Sarah Coakley (eds.), *Religion and the Body* (Cambridge: Cambridge University Press, 1997).
Geldhof, Joris, *Liturgical Theology as a Research Program* (Leiden: Brill, 2020).
  Liturgy and Secularism: Beyond the Divide (Collegeville, MN: Liturgical Press, 2018).
  "The Philosophical Presuppositions and Implications of Celebrating the Liturgical Year," *Studia Liturgica* 40 (2010): 197–207.
Gelineau, Joseph, *Dans vos assemblées: Manuel de pastorale liturgique* (Paris: Desclée, 1989).
  Les chants de la messe dans leur enracinement rituel (Paris: Cerf, 2001).
Getcha, Job, *Participants de la nature divine: La spiritualité orthodoxe à l'âge de la sécularisation* (Paris: Apostolia, 2020).
Giraudo, Cesare, *In Unum Corpus: Traité mystagogique sur l'Eucharistie*, trans. Éric Iborra and Pierre-Marie Hombert (Paris: Cerf, 2014).
Gittos, Helen, and Sarah Hamilton (eds.), *Understanding Medieval Liturgy: Essays in Interpretation* (Burlington, VT: Ashgate, 2016).
Glibetić, Nina, "History of Orthodox Worship," in *Historical Foundations of Worship: Catholic, Orthodox, and Protestant Perspectives*, ed. Melanie Ross and Mark Lamport (Grand Rapids, MI: Baker Academic, 2022), 85–97.
The Global Luther: A Theologian for Modern Times, ed. Christine Helmer (Minneapolis, MN: Fortress, 2009).
Goyvaerts, Samuel, "Moving between Liturgical Theology and Liturgical Pastoral: On Theology, Liturgy, and Christian Life," *Questions Liturgiques* 100 (2020): 294–312.
Grillo, Andrea, *Eucaristia: Azione rituale, forme storiche, essenza sistematica* (Brescia: Queriniana, 2019).
Grüter, Verena, *Klang – Raum – Religion: Ästhetische Dimensionen interreligiöser Begegnung am Beispiel des Festivals Musica Sacra International* (Zurich: Theologischer Verlag Zürich, 2017).
Hahn, Cynthia, *Strange Beauty: Issues in the Making and Meaning of Reliquaries, 400–circa 1204* (University Park: Penn State University Press, 2013).

Harmon, Katharine E., *There Were Also Many Women There: Lay Women in the Liturgical Movement in the United States, 1926–59* (Collegeville, MN: Liturgical Press, 2013).

Harper, John, *The Forms and Orders of the Western Liturgy from the Tenth to the Eighteenth Century: A Historical Introduction and Guide for Students and Musicians* (Oxford: Clarendon Press, 1991).

Heil, Uta (ed.), *From Sun-Day to the Lord's Day: The Cultural History of Sunday in Late Antiquity and the Early Middle Ages* (Turnhout: Brepols, 2022).

Hoffman, Lawrence A., *Beyond the Text: A Holistic Approach to Liturgy. Jewish Literature and Culture* (Bloomington, IN: Indiana University Press, 1995).

Holcomb, Justin S., and David A. Johnson (eds.), *Christian Theologies of the Sacraments: A Comparative Introduction* (New York: New York University Press, 2017).

Iogna-Prat, Dominique, *Cité de Dieu, cité des hommes: L'Eglise, l'architecture et la société* (Paris: Presses Universitaires de France, 2016).

Irving, Andrew J. M., and Harald Buchinger (eds.), *On the Typology of Liturgical Books from the Western Middle Ages. Zur Typologie liturgischer Bücher des westlichen Mittelalters*, LQF 115 (Münster: Aschendorff, 2023).

Irving, Andrew J. M., and Daniel DiCenso (eds.), *Medieval Latin Liturgy: A Research Guide* (Leiden: Brill, forthcoming).

Ivanic, Suzanna, *Catholica: The Visual Culture of Catholicism* (London: Thames & Hudson, 2022).

Jennings, Nathan G., *Liturgy and Theology: Economy and Reality* (Eugene, OR: Cascade Books, 2017).

Jensen, Robin M., *The Cross: History, Art, and Controversy* (Cambridge, MA: Harvard University Press, 2017).

Understanding Early Christian Art (London: Routledge, 2000).

Johnson, Maxwell E. (ed.), *Between Memory and Hope: Readings on the Liturgical Year* (Collegeville, MN: Liturgical Press, 2000).

Jungmann, Joseph A., *The Mass of the Roman Rite: Its Origins and Development (Missarum Sollemnia)*, 2 vols. (Notre Dame, IN: Ave Maria Press, 2012).

Pastoral Liturgy (Notre Dame, IN: Christian Classics, 2014).

Kalaitzidis, Pantelis, et al. (eds.), *Orthodox Handbook on Ecumenism: Resources for Theological Education* (Minneapolis, MN: Fortress Press, 2014).

Kavanagh, Aidan, *On Liturgical Theology: The Hale Memorial Lectures of Seabury-Western Theological Seminary, 1981* (Collegeville, MN: Pueblo, 1984).

Kearney, Richard, *Touch: Recovering Our Most Vital Sense* (New York: Columbia University Press, 2021).

Kelleher, Margaret Mary, "Sacraments and the Ecclesial Mediation of Grace," *Louvain Studies* 23 (1998): 180–97.

Kieckhefer, Richard, *Theology in Stone: Church Architecture from Byzantium to Berkeley* (Oxford: Oxford University Press, 2004).

Kilmartin, Edward J., *The Eucharist in the West: History and Theology*, ed. Robert J. Daly (Collegeville, MN: Liturgical Press, 2004).

Klöckener, Martin, and Heinrich Rennings, *Lebendiges Stundengebet* (Freiburg: Herder, 1989).

Klomp, Mirella, *The Sound of Worship: Liturgical Performance by Surinamese Lutherans and Ghanaian Methodists in Amsterdam* (Leuven: Peeters, 2011).

Koester, Anne Y., and Barbara Searle, *Vision: The Scholarly Contributions of Mark Searle to Liturgical Renewal* (Collegeville, MN: Liturgical Press, 2004).

Kreinath, Jens, "Infrastructures of Interrituality and the Aesthetics of Saint Veneration Rituals among Orthodox Christians and Arab Alawites in Hatay," in *The Palgrave Handbook of Anthropological Ritual Studies*, ed. Pamela J. Stewart and Andrew J. Strathern (Cham: Palgrave Macmillan, 2021), 345–71.

Larson-Miller, Lizette (ed.), *Medieval Liturgy: A Book of Essays* (New York: Garland Publishing, 1997).

Sacramentality Renewed: Contemporary Conversations in Sacramental Theology (Collegeville, MN: Liturgical Press, 2016).

Lathrop, Gordon W., *Holy People: A Liturgical Ecclesiology* (Minneapolis, MN: Fortress, 1999).

Holy Things: A Liturgical Theology (Minneapolis, MN: Fortress Press, 1993).

Levy, Ian Christopher, Gary Macy, and Kristen Van Ausdall (eds.), *A Companion to the Eucharist in the Middle Ages* (Leiden: Brill, 2012).

Lossky, Vladimir, *À l'image et à la ressemblance de Dieu* (Paris: Cerf, 1967).

MacMullen, Ramsay, *The Second Church: Popular Christianity a.d. 200–400* (Atlanta: Society of Biblical Literature, 2009).

Mayer, Wendy, "The Changing Shape of Liturgy: From Earliest Christianity to the End of Late Antiquity," in *Liturgy's Imagined Past/s: Methodologies and Materials in the Writing of Liturgical History Today*, Teresa Berger and Bryan D. Spinks (eds.) (Collegeville, MN: Liturgical Press, 2016), 275–302.

Mazza, Enrico, *Mystagogy: A Theology of Liturgy in the Patristic Age* (New York: Pueblo, 1989).

The Celebration of the Eucharist: The Origin of the Rite and the Development of Its Interpretation, trans. Mathew J. O'Connell (Collegeville, MN: Liturgical Press, 1990).

The Eucharistic Prayers of the Roman Rite, trans. Mathew J. O'Connell (Collegeville, MN: Liturgical Press, 2004).

McCarthy, Daniel, and James Leachman (eds.), *Appreciating the Collect: An Irenic Methodology* (Farnborough: St Michael's Abbey Press, 2008).

McGowan, Andrew B., *Ancient Christian Worship: Early Church Practices in Social, Historical, and Theological Perspectives* (Grand Rapids, MI: Baker, 2014).

Meßner, Reinhard, "Der Gottesdienst in der vornizänischen Kirche," in *Die Geschichte des Christentums: Religion – Politik – Kultur. Band 1: Die Zeit des Anfangs (bis 250)*, Luce Pietri (ed.) (Freiburg: Herder, 2003), 340–441.

"Über einige Aufgaben bei der Erforschung der Liturgiegeschichte der frühen Kirche," in *Liturgie verstehen. Ansatz, Ziele und Aufgaben der Liturgiewisssenschaft*, ALW Jubiläumsband 50, eds. Martin Klöckener, Benedikt Kranemann, and Angelus A. Häußling (Fribourg: Academic, 2008), 207–30.

Meyer, Barbara U., "Not Just the Time of the Other – What Does It Mean for Christians Today to Remember Shabbat and Keep It Holy?," *Religions* 13 (2022): 736.
Mikalson, John, *Honor Thy Gods: Popular Religion in Greek Tragedy* (Chapel Hill, NC: University of North Carolina Press, 1991).
Mitchell, Nathan, *Liturgy and the Social Sciences* (Collegeville, MN: Liturgical Press, 1999).
Monti, James, *A Sense of the Sacred: Roman Catholic Worship in the Middle Ages* (San Francisco, CA: Ignatius Press, 2012).
Morrill, Bruce T., *Practical Sacramental Theology: At the Intersection of Liturgy and Ethics* (Eugene, OR: Cascade Books, 2021).
Morrill, Bruce T. (ed.), *Sacramental Theology: Theory and Practice from Multiple Perspectives* (Basel: MDPI, 2019).
Moschella, Mary Clark, *Ethnography as a Pastoral Practice: An Introduction*, 2nd rev. ed. (Cleveland: Tpp, 2023).
Moyaert, Marianne, *Interreligious Relations and the Negotiation of Ritual Boundaries: Explorations in Interrituality* (Cham: Springer International Publishing, 2019).
Moyaert, Marianne, and Joris Geldhof (eds.), *Ritual Participation and Interreligious Dialogue: Boundaries, Transgressions and Innovations* (London: Bloomsbury Academic, 2015).
Neunheuser, Burkhard. "Odo Casel and the Meaning of the Liturgical Year," *Studia Liturgica* 15 (1983): 210–13.
Nichols, Bridget (ed.), *The Collect in the Churches of the Reformation* (London: SCM Press, 2010).
Nocent, Adrian. *The Liturgical Year*, trans. by Matthew J. O'Connell. 4 vols. (Collegeville, MN: Liturgical Press, 2013).
O'Donnell, Emma, *Remembering the Future: The Experience of Time in Jewish and Christian Liturgy* (Collegeville, MN: Liturgical Press, 2015).
O'Loughlin, Thomas, *Eating Together, Becoming One: Taking Up Pope Francis's Call to Theologians* (Collegeville, MN: Liturgical Press, 2020).
O'Loughlin, Thomas (ed.), *Shaping the Assembly: How Our Buildings Form Us in Worship* (Dublin: Messenger, 2023).
Ouspensky, Leonid, and Vladimir Lossky, *The Meaning of Icons* (Crestwood, NY: St Vladimir's Seminary Press, 1999).
Palazzo, Eric, *A History of Liturgical Books from the Beginning to the Thirteenth Century* (Collegeville, MN: Liturgical Press, 1998).
Pauly, James C., *Liturgical Catechesis in the 21st Century: A School of Discipleship* (Chicago: Liturgy Training Publications, 2017).
Pecklers, Keith F., *The Unread Vision: The Liturgical Movement in the United States of America: 1926–1955* (Collegeville, MN: Liturgical Press, 1998).
Ploeger, Mathijs, *Celebrating Church: Ecumenical Contributions to a Liturgical Ecclesiology* (Groningen: Liturgisch Instituut, 2008).
Poorthuis, Marcel, *Rituals in Interreligious Dialogue: Bridge or Barrier?* (Cambridge: Cambridge Scholars Publishing, 2020).
Pott, Thomas, James Hawkey, and Keith F. Pecklers (eds.), *Malines: Continuing the Conversations* (London: SPCK, 2023).

Prétot, Patrick, "La Liturgie: Une Expérience Corporelle: Jalons pour une grammaire du corps en liturgie," *La Maison-Dieu* 247 (2006): 7–36.

Pui-lan, Kwok, "Postcolonial Preaching in Intercultural Contexts," *Homiletic* 40 (2015): 8–21.

Rempel, John D., *The Lord's Supper in Anabaptism: A Study in the Christology of Balthasar Hubmaier, Pilgram Marpeck, and Dirk Philips* (Waterloo, ON: Herald Press, 1993).

Rijken, Hanna, *My Soul Doth Magnify: The Appropriation of Choral Evensong in the Netherlands* (Amsterdam: VU University Press, 2020).

Robert, Philippe, *Chanter la messe* (Paris: Bayard, 2016).

Ross, Melanie C., *Evangelical Worship: An American Mosaic* (New York: Oxford University Press, 2021).

Ross, Melanie C., and Mark Lamport (eds), *Historical Foundations of Worship: Catholic, Orthodox, and Protestant Perspectives* (Grand Rapids, MI: Baker Academic, 2022).

Rouwhorst, Gerard, "Christlicher Gottesdienst und der Gottesdienst Israels. Forschungsgeschichte, historische Interaktionen, Theologie," in *Theologie des Gottesdienstes, GDK 2/2*, Martin Klöckener, Angelus A. Häußling, and Reinhard Meßner (eds.) (Regensburg: Pustet, 2008), 491–572.

"Vielfalt von Anfang an. Pluralität in der Liturgiegeschichte," *Archiv für Liturgiewissenschaft* 57 (2015): 1–23.

Ruth, Lester, and Swee-Hong Lim, *A History of Contemporary Praise and Worship: Understanding the Ideas That Reshaped the Protestant Church* (Grand Rapids, MI: Baker Academic, 2021).

Schmemann, Alexander, *Introduction to Liturgical Theology*, trans. Asheleigh E. Moorehouse (Crestwood, NY: St. Vladimir's Seminary Press, 2003).

For the Life of the World: Sacraments and Orthodoxy (Crestwood, NY: St Vladimir's Seminary Press, 1973).

The Eucharist: Sacrament of the Kingdom. Trans. Paul Kachur (Crestwood, NY: St Vladimir's Seminary Press, 1988).

Seasoltz, R. Kevin, *A Sense of the Sacred: Theological Foundations of Christian Architecture and Art* (New York: Continuum, 2007).

Senn, Frank C., *Embodied Liturgy: Lessons in Christian Ritual* (Minneapolis, MN: Fortress Press, 2016).

Spurrier, Rebecca F., *The Disabled Church: Human Difference and the Art of Communal Worship* (New York: Fordham University Press, 2019).

Stjerna, Kirsi Irmeli, *Women and the Reformation* (Malden, MA: Blackwell, 2009).

Stuflesser, Martin, *Eucharistie: Liturgische Feier und theologische Erschließung* (Regensburg: Friedrich Pustet, 2013).

Taft, Robert F., *Beyond East and West: Problems in Liturgical Understanding* (Rome: Pontifical Oriental Institute, 2001).

The Byzantine Rite: A Short History (Collegeville, MN: Liturgical Press, 1992).

"The Liturgical Year: Studies, Prospects, Reflections," *Worship* 55 (1981): 2–23.

The Liturgy of the Hours in East and West: The Origins of the Divine Office and Its Meaning for Today, 2nd ed. (Collegeville, MN: Liturgical Press 1993).

Talley, Thomas J., *The Origins of the Liturgical Year* (New York: Pueblo, 1986).
Thibodeau, Timothy, "Western Christendom," in *The Oxford History of Christian Worship*, edited by Geoffrey Wainwright and Karen B. Westerfield-Tucker (Oxford: Oxford University Press, 2012), 216–53.
Travis, Sarah, *Decolonizing Preaching: The Pulpit as Postcolonial Space* (Eugene, OR: Cascade Books, 2014).
Uro, Risto, Juliette J. Day, Richard E. DeMaris, and Rikard Roitto (eds), *The Oxford Handbook of Early Christian Ritual* (Oxford: Oxford University Press, 2019).
US Conference of Catholic Bishops, *Built of Living Stones: Art, Architecture, and Worship – Guidelines of the National Conference of Catholic Bishops* (issued 16 November 2000 by NCCB/USCC [Now USCCB]), https://nyliturgy.org/wp-content/uploads/BOLS.pdf.
Vogel, Cyril, *Medieval Liturgy: An Introduction to the Sources*, trans. William G. Storey and Niels Krog Rasmussen (Washington, DC: The Pastoral Press, 1986).
Vogel, Dwight W., (ed.), *Primary Sources of Liturgical Theology: A Reader* (Collegeville, MN: Liturgical Press, 2000).
Wainwright, Geoffrey, and Karen B. Westerfield-Tucker (eds.), *The Oxford History of Christian Worship* (Oxford: Oxford University Press, 2012).
Westerfield Tucker, Karen, *American Methodist Worship* (New York: Oxford University Press, 2011).
White, James F., *Introduction to Christian Worship* (Nashville, TN: Abingdon Press, 2000).
  Protestant Worship: Traditions in Transition (Louisville, KY: Westminster/John Knox Press, 1989).
Wilson, Paul Scott, et al., *The New Interpreter's Handbook of Preaching* (Nashville, TN: Abingdon, 2008).
Wolterstorff, Nicholas, *The God We Worship: An Exploration of Liturgical Theology* (Grand Rapids, MI: Eerdmans, 2015).
Woolfenden, Gregory W., *Daily Liturgical Prayer: Origins and Theology* (Aldershot: Ashgate 2004).
Zimmerman, Joyce Ann, *Liturgy and Hermeneutics* (Collegeville, MN: Liturgical Press, 1999).
Zizioulas, John, *L'Eucharistie, l'Évêque et l'Église* (Paris: DDB, 1994).

Names Index

Abraham, 242, 244, 341, 348
Adam, 280
Afanassieff, Nicolas, 273
Alcuin of York, 34
Al-Ghazali, 349
Allmen, Jean-Jacques von, 299, 301–2, 306, 308–9, 314–15
Amalarius, 29, 34
Ambrose of Milan, 11
Aristotle, 28, 30, 119, 138
Asad, 379
Athenagoras, 338–39
Augustine of Hippo, 18, 30, 38, 55, 119, 131, 135–36, 196, 284

Barnard, Marcel, 294, 296, 306, 315, 375, 384
Barth, Karl, 299, 307, 349
Basil of Caesarea, 124, 265, 280
Baudelaire, Charles, 230
Baumstark, Anton, 82–83, 333
Bell, Catherine, 372–73, 375, 380
Benedict of Aniane, 30, 34, 169
Benedict of Nursia, 21, 30, 160, 169
Benedict XVI, 118, 127, 325, 344, 347
Boethius, 30
Bonaccorso, Giorgio, 196–97, 203
Bouyer, Louis, 104–5, 117–18, 126, 218
Bradshaw, Paul F., 86, 88, 113, 120–21, 157, 159, 176–77, 182–83, 328, 396, 399
Brown, David, 255, 263, 267
Brueggemann, Walter, 309–10
Bucer, Martin, 43, 48, 50, 55

Cabasilas, Nicholas, 85, 91–92, 269, 272
Calvin, Jean, 43, 45, 48, 51, 55–56, 66, 209, 238, 240, 243, 285, 309, 314
Carvalhaes, Claudio, 300, 337
Casel, Odo, 101, 103, 120, 139, 216

Charlemagne, 27, 33, 238
Charles III, 331
Chauvet, Louis-Marie, 217, 271, 289–90
Chupungco, Anscar J., 86, 98, 175, 185, 259, 285, 361
Cilliers, Johan, 306, 309, 312, 315, 384
Clement of Alexandria, 275, 277
Clovis, 38
Collins, Mary, 377
Columbanus, 30
Congar, Yves, 126, 129, 140, 224
Constantine (the Great), 14, 176, 184, 278
Constantine V, 236
Cosse, Jean, 229
Cranach, Lukas, 243
Cranmer, Thomas, 43, 45, 49–50, 53, 56, 358, 362
Cyril of Alexandria, 87, 274
Cyril of Jerusalem, 86, 119, 279

Day, Dorothy, 110
Debuyst, Frédéric, 226–27
Diego, Juan, 246
Diekmann, Godfrey, 110, 113
Dionysius the Areopagite, pseudo-, 30, 226, 228, 269
Dix, Gregory, 123, 175, 178, 295, 393
Douglas, Mary, 375, 378
Drey, Johann Sebastian (von), 285–86, 289, 293
Duchesne, Louis, 103, 366
Duns Scotus, 85, 138
Durandus of Mende, William, 36, 234
Duthilleul, Jean-Marie, 224

Egeria, 86, 157, 274, 276, 280
Eliade, Mircea, 375
Eusebius of Caesarea, 11, 232

Fagerberg, David W., 196, 389, 395–97, 403
Farwell, James, 255, 350–51
Fëdor I Ivanovic, 331
Ferrone, Rita, 294–95
Fox, George, 62
Francis I (pope), 118, 123, 134, 136, 154, 216, 225, 343–44, 351

Gelasius, 362
Geldhof, Joris, 100, 130, 258, 336, 346
Gelineau, Joseph, 292
Gibson, Mel, 241
Giraudo, Cesare, 35, 81, 118
Gregory of Nyssa, 233
Gregory of Tours, 361–62
Gregory the Great, 25, 36, 176, 219
Gregory VII, 20, 25
Grimes, Ronald, 252, 313, 371–72, 374–75, 378, 382
Grünewald, Matthias, 299–300
Guardini, Romano, 205, 211, 216, 292
Guéranger, Dom Prosper, 102–3, 174

Henry VIII, 49
Herwegen, Ildefons, 103–4
Hoffman, Lawrence, 370, 378
Hugh of Saint Victor, 138
Hugo, Victor, 214, 215

Irenaeus of Lyon, 179
Irwin, Kevin W., 134, 136, 140, 258, 266
Irwin, Sara, 357
Isaac, 242, 244, 247
Isaiah, 188, 236, 261
Isidore of Seville, 30

Jacob, 245
Jeggle-Merz, Birgit, 288
Jenkins, Philip, 305
John Cassian, 261
John Chrysostom, 49, 119, 317, 363
John of Damascus, 236
John Paul II, 81, 216, 343–46
John XXIII, 118, 341
Johnson, Elizabeth, 263
Jungmann, Joseph Andreas, 162, 176, 286, 292
Justin Martyr, 265, 360
Justinian I, 188

Kavanagh, Aidan, 377, 389, 394, 396, 402
Kiesgen, Agape, 103
Kilmartin, Edward J., 134, 140

Klauser, Theodor, 25, 38
Knox, John, 43

Lathrop, Gordon, 98, 100, 104, 251–52, 295, 320, 329, 389, 397–98, 403
Leo III, 236
Leo the Great, 135, 362
Leo XIII, 99, 106, 327
Lévi-Strauss, Claude, 375
Löhr, Aemiliana, 101, 103
Lukken, Gerard, 375, 377
Luther, Martin, 42–46, 48, 50–57, 66, 208, 241, 243

Maimonides, 349
Mary, 93, 183–86, 188–89, 235, 238, 245–46, 277
Maximus the Confessor, 226, 228, 255, 269
Mazza, Enrico, 118, 402
Metzger, Marcel, 25–26, 28, 36, 38
Michel, Virgil, 106–7, 110, 114
Morrill, Bruce T., 290
Moses, 187, 280

Ommen, Léon van, 265, 283, 291, 386
Origen, 10–12, 275, 365–66
Orsi, Robert, 375, 381

Parsch, Pius, 292
Pascal, Blaise, 225–26
Paul VI, 122, 150, 185, 338–39
Paulinus of Nola, 234
Pauly, James, 293–94
Pepin the Short, 331
Pius V, 119
Pius X, 105–7, 147, 163, 292
Pius XI, 107
Pius XII, 112–13
Plato, 28
Polycarp of Smyrna, 232
Prétot, Patrick, 133, 139, 255–57, 276–77, 292
Prosper of Aquitaine, 292, 396

Rahner, Karl, 135, 139, 294
Rappaport, Roy, 374
Rembrandt, 242–45
Ricoeur, Paul, 356

Saberschinsky, Alexander, 296–97
Schillebeeckx, Edward, 57, 139
Schleiermacher, Friedrich D.E., 104

Schmemann, Alexander, 177, 181–82, 196, 270–74, 276, 289–90, 319, 389–95, 397, 399, 403
Schwarz, Rudolf, 216
Searle, Mark, 101, 288, 375, 377
Senn, Frank, 48–49, 98, 100, 253–54, 378
Serapion of Thmuis, 342, 363
Sidonius Apollinaris, 361
Soskice, Janet M., 263
St. Dominic, 31
St. Francis, 31, 345
St. Mark, 88
St. Martin of Tours, 40, 183
St. Michael, 181, 189
St. Paul, 30, 34, 53, 74, 268, 275, 281, 317–18
St. Stephen, 279
Suger, 226

Taft, Robert F., 21, 82–84, 87–88, 91, 159, 167, 275, 317, 333
Talley, Thomas J., 174, 277
Teilhard de Chardin, Pierre, 226

Theodore of Mopsuestia, 119
Theodore the Studite, 237
Theophilos III, 331
Thomas Aquinas, 29, 38–39, 57–58, 127, 138, 224, 270, 285, 349
Turner, Edith, 375–76
Turner, Victor, 375–76

Urban IV, 38

Vagaggini, Cipriano, 287, 289
Vigilius, 362

Welby, Justin, 331
Wesley, Charles, 69
Wesley, John, 69–72
White, James F., 61–62, 64, 70–72, 98, 302
Williams, Rowan, 236, 324
Wintersig, Athanasius, 285–86

Zwingli, Huldrych, 43, 45, 48, 51, 55–56, 68, 209, 243

Concepts and Places Index

abbey, 27, 31, 37, 102–3, 106, 227, 331
absolution, 46, 146, 262
active participation, 100–1, 104, 109, 111, 113, 120, 129–30, 140, 221, 224–25, 288, 292, 294, 304
Advent, 102, 147, 183, 185, 188, 281, 384
aesthetics, 114, 198, 234, 242, 246, 257
Africa, 88, 118, 375
Agnus Dei, 34, 47
Alexandria, 10, 16, 87–88, 275, 277
Anabaptism, 52, 62, 66–69, 78, 137, 142
anaphora, 16, 21, 81, 121, 124, 361, 364, 380
Angelus, 158
Anglicanism, 50, 61, 70–71, 98, 112, 137, 163, 166, 168, 170, 195, 209, 262–63, 321, 327–28, 331, 357–59, 398
Annunciation, 183–84, 187, 189
Anointing of the Sick, 36, 136, 141, 147–49, 252, 270, 290
anthropology, 2, 59, 140, 199, 204, 215, 272, 294, 312, 321, 338, 369, 375, 377–78, 381, 386, 389, 391, 393, 397, 400
Antioch, 9, 16, 19, 87, 89, 218
Antiquity, 7, 15, 19, 24–26, 28, 39–40, 119, 220, 234, 268
anti-Semitism, 240, 242, 370
Apocrypha, 7, 12
apostles, 7, 12, 46, 51, 93, 123–24, 144, 153, 187, 189, 279, 281, 329, 360
Apostolic Tradition, 12, 14, 121, 124, 152
Apostolicae Curae, 327
Aquileia, 217
Arabic, 88, 90, 189
architecture, 37, 77, 90, 103, 207–8, 215, 218–19, 225, 271, 377, 380
Arianism, 182, 236

Armenia, 7, 20, 22, 82–83, 85–87, 94, 188
Ascension, 124, 135, 180, 191, 260, 277–79
asceticism, 95, 268, 280, 282, 403
Ash Wednesday, 49, 114, 179, 186
assembly, 16, 42, 44–45, 49, 53, 58–59, 72, 74, 119, 123–24, 126, 128–29, 131, 133, 139, 143, 152–53, 156, 158, 160, 168, 177, 196, 198, 216–17, 220–21, 223–25, 229–30, 251–53, 255, 257–58, 260–61, 264–65, 273–74, 296, 324–25, 329, 357, 369, 393, 395, 397
Assisi, 31, 100, 108, 345–47
Assumption, 184, 188, 281

Babylonia, 50, 301–2
baptism, 11, 13, 15, 18, 26, 36, 38, 43, 48–53, 56, 58–59, 62, 65–68, 71, 74, 78, 85, 92, 101, 105, 114, 136–39, 141–45, 151, 171, 177–80, 182–83, 186, 222–24, 252, 259, 265–66, 270–71, 273–74, 282–83, 287, 294, 296, 327, 329–31, 362, 370, 391, 398, 402
Baptists, 61, 66, 73, 137, 304–5
Benedicite, 157
Benedictus, 47, 170
Bible, 10, 17, 19, 32, 34, 48, 69, 84, 86, 94, 119, 125, 128, 158, 168, 170, 173, 176, 243–44, 262, 268, 299–300, 303, 313, 331, 341, 364, 399, 403
bishop, 10, 16, 18, 20–21, 28, 36, 49, 58, 108, 110, 142, 144–45, 148, 152–53, 218, 235, 238, 246, 257, 275, 294, 323, 325, 327–29, 331, 360–64, 402
blessing, 12, 15, 36, 77, 85, 145, 148, 151, 153, 233, 252, 255, 264, 266, 290, 339–40, 366

419

Body of Christ, 55–57, 109, 114, 119, 131, 133, 140–41, 143, 217, 221, 225–26, 228, 233, 251–53, 257, 273, 317–20, 322, 325–26, 330–31, 334, 370, 376, 392–94, 398–99
Book of Common Prayer, 43, 46, 49–50, 63, 70–72, 112, 262, 358–59, 396
bread, 9–10, 12, 48, 53, 55, 57, 92–95, 123, 126, 130, 134, 176–77, 225, 258–60, 265, 284
bread and wine, 12, 40, 53, 55–57, 68, 122, 124, 251, 257, 259, 280, 318, 360, 398
breviary, 35, 107, 155, 157, 163–64
Buddha, 340, 350
Buddhism, 203, 340, 348, 350–51
Burg Rothenfels, 216
Byzantine Rite, 20, 22, 81, 83, 87–88, 169, 189, 281, 391

Calvinism, 61, 362
canon law, 143, 150, 153, 322
Canterbury, 43, 46, 49, 331
canticle, 47, 156, 169–70, 255
Cappadocia, 86
catechism, 50–52, 57, 128, 133, 274, 292
catechumenate, 11, 15, 142, 223, 274, 297, 375
cathedral, 21, 87, 152–53, 168, 195, 210, 215, 219, 228, 266, 383
cathedral office, 18–19, 156, 159, 167–70, 176
Catholicism, 50, 63, 66, 99–100, 102, 106, 109–10, 114, 137, 148, 163, 210, 220, 230, 239, 323, 327, 339, 342, 345, 383
chants, 16–17, 21–23, 35, 102, 126, 157, 199, 202–3, 361, 383
charismatic, 73–74, 77, 357, 383–84
Chevetogne, 332
children, 39, 75, 107, 112, 130, 142, 144, 147–48, 150–51, 179, 199–200, 204–5, 257, 261, 304, 307, 340
choir, 48, 63, 156, 170, 199, 201, 210, 238, 362
Chrism, 92, 143, 145, 153, 259, 329–31
Chrism Mass, 148
Christ-event, 185
Christian initiation, 7, 11, 15, 26, 37–38, 50, 52, 142, 144, 223, 230, 271, 282, 330, 375–76,

Christmas, 18, 110, 173, 181–83, 186, 189–90, 281, 340
Christology, 68, 85, 87–91, 93, 157, 226, 228, 236–37, 299, 321
Christus totus, 224, 228
Church of England, 49–50, 56, 62, 69–72, 99, 260–61, 328, 358, 364
Church Orders, 7, 12, 152, 360
Cîteaux, 31
clergy, 10, 14, 17, 37, 84, 99, 105–6, 274, 315, 392
Cluny, 31, 225
Code of Canon Law, 137, 318
commemoration, 2, 17–18, 160, 175, 178, 180, 182, 184–86, 189, 277, 302, 361, 387
Common Worship, 260, 358, 364
communion, 12, 16, 21, 45, 48–50, 53, 56, 65, 69–70, 82, 84, 87, 103, 105, 122–24, 130–31, 135, 137, 141–42, 145–47, 149, 152–53, 180–81, 189, 221, 254, 256, 262, 280, 282, 296, 304, 317–18, 320–26, 328–29, 331, 333, 339, 378, 383, 398
communion of saints, 317
communion song, 34
Communion, Anglican, 262
comparative liturgy, 8, 21, 82, 333
Compline, 18, 49, 165, 167, 170
confession, 15, 39, 46, 50, 68, 82, 125, 146, 273, 392
confessional, 222
Confirmation, 49, 71, 136, 139, 141–42, 144–45, 180, 259, 270, 273, 304, 327, 375
Confiteor, 146
consecration, 36, 47, 57, 85, 91, 122, 124, 281, 327–29, 361–62
Constantinople, 20, 25, 33, 81, 87–88, 281, 331
consumerism, 95, 129, 132, 307, 379
Coptic, 20, 82–83, 85, 88, 91, 93, 167–68, 189
Corpus Christi, 38, 183, 239
Councils
  of Chalcedon, 20, 88, 90–91, 226
  Chalcedon, 20, 88, 91, 237
  of Constantinople, 329
  of Ephesus, 82, 89
  of Florence, 136
  Fourth Lateran, 57
  of Laodicea, 329
  of Lyons II, 136
  of Nicaea, 179, 182, 188, 328

of Nicaea II, 236–37
of Trent, 20, 36, 57, 120, 122, 136, 139, 210, 221
Covid-19, 118, 251, 296, 304, 382–83
Creed, 46, 48, 63, 73, 145, 256, 278, 304, 322, 349, 357, 392, 396
cross, 94, 103, 110, 120, 123, 130, 143, 145, 180, 187–88, 190, 229, 233–35, 239–42, 247, 252, 279
Crucifixion, 9, 13, 175, 182
cult, 8–10, 14, 30, 40, 123, 127, 173, 175, 184–85, 285, 301, 396

Dei Verbum, 125, 127, 337
deification, 269, 282
denomination, 62, 69, 72–73, 100, 105, 113, 120, 137, 142, 145, 158, 161–62, 195, 206–7, 209–11, 304, 365
Desiderio desideravi, 123, 136, 225
Deutsche Messe, 43–46, 59
devotion, 14, 38–40, 130, 183, 219, 234, 244, 268, 274
diakonia, 152, 284, 289–91, 295
Didachè, 10, 12, 177, 280, 360
Divine Liturgy, 21, 83, 86, 238, 317
Divine Office, 102, 155, 158–59, 276
Dominicans, 31, 110, 126, 220
Dormition, 184, 189, 281
doxology, 166, 367, 396

Easter, 13, 17–18, 38, 132, 181, 184, 186, 188, 190, 229, 241, 257, 281–82, 355
Easter Vigil, 113, 142, 144, 166, 177, 259, 274
East-Syrian, 82, 84–85, 89–90, 183–84, 186
Ecclesia orans, 104, 155–56, 170
ecclesiology, 129–30, 218, 221, 273, 288, 294–96, 320–21, 324, 327–28, 332, 378, 386
Ecumenical Movement, 80–81, 221, 319, 326, 331–32
ecumenism, 81, 106, 108, 319–20, 322, 324, 326, 328–29, 331, 333–34, 383
Edessa, 86, 89
editio typica, 117, 147, 358–59
Egypt, 19, 88, 361
encounter, 31, 43, 75, 92, 139, 148, 191, 209, 254, 262, 287, 293, 307, 311, 314, 394–95, 398, 401, 403
epiclesis, 16, 124, 131, 151, 303, 314

Epiphany, 18, 85, 175, 182–83, 186–87, 190, 279
epistle, 46, 49, 111
Eritrea, 82, 89
Ethiopia, 19, 82, 88, 183–84
ethnography, 371, 374, 377–78, 380–86, 389, 391
euchology, 22, 83, 120, 366
Europe, 1, 24, 26–28, 30–31, 33, 39–40, 42, 66, 102, 106–7, 109, 118, 163, 239, 288–89, 340, 384
Evangelicalism, 61, 63, 73, 75, 78, 242, 383–84
Evensong, 49, 165–66
ex opere operato, 54, 138

fast, 12–13, 95, 179–81, 187, 189, 280–82, 385
festival, 48, 174, 177–78, 180–83, 205–6, 266, 277, 281
forgiveness of sins, 45, 54, 67, 149
funeral, 14, 49, 85, 144, 252, 266, 384

Gallican, 20, 33
Gaul, 22, 33, 218, 361
Geneva, 42, 46, 48, 103, 209
Georgia, 7, 22, 86
gestures, 3, 14, 74, 122, 158, 255, 271, 290, 334, 349, 371, 378
gifts, 10, 12, 16, 40, 59, 122–24, 131, 290–91, 317, 324
Gifts of the Spirit, 74–75
Gloria, 34, 46–47, 50
glorification, 178, 270, 287
Good Friday, 179–80, 240, 282, 341–42
gospel, 13, 34, 43, 46, 49, 53, 58, 68, 78, 80, 96, 111, 126–27, 152, 167, 240, 255, 284, 287, 289, 291, 300, 308, 314, 360, 362, 366, 398
Greco-Roman culture, 10, 12, 14, 24, 235
Greek, 7, 22, 29, 81, 84, 86, 88–91, 176, 207, 268, 360
Guadalupe, 245–47

Hesychasm, 276
Hinduism, 348
Holy Family, 183
Holy Land, 233, 278, 331
Holy Orders, 136, 139, 141, 152–53, 273
Holy Saturday, 38, 142, 188, 278, 282
Holy Sepulcher, 233, 276
Holy Thursday, 240

Holy Week, 113, 148, 179, 190, 239, 383–84
Homiletics, 307–8, 310, 312, 380
homily, 7, 35, 64, 70, 125–26, 143, 145, 149, 152, 233, 257, 274, 277, 279
hospitality, 227–28, 230, 265, 321, 326, 338, 343, 349
hymn, 7, 14, 35, 64, 69–71, 94, 103, 111, 157–59, 163, 169–71, 195, 211–12, 258, 275–77, 315, 361, 366

iconoclasm, 88, 233, 236–37, 240, 243
iconostasis, 237
icons, 207, 232, 235–38, 271, 351
idolatry, 236, 386
incarnation, 83, 134, 178, 182, 191, 226, 237, 269, 277–78, 281, 285, 314, 334, 400
incense, 14, 19, 157, 257, 271
infants, 142–44, 200, 257
institution narrative, 16, 44, 81, 121, 124, 360
instrumental music, 196, 202, 205, 207, 209–10
Isenheim Altarpiece, 299
Islam, 164, 346, 351, 379
Israel, 9, 74, 119, 157, 275, 301–2, 340–42, 344

Jesuits, 286
Jews, 8, 176, 240, 336, 341–44, 348–49, 370
Judaism, 9, 11, 277, 280, 341
justification, 43–44, 50, 53, 197, 211, 244, 278, 367

kerygma, 284, 289, 295, 392
Kingdom of God, 67, 99, 181, 272, 277–78, 284, 287, 314
koinonia, 73, 283–84, 289, 295–97
Kyrie, 34, 46

laity, 53, 59, 105–6, 111, 150, 164, 221, 244, 276, 315, 362
lamb, 13, 259, 262
Latin, 7, 22, 28, 30, 44, 81, 86, 90, 103, 105, 107, 119, 122, 124, 126, 136, 157, 162–63, 165–66, 169, 176, 268, 323–24, 333, 342, 355, 358, 360, 396
Latin America, 118, 241, 246
Latin Mass, 48, 359
Latinx, 245, 247
Lauds, 18–19, 49, 166–67, 169–70

laying on of hands, 14, 148, 151, 153
lectionary, 22, 34, 48, 86, 103, 125, 303–4, 361, 365
Lent, 10, 34, 95–96, 147, 169, 179, 181, 184, 187, 190, 253, 259, 261, 274, 281, 391
Leuven, 304–5
lex orandi, 117, 300, 396
lex orandi, lex credendi, 292, 300, 346, 396–97
liminality, 206, 305, 313, 375–77, 385
litany, 49, 70, 72, 143, 147, 149, 152, 263, 366
Little Hours, 18, 167, 169
Liturgy of the Word, 12, 16, 21, 118, 120, 125–26, 128, 145–46, 180, 223, 301, 303–4
lived religion, 8, 14–15
Lord's blood, 123
Lord's body, 123, 130
Lord's Day, 13, 48, 71, 175–76, 276, 278
Lord's death, 120, 174
Lord's Prayer, 46, 50, 143, 145, 147, 149, 304, 355, 357
Lord's presence, 127–28
Lord's supper, 13, 55, 62, 66, 68, 70–72, 101, 105, 287, 317
Lucernarium, 157, 159, 169
Lumen gentium, 130, 135, 324, 337
Lutheranism, 45, 54, 61, 66, 73, 137, 168, 206, 208, 305, 358, 398

Magnificat, 157, 165, 170
Maria Laach, 103–4
Maronite, 80, 82, 85, 90, 94, 189
marriage, 49, 71, 85, 150–51, 252, 264, 266, 273, 321
martyrdom, 13, 18, 39, 66, 84, 95, 184, 189, 232, 279, 361
Matins, 35, 49, 166
matrimony, 136, 141, 149–51, 270
Maundy Thursday, 290
Mediator Dei, 112
megachurches, 75–77
Melbourne, 304–5
Menorah, 344
Methodism, 62, 69–73, 78, 101, 112, 137, 358, 400
Metropolitan, 153, 325
Mexico, 245–46
Milan, 14, 20, 22, 34–35, 361
Missale Romanum, 35, 117, 131

CONCEPTS AND PLACES INDEX 423

modernity, 40, 220, 225, 306, 320, 378, 397
monastery, 27, 30–31, 36–37, 39–40, 87–88, 102, 160, 162–65, 219, 227, 276, 332, 345, 362
monasticism, 7, 18, 21, 30–31, 37, 86, 88, 95–96, 158, 162–63, 165–66, 168–70, 224, 254, 276, 332
Monophysitism, 236
Mont César, 105
Mother of God, 184–85, 281
Mount of Olives, 278, 331, 338
Muslim, 336, 339, 346, 348–50
mustèrion, 319, 332
mystagogy, 7, 15, 86, 118–19, 142, 226, 228, 257, 293–95, 361, 389–90, 402–3
Mystical Body, 109, 111, 269

Nativity, 17, 175, 182–85, 187, 189, 278–79
neophyte, 142, 274, 294
Nestorianism, 236
neuroscience, 196, 198
New Testament, 10–11, 14, 121, 123, 157, 165, 268, 360
Nisibis, 89, 184
None, 18, 167
Nostra Aetate, 337, 340–41, 345
Nunc dimittis, 157, 165, 170

Oberammergau, 240–41
offering, 10, 12, 16–17, 46, 95, 123–24, 129–30, 281, 291, 303
oil, 15, 134, 143, 147–49, 225, 257–59, 281, 331, 361
Old Catholic Church, 160, 168, 295, 321, 328
Old Testament, 10, 51, 89, 157, 169, 180, 222, 237, 340
Orate Fratres, 106–7, 112, 114
ordination, 10, 14, 36, 71, 85, 122, 152–53, 328, 362
Ordines Romani, 35–36
ordo, 113, 252, 390, 393, 397–98, 400–1
Ordo Lectionum Missae, 125
Ordo Missae, 35, 117, 121, 126, 342
Ordo paenitentium, 39
organ, 195, 207, 210
Oriental Orthodoxy, 82, 88
Orthodox Church, 87, 188–89, 207, 237, 280, 323, 325–26, 329, 331, 355, 383, 392

orthodoxy, 8, 14, 16, 80, 85, 136, 182, 207, 237, 273, 319, 323, 361
Orthros, 169
Our Lady, 238, 246
Oxford, 69, 99
Oxford Movement, 98–99, 210

papal liturgy, 22, 33, 160
Paris, 215, 227–28
parish, 33, 37, 70, 99, 106, 109, 162, 168, 227, 276, 304, 306
Pascha, 13, 175, 178–81, 184
Paschal Mystery, 120, 125, 133, 173–76, 184, 191, 222, 281, 290
passion, 9–10, 124–25, 149, 161, 167, 176, 178, 185, 239–43, 278
Passover, 9–10, 13, 128, 130, 132, 178–79
pastor, 73, 76–77, 228, 242, 292–93, 303–4, 306, 320, 325, 402
pastoral, 27
pastoral care, 26, 147
pastoral liturgy, 100, 160, 283, 285–89
pastoral ministry, 254, 283–85, 288–89, 291, 294–98
pastoral practice, 283
pastoral staff, 153
pastoral theology, 288
patriarch, 81, 237, 242, 245, 325, 330–31, 338
patriarchate, 87
penance, 14, 26, 37, 39–40, 85, 136, 141, 145–47, 149, 254, 256, 270
penitence, 256, 261, 365
Pentecost, 13, 18, 144, 175, 180, 186–87, 189–91, 277, 279, 281
Pentecost vigil, 177
Pentecostalism, 61, 72–74, 78, 137, 303, 305, 357, 384
Philokalia, 276
Phos hilaron, 157, 169
piety, 15, 52, 54, 70, 83, 99, 103, 128, 183, 239–40, 244, 247, 268, 270–71, 273, 279, 281–82, 380
pilgrim church, 161, 256
pilgrimage, 15, 17, 33, 40, 85–86, 167, 245, 254, 261, 338–39, 376, 385
pilgrims, 17, 129, 233, 246, 272, 279, 305, 315
pneumatology, 15, 124, 296, 313–14, 346
Pontificale, 36
pope, 27–28, 33, 36, 212, 339, 343–44
popular piety, 183, 268
postcolonial preaching, 311

postcolonialism, 300, 305–6, 310, 315, 338, 378–80, 384
Praenotanda, 141
prayer of the faithful, 126–27, 143
Presbyter, 10, 16, 21, 152, 218, 361–62
Presbyterianism, 73, 112
presence of Christ, 40, 55–57, 122, 127–29, 135, 216, 223, 225, 230, 236, 267, 332
presence of God, 75, 78, 84, 173, 257, 260
Prime, 18, 167
Protestantism, 42, 61, 63, 67, 73, 78, 81, 98, 122, 137, 163, 199, 238–39, 241, 243, 245, 247, 338, 357, 397–99
psalmody, 16–17, 19, 170, 276, 366
psalms, 17, 19, 35, 48–49, 71, 94, 156, 158–60, 163, 165–69, 171, 222, 255, 258, 260, 275–76, 344, 365
psalter, 19, 35, 43, 48, 103, 168, 209, 276, 362, 366
psychology, 140, 203, 244, 369
Puritanism, 50, 62–63, 209

Quakers, 61–62, 64–65, 78
queer, 379
Qurbana, 83

rabbi, 343–44
Ramadan, 164, 339
Ravenna, 217, 323
Ravenna Document, 323–24, 326, 328
RCIA (Rite of Christian Initiation of Adults), 142, 144, 147, 294–95, 298
readings, 16–17, 34, 49, 126, 157, 166–67, 170, 179, 189, 302–4, 361
real presence, 40, 53, 57, 120, 127, 222
reconciliation, 14, 68, 147, 190, 222, 254, 318–20, 330, 340–41, 385
Redemptoris Missio, 346
Reformation, 42, 44–45, 52–54, 58–59, 61–62, 81, 99, 103, 121, 207–9, 220, 238, 240, 243–44, 258, 285, 324, 326, 362
Reims, 38, 331
relics, 15, 26, 40, 219, 232–34
remembering, 124, 302–3
responsorial psalm, 34, 125, 143
resurrection, 8–9, 18, 52, 68, 124–25, 134, 141, 161, 166, 176–80, 185, 187, 189–90, 217, 241, 256, 278–79, 282, 327
ritual studies, 83, 140, 288, 290, 294, 306, 313, 369–71, 374–77, 380–83, 386–87

rituale, 36
Roman Catholic Church, 90, 112, 117, 142–43, 155, 163–64, 166–68, 189, 210, 238, 283, 294, 318, 323–24, 326–27, 335–36, 343, 355, 358, 383
Roman Catholicism, 73, 100, 104, 133, 158, 206, 262, 359
Roman Empire, 8, 24, 27, 188, 327
Roman rite, 20–23, 32–33, 42–43, 45, 53, 58, 174, 185
Romanticism, 98, 100, 103, 214, 285, 293
Rome, 18–19, 22, 27, 33, 35–36, 82, 108, 110, 160, 169, 182–83, 219, 329, 343–44, 362
Russia, 110, 238, 331

Sabbath, 164, 176–77, 277–78
sacramental theology, 26, 39, 61, 84, 137, 139–40, 266, 290, 319, 321, 324, 398
sacramentality, 127, 133–34, 230, 255–56, 259, 273, 285, 378
sacramentary, 361–63, 365, 367
Sacred Heart, 183, 238
sacrifice, 9–10, 16, 19, 44, 53, 120, 123–24, 128–30, 140, 218, 220, 222, 228, 242, 244, 247, 269, 287, 329
Sacrosanctum Concilium, 118, 125, 130, 137, 161, 164, 175, 210, 218, 223–24, 269, 274, 277, 283, 286, 320
saints, 15, 33, 39–40, 84, 128, 143, 152, 169, 184, 234, 238, 275, 289, 318, 324, 357, 369
sanctification, 73, 123, 160, 171, 187, 197, 211, 233, 269–70, 276, 287, 290
sanctorale, 186, 362
Sanctus, 16, 34, 45, 47, 50, 123, 259
scholasticism, 29, 85, 119, 138–39, 228, 391, 393–95
senses, 55, 57, 75, 128, 138, 140, 233, 252, 257–59, 309, 312
Sext, 18, 167
Shoah, 341
silence, 62–65, 102, 122, 127, 149, 152, 165, 168, 233, 267, 304, 339, 367
simony, 28
sin, 39, 50, 52, 54, 68–69, 141, 143, 145–47, 149, 179, 190, 244, 386
sociology, 140, 205, 369, 381
Solesmes, 102
soteriology, 320, 341–42
South Africa, 112, 303, 311, 385

spiritual gifts, 67, 145
spirituality, 83–84, 95, 99, 102, 111, 113, 118, 159, 228, 268, 270, 280, 282
Stations of the Cross, 239, 241
Strasbourg, 42, 44, 46, 48, 55, 209
Summorum Pontificum, 118, 342–43
synagogue, 188, 217–18, 301–2, 342–44, 359
syncretism, 345, 347
synod, 364
Synod of Constantinople, 330
Synod of Moscow, 330
Syria, 11, 86, 89–90
Syriac, 7, 10, 20, 81–83, 89–90, 176, 189

Taizé, 168
Te Deum, 153, 157
technology, 75, 307, 356
temple, 8–9, 11, 16, 120, 142, 217–18, 220, 284, 301–2
temporale, 103, 186, 362
Terce, 18, 167
theologia prima, 117, 196, 394, 396–97, 401–2
Traditionis custodes, 118, 343
Transfiguration, 182, 187
transubstantiation, 53, 57, 122
Tria munera, 283, 285–86
Trinity, 15, 134, 138, 142, 183, 237, 260, 263, 297, 314, 327, 348, 370, 379, 402–3

unction, 11, 15
Unitatis Redintegratio, 81, 320, 326, 331, 334, 339

unleavened bread, 10, 178
Upper Room, 180, 217, 378

Vatican II, 25, 81, 90, 111, 113, 118, 120–21, 125–26, 129–30, 136–37, 139–41, 155, 161, 163–64, 166–67, 169, 171, 185, 210, 218, 221–23, 269–70, 272, 276, 282–83, 286, 288, 293, 320, 324, 334, 337, 341–42, 351
veneration of the saints, 17–18, 26, 39, 48, 173, 178, 184–86
vernacular, 35, 44, 48–49, 59, 108, 111, 120, 125–26, 157, 164, 189, 358–59
Vespers, 18–19, 49, 165–67, 169–70, 208
viaticum, 147–48
Vigil, 18–19, 166–67, 178–81, 266, 384
voice, 42, 95, 127, 156, 200, 208

water, 11, 15, 51–52, 67, 85, 92–93, 122, 134, 138, 141–43, 149, 225, 235, 252, 258–59, 265, 327, 360, 385, 391, 393
Westminster Abbey, 331
West-Syrian, 20, 82, 85, 89–90, 183, 186–87, 189
wine, 53, 93–94, 134, 225, 258, 280, 393
Wittenberg, 42, 44–46, 303, 305
Word of God, 52, 59, 118, 125–27, 130, 136, 143, 149, 159, 163, 171, 211, 234, 254, 289, 299, 312, 314–15, 341, 392
words of institution, 45, 47
World Council of Churches, 65, 113, 335
World War II, 108, 111

Zurich, 42, 46, 48

CAMBRIDGE COMPANIONS TO RELIGION *(continued from page ii)*

Other Titles in the Series

CHRISTOLOGY Edited by Timothy J. Pawl and Michael L. Peterson
THE CISTERIAN ORDER Edited by Mette Birkedal Bruun
CLASSICAL ISLAMIC THEOLOGY Edited by Tim Winter
THE COUNCIL OF NICAEA Edited by Young Richard Kim
JONATHAN EDWARDS Edited by Stephen J. Stein
EVANGELICAL THEOLOGY Edited by Timothy Larsen and Daniel J. Treier
FEMINIST THEOLOGY Edited by Susan Frank Parsons
FRANCIS OF ASSISI Edited by Michael J. P. Robson
GENESIS Edited by Bill T. Arnold
THE GOSPELS Edited by Stephen C. Barton
THE GOSPELS, 2ND EDITION Edited by Stephen C. Barton and Todd Brewer
THE HEBREW BIBLE/OLD TESTAMENT Edited by Stephen B. Chapman and Marvin A. Sweeney
HEBREW BIBLE AND ETHICS Edited by C. L. Crouch
THE JESUITS Edited by Thomas Worcester
JESUS Edited by Markus Bockmuehl
JUDAISM AND LAW Edited by Christine Hayes
LAW IN THE HEBREW BIBLE EDITED BY Bruce Wells
C. S. LEWIS Edited by Robert MacSwain and Michael Ward
LIBERATION THEOLOGY Edited by Chris Rowland
MARTIN LUTHER Edited by Donald K. McKim
MEDIEVAL JEWISH PHILOSOPHY Edited by Daniel H. Frank and Oliver Leaman
MODERN JEWISH PHILOSOPHY Edited by Michael L. Morgan and Peter Eli Gordon
MUHAMMAD Edited by Jonathan E. Brockup
THE NEW CAMBRIDGE COMPANION TO BIBLICAL INTERPRETATION Edited by Ian Boxhall and Bradley C. Gregory
THE NEW CAMBRIDGE COMPANION TO CHRISTIAN DOCTRINE Edited by Michael Allen
THE NEW CAMBRIDGE COMPANION TO JESUS Edited by Markus Bockmuehl
THE NEW CAMBRIDGE COMPANION TO ST. PAUL Edited by Bruce W. Longenecker
NEW RELIGIOUS MOVEMENTS Edited by Olav Hammer and Mikael Rothstein
NEW TESTAMENT Edited by Patrick Gray
PENTECOSTALISM Edited by Cecil M. Robeck, Jr., and Amos Yong
POSTMODERN THEOLOGY Edited by Kevin J. Vanhoozer
THE PROBLEM OF EVIL Edited by Chad Meister and Paul K. Moser
PURITANISM Edited by John Coffey and Paul C. H. Lim
QUAKERISM Edited by Stephen W. Angell and Pink Dandelion
THE QUR'AN Edited by Jane Dammen McAuliffe
KARL RAHNER Edited by Declan Marmion and Mary E. Hines
JOSEPH RATZINGER Edited by Daniel Cardó and Uwe Michael Lang
REFORMATION THEOLOGY Edited by David Bagchi and David C. Steinmetz
REFORMED THEOLOGY Edited by Paul T. Nimmo and David A. S. Fergusson

RELIGION AND ARTIFICIAL INTELLIGENCE Edited by Beth Singler and Fraser Watts
RELIGION AND TERRORISM Edited by James R. Lewis
RELIGIOUS EXPERIENCE Edited by Paul K. Moser and Chad Meister
RELIGIOUS STUDIES Edited by Robert A. Orsi
FRIEDRICH SCHLEIERMACHER Edited by Jacqueline Mariña
SCIENCE AND RELIGION Edited by Peter Harrison
ST. PAUL Edited by James D. G. Dunn
SUFISM Edited by Lloyd Ridgeon
THE *SUMMA THEOLOGIAE* Edited by Philip McCosker and Denys Turner
THE TALMUD AND RABBINIC LITERATURE Edited by Charlotte E. Fonrobert and Martin S. Jaffee
THE TRINITY Edited by Peter C. Phan
HANS URS VON BALTHASAR Edited by Edward T. Oakes and David Moss
VATICAN II Edited by Richard R. Gaillardetz
JOHN WESLEY Edited by Randy L. Maddox and Jason E. Vickers
WOMEN AND ISLAM Edited by Masooda Bano

For EU product safety concerns, contact us at Calle de José Abascal, 56–1°, 28003 Madrid, Spain or eugpsr@cambridge.org.

www.ingramcontent.com/pod-product-compliance
Ingram Content Group UK Ltd.
Pitfield, Milton Keynes, MK11 3LW, UK
UKHW020049040426
469672UK00019B/381